The Economy of Western Xia

The Economy of Western Xia

A Study of 11th to 13th Century Tangut Records

By

Shi Jinbo

Translated and Edited by

Li Hansong

BRILL

LEIDEN | BOSTON

This book is published with financial support from the Chinese Fund for the Humanities and Social Sciences.

社会科学文献出版社
SOCIAL SCIENCES ACADEMIC PRESS (CHINA)

The original Chinese version was published by Social Sciences Academic Press (China).

Cover illustration: Yulin cave mural: original image in Shi, Jinbo; Bai, Bin; Wu, Fengyun (eds.). *Xixia Wenwu* (*Tangut Cultural Relics*). Beijing: Cultural Relics Publishing House, 1988. The image appeared black and white in the 1988 book; this is the original coloured version. (background) Tangut Contract of Land Sale, the 22nd Year of Tiansheng (1170), previously appeared as image 1, pp. 1–2, in Shi, Jinbo; Wei, Tongxian; Кычанов, Е.И. (eds.). *Russian Collection of Khara-Khoto Manuscripts* [俄藏黑水城文獻]: vol. 14. Shanghai: Shanghai Chinese Classics Publishing House, 1996–2011.

The Library of Congress Cataloging-in-Publication Data is available online at http://catalog.loc.gov

Typeface for the Latin, Greek, and Cyrillic scripts: "Brill". See and download: brill.com/brill-typeface.

The copyright of the Tangut Yinchuan font used in this publication resides with Prof. Jing Yongshi 景永时 of the Beifang Ethnic University (北方民族大学) in Yinchuan. For more information about this font see http://www.babelstone.co.uk/Fonts/Yinchuan.html.

ISBN 978-90-04-46129-1 (hardback)
ISBN 978-90-04-46132-1 (e-book)

This book is printed on acid-free paper and produced in a sustainable manner.

Contents

Translator's Preface

This book is a comprehensive introduction to the economic policies and practices in Western Xia (1038–1227). To economic historians and expert Tangutologists alike, it sketches the outer shapes and inner lives of the Tanguts and their society, offering an interwoven account of economic norms and laws in speech, and economic activities and experiences in action. The key to this productive tension between the macroscope of institutions and the micro-history of individuals is the author's synthetic reading of traditional historical sources: law codes, chronicles, and reference books, in the light of social, legal, and economic records: accounts, contracts, and registers. These extensive manuscripts, primarily from the north-western city of Khara-Khoto, or Heishuicheng, feed the raw material, data, and information to the quantitative and qualitative analyses of the Tangut economy. Still, the focused study of Khara-Khoto documents does not lose sight of the fewer, but equally important surviving primary sources elsewhere in Tangut territories, from Dunhuang to Wuwei, from the capital to Song-Xixia frontiers. At times, comparisons to social documents from earlier and later eras, from Tang, Song, to Yuan dynasties, reveal both contrasts and consistencies in the economic conditions of the same area through the ages. In these and many ways, this book fills a void in existing historiographies of Tangut studies, histories of books, records, and manuscripts, as well as the economic histories of medieval Inner Asia, East Asia, and beyond.

Command of Tangut is not a prerequisite for reading *The Economy of Western Xia*. Chapter 1, a general outline of the social, political, and economic history of the Tanguts and their empire, and Chapter 2, a parade of diverse economic records of Western Xia, are introductory discussions fully accessible to general readership. Chapters 3–7 analyse Tangut household registers, tax records, grain and property accounts, trade and transaction documents, and crucially, Tangut contracts for various purposes. Despite the density of the five main chapters, all primary sources are presented in English translation. Charts, diagrams, and images, are also deployed to aid comprehension. Finally, Chapter 8 on the economic records of Xixia written in Chinese may be useful to Sinologists at large. That said, readers are encouraged with the utmost enthusiasm to pick up the Tangut tongue. A full introduction to the Tangut language is available in *Tangut Language and Manuscripts: An Introduction*. Students and scholars are expected to benefit from a rapidly growing body of English, French, Russian, and Chinese scholarly literatures on the cultural, textual, and linguistic traditions of Western Xia. In contemporary anglophone academia and beyond, examples abound: the scholarships of Ruth Dunnell, Imre Galambos, Kirill Solonin, Guillaume Jacques, Shintarō Arakawa, and Andrew West, to name only a few. Today, Tangut primary sources are photocopied, printed, and digitised en masse. Still more texts and artefacts may come to light. Historical and archaeological sites are recipients of generous funding, maintenance, and public interest. The Western Xia Mausoleums, for instance, remain an ever competitive and promising candidate to UNESCO World Heritage status. A golden era of international Tangut Studies is a prize within reach.

The present book is the English edition of Shi Jinbo's award-winning treatise on the economic records of Western Xia. In a number of aspects, the translation differs from the original text. The illustrations include 27 statistical charts and 219 images, 117 of which are photocopies of Tangut manuscripts of economic documents. An extensive cursive-to-standard transcription in the Chinese appendix is omitted in the present edition, in order to optimise both the length of the book and its accessibility to the general readership. The most important of these manuscripts, however, are presented, translated, and analysed in the main text. References, both translated and left in the original, are compiled into a full bibliography toward the end of the book. Naturally, a new index is prepared for the present edition. Readers may assume that footnotes labelled "TN" (Translator's note) are clarificatory remarks by the translator, whereas those without are comments by the author. A number of repetitive passages are condensed or reorganised. Where formatting, typological, and interpretive errors are identified, I have either corrected them, or spelled out my concerns in footnotes, especially when the confusions outweigh my confidence. Throughout the main text and the footnotes, I have supplied phonetic notations, based on Gong Hwang-cherng's reconstruction, to key terms, expressions, and citations in the Tangut Unicode font. As for scripts of Indo-European languages, both the Devanāgarī and the IAST are used for Sanskrit and Pali; the Cyrillic script is used in references to Russian scholarships; Pinyin is the default romanisation scheme for Chinese terms, titles, and bibliographies. Readers will not fail to notice, perhaps to their disrelish, that many Tangut names are kept in the original with phonetic notations. After much scrutiny, I find that many of the cursively-scribbled Tangut names have been converted to the standard script with inconsistencies. Errors multiply, as half-baked names are translated into Chinese characters. Even if all constituent characters of a particular Tangut name are self-evident in meaning, I hesitate to speculate on their exact 'syntactical' order, function, and relationship, without the aid of further evidence. Here, the difficulty of Latinisation lies more in cursive-to-standard transcriptions than in Romanisation. In order to minimise loss in energy flow along the chain of translations—to use an ecological metaphor—I have decided to leave most names in Tangut characters, with additional phonetic notations. But occasionally, I rely on Pinyin (e.g. Liang Lama), or translate the general sense of the name (e.g. Liang "the greatly benevolent"), or resort to a combination of multiple representations. For the most part, however, I have sought to maintain a level of consistency throughout the book.

I have prepared this translation over the past three years, from 2017 to 2020, from *Cantabrigia antiqua* to *Cantabrigia nova*. I am grateful for the library staff at both institutions, Christ's College Library, Cambridge's East Asian Reading Room, and the Yenching and Fung Libraries. A significant amount of the work was done on the Upper West Side during the Covid-19 lockdown in New York, the epicentre of the pandemic in the United States. Wherever I end up in exile, my correspondence with Shi Jinbo is a constant source of delight and discoveries. Time and again, I have counted on the prudence and percipience of young Harvard scholars, Aurelia Han and Alex Koller, thanks to the generous support of Mr. Michael Weishan at the Franklin Delano Roosevelt Foundation. I am deeply indebted to my marvellous instructors of ancient and modern languages from the near and distant pasts, to historians who urge me to think at the nexus of book history, material history, and intellectual history, at the crossroad of economic thought, institutions, and activities, and to fellow political philosophers who graciously tolerate my Tangut musings by ignoring them. I am gratified that this book is published during my tenure of affiliation at the Centre for History and Economics. I wish to offer it as a humble gift to like-minded colleagues in this space of intellectual cross-pollination on the premise of disciplinary equality, fluidity, and solidarity. Last but not least, I wish to reiterate my profound thanks for both Brill and Social Sciences Academic Press (SSAP) editors, especially Irene Jager, Qiusha Lü, Chunyan Shu, and Yanling Li, for their unwavering support. Equally convinced of the desirability and impossibility of *interpretatio*, I assume full responsibility for all errors, and welcome all critiques and corrections.

Hansong Li
11 November 2020
At Harvard University

Illustrations

Figures

Charts

Introduction

Shi Jinbo

Western Xia (1038–1227) was a dynastic empire in medieval China, based in the city of Xingqing, later Zhongxing (modern-day Yinchuan of Ningxia Hui Autonomous Region). At its height, the Tangut imperium encompassed most of Ningxia, Gansu, northern Shaanxi, western Inner Mongolia, as well as parts of today's Qinghai and Xinjiang.

In the eyes of a historian, one of the most crucial aspects of a bygone empire is its socio-economy. However, when Mongol officials in the Yuan government followed the Chinese historiographical convention to compile chronicles for the preceding Song, Liao and Jin dynasties, they left the history of Western Xia alone unattended. Although the *History of Song*, *History of Liao* and *History of Jin* devoted chapters to the Tanguts, they offer a far too concise account of so complex a regime. This lack of chronicling also means the absence of any specific historical treatise on various aspects of the Tangut society, notably the genre of economic history, known in Chinese historiography as the *Records of Food and Goods* (*Shihuo Zhi*). It is also not surprising that references to Western Xia in Chinese archives are made mostly in the contexts of dynastic changes, military conflicts, and inter-state relations between the Song, Liao, Jin, Huihu (Uyghur) and Tubo (Tibetan) regimes. Very little is addressed or even known about the socio-economic history of Western Xia. In the meantime, most of the scarce narratives on the Tangut economy available to historians have been exhausted and regurgitated into common knowledge by Tangutologists throughout the past decades. As early as the 1980s, Wu Tianchi offered a comprehensive and commendable analysis of the Tangut economy in his *Xixia Shigao* (*A History of Western Xia*), which was based on surviving literatures documented in Chinese archives.[1] Further progress was made in 1994 when Qi Xia and Qiao Youmei published their study, *Liao Xia Jin Jingjishi* (*An Economic History of Liao, Xia, and Jin Dynasties*), where the Dangxiang Tangut economy is discussed within the compass of a chapter.[2] The ensuing years, however, witnessed a stagnation in this field of study. Handicapped by a remarkable lack of

1 Wu, Tianchi: *Xixia Shigao* [西夏史稿]. Chengdu: Sichuan People's Publishing House, reprinted 1983.

2 Qi, Xia; Qiao, Youmei. *Liao Xia Jin Jingjishi* [遼夏金經濟史]: *An Economic History of Liao, Xia and Jin Dynasties*. Baoding: Hebei University Press, 1994.

 | DOI:10.1163/9789004461321_002

primary sources, experts in Tangut Studies struggled to break the ground. As a result, our understanding of many aspects of the Tangut economy remained vague, if not altogether void.

In the early 20th century, a team of Russian explorers discovered a large pile of manuscripts at the site of Khara-Khoto (part of modern-day Ejin Banner, Inner Mongolia) in north-western China, most of which are written in the Tangut script. The Russians took the entire corpus home, a tragic loss of precious archaeological finds for the Chinese. Nonetheless, this event proved a key catalyst in the birth of the modern field of Tangutology.

It turns out that a significant amount of records on the Tangut economy lurks inside this corpus of medieval texts. The Tangut law code excavated in Khara-Khoto, the *Revised Laws of Heavenly Prosperity*, with its many rules and regulations on trade and transactions, has significantly enriched existing sources on Tangut social and economic history.[3] The subsequent publication of a Chinese translation of this important Tangut law code breathed life into new approaches to reimagining the historical economy of Western Xia. Since then, Du Jianlu made important advancements in the study of the Tangut economy with his publications of *Xixia Jingjishi Yanjiu* (*A Study of the Economic History of Western Xia*) and *Xixia Jingjishi* (*An Economic History of Western Xia*), both of which use not only Chinese archives, but also sources from the Tangut laws.[4]

Notwithstanding sound and steady progress, the dearth of primary materials on the Tangut economy remained a major obstacle to scholarship. Not only was the like of a *Record of Food and Goods* nowhere to be found, sources on the social and economic lives of the ordinary Tanguts, which would have enabled case studies of this kind, remained unheard of and unseen. To decode the mysteries of the Tangut Empire, there was no shortcut but to discover more primary sources, especially those written by the Tanguts themselves. By good fortune, this turned into a reality in a dramatic turn of events in the process of preparing and editing the *Russian Collection of Khara-Khoto Manuscripts*.[5]

3 Shi, Jinbo; Nie, Hongyin; Bai, Bin (eds.). *Xixia Tiansheng Lüling* [西夏天盛律令]: *The Tangut Laws of Heavenly Prosperity. Zhongguo Zhenxi Falü Dianji Jicheng* [中國珍稀法律典籍集成]: *A Collection of Rare and Precious Chinese Codes of Law*, vol. 5. Beijing: China Science Publishing & Media, 1994. Shi, Jinbo; Nie, Hongyin; Bai, Bin (eds.). *Tiansheng Gaijiu Xinding Lüling* [天盛改舊新定律令], hereafter *Revised Laws of Heavenly Prosperity*. Series: *Zhonghua Chuanshi Fadian* [中华傳世法典]: *Law Codes in the Chinese Civilization*. Beijing: Law Press of China, 2000.

4 Du, Jianlu. *Xixia Jingjishi Yanjiu* [西夏經濟史研究]: *A Study of the Economic History of Western Xia*. Lanzhou: Gansu Culture Publishing House, 1998. Du Jianlu. *Xixia Jingjishi* [西夏经济史]: *An Economic History of Western Xia*. Beijing: China Social Sciences Press, 2002.

5 Shi, Jinbo; Wei, Tongxian; Кычанов, Е.И. (eds.). *Ecang Heishuicheng Wenxian* [俄藏黑水城文獻], hereafter *Russian Collection of Tangut Manuscripts*. Институт восточных рукописей

The new historical materials discovered towards the end of the 20th century are known as the Tangut social documents. The academia has devoted much attention to these manuscripts in recent years. I am fortunate to have witnessed and taken part in the search, discovery, compilation, registration and study of these documents, which lasted for a total of almost 20 years. The transcription (from cursive to standard script), translation, and interpretation of the Tangut social documents have unveiled many mysteries surrounding the imperial history of Western Xia.

The discovery of this world-class corpus of historical materials is a matter of great fortune. In 1992, the Chinese Academy of Social Sciences delegated me to collaborate with experts at the Institute of Oriental Manuscripts (IOM, St. Petersburg) to publish an exhaustive collection and translation of the Tangut manuscripts first discovered at the site of Khara-Khoto in the early 20th century. An agreement was reached in the spring of 1993, and in the following years of 1994, 1997 and 2000, a Chinese team paid four visits to the IOM to compile the manuscripts, most of which had been organised and registered by generations of Russian scholars.

However, given the enormous size of this collection and the presence of many fragments and single pages scattered across and alongside the better-preserved texts, I could not help but wonder whether the Russian experts had left a number of pages unregistered. After repeated requests, I was informed that there had indeed been some broken and disjointed volumes, but that they would unnecessarily burden our already overwhelming workload in the duration of the short research trip. Finally, on our third visit to the IOM in 1997 and at my insistence, the team was granted access to the unregistered manuscripts. It turned out that the Russian experts had assorted the manuscripts that either lacked fronts and ends, or could not be easily named, identified or classified, into a total of 110 boxes. When I opened these boxes, what I saw was indeed a pile of diverse and disjoined Tangut texts, most of which seemed to be Buddhist scriptures. But in the same collection was a large number of social documents that reflected various aspects of the Tangut society. Most of these documents are written in the cursive script. Fortunately, some prior exposure to the cursive style enabled me to recognise enough to tell the types and traits of these texts. Their potential significance to the field of Tangutology appeared increasingly clear as I identified a wide array of records, ranging from household

---

Российской академии наук, formerly the St. Petersburg Branch of the Institute of Oriental Studies of the Russian Academy of Sciences. Institute of Ethnology and Anthropology, formerly Institute for Ethnology of the Chinese Academy of Social Sciences. Shanghai: Shanghai Ancient Books Publishing House, 1996–2011.

registers, financial accounts, contracts, military documents, legal complaints, announcements, official records, to private letters. In the end, I picked out the social documents, registered them in detail and arranged for the professional production of a collection of photocopies, resulting in 50 boxes of primary materials, index cards and several hundred photocopies of primary materials.

This unexpected reward of invaluable, albeit incomplete manuscripts also greatly impressed another member of the team to the IOM: Dunhuang expert and senior editor of the Shanghai Ancient Books Publishing House, Mr. Jiang Weisong. It is no secret to any historian that these documents may be rightfully considered social archives, indispensable to any reliable historical narrative. Primary materials such as historical archives are the core and foundation of historical research, for these first-hand accounts are more trustworthy than various kinds of secondary literatures, such as the narratives of historians, research findings abroad, and memoirs of later generations. Uncompromised by artificial or arbitrary editing, and untainted by falsifications or fabrications, primary sources provide a more authentic and straightforward gateway to history. In other words, these social documents are critical to any proper understanding of the Tanguts and their history.

During my fourth visit to St. Petersburg in 2000, I worked through the remaining 50 boxes of materials. An additional discovery was made of numerous social documents pasted to the inner covers of Buddhist sutras. The result was a total of 1,000 registers and more than 1,500 documents. The sheer size testifies to the significance of this historical source.

In the aftermath of the discovery of the Tangut social documents, I was equally fortunate to take part in the interpretive work that ensued from the research trips. Given the sudden appearance and acquisition of a large number of additional materials, much more time is required to reorganise the photocopies. Therefore, the scheduled publication date of the *Russian Collection of Khara-Khoto Manuscripts* was postponed. According to the original plan, based on both the bibliography provided by the Russian experts and the quantity of materials photographed, the secular texts of the Tangut corpus would be printed in 5 books, from volume 7 to 11. The unexpected identification and inclusion of as many as 1,000 secular texts, however, changed our timetable. In fact, this body of social documents were estimated to fill up to three full volumes: 12, 13 and 14, which we duly added to the plan for publication.

Since the social documents were at the time completely new to academia, they had never been edited or studied. It was a daunting task to name each single document, in order to ensure that it appears with a valid caption and description in the forthcoming *Russian Collection of Khara-Khoto Manuscripts*. Surely, to give a fitting title to a document presupposes an accurate interpretation of its content. Most of these cursive writings would have been difficult to translate even if they had been written stroke by stroke, with perfect clarity, in the standard script. At times, the characters are continuously and ceaselessly cursive, like soaring dragons and fluttering phoenixes; other lines are schematically styled and simplistically scribed. Blurred and damaged parts are spotted throughout the manuscripts. Some texts are written with brush-strokes on both sides, which explains why the ink seeps through the page and ruins another text, only to exacerbate the plight of scholars trying to identify the words. Therefore, the first step to interpret and transform the social documents into user-friendly primary sources is to decipher the code of the Tangut cursive script. But there is no systematic approach to decoding the highly idiosyncratic cursive script other than repeated conjectures and prolonged inferences. Attempting and failing at identifying a character hundreds of times is a kind of work both strenuous and entertaining. In fact, my interest in interpreting the Tangut social documents only intensified over time.

Reading through the social documents repeatedly over the years, I have tracked the shapes and patterns of the Tangut cursive characters in reference to, and by comparison to the standard script. After a long eight years, in 2005, I completed the annotated bibliography of the Tangut social documents for the *Russian Collection of Khara-Khoto Manuscripts*, which range from volume 12 to 14. Throughout this process, I gradually decrypted the abstruse system of Tangut cursive writing. With this knowledge, I then translated a number of the more important documents for the convenience of scholars interested in using these sources for their studies.

The third phase of my research was devoted to a systematic examination of the Tangut social documents. Amongst the approximately 500 registers of economic records excavated in Khara-Khoto, there are household registers, *shoushi* self-reports, demographic accounts and registers by *liliu* and gender, which altogether furnish us with first-hand demographic information on Tangut Khara-Khoto. There are also tax records, including accounts of land and grain taxes, grain loans by *liliu* & households, hay loans, as well as capitation and irrigation taxes, which give us a comprehensive view of the tax system in Tangut-ruled Khara-Khoto. Also available in large numbers are accounts of grains and properties, including grain accounts of the military supervisory district and by *liliu*, accounts of cash and property, livestock, and other miscellaneous materials, which reflect the government's practice of registering, calculating, preserving and storing food and properties. Last but not least, there are documents concerning trade and transaction, such as sales records (sell & purchase taxes, accounts of grain, livestock, and alcohol) and loan records (monetary loan interests, grain loans, and land sales), which tell us as much about commercial activities and commodity prices in local markets. Contracts constitute the majority of Tangut economic documents. Prior to this discovery, few Tangut contracts had been known: 15 pawning contract fragments in Chinese and 2 other contracts written in Tangut. The newly discovered contracts are much more numerous and diverse, including loan contracts (grains, properties and cash), transaction contracts (land, livestock and human beings), lease and rent contracts (land and livestock), pawning contracts (livestock and properties), employment contracts (human and animal labour), exchange contracts and communal contracts. The size and scope of these materials show the omnipresence and importance of contracts in the daily economic activities of the common people at the base level of Tangut society. The more research done on these social documents reveals more evidence of the value and significance of these historical sources, in and beyond the field of Tangutology.

The Tangut social documents are a novel area of study. First of all, it presumes a high level of familiarity with Chinese economic history, in both primary sources and secondary literature, alongside a wide range of topics: household registration, taxation, pawning and loaning, commerce and contracts. It also requires a thorough engagement with the existing scholarship on social documents excavated at two other archaeological sites: Dunhuang and Turpan. It is on these studies that I spent the past ten years, in which I wrote and published a number of papers on Tangut household registers, taxes and contracts.

In 2007, my research proposal for the *Economic Records of Western Xia* received sponsorship from the National Social Science Fund of China. Thereafter, I continued to uncover more Tangut social documents. Due to the increasing quantity of archives, the project did not come to a conclusion until 2012. The next four years witnessed further research in this field, with the main body of Tangut economic records interpreted, the content of this book enriched, its structure optimised and viewpoints further clarified. Academic research takes place over a long stretch of time, punctuated by a sequence of temporary findings that improve on previous results. For example, in an article published in 2010 titled "Preliminary Discussions on the Appellations and Revisions of the *British Collection of Khara-Khoto Manuscripts*," I presented and translated a number of Tangut materials then freshly discovered in the British archive.[6] Some of them were identified for the first time of their type, and had not yet been interpreted with precision, due to excessive loss and damage of

6 Xie, Yujie; Wu, Fangsi (eds.). *Yingcang Heishuicheng Wenxian* [英藏黑水城文獻]: *British Collection of Khara-Khoto Manuscripts*. Second Northwest University for Nationalities, Shanghai Ancient Works Publishing House, and the British Library. Shanghai: Shanghai Ancient Works Publishing House, 2005.

the manuscript. Within the span of a few years, however, those texts made their ways into the present work, where they are interpreted anew. Thanks to the discovery of an important printed text on the 'junior accounting magistrate' and related topics in the *Laws of Heavenly Prosperity*, the then-unknown document was finally identified as a grain tax receipt. Recent studies have shown that this fragment, only 20 words long, could be the earliest block-printed economic document hitherto known to the world. It has added new materials to both the economic history of China and the history of block-printing, within the larger history of science and technology.

The *Economy of Western Xia* provides new primary sources to Tangut studies, archaeology, linguistics and medieval history. It seeks to add some fresh and well-grounded insights to our existing knowledge of the medieval economy of Western Xia. In this way, it may contribute to not only the social historical scholarship on Western Xia but also the economic history of East and Inner Asia as a whole during this period. From the perspective of palaeography, this work may also serve as a textbook or a source of reference for those interested in acquiring the ability to read the Tangut cursive script.

Classifying a pile of fragmented documents may be demanding and exhausting, but to cultivate a barren land into a fertile soil, and to turn broken pages into a legendary tale, is not a mission to be taken lightly. Twenty years have passed since the discovery of this precious archive in 1997. Throughout these years, I have intermittently taken up other projects, but the interpretive study of the Tangut social documents has always preoccupied the bulk of my time. It is after all the duty of a historian to weave the fragments of the past into a fair tapestry of historical narrative.

Due to both the large quantity of economic records and the difficulty in deciphering the Tangut cursive script, this book may be considered at its best a work-in-progress. Where it commits an error or exposes an insufficient analysis, I am most eager to receive critiques from the readers. It is also my hope that experts in the relevant and allied fields would engage with these sources and produce better research. In this way, we collaborate to deepen our common understanding of Tangut society. Apart from the economic records, there are also a variety of other texts, ranging from military and government records to those in the private sphere.

In 2007, I visited Mr. Ji Xianlin at the 301 Hospital, where I informed him on the selection, compilation, and interpretation of the Tangut social documents, and updated him on the progress and prospect of this research. Praising the work, Mr. Ji handwrote a title, *Xixia Wenshu Yanjiu* (*A Study of Tangut Documents*) for this book in a show of support and encouragement. He passed away only about a year later. Now, eight years have elapsed since our tremendous loss. This book is published in fond and profound memories of Mr. Ji.

CHAPTER 1

The Empire of Western Xia and the Tangut Economy

Contemporary to the Song Empire, a dynastic regime of mighty power and lasting influence emerged in what is today the northwest of China. The inhabitants of the land named their regime the 'Great Xia Kingdom White and High,' or simply the Kingdom of Great Xia. And since it was located to the west of the Song, it is by convention referred to in the Chinese historiographical tradition as Western Xia (1038–1227 AD). The imperial dynasty was ruled by a total of ten emperors, spanning a history of 190 years. The Tanguts stood off against the Northern Song and Khitan Liao in its early history, and later against Southern Song and Jurchen Jin. In each of the two 'three-kingdom' periods, it constituted a major force and played a critical role in a delicate balance of power in medieval China. Further adding to the complexity of imperial diplomacies in this period was the presence of the Uyghurs, Tibetans, and other ethnic groups with overlapping territories, mutual goals, and conflicting interests. The majority of the population in Western Xia was the prominent Tangut tribe of Dangxiang Qiang. During their rule, the Tanguts excelled in military power, steered a large economy, and prospered in all aspects of cultural life.

Although the Tanguts built an empire not inferior to the Song, Liao, and Jin Dynasties, imperial historians of the Yuan Dynasty left the history of Xixia unchronicled. As a result, unlike the *History of Song*, *History of Liao*, and *History of Jin*, the vast number of Tangut historical records have not survived in the form of imperial chronicles. Furthermore, when the Mongol army breached the walls of Xia, a sizeable portion of Tangut publications and cultural artefacts were destructed in war. Whilst some precious materials have luckily survived, they have been buried deep in the dust of history over many centuries. All of these misfortunes have added to the aura of mystery around the Tangut Empire. Nevertheless, the main contour of the history of Xia has remained accessible to those who consult the brief and cursory portrayals of the Tanguts within the pages of the Histories of Song, Liao, and Jin.

The geography and natural environment of a historical regime is a key factor in its socio-economic experiences. Therefore, it is fitting and proper to first investigate the natural conditions of Western Xia before proceeding to discuss the state of its economy.

1 Natural Conditions of Western Xia

The Tanguts inhabited a territory that encompassed a diverse range of geographic features, which are the main factors in the formation of the Tangut society. Especially noteworthy are the landscape, waters, and climates.

The territories of the Tangut empire encompassed a wide range of landscapes and diverse geographic features: plains, steppes, mountains, and deserts. After the Dangxiang tribe migrated north from the medieval Songzhou (prefecture of Song, Songpan of Sichuan province) in the Tang Dynasty, they scattered and settled on the Loess plateaus of the Shaanxi and Gansu areas. By the time the Tangut empire was proclaimed in the early 11th century, the Tanguts had significantly expanded their territory. The east and south were the Loess plateau, with the Liupan mountains as its southernmost barrier. To the north were the Ordos and Alashan areas of the Mongolian Plateau, featured by its long-stretching deserts dotted by pastures, including the Mu Us Sandyland, the Tengger Desert, and the Badain Jaran Desert. To the west are the northern borders of the Tibetan plateau, where the Qilian mountains stand as a shield to the Hexi corridor. The Helan Mountains are embedded in this landscape like a piece of beautiful Sapphire. Here are the fertile Hetao plain and the thin stretch of oasis across the otherwise sandy Hexi corridor.

A broad sketch of the Tangut landscape reveals the predominance of high mountains, bleak deserts, and limited arable land. In a sharp contrast to the

FIGURE 1 The Helan mountains

Central Plains covered with a higher proportion of hills and plains suitable for agriculture, Western Xia suffered obvious geographical disadvantages in the production of grains. Chronicles from the Song Dynasty record that "The Xia relied on the fertile land south of the River, bound by the Heng mountains on the right, and by the Tiandu and Maxian mountains on the west. The rest of its land is insufficient for cultivation or animal-husbandry."[1]

Not only does the Yellow River flow across the entire Tangut territories, but some of its branches upstream and midstream also fall within the Tangut realm, such as the Rivers Huangshui, Tao, Qingshui, Kuye, and Wuding. Since time immemorial, the Yellow River has been exploited for the purpose of irrigation and remained a lifeline for local agriculture throughout the life of Western Xia. Irrigation by river was especially important for Tangut peasants dealing with persistent draught, who could afford to count much less on natural precipitation as a reliable water supply. The Hetao area "enriched the five grains, especially in the growing of rice and wheat. Between Gan (zhou) and Liang (zhou), however, irrigation relied on the many rivers nearby. As for Xing (zhou) and Ling (zhou), there are ancient waterways: the Tanglai and Hanyuan canals, both diverted from the Yellow River. With the benefit of irrigation enjoyed, there is less risk of flood, or peril of draught."[2] Although the Yellow River has earned for what is present-day Ningxia the reputation of the "Prosperous Jiangnan beyond the Northern Frontiers," it also furnishes the area with natural catastrophes. With an unexpectedly heavy rainfall, dams break, unleashing floods upon the humans and livestock of the farmlands.

There are also endorheic rivers within the Tangut territory, which form an area of inland waters in the Hexi-Alashan and another near Ordos. The most renowned is the 'Black Water' from the melting snow of the Qilian mountains, which flows into the Juyan Lake (Mongolian: Gashuun Nuur), nourishing a trail of oases along its way, thus providing an ideal base for Tangut agriculture. By "between Gan and Liang, however, irrigation relied on the many rivers nearby,"[3] the chronicle refers to rivers formed by the convergence of meltwaters from the Qilian mountains. One of the oases was Shazhou (modern-day Dunhuang, Gansu) where "residents relied on locally-produced wheat as their

1 Li, Tao (Song Dynasty). *Xu Zizhi Tongjian Changbian* [續資治通鑒長編], hereafter *The Extended Zizhi Tongjian*. Book 466, Sixth Year of Yuanyou (1091), Ninth Month, Renchen. Emended Critical Edition. Beijing: Zhonghua Book Company, 1979.

2 Tuo Tuo, et al. (Yuan Dynasty). *Songshi* [宋史], hereafter *History of Song*. Book 486. "The State of Xia" Part II. Emended Critical Edition. Beijing: Zhonghua Book Company, 1977.

3 *History of Song*, Book 486, "The State of Xia" Part II.

FIGURE 2 The Yellow river near Yinchuan, Ningxia

FIGURE 3 The Yellow river near Zhongwei, Ningxia

principle source of nourishment."[4] This demonstrates beyond doubt the existence of developed agricultural zones along the Hexi corridor. The very city of Khara-Khoto, where the largest corpus of Tangut manuscripts was discovered, was one of the oases along the downstream of the 'Black Water.'

The climate in Western Xia is typically continental, with long winters of low temperature and dry air that allow a short time for crops to grow. Some areas are plagued by chronic draught and negligible rainfall, which cause enormous challenges to farming lands and raising livestock. The Tanguts did, however, enjoy nature's gift of ample sunlight, since adequate heat, strong solar radiation, and high diurnal temperature variation are all favourable conditions for agriculture. With that said, in those areas farther away from the natural waters, draught alone is able to cripple the economy. Thus, where rainfall in the spring and autumn are indispensable for sowing and harvesting, the Tanguts depended solely on the mercy of heaven and their own fortune for their livelihood.

4 A.J.H. Charignon, *Le Livre de Marco Polo*. Pékin: Albert Nachbaur, Vol. 1. 1924, Vol. 2. 1926, Vol. 3. 1928. Ch. 57.

FIGURE 4 Juyan Lake Basin, Ejin Banner, Inner Mongolia (near Khara-Khoto)

FIGURE 5 Badain Jaran Desert, Inner Mongolia

In sum, the natural condition of Western Xia is inferior to that of the Central Plains. Lands naturally favourable for habitation such as the Hetao area are extremely rare. Although in more than a few regions, it may be said that vegetation used to be more plentiful than now, it should also be observed that water and land resources had already been overly exploited under the Tanguts. The frequency of war and the forced exile of the people further exacerbated the deterioration of the natural environment.

2 Dangxiang People and Their Economy before the Tangut Empire

The early Dangxiang Tanguts, a branch of the Western Qiang ethnics—as they were known in the Han Dynasty—lived between expansive steppes and hills in what are modern-day south-eastern Qinghai and north-western Sichuan. According to the *Old Book of Tang*, "as the Western Qiang weakened after the Wei and Jin dynasties, its tribes either succumbed to the central power, or fled to the fields and mountains. It is only after Zhou destroyed Tanchang and Dengzhi,[5] that the Dangxiang gained strength. Their territory sets its eastern boundary near Songzhou, borders Yabghu to the west, reaches the Chongsang, Misang and other Qiangtic tribes in the south, and connects with the Tuyuhun in the north. They are situated in the middle of hills and valleys, and stretches across three thousand *li* of land."[6] To the west of the Dangxiang ethnics were the Tibetans, and to its northwest lied the regime of Tuyuhun. At the time, Dangxiang was comprised of multiple clans by their unique family names, of which the most powerful was Tuoba. In the early Tang period, Tuoba Chici, the Dangxiang chief of the Tuoba clan, paid tribute to the Empire. Honoured by the bestowment of the Tang imperial name, Li, the leader was named the Xirongzhou Dudu, or Commander of the Prefecture of Western Rong.

Originally, the Dangxiang were a people of herdsmen. And up to the times of Sui and Tang, they knew only how to raise livestock and engaged in no agriculture. The *Book of Sui* states plainly that the Dangxiang "herded yaks, sheep and swine for food, and knew not how to sow and reap."[7] Even during the Tang

5 TN: Tanchang (Chinese: 宕昌), a Qiangic regime based in southern Gansu, near modern-day Tanchang county; Dengzhi (Chinese: 鄧至), a Qiangic power established in present-day northern Sichuan, to the west of Jiuzhaigou.

6 Liu, Xu, et al. *Jiu Tang Shu* [舊唐書]: *Old Book of Tang*. Beijing: Zhonghua Book Company, 1975, Book 198, "Dangxiang Qiang"; see also, Li, Yanshou, et al. *Bei Shi* [北史]: *History of the Northern Dynasties*. Beijing: Zhonghua Book Company, 1974, Book 96, "Dangxiang"; Wei, Zheng et al. *Sui Shu* [隋書]: *Book of Sui*. Beijing: Zhonghua Book Company, 1977. Book 83, "Dangxiang."

7 *Book of Sui*, Book 83. "Western Regions: Dangxiang."

Dynasty, the Dangxiang "raised yaks, horses, donkeys and sheep as a source of nourishment. But they knew not how to sow and reap, and grew not the Five Crops in their fields." At that time, all that the Dangxiang relied on for food, clothing, and other utilities came directly from animal husbandry: they consumed meat and milk, and fabricated clothes using the fur and skin of their livestock. Even their internal chambers were "covered with woven wool of sheep and hairs from Yak tails."[8]

However, with the rise of the neighbouring Tibetan power, the Dangxiang tribes came increasingly under pressure. Scattered around present-day northern Sichuan, southern Gansu, and Qinghai, they finally migrated closer to the Central Plains in the early 8th century. The Tang Empire moved the Commandership of the Jingbian Prefecture, originally established in the Longxi area, to the Qing Prefecture (modern-day Qingyang, Gansu), and appointed the Dangxiang chief, Tuoba Sitai, as the Commander in effective control of twelve prefectures. In mid-8th century, the Tibetans seized the moment of the Anshi Rebellion (755–763 AD) to invade the poorly-guarded Hexi and Longyou, forcing the Dangxiang tribes in these areas to once again move eastward, to an area north to Yinzhou (modern-day Mizhi county of Shaanxi), and east to Xiazhou (today's Baichengzi, north of Jingbian county, Shaanxi). The Commandership of Jingbian Prefecture relocated to Yinzhou. Over time, a large number of Dangxiang clans arrived in Suizhou (present-day Suide county of Shaanxi) and Yanzhou (Yan'an, Shaanxi). Some of the tribes aided the Tibetans in their assault on Tang cities, culminating in the fall of Chang'an. In the second wave of Dangxiang migrations, the clans dwelling near the Qing prefecture were commonly referred to as the "Tribes of the Eastern Mountains" (Dongshan-bu) whereas those that entered the Xia prefecture were called the "Tribes of the Plain Xia" (Pingxia-bu). The southern borders of Pingxia are marked by the Heng mountains, which was known to the Tang as the Southern Mountains, hence the name for the Dangxiang clans that settled down in this area, "The Tribes of the Southern Mount" (Nanshan-bu). The Dangxiang tribes that migrated inland still maintained their habitual practice of herding. As their wealth accumulated and population bloomed, a process of social stratification based on ownership and proprietorship gradually took shape within the clans.

In the First Year of Guangming during the Tang Dynasty (880 AD), Huang Chao's peasant rebels captured the imperial capital, Chang'an (Xi'an, Shaanxi). In the First Year of Zhonghe (881 AD), the Dangxiang chief Tuoba Sigong, then Regional Inspector (Cishi) of the You Prefecture, joined other Regional Commanders (*Jiedushi*) in answering Xizong Emperor's call to suppress

8 *Old Book of Tang*. Book 198, "Dangxiang Qiang."

FIGURE 6 Site of Tongwan city, prefecture of Xia

the Huangchao rebels. After Chang'an was recovered in the Third Year of Zhonghe (883 AD), Tuoba was awarded the title of *Dingnan Jiedushi* (Regional Commander of the Dingnan Circuit), and once more conferred the imperial name of Li, ruling five prefectures from his government in Xiazhou. The place was, a few centuries ago, the capital of the Xiongnu Xia state (407–431) founded by Helian Bobo during the Sixteen Kingdoms period of Eastern Jin Dynasty. The other four prefectures were Yin, Sui, You (Jingbian county, Shaanxi), and Jing (Mizhi county, Shaanxi). Since then, Tuoba exercised *de facto* autonomous rule in the region. Throughout the Five Dynasties period (907–960), the Dangxiang regime based in Xiazhou attached itself to Liang, Tang, Jin, Han, and Zhou, assorted dynasties that rose and fell in rapid succession in the Central Plains. At the same time, it fought a series of wars with neighbouring cities and emerged from these struggles an even greater power than before.[9]

9 Xue, Juzheng, et al. *Jiu Wu Dai Shi* [舊五代史]: *Old History of the Five Dynasties*. Beijing: Zhonghua Book Company, 1976. Book 138, "Dangxiang"; *History of Song*. Book 485–486. "State of Xia" (Parts I & II); Tuotuo, et al. *Liao Shi* [遼史]: *History of Liao*. Beijing: Zhonghua Book Company, 1974. Book 115, "Extra Sources on Western Xia"; Tuo Tuo, et al. *Jin Shi* [金史]: *History of Jin*. Beijing: Zhonghua Book Company, 1975. Book 134. "Western Xia." See also Wu, Guangcheng (Qing Dynasty). *Xixia Shushi* [西夏書事]: *Book of Western Xia*. Fifth Year of Daoguang (1835) printed edition (TN: see also Beijing: Wenkuitang, 1935; Taipei: Guangwen, 1968).

FIGURE 7 Tangut mural of ploughing oxen, in Yulin cave, No. 3

The great migration in the Tang Dynasty did not significantly alter the Dangxiang reliance on herding as the main pillar of its economy. The Dangxiang Tanguts traded their animal products for grains, cloths, and other commodities from the Central Plains. A main Tangut export was the famed breed of Dangxiang steeds, favoured by the inlanders and traded at extravagant prices.

A sizable number of Dangxiang Tanguts, however, did resort to farming once they settled on cultivated lands. These families thus began a historical process of transitioning from nomadic herding to settled agriculture, eventually becoming farmers. This change in economic production greatly enriched the Dangxiang social life. Historically, many areas which came under Dangxiang rule had already preserved a base of agriculture with a high speed of development and economic production. The joint cultivation efforts by both Dangxiang and Han Chinese peasants in the area unleashed a long-lasting impact on the shape of the Tangut society.

The Anxi Yulin Cave No. 3, west of Dunhuang, Gansu, is a reservoir of Tangut art. In its mural portraying the Fifty-one-faced, Thousand-armed Bodhisattva Avalokiteśvara, is an image of ploughing: two oxen bear a horizontal frame connected to the plough shaft—the so-called 'two oxen drawing the plough' method—whilst the peasant lays one hand on the plough and has the other clutch the whip, a vivid depiction of the ploughing field in Western Xia.

3 Founding of Western Xia and Its Economy

In the early years of Northern Song, the Dangxiang ethnarchs were tributary kings to the Song Empire. Li Jipeng's succession to his elder brother in 980 AD, however, catalysed conflicts within the tribes. In the end, he resorted to surrendering the five prefectures to direct rule by Song officials. In the seventh year of Song Taiping Xingguo (982 AD), Song bestowed on Li Jipeng the title of Regional Commander of Zhangde Circuit (*Zhangdejun Jiedushi*)[10] and sent an army to Xiazhou to take control over the Tangut prefectures. The imperial edict required not only the settlement of Jipeng in Kaifeng but also the presence of all Tangut Li royalties within the *Sima* range of family relatives in Bianjing.[11] Li Jiqian, a younger cousin of Li Jipeng and at the time in charge of Dangxiang internal affairs within the *Dingnan Jiedushi* (*Duzhi Fanluoshi*), vehemently opposed the transfer of the five prefectures and the Song demand for the Li family as virtual hostages. He led a cohort to flee to Dijinze, in modern-day Ordos, Inner Mongolia, where he proclaimed autonomous rule from the Song Dynasty.

Li Jiqian stood fast against Song summons of surrender and offers of recruitment, to which he responded with more looting. In the First Year of Yongxi (984 AD), Jiqian reached the Xiazhou area, where he suffered a major defeat by Yin Xian (932–994), the Song prefect of Xiazhou (*Zhizhou*), and Cao Guangshi (931–985), the inspector-commissioner (*Duxunjianshi*) whose thousand-strong cavalry dashed into the Tangut camps in Dijinze. The Song army prevailed decidedly against Jiqian's force, captured the chief's mother and wives, and forced him into dormancy, waiting for fortune to turn her tide. In the following year, however, Jiqian maneuvered a deceptive surrender, where he surprised Cao Guangshi in an ambush, killing the general and his followers before capturing Yinzhou. Now with a prefecture, Jiqian assumed the position of *Dingnan Liuhou*, giving him temporary command of affairs within the Jiedushi, and appointed officials who formed a new bureaucracy around him. Enraged, Emperor Taizong of Song dispatched four armies to besiege Jiqian, but although serious damages were inflicted, the expedition was not able to uproot the foundation of the new Dangxiang regime in Xiazhou, due to the lack of effective military coordination on the frontiers.

---

10 TN: Zhangdejun (彰德軍) was a circuit near present-day An'yang, established by the Later Liang as a strategic post, and abandoned after mid-10th century. It was an empty title recycled as an honorary status for Li Jipeng.

11 TN: Sima (緦麻): the funerary costumes worn for the deaths of cousins, grandparents and children, married aunts, and in-laws. Here, it specifies the range of family relatives.

Jiqian, fully aware that his emerging power was far from a full-fledged kingdom, came to the strategic decision to submit to Khitan rule in a diplomatic effort to leverage support against the Song Dynasty. He was subsequently dubbed the King of Xia by the Liao emperor, the archenemy of Song, and was given a Khitan princess as wife. The deal was within his reach: in a fierce rivalry between Liao and Song, the rise of a Dangxiang power within Song's western gates was all benefit and no menace to Liao. For the court in Bianjing, which sees itself as the only orthodox and legitimate heir of the Central Plains, the Dangxiang lands had been former Song territories. For the Song Empire to recognise Tangut independence, therefore, was as painful as cutting off its own flesh and bones. Even worse was the prospect of an alliance between the Dangxiang and the Khitan, which would have placed Song between two formidable enemies. For these reasons, the Song court resolved to forestall the growth of Tangut power. So, whilst Jiqian was exploiting Song-Liao hostilities to carve out a space for his ambitions in the west, Song tried to leverage Jipeng to check and undermine Jiqian by re-appointing the elder cousin as the *Dingnan Jiedushi* in the First Year of Duangong (988 AD), with a new imperial name of Zhao Baozhong, to prepare for a campaign against Jiqian. Jipeng, however, compliant overtly but, considerate of his own interests covertly, wavered in his thoughts and oscillated back and forth between the two sides. Furthermore, Liao again crowned Jiqian as King of Xia, pressing him to launch an offensive against Song.

Amongst all Chinese dynasties, Song is known for its suboptimal military power. The inadequacy of its army was aggravated by the lack of prudent command. These are the reasons that there are many more losses than victories in Song's war records. In the Third Year of Zhidao (997 AD), Li Jiqian forced the Song Dynasty to recognise his status as *Dingnan Jiedushi* based in Xiazhou. All the five prefectures were recovered to Dangxiang rule.

Li Jiqian then set his eyes on Lingzhou, modern-day Wuzhong, as his new strategic focus. Through repeated interceptions of Song deliveries of supplies and munitions, he reduced the prefecture to isolation. By this time, years of attrition had witnessed the rise and fall of Li Jiqian's fortune. His Dangxiang regime finally emerged from a succession of surrenders and revolts, and proved itself a major threat to the Song Dynasty. After another disappointing campaign five contingents strong, Song officials sank into a quagmire of hesitations and debates over the cost of giving up Lingzhou. Those who opposed the abandonment considered the prefecture "a strategic location for herding, farming and campaigning," a barrier against barbarians from across the borders. Indeed, as the Central Plains' gateway to purchase horses from the Hexi areas, Lingzhou was important for not only military but also economic reasons.[12]

In the Third Year of Xianping (1000), Li Jiqian again seized grains and provisions from a Song division, and besieged Lingzhou with a cavalry force of 50,000 in the following year. With key outposts and strategic locations occupied, he ordered soldiers to cultivate more fertile lands around the outskirt of the city, showing determination for a long-term siege. As large towns near Lingzhou fell to Jiqian one after another, the lifeline between Lingzhou and the rest of the Song Empire was cut off completely. It was only a matter of time before the entire city collapsed. In the spring of the Fifth Year (1002 AD), Jiqian concentrated his picked troops in a swift assault on Lingzhou. Prefect Pei Ji, desperate for aid, fell together with the wall.

After capturing Lingzhou, Jiqian immediately reported the victory to Liao. For the first time, there was a large, central city within Tangut territory. The next year, he renamed the Ling prefecture 'Xipingfu,' transforming it into a new centre of Dangxiang rule. This is followed by the capture of Xiliangfu, in present-day Wuwei, Gansu.

Immediately after the victory at Lingzhou, the coupled effect of political instability and a severe draught convinced Li Jiqian of the importance of agriculture in consolidating Tangut power. For a long-term politico-economic policy, he promoted water conservation and irrigation projects in support of agricultural production.

Just as the Dangxiang leader's ambition grew in the flames of two conquered imperial cities, the Tibetan chief Pan Luozhi, who recently received a commission from Song in the Sixth Year of Xianping (1002 AD), devised a stratagem against the Tanguts. In a feigned surrender, he surprised the Dangxiang army in a sudden attack, leaving Li Jiqian fatally wounded. As a result, Song's emergent threat from the northwest was temporarily alleviated. In the ninth month of the same year, the Khitans sent a massive army against Song, but meeting tenacious resistance, they settled for peace in the famous 'Chanyuan Treaty.' Song thus gained relief in both the Midwest and most of the North within the same year. This relative stability laid the foundation for a period of successful development.

After Li Jiqian died in battle, his son Li Deming succeeded the kingship. In a general state of amity between Liao and Song, he continued the Pro-Khitan

12 *Zizhi Tongjian* Book 44. Second Year of Xianping in Zhenzong's Reign (999), Sixth Month, Wuwu.

policy of his father, but also tried to amend ties with the Song Dynasty, resulting in rather cordial diplomatic relations between the two regimes. The Song emperor honoured Deming as the *Dingnan Jiedushi* and King of Xiping, in addition to annual gifts of silver, silk, and tea: the imperial award bestowed reached as much as 40,000 in silver, cloth, and coins, as well as 20,000 *jin* of tea leaves. A further testament to the bilateral friendship was the establishment of trading markets in *Bao'an jun*, an area in modern-day Zhidan county of Shaanxi province. The Song empire traded economic benefits in return for quietness on the western front, whilst the Tanguts further secured and strengthened their power.

The Deming regime, rather isolated on the periphery of trade and production hubs in the Central Plains, still fell short of a well-rounded economy. Indeed, it still remained in need of exchanges, subsidies, and complements from the Song Dynasty. Through markets established along the frontiers, the Tanguts were able to trade a wide array of livestock and other local produces for goods such as silk and handicraft merchandises:

> Since the Fourth Year of Jingde, Western Xia trading markets are set up in *Bao'an jun*, where silk clothes and fabrics are exchanged for camels and horses, cattle and sheep, jade, fur-felt carpets, and *gancao* herbs; perfume and spices, porcelains and lacquerwares, ginger and cinnamon, etc. are traded for *mila* amber, *sheqi* musk, fur and hemp shirts, goat-antelope horns, the mineral *sal ammoniac*, bupleurum herbs, cistanche, safflower, and plume. Those outside the official markets are free to trade with each other, and so are those paying tributes in the imperial capital allowed to trade their goods.[13]

Given the many and mutual economic benefits of commerce, there also arose private initiatives of cross-border trade. Song officials in those prefectures reported these incidents to the emperor, who nonetheless showed a spirit of magnanimity and reconciliation:

> The Hedong border-pacification commission (*Yuanbian Anfusi*) reports: "Civilians in the Prefectures of Lin and Fu engage in frequent transactions of goods on their own initiatives and set up unauthorised markets near the borders of Xia prefecture. It is hereby hoped that the Imperial Majesty grants a permission to arrest the miscreants, and to establish a system of prize and punishment in order to dissuade them from further

13 *History of Song*. Book 186, Eighth Chapter on Food and Goods, On Mutual Trade.

> pursuing such activities." The emperor replies, "I have heard that the roads in yonder lands are rugged and hazardous. As for those who trade amongst themselves, so long as the quantity is not large, it is sufficient to apply the previous edict, with an additional, reasonable amount of alert and attention into this matter."[14]

Deming's territory covers stretches of lakes and lands teeming with the famed 'dark and white salt' (*qingbaiyan*). Both of high quality and at low prices, Tangut salt threatens the sales and profits of Xiechi salt (Yuncheng, Shanxi) in the Song Dynasty. Whether to tighten or to relax imperial sanctions against Tangut salt was the subject of numerous debates within the Song court.[15] It was also true that sometimes, Deming's envoy tasked with paying tributes visited Song cities to purchase contraband goods and weapons to make up for his own needs.[16]

When natural disasters befell the Tanguts, Deming requested a large sum of grains for famine alleviation, both out of economic concerns and intention to force the Song emperor into a difficult decision. Wang Dan, then premier of Song, offered his counsel:

> Zhao Deming once requested grains in the number of millions under the pretext of a famine. The emperor circulated the memorial to the officials. All are enraged, "Deming has just agreed to his share of the treaty, and now he breaks his oath by such an outrageous request. We humbly entreat Your Majesty to issue an edict to scold him." Wang Dan alone remains silent. The emperor asks him, "What then is your opinion?" Dan replies, "It is my wish that an edict be issued to Deming, saying that in such a crisis of famine on your territories, the imperial court which always pacifies and defends faraway lands would as a matter of course grant aids to those in need. And yet, since grains stored in border cities as provisions for the army are the source on which too many imperial guards depend, they cannot be easily appropriated for other purposes. Therefore, the Emperor has demanded that the three main Bureaus hoard grain, in the number of a million, in the imperial capital Bianjing, and that Deming dispatch his own men to come in order to fetch them." The emperor, delighted,

14 *Zizhi Tongjian*. Book 72. Second Year of Dazhong Xiangfu in Emperor Zhenzong's Reign (1009). November, Yimao.

15 *Zizhi Tongjian*, Book 73. Third Year of Dazhong Xiangfu in Emperor Zhenzong's Reign, (1010), Fifth Month, Renwu.

16 *Zizhi Tongjian*, Book 79. Fifth Year of Dazhong Xiangfu in Emperor Zhenzong's Reign (1012) Eleventh Month, Bingwu.

> adopts the advice. When Deming received the imperial edict, he paid his worship on bended knees, "There is real talent in the Imperial Court, and it is not appropriate for me to act in this manner."[17]

Over time, Deming moved his base from Lingzhou near the Song border farther north. In the Fourth Year of Tianchi in Northern Song (1020 AD), Li Deming officially designated the town of Huaiyuan by the Helan mountains as his new capital, which he then renames Xingzhou (today the city of Yinchuan, in Ningxia Hui Autonomous Region). The new 'Prefecture of Prosperity' gradually grew into the magnitude of a grand metropolis in the northwest, and the fertile land around this area formed the base and lifeline of the Tangut economy.

With the increase of his power over the years of rest and restoration, Deming shifted from his father's policy of eastward expansion into Song territories to focus instead on the western frontiers, scheming against the weaker Tibetans and Uyghurs along the Hexi corridor. In fact, Li Jiqian himself arranged an army to take over Liangzhou, an effort that was quickly lost. Deming's own campaigns against the Uyghur regime in Ganzhou was thwarted and relaunched several times without much progress. By this time, however, the Tangut kingdom had eclipsed the Uyghurs with respect to both their military and economy.

In the Sixth Year of Tiansheng (1028), Deming placed his son, Yuanhao, at the head of an army sent to once more test the strength of Ganzhou (modern-day Zhangye, Gansu). In horror and haste, the Uyghur Khan fled the city at night, handing Yuanhao an achievement which earned him the official title of the Crown Prince.

During Deming's reign in Western Xia, the Prefecture of Liang (present-day Wuwei, Gansu) came under the occupation of the Tibetans, Dangxiang, and the Uyghurs. Dispatched there in September of the First Year of Mingdao (1032), Yuanhao first lulled the Uyghurs to rest by the delusive appearance of engaging the Song army in Huanqing but then attacked Liangzhou in a sudden strike. After capturing this strategic post in the Hexi area, the Tanguts received the surrender of Guazhou (today's Guazhou county, Gansu) and Shazhou.

In this way, Dangxiang power under the leadership of Li Deming claimed the entire Hexi corridor, effectively replacing the Tibetan and Uyghur supremacies in the region. The dramatic expansion of Tangut territory not only laid the blueprint for the foundation of Western Xia but also invigorated its economy in the long run by claiming the rich and moist Hexi lands suitable for

17 *Zizhi Tongjian*. Book 68. First Year of Dazhong Xiangfu in Emperor Zhenzong's Reign (1008), First Month, Renshen.

both pasturing and harvesting.[18] Indeed, given the double-edged legacy of the Yellow River as the source of both irrigation and inundation throughout the history of imperial China, it is worth noting that the Hetao region between Ling, Xia, and other prefectures alone enjoys all benefits and little harm from the "Mother River." Naturally, this plain proved to be the lifeline of the Tangut economy. Overall, during this period, both Fan and Han populations dwelled and flourished on Tangut lands with general stability, where they produced and traded in large quantities, building an economic and military backbone for the future empire.

As king, Li Deming showed moderate ambitions. Mindful of the cost and futility of excessive military campaigns, he hoped instead to leverage Song's economy to improve Tangut livelihood. Historical archives have passed down an interesting conversation between Deming and his heir, Yuanhao:

> [Yuanhao] many times remonstrated Deming against submission to the Central Empire. Deming then admonished him, "We have been in wars for too long, which is ultimately counterproductive. In vain, we exhaust ourselves. Our tribes have for thirty years received fine silk clothes thanks to the benevolence of the divine Song emperor, a grace we shall not betray." Yuanhao replies, "To herd in fur clothes is the nature of the Fan people. The destiny for such heroes is kingly hegemony, so what use is there for fine silk?"[19]

This conversation vividly contrasts the distinct characters and ambitions of Deming and Yuanhao, as well as the different emphases in their economic policies: whereas the father aimed to invigorate trade and receive benefits from Song, the son preferred to revitalise the traditional economy based on raising livestock. Indeed, this conversation was a symbolic prelude to the eventual separation of Western Xia and its resistance against Song under Yuanhao's reign.

4 Tangut Politics and Economy in the Early Period of Western Xia

Ever mightier than before, the Western Xia after Yuanhao's succession saw ripening conditions to proclaim an independent empire. With a far-reaching vision and an unrelenting spirit of innovation, the new King enacted a series

18 *History of Song*. Book 486. "Western Xia" Part II.

19 *Zizhi Tongjian*. Book 111, First Year of Mingdao in Emperor Renzong's Reign (1032), Eleventh Month, Renchen.

of political, military, and cultural policies in preparation for the establishment of a new regime.

With respect to titles, Yuanhao replaced the Tang and Song imperial surnames of Li and Zhao with Weiming (𘟣𘝚 [ŋwe mji]), meaning 'the close family of Dangxiang.'[20] He altered his own title to 'Wuzu,' the Tangut word for 'emperor.' Regarding literacy and literature, the king ordered his reliable adviser, Yeli Renrong, to create an entirely new script to record the Tangut language. The Fan and Han Academies were established and placed in charge of printing texts in the Tangut and Chinese languages. Buddhist in faith, the Dangxiang royalty set up translation bureaus that interpreted and printed sutras.

Yuanhao's institutional reforms integrated ethnic customs with the imperial model of the Central Plains. The emperor established an elaborate bureaucracy, where officials were assorted into the Departments of Literary and Military affairs, respectively. Below the ranks of the Central Secretariat (*zhongshu*), Grand Chancellery (*zaixiang*), Council of Military Affairs (*Shu*[*mi*]*shi*), Grandees (*dafu*), Palace Commanders (*shizhong*), and Grand Commandants (*taiwei*), both Fan and Han officials held a variety of positions. The city of Xingzhou was elevated to the status of a great metropolis, Xingqingfu: The Capital of Prosperity and Festivity.

Culturally, however, Tangut customs and mores prevailed in the new empire. A new edict was passed, requiring all Dangxiang adults to shave their heads to match the Tangut hairstyle. Administrators and generals wore different costumes both on duty and in private, leaving the commoners in blue and green dress in order to distinguish the noble from the vulgar.

Yuanhao launched ambitious reforms in the military. Within the Tangut territories, the emperor established a number of military districts with their own supervisory commissions:

> [The Emperor] established twelve supervisory military districts under the commands of appointed aristocrats: 70,000 strong from the North of the Yellow River to the Wularuo mountains,[21] on guard against the Khitans; an army of around 50,000 is on duty south of the Yellow River

20 Shi, Jinbo. "Xixia Minghao Zakao" [西夏名號雜考] (Miscellaneous Studies on Tangut Titles). *Zhongyang Minzu Xueyuan Xuebao* [中央民族學院學報]: *Academic Journal of the Minzu College (University) of China*, issue 4, 1986.

21 TN: Wula or Moni mountains is a part of the Yin Mountains in present-day Inner Mongolia.

> in Hong,[22] Baibao,[23] An and Yan Prefectures,[24] Luoluo,[25] Tiandu and Weijing Mountains, on alert against Huan, Qing, Zhenrong and Yuan prefectures;[26] The left-wing Youzhou district boasts 50,000 men,[27] in defence against Lin, Yan, Lin, and Fu Prefectures;[28] The right-wing Ganzhou district deploys 30,000 men to keep a watchful eye on the Tibetans and Uyghurs; Helan is protected by a legion of 50,000 in size, Lingzhou by another force of 50,000, and finally, 70,000 more are stationed in the Xingqing city of Xingzhou. The total number amounts to more than 500,000.[29]

Yuanhao launched a series of military campaigns against Northern Song, Tibet, and the Uyghur Khanate to expand the Tangut territory. At his time, the map of Western Xia encompassed present-day Ningxia, most of Gansu province, northern Shaanxi, western Inner Mongolia, as well as vast lands in eastern Qinghai. Western Xia emerged a third major force in the game of great powers, competing on equal terms with Song and Liao empires. And although Tangut-owned lands were generally on the more barren peripheries of the Central Plains not known for the best environmental conditions, there were still plenty of arable lands for agriculture and livestock to flourish.

On the 11th day of the 10th month in the first year of Song Baoyuan (1038 AD), Yuanhao ascended the throne and claimed the heavenly mandate for imperial rule. After he officially proclaimed the founding of the Great Xia and himself as its emperor, Yuanhao submitted a public memorandum to the Song to notify

22 TN: Hongzhou (洪州) is a Tangut prefecture in an area southwest to modern-day Jingbian county, Shaanxi province.

23 TN: Baibao (白豹), a strategic fort along the Song-Xia frontier, near present-day Baibao town of Wuqi, Shaanxi.

24 TN: Anzhou and Yanzhou (安鹽州), near modern-day counties of Dingbian, Shaanxi and Yanchi, Ningxia. Two cities south of the Yellow River.

25 TN: Luoluo (羅洛), an area.

26 TN: Prefectures under Song control: Huanzhou (環州), modern-day Huan county, Gansu; Qingzhou (慶州), today's Qingyang and other parts of southern Ningxia; Zhenrong (鎮戎), the site of a major Xia victory over Song, designated as a post-war trading city, near present-day Guyuan, Ningxia; Yuanzhou (原州), today's Zhenyuan and Pingliang.

27 TN: Youzhou (宥州), in the time of Western Xia, was an area named Changze to the northwest of Xiazhou, along the modern-day border between the south of Inner Mongolia and Shaanxi province.

28 TN: Linzhou (鄜州), Shaanxi District under Song control, encompasses modern-day Ganquan, Fu and Luochuan counties; Yanzhou (延州), near Yan'an; Linzhou (麟州) and Fuzhou (府州), today's Shenmu, and Fugu counties of Shaanxi, respectively, would both be conquered and annexed by the Tanguts around 1148 AD.

29 *History of Song*. Book 485. "State of Xia" Part II.

FIGURE 8 Geography of Western Xia in the era of Northern Song

his former patron of his independence.[30] The new kingdom would stand firm in the northwest and prove a fierce rival in a two-century standoff against the empires of the Central Plains. With *de facto* imperial status along with new modes and orders modelled after the example of the celestial empire, the Tanguts effectually moved into a 'feudal' order characterised by the system of 'lordship' and 'fiefdom:' the royalty, nobility, and upper stratum of the clergy constituted the three major pillars of the ruling estates, with a vast base population composed of common peasants and herdsmen and an additional class of serfs and semi-slaves regularly traded as 'shijun' and 'nupu' in the market.[31]

30 *Zizhi Tongjian*. Book 122, First Year of Baoyuan in Emperor Renzong's Reign (1038). Tenth Year, Jiaxu.

31 Wu Tianchi, 1983, pp. 151–159; Shi, Jinbo. *Xixia Shehui* [西夏社會]: *Tangut Society* (vol. 1). Shanghai: Shanghai People's Press. Aug. 2007, pp. 211–229; Shi, Jinbo. "Heishuicheng Chutu Xixiawen Mai Renkou Qi Yanjiu" [黑水城出土西夏文賣人口契研究]: "A Study of the Tangut Contracts of Human Transaction Excavated in Khara-Khoto" in *Zhongguoshehuikexueyuan Yanjiushengyuan Xuebao* [中國社會科學院研究生院學報]: *Academic Journal of the Graduate School of the Chinese Academy of Social Sciences*, Issue 4, 2014.

At his ascension to the imperial throne, Yuanhao recognised and endorsed new modes of economic productions. With equal emphasis on herding and farming, he enacted a dual policy of maintaining traditional animal-husbandry whilst advancing agriculture. Moreover, the emperor resorted to and relied on benefits from the neighbouring Song Empire, especially to compensate for the weaknesses of the Tangut economy.

Due to its chronic dearth of grain, Western Xia cultivated its agricultural economy with care and eagerness. The Tanguts not only fully exploited the expediency of the Yellow River for the purpose of irrigation, but also took over the Qin (*qinjia*), Han (*hanyan*), and Tang (*tanglai*) canals, in addition to projects of their own. The "Canal of King Hao" (*haowangqu*), a site that remains to this day in Yinchuan, Ningxia, is reputed to have been built during Yuanhao's reign.

As one of Xia's patron states, the Liao empire often acted as the mediator between Song and Xia. However, the founding of the Tangut Empire, significant as it must have been, did not find itself into the "Annals" (*Benji*) and the "Book of Xixia" in the *History of Liao*. What is certain is that Yuanhao's coronation exacerbated an already flimsy ground for diplomatic relations between the states, adding more tension to their frigid relations. As expected, the Song Court, in a spur of fury, lashed out against Yuanhao, depriving him of titles and imposing a sanction against all cross-border markets. Announcements were posted on walls near the border, declaring anyone who captures or beheads Yuanhao to be the next Dingnan Jiedushi,[32] at which point the frozen bilateral relation dipped to its nadir. The Song government first adopted a policy of yanking exchange markets (*hushi*) and removing trading posts (*quechang*) in an attempt to choke the Tanguts into submission.

At the time of Yuanhao's revolt, the Emperor ordered the Shaanxi and Hedong to cease their trade activities and abolish the Bao'an district markets; later, military authorities in Bingbian, Shaanxi were also prohibited from exchanging with the Qiangic people. After a long period of time, Yuanhao voluntarily submitted himself again as a subject, and dispatched several emissaries to request the restoration of the markets.[33]

But before that, the begrudged Song, eager to punish the ungrateful client, and the ambitious Xia, intent on marching into the Central Plains, contended in three successive battles near Sanchuankou (to the northwest of modern-day Yan'an), Haoshuichuan (to the north of Longde county, or at the town of Xinglong in Xiji county, Ningxia), and Dingchuanzhai (to the northwest of today's Guyuan, Ningxia). In 1040 AD, the third year of Jingzong's new reign,

32 *History of Song*. Book 485. "State of Xia" Part 1.

33 *History of Song*. Book 186. Eighth Section on Food and Goods, Laws on Mutual Trade.

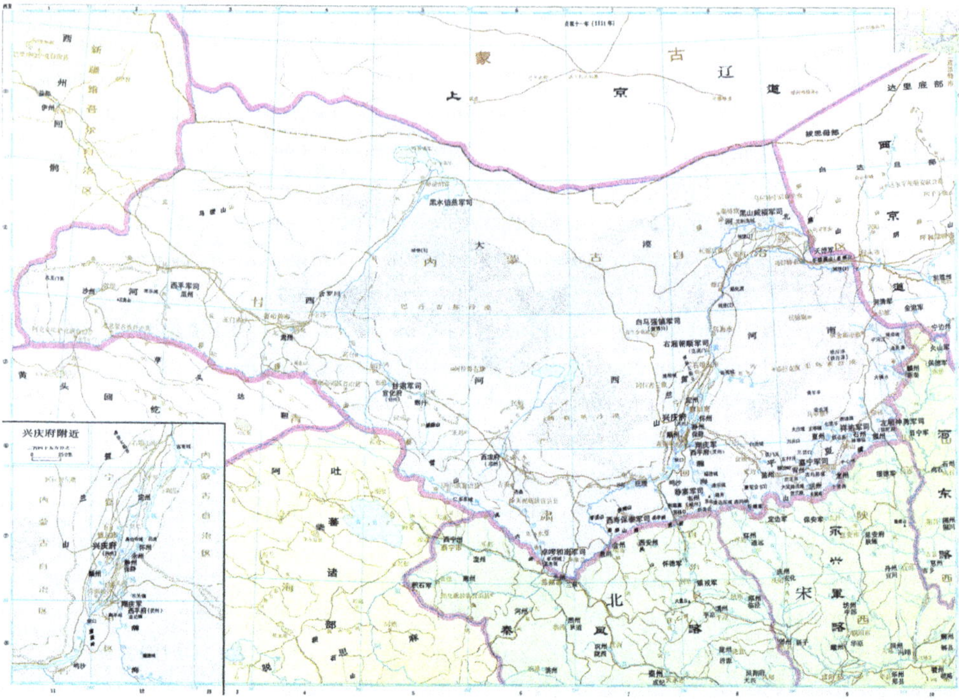

FIGURE 9 Territories of Western Xia

some of Song's most eminent generals were captured, leaving Yanzhou in a precarious condition. The next year, numerous military leaders including Ren Fu, the Song general in command of the camp, along with soldiers in the tens of thousands fell in the Battle of Haoshuichuan. The catastrophe shook Song cities in the Guanyou area—to the east of Hangu and Tong fort—and left the Renzong emperor with hardship. The next year was marked by another disaster for Song, this time in Dingchuanzhai, where Ge Huaimin, the associate general of Jingyuan district,[34] and another forty high-ranking officers died in battle, with nearly ten thousand soldiers also captured alive by the Tanguts. Pursuing the rout deep into the enemy's territory, Yuanhao's legions looted Weizhou (present-day Pingliang, Gansu), terrorising a large number of Guanfu populations into the mountains.[35] All three campaigns ended with resounding Song defeat. Ever more hubristic, Yuanhao posted public notices to the people announcing his imperial majesty's desire "to arrive myself at the Wei River, and

34 TN: Jingyuanlu (涇原路): a politico-military district under Song and Jin rule, which lasted from 1041–1142 AD. The territory included modern-day Longde, Guyuan, Jingyuan and Xiji.

35 TN: Guanfu: Guanzhong and Sanfu, refers to the area surrounding Chang'an.

march straight into Chang'an."[36] Moreover, inscription fragments unearthed in the Tangut Mausoleum provide corroborating evidence with such lines as "… could launch straight into the Central Plains."[37]

The ensuing years were punctuated by intermittent offensive and defensive moves, as well as bargains and negotiations. Wars and diplomatic contentions revealed the weaknesses of Song armies, from their overly stretched supply lines to suboptimal military leadership. Losses on the battlefield also led to repercussions in the Chinese economy, "trapping the impoverished and infirm in tax and debt."[38] The imperial exchequer, emptied over time, proved the root cause of rampant peasant rebellions, which shook the foundation of the Song Empire. The Tanguts, however, benefited less than expected from the Song-Xia wars. Farmlands lied in waste, agriculture suffered losses, tea evaporated from the market, and cattle and sheep were sold en masse at low prices to the Khitans in exchange for cash to fund the war effort. Adding to the plight of the poor peasants was the compulsory military draft, which gave rise to public complaints against the imperial policy. This is evident in the folk ballad chanted in protest of the war: *Shi Buru*, or *The Ten Ways it is Worse*.[39] A slightly subdued Yuanhao eventually agreed to come back to the negotiating table. Besides the principle issues of title and territory, most of the eleven items of memoranda raised by the Tangut envoys to the Song emperor concern economic interests. The most important ones are a proposed increase in Song's annual monetary reward to the Tanguts, an expansion of trade zones, and an additional Tangut export of 'dark and white salt' to the Central Plains.[40] Both sides reached an agreement in the fourth year of Song's Qingli reign (1044), by which "Yuanhao finally submitted himself to Song as an imperial subject, and entitled himself the king of his regime."[41] With an annual gift of 255,000 *liang*, *pi* and *jin* of silver, fine silk, and tea lavished on the Tanguts, the Song Dynasty recognised the *de facto* independent status of the Tangut Empire. This peace settlement, commonly referred to as the Qingli Treaty, proved yet another

36 Wang, Gong (Song Dynasty). *Wen Jian Jin Lu* [聞見近錄]. Beijing: Zhonghua Book Company, 1984.

37 Li, Fanwen and Museum of Ningxia (eds.). *Xixia Lingmu Chutu Canbei Suibian* [西夏陵墓出土殘碑粹編]: *Inscription Fragments Excavated in the Tangut Tombs*. Beijing: Cultural Relics Publishing House, 1984. See image 98, M108H:145.

38 TN: Fan Zhongyan, "Da Shou Zhao Tiao Chen Shi Shi" (答手詔條陳十事): "Statement of Ten Affairs in Response to the Emperor's Hand-written Edict."

39 *History of Song*. Book 486. "State of Xia" Part 1.

40 *Zizhi Tongjian*. Book 163. Eighth Year of Qingli in Emperor Renzong's Reign (1048). Second Month, Xinhai. History of Song, Book 330. "Biography of Renzhuan."

41 *Zizhi Tongjian*. Book 149. Fourth Year of Qingli in Emperor Renzong's Reign (1044). Fifth Month, Jiashen.

monumental diplomatic feat some 40 years after the Liao-Song Chanyuan Treaty of 1005 AD. Thereafter, the extended Song-Xia frontiers finally breathed the air of peace, and in the midst of recuperated bilateral relations, flourished in trade at least for a period of time. Two years after the treaty was signed, Song and Xia reached the decision to re-establish trade posts out of their own economic interests and considerations.

> In the sixth year of Qingli, trade markets were restored in the two districts of Bao'an and Zhenrong. Since there was a lack of pasture land for horses and sheep driven to the area near the markets, an additional trade post was established at the Shunning fort.[42]

Historically, Tangut rulers placed great emphasis on economic production within their realm. With a solid base of the livestock industry, the Tanguts profited mainly from exporting extra animal products to Song merchants in the trade markets. The Song Dynasty, on the other hand, relied heavily on Tangut horses and sheep, to the point that the court would designate specific quotas at which local markets should import them. For example, in December of the sixth year of Renzong's Qingli reign (1046):

> In the Jiyou month, [the emperor] issued an edict, by which he orders the markets at Bao'an and Zhenrong to each exchange for 2,000 horses and to purchase 10,000 sheep.[43]

Although in name, Western Xia was a tributary state of the Khitan Liao Empire, serious conflicts emerged between the two sides over time as Yuanhao painstakingly maneuvered to pit the two other empires against each other in a strategy of self-protection. He even rallied the support of ethnic Tangut tribes living within the Khitan border, inciting them to resist the Liao order and providing them with critical aid in their rebellion. Consequently, in the thirteenth year of Chongxi (1044 AD), not long after Song and Xia reached a peace treaty, the Xingzong Emperor of Liao, Yelü Zongzhen (personal name: Zhigu) (1016–1055 AD) himself led an army 100,000 strong and divided into three legions, crossed the Yellow River, and invaded the newly founded Western Xia. In response, Yuanhao applied a mixed strategy: he deceived the enemy with feigned signs of weaknesses, fortified the walls, cleared the fields of any

---

42 *History of Song*. Book 186. Eighth Section on Food and Goods, Laws of Mutual Trade.

43 *Zizhi Tongjian*. Book 159. Sixth Year of Qingli in Emperor Renzong's Reign (1046). Twelfth Month, Jiyou.

resources, and surprised the Khitan camps with strikes at night. The Liao army suffered inestimable casualties and a complete rout. The Tanguts captured dozens of illustrious Khitan officials, including the escort-commandant (*fuma duwei*) Xiao Hudu. In a frenzied hurry, Zongzhen managed to escape the battlefield. However, as soon as Yuanhao turned the initial defeat into an ultimate victory, he pressured Liao into a peace agreement on the best terms. Because the main battle was fought in Hequ (within the modern-day city of Ordos, Inner Mongolia), it is also known as the Battle of Hequ.

Yuanhao spent almost the entirety of his life in the midst of wars. For this reason, he won a great name for himself in written history. In his late years of indulgence in pleasure, he was assassinated in a palace coup. His reign lasted for a total of 11 years. He is known as the Jingzong Emperor of Western Xia.

After the death of Yuanhao, his young son inherited the throne while literally still 'in swaddling,' at the age of only one. Western Xia at the time found itself in a precarious situation. With the emperor infantile and ineffectual, political power fell into the hands of the maternal clan. The Mozang family, with lady empress Mozang and her brother Mozang Epang in command, tended to both administrative and military affairs. The duo of the Empress and the 'imperial maternal uncle' calmed and coordinated the numerous Dangxiang tribes, amassed soldiers and trained the forces regularly in preparation for war. During this period of regency, the Tanguts embarked on a series of campaigns against both the Liao and Song with advances and setbacks on all sides.[44]

Within two years of Yuanhao's death and in the first year of Yansi Ningguo (1049 AD), Xingzong Emperor of Liao seized the moment to dispatch three armies against Xia. The southern and middle crusades proved unavailing, whereas the northern campaign sent to the Helan mountains successfully trounced a cavalry force of three thousand led by Mozang Epang himself and thus captured the wives of Yuanhao, families of Tangut nobles, as well as a large sum of livestock.

Fully aware of the strategic and economic importance of farmlands, the imperial minister Mozang Epang launched repeated incursions into heavily cultivated agricultural zones on the other side of the border. Territorial disputes over the fertile fields of Quyehe[45] caused major rifts between the two sides, and bilateral relations steadily deteriorated. According to the *Zizhi Tongjian*:

---

44 *Zizhi Tongjian*. Book 162. Eighth Year of Qingli in Emperor Renzong's Reign (1048). First Month in the Spring, Xinwei.

45 TN: Quyehe (屈野河), historically known as a fertile territory near present-day Shenmu, Shaanxi. Its ownership was the cause of much dispute within Song and between Song and Xia.

> The Regulatory Commission (*jingluesi*) then reported to the emperor, that the palace-attendant officer (*dianzhi*) Zhang Anshi and Jia En be appointed as special inspectors, in order to thwart [the incursion]. However, by then the enemies had occupied and cultivated the lands for an extended period of time, pretending as if the territory were their own. Furthermore, all the economic benefits of agricultural production were reaped by their chief, Mozang Epang. As a result, the invaders would resort to fighting if Anshi and others forced their case, but when the officers adopted a softer approach, they would simply refuse to leave. The Regulatory Commission repeatedly demonstrated records of past territorial boundaries and ordered the Tanguts to return the farmlands. The sister of Mozang Epang sent her confidant *Buqu* Jiayike to inspect the fields, who returned and reported [to the Empress] that the concerned territories were originally owned by the Han. [She] then ordered Epang to return, with the intention to give the encroached lands back [to their proper owners]. But it fell upon the occasion that the Empress died in a civil strife of Jiayike. And thereafter, Epang indulged even more in his misdeeds.[46]

The Song court, on its part, adopted the policy of economic sanctions to curb Tangut encroachments:

> The Regulatory Commissioner Pang Ji commented, "For the westerners (Tanguts) to trespass on Quyehe and to cultivate the fields illegally was originally the scheme of Mozang Epang. Unless the markets are closed down [in retaliation], I fear that the incursion into our interior lands shall never end. [I therefore] beseech [your Imperial Majesty] to temporarily halt the trade posts along the Shaanxi borders, in order that the Tanguts lay blame on Epang. If so, then negotiation may be again on the table within years." [The Emperor] thus issued an edict whereby he orders punishment to all in the four districts of Shaanxi who dare to engage in private trade with the westerners.[47]

46 *Zizhi Tongjian*, Book 185. Second Year of Jiayou in Emperor Renzong's Reign (1057). Second Month, Renxu.

47 *Zizhi Tongjian*, Book 185, Second year of Jiayou in Emperor Renzong's Reign (1057), Second Month, Jiaxu. See also *History of Song*. Book 186, On Food and Goods, Laws on Mutual Trade.

When at last the two sides opted for peace, they established the border line, restored the markets, and resumed trade. At that time, the Tanguts vied with the Tibetans for control over Qingtang (Xining, Qinghai), and successfully subdued the areas encompassing the cities of Xishi (Dingxi county, Gansu) and Qingtang. As a result, Tangut power extended all the way to Hezhou (today the city of Linxia, Gansu).

At the impressive age of fourteen, Liangzuo rallied support from his court officials to quell the rebellion of Mozang Epang, whose execution marked the beginning of the young emperor's sovereign rule. However, he was fatally wounded in the Fourth Year of Gonghua (1066 AD) during a siege of Song's Qingzhou. Pining away in anguish in the following year, Liangzuo ended his nineteen years of reign as the Emperor Yizong.

As the economy of Western Xia grew over time, the role of currency proved more salient in the hustles of trade activities. Ever since Deming's reign, coins had been on the list of annual imperial gifts from the Song Dynasty. Song coins were the most highly circulated currency within the territories of Western Xia. According to the author's own field research, Song coins are unearthed on a massive scale, not only along the Song-Xia frontiers in northern Shaanxi and southern Ningxia, but also in the Tangut hinterlands and even remote areas of the Hexi corridor never reached by Song power. Most of these excavations date to Northern Song, representing nearly every reign period of the dynasty. It is worth mentioning that in the discovery of depositories of coin hoards, the vast majority were Song coins, whereas Tangut mints only constituted a minority. Such a proportion further illustrates the wide circulation and employment of Song currency in Western Xia. For a while, when copper coins were temporarily placed on prohibition in Wang Anshi's economic reforms, they flooded on an even greater scale and sped into western territories of the Tanguts.[48] Although the Tanguts also regularly exchanged goods with their own currency, exactly when they minted coins is nowhere to be found in written records available today. Amongst excavations dated to the early imperial period, archaeologists have found coins with the inscription, "Treasured Coins of Divine Fortune," (*Fusheng Baoqian*) which echoes the reign title, "the legacy of the true way by divine fortune" (*Fusheng Chengdao*) in the time of Yizong (1053–1056 AD). In context, the significance of claiming a separate coinage unable to replace the Song currency was perhaps more political and economic. For the Tanguts

---

48 Su Shi. *Dongpo Quanji* [東坡全集]: *Complete Works of Su Dongpo*. Shanghai: Shanghai Ancient Books Publishing House, 1987. Book 88. *Memorial Inscription for Sir Zhang Wending* (TN: canonized name of Zhang Fangping, 1007–1091).

to mint their own coins was a symbol of imperial independence more than a spontaneous sign of economic expansion.

At the demise of Yizong, his son Bingchang inherited the throne, again at an infantile age. This time, Empress Liang and her own brother Liang Yimai assumed the highest command of the empire. They devised a policy of rapprochement with the Khitans and contended with the Song over the border towns of Suide and Luowu (to the west of modern-day Mizhi, Shaanxi), where the Tanguts erected new boundary stones to mark the border. At the time, the Tibetan Qingtang regime fell into factions. Empress Liang took the opportunity to revise her foreign policy by entertaining a new diplomatic alliance with Tibet. In the third year of Tianci Lisheng ('Divinely Endowed Prosperity of Customs': 1072 AD), the regentess married her own daughter to Lin Bibu, son of the Tibetan chief Dong Zhan.[49] With Tibetan-Tangut relations improved, the Empress imprisoned Bingchang when the sixteen-year-old young emperor assumed the throne and proceeded immediately to sue for peace with Song. Under the pretext of succouring the Tangut emperor unjustly detained, Song launched five large legions to Western Xia, none of which won a decisive battle due to ineffective command and defective coordination. The Tanguts again resorted to fortifying their strongholds and razing the field so that no provision was left to the enemies. For this reason, the Song army was unable to retain cities in preparation for further advances.

> Along the seven to eight hundred *li* of lands in the Hengshan area, in at least more than two hundred, peasants feared too much to farm. As the annual gifts ceased, trade also came to an end. Silk and cloth amongst the barbarians dwindle to little more than fifty thousand. The elderly and infirm are relocated, cattle and sheep ruined, and the total losses are innumerable.[50]

The text shows that the Song-Xia wars wreaked havoc on the economy of the Hengshan areas. Commodity prices flared up, and local residents had no choice but to leave their homeland. Then in the eighth year of Xia's Da'an reign (1081 AD), the battle of Yongle (to the west of Mizhi, Shaanxi) witnessed yet another miserable defeat of Song at the hands of the Tangut army.

49 TN: Dong Zhan (1032–1083), son of Gusiluo (997–1065), second Khotan Tsenpo of the Tibetan Tsongkha regime (997–1099).

50 Su Shi. *Dongpo Quanji*, vol. 54. "Eighteen Verses of expostulation" [奏議十八首], "Comments on the Affairs concerning the Xia People of Western Qiang on the Occasion of the Capturing of Guizhang" (因擒鬼章論西羌夏人事宜劄子).

There is no doubt, however, that decades of settled cultivation furnished Western Xia with a booming agriculture. Some areas of the Tangut empire even managed to maintain large storages of grains. The prosperity of Tangut agriculture finds its most convincing record in Song archives that document the seizure of Tangut provisions. In the eighth month of 1081, the Song general Li Xian conquered Kangu.[51]

> Our great army passed by the valley of Kangu, which Bingchang unduly refers to as the 'imperial manor.' It houses an exceedingly large storage … [I have] already dispatched my lieutenants to each lead a force to seize the grains, as well as bows and arrows for the defence of the city.[52]

In the tenth month of the same year, "In the tenth month of the year *bingyin*, the [surrendered] Fan (Tangut) official Maye Eshang and others seized more than a hundred of the westerners' (Tanguts') large and small granaries on a hill seven *li* from the town of Jingde along the western borders. The 80,000 or so *dan* of grains are transferred to the Commission of Transport and the Commission in Hedong." When Chong E captured Mizhi,[53] "he also claimed that he seized more than 19,500 *dan* of grains."[54] Indeed, as Tangut food supplies accumulated over time, the more fertile lands were able to bring relief to the more barren in events of natural disasters. In the eleventh year of Da'an (1084), for example, when Yinzhou and Xiazhou suffered severe droughts, Emperor Huizong ordered the transportation of grains from the western areas of Ganzhou and Lingzhou to the east in order to manage the crisis.[55]

In terms of coinage, archaeological finds reveal that the Tanguts minted coins inscribed in both Tangut and Chinese characters. The Tangut reads, "Treasured coins of Great Peace" (which corresponds to the Chinese *Da'an Baoqian*), and the Chinese reads, "Circulated Treasure of Great Peace" (*Da'an Tongbao*). Bingchang reigned as Emperor Huizong for a total of 18 years.

The story seems to repeat itself. Bingchang's son Qianshun assumed the throne at the age of three. His own mother, Empress Liang—the niece of

51 TN: Kangu (龕谷), a fortress south of present-day Yuzhong county, Gansu, near the city of Lanzhou.

52 *Zizhi Tongjian* Book 316, Fourth Year of Yuanfeng in Shenzong's Reign (1082), Yiwei in the Ninth Month.

53 TN: Chong E (种諤, 1017–1083), a major general of Northern Song, known for his 1081 victory in Mizhi.

54 *Zizhi Tongjian* Book 318, Fourth Year of Yuanfeng in Emperor Shenzong's Reign (1082), Bingzi & Yimao, Tenth Month.

55 Wu, *Xixia Shushi*, Ch. 27.

the elder Empress Liang—and her brother Liang Qibu—son of the aforementioned Liang Yimai—proclaimed themselves as regents. It is no surprise that the maternal clan continued the policy that favoured the Tangut-Khitan alliance. And as in the time of the elder Liangs, the imperial minister Liang Qibu arranged a marriage for his son with the family of Aligu, then chief of the Tibetans.[56] The fifth Tsenpo, Longzan,[57] arranged another marriage with the Tanguts. It may be said that towards the middle and later periods of Western Xia, Tibetan-Tangut relations improved slowly and steadily. In the tenth year of 1092 AD, the third year of Tianyou Min'an ("Divinely-blessed peace for the people") period, Empress Liang herself led 100,000 men to besiege Huanzhou for seven days without success. She then turned to the Hongde fort and suffered tremendous losses at the fierce resistance of the ethnic-Tangut Song general, Zhe Keshi.[58] When friction arose between Empress Liang and Liang Qibu, the lady ordered royal officials to arrest and execute the minister in 1094, the fiftieth year of Tianyou Min'an. Since then, she presided over both civil and military affairs of the state. Remembered as a heroine figure, Empress Liang not only held the supreme command of a formidable army but also presented herself at the front lines of the battlefield. In the seventh year of Tianyou Min'an (1096), Qianshun and his mother led an alleged army of 500,000 to the walls of Yanzhou, battered through the Jinming fort, and seized 50,000 *dan* of grains stored in the city and tens of thousands bundles of forage. Then in the first year of Yong'an (1098), she again spearheaded a campaign of supposedly 400,000 men to contest domination in Pingxia. Song and Xia armies fired missiles against each other's fortresses in a war of attrition until a strong wind blew in the unfavourable direction and disbanded the Tanguts.[59]

The empress died in the second year of Yong'an (1099), paving the way for Emperor Qianshun to finally assume official duties of the crown. Three dynasties of regency and hegemony left the Tangut elites embattled in a civil strife between the aristocracies and the maternal clans. Conflicts within the ruling class between the two camps at times translated into a struggle between Fan (Tangut) and Han (Chinese) customs. During the same time, the Tangut economy was further entangled with its surrounding neighbours. For one, the exchange of goods and cultures was booming along the Song-Xia borders.

56 TN: Aligu (1040–1096), foster son of Dong Zhan, third Khotan Tsenpo of the Tibetan Tsongkha regime.

57 TN: Longzan, son of Xibawen, fifth Tsenpo. After a rebellion of Tibetan nobilities, he succeeded Xiazheng (or Bangbiaojian) as Tsenpo in 1099 AD.

58 *Zizhi Tongjian* Book 478, Seventh Year of Yuanyou in Emperor Zhezong's Reign (1092), Tenth Month, Xinyou in the Winter.

59 *Zizhi Tongjian* Book 503, First Year of Yuanfu, Emperor Zhezong's Reign (1098), Tenth Month, Yihai in the Winter.

Whenever the Tanguts initiated military conflicts, Song always countered with various measures of economic sanctions, ranging from cutting the supply of coins to the halting of markets, which invariably affected the quotidian lives of local residents. Insofar as this is true, the efficacy of such punitive sanctions speaks to imbalances of economic productions in Western Xia, hence its reliance on the Song economy.

5 Tangut Politics and Economy in the Middle Period of Western Xia

When Qianshun assumed imperial command at the age of fifteen, Liao sent a delegation to Song to request peace on behalf of the Tanguts. Xia emissaries also arrived in the imperial capital to report public mourning for the deceased empress and to express gratitude for the Song emperor's generosity. The Tangut emperor also appointed his trusted official, Weiming Jijin, as an envoy, to explain the tyranny of the maternal clans and to apologise for border conflicts:

> Our country, your client state, has suffered misfortunes for too long. While it endured through the two tyrannies of maternal clans, and that treacherous officials usurp power regularly from the crown, the kingdom has met many dangers and atrocities. During this time, the border areas often plunged into perils, which further exacerbated our hot temper. As a result, the discord between us has run so deep, that my words of plea and argument appear insufficient. Fortunately, the vicious clan has died out, and my humble and youthful self has been able to restore justice.

The Song Emperor, on his part, also assumed a tone of reconciliation:

> It is due to the conspiracies of vicious factions, that your country has repeatedly disturbed our borders. Fortunately, you now regret the past, apologise for the harm, and restore our previous oath of alliance. Considering that all your people are also my good-natured subjects, your settlement in peace accords best with my intention. I commend your effort to correct yourselves and to turn over a new leaf. Let us follow our faithful purpose: so long as you do not violate the terms, I shall never renege my words. From now on, the annual imperial gifts shall resume.[60]

60 *Zizhi Tongjian* Book 519, Second Year of Yuanfu in Emperor Zhezong's Reign (1099), Renyin Twelfth Month; *History of Song* Book 485. "On the State of Xia" Part 1.

The new foreign policy placed equal emphasis on Tangut-Khitan ties, for after all, the Tanguts often counted on Liao deterrence, if not interventions, in its conflicts with Song. As mentioned, Liao envoys proposed a truce on behalf of the Tanguts. Qianshun followed up the friendly gesture with a proposal of marital alliance. In the third year of Zhenguan (1103), the Liao princess Cheng'an married the young Tangut emperor, an arrangement which further bonded the two peoples.

But when Cai Jing dominated Song politics, he lured the Tangut general and then supervisory commander of the right-wing Zhuoluo army, Renduo Baozhong, into defection. Tong Guan, the Hedong Jiedushi of the Song Dynasty at that time, intruded several times into Tangut territories, which caused tensions to flare again along the frontiers. In the first year of Yuande (1119), Tong Guan again forced Liu Fa, regulatory commander of Xihe, to invade Western Xia. Unable to refuse the order, Liu Fa assembled an army and marched to the Tong'an city (to the west of Yongdeng county, Gansu), where he met a combined force of infantry and cavalry at the command of Chage Langjun, brother of the Chongzong emperor of Xia. As the two armies clashed, an elite Tangut cavalry mounted the hills, blocked the Song army, and attacked from behind. In the span of an entire horrid day, many men and horses in the Song army starved and thirsted to death. Song casualties are calculated to have reached 100,000.

In the beginning of the 12th century, the Jurchens in the far north rose to establish the Jin Empire. As Liao and Jin doubly plunged into war, Western Xia first threw its weight behind its Khitan patrons. When the Liao Empire spiralled into the abyss of destruction, the Khitan emperor hurried to bestow Qianshun with an imperial title. In the sixth year of Yuande (1124), however, as it became clear that Liao was on the verge of final collapse, the Tangut emperor abandoned his old patron and submitted instead to the Jin Empire. By expanding its territories further to the northwest, the Tanguts also schemed and laboured to profit from the Jin-Liao wars. A new tripartite balance of power of Jin, Song, and Xia gradually emerged, took shape, and consolidated. At first, when Southern Song still actively sought to recover northern China, Wu Jie, then associate Commissioner of Pacification (*Xuanfushi*) of Sichuan and Shaanxi, was regularly in touch with the Tanguts to coordinate a joint campaign against the Jin Dynasty.

Emperor Qianshun appointed his half-brother Chage as the commander-in-chief, honoured him as the King of the Jin estate, and stationed him in the empire's general headquarter (*yatou*). Chage's proposal to collect elite conscripts trained in both high-range crossbows and rattan shield won the approval of the Emperor.[61]

---

61 Wu, *Xixia Shushi*, Ch. 31.

FIGURE 10 Western Xia in the era of Southern Song

The Tangut economy progressed in the reign of Chongzong. Archaeological finds show that Tangut coins *Zhenguan Baoqian* were circulated alongside the Chinese *Yuande Zhongbao* and *Yuande Tongbao*. Tangut mints increased in number. The government also undertook a project to renovate the capital city Zhongxing. According to Chinese inscriptions excavated in the Tangut Mausoleum, "Chongzong ascended the throne and ruled the world … capital Zhongxing … changed the reign title to Zhenguan, in the fourth year …"[62] Such a large project speaks to the economic prowess of the empire.

Highly reverential of literary education, Chongzong established in the first year of Zhenguan (1101) an imperial academy that hosted three hundred students and a state-sponsored bureau of civil service in support of the talented. 'State academies' had existed long ago in Chinese dynastic empires, where the highest academic institutions of the country were known as the 'School

62 Shi, Jinbo and Chen, Yuning (eds.). Centre for Tangut Studies at Ningxia University, National Library of China & Gansu-Wuliang Centre for the Compilation of Historical Manuscripts (五涼古籍整理研究中心). *Zhongguo cang Xixia Wenxian* (中國藏西夏文獻), hereafter *Chinese Collection of Tangut Manuscripts* vol. 19. Lanzhou: Gansu People's Press & Dunhuang Wenyi Press, 2005, p. 321.

of the Greatest Studies' (*Taixue*) or 'Imperial College of the State' (*Guozijian*). Both spaces were designated for the preservation and promotion of Confucian teachings. Founded in western territories under ethnic Tanguts, Western Xia's 'national' academy devoted to Sinology was by all measures a revolutionary event in the cultural history of Western Xia. Politically, it represented a policy change aimed at reordering Fan-Han relations within the bounds of the empire. Thereafter, prospective state officials prepared for civil duties by trainings in both Tangut and Chinese traditions. At the same time, it is worth noting that Qianshun did not neglect Buddhism, either. In the third year of Zhenguan (1103), he ordered the construction of a new Temple of the Recumbent Buddha in the western prefecture of Ganzhou.

Because the eastern and southern borders of Western Xia were enveloped by Jurchen territories, the Tangut-Song frontiers were barely existent. The Tanguts had no choice but to depend on the Jurchen economy for trade. At the request of the Xia emperor, Jin opened markets along the frontiers and relaxed the prohibition of iron sales to Western Xia.[63] During the twelfth year of Dading (1172), the Shizong emperor of Jin had a conversation with his minister that had lasting impact on Jurchen-Tangut trade:

> Twelfth year (of Dading), the Emperor speaks to his minister, "Xia exchanges its jewels and jade for our silk and cloth: this is to trade their useless for our useful." He thus reduced and abolished the trade markets in Bao'an and Lanzhou.[64]

However, the Tangut economy gained considerable strength over the years despite the vicissitudes of imperial geopolitics. When natural disasters ruined the crops, for example, the Tanguts relied mainly on themselves. In the tenth year of Zhenguan (1110), when large Tangut populations dispersed in exile to escape severe draughts in Guazhou and Shazhou, Chongzong ordered disaster relief from Lingzhou and Xiazhou:

> Historically, lands in prefectures such as Guazhou and Shazhou are rarely cultivated for agriculture, but are mainly used for raising livestock. Since March, there has been no rain. Till this present month, the pasture has withered away, and barren lands now stretch to hundreds of *li*. Cattle and sheep are left with nothing to feed on, and a vast number of the Tanguts are forced into exile. When the news reaches the supervisory military

63 *History of Jin*, Book 4. "Biography of Xizong Emperor."
64 *History of Jin*, Book 134, "Western Xia."

> commission, Qianshun issues an edict requiring that officials release grains from Ling and Xia prefectures to alleviate the famine.[65]

Qianshun's 54 years on the throne were passed down as the reign of Chongzong. The early phase of this reign is marked by the supreme command of the empress's regency, followed by nearly 40 years of Qianshun's own imperial rule. Although these years were not free of wars, military operations were not so frequent. Moreover, the emperor placed literature and education as his priorities, and his promotion of Chinese classical culture laid the foundation for the extensive development of Tangut Confucianism in the reign of his son Renxiao.

Renxiao's reign was marred, however, by the internal chaos in a succession of political incidents. The Khitan defect, Xiao Heda, roused an insurrection within Tangut territories. As the economy suffered losses, a severe famine plagued the empire. Rice prices skyrocketed to hundreds per *sheng*, further straining the destitute lives of the common folk. Even worse was the earthquake in capital Xingqing; the loss of human and animal lives was in the tens of thousands. In the fourth year of Daqing (1143), Renzong issued the following edict after the earthquake in Xiazhou,

> In the two prefectures, in cases where lives are lost to the earthquake, two are compensated with exemption of taxes for three years, and one with waiver of taxes for two years; the injured are exempt from taxes for two years; let collapsed houses and walls be repaired by the relevant commission.[66]

Tax exemptions alone, however, could not have reversed the dire situation of food shortage. Starvation was one of the root causes of the large-scale peasant uprising led by Duo'e. In quelling the rebellion, the maternal-clansman Ren Dejing seized political power and rose to the position of imperial minister.

Notwithstanding economic downturns and social unrests, Renxiao's reign witnessed improved means of production in both pasturing and farming. Renxiao followed his father's legacy to advocate for classical education. He promoted the system of civil examination, oversaw the revision of imperial laws by able officers, and patronised the printing of emended sutras in Buddhist temples. During this period, scholars enjoyed a high rate of publication,

65 Wu, *Xixia Shushi*, Vol. 32.
66 Wu, *Xixia Shushi*, Ch. 35.

and the cultural industry reached its greatest height in the imperial ages of Western Xia.

Renxiao's achievements lied more in the cultural sphere than in the military realm. Unobservant of the unfolding crises, Renxiao was late to check the hubris of his once trusted officer. Honoured as the king of Chu and Qin-Jin, Ren Dejing schemed to secede from Western Xia to establish an independent kingdom. With support from the Jurchens, Renxiao executed Ren and his clans, temporarily reining back a simmering calamity. The emperor then appointed the renowned scholar Wo Daochong as minister, who led the empire onto the course of recovery.

Although official archives record that the Tanguts "first established the Commission of Exchange (*Tongjijian*) to mint coins" in the tenth year of Tiansheng (1158) during Renzong's reign,[67] archaeologists have discovered Tanguts coins that date back to the second emperor Yizong, which precedes the Tiansheng period by almost a century. Evidence then points to long-time establishment of governmental institutions in charge of minting and regulating the circulation of coins. The Tangut legal codex, the *Laws of Heavenly Prosperity* (or the *Tiansheng Laws*), mentions a 'Supervisory House of Currency' which could have been another name for the Commission of Exchange.[68] Since Southern Song and Western Xia territories barely shared a border during the reign of Renzong, being cut off by the vast Jin Empire, it was impossible to obtain large quantities of Song coins. It is also worth noting that, with the Jurchen occupation of the Guanyou area and establishment of markets in Lanzhou and other cities, the Tanguts would have suffered to pay higher real prices, had they insisted on trading goods with Song currency. As a result, the Tanguts casted cash coins at a significantly larger scale. For a while, the Tangut "Tiansheng" was circulated simultaneously as the Jurchen "Zhenglong" coins. At first, the Jin emperor grudged the Tangut currency. But at the repeated entreaty of Renxiao, he at last granted permission.[69] Recent archaeological discoveries of Tangut coin hoards, some of them containing more than a hundred thousand (around 600 *jin*) of coins, reveal that Song, Jin, and Tangut coins circulated at the same time.[70] However, it is also right to point out that the Tanguts first relied on

67 *History of Song* vol. 486, *On the State of Xia*, Part II.

68 *Revised Laws of Heavenly Prosperity*. No. 5: "On the Supply of Weaponries," p. 224.

69 Wu, *Xixia Shushi*, Ch. 36.

70 Niu, Dasheng. "Yizuo Zhongyao de Xixia Qianbi Jiaocang—Neimenggu Wushenqi Taoli Jiaocang" [一座重要的西夏錢幣窖藏—內蒙古烏審旗陶利窖藏]: "An Important Tangut Coin Hoard: Depository of Tangut Coins in Uxin Banner, Inner Mongolia" in *Gansu Jinrong Qianbi Zhuanji* (甘肅金融錢幣專輯), 1989. See also, Niu, Dasheng. "Xixia

Song coins, and then depended on Jurchen cash. Therefore, the Tanguts lacked real autonomy in currency.

Although the diplomacy of Western Xia in this period was largely defined by a foreign policy of self-protection, the Tanguts fell short of faithful allies and subjects. Although nominally, the Tanguts submitted to Jin paramountcy, sending one delegation after another to proclaim friendship and alliance, Renxiao responded positively and enthusiastically to Song requests of an anti-Jurchen alliance by writing a letter featuring the gravest insults to the Jin Empire and vows to 'dutifully follow the heavenly order to combat the infidels.'[71] And yet, before the ink had barely dried, he ordered skirmishes against Song territories. Two months later, when a new Jin emperor succeeded the throne, Renxiao first attacked Jin and then pledged the most solemn oath to pronounce Jin and Xia as brotherly kingdoms. The fickle emperor's inconstant geopolitical strategy served particular interests. Although the illustrious minister Wo Daochong remained in command of administrative duties, the empire by that time had for too long neglected its defence capability. Signs of a spent force appeared increasingly evident. Renxiao remained in throne for 54 years, known as the Emperor Renzong of Xia.

6 Tangut Politics and Economy in the Late Period of Western Xia

After Renxiao's decease, the once mighty empire of Western Xia was plagued by both internal crises and external threats. In the late period of Xia, the Mongols rose as a formidable foe from the north of the Gobi Desert and repeatedly raided into Tangut territories. In the last thirty years of Western Xia, the imperial authority also weakened significantly. Five emperors ascended the throne in rapid succession: Emperor Huanzong, Chunyou ruled for 13 years; Emperor Xiangzong, Anquan, 4 years; Emperor Shenzong, Zunxu, 13 years; Emperor Xianzong, Dewang, 3 years; and Emperor Mo, Xian, for only one year. The entire length of this time was enveloped by the smokes of war amidst six Mongol invasions. Although the Mongols assailed both Tangut and Jurchen walls, Xia and Jin squandered their resources and energy in a war of attrition against each other. In the fourth year of Yingtian (1209), when capital Zhongxing fell under siege, Emperor Xiangzong finally arranged to marry his daughter away in exchange for peace and alliance with the Jurchens.

Qianbi Lunji" [西夏錢幣論集]: *Collected Essays on Tangut Coins. Ningxia Jinrong* [宁夏金融]: Ningxia Finance, Supplementary Issue, 2007.

71 Wu, *Xixia Shushi*, Ch. 36.

Both the political unrests at home and the wars abroad exacerbated the economic decline of Western Xia. According to the narrative of then imperial censor-in-chief Liang Deyi,

> The country has plunged in war for more than a decade, the fields are bleak and desolate, human lives are ruined and lost, even women and maidens know that the fate of the country is in grave peril, but the officials in the Court sing light-hearted songs, feast joyfully at night, and have nothing to say.[72]

In the second year of Qianding (1225), imperial censor-in-chief Zhang Gongfu submitted a proposal to revitalise the country in seven ways. His economic policy states the following,

> In the flames the war, human lives are reduced to destitution. In the absence of farming and weaving, wealth and resources are in dire shortage. With regard to wasteful practices in the palaces and offices, let meritorious statesmen and royal clansmen be rewarded justly so that they abandon luxury in favour of simplicity, and wait to be assigned their duties. In these ways, the grains will be sufficient, and the army will regain its strengths.[73]

The emperor himself testifies to the depletion of imperial treasury and the general paucity of resources across the empire. In an illustrated Tangut edition of the *Supreme Sovereign Sutra of Golden Light* (*Suvarṇaprabhāsa-uttamarāja-sūtra*) curated in the Institute of Cultural Relics in Xi'an, the sutra ends with the prayer of Emperor Shenzong dated to the fourth year of Guangding (1214), thirteen years prior to the fall of the empire. The text mentions that the emperor felt "as if standing on the brink of an abyss, and as if walking on a thin layer of ice," and prays that "the people and the state may enjoy peace and prosperity."

Although the late period of Western Xia proved short-lived, Tangut currency still enjoyed a steady rate of production and circulation. Excavated coins dating back to this period include the Chinese *Tianqing Yuanbao*, *Huangjian Yuanbao*, and *Guangding Yuanbao*, minted during the reigns of Huanzong, Xiangzong, and Shenzong, respectively.

When finally, Jin and Xia were on the verge of mortal danger, the two sides arranged for a détente, reaching a peace agreement in the first year of Xia's

72 Wu, *Xixia Shushi*, Ch. 41.

73 Wu, *Xixia Shushi*, Ch. 42.

Qianding (1224). By this treaty, the Tanguts and Jurchens vowed (again) to be brothers, in coordinated defence against the Mongols. The alliance, however, came only too late.

The last Mongol campaign against the Tanguts took place in 1226, when Genghis Khan himself led the army south to conquer Western Xia. With a dual strategy of launching siege operations and inciting defections, the Mongols quickly captured a number of cities and prefectures, from Khara-Khoto to Shazhou, Suzhou (present-day Jiuquan city, Gansu), Ganzhou, and Xiliangfu, effectively bringing the entire Hexi corridor under their control. By this time, vast territories of Western Xia had been lost. The Mongol army then besieged the imperial capital Zhongxing. Seeing that his fortune had come to an end, Emperor Mo, Li Xian, surrendered to the Mongols. Although Genghis Khan passed away on the eve of the final victory, the Mongols followed his will to execute the Tangut emperor. The once great power of Western Xia came to its end.

CHAPTER 2

Economic Records in the Corpus of Tangut Manuscripts

For generations, the main sources of knowledge and historical evidence on the Tangut economy were archives in the Chinese tradition, such as memorials and documents that court authorities and local officials had submitted to the Song, Liao and Jin emperors, as well as a range of literary works found in these regimes, which touch on the economic lives of the Tanguts. These materials, neither systematic nor 'primary' statistical records, are at best second-hand reports. The general lack of economic-historical sources resulted in tremendous obstacles to scholars interested in the economy of Western Xia.

Archaeology in the past century has yielded a considerable body of manuscripts dating back to the Tangut imperial period, all of which were recorded by the Tanguts themselves. Among them is the imperial law code of Xixia, which offers a wealth of information on the legal regulations of the empire's economy. Also excavated are social documents, such as household registers, accounts and contracts. These materials produced and maintained by the rulers and residents of Western Xia are authentic, reliable and worthy of historians' trust. They constitute the main corpus of primary resources, not only on the history of Tangut economic life and productions, but also on Western Xia, in general. Therefore, these sources deserve our special attention and appreciation.

1 Economic Regulations in the *Laws of Heavenly Prosperity*

The *Laws of Heavenly Prosperity*, first excavated in Khara-Khoto, is a comprehensive imperial law code compiled and revised during the reign of Emperor Renzong of Xia (1124–1193), based on existing materials from previous generations. As the fundamental legal document of the country, it set forth items of laws pertaining to the economic life.

1.1 *Compilation and Content of the* Laws of Heavenly Prosperity

The surviving copy of the legal text is the Tangut block-print edition of the work. As the majestic walls of Western Xia crumbled, the law code was also buried deep underground for as long as seven centuries. Today, it is preserved

DOI:10.1163/9789004461321_004

at the Institute of Oriental Manuscripts (IOM) in the Russian Academy of Sciences. Russian experts have conducted research on the text and translated it into Russian. In subsequent years, the original Tangut has also been translated into Chinese, supplemented with annotations and commentaries by Chinese scholars. But already in the *Russian Collection of Khara-Khoto Manuscripts* (1998), a complete and generally clear original text has been made accessible to the public.[1]

The *Laws of Heavenly Prosperity* is prefaced by a "Proclamation of Legislations," which details the historical facts about the revision, entitlement, carving and printing, imperial sanction and establishment of the laws. It bears a certain degree of resemblance to such similar Tang and Song documents as Zhangsun Wuji's 進疏律表 for the *Tang Code* and Dou Yi's 進刑統表 for the *Compendium of the Song Laws*, except that the latter two only mention the history of compilation and submission of the law code therein concerned, but nothing related to the enactment of the laws.

As suggested by the full title of the laws, the *Revised and Newly Enacted Laws of Heavenly Prosperity*, there had been laws in Western Xia prior to the birth of this monumental code. A series of references in the proclamatory preface, "with the meanings from the righteous and great laws," "by comparison between the old and new laws and orders," and "to conduct in accordance with the new law," reveal the pre-existence of laws before their eventual codification. It is further mentioned in the "Proclamation of Legislations" that 'obscurities, ambivalences and other confusions and obstacles' also demand revisions. In other words, the Tanguts amended their laws according to practical needs in order to render laws and regulations clear and consistent, and thus easier to enact and enforce. The excavation of the *New Laws* and the *New Laws of Year Hai* in Khara-Khoto alongside the *Laws of Heavenly Prosperity* shows that neither the codification nor the revision of laws was a one-time project.

The *Laws of Heavenly Prosperity* was compiled and edited by the Tangut royalty, Lord of the North and Central Secretary Weiming Dibao. A high-ranking official, he was probably the first premier of the court, but for some reason remains unspecified in Chinese archives. Amongst the editor-legislators under his directorship were up to nine affiliated officials in the Central Secretariat

1 Кычанов, Е.И. Измененный и заново утвержденный кодекс девиза царствования Небесное процветание (1149–1169). В 4-х кн. М.: Издательство «Наука», ГРВЛ, 1987–1989 (Памятники письменности Востока LXXXI, 1–4). Shi, Jinbo; Nie Hongyin; Bai Bin (eds.). *The Laws of Heavenly Prosperity*. Beijing: Science Press, 1994. Shi, Jinbo; Nie, Hongyin; Bai, Bin. *Revised Laws of Heavenly Prosperity*. Beijing: Law Press, 2000. For the original text, see also Shi, Wei and Kychanov (eds.). *Russian Collection of Khara-Khoto Manuscripts* Vol. VIII. Vol. IX, pp. 1–52.

and the Council of Military Affairs. Others included chiefs of bureaus, scholars and fellows of the imperial academy. Indeed, the project gathered the most authoritative political, cultural and literary figures of the time, and, even upon its completion, was not enacted until approved by Emperor Renzong himself.

Listed right after the authors of the "Proclamation of Legislations" are about four additional officials, imperial scholars and academicians, who joined the team not as editors but as Tangut-Chinese translators. It may be inferred from this arrangement that both Tangut and Chinese editions of the *Laws of Heavenly Prosperity* circulated in Western Xia, a fact marvellous but not strange, given that large communities of Han and Fan people in the Tangut regime would both have resorted to consulting the laws.

"Heavenly Prosperity" (Tangut: 𗼃𗗙 [ŋwər lji.j]; Chinese: 天盛), a period which lasted for 21 years, was the era-name of Emperor Renzong of Western Xia. Because no specific year or sexagenary cycle (stem-and-branch) is referred to in the *Laws of Heavenly Prosperity*, it is rather difficult to infer the exact time of its publication and enactment. But we know that the era of "Heavenly Prosperity" was about the time when the ambitious Ren Dejing entered the court, eventually divided up the country and sought his own ruin. This context of tense court politics sheds special light on possible reasons why the content of the *Laws of Heavenly Prosperity* emanates an ardent defense of imperial power. In addition to extremely harsh penalties for potentially subversive activities, the legal codex also restricts the eligibility of royal status to the Weiming clan, and stipulates that concerning office-holders at the same bureaucratic rank, the Fan (Qiangic Tanguts) always come before the Han (Chinese in the Central Plains). To the Han-ethnic Ren Dejing, these are formidable obstacles to his path of promotion and eventually, attempted usurpation. In fact, it is quite possible that the *Laws of Heavenly Prosperity* was enacted in the early years of Ren Dejing's tenure in the court, when he was still cultivating his political clout. The best we can do to pin down a specific time is to narrow it down to any point between the first year of the era (1149 AD) and the eighth year of "Heavenly Prosperity"—when Ren finally rose to the rank of Premiership. It is not rash to conclude, based on the list of legislating editors in charge of the *Laws of Heavenly Prosperity*, that the laws were the doings of the Weiming royalties: amongst the first nine titled officials, six enjoy the honour of the family name Weiming. Even in the entire crew of 19 editors, most are Dangxiang Tanguts, and not even one of them is from Ren's family. All the evidence seems to suggest that this revision was accomplished when the Tangut royalties had not yet been significantly weakened.

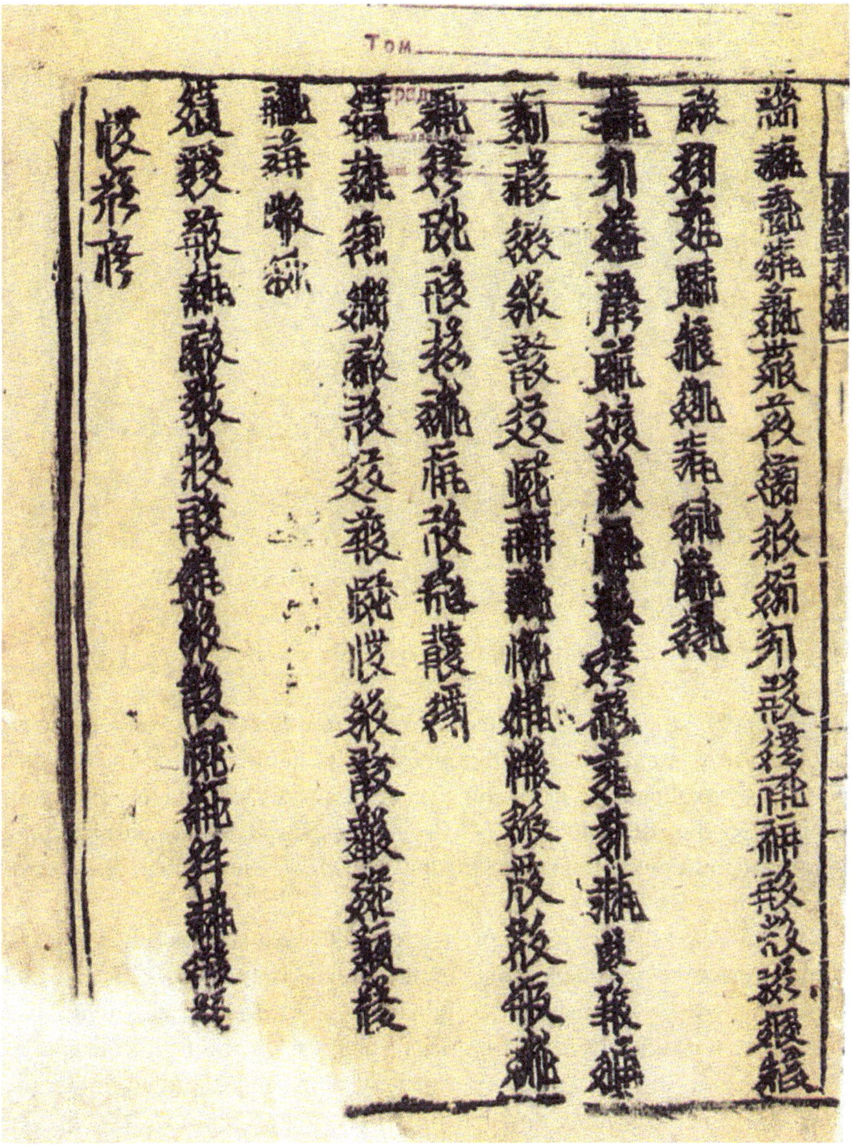

FIGURE 11 The "Proclamation of Legislations" in the *Laws of Heavenly Prosperity* (1)

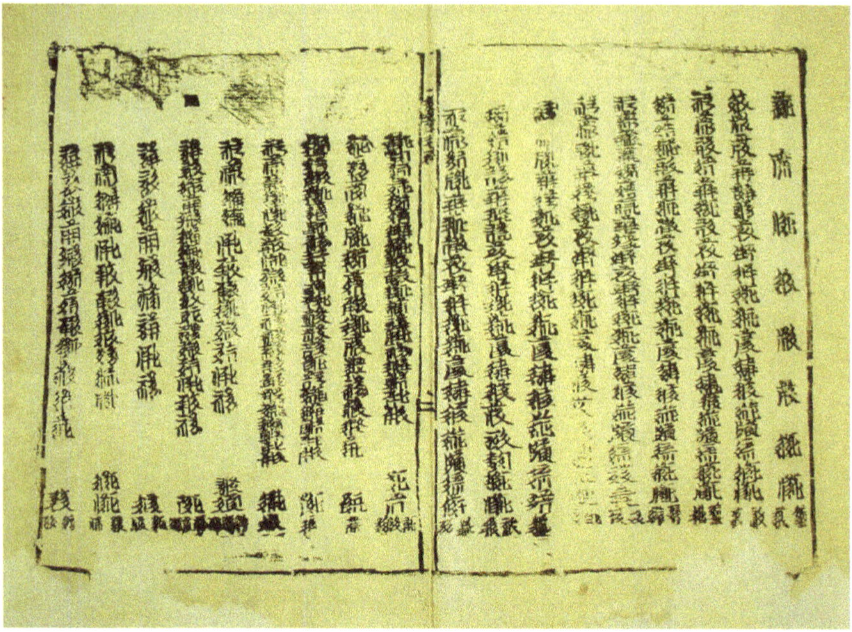

FIGURE 12 The "Proclamation of Legislations" in the *Laws of Heavenly Prosperity* (2)

There is no doubt that the Tanguts borrowed from the Chinese imperial laws, but the process was one of adaptive reception, rather than mechanical appropriation. The ruling elites of Western Xia by no means resorted to simply copying and pasting established Chinese legal codes. Instead, they considered the practical conditions of their own kingdom, and creatively enacted laws according to their needs.

The *Laws of Heavenly Prosperity* encompassed criminal laws, litigation laws, administrative laws, civil laws, economic laws and military laws. Diverse and comprehensive, it was meant to be a universal collection of all legal iterations.[2] The codex not only absorbed from legal theories based on the concepts of political loyalty and filial piety, the essential philosophies underpinning the Tang and Song legal traditions, and from the effective and enforceable "Ten

2 Shi, Jinbo. "Yibu You Tese de Lishi Fadian: Xixia Tiansheng Gaijiu Xinding *Lüling*" [一部有特色的歷史法典: 西夏天盛改舊新定律令]: "A Historical Law Code with Characteristics, the Tangut *Revised Laws of Heavenly Prosperity*" *Zhongguo Falüshi Guoji Xueshu Taolunhui Lunwenji* [中國法律史國際學術討論會論文集]: *Proceedings of the International Conference on Chinese Legal History*. Xi'an: Shaanxi People's Press, Sep. 1990; Shi, Jinbo. "Xixia Tiansheng Lüling Luelun" [西夏天盛律令略論]: "A Cursory Discussion on the Tangut *Laws of Heavenly Prosperity*" *Ningxia Shehui Kexue* [寧夏社會科學]: Ningxia Social Sciences, issue 1, 1993.

Evils,"[3] "Eight Deliberations"[4] and "Five Penalties,"[5] but also inherited a rich and rigorous legal system in criminal law and litigation from their rivals and neighbours in the Central Plains. In learning from the Chinese Empire, the Tanguts were as studious as innovative, and in this way, they even developed and enriched the Tang and Song laws.

Unlike the imperial laws of previous dynasties, which, for the most part, only detail the penalties for violations of the laws, the *Laws of Heavenly Prosperity* first expounds on what are and are not to be done, before it establishes the punishments of wrongdoings. In this regard, the Tangut law code inches closer to the form of a universal legal codex, even when compared to Tang and Song laws. On the other hand, the Tangut Empire never transcended its identity as a conventional medieval empire, for which the laws were meant to defend the imperial authority, to uphold the feudal social order and hierarchy, and as is the case in Chinese laws, to place its heaviest emphasis on traditional values of filial piety and righteousness.

The *Laws of Heavenly Prosperity* boasts its own distinctions, makes noteworthy contributions to the tradition of written law, and points to new conceptual and practical paradigms in and beyond medieval Chinese legal history. Through the lens of the *Laws of Heavenly Prosperity*, it is possible to gain a thorough understanding of the multifarious sides of the socio-economic lives of the Tangut people, and thus to further investigate the political institutions, class relations, social structures, economic systems, military organisations, religious policies and ethnic relations of this medieval Asian kingdom.

Given the paucity of Chinese primary sources on Tangut society 'in the streets' and 'on the ground,' materials in Tangut are valuable to the point of irreplaceable. Amongst all the available sources authored by the Tanguts themselves, the *Laws of Heavenly Prosperity* is the most concentrated, comprehensive and

3 TN: Or ten abominations, included Plotting Rebellion [謀反], Plotting Great Sedition [謀大逆], Plotting Treason [謀叛], Contumacy [惡逆], Depravity [不道], Great Irreverence [大不敬], Lack of Filial Piety [不孝], Discord [不睦], Unrighteousness [不義], Incest [內亂].

4 TN: In traditional Chinese criminal laws since the time of Zhou (enacted since Wei), the "Eight Deliberations" are the Deliberation for Relatives of the Emperor [議親], Deliberation for Old Retainers of the Emperor [議故], Deliberation for the Morally Worthy [議賢], Deliberation for Ability [議能], Deliberation for Achievement [議功], Deliberation for High Position [議貴], Deliberation for Diligence [議勤], Deliberation for Guests of the State [議賓]. These privileged conditions are the prerequisites for further discussions on possible commutations of sentences.

5 TN: Tattooing on the face or forehead [墨], amputation of the nose [劓] or feet [刖] (sometimes kneecap: [臏]), removal of the reproductive organs [宮] and death [大辟]; or, lashes [笞], strokes [杖], penal servitude [徒], exile [流] and death [死].

consequential. The discovery, translation and interpretation of manuscripts such as the *Laws of Heavenly Prosperity* pave new ways for historical research on Tangut society.

1.2 *Economic Regulations and Legislations in the* Laws of Heavenly Prosperity

Of the 20 volumes of the *Laws of Heavenly Prosperity*, volumes 15 to 19 concern economic laws. Volumes 15 and 16 are devoted to agriculture, with 19 categories and 132 items in total. Volume 15 alone contains more than 10,000 characters. Regrettably, the malignity of fortune leaves us hardly anything in volume 16. Contents on agriculture and land tax in Tangut laws dwarf those in Tang and Song codes. Volume 15, which concerns such matters as levying land taxes, cultivating barren lands, opening canals and applying irrigation, is detailed and exhaustive. The chapter on waterways, for instance, not only commands that 150 deputy supervisors and 'canal-officers' be sent along all the water routes from the Central Commander's Region to the county of Dingyuan, but also elaborates on how they should oversee the watercourses:

> All the heads of canals, canal-officers, canal-supervisors and junior supervisors should proceed along the waterways in their due territories, and in overseeing the watersheds, let them take caution. In case parts of the plates and water gates are unstable, let the concerning bureau repair and reinforce them. If out of negligence or carelessness, the officers do not report such problems to the local bureau, and due to the lack of renovation and consolidation, the canals break and the water is cut off, the monetary assessments of all the resulted losses of houses, either private or state-owned, sprouts in the field, stored grains, temples and roads, as well as incurred labour and other costs will be duly calculated, the sum of which will provide the basis for the judgment of the crime and due prosecution.[6]

It is followed by five further items of about 600 characters assuring the accuracy and the standards of credit and oversight for these officials. Such detailed accounts of the plate and water gate are found perhaps nowhere else than the unique law code of Western Xia.

The Dangxiang Tanguts were originally a nomadic race on the steppe and did not cease their herding activities even after the founding of the empire. In addition, the Uyghurs and Tibetans within Tangut territories relied just as

6 *Revised Laws of Heavenly Prosperity* 15, p. 499.

much on animal husbandry. In the *Laws of Heavenly Prosperity*, there is considerable mentioning of stock-raising in volume 19, which is divided into 13 categories and 78 items, about 13,000 characters in total (the surviving manuscript is partly damaged). Similar topics are also found scattered in other volumes. The items and word count of this topic outnumber those in the Tang laws by five and ten times, respectively. Such descriptions are also richer and more diverse than in the *Tang Code*. In fact, it is still possible to learn everything about how to care for animals giving births, and to reward and punish the personnel in charge:

> The youngsters of the Four Herds should be counted in the prescribed manner, and the actual number should be registered. If there is a gap, then ask the people concerned to compensate for it. Each year, let the extras be given to the herdsmen. When the babies die, do not cancel the record. Do not give the foals to the stallions, but to the mares.
>
> A hundred adult female camels are expected to produce thirty youngsters, and this should be checked by a *Yingneng* magistrate on the first day of April. Let a magistrate examine it and an official confirm it, and register it as newly obtained and collectively produced. Sixty youngsters are expected for two years, and the number should be met accordingly. The foals on the record should be registered in order.
>
> A hundred mares are expected to give birth to fifty foals per year.
> A hundred cows are expected to give birth to sixty calves.
> A hundred ewes are expected to give birth to sixty lambs.
>
> Yaks roam the Yanzhi and Helan mountains. The Yanzhi mountains offer excellent earth thanks to the yaks. Each year, five calves are expected from ten yaks. When deaths are compensated, real yaks should be repaid. As for the number of yaks in the Helan mountains, each year around the time of July and August, let someone honest and reliable from the imperial household be sent to examine it. Register all matured calves in the record. When there are deaths, repay by calves. In case of any violation of the law, for instance, should the yak-examiner not fulfil this duty according to the prescribed time, all concerned Senior Officials (*daren*), Order-bearers (*chengzhi*), Administrators (*du'an*), Clerks (*antou*), agents (*sili*) and other functionaries with titles should yield a horse as a way of punishment. For commoners, thirteen strokes await. If the yak-examiner purposefully conceals the number of calves, or if the examiner and the

> herdsmen are bribed, then an analogy to the crimes of corruption and theft is applied. In severe cases, the criminals are tried. If there is neither bribery nor ignorance, let the examiner not be sentenced, but the herdsmen punished as if in cases of theft.[7]

The "Four Herds" refer to horses, camels, cows and sheep. *Yingneng* is the title of a low-ranking official. In these items, the expected number of youngsters is properly distinguished for each animal, and the law devoted a specific passage to the examination of yak calves in Yanzhi and Helan mountains.

The *Laws of Heavenly Prosperity* focuses on the regulation and maintenance of storage in volume 17, in 7 categories and 58 items, about 14,000 in words in total (despite some loss and damage). The sheer number of storage laws here are more than 10 times the number in the *Tang Code*. For example, concerning transfers between different storage departments, there are specific rules about the number of agents and office employees, overseers (monitors) and cashiers to be dispatched by each storage house, as well as the proper procedures for local tax-collecting agencies to report taxes to the three main bureaus:

> All the taxes and alcohol taxes on each day are collected to the treasury in capital Zhongxing at night; land taxes from the five prefectures are collected once per month. Such information is to be reported to the three bureaus, and should be regulated according to another law of supervision.[8]

The chapter on the delivery of supplies details the procedures, management and registration of the retrievals and expenditures of supplies from the storages:

> All the officials in charge of the storages, their paid, distributed and slaughtered livestock, and grain of government ownership, the receipts of such incomes and expenditures should be urged at speed by the personnel of the storages. From the day of the reception of government-owned livestock and grain, receipts should be available within ten days. The bureaus in charge of the storages should make the calculation, and are prohibited from soliciting briberies. If any violation of the law is discovered, or if the bureau's officials do not urge the people, or if they do not issue the due receipts, or if they solicit bribes, delay the time, and in this

7 *Revised Laws of Heavenly Prosperity* 19, pp. 576–577.

8 *Revised Laws of Heavenly Prosperity* 17, p. 529. Some revisions have been applied to the original text.

> way, exceed the time limit, the concerned administrators (*du'an*), clerks (*antou*), and agents (*sili*), overseer of room and board, head of the storage and the cashiers will be duly prosecuted for their delay and negligence of public affairs. Those who furthermore accepted briberies will be prosecuted on the charge of corruption, which will then be compared to the charge of delay and negligence of public affairs, and whichever is more severe will be the charge to be applied.[9]

There is also a section on urgent necessities and those prohibited from governmental purchase, which clarifies the procedures of purchasing items for governmental use and regulations of their supplies and transactions:

> In case each bureau should dispatch men to purchase diverse products, miscellaneous properties and such things as peat, as well as temporary needs for livestock and produce, the transaction could only take place if both parties are willing. It is strictly prohibited to purchase by force. Should such an instance occur, the senior officials (*daren*), order-bearers (*chengzhi*), administrators (*du'an*), clerks (*antou*), and the other employees in political office will be prosecuted on the charge of forced transaction: the price at which the officials forcefully bought the products will be compared to the original price, to calculate the loss incurred to the seller. Then the concerned individual should be sentenced to at least one year in prison. If, moreover, an official should flaunt his political power to commit fraud in a forced transaction, such as to appropriate for private use or to lower the price of the products and thus incur loss to the owner of the properties, the crime will be deemed to be one level below that of theft. If out of personal greed the official consumes it in private, even though he allegedly purchased it for the public and thus lowered the price, the gap will be calculated, and he will be prosecuted on a charge one level further below that of appropriation for private use.[10]

The section on the transmission and departure of stored properties sets the procedures and times for the director of the storage to transfer and examine such products as grains, gold, silver, bronze, threads, coins, paper, vases, grass, oil, alcohol, medicine, linen, butter, coal, thick and thin liquor ferments, rush used as lamp wick and raw silk. It records the precise amounts of these supplies to be consumed, to the extent that it lists more than 200 names of

9 *Revised Laws of Heavenly Prosperity* 17, p. 536.
10 *Revised Laws of Heavenly Prosperity* 17, p. 540.

herbal medicine in its discussion on the consumption of raw medicine.[11] That a 'national,' imperial legal code contains such meticulous details demonstrates the fullness and thoroughness of the Tangut code, and the Tanguts' attachment of great importance to the regulation of its own economy. Historians also derive from these primary sources the major goods and necessities, and the state of the manufacturing industry in the Tangut Empire. The laws are also instrumental to the general study of Tangut society.

In the same category was found a list of rules for government-regulated pawning:

> In government-owned pawnshops, properties are allowed to be pawned only if the capital and the interest are calculated to be cancelled out. Nothing should be pawned without such careful calculation. If there is any violation of the laws, the concerned individuals will be condemned on the charge of corruption and violation of law. Among those who have not accepted bribery, officials should yield a horse as punishment, while commoners should receive thirteen strokes. The gap between the capital and the interest should be repaid by the owner of the pawnshop. Should the junior overseers of the shop and other great officials including the premier use their political power to force the transaction, to not consider the capital and the interest of the government-owned pawnshop, or to pawn only because of wealth; also let the concerned individual forcing the pawning repay the capital, and be prosecuted according to the prescribed law.[12]

To the legal issues of debt, market transactions and transaction taxes, the Song lawmakers devoted about 13 items in volume 26 in the *Compendium of Song Laws*, whereas in the Tangut *Laws of Heavenly Prosperity* the entire volume 18 is devoted to business transaction and taxes, divided into 9 categories and 56 items. They encompass a wide range of topics, including sales taxes, shipping, liquor ferments, salt pond, dispatch of overseers (monitors), and lowering taxes for foreign trade. One example is an account of the 12 levels of fines for unlicensed productions of liquor ferments, varied according to the monetary values of the ferments produced. First-degree crimes in ferment-production even leads to the sentence of imprisonment for life:

---

11 *Revised Laws of Heavenly Prosperity* 17, pp. 547–556.

12 *Revised Laws of Heavenly Prosperity* 17, p. 542.

All men are prohibited from producing liquor ferment in secret. If a violation of the law is uncovered, let the total of ferments produced be weighed. Within a thread of ferments, the principal offender deserves thirteen strokes, and the accomplices ten strokes; between one to two threads, the principle criminal is to be sentenced to prison for six months, the accomplices three months; between two to four threads, the prime culprit will be imprisoned for a year, and the accomplices six months; between four to six threads, the principle will be imprisoned for two years, and the accomplices one year; between six to eight threads, the principle will be imprisoned for three years, and the accomplices two years; between eight to ten threads, the principle will be sentenced to four years, and the accomplices three years; between ten to twelve threads, the principle will be sentenced to five years, the accomplices four years; between twelve to fourteen threads, the principle will be sentenced to six years, and the accomplices five years; between fourteen and sixteen threads, the principle will be sentenced to eight years, and the accomplices six years. Between sixteen and eighteen threads, the principle will be sentenced to ten years, and the accomplices eight years; between eighteen and twenty threads, the principle will be sentenced to twelve years, and the accomplices ten years. Above the quantity of twenty threads, all the principle criminals who intended the production will be imprisoned for life, and the accomplices for twelve years. If the buyer was aware of the illegality of the transaction, then his guilt is one level lower than that of the accomplice. If the buyer is ignorant, then let no charge be brought against him. To those who report the name of an offender, let there be reward: five threads are rewarded to the reporter of a crime in the range from punishment by strokes to six months of imprisonment; ten threads rewarded for the level of one year of imprisonment; twenty threads rewarded for the level of two years of imprisonment; thirty threads rewarded to the level of three years of imprisonment; forty threads rewarded to the level of four years of imprisonment; fifty threads rewarded to the level of five years of imprisonment; sixty threads rewarded to the level of six years of imprisonment; seventy threads rewarded to the level of eight years of imprisonment; eighty threads rewarded to the level of ten years of imprisonment; ninety threads rewarded to the level of twelve years of imprisonment; a hundred threads rewarded to the level of life imprisonment. Let the rewards be obtained from the criminals who committed various degrees of crimes. In case a price of the liquor ferments has already been applied,

> let the price of the time be adopted for calculation, and let them be confiscated to the palace.[13]

The Tangut Empire was a main exporter of salt, one of the most critical components of its trade and economy. It is therefore no surprise that this volume painstakingly details the prices and taxes of salt:

> Concerning all salt dealers, the salt from the *Wu* Pond should be sold at the price of a hundred and fifty maces per *dou*; for salt extracted from other salt ponds, the price is a hundred maces per *dou*. Let all taxes be levied and leave no tax evaded. In case of a violation of law, the amount of taxes evaded is to be calculated, and the concerned individuals will be prosecuted on the charge of theft.[14]

Furthermore, there are as many as 22 items in the discussions on pawning and pursuit of debt and interest in the third volume. Here is a piece of legislation on pawning:

> Pawning should only occur if both parties, the owner of the property to be pawned and the pawnbroker, are perfectly voluntary. In case that the pawned property is of greater value than the loan received, it is possible to demand that the property not be sold once the principle equals the interest, provided there is a witness; in the opposite case, if the value of the pawned property is less than that of the loan, it is possible to set a date, beyond which the pawnbroker would be allowed to sell the property. The two parties may conduct such plans upon mutual agreement. In addition, if the discussed and set date is not made clear to the pawning party, and the principle and interest are equal, but the property owner does not come to reclaim his belonging, the shop owner may sell it as he wishes. If the property owner violates the law in the litigation, his punishment would be a horse if he is an official, and thirteen strokes if a commoner.[15]

But to pawn more valuable assets such as houses and lands, there are more specific laws and regulations to consider:

---

13 *Revised Laws of Heavenly Prosperity* 18, p. 564.
14 *Revised Laws of Heavenly Prosperity* 18, p. 566.
15 *Revised Laws of Heavenly Prosperity* 3, p. 186.

> There should be no confusions or disagreements between the parties about to pawn houses and lands in exchange for loans. Let them estimate the total value of the sprouts and houses in the field, see to it to be written in a signed record, and pay back once the money is in place. Moreover, if interest arises from the sum of money, and the houses and lands are returned to the owners, let the interests, and the prices of the houses, sprouts in the fields, and the fruits born be re-calculated. No extra interest should be demanded once the principle and interest should equal. If there is a delivery of interest against the law when the land and houses do not belong to the owners, officials will pay the penalty of a horse, and commoners will suffer thirteen strokes.[16]

There are also specific rules to follow when it comes to borrowing and lending, pressing your debtors for payments, and covering debt by means of labour:

> Throughout the country, concerning public loans of money and grains, the interest rate of each thread should be below five maces, that of each *gong* of grain should be below a *gong*; interests should be set voluntarily, and no further increase is allowed. If the principle equals the interest, but there is no repayment, the relevant party should report to the government to urge the debtor to pay the loan back to the creditor. If the debtor is unable to pay it, urge the ones who went along to repay the loan. If neither were those who went along able to cover the sum, let the two kinds of men's wives, daughters-in-law and unmarried daughters pawn their belongings in exchange for money, in order to pay the debt. If the ladies receive insufficient money from pawning, or if they have nothing to pawn, the current owner should pay the debt. If he is unable to, and he received the loan before he divides his meals, let his families contribute to the payment; if the debt is incurred when the meal is not divided, let him not enter the house. If neither is possible, let the borrower pay back in the form of physical labour. After the principle equals the interest, he is still not to obtain payment of debt from the interest or the grains. If there is any violation of the law, the officials are punished a horse, commoners thirteen strokes, and all the debts are to be paid on that exact same day. As for those who went along to claim the loans, they should, if they are able to, contribute to the repayment.[17]

16 *Revised Laws of Heavenly Prosperity* 3, p. 187. Revisions have been applied to the original text.

17 *Revised Laws of Heavenly Prosperity* 3, pp. 188–189.

These legislations on commercial activities are proofs of a highly advanced and well-managed economy in the Tangut Empire. It also reveals information on the situations of debt and pawning in the regime, increased regulations of transactions at home and trade from abroad, as well as tremendous influence of Chinese economic laws and of Song-Tangut trade.

To a large extent, such primary texts from the Tangut legal codex, the *Laws of Heavenly Prosperity* as presented above, are critical sources of information on Tangut society and economy. They are of paramount importance, especially because they filled the want, if not vacancy, of archival materials on the Tangut economy. But since these items were established according to legal norms, it is still necessary to consult economic documents that directly reflect social realities in order to paint a more detailed and vivid portrait of the Tangut economy.

2 Economic Documents in the Corpus of Tangut Social Documents

The social and economic documents excavated in the past century have caught the attention of academia, for these realistic and vivid sources are enough to enrich, and even to evolve studies of economic history, in general. For instance, the many social documents discovered in the Dunhuang cave made a priceless contribution to historical research on the economy of the medieval world centred around the Tang imperium. However, it is unfortunate that little progress had been made in the economic histories of Song, Liao and Jin, due to the lack of social documents as primary sources, until the excavation of the Khara-Khoto manuscripts, which helped launch Tangutology as a modern discipline. Published in the 1990s, these once hidden manuscripts have come to public light and greatly transformed Tangut studies and allied fields. The discovery and publication of social documents, in particular, gave birth to "Tangut social document studies" as a viable and productive subfield in Tangut Studies. This sizable collection of social documents added a new library of invaluable materials to a field of study long plagued by the deficiency of primary sources. As if a gift from heaven, this wealth of historical documents brought great joy to the scholars, for it is critical not only to studying Tangut society and economy, but also to gaining a more accurate understanding of the close interactions between states such as the Chinese, Khitan and Jurchen dynasties.

Barely known to the world, Tangut social documents did not always feature prominently in academic research. There were only 15 known Chinese pawning contracts before the 1990s, obtained by British archaeologist Aurel Stein. Amongst these, only 11 are still legible, of which the numbers of the pawned properties could be identified.[18] It was also known that 2 Tangut transaction and loan contracts emerged from the Khara-Khoto site. Pyotr Kuzmich Kozlov (Пётр Кузьми́ч Козло́в) brought them home, where they were studied and published by the renowned Soviet Tangutologist Evgenij Ivanovich Kychanov (Евгений Иванович Кычанов).[19] Though small in quantity, the information contained in these precious manuscripts reflects the fascinating realities of Tangut economic lives and activities. The early study and publication of these texts initiated the research on Tangut social documents. But as said previously, due to the limited types and numbers of social documents, it did not then seem likely that the path to a thorough investigation of the Tangut economy was underway.

Then came the good news. In collaboration with Russian experts on the publication of the *Russian Collection of Khara-Khoto Manuscripts* in Chinese, we found a pile of unregistered social documents at the Institute of Oriental Manuscripts (IOM) in St. Petersburg. It turns out that although Russian experts had already sorted out a group of social documents, most of which we identified in 1997 and 2000 from 110 boxes of manuscript fragments, as if sifting gold through sand, some other documents were used as sutra covers—some had their words exposed, whilst others had already fallen off. We registered and photocopied all of them, which counted up to 1,000 numbers and 1,500 pieces. Amongst them, most are written in Tangut, others in Chinese, including household and military registers, accounts, contracts, official documents and epistles. These precious primary sources outnumber even those found in the Dunhuang Grottoes. Moreover, the proportion of completely legible manuscripts is also impressive.[20]

In recent years, more Tangut and Chinese social documents have been found and stored in Khara-Khoto, Dunhuang, Wuwei, Yinchuan and the National Library of China.

---

18 Chen, Guocan. "Xixia Tianqing Diandang Canqi de Fuyuan" [西夏天慶典當殘契的復原]: "Restoration of the Remnant Pawning Contracts from the Era of the Heavenly Celebration (Tianqing)" in *Zhongguoshi Yanjiu* [中國史研究]: *Journal of Chinese Historical Studies*, issue 1, 1980. For the original, see Maspero, Henri. "Les Documents chinois de la Troisième Expédition de Sir Aurel Stein en Asie Centrale" London: Trustees of the British Museum, 1953.

19 Кычанов, Е.И. Тангутский документ 1170г. о продаже земли, "Письменные памятника Востока.Ежгодник. 1971" М., 1974, pp. 196–203. Е.И. Кычанов Тангутский документ о займе под залог из Хара-хото Письменные памятника Востока.Ежгодник. 1972, М., 1977, pp. 146–152.

20 *Russian Collection of Tangut Manuscripts*, vol. 12–14, 2006–2011.

The value of the Tangut social documents mentioned above is obvious to experts in the humanities and social sciences in general, and especially to those interested in historical social studies. They are the gateway to research on the concrete social realities of the Tangut regime. To compile, translate and study them, therefore, leads to not only progress in Tangut history but also the enrichment of historical references to the societies of Song, Liao and Jin empires, whose residents lived contemporaneously to the Tanguts. It is therefore no exaggeration that this collection was the key to the theretofore impenetrable gates of Tangut society, with which it now seems possible to create new paradigms and subfields on the increasingly fertile soil of Tangut Studies.

In this book, I try to recreate a sketch of Tangut populations, lands, taxes, commodity prices, loans, transactions, leases, exchanges and mutual supports, based on substantial translations of Tangut social documents and resources from Tangut laws and other materials. The goal is to further analyse the organisations of Tangut communities, basic units of the military, as well as agriculture, animal husbandry and manufacture, and in this way, reach a more refined perspective on the Tangut society. In the following section, I will present a brief introduction to the Khara-Khoto social documents and current research on these historical sources.

2.1 *Tangut Household Registers and Demographic Records*

Household registers and population records number to more than 110 pieces, including brief household registers, self-reported *shoushi* (records on registered residence, population, ownership of land, and taxation reported by families themselves), *liliu* (unit of distance, equivalent to the Chinese *li*) registration, and household registers of male and female populations. These materials preserve the most authentic information on the demographics in the Khara-Khoto area under Tangut rule. For example, household register Инв. No. 6342-1, as long as 300 cm, contains a brief account of nearly 30 households, including the demographics, the name of the patriarch of the house, and each family member's name, gender, age and relationship to the patriarch. These records provide us with enough data to carry out further analysis of family types, populations, male-to-female gender ratio, residence and marriage status of the Tanguts in the Khara-Khoto area, and to confirm the occurrences of Fan (Tangut)-Han (Chinese) intermarriage, polygamy, and cross-cousin marriage.[21] Also available are data on household ownerships of lands and livestock, and

21 Shi, Jinbo. "Xixia Huji Chutan: 4 Jian Xixiawen Caoshu Huji Shiyi Yanjiu" [西夏戶籍初探4 件西夏文草書戶籍譯釋研究]: "Some Initial Discussions on the Interpretation of Four Tangut Household Registers in the Cursive Script" in *Minzu Yanjiu* [民族研究]: *Ethno-National Studies*, issue 5, 2004.

with *Laws of Heavenly Prosperity* as a point of reference, we can inquire into the modes of organisation at the village level, and other matters such as the close relationship between Tangut household registers and the military *chao* system. The *Laws of Heavenly Prosperity* mandates that all families report promptly any demographic change in their houses to the government, to avoid falsities and confusions, in order to keep the "records clean, and updated every three years."[22] These documents suggest that the Tanguts had indeed formulated, established and enforced a robust institution of household registration. The discovery of these sources therefore filled the vacancy of Tangut household records and now assuredly provides the best primary sources to conduct research on Tangut family and society.

2.2 *Tangut Land Taxes*

More than 140 registers of Tangut accounts of land taxes survived, of which there are accounts of farming, grain loans, hay and forage loans, *liliu* grain loans, poll taxes, irrigation taxes, warranties for grain debt, accounts of grains owed to the government, and deficit supply accounts. Khara-Khoto Инв. No. 5949-33, 34, 35, 36 and 37, for example, are accounts of farmlands. One of the records, which measures land size by the amount of seeds sowed, records the farmlands owned by 20 households within 1 *liliu* of distance. Another example is Инв. No. 4808, an account of grain loans by *liliu*, a long roll of 255 lines—with the 6 additional fragmented lines, it would be 261 in total—stitched by 4 sections. The first and second are statistics on grain taxes; the third and fourth are accounts of grain taxes paid. All of them indicate that the Tanguts resorted to a fixed agricultural taxation system based on the amount of land owned. Historians could also infer from these data the types of grains substituted for taxes, and the ratio between barley and wheat as taxes. For instance, Инв. No. 1755-4, an account of grain taxes by household, includes both the quantities of land in *mu* and of grains, from which it is possible to calculate the land taxes in the form of grains to be 1.25 litres per *mu* in the Khara-Khoto area. Similarly, Инв. No. 4067 and 5067 are both accounts of peasants' payment of land taxes, labour and hay based on their ownership of land. Some of them even recorded the location and four borders of their land. Another booklet, Инв. No. 8372, collects statistics based on units of *liliu*. There is also Khara-Khoto Инв. No. 4991, a record of poll taxes that assembles data on the demographics and grain taxes of 59 households based on the number of family members—males, females, adults and children—in each household. This is a kind of *tributum capitis* ("capitation tax" or "head tax"). It is obvious from the data that the standard tax rate was fixed, despite gender differences, albeit with reasonable variations

22 *Revised Laws of Heavenly Prosperity* 15, p. 514.

between the adults and the underage: 3 *dou* per adult versus 1.5 *dou* per child, by all means a heavy poll tax.[23] Besides, there were also "water taxes" such as the irrigation tax record Инв. No. 1454-2V, which mentions not only the areas and due taxes of three irrigated fields, but also the specific locations of these fields. It belongs to a group of special taxes in Western Xia. The tax on water for agricultural use subtly reveals the dire situation of irrigation in Khara-Khoto.

2.3 *Tangut Accounts of Grains and Properties*

Apart from grain accounts, there were amongst the excavated manuscripts some fragmented statistical records of grains and other properties, which disclose some curious materials otherwise unfound in the aforementioned long rolls. For example, some were accounts of subsidies to soldiers in the camps. Others were records of grains assigned to local residents to transport. They add to our existing materials and point to new ways to study the Tangut society.

These documents also make records of iconic properties about which, nonetheless, we knew little in the past. For example, some texts mention the words "Fan cloth" and "Han cloth," suggesting that the Tanguts had their own textile industry before entering traditionally Han territories and continued to manufacture cloths 'with ethnic characteristics,' perhaps to complement Chinese cloths, well into the final years of the empire. This discovery corrects our previous assumption that the Tanguts had been ignorant of textile manufacture until they settled down in the northwest and learnt from their more industrially advanced Chinese neighbours.

2.4 *Tangut Commercial Documents*

Commercial documents number up to 90 registers, of which are accounts of properties sold and purchased, transaction prices, grain prices, grain loans, interest of grain loans, transaction taxes, money and properties, as well as other financial statistics.

It is now possible to work out the commodity prices in the Tangut Empire. Transaction accounts Инв. No. 1219-1, 2 and 3, for example, reveal the price of sheep; Инв. No. 3858 tells us the price of silk; Инв. No. 4696-8, an account of alcohol sales, features quite a few transaction records, from which we could infer that the price of rice wine per *dou* was roughly equivalent to that of 1.5 *dou* of barley. Nor is it impossible to compute a price directly: the remnant

23 Shi, Jinbo. "Xixia Nongye Zushui Kao—Xixiawen Nongyeshui Wenshu Yishi" [西夏農業租稅考: 西夏文農業稅文書譯釋]: "Agricultural Taxes in Western Xia: Interpretations of Tangut Documents of Agricultural Taxes" *Lishi Yanjiu* [歷史研究]: *Historical Research*, issue 1, 2005.

pages, Инв. No. 1366-6, 7, 8 and 9, record the prices of alcohol to be 250 maces per *dou*.

Other documents are accounts of sales taxes. Khara-Khoto Инв. No. 6377 tells us that the transaction tax rate of purchasing a sheep was 5%–10% of the original price, whereas that of a cow was as much as 8%.[24]

Still, others are accounts of money and grains in both Tangut and Chinese, such as Khara-Khoto Инв. No. 2851, essentially a thirty-page book, which has on its back the following grain accounts: "153 *dan*, 7 *dou*, 2 *sheng*, 8 *ge*" on the first page, "grains 50 *dan*, 1 *dou*, 3 *sheng*, 3 *ge* and a half" on the second page, "grains 175 *dan*, 1 *dou*, 6 *sheng*" on the fourth page, "584 *dan*, 1 *dou*, 9 *sheng*, 2 *ge*" on the seventh page, and "grains 529 *dan*, 2 *dou*, 1 *sheng*, 6 *ge* and a half" on the eighth page, with each item followed by more detailed comments.[25]

2.5 *Tangut Contracts*

Thus far, we have identified and preserved contracts—as many as 150 registers and 500 pieces, 200 of which are dated to specific eras. Only a handful of Tangut contracts was known in the past: 15 fragmented pawning contracts written in Chinese and 2 Tangut contracts published by Russian experts. The newly discovered batch of materials, on the other hand, are impressive not only in quantity but also in variety, including contracts of grain loans, property loans, monetary loans, land sale, transaction of human beings and livestock, land lease, employment of human and animal labour, as well as communal contracts. In any sense, the Tangut contracts are comparable, if not superior to those discovered in Dunhuang. Zhang Chuanxi, an expert on contracts, once commented on the scarcity of early Chinese contracts, "Contracts dated between Western Han and Yuan Dynasties are rare, so every single one of them is a treasure."[26] It is therefore no exaggeration that our collection of Tangut social contracts is a priceless treasure-trove.

2.5.1 Loan Contract

Contracts of grain loans feature most prominently among loan contracts, numbering up to 110 registers and 300 pieces. They contain detailed information on

24 Shi, Jinbo. "Xixia de Wujia, Maimaishui he Huobi Jiedai" [西夏的物價、買賣稅和貨幣借貸]: "Commodity Prices, Transaction Taxes and Loans in Western Xia" in *Songshi Yanjiu Lunwenji* [宋史研究論文集]: *A Collection of Papers on Song History*. Shanghai: Shanghai People Publishing House. July 2008.

25 *Russian Collection of Khara-Khoto Manuscripts* 13, pp. 120–131.

26 Zhang, Chuanxi (ed.). *Zhongguo Lidai Qiyue Huibian Kaoshi* [中國歷代契約彙編考釋]: *Studies and Interpretations of Contracts in All Chinese Dynasties*. Beijing: Peking University Press, 1995, p. 7.

the time of the loan, the names of the borrowers and the lenders, the types and quantities of the grains loaned, interest rates, expected duration and frequency of repayments in instalments, penalties of the debtor in case of default or a breaching of contract, as well as the signatures, finger stamps and numerical notations of both parties. These contracts of grain loans vary greatly in terms of their types and extensiveness. Many of them were usurious loans at unstable times. Once again, with comparative and connective reference to *Laws of Heavenly Prosperity*, we are able to analyse the terms of grain loans in Western Xia, and in this way, to refine our perceptions of the living standards, economic conditions and social inequalities at the bottom level of the Tangut society.[27]

2.5.2 Transaction Contract

Transaction contracts concern the transfers or sales of land, livestock, house, and even human beings. At least 12 land lease contracts in acceptable conditions have been found in Khara-Khoto, with all necessary information such as the amount, price, arable fields, irrigation, agricultural taxes and the four borders of the land sold. They are undoubtedly the best primary sources to consult in research on Tangut agriculture and transfer of arable land.[28]

In addition, 20 of the Khara-Khoto manuscripts were transaction records of livestock, and similar contracts were found in the city of Wuwei. All of them are dated to the late imperial ages, of which about ten remain well-preserved. They reflect the realities of the Khara-Khoto and Wuwei economies during this period, through the sales of camels, horses and cows, in light of fluctuating prices of these steeds and livestock. Other records have to do with the pawning and mortgaging of animals.[29]

Three of the Khara-Khoto contracts concern terms of agreements on the transaction of actual human beings, an accurate portrayal of this particular social reality of the Tangut Empire. They show that although the Tanguts entered what some historians still refer to as the 'feudal' age, there were still remnants of slavery, though in the moderated forms of *shijun* (acquired

---

27 Shi, Jinbo. "Xixia Liangshi Jiedai Qiyue Yanjiu" (西夏糧食借貸契約研究): "A Study of Tangut Contracts of Grain Loans" in *Zhongguoshehuikexüeyuan Xüeshu Weiyuanhui Jikan* (中國社會科學院學術委員會集刊): *A Collection of Papers by Fellows of the Chinese Academy of Social Sciences*, issue 1. Beijing: Social Sciences Academic Press, March 2005.

28 Shi, Jinbo. "Heishuicheng Chutu Xixiawen Maidiqi Yanjiu" [黑水城出土西夏文賣地契研究]: "A Study of Tangut Contracts of Land Sales Excavated in Khara-Khoto" *Lishi Yanjiu* [歷史研究]: *Historical Research*, issue 2, 2012.

29 Shi, Jinbo. "Xixiawen Maichuqi he Guchuqi Yanjiu" [西夏文賣畜契和雇畜契研究]: "A Study of Tangut Contracts of Livestock Transaction and Employment" *Zhonghua Wenshi Luncong* [中華文史論叢]: *Series on Chinese Literature and History*, issue 3, 2014 (a).

through military) and *nupu* (domestic servants) till the very end of its history. These documents tell us much about the bottom level of the Tangut social hierarchy, a kind of knowledge impossible to acquire through the reading of archives, annals and political texts.[30]

2.5.3 Land Lease Contract

The long roll registered as Khara-Khoto Инв. No. 5124 features 8 Tangut land lease contracts dated to the late Tangut period of Tianqing (1194–1206), which for the first time reveal the secrets of the living standards and conditions for ordinary Tanguts, lease and cultivation of arable land, and how religious establishments and temple authorities in Khara-Khoto encroached upon farmlands.[31]

2.5.4 Employment Contract

The labour 'employed' came either from humans or livestock. Only one single contract of human employment is still preserved intact—rare, as people say, as the hair of a phoenix and the horn of a unicorn. And this is not an exaggerated metaphor, because nothing of its kind remains of Song, Liao, and Jin, regimes contemporaneous to Western Xia. This manuscript therefore almost single-handedly fills the gaps in Chinese labour contracts of the 11th–13th centuries. Registered as Инв. No. 5949-32, this document is dated to 1219 of the Guangding era. Still legible are the time of signing, the names of the labourers employed, the employer, wage, requirements, and terms of agreements and penalties reserved for the employed, in case the contract was breached and the promise reneged. Then both parties involved in the agreement, together with the witness, gave their signatures and finger stamps. The format of this contract is therefore accurate and complete. Though admittedly a minuscule record of a specific case, this piece of contract allows us to peek into the modes and orders of Tangut agriculture. It also indicates that the Tanguts both imitated and simplified Chinese labour contracts.[32]

---

30 Shi Jinbo, 2014 (b).

31 Shi, Jinbo. "Heishuicheng Chutu Xixiawen Zudiqi Yanjiu" [黑水城出土西夏文租地契研究]: "A Study of Tangut Contracts of Land Lease Excavated in Khara-Khoto" *Wu Tianchi Jiaoshou Bainian Danchen Jinian Wenji Papers* [吳天墀教授百年誕辰紀念文集]: *Essays Dedicated to the Hundredth Year Anniversary of Professor Wu Tianchi*. Chengdu: Sichuan People's Publishing House, Nov. 2013.

32 Shi, Jinbo. "Heishuicheng Chutu Xixiawen Gugongqi Yanjiu" [黑水城出土西夏文雇工契研究]: "A Study of Tangut Contracts of Employment Excavated in Khara-Khoto" in *Zhongguo Jingjishi Yanjiu* [中國經濟史研究]: *Research in Chinese Economic History*, issue 4, 2016.

A long roll of contracts registered as Khara-Khoto Инв. No. 5124 reveals a curious phenomenon. Three contracts of livestock transaction are each followed by a contract of livestock employment—to 'employ' an animal is, basically, to rent it. We know also that the large-sized livestock concerned in the contracts had just been purchased from impoverished peasants. It is not difficult to infer from these contracts that the Pudu Temple in Khara-Khoto engaged in the sketchy business of purchasing large livestock from grain-deprived peasants at lower prices, and immediately leasing them to needy peasants at higher prices. In this back-and-forth extraction from the poor, the dealers profited enormously.[33] There were additionally some more specific contracts of livestock employment, such as Khara-Khoto Инв. No. 19-2, which concerns the temporary loan of five camels, and thus has little to do with the transaction of livestock.

2.5.5 Contracts of Exchange and Mortgage

Some contracts found in Khara-Khoto were signed by two individuals with the intention to exchange livestock, who agree that any gap in price would be filled in by the appropriate amount of grains. Contract Инв. No. 4195, for instance, uses the word "exchange" to describe the transaction of livestock, but "add" and "pay" for the supply of grains. Other contracts at times replace these expressions with "sell." Rare amongst excavated manuscripts, and much more complicated than the mere selling and purchase of livestock, this type of contract reflects the diverse economic lives of the Tanguts.

Khara-Khoto contracts Инв. No. 2996-1 and Инв. No. 4079-1 seem to suggest that farmers sometimes had to mortgage their livestock in order to obtain the desired loan of grains. Economic activities such as these, at once borrowing and mortgaging, are also more complex than regular contracts of grain loans. The two contracts demand that, if grains and interests were not paid back in full after autumn, the livestock would have to be foreclosed—taken possession as a result of the mortgagor's failure to keep up his payments. In this way, the lender is guaranteed a high level of financial security. There have been found in Khara-Khoto at least 8 pieces of contracts that both loan grains and mortgage livestock, which are still subtly different. In short, this is a diverse and precious collection of contracts.

2.5.6 Communal Contracts

Two pieces of communal contracts were found in Khara-Khoto, equivalent to the "community and neighbourhood contracts" (*sheyi*) in Dunhuang. These

33 Shi Jinbo, 2014 (a).

documents show the many ways the Tangut folks gathered, organized and supported themselves at the grassroot level. Among them is Инв. No. 5949-31, first signed in 1218. It records the rules and regulations of communal activities agreed upon, established and dutifully obeyed by all members of the societal organisation. A basic sense of equality between all involved members permeates this arrangement. The names seem to suggest that most active members were Han Chinese, though there were also participating Khitans. From the perspective of interactions between ethnic groups, these Tangut communal contracts shed a new light on Chinese communal history. It is in this broad sense that the two pieces of Tangut communal contracts are said to have filled the gap in 12th century communal records. Khara-Khoto Инв. No. 5949-31 is particularly well-preserved and of great value from the perspective of the history of books and manuscripts.[34]

2.6 *Economic Documents in Chinese*

Apart from the Tangut social documents excavated in former Tangut territories, there are also, quite expectedly, manuscripts in Chinese. Though less numerous, the Chinese documents are also varied and valuable. And to Chinese scholars such as myself, they are ready for interpretation without any major linguistic hurdles.

Of the Chinese documents, most were found by Kozlov in Khara-Khoto. Amongst them are an account of timber taxes in 1171 AD (2nd year of *Qianyou*), a loan contract dated to 1163 (15th year of *Tiansheng*), a mortgage loan contract by Linghu E dated also to 1163 (15th year of *Tiansheng*), a grain-pawning contract by Pei Songshou dated to sometime between 1194 and 1206 (*Tianqing* era), a sale contract of a bakery shop by Li Chungou and others dated to January of 1222 (12th year of *Guangding*), as well as correspondences on land sale, a land-pawning contract, a monetary loan contract, a contract of clay payment, flax, old bags and accounts of income and payment.

The British Mùseum also holds a certain number of Khara-Khoto documents thanks to donations by Stein. Amongst them are Chinese economic documents such as Pei Songshou's grain-pawning contract and accounts of hay.

Quite a few Chinese economic documents have been excavated in the north zone of the Mogao caves and are now preserved at the Dunhuang Academy. One of them is Weiming Fabaoda's land sale and grain loan contract.

---

34 Shi, Jinbo. "Heishuicheng Chutu Xixiawen Zhonghui Tiaoyüe (Shetiao) Yanjiu" [黑水城出土西夏文眾會條約(社條) 研究]: "A Study of Tangut Communal Contracts Excavated in Khara-Khoto" in *Xixiaxue* [西夏學] *Tangut Studies*, issue 10. Shanghai: Shanghai Ancient Books Publishing House, 2014 (c).

Other Chinese economic documents such as IOUs (documents acknowledging debt) have been unearthed and identified in Wuwei, along with manuscripts in Tangut, as well. Some of them are today preserved at the Museum of Gansu.

The Chinese and Tangut economic documents are best studied in comparison with each other. It is most productive to consult the content of both simultaneously in scholarly research. In doing so, we not only elevate their importance in their respective traditions, but also benefit the development of Tangutology as a field of study.

CHAPTER 3

Tangut Documents of Household Registrations

Chinese historical archives are generally short of information on Tangut social conditions such as demographics, households and families. For this reason, work on Tangut families and populations long remained virtually non-existent. Although it is true that the *Revised Laws of Heavenly Prosperity* provides generations of scholars with important legislations on Tangut households and families, as a general code of law it could not possibly offer any detail on the social realities in Western Xia. It is in this historiographical context that the more than 100 registers of households and demographic documents, though fragile and fragmented, are celebrated as a breakthrough in the field and are marvelled at for their vast number of primary materials on the demographics of Khara-Khoto.

Household registration, a tradition of more than 2,000 years, may be traced back to the Qin Dynasty, and is said to have matured under the Tang Empire. Chinese household records are oftentimes mentioned in archives but seldom preserved in physical forms. The only exceptions are the Dunhuang and Turpan household registers and self-reports (*shoushi*), our main sources of knowledge on local demographics from Western Liang to the Five Dynasties. The discoveries of these documents transformed social and economic studies on these areas, and shed light on the evolving history of household registrations over the course of six centuries.

The discovery of Tangut household registers, long unknown to historians, not only fills the gap in knowledge on Tangut household registration itself, but also revolutionizes research on the society and economy of Xia. They also serve as references for the contemporaneous Liao, Song and Jin—the studies of which all suffer a lack of material sources.

1 Household Registers and Accounts

Most of the numerous household registers and accounts from Khara-Khoto are today housed at the Institute of Oriental Studies at the Russian Academy of Sciences. Few of them are preserved at the British Museum. Most Tangut household records are written in the cursive or the running script, and are unfortunately only in fragments.

DOI:10.1163/9789004461321_005

1.1 *Household Registers*

Tangut manuscripts excavated at Khara-Khoto might not necessarily have been produced in that city. In fact, they are likely to have come from all parts of the empire. The books printed by the Bureau of Character-Carving, for example, were brought over from the capital city Zhongxing (today the city of Yinchuan in Ningxia). But the hand-written social documents—household registers, contracts, accounts, enlistment records, official documents and letters—unlikely to be highly circulated texts, were from local sites of Khara-Khoto, according to the locations indicated on the manuscripts. Инв. No. 2736, an official document by the commander of Khara-Khoto dated to 1224, Инв. No. 2775-6, an official document by the deputy commander of Khara-Khoto, Инв. No. 2851-26, and another 14 military documents (e.g., Инв. No. 7916), are all labelled "belonging to Khara-Khoto." Likewise, household records and contracts excavated in Khara-Khoto were also locally used and circulated documents.

The Tangut character for "household" is [illegible] [ɣa]. Some fragments of manuscripts seem to suggest that, at least in the city of Khara-Khoto, the Tanguts counted households by the unit of [illegible][illegible] [tśji-. rer], or *liliu*. The first character means "to move or migrate," and the second, "a line." The term is translated in Chinese as *liliu*—roughly equivalent to the Chinese *li* or *lijia*—according to its definition in *Revised Laws of Heavenly Prosperity*. *Liliu* constitutes the basic level of social organization in Western Xia. Households in Khara-Khoto registered under the category of *liliu*, reporting first the name of the patriarch, then the number of family members in the house, and finally details of their gender, age and relationship to the patriarch, or "head of the household." Инв. No. 4991-4, for example, is a fragment of a *liliu* register. The 11 lines in total, with some corrections and markings, are handwritten in the Tangut running script on a piece of hemp paper, which is 18 cm in length and 28.5 cm in width.[1]

The un-indented first line records the name of the head of the *liliu*, below which is the population size in each household, and further down, the numbers of males and females, numbers of adults and children, and at last, their own names.

Translation:[2]

---

1 *Russian Collection of Khara-Khoto Manuscripts*, vol. 13, p. 322. Lit. "*qianliu* accounts of poll tax," now translated as "*liliu* register accounts."

2 Tangut characters are written vertically, from top to bottom. In the following translation, the best approximation is to write the vertical lines horizontally, but have the format and content remain the same. The insertions of "……" represent missing lines. The squares "□" are missing characters, and the characters inside the □ are inferred from context. The shaded □ suggests that the original characters had been blotted out in the original text. "?" indicates that the character is either unclear or illegible. The same format applies to the translation of

FIGURE 13 Инв. No. 4991-4: *Liliu* household register

Liliu, [illegible] [ŋwe zjwi. śjow sjwij] administrative unit:[3]
(lit.) dark, lone man,[4] no livestock, previously, Chen?
One, household, [illegible] [dej ljo lhu khjwi-], 5 members
Males, 3 2
Adult 1, [illegible] [ljo lhu khjwi-]
Child 2 1, son

---

social documents in the rest of the book. For the sake of convenience, the English translation of Tangut names features the Chinese pinyin transcriptions of the Tangut characters, rather than the phonetic symbols designed for Tangut characters by Dr. Gong Hwang-cherng, which are found elsewhere in the book for the specific purpose of introducing phonetics. Some of the transcripts are followed by literal translations of the names in the parentheses, whose meanings are then discussed in the main body of the text.

3 Tangut, [illegible] [tśju lji.j] in the *Fan-Han Pearl in the Palm* is literally translated as "department/bureau, division." Based on its use in multiple Tangut manuscripts, the phrase means an administrative area or division. See also the *Russian Collection of Khara-Khoto Manuscripts*, vol. 10, p. 15.

4 The original character is [illegible] [lu.] (poor, impoverished) or [illegible] [mjo.] (alone, widowed). Despite morphological similarities to the left, the character as shown and used in the context of the document is best interpreted as the latter.

[lji-. we sjwij], [gju_rjur khjwi-][5]

Females 3

Adult 2

Wife, Lady [ljow] (Liang) [mja mji- wejr]

Female□□□[6]

Child 1

……

According to *Revised Laws of Heavenly Prosperity*, a *liliu* comprises nearly a hundred households.[7] The head of the *liliu* referred to in the manuscript above is called [ŋwe zjwi. śjow sjwij] (Weiyi Tieming)— (Weiyi) being a prominent Tangut surname. The mentioning of the local "administrative unit" indicates that the territories to be enumerated fall under this man's political authority. Line 2 begins with the name of a special individual in this *liliu*, the first three words being [dzjwo] (man), either [lu.] (lit. poor) or [mjo.] (alone, single, widowed)—the left part of the character resembles the former, but the latter makes more sense in this context—and [nja_] (dark, black). Put together, the name reads, "a dark, lonely man," one without livestock, possibly surnamed Chen, and, because there is no "one household" noted before his name, probably someone who has family members but not a settled house. Then follows the registration of each household. The first line starts with [lew ɣa] (one household). Unfortunately, only the information on the first household survived, whose patriarch is [dej ljo lhu khjwi-]. The man used to be in the company of six family members, but as shown on the manuscript, the number [tśhjiw] (six) was crossed out and corrected to [ŋwə] (five). One of them was supposedly, and sadly, lost to the family. Likewise, though there used to be three males, as [so.] (three) was crossed out and updated to [nji-] (two), only two of them seem to have survived. Among the men, the adult is the patriarch [dej ljo lhu khjwi-] and the child is his son. In the records on the two children, the [nji-] (two) is updated to [lew] (one), leaving Xiao Luming (lit. little bright donkey) as the

5 TN: The names of the two children literally mean, "a manifest donkey" and "a lucky dog."

6 The four characters in the 11th line all suffer the loss of their left parts. The first character seems to be the right part of [mji.j] (woman). The next three characters are a person's name. And the rest of it is lost. It is inferred from context that the next line is "child, one," followed by the name of the second daughter.

7 See the *Revised Laws of Heavenly Prosperity* 15, pp. 514–515. There it is translated as *qianliu*, now corrected to *liliu*.

only child, and the name of the second son, Ji Xiang Quan (lit. "blessed dog"), is crossed out. He possibly passed away.

There are three women: the wife of the patriarch, née Liang (maiden name), whose name is Mu Niang Sheng (lit. "prosperous mother"), and their two daughters. The elder daughter is a grown-up (only half a line remains legible), and though the rest of the piece is lost, we infer that the other daughter is still underage. Despite the damages, this register preserves the first page of the *liliu* record, offering a wealth of information on Tangut household registration.

One of the registers that records rather numerous households is Инв. No. 6342-1, a long roll of considerable width and rich in content. The register, 19.1 cm long, 312 cm wide and somewhat damaged in the front, is handwritten in the Tangut running-cursive script on a piece of hemp paper. The three-meter document is divided into two parts—117 lines in the first and 47 lines in the second—164 lines total.[8] On this precious manuscript are found the demographics of 30 households.

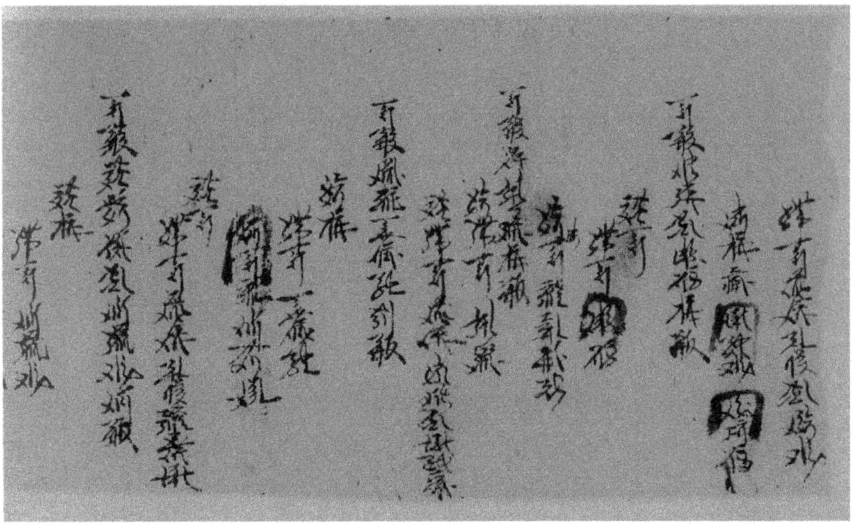

FIGURE 14 Инв. No. 6342-1: Register fragment (1)

8 *Russian Collection of Khara-Khoto Manuscripts*, vol. 14, pp. 118–123.

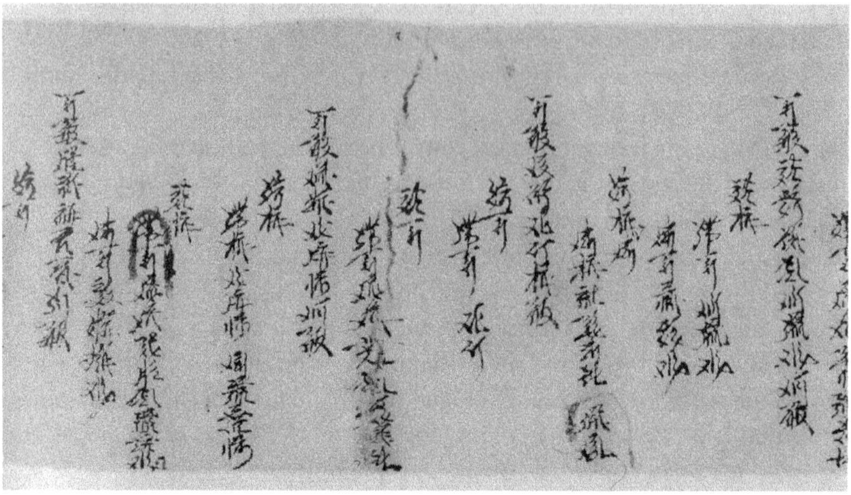

FIGURE 15 Инв. No. 6342-1: Register fragment (2)

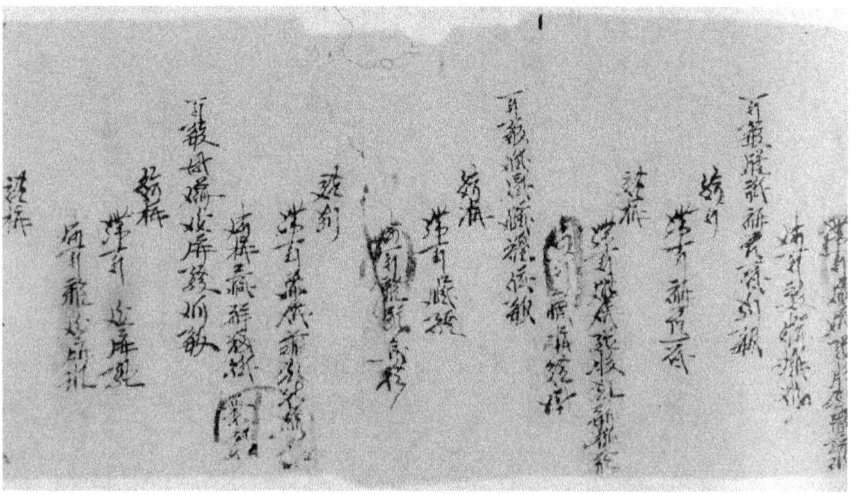

FIGURE 16 Инв. No. 6342-1: Register fragment (3)

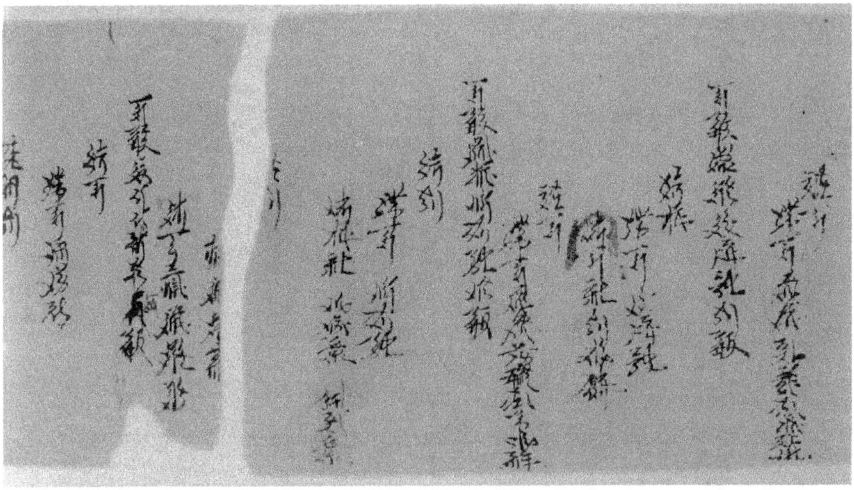

FIGURE 17 Инв. No. 6342-1: Register account (9)

Translation into English:[9]

(one household ……) (1)
  Adult, one, wife, [Tangut] [·ja xwa ne_w lji-.][10]
  Children, two, [Tangut] [mji.j mja wejr lji-.], [Tangut] [da kia swew]
One household, [Tangut] [phjij śjo ·ja swew], two members (2)
  Female, one
    Adult, one, [Tangut] [·ja swew]
  Male, child, one, son, [Tangut] [zjo. dźjo ·jiw]
One household, [Tangut] (Liang) (?)[Tangut] [ljow ne. khjwi-], 2 members (3)
  Male, adult, one, (?)[Tangut] [ne. khjwi-]
  Female, adult, one, wife [Tangut] [gjwi- dji mja wejr khjwi-]
One household, [Tangut] [lwər ze śja lhji. wejr], 3 members (4)
  Male, two
    Adult, one, [Tangut] [śja lhji. wejr]
    Child, one, son, [Tangut] [ljo dju bie_j]
  Female, one
    Adult, one, wife, [Tangut] [·ja xwa pa rya mja]

9 The numbers in the parentheses given on the first line of each household are labels added by the author.

10 TN: lit. "benevolent treasure."

One household, widow [Tangut] [·jow] (Yang) [Tangut] [·jow ljo dju lji-.],[11] four members (5)

Female, two

Adult, one, [Tangut] [ljo dju lji-.]

Child, one, daughter, [Tangut] [mju][12] [Tangut] [lji-]

Male, two, children

Children, two, sons, [Tangut] [tsja tsji- wejr],[13] [Tangut] [khjwi- bie_j][14]

One household, [Tangut] [tshja ślo_w wa gju_], 2 members (6)

Male, one

Adult, one, [Tangut] [wa gju_]

Female, one

Adult, one, wife, née Jiao ([Tangut] [tsew])???

One household, [Tangut] [lwər ze da kia śia~],[15] four members (7)

Male, two

Adult, two, [Tangut] [da kia śia~], brother [Tangut] [pa rya śia~][16]

Female, two

Adult, one, wife, née [Tangut] [·o mji_] (Emi) [Tangut] [pa rya lji-][17]

Child, one, younger sister, [Tangut] [lja nji lji-][18]

One household, [Tangut] [mə rar dow dźjij gjow], three members (8)

Male, one

Adult, one, [Tangut] [dow dźjij gjow]

Female, two

Adult, one, wife, née [Tangut] [·o mji_] (Emi) [Tangut] [wjor lhej kie.][19]

Child, one, daughter, [Tangut] [lji-.j sji bie_j][20]

---

11 TN: lit. "blessed with treasure."

12 It is a one-character word in Tangut meaning "brother" (TN: or maternal uncle) commonly used for a woman's reference to her brothers. Here, "the brother's treasure" is the name of the girl.

13 TN: lit. "sister, prosperous" (Chinese edition: "beautiful son").

14 TN: lit. "a joyful dog."

15 TN: lit. "the mountain of/by the old house," etc., depending on how one reverse-transliterates [Tangut].

16 TN: lit. "mountain of wisdom (Prajñā)."

17 TN: lit. "the wise treasure."

18 TN: lit. "treasure of auspicious sign" ([Tangut] is a fixed expression for auspicious signs and good fortune).

19 TN: lit. "nest, change, gold."

20 TN: lit. "joyful and delighted maiden."

One household, [Tangut] [ŋwe zjwi. dzju. we][21] five members (9)

  Male, two

    Adult, one, [Tangut] [dzju. we]

    Child, one, son, [Tangut] [tśjow lhji. ·jiw][22]

  Female, three

    Adult, one, wife, née [Tangut] [la] (Luo) [Tangut] [·jiw dju]

    Child, two, daughter, [Tangut] [phiow bju nja_][23]

One household, [Tangut] [mja dzow da kia wejr],[24] four members (10)

  Male, two

    Adult, one, [Tangut] [da kia wejr]

    Child, one, son, [Tangut] [da kia lji-][25]

  Female, two

    Adult, one, wife, née [Tangut] [ljow] (Liang) [Tangut] [tsja tsji- lji-][26]

    Child, one, daughter, [Tangut] [mju][27]

One household, [Tangut] [pu. śja phji], two households (11)

  Male, one

    Adult, one, [Tangut] [śja phji]

  Female, one

    Adult, one, wife, [Tangut] (name)? [lwər ze ? ka]

One household, [Tangut] [mjij pu. da kia khjwi-][28] two members (12)

  Male, one

    Adult, one, [Tangut] [da kia khjwi-]

  Female, one

    Adult, one, wife, [Tangut] [phjij śjo nio. mja kie.][29]

One household, widow, [Tangut] [xwe~] (Hun), [Tangut] [lji-. mja], three members (13)

  Female, one

    Adult, one, [Tangut] [lji-. mja]

21 TN: lit. Weiyi "the rainbird."

22 TN: lit. ? (the Year of You/the one born in ...) the first month, depending on how [Tangut] is reverse-transliterated.

23 TN: lit. "white, bright, dark."

24 TN: lit. Maze "the prosperity of the old house."

25 TN: lit. "treasure of the old house."

26 TN: lit. "sister, little, treasure."

27 TN: lit. "brother/maternal uncle of the old house."

28 TN: lit. "dog of the old house."

29 TN: lit. "sister/aunt, mother, gold."

Male, two

Child, two, son, [bə ku. lji-.],[30] [phə sa lji-.][31]

One, household, [gjwi- dji ne_w lhji. tśhjwor], three members (14)

Male, one

Adult, one, [ne_w lhji. tśhjwor][32]

Female, two

Adult, two, mother, [phiow tshji-j lja. mja]

Wife, [phiow tshji-j wejr dju]

One household, [·ja ·jiw śjow wejr], two members (15)

Male, one

Adult, one, [śjow wejr]

Female, one

Adult, one, wife, [ljow tsja tsji- phiow][33]

One household, [zar śja kia gju_], four members (16)

Male, three

Adult, one, [śja kia gju_]

Children, two

Son, [tśjow lhji. wejr], [ɣa. wa. wejr]

Female, one

Adult, one, wife, [o da ŋwə tśjow mja]

One household, [le tśhjwor lji-.], four members (17)

Male, two

Adult, one, [tśhjwor lji-.]

Child, one

Son, [kia nja_]

Female, two

Adult, one, [zjwi. o śja~ dji-j kie.][34]

Child, one, daughter, [wa lji-. kie.]

One household, [le ne_w lhji. wejr], two members (18)

Male one

Adult, one, [ne_w lhji. wejr]

Female, one

Adult, one, wife, [ja xwa] …

30 TN: lit. "a treasure behind the pagoda."

31 TN: lit. "Qiang/fan, receive, treasure."

32 TN: lit. "benevolent, month, servant."

33 TN: lit. "white maiden."

34 TN: lit. "Golden Samādhi."

One household, [illegible] [le śjow lji-.], four members (19)

Male, one

Adult, one, [illegible] [śjow lji-.]

Female, three

Adult, two

Wife, [illegible] [ŋwə_rar tsja tsji- gjow]

Mother, [illegible] [śiə nji_j lji-.j lji-.][35]

Child, one

Daughter …

One household, [illegible] [pha~ lji-. we ·jiw],[36] two members (20)

Male, one

Adult, one, [illegible] [lji-. we ·jiw]

Female, one

Adult, one

Wife, [illegible] [rjijrs pa rya mja]

One household, [illegible] [la wejr rjijr pu.], four members (21)

Male, three

Adult, one [[illegible]]

Children, two …

Female, one, adult, one, wife …

One household … two members (22)

Male, one

Adult, one, [illegible] [lu. zji-_r śia~][37]

Female, one, adult, wife [illegible] ? [phjij śjo ? lji-.]

One household, [illegible] [ljow gju_rjur ɣwie], five members (23)

Male, three

Adult, two, [illegible] [gju_rjur ɣwie], brother [illegible] [da kia śia~]

Child, one, son, [illegible] [śja. lhji. khjwi-][38]

Female, two

Adult, two, wife [illegible] [lwər ze phiow bie_j][39]

Wife, [illegible] [gjwi- dji ne_w lhji. kie.]

One household, [illegible] [gjwi- dji dju wejr], two members (24)

Male, one

Adult, one, [illegible] [dju wejr]

35 TN: lit. "treasure of/with a joyful heart."

36 TN: lit. "the one with a donkey."

37 TN: lit. "joy, water, mountain."

38 TN: lit. "dog of the seventh month."

39 TN: lit. "white and joyful."

- Female, one
  - Adult, one, wife [Tangut] [njij no kə ta mja]
- One household, [Tangut] [gjwi- dji da kia zji][40] three members (25)
  - Male, two
    - Adult, one, [Tangut] [da kia zji]
    - Child, one, son, [Tangut] [so. lji-. wejr]
  - Female, one
    - Adult, one, wife, [Tangut] [ji- ·ji-r śja. lji-. phiow][41]
- One household, [Tangut] [lwər ze ljo dju wejr],[42] six members (26)
  - Male, three
    - Adult, one, [Tangut] [ljo dju wejr]
    - Children, two, son, [Tangut] [gji-_ lhji. śjow],[43] [Tangut] [tśhjwiw śiə śjow]
  - Female, three
    - Adult, two, wife ......
      - Daughter ...
    - Child, one, daughter, [Tangut] [khjwi- mja lji-.]
- One household, [Tangut] [tshja gju_ gju_ rjur ·jiw], four members (27)
  - Male, one
    - Adult, one, [Tangut] [gju_ rjur ·jiw]
  - Female, three
    - Adult, three, wife, [Tangut] [khju_] [Tangut] [ŋwə lhji. kie.]
      - Wife, [Tangut] (Liang) [Tangut] [ljow ljo ta]
      - Daughter, [Tangut] [śjow mja]
- One household, [Tangut] [ŋwe zjwi. śja. lhji. ·jiw] four members (28)
  - Male, one
    - Adult, one, [Tangut] [śja. lhji. ·jiw]
  - Female, three
    - Adult, one, wife [Tangut] [ŋwə_gjwi- da kia mja]
    - Children, two, [Tangut] [wjor lhej mju] [Tangut] [da kia ne_w]
- One household, [Tangut] [ja xwa wa ɣwie] two members (29)
  - Male, one
    - Adult, one, [Tangut] [wa ɣwie]
  - Female, one
    - Adult, one, wife, [Tangut] [mjij pu. tśjow lhji. kie.]

40 TN: lit. "son/man of the old house."

41 TN: lit. "seven, treasure, white."

42 TN: lit. "the one blessed with great fortune."

43 TN: lit. "iron of the ninth month."

One household, [illegible] [ljow lu. zji-_r śia~], two members (30)

……

The records of 26 out of the 30 households are complete. Household record (1) is damaged on the front, whereas the 30th register has lost its end. It is therefore difficult to gain precise numbers on these two families. As for (21), we can still compute the numbers of males and females. Also, that the name of the patriarch on register (22) is lost does not affect our use of the data. The following is the statistics on the 28 households:

CHART 1 Инв. No.6342-1: household registers and demographics

No. 6342-1	Total numbers	Male			Female		
		Total	Adult	Child	Total	Adult	Child
(2)	2	1		1	1	1	
(3)	2	1	1		1	1	
(4)	3	2	1	1	1	1	
(5)	4	2		2	2	1	1
(6)	2	1	1		1	1	
(7)	4	2	2		2	1	1
(8)	3	1	1		2	1	1
(9)	5	2	1	1	3	1	2
(10)	4	2	1	1	2	1	1
(11)	2	1	1		1	1	
(12)	2	1	1		1	1	
(13)	3	2		2	1	1	
(14)	3	1	1		2	2	
(15)	2	1	1		1	1	
(16)	4	3	1	2	1	1	
(17)	4	2	1	1	2	1	1
(18)	2	1	1		1	1	
(19)	4	1	1		3	2	1
(20)	2	1	1		1	1	
(21)	4	3	1	2	1	1	
(22)	2	1	1		1	1	
(23)	5	3	2	1	2	2	
(24)	2	1	1		1	1	
(25)	3	2	1	1	1	1	

CHART 1 Инв. No.6342-1: household registers and demographics (*cont.*)

No. 6342-1	Total numbers	Male			Female		
		Total	Adult	Child	Total	Adult	Child
(26)	6	3	1	2	3	2	1
(27)	4	1	1		3	3	
(28)	4	1	1		3	1	2
(29)	2	1	1		1	1	
Total	89	44	27	17	45	34	11

As shown in the table above, there is a total population of 89 living in 28 households, or 3.18 per house, on average. These are relatively small families. There are 44 males and 45 females—almost a 1:1 ratio. With 61 adults and 28 children, there are 2.2 times as many grown-ups as there are underage residents. It is by no means a large population of children.

Other relatively small register fragments, with few households recorded, have also been found. But they do reflect the demographics in the area. An example is Инв. No. 4761-4, handwritten on hemp paper, damaged both in the front and at the end, 17.7 cm long and 43.5 cm wide. With some markings, crossings and corrections, the record features 27 lines of Tangut in the running script concerning the registration of only four households.[44]

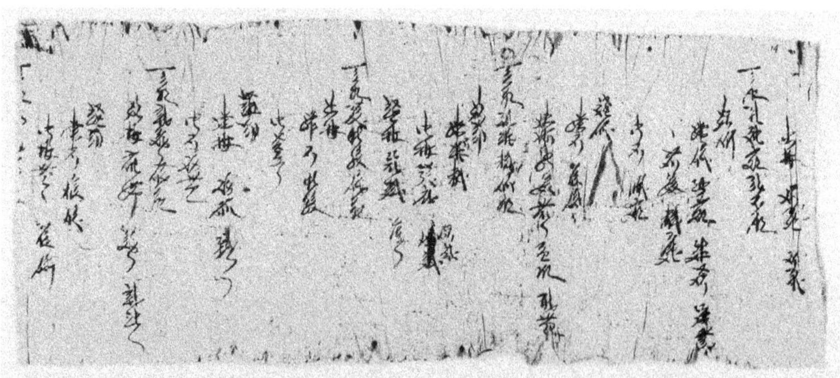

FIGURE 18 Инв. No. 4761-4: Register fragment

44 *Russian Collection of Khara-Khoto Manuscripts*, vol. 14, p. 273.

Each register begins with the name of the patriarch and size of the family, followed by the numbers of males and females in the line below, and finally, the numbers and names of adults and children further down in the last lines.

Here are the statistics on the registered households:

CHART 2 Инв. No. 4761-4: demographic data

No. 4761-4	Population size	Male			Female		
		Total	Adults	Children	Total	Adults	Children
(1)	11	6	5	1	5	1	4
(2)	5	3	1	2	2	2	
(3)	5	2	1	1	3	2	1
(4)	5	2	2		3	1	2
Total	26	13	9	4	13	6	7

As shown in Khara-Khoto No. 4761-4, one of the four households is as large as 11 in size, while the other three have five members each. The four households have 26 residents in total, about 6.5 per house. There are 13 males and 13 females, in a perfect 1:1 ratio. In contrast to the first set of registers, the children here make up a larger proportion: for the 15 adults, there are 11 children.

Another register fragment is the Khara-Khoto manuscript Инв. No. 4761-5, written on hemp paper, damaged in the front and in the back, and measuring 17.7 cm in length and 34.5 cm in width. There are 22 lines of Tangut in the

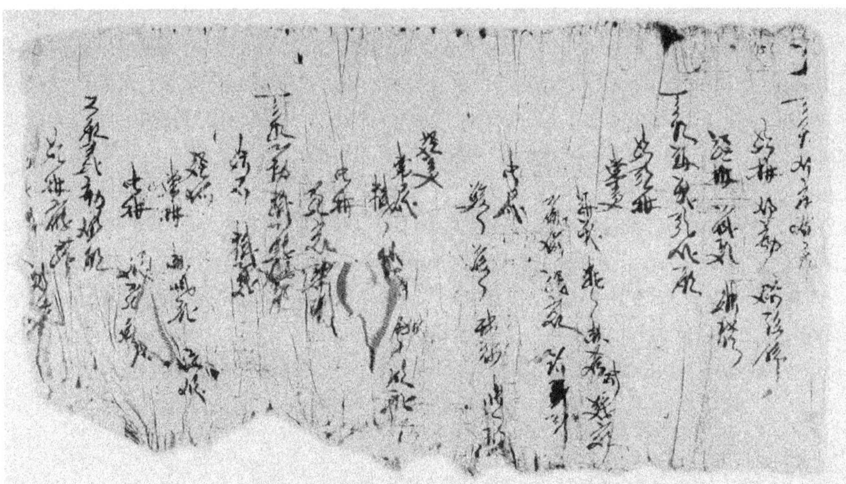

FIGURE 19 Инв. No. 4761-5: Register fragment

cursive script. It also has data on four households, though the record on the last one is damaged.[45]

This household register is similar in form to the previous one. Here is a table of its demographics:

CHART 3 Инв. No. 4761-5: demographic statistics

No. 4761-5	Population Size	Male			Female		
		Total	Adults	Children	Total	Adults	Children
(1)	4	2	2		2	2	
(2)	19	12	7	5	7	5	2
(3)	5	1	1		4	2	2
(4)	6	2	2		4	2?	2?
Total	34	17	12	5	17	11	6

As shown in No. 4761-5, there are three families of four, five and six members, respectively. One household is quite large, with 19 members. The total population living in the four houses is 34—on average, 8.5 per family—a large number, indeed. There are 17 men and 17 women, also in a perfect 1:1 ratio. However, there are only 11 children for the 23 adults, or 2.1 times more adults than children.

From all of this demographic data, it is fair to conclude that at least in Khara-Khoto, small families dominated local communities. Still, there were occasionally prosperous families of more than 10 members as well, like the one large enough to house almost 20 members at the same place. Curiously, it happens to be the case that in the two fragments analysed above, the number of males equals that of females. Perhaps the male-female ratio at the local level was indeed in balance. But of course, we couldn't responsibly make that statement without assembling more demographic data.

1.2 *Household Accounts*

Next to the register above is a fragmented page labelled Инв. No. 6342-2. Although physically broken off from Инв. No. 6342-1, the two are inferred to have once been attached to each other, given their uniform paper material, writing style and shared peculiarities of cursive script. This piece functions as the statistical summary of the previous register. It could therefore be seen as

45 *Russian Collection of Khara-Khoto Manuscripts*, vol. 14, p. 273.

an account. Also written on hemp paper, it is identical in size to the previous one: 19.1 cm in height and 64.7 cm in length. There are 21 lines of Tangut in the cursive script, accompanied by markings and signatures.[46]

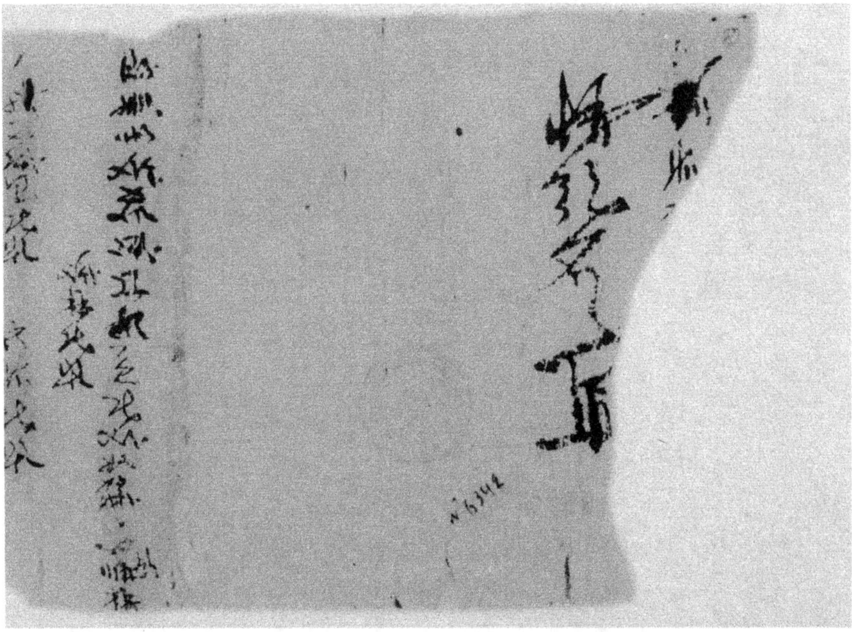

FIGURE 20 Инв. No. 6342-2: Register account (1)

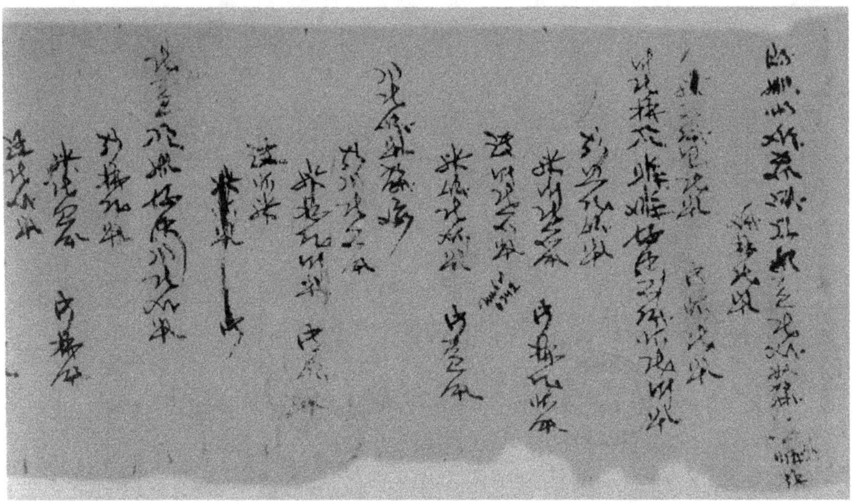

FIGURE 21 Инв. No. 6342-2: Register account (2)

46 *Russian Collection of Khara-Khoto Manuscripts*, vol. 14, pp. 123–124.

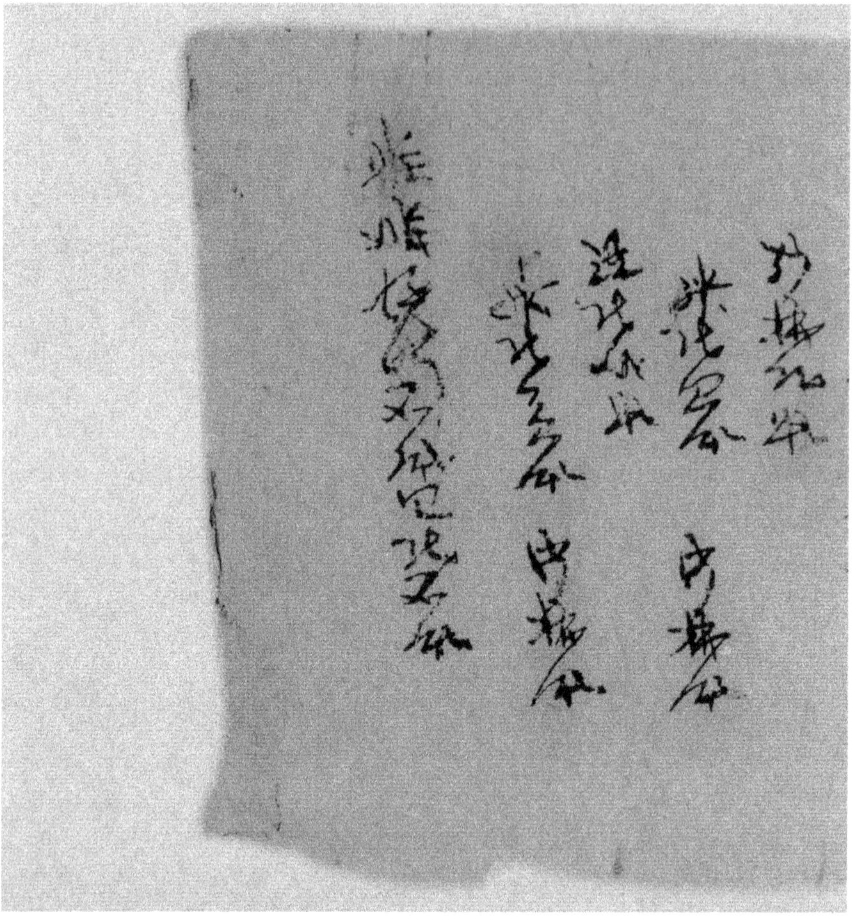

FIGURE 22 Инв. No. 6342-2: Register account (3)

Here is an English translation of the account:

> ……
> Twenty-one (in large characters, with signature)
> *Liliu*, [illegible] [rjir śjow pow ·jir], administering seventy-nine households?? In total two
> Hundred and twenty persons
> Adults, one hundred and eighty persons, children, forty persons
> Sixty-two households, original size, adults and children one hundred forty-six persons
> Males eighty-five persons
> Adults sixty-one persons, children twenty-four persons

Females, sixty-one persons
Adults, fifty-four persons, children, seven persons
Thirty-five persons single
Male, thirty-one persons
Adults, twenty-six persons, children five persons
Females, four, adults
Seventeen households? Adults and children, forty-nine
Males, twenty persons
Adults, eighteen persons, children, two persons
Females, nineteen persons
Adults, seventeen persons, children, two persons
Adults and children, one hundred eighty-one persons

We now know that the long roll Инв. No. 6342-1 records 79 households—much more than just 30—and all fall under the administrative authority of one *liliu*. In Sui and Tang times, Tangut communities still retained traits of tribal organizations.[47] *Revised Laws of Heavenly Prosperity* establishes specific legislations for local communities:

> Under proper leadership, all landed households should gather by the proximity of distance: Ten households form a small unit under the local administration of *jia*, and five small *jia* units come under a junior supervisor, two of whom are under the authority of a rural *liliu*. The commands should be given to excellent and leisurely individuals in the positions of junior officials, local bureaucrats, junior administrators, standard soldiers and assistant soldiers.[48]

The owners of the "landed households" are patriarchs of the "taxable households"—peasant families in possession of arable lands and obliged to pay land levies. The "*jia*, small supervisory unit, and rural *liliu*" is a tripartite organisation of Tangut rural communities. One rural *liliu* is placed in charge of two small supervisory units, 10 *jia* and about 100 households. This complex structure demonstrates that Tangut rural villages were ruled and regulated at multiple levels in systematic governance.

Although Tangut rural communities are scarcely mentioned in Chinese sources, their eastern neighbours are keen to understand the basic organisation of the Tangut military, for obvious reasons. According to Song accounts

47 *Old Book of Tang*, Bk. 198: History of Dangxiang Qiang.
48 *Revised Laws of Heavenly Prosperity* 15, pp. 514–515.

and analyses, Tangut soldiers "under the command of the generals of the chief are referred to as one *liu*."[49] It is also said that "each family in the tribe is called a *tent*; a male above fifteen years of age, or *ding*, may be enlisted. Of two such men, one is chosen as a 'standard soldier,' the other a 'bearing soldier,' and the two make a unit of *chao*."[50] It seems that *liu* in the military sense is in some way related to *liliu*. It could be that the rural "*liliu*" in times of peace was turned into the "military *liu*" when the Tanguts were at war.[51]

Manuscript Инв. No. 6342-2 proves the existence of the rural *liliu*. As shown in this account, Raoshang Banbai ([illegible] [rjir śjow pow ·jir]) is in charge of this *liliu* of only 79 households. This means that "100 households per *liliu*" was no more than a principle established by the government. The actual numbers of families under the authority of one *liliu* varied on a case-by-case basis. Oftentimes, the numbers were smaller than prescribed in the laws.

A register account fragment in the manuscript Инв. No. 4384-9 features texts written in the cursive script on both sides of the hemp paper, which are unfortunately illegible due to water stain. Damaged in the front, it is 20.7 cm in length and 24.7 cm in width. Of the 14 lines in cursive Tangut, 1–10 are records of four households, and the 11th contains four un-indented characters, "ten houses, one *jia*," followed by details on each family.[52]

And there is also Инв. No. 4762-3, a list of names of all residents in their own *jia* in one *liliu*. Damaged both at the front and at the end, it is handwritten on a hemp paper 20.2 cm long and 43.2 cm wide, with 23 lines in the Tangut cursive style.[53]

Six *jia* are listed in this document, each one preceded by the character [illegible] [kia] (*jia*) and followed by series of names. The first name after "[illegible]" should be the administrator of the *jia*, the others being members of the group. Some *jia* communities noted their locations, though the last *jia* is partly lost. There are around 10 persons in each of the first five *jia*. This document reveals that rules in the *Revised Laws of Heavenly Prosperity* concerning households, *jia*, and *liliu* were basically enforced in practice.

---

49 *Zizhi Tongjian* vol. 132, First year of Qingli Era, Emperor Ren of Song (1041), Jiazi, fifth and twelfth months.

50 Zeng, Gong (曾鞏: 1019–1083). *Long Ping Ji* [隆平集] Bk. 20. "On Foreign States" Wenyuange Sikuquanshu edition (文淵閣四庫全書本). Rpt. Beijing: Airusheng, 2009; Taipei: Taiwan Commercial Press, 1983, Bk. 20, "On Foreign States."

51 TN: A soldier carries provisions and weapons for his partner in the same *chao*. For more on the military & civil organisations of *liu* of Western Xia, see Shi, Jinbo; (transl.) Li, Hansong. *Tangut Language and Manuscripts: An Introduction*. Leiden: Brill, 2020, pp. 23–24, 452, 474, 476 (military); 21, 452, 469–471, 500 (civil).

52 *Russian Collection of Khara-Khoto Manuscripts*, vol. 13, p. 209.

53 *Russian Collection of Khara-Khoto Manuscripts*, vol. 13, p. 277.

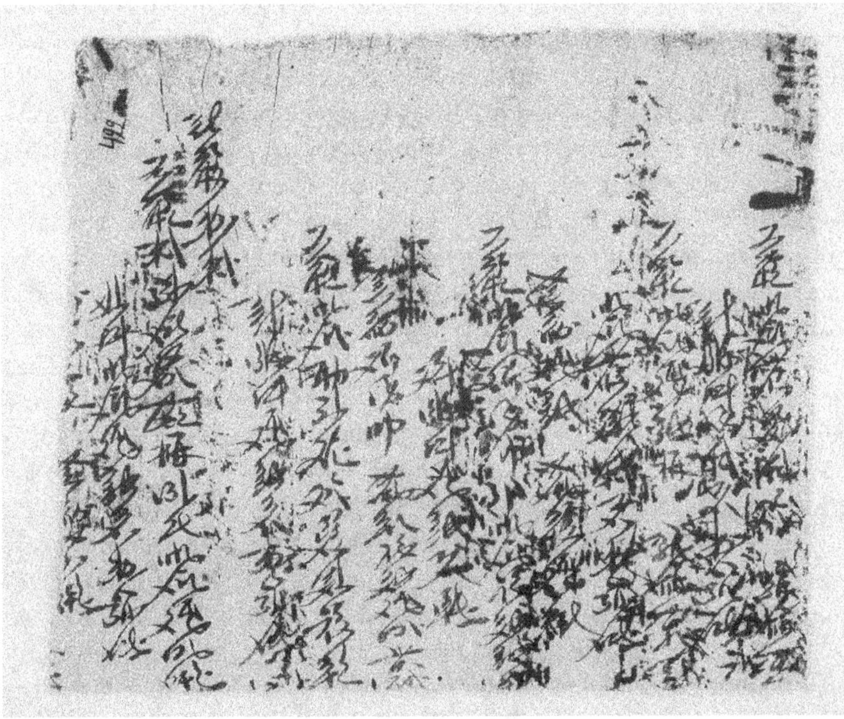

FIGURE 23 Инв. No. 4384-9: *Jia* register accounts fragment

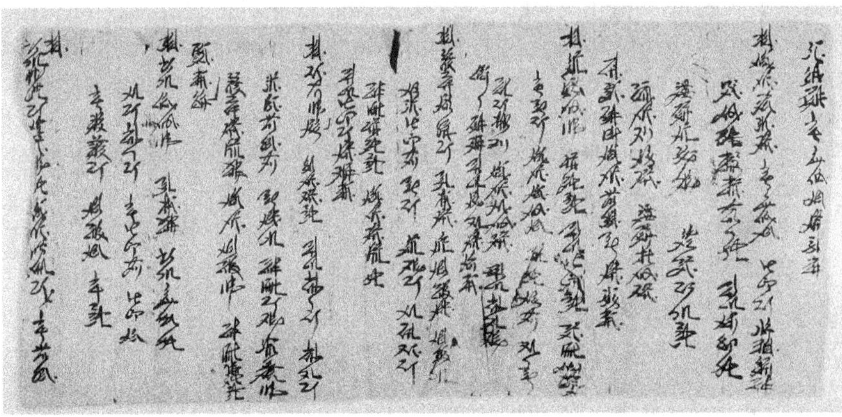

FIGURE 24 Инв. No. 4762-3: *Liliu jia* list of household registers

In ancient China, rural villages never constituted a level of government. The imperial dynasties chose not to rule at the bottom level in order to reduce both governmental expenditure and the burden on local peasants. The Tanguts also adopted this measure and made some adjustments to their own conditions. We know from the Tangut laws that *liliu* is not actually a governmental agency, but a self-governed organisation of communities under the guidance of the government. Those in charge of a *liliu* were not experienced, government-appointed officials, but men with some governing skills chosen from amongst the folks. In the Tang Dynasty, a hundred households made a *li* [里] and five *li* formed a *xiang* [鄉].[54] During the Song Dynasty, the *xiang-li*, still in use in the early period of Song, gradually evolved into the *bao-jia* system, which dominated the scene in mid and later Song. Under the latter system, 10 households constitute one *bao*: 50 houses are one *dabao*, and 500 a *dubao*. As time went on, a *bao* shrank to five, a *dabao* to 25, and one *dubao* to 250 households. Each *bao* is headed by an elder, and a *dubao* by an officer and a deputy officer.[55] There is little doubt that the organisation of local communities in the Tangut Empire was borrowed from the Chinese *xiang-li* system and, after the legal reforms of Northern Song, the *bao-jia* laws. Furthermore, the Tangut character 𗣫 [kia] is almost phonetically identical to the Chinese *jia* 甲. It is reasonable to surmise that the concept of *kia*, a transliterated word, had been unknown to the Tanguts until it was introduced from the Central Plains to the northwest.

The socio-political functions of the *xiang-li* system in China expanded over time. The *bao-jia* was responsible for monitoring demographic changes in rural areas, compiling household registers, and overseeing the levy of taxes. Likewise, the Tangut *liliu* assumed expansive roles. It registered the households, lands, livestock and other properties, compiled and reported the accounts from the area, commissioned and coordinated the building and repairing of canals. Another important role of the Tangut *liliu* was registering and managing *junchao*, the basic units of the Tangut military. This function, unique to the Tanguts and unheard of elsewhere in China, was closely linked to the Tangut institution of enlistment at that time.[56]

54 *Old Book of Tang*, Book 43, 2: Bureaucratic System.

55 *History of Song*, 192, 6: Military System.

56 Shi, Jinbo. "Xixiawen Junji Wenshu Kaolue: Yi Ecang Heishuicheng Chutu Junji Wenshu Weili" [西夏文軍籍文書考略：以俄藏黑水城出土軍籍文書為例]: "Studies on Tangut Military Records: Taking the Military Records from the *Russian Collection of Khara-Khoto Manuscripts* as Examples" in *Zhongguoshi Yanjiu* [中國史研究]: *Journal of Chinese Historical Studies*, issue 4, 2012.

As shown in the register account Инв. No. 6342-2, there was a population of 146 amongst the 79 households (previously 62), and 35 were single.[57] The latter 17 houses are recorded to have 49 men and women, but a quick addition of the numbers yields 39 instead of 49. It could be an error that the Tangut "three" was written as "four." But in any case, the total population of this *liliu* should be 220. The "singles," as illustrated above, are a special group, both included in the total number and excluded from the 79 households. They might be similar in status to the "dark, poor man" mentioned in No. 4991-5: he roams the area, without a household or settlement. One possibility is that they were *shijun* or *nupu* slaves who had not achieved full status as free men.[58] Whichever case it is, the seemingly homeless Tanguts revealed in this document are worth further study. The final line notes that originally there were 181 adults and children, exactly the sum of the 146 persons in the original 62 households and the 35 singles. Again, it suggests that the 17 households were later added to the list. As for where the additional families were from and why they were listed separately from the original 62 households, we do not have a clue. But it is the case that the household registers found in Dunhuang also distinguished new from old households.

The average household size in this rural *liliu* is less than three: These are notably small families. There are 180 adults and 40 children—not a community of many children. Amongst the residents, there are 136 men and 84 women, a ratio of 1.62:1. Compared to other registers, the men in this place are out of proportion, and definitely beyond the limit that is required for sustainable social development. But amongst the individuals of single status, there are 31 males and only 4 females, an enormous difference that greatly affected the overall male-to-female ratio of the population. If, for a moment, we disregard the outlying data points of the 35 singles, the male-to-female ratio drops to 1.2:1. And if we only take the numbers of adult males (61 men in 62 households) and females (54 women in 62 households), the ratio turns out to be even closer: 1.13:1. At last, among the 17 new households, there are 20 adult males and 19 adult females, with a ratio of 1.05:1. In short, with a more rigorous approach and a sufficiently narrow scope of analysis, the male-to-female ratio appears more in order.

Additionally, there are some register fragments that also deal with statistics on households. Инв. No. 7893-18 is a list of names of individuals under the

57 Single status in Tangut is 𗦧𗺉 [ta~ śji~], transliteration of the Chinese: 单身.

58 *Revised Laws of Heavenly Prosperity* 12, p. 417; 20, p. 606.

administration of a particular *liliu*.[59] Инв. No. 5949-41 and Инв. No. 7922 are lists of names under the authority of a *lizheng* (commander in charge of a *li*).[60]

2 Household Self-Reports (*Shoushi*)

In the tradition of Tang and Song local administrations, residents would report their own demographics, land ownership and burden of taxation to the government in self-declared documents that we call *shoushi*. Tangut *shoushi*, or 'self-reports,' constitute a part of the corpus of Tangut social documents. For example, manuscript Инв. No. 7629-1 is the record of a rather large family. It is written on hemp paper, 19.9 cm long and 50 cm wide, with 28 lines in Tangut: 25 lines of main text, and 3 lines in a smaller font, noting the ages of the individuals next to their name.[61]

We are also surprised to find a piece of self-report written in the Tangut running-standard script: the manuscript Инв. No. 8203, which happens to be the fair copy of 7629-1 (reproduced for more clarity). It is also written on hemp

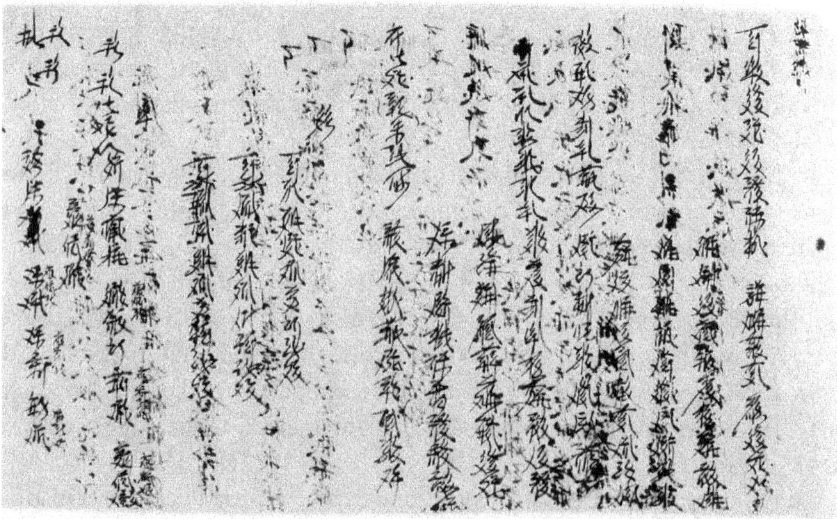

FIGURE 25 Инв. No. 7629-1: Self-reports (*shoushi*) (1)

59 *Russian Collection of Khara-Khoto Manuscripts*, vol. 14, p. 217.

60 *Russian Collection of Khara-Khoto Manuscripts*, vol. 14, pp. 100, 227. In Tangut and Chinese, the term means "commander in charge of *li*," i.e. a person who has authority over the households within the range of a *liliu*.

61 *Russian Collection of Khara-Khoto Manuscripts*, vol. 14, pp. 183–184.

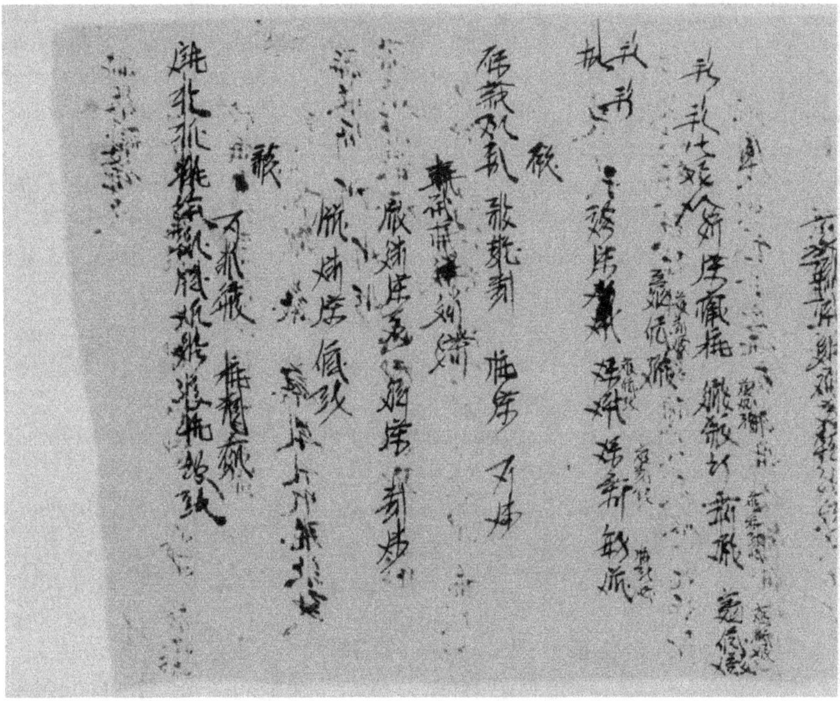

FIGURE 26 Инв. No. 7629-1: Self-reports (*shoushi*) (2)

FIGURE 27 Инв. No. 8203: Household self-report

paper, 20.2 cm long and 53.6 cm wide, with 22 lines of text and 3 lines of small characters noting the age of the person next to each name.[62]

The patriarch of this household formerly held the title of "standard soldier of the Imperial Sentinels." The "imperial sentinel," which literally translates

62 *Russian Collection of Khara-Khoto Manuscripts*, vol. 14, pp. 256–257.

as "front, internal guard," is the title of a Tangut soldier or official who both watches over the imperial household (the private and internal part of the palace housing all the wives and concubines of the emperor and his families) and is sometimes sent out to preside over civil affairs. A "standard soldier" is the main combat soldier in a *chao*, the most basic unit of the Tangut military. His assistant is an associate or assistant "main force," and the person bearing the burden or responsibility for miscellaneous physical labour is called the "burden man." This is a rather literal English translation of the *shoushi* Khara-Khoto Инв. No. 8203:

> One man, [zjwi. ·o tshja zji], used to, with imperial sentinel
> [zjwi. ·o gju_rjur khjwi-], brother
> [tshja wja], [used to] be in one unit of *chao*. First because [he was] physically weak, under
> supervisor [ŋwe zjwi. ne_w wejr], shared the same old *chao*. [tshja wja] and
> military chief [ŋwe zjwi. gju_rjur śia~], and [ŋwe zjwi. pa rya]
> [lji-.], the three men formed one *chao*. [tshja zji] now, uncle
> by law transfer, [zjwi. ·o gju_rjur ne_w], dead, [his] adopted
> son. All the livestock are clear, as listed below:
> Land:
> One patch bordering the new canal, sowed seven *dan*, place.
> One patch bordering Lüyi canal, sowed six *dan*, place.
> One patch bordering Xipan canal, sowed seven *dan*, place.
> One patch, mixed lands at the field's opening, sowed seven *dan*, place
> Persons:
> Age forty age twenty-five age five
> Male, adult, children, two, [ɣa. wa. gju_], [śji-j khjwi-],
> [śja. lhji. bie_j]
> Age three
> [śja lhji. khjwi-]
> Woman, adult
> Age fifty age thirty age twenty-five
> [gju_mja] [gju_kie.] [sa~ tsjij]
> Livestock:
> Camels, three, two adults, one young (calf)
> Cows, adults and young ten, four adults six youngsters (calves)
> Sheep, adults and young eighty

Properties

One blanket, two rolls of knots.[63]

This document declares the origin and history of the patriarch's military *chao*, the population size, and property ownership of the household. It provides details on the precise location (in terms of the four borders) and the amounts of his land, the names of family members, their age, the types and quantities of livestock, as well as other properties of considerable value. It is an important source for studies on both Tangut military (i.e., the *chao* system) and families.

The declarer of the form, [Tangut] [zjwi. ·o tshja zji] is the patriarch of the family. "Yi'e" ([Tangut] [zjwi. ·o]) is a Tangut surname, and [Tangut] [tshja zji] is his given name. He may have been re-registering his household, along with his land, family members and livestock, as the foster son of his uncle Yi'e "the blessed and benevolent" ([Tangut] [zjwi. ·o gju_rjur ne_w]). The other parties mentioned in this document, such as Yi'e "the lucky dog" ([Tangut] [zjwi. ·o gju_rjur khjwi-]), Weiyi "the greatly benevolent" ([Tangut] [ŋwe zjwi.]) [Tangut] [ŋwe zjwi.] Weiyi "the treasure of wisdom," were all related to the man in one way or another, and their names suggest that all of them were members of Dangxiang Tangut clans.

An analysis of the self-reports Khara-Khoto Инв. No. 7629-1 and Инв. No. 8203 yields some interesting numbers: We know that the family has four patches of farmlands, three of which were each large enough for seven *dan* of seeds, and one fit for six *dan* of seeds. The corpus of Tangut social documents reveals a variety of ways to measure land in the Tangut tradition, in addition to the Chinese *mu* (614.4 m^2) and *qing* (100 *mu*, or 15.18 acre). The Tanguts evaluated the size of land by the amount of seeds to be sowed. This measurement is adopted in the accounts of water taxes, contracts of land sales, and land lease excavated in Khara-Khoto. It is quite similar to the Tibetan practice of measuring land by the amount of seeds (in grams) that could be sowed in it. I have concluded, based on some statistical studies on the measurement of weight, that 1 *hú* (51 L, ½ *dan*) of seeds is roughly equivalent to 10 Tangut *mu* (2.4 Song *mu*) of farmlands.[64] Given this family's land in terms of 27 *dan* of seeds, they owned about 270 Tangut *mu* farmlands.

63 [Tangut] [ɣjwi-], unclear in meaning, is translated as "knot."

64 Shi, Jinbo. "Xixia Duliangheng Chuyi" [西夏度量衡芻議] "Some Initial Discussions on the Tangut System of Measurement" *Journal of Guyuan Teacher's College* [固原師專學報], now *Journal of Ningxia Normal University*, issue 2, 2002.

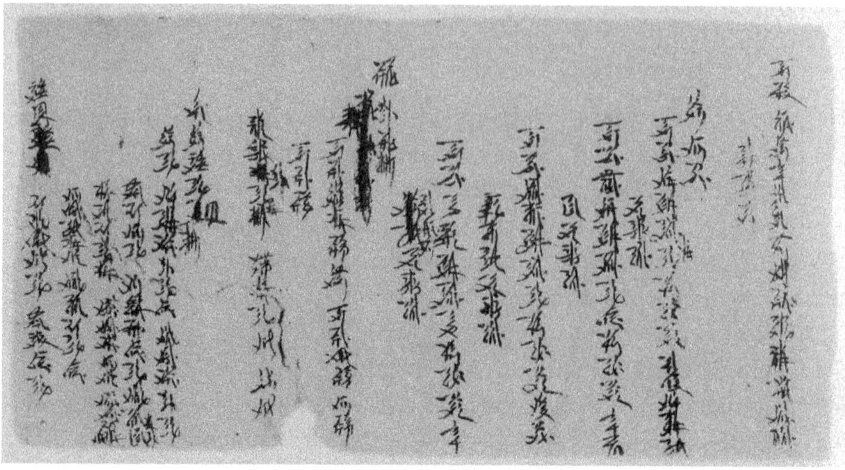

FIGURE 28 Инв. No. 7893-9: Household self-report

In addition to the patriarch himself, there are 2 adult males (40 and 25 years old, respectively), 2 boys (5 and 3 years old), and 3 adult females (50, 30 and 25 years old) in this rather large family. On average, each family member owns 3.37 *dan* seeds of land—equivalent to 33.7 Tangut *mu*. Their wealth is also seen in the possession of 3 camels, 10 cows and 80 sheep. The only missing information seems to be the family members' relationships to each other.

Another self-report (*shoushi*), Khara-Khoto Инв. No. 7893-9, records the data on the household of a mid-level military officer. It is written on hemp paper, 20.2 cm long and 39.8 cm wide, with 23 lines in Tangut cursive script and some damages near the end.[65]

This is an English translation of the document:

> One household, *xingjian* Liang? Zhu, owned livestock, properties are registered and listed below:
>
> Land, four patches:
>
> One patch, borders Yang canal, fit to sow twenty *dan*, borders [illegible] [·ja xwa nji_j lji-.j wejr] (place)
>
> One patch, borders Daoli canal, fit to sow fifteen *dan*, borders [illegible] [ljow kie.j bie_j] (place)
>
> One patch, borders Lüyi canal, fit to sow ten *dan*, borders [illegible] [zjwi. ·o tsja tsji- wejr] (place)

65 *Russian Collection of Khara-Khoto Manuscripts*, vol. 14, p. 213.

One patch, borders Qihu canal, fit to sow seven *dan*, borders [illegible] ? [ljow njij ?] (place)

Of the three horses (livestock):

One stallion of two teeth, one mare of four teeth

One foal

Camels thirty-two, adults twenty-six, calves six

Of the eighteen persons, male and female:

Males, ten. [illegible] [nji_j lji-.j khjwi-], thirty-five [years old]; [illegible] [tśjow lhji. khjwi-], thirty.

[illegible] [śjow gju_] forty. [illegible] [ɣwie xwe kji~], fifty. [illegible] [ɣa. wa. bie_j], thirty.

[illegible] [kə ta gju_], twelve. [illegible] [lhji. lhji. khjwi-], four years old. [illegible] [tśjow lhji. gju_]

[illegible] [lji-r lhji. wejr], two years old. [illegible] [ɣa. wa. gju_], fifteen.

Females, eight. [illegible] [gju_ rjur bie_j], sixty. [illegible] [zji-_r tśju.], fifty.

……

Xingjian (a local supervisor in the military) is lower in rank than *bianjianjiao* (a secretary, magistrate or censor), but higher than *yingneng* and *liliu* chiefs, and certainly high enough to be furnished with military tallies and signs.[66] We could tell from the population and wealth of this household that it is well-established and well-to-do. The family owns four patches of lands, the sizes of which are: 20 *dan*, 15 *dan*, 10 *dan* and 7 *dan*, totalling 52 *dan* in terms of sowed seeds. They also own 3 horses and 22 camels—not a small amount for a local family. The family comprises 19 members: 10 males including the patriarch (five are adults, three children, and one unclear) and 8 females (though only records on 2 of them, both adults, still remain legible). It is obviously a large and prosperous family, whose 19 members own 52 *dan* seeds (in size) of land, about the equivalent of 520 *mu* (approximately 86 acres), and on average 22.8 *mu* (approximately 3.8 acres) of farmlands per person.

Although data in both this and the previous form seem to suggest that the Tanguts enjoyed vast farmlands, it should be noted that Khara-Khoto is far up in the northwest, where land is expansive and scantly populated. Moreover, the two families certainly do have some social connections and considerable wealth. They are by no means representative of the many impoverished peasants who presumably owned much less land.

66 *Revised Laws of Heavenly Prosperity* 6, p. 266.

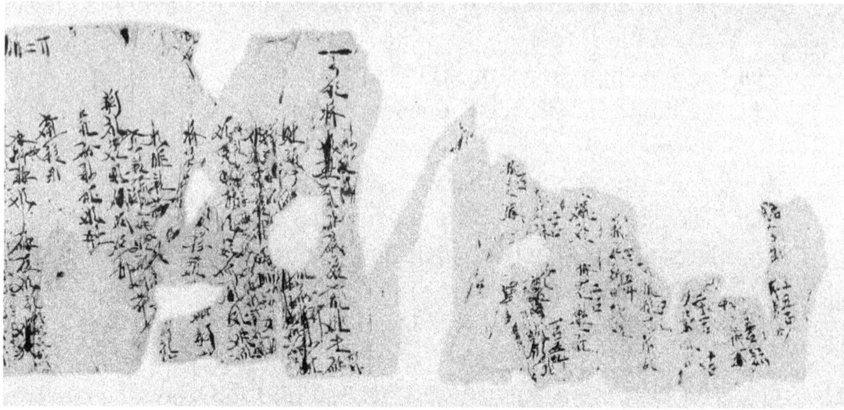

FIGURE 29 Инв. No. 4761-10V: Household self-report (1)

FIGURE 30 Инв. No. 4761-10V: Household self-report (2)

There is also a bilingual fragment of a self-report, Инв. No. 4761-10V, handwritten on hemp paper, 19 cm long and 70.8 cm wide, with 56 lines in cursive Tangut, as well as occasional markings and corrections.[67]

This self-report is fragmented and blurred, and the Tangut text is difficult to read. The patriarch of the household is Hun, [illegible] [xwe~] (渾), one of the major Han names in the northwest. So, it could have been because the family was Han that they labeled key words in Chinese, hence the Tangut-Chinese bilingual self-report.

67 *Russian Collection of Khara-Khoto Manuscripts*, vol. 13, p. 270.

Apart from being bilingual, the *shoushi* is also noted for the following features:

1. *Standard and Assistant Soldiers Listed.* As we know, Tangut household and military registers are closely associated. In this document one standard soldier and three assistant soldiers within the family are identified, details rarely and for the first time seen in self-reports.
2. *Numerous Items of Properties.* Among the registered properties, in addition to farmlands and livestock, there are also houses and clothes listed separately. It is in this way more meticulously recorded than the Tangut self-report we have already seen.
3. *Values of Noted Properties.* When registering one's properties, the declarants sometimes write down not only the titles of the property but also its estimated value in Chinese right next to the item. The values of properties are commonly evaluated in terms of grains in *dan*. For example, a side note to "one patch of land, the place where six *dan* may be sowed" reads in Chinese, "eighteen *dan*," which is likely to be the value of this patch of land. Another example is the note in Chinese "twenty *dan*" written to the side of a mentioned horse, to denote the monetary value or market price of the concerned horse. Likewise, "twenty-five *dan*" noted next to a "full-teethed" (mature) camel informs us of the value of the camel. And "fifteen *dan*," "fifteen *dan*" and "four *dan*" written in Chinese by the side of the mentioning of three cows are probably their respective prices.[68] Also, such labels as "ten *dan*" for a property, and "two *dan*," "three *dan*," "six *dan*" and "four *dan*" for clothes are all listings of their prices.

But the prices listed above tend to be higher than those indicated in contracts of land and livestock sales also excavated in Khara-Khoto.[69] One may explain this gap by speculating that owners of properties sold their lands and livestock in a hurry, or out of emergencies, and therefore had to lower their prices to process the transactions and receive the payments in time.

3 Analysis of Khara-Khoto Household Registers

Household registers excavated in Khara-Khoto shed light on the region's demographics under the Tangut regime, with which we may inquire into many social realities of the Khara-Khoto city. These surviving manuscripts are also precious

68 Compared to prices in Khara-Khoto livestock sales contracts, the prices of horses, camels and cows here seem be rather high.

69 See Chapter 7 for more on contracts of land sale and livestock sale.

because they alone tell us about the lives of the Tanguts at the bottom of the social hierarchy.

First, the Khara-Khoto household accounts are evidence of a highly developed household registration system in Western Xia. Registers are referred to as 𗏁 [dźjij] in *Revised Laws of Heavenly Prosperity*, which could be either household or military records. Household registration played important roles in the regime. For example, in the case of an indicted adopted son, courts of law considered pursuing charges on his family members based on whether the criminal was registered under the household of his biological parents or his foster parents.[70] *Revised Laws of Heavenly Prosperity* require that Tangut peasant families report demographic changes in their households on time, to avoid any inaccuracies and confusions, and in this way to "keep the records clean and updated every three years."[71] On the other hand, registers were directly linked to land taxes. These household records show that the Tanguts had already practiced a certain kind of census, and, after the Chinese tradition, updated their statistics every three years. It is also interesting to note that the data on *liliu* and *jia* as shown on the actual registers correspond accurately to the legislations in *Revised Laws of Heavenly Prosperity*. This showcases how the Tangut legal code was not only theoretically sophisticated, but systematically enforced.

Secondly, the archaeological finds in Khara-Khoto have furnished us with diverse materials, not only household registers but also accounts and forms declared by families (*shoushi*). Some of them are more elaborate than others. Some are more demographical, others more concerned with data on grain taxes, livestock and enlisted soldiers. In short, the Tangut registers are a microcosm of the diverse registration in medieval China.

At last, I should mention that the Khara-Khoto documents are rich in information, with names of patriarchs, all family members identified by gender, age and their relationships to the patriarch of the household. Sometimes even their specific ages at the time of the registration are given to us. More exhaustive is the content of a self-self-report, or *shoushi*, which reports the origin of *junchao* in the family, the identities of the patriarch, family members, owned lands, livestock and assets, even houses and clothes. Occasionally, properties such as land, livestock and clothes are evaluated in terms of grains, data that would enable us to estimate the commodity prices in the area. Therefore, that these comprehensive and manifold Tangut registers and accounts survived to this day is fortuitous for modern historians interested in Tangut families and

70 *Revised Laws of Heavenly Prosperity* 1, pp. 112–113.

71 *Revised Laws of Heavenly Prosperity* 15, p. 515.

society. They occupy an extraordinary seat in the hall of medieval archives. Thanks to these documents, it has for the first time become possible to carry out rigorous inquiries into many previously unknown topics on the social conditions of Western Xia.

For example, the Russian Khara-Khoto manuscript Инв. No. 6342-1 tells us the population of 28 households to be 89 in total, which is on average 3.18 per household. Families appear to be quite small, for 10 of them are families of two comprised of only a man and his wife, which are 35.7% of the total number of households. This phenomenon deserves our attention. It could be that men leave to found their own household as soon as they are married. There are, moreover, 10 of what we may call 'nuclear families'—a couple and their children—also 35.7% of the total number. Given that this is the default pattern among youthful families, the percentage may appear to be small. Only one 'stem family'—with three generations living in the same household—has been identified. By contrast, households (2), (5) and (13) are single-parent families, constituting 11% of the total. In each of these three cases, an adult woman alone raises the children: one, two and three, respectively. The single mother in household (2) is identified as widowed. It is of legal importance that the families, though deprived of a patriarch or other adult males, still have boys: one boy, a boy and a girl, and two boys, respectively. According to *Revised Laws of Heavenly Prosperity*:

> If all men of a household have perished, the law considers the family to be broken in its lineage. As for the properties belonging to the household, such as livestock, grain, treasures, house and lands, if there are surviving wives, daughters and sisters of the dead, as well as the married daughters and unmarried in-laws, let the wife gather the livestock, grains, and treasures, so that the women may receive their dowries as needed, according to the laws; but the rest of the livestock, grain, and treasures are not in the wife's disposal. They are, instead, to be monitored and managed in collaboration with another household that is close in lineage. If the women remarry or die, half of the properties they leave behind are to be distributed as dowries to the living daughters and sisters in the household in accordance with the prescribed laws mentioned above, with an increase to the sum; whereas the other half of the properties should be granted to different houses that do not share the same livestock, but are close in lineage to the descendants of grandparents, parents, uncles, aunts, brothers, nephews and grandsons.[72]

72 *Revised Laws of Heavenly Prosperity* 10, p. 355.

In other words, a household without male family members is "broken in lineage"—its properties are not inherited by the widow. Such a family barely survives in the legal sense of the term. The three families mentioned above, however, are not 'depleted' yet, thanks to the presence of the boys. They still have a chance to struggle and support themselves.

Most male heads of households have two-character surnames, whilst others have monosyllabic family names. Historically, traditional Tangut clans give themselves compound surnames. Some examples from the documents analysed in this chapter include: [illegible] [phjij śjo] (Pingshang), [illegible] [lwər ze] (Lüyi), [illegible] [tshja ślo_w] (Qianshu), [illegible] [mə rar] (Moluo), [illegible] [ŋwe zjwi.] (Weiyi), [illegible] [mjij pu.] (Mingbu), [illegible] [gjwi- dji] (Judi), [illegible] [·ja ·jiw] (Yeyou), [illegible] [tshja gju_] (Qianyu), [illegible] [·ja xwa] (Yehe), all being characteristically Dangxiang-Tangut family names. Three heads of households are named Lüyi, three Judi, two Qianshu, and two Weiyi. The name Liang is a more complicated story to tell. When it comes to Tangut royalties, the maiden name Liang often refers to the elder Empress Liang—wife of Liangzuo (Yizong), the second emperor of the Tangut Empire—and the younger Empress Liang—wife of Bingchang, the third emperor of Western Xia. Although there are Han Chinese Liangs, the Tangut classic *Golden Fragments* lists 'Liang' as one of the Fan (Tangut) surnames.[73] The name "Le," rather unlikely to be of Han origins, might be an abbreviation of the Tangut name "Gule." More research is due to solve this and other riddles. Compound names such as [illegible] [mja dzow] (Maze) and [illegible] [·ji- ·ji-r] (Yiyi) are absent in summaries of Tangut names in the *Assorted Words*, the *Golden Fragments*, or any other surviving Tangut manuscript. So, they may be newly-discovered Tangut surnames. Obviously, there are also a number of Han Chinese names in household registers, such as Yang, Hun, Pan, Luo and Han. Still, the documents are dominated by Fan names. In other words, households in this area of Khara-Khoto were mostly ethnic Tanguts. Given that no pattern of surname 'clusters' has been discerned, scholars could establish the weakness, if not absence, of family-based, clan-based domination at the local level. That is to say, ordinary Tangut villages might by this time have already evolved beyond or simply abandoned the shackles of clan-based social organisations. Instead, they formed mixed communities of different surnames and ethnicities. Historically, this was especially the case in mixed economies of farming and pasturing, where it is much more common to live alongside, and even to intermarry with Fan and Han neighbours.

73 Nie, Hongyin and Shi, Jinbo. "Xixiawenben Suijin Yanjiu" [西夏文本碎金研究]: "A Study of the Tangut *Golden Fragments*" in *Ningxia Daxue Xuebao* [寧夏大學學報]: *Journal of Ningxia University* (Humanities & Social Sciences Edition), issue 2, 1995.

There are, however, 'clusters' of given names, if not surnames. And it is here that the ingenuity and creativity of the Tangut mind is on full display. Some names pray for blessings and peace: [illegible] [zjo. dźjo ·jiw] (to enjoy longevity), [illegible] [ljo dju lji-.] (blessed with treasure), [illegible] [gju_ rjur] (bliss); others feature various months: [illegible] [mjij pu. tśjow lhji. kie.] (gold of the first month), [illegible] [ŋwə lhji. kie.] (gold of the fifth month), [illegible] [gji-_ lhji. śjow] (iron of the ninth month), [illegible] [śja lhji. wejr] (prosperity of the tenth month). They could well be the months in which the children are born, though so far, there is no conclusive evidence in support of hypothesis. Still others are clearly influenced by Buddhist ideas, such as [illegible] [pa rya śia~] (mountain of prajñā, or wisdom), [illegible] [rjijrs pa rya mja] (delight of prajñā), and [illegible] [so. lji-. wejr] (flourishing of the triratna, or 'three treasures'). There are also some curious names with derogatory epithets, or names of animals that do not sound so glorious: [illegible] [ne_w lhji. tśhjwor] ("servant of the benevolent moon/month"), [illegible] [tśhjwor lji-.] (precious slave), [illegible] [wa. khjwi-] (a blessed dog), [illegible] [da kia khjwi-] (dog of the old house), [illegible] [lji-. we ·jiw] (with a donkey), [illegible] [dzju. we] (rainbird). Even women are given such names: [illegible] [mja wejr khjwi-] (joyful, prosperous dog), [illegible] [khjwi- mja lji-.] (dog, lady, treasure). We know for certain that in Chinese folk culture, a derogatory name is thought to calm the jealousies of spirits and ghosts, thereby increasing the chance of the child's survival. Whether the Tanguts thought similarly is up for debate. Another revelation of the registers is that Tangut siblings rarely share "generation names." Quite the contrary, fathers and sons, mothers, and daughters do not shun the same characters in their names, despite their generational gap. An obvious example is household (10), where the names of the father [illegible] [da kia wejr] (prosperity of the old house) and the son [illegible] [da kia lji-] (treasure of the old house) are strikingly similar. Likewise, in household (28), the mother [illegible] [da kia mja] (delight of the old house) and the son [illegible] [da kia ne_w] (the benevolent old house) share two overlapping characters. Apparently, it is no offense to the seniors to be 'ranked' the same as their children.

Although the majority of Khara-Khoto residents seem to be ethnic Tanguts, and the registers suggest that most marriages are between Tanguts families, intermarriage was by no means a rarity. In household (6), for example, the wife of [illegible] [tshja ślo_w wa gju_] has the maiden name 'Jiao' ([illegible] [tsew]); Weiyi "the rainbird" in household (9) is married to lady 'Luo'; in (27), the wife of [illegible] [tshja gju_ gju_ rjur] is from the Han Chinese family of "Qu." These inter-ethnic marriages registered in official documents show that there was no legal barrier to Fan-Han intermarriage.

Polygamy is occasionally on display in the registers. In most cases, one man is married to two wives. In Household (23), for instance, there are two wives and two adult males in the family. But it remains unclear whether each man is married to one woman, or if one of the brothers is married to two wives. There is no doubt, however, that in household (27), the patriarch and sole adult male in the family [illegible] [tshja gju_ gju_ rjur ·jiw] is in the company of two wives, [illegible] [khju_ ŋwə lhji. kie.] and [illegible] [ljow ljo ta]. The Tangut law code the *Revised Laws of Heavenly Prosperity*, especially in Book II on family relations, frequently refers to the "secondary mother"—in the sense of a "father's concubine" (equivalent to the Chinese *shumu*)—in regulations on mourning apparels honouring the deaths of family members. According to the laws, children are obliged to observe mourning rituals for their parents and "father's concubine" (considered a "secondary mother") for three years.[74] In a way, Khara-Khoto social documents have verified the statements in the legal code, showing for certain that polygamy did exist in Western Xia. Previously, we only knew for a fact that Tangut emperors married multiple wives. Now, Khara-Khoto household registers convince us that commoners also engaged in this practice.

One of the two registers that mention the mother and daughter-in-law is worth some additional attention. In household (14), two adult females, the mother and wife of the patriarch, share an identical maiden name [illegible] [phiow tshji-j] (Pangqing). In other words, the mother-in-law is the aunt of the daughter-in-law, and the father-in-law of the patriarch is also his uncle. This is a case of cross-cousin marriage, a widespread social phenomenon in Tangut communities. In the Tangut language, the word for "marry" is a homophone of "nephew-uncle," and "mother-in-law" is homophonic to "aunt." This is a telling piece of historical-linguistic evidence on the social practice of cross-cousin marriage.[75] The custom was also present in the imperial court. After all, the first emperor of Western Xia, Li Yuanhao, the second emperor Liangzuo, and third emperor Bingchang all married daughters of their maternal uncles. The kind of cross-cousin marriage as practiced in Western Xia was in fact an ancient marital custom, once popular amongst many ethnic communities. Therefore, the surfacing of specific scenarios of cross-cousin marriage from the Tangut household registers is neither surprising nor coincidental.

Western Xia is a multi-ethnic empire. Each ethnic group is organised along the lines of social classes. For the same reason, family structures are highly diverse. Overall, Tangut families are patriarchal. By the *Revised Laws of*

74 *Revised Laws of Heavenly Prosperity* 2, pp. 134–135.

75 Shi, Jinbo, "Xixiayu de Maimai he Jiaqu" [西夏語的買賣和嫁娶]: "Tangut Words for 'Buy,' 'Sell,' 'marry (to a husband),' 'marry (to a wife).'" Minzu Yuwen [民族語文]: *Minority Languages of China*, issue 4, 1995.

Heavenly Prosperity, a couple may jointly form a "co-habited household" with their elders: great grandparents, grandparents, parents and unmarried aunts, kinsmen of the same generation, such as unseparated brothers and unmarried sisters, as well as the youths: sons, daughters-in-law, unmarried daughters, grandsons and granddaughters. Of course, a family comprised of all the above kinships is rare, if not non-existent. Most households are only parts and branches of their extended family tree. The demographics disclosed in the self-reports (*shoushi*) reflect the diversity and complexity of Tangut families in the Khara-Khoto area. In short, the excavation of household registers in Khara-Khoto has furnished us with sources of unprecedented depth and detail, and greatly advanced our knowledge in many aspects of the Tangut society.

CHAPTER 4

Tangut Tax Records

As a major pillar of Tangut economy, agriculture not only provided the lifeline of livelihood on which so many depended, but it also constituted the main source of tax revenue for the government. Indeed, tax levied on agricultural production was an indispensable income that sustained imperial, governmental, and military expenditures. In fact, the Chinese empire in the Central Plains likewise relied on agriculture for government spending, as "funding for the army and the state all comes from taxation."[1] There are some, though very scare, Chinese documentation on the taxation system of Western Xia, mainly in the larger context of tax exemption in disaster relief. As mentioned in Chapter 1, the Renzong Emperor approved his ministers' proposal to reduce or eliminate taxes for those injured in the great earthquake of Xingzhou (Yinchuan) and Xiazhou (Jingbian county, Shaanxi) in April of the fourth year of Daqing (1143):

> In the two prefectures, in cases where lives are lost to the earthquake, two are compensated with exemption of taxes for three years, and one with waiver of taxes for two years; the injured are exempt from taxes for two years; let collapsed houses and walls be repaired by the relevant commission.[2]

The abundance of historical sources on Tangut taxation, however, is found in the *Laws of Heavenly Prosperity*, the law code of the empire, and specifically in Book XV, which contains a list of items on agricultural taxes. Section titles reveal the classification of content in this chapter, such as "To Press for Payment" and "Misbehaviours and Merits in Pressing for Payment." The *Tiansheng Laws* require that:

> Let the authority command the heads of the taxable households to register for their cultivated lands, including the size in *qing* and *mu*, the harvest in *sheng* and *dou*, as well as the amount of forage. Let staff members from the Bureau of Transfer and Transportation issue the owners of the

1 Ma, Duanlin. *Wenxian Tongkao*, "Tianfukao" [文獻通考 田賦考]: *Comprehensive Examination of Literature* (1317). Beijing: Zhonghua Book Company, 1986, "Examination of Farmland Taxes" Part 4, "Institutions of Taxation in Previous Dynasties."

2 *Xixia Shushi*, Ch. 35.

> properties their receipts, in order that the heads of the households pay the due amount according to the number indicated on the documents.[3]

The so-called head or owner of a household refers to a subject who legally owned farmlands under tax obligations. Peasants typically paid a variety of land taxes, which are fastidiously registered in official records. In the same section of the law code, it is indicated that late payments were subject to penalties:

> In case the head of a household is liable for a variety of taxes on land, labour and forage, and yet delays the payment even when pressed by the authorities, let the concerned farmer and other members of his household be arrested, and based on the severity of the violations, let them be punished by the right number of strokes, and urged again to the speedy payment of their taxes.[4]

The *Laws* also require that each year, all prefectures and counties submit registers of land taxes and receipts to the Bureau of Transfer and Transportation on the first day of November. In late November, the staff at the Bureau of Transfer and Transportation would then deliver the records to the Bureau of Review (*Mokansi*) whose officials will proofread them within a month, in other words from the first day of December till the end of the month. Any delay in the review process would have implicated the governmental staff in criminal negligence.[5] Book XVI in the *Laws of Heavenly Prosperity* also concerns agricultural taxes. Unfortunately, this volume of the manuscript survives only in fragments, so it is only possible for scholars to speculate on the original content based on the titles in the table of contents. Although a relatively large corpus of written records on Tangut agricultural taxation have survived to the twentieth century, for a while, scholars neither retained sources on the precise amounts paid nor fully understood the formality and materiality of the tax registration. The answer to these questions, however, has recently emerged from the cloud as new materials have appeared. A diverse range of tax records

3 *Revised Laws of Heavenly Prosperity* 15, "On the Miscellaneous Taxes of Irrigation for Farmland," p. 508. The text operates on a distinction between the idea of state-imposed 'rent' (i.e. taxes) on land leased out for farming, and the conventional notion of 'rent' as transferred in contracted use of land between and amongst households. "Household" in the context of the *Revised Laws of Heavenly Prosperity* refers to the farming households that pay land taxes to the state, rather than landowners who farm the land out, or tenants who sharecrop the land.

4 *Revised Laws of Heavenly Prosperity* 15, "On the Miscellaneous Taxes of Irrigation for Farmland," p. 508.

5 *Revised Laws of Heavenly Prosperity* 15, "On Urging the Payments of Taxes," p. 490.

have recently been identified in the corpus of Khara-Khoto social documents, which now constitute the bulk of primary source on Tangut taxation. These texts not only offer a close look at the system of taxation in Western Xia but also open the gateway to inquiries on a wide array of social issues related to the Tangut economy.

1 Accounts of Agricultural Taxes

In the Russian collection of Khara-Khoto manuscripts, Инв. No. 4808 is a 20.4 × 575 cm hemp-paper scroll of signed grain taxes (by *liliu* and household) in 259 lines of cursive Tangut writings, comprised of four stitched fragments. The beginning and ends of the manuscript are missing, and two additional patches, one with six lines and the other with one line, are fractured. Furthermore, since the back of the manuscript is covered with the text of a Buddhist sutra, overlapping ink from the two sides have obscured some of the characters. The first two sections are statistical accounts of grains levied as taxes, while the third and fourth are registers of household grain taxes.

The following is a translation of the grain tax accounts of the first five households indicated in the third section (line 6–15):[6]

House of [illegible] [źjiw pa rya bie_j] (1)
  Barley 1 *dan*, 1 *dou* 5 *sheng*; wheat 2 *dou*, 8 *sheng*, 7.5 *ge*
House of chief? ?[illegible]? [? wejr] (2)
  Barley 4 *dou* 3 *sheng*; wheat 1 *dou* 7 *ge* and a half

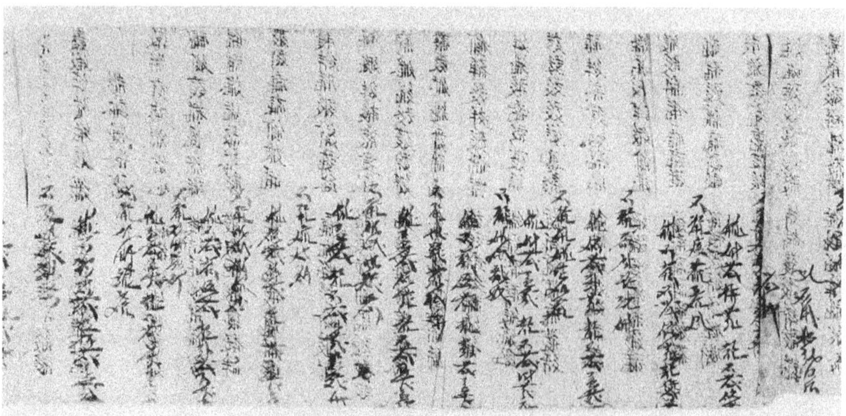

FIGURE 31 Инв. No. 4808 (6): Grain tax account

6 *Russian Collection of Khara-Khoto Manuscripts* 13, pp. 291–298.

House of [illegible] [ŋwe sji gji-_śjow] (3)
Barley 6 *dou*, 7 *sheng*; wheat 1 *dou*, 6.5 *sheng*
House of [illegible]? [ŋwe zjwi. ? wejr] (4)
Barley 1 *dou* 5 *sheng*; wheat: 3 *sheng* 7 *ge* and a half
House of [illegible]? [mja dzow kie. gju_] (5)
Barley 6 *dou* 7 *sheng*; wheat 1 *dou* 8 *sheng* 7 *ge* and a half[7]

The five registers show that these Tangut households paid 'taxes-in-kind' in the form of barley and wheat, rather than in money. In fact, more than 20 households registered in this section pay taxes in these two kinds of grains. Indeed, the Tangut government designates different crops as taxes for the various regions of its territory. According to its laws:

> Residents of the Lingwu county are obliged to pay wheat; Barley is levied on the Baojing county; both hemp and soybean are paid by the heads of households in Huayang county; the (glutinous) sorghum is levied on the residents of Linhe county; *Su*, the (foxtail) millet, is taxed from the Zhiyuan county; *Mi*, the proso millet, is paid by the two counties of Dingyuan and Huaiyuan.[8]

The list of multiple kinds of crops and grains includes the taxes-in-kind paid by households in the larger area surrounding the imperial capital. Absent on this list are the kinds of grain taxes levied on faraway regions on the periphery of the empire, such as the city of Khara-Khoto. However, from the above manuscript, we have learned that the Tanguts in Khara-Khoto paid taxes in both barley and wheat. Similar texts also show that occasionally, taxpayers turned in proso millet along with barley and wheat. For historians, these primary sources shed light on the main types of agricultural produces in Khara-Khoto under Tangut rule.

If we pay close attention to the ratio of wheat to barley mentioned in the manuscript, it is easy to notice that the amount of wheat is roughly quarter that of barley. Although the bottom part of the text is not in good condition and the end digits of wheat statistics for households 1, 2, 4, and 5 are incomplete, the numbers of both crops in the case of household 3 is a clear indication of the ratio: 6 *dou* and 7 *sheng* of barley, 1 *dou* and 6.5 *sheng* of wheat. In other words, the amount of barley is almost precisely four times that of wheat. This evidence supports the hypothesis that the Khara-Khoto authorities levied the

---

7 *Russian Collection of Khara-Khoto Manuscripts* 13, p. 293.
8 *Revised Laws of Heavenly Prosperity* 15, "On Urging the Payment of Taxes," pp. 489–490.

FIGURE 32 Инв. No. 4808 (9): Household grain tax accounts

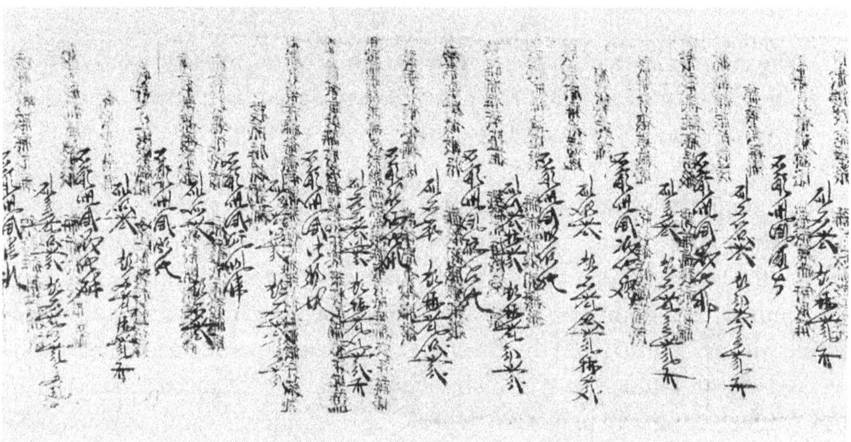

FIGURE 33 Инв. No. 4808 (10): Household grain tax accounts

two grains from local households in the ratio of 4:1. If so, then it becomes also possible to speculate on the missing numbers in the manuscript.[9]

The fourth section of the same account features a different category of produce: (miscellaneous) grains.

The following is a translation of the first ten household registers in section 4, Инв. No. 4808 (the last six lines of the first to the second image):[10]

9 The numbers within the soft brackets () are numerical orders of households added by the author for purposes of convenience and reference.

10 *Russian Collection of Khara-Khoto Manuscripts* 13, p. 295.

House of [Tangut] [dji djij gju_ rjur dju] (1)
Grains 2 *dou*; wheat 5 *sheng*
House of [Tangut][?][Tangut] [ŋwe ze tśjo. wejr] (2)
Grains 1 *dou*; wheat 2.5 *sheng*
House of [Tangut] [ŋwe zjwi. we tsji-] (3)
Grains 1 *dan* 5 *dou*; wheat 3 *dou* 7.5 *sheng*
House of [Tangut]??[Tangut] [ŋwe zjwi. ?? lji-.] (4)
Grains 7 *dou*; wheat 1 *dou* 7.5 *sheng*
House of [Tangut]??[Tangut] [ŋwe zjwi. ?? lju] (5)
Grains 6 *dou*; wheat 1 *dou* 5 *sheng* 2 *ge*
House of [Tangut]? [ŋwe zjwi. ? wejr] (6)
Grains 9 *dou* 2 *sheng*; wheat 2 *dou* 3 *sheng*
House of [Tangut]? [ŋwe zjwi. dow dźjij] (7)
Grains 1 *dan*; wheat 2 *dou* 5 *sheng*
House of [Tangut]?? [·jiw dji.j] (8)
Grains 1 *dan*, 1 *dou*, 8 *sheng*; wheat 2 *dou* 9.5 *sheng*
House of [Tangut] (the blessed)?? (9)
Grains 6 *dou* 8 *sheng*; wheat 1 *dou* 7 *sheng*
House of [Tangut] [ŋwe zjwi. tśjow lhji. śia~] (10)
Grains 4 *dou*, wheat 1 *dou*

The ten households indicated above, and another 50 or so, pay the so-called (miscellaneous) grains in addition to wheat. The 'grains' might have been simply another term for barley, for the grain to wheat ratio in all 9 houses was 4:1, with only the fifth house paying an additional 2 *ge* of wheat, possibly due to calculation or transcription errors. This account registers crop taxes by the unit of distance, *liliu*. With some margin of error in the case of the fifth house as mentioned above, the account of taxes paid by up to 18 houses confirms the grain to wheat ratio to be about 4:1.

Similar social documents include the Инв. No. 1222 and 1460-1. From these manuscripts, we know the actual amount of taxes-in-kind that each household paid but not the category of tax nor tax rate. Another kind of document offers some insights to answer these questions.

Инв. No. 1755-4 is a fragment page of a grain tax document. This 16.8 cm × 31.9 cm hemp paper with damages on all four sides contains the following 14 lines in Tangut cursive:

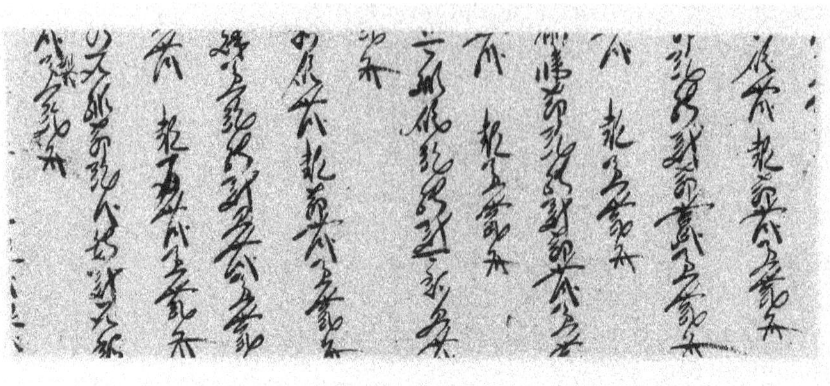

FIGURE 34 Инв. No. 1755-4: Account of grain tax by land size

Translation:[11]

...... 5 *dou*; wheat 3 *dou* 7 *sheng* and a half (1)
...... 10 *mu*, tax: 3 *dou* 7 *sheng* and a half (2)
...... *dou*; wheat 7 *sheng* and a half
...... shan 30 *mu*, tax: 3 *dou* 7 *sheng* and a half (3)
...... *dou*; wheat 3, 7 *sheng* and a half
...... 1 *qing* 50 *mu*, tax: 1 *dan* 8 *dou* and 7 (4)
sheng and half
...... dan 5 *dou*; wheat 3 *dou* 7 *sheng* and a half
...... ji, 70 *mu*, tax: 8 *dou* 7 *sheng* & half (5)
...... *dou*; wheat 1 *dou* 7 *sheng* and a half
...... 1 *qing* 39 *mu*, tax: 1 *dan* (6)
...... *dou* 3 *sheng* 7 *ge* and a half

This text documents the size of the farmland and the amount of grains paid as tax-in-kind. Quite obviously, this is a grain tax account by the size of household-owned land. Line 1 is in fact the last line in the register of household #1; lines 2–3 are the tax account of household #2; lines 4–5 correspond to household #3; lines 6–8, household #4; lines 9–10, household #5; lines 11–12, household #6. Most names of the household heads are missing, but the first character in line 4 for 'hill,' and 'fortune' in line 9 are what remains of two such names. With the imperfect data on tax and land size, it is now possible to calculate the rate of taxation by farmland. Take household #4 as an example. The

11 *Russian Collection of Khara-Khoto Manuscripts* 12, p. 306.

family owns 150 *mu* of land and pays one *dan*, eight *dou* and seven and a half *sheng* of grains as tax. Although the precise number of assorted grains are lost, there remain the characters for "... *dan* 5 *dou*" and "(taxed) wheat 3 *dou* 7 *sheng* and a half." With the performance of a simple deduction of the wheat taxed (3 *dou*, 7.5 *sheng*) from the total crops taxed (1 *dan* 8 *dou* and 7.5 *sheng*), we arrive at the number of assorted grains taxed as 1 *dan* and 5 *dou*, which matches the remnant information in the manuscript (the indication of 'dan' before and the absence of any remainder in *sheng* or *ge* after the 5 *dou*). If we then divide the tax by the size of the land, it is possible to gain the tax rate at 0.1 *dou* (i.e. 1 *sheng*) of assorted grains and 0.025 *dou* of wheat (i.e. a quarter of *sheng*) per *mu* of land. This tax rate is confirmed in the data on land and grains from other households. The moral of this story is the existence of a well-enforced system of agricultural taxation in the Western Xia, by which the grains are levied in proportion to the size of house-owned farmland. The discovery of this well-documented institution of fixed tax rates generates significant insights on Tangut agriculture. It shows at least that the Tanguts inherited the land tax system typical of the imperial institution of taxation in many dynasties.

Furthermore, once the tax rate is ascertained, it becomes possible to regain access to the numbers on both land and grain now missing in manuscript Инв. No. 1755-4, and thus to expand the text to a total of 14 lines:

...... 1 *qing* 50 *mu*, tax: 1 *dan* 8 *dou* 7 *sheng* and a half (1)
Grains: 1 *dan* 5 *dou*; wheat 3 *dou* 7 *sheng* and a half
...... [thir]ty *mu*, tax: 3 *dou* 7 *sheng* and a half (2)
Grains 3 *dou*; wheat 7 *sheng* and a half
...... shan [thir]ty *mu*, tax: 3 *dou* 7 *sheng* and a half (3)
Grains 3 *dou*; wheat 3, 7 *sheng* and a half
...... 1 *qing* 50 *mu*, tax: 1 *dan* 8 *dou* 7 (4)
sheng and a half
Grains 1 *dan* 5 *dou*; wheat: 3 *dou* 7 *sheng* and a half
...... ji, 70 *mu*, tax: 8 *dou* 7 *sheng* & half (5)
Grains 7 *dou*, wheat 1 *dou* 7 *sheng* and a half
...... 1 *qing* 39 *mu*, tax 1 *dan* (6)
7 *dou* 3 *sheng* 7 *ge* and a half
Grains 1 *dan* 3 *dou* 9 *sheng*; wheat 3 *dou* 4 *sheng* 7 *ge* and a half

There exist numerous similar accounts of grain taxes by land size, such as the manuscript Инв. No. -2-1. This 12.9 × 31.8 cm document is originally a layering paper for a book cover. The text features an upper and lower section of grain tax registers in fragments. The lower part contains grain tax accounts of seven

FIGURE 35 Инв. No. 1178-2: Account of grain tax by farmland size

households in 12 lines of Tangut cursive writings, but the tax payment registers are missing. Another example is the 12.7 × 32.3 cm manuscript Инв. No. 1178-2, with its 11 lines in Tangut cursive scribbled over another layering paper of a book cover.[12]

Translation of the text with emendation:

> …… Grains 1 *dan* 5 *dou*; wheat 3 *dou* 7 *sheng* and a half (1)
> …… le 1 *qing* 48 *mu*, tax: 1 *dan* *dou* (2)
> 5 *sheng*
> Grains 1 *dan* 4 *dou* 8 *sheng*, wheat 3 *dou* 7 *sheng* ……
> …… [illegible] [sji- twe. gji pa rya wejr], 1 *qing* 43 (3)
> *mu*, tax: 1 *dan* 7 *dou* 8 *sheng* 7 *ge* & a half
> Grains 1 *dan* 4 *dou* 3 *sheng*; wheat 3 *dou* 3 *sheng* 2
> …… ji, 28 *mu*, tax: 3 *dou* 5 *sheng* (4)
> Grains 1 *dan* *dou* 8 *sheng*; wheat 7 *sheng*
> …… you, 72 *mu*, tax: 9 *dou* (5)
> Grains 7 *dou* 2 *sheng*; wheat 1 *dou* 8 *sheng*

The calculated tax rates for household # 1, 2, 4, and 5 are identical to the standard rate that was calculated based on data from the previous manuscript: one *sheng* of grains and about a fourth of *sheng* of wheat per *mu* of land. In the lone of household #3, however, the wheat count is three *dou* 3.2 *sheng*, which could have been a calculation or transcription error from the correct amount of three *dou*, five *sheng*, and 7.5 *ge*. Indeed, an additional number of grain-to-land tax accounts such as Инв. No. 324-2, 5809-2 and 5940 demonstrates consistency

12 *Russian Collection of Khara-Khoto Manuscripts* 12, p. 211.

in the grain tax rate that we have determined, with a result that deviations from the number may be treated as minor mistakes or discrepancies. Scholars are also able to conclude that the manuscript Инв. No. 4808, which only shows the number of crops taxed but not the size of farmland, to be likewise a grain-to-land tax account.

According to the *Laws of Heavenly Prosperity*, those who clear wastelands for agriculture in the peripheral regions of the empire are exempt from taxes for three years: "after three years, if the area proves arable, then three *sheng* of miscellaneous grains are taxed for one *mu* of land."[13] It then seems that the tax rate applied to local communities in Khara-Khoto was lower than the rate for newly-farmed lands as indicated in the code of law. But it is also worth noting that the agricultural taxes in Khara-Khoto are not necessarily representative of those in the majority of areas in Western Xia. Consider another set of rules and regulations in the same *Laws of Heavenly Prosperity* where the government may apply an adjusted measure of grain-to-land taxation in the areas surrounding the imperial capital: the farmlands concerned are sorted into five ranks based on quality, with a slightly modified tax rate for each. As a result, the tax rate sometimes exceeds that in Khara-Khoto by a significant margin.

> Concerning the taxpaying households in the seven neighbouring counties near the imperial capital, lands are ranked according to their fertility: the highest, 1 *dou*; the second best, 8 *sheng*; the middle, 6 *sheng*; the lower, 5 *sheng*; the bottom, 3 *sheng*; hence a total of 5 ranks.[14]

It is not difficult to see the underlying message of this piece of legislation: the fertile and irrigable lands near the imperial capital are progressively taxed, at

13 *Revised Laws of Heavenly Prosperity* 15, "On Land Taxes," pp. 495–496.

14 *Russian Collection of Khara-Khoto Manuscripts* 8, pp. 300, 307, 301. Only the second half of this item is published in Professor Kychanov's Russian edition of the *Revised Laws of Heavenly Prosperity* (*Изменённый и заново утверждённый кодекс девиза царствования Небесное процветание*, 1149–1169) Vol. 4. Three earlier leaves were missing. Nor is the missing half present in the Chinese edition (Shi, Jinbo, et al.) of the *Revised Laws of Heavenly Prosperity*. However, the missing piece was discovered amongst the manuscripts in Russia, just in time for the Sino-Russian collaboration in the publication of the *Russian Collection of Khara-Khoto Manuscripts*. In another unfortunate turn of events, page 2 in Volume 8 of the *Russian Collection of Khara-Khoto Manuscripts* was mistakenly placed at the end. See Pan, Jie. "Tiansheng Gaijiu Xinding Lüling Cuijiaozumen Yiduan Xixiawen Zhuihe" [天盛改舊新定律令·催繳租門一段西夏文綴合]: "Conjoining a piece of Tangut writing in the Section on Urging the Payment of Taxes in the *Revised Laws of Heavenly Prosperity*" in *Ningxia Shehui Kexue* [寧夏社會科學]: *Ningxia Social Sciences*, issue 6, 2012.

some rates much higher than in Khara-Khoto in order to extract maximal government revenues.

2 Accounts of Land and Forage Taxes

Agricultural taxes in Western Xia are hardly limited to the fixed grain-to-land imposts. According to the *Law of the Heavenly Prosperity*:

> All the counties are obliged to transfer the imposts, so they are required to urge and monitor the payment of levies on land, labour and forage. They are then supposed to collect all the receipts, one round per month, to be fetched by appointed officials and delivered to the Transfer Commission.[15]

In fact, there are more than a few accounts of taxes on land, labour, and forage in the corpus of Tangut economic records. Altogether, they document all three kinds of taxes that sustained the imperial revenue.

2.1 *Land, Labour and Forage in Tax Accounts*

The term 'land tax' is captured by the Tangut character [illegible] [zji.j], which means 'rent' and 'tax.' It refers both to the 'rent' that a taxpayer submits to the state, and to the lease rent that any private farmer has to pay the landowner. In this context, however, it means the land tax levied by the empire. The Tangut character for 'labour' is [illegible] [tśju], an equivalent of the Chinese character '役,' which literally means 'occupation.' In the context of the *Laws of Heavenly Prosperity*, the word is customarily translated as 'employment' (i.e., the service of labour contributed to a particular project), which may be an extension of the Song-era Chinese term for 'employment,' "職役."[16] As for 'forage,' or 'hay' in particular, the Tangut word is that for 'grass' [illegible], or the bundles of hay levied as a tax-in-kind. The tax laws cited at the beginning of the section convey a very clear message: The Tanguts paid not only crops in proportion to their lands and harvests, but also labour services and forages. According to the regulations of agricultural profits in Book 16 of the *Laws of Heavenly Prosperity*, there are

---

15 *Revised Laws of Heavenly Prosperity* 15, "On the Miscellaneous Taxes of Irrigation for Farmland," pp. 507–508.

16 Pan Jie changed the translation of 'employed labour' to 'taxed labour,' which is adopted in this book. See Pan, Jie. "Xixia Zuyicao Kaoshu" [西夏租役草考述]: "A Critical Survey of Tax, Labour, and Hay in Western Xia" (unpublished manuscript).

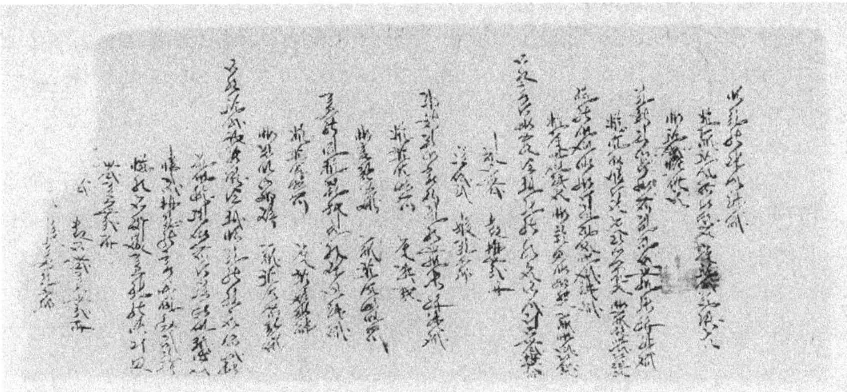

FIGURE 36 Инв. No. 4067: Household account of farmland and labour taxes

items that specify the procedures of "landowners' registration of taxes," "the forage obligations of farmers in the Mingsha and imperial capital" and "the distribution of ryegrass duties to the farm owners." Although the content of these legislations remains unknown to scholars, for none of the relevant manuscripts have survived to this day, it is now possible to catch a detailed and realistic glimpse of the land, labour and forage taxes through the lens of excavated Tangut social documents.

The manuscript Инв. No. 4067 is a tax payment account on a piece of 19.5 × 46.2 cm hemp paper. Although the beginning and end are both missing, there are 23 lines of legible Tangut in the cursive style, which provide data on three households: their payment of taxes, location and boundaries of owned lands. The only register preserved in complete form is in the middle. The first 3 of its 9 lines (lines 8–16) concern the size of land and amount of tax, whereas the next 6 lines describe the locations and boundaries of the two farmlands owned by this house.[17]

The following is a translation of three lines (8–10) on the land and tax:

> House of 𗁅𗼑𗶷𗡟 [ljow gju_ rjur dju], owns ten *mu* of land on the register; tax: 1 *dou* 2 *sheng* and a half
> Miscellaneous grains 1 *dou*; wheat 2 *sheng* and a half
> Labour services: 5 days; forage: 10 bundles of hays

The land-to-grain tax rate here is patently identical to the calculated number in the previous sections: For 10 *mu* of land, a tax rate of 1 *sheng* (0.1 *dou*)/*mu*

17 *Russian Collection of Khara-Khoto Manuscripts* 13, p. 180.

yields a total payment of 1 *dou* of tax; as for wheat, 10 *mu* × 0.025 *dou*/*mu* = 0.25 *dou* = 2.5 *sheng*. But this account differs from what has been seen so far in that it lists 5 days of labour services and 10 bundles of hay. This rule in the *Laws of Heavenly Prosperity* states:

> When large or small-scale labour projects take place within and at the borders of the realm, let labourers be gathered and dispatched according to law. If labourers are not sent, in violation of the law, let a man of status be punished with the confiscation of a horse, and a commoner by thirteen strokes.[18]

There were a wide variety of labour services in Western Xia. The government drafted labourers to construct and repair canals and to transport goods and provisions across the territorial domain of the vast empire. Labourers summoned to work were scattered at the end of the project. If an unfinished assignment required the continued service of labourers, the government asked for and approved a special report on the status of the commission. The household listed above offered five days of services, which is about the amount of labour required for a year.

The manuscript Инв. No. 5067 is a tax record of the same kind, written on the back of a Buddhist sutra. Despite damages in the beginning and at the end, the 19.2 × 238 cm long scroll features a total of 119 lines of Tangut in the cursive. The section on each household's land and labour tax begins at the top without indentation, followed by lower indented lines on the names of the household patriarch, changes in land conditions, the current size of cultivated lands, as well as the total amount of grains taxed. The final two lines rise up two spaces, which record the numbers of mixed grains, wheat, labour (in days) and hay (in bundles) in four parts. Occasionally, this section also documents the location and four boundaries of the piece of farmland concerned.[19]

Of the 14 household records, #1 suffers an illegible beginning and a loss of information on land size, while households #2, #9 and #12 seem to have sold their lands, hence the absence of records on their payments of land, labour and forage taxes. The other 10 households, however, have complete sets of records sufficient for us to calculate and analyse the relationship between land and labour taxes.

---

18 *Revised Laws of Heavenly Prosperity* 7, "On Conducting Taxed Labour," p. 288.

19 *Russian Collection of Khara-Khoto Manuscripts* 14, pp. 5–7.

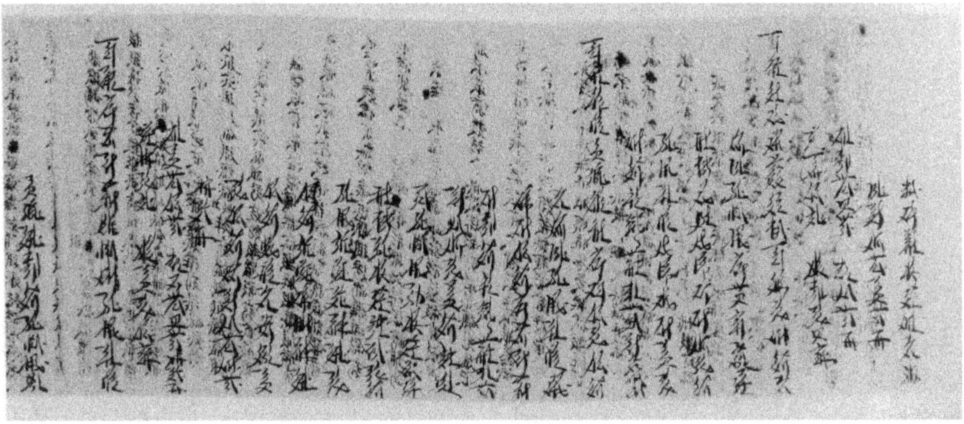

FIGURE 37 Инв. No. 5067 (1): Household account of farmland and labour taxes

FIGURE 38 Инв. No. 5067 (2): Household account of farmland and labour taxes

The following is a translated excerpt of Инв. No. 5067 on the land size (in *mu*) and labour service (in days) of the ten households:

> Household #3: land 75 *mu*, labour service 20 days;
> Household #4: land 10 *mu*, labour service 5 days;
> Household #5: land 10 *mu*, labour service 5 days;
> Household #6: land 38 *mu*, labour service 15 days;
> Household #7: land 10 *mu*, labour service 5 days;
> Household #8: land 35 *mu*, labour service 15 days;
> Household #10: land 73 *mu*, labour service 20 days;
> Household #11: land 63 *mu*, labour service 20 days;
> Household #13: land 15 *mu*, labour service 15 days;
> Household #14: land 40 *mu*, tax levied 15 days.

At first glance, owners of ten *mu* of land typically contributed five days of labour. Fifteen days of work, however, correspond to a range of land sizes, from 15 to 35, 38 and 40 *mu*. Those who owned 63, 73 and 75 *mu* of land paid 20 days of labour. In general, land size and labour output are positively correlated. It is likely, therefore, that the amount of labour taxes was also partly determined by land ownership.

Labour service as a form of taxation is mentioned in the statements on springtime canal constructions in the *Laws of Heavenly Prosperity*:

> For taxable households within the vicinity of the imperial capital, which contribute to the great canal construction in the spring, those who own 1–10 *mu* of land work for 5 days; owners of 11–40 *mu* of land, 15 days; 41–75 *mu*, 20 days; 75–100 *mu*, 30 days; from 100 *mu* to 1 *qing* and 20 *mu*, 35 days; from 1 *qing* and 20 *mu* to 1 *qing* and 50 *mu*, 40 days. Days are calculated based on land size in *qing* and *mu*. Those who fulfil the requirement sooner may be released of their duty earlier.[20]

The law stipulates that for the canal-building project in the spring, each household unit is to contribute labour services for five varying lengths of duration: 5, 15, 20, 30, 35 or 40 days, respectively. The numbers indicated in the law code agree with the data from the manuscript studied above, except for the lack of examples for 35 and 40-day periods. However, this is partly compensated, by a similar record, Инв. No. 7415-1, a 20.5 × 28.9 cm manuscript account of household land, labour and forage tax also marred at the two ends. Its first two lines indicate a tax amount of 1 *dan*, 1 *dou* and 2 *sheng* of miscellaneous grains, which allow us to calculate the land size to be 1 *qing* and 12 *mu*. This family paid "1 month and 5 days of labour service"—exactly 35 days.[21]

Yet another land, labour and forage tax of the same type deserves our attention. The 19 × 37.5 cm Russian manuscript Инв. No. 5252 contains 22 lines of cursive Tangut, despite loss of information at the two fronts. One of the households recorded in this document (see lines 10–15), which owns 1 *qing* and 50 *mu* of farmland, pays 1 *dan* and 5 *dou* of assorted grains, 3 *dou* 7.5 *sheng* of wheat, as well as "one full range" of labour.[22]

---

20 *Revised Laws of Heavenly Prosperity* 15, "On the Affairs of Opening Canals in the Spring," pp. 495–496.

21 *Russian Collection of Khara-Khoto Manuscripts* 14, p. 177.

22 *Russian Collection of Khara-Khoto Manuscripts* 14, p. 30.

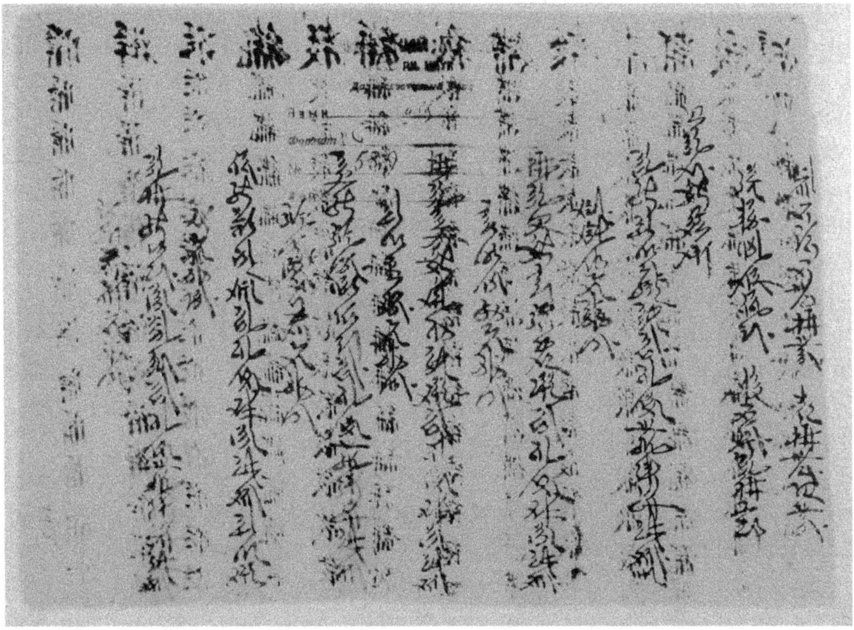

FIGURE 39 Инв. No. 7415-1: Household account of land, labour and hay taxes

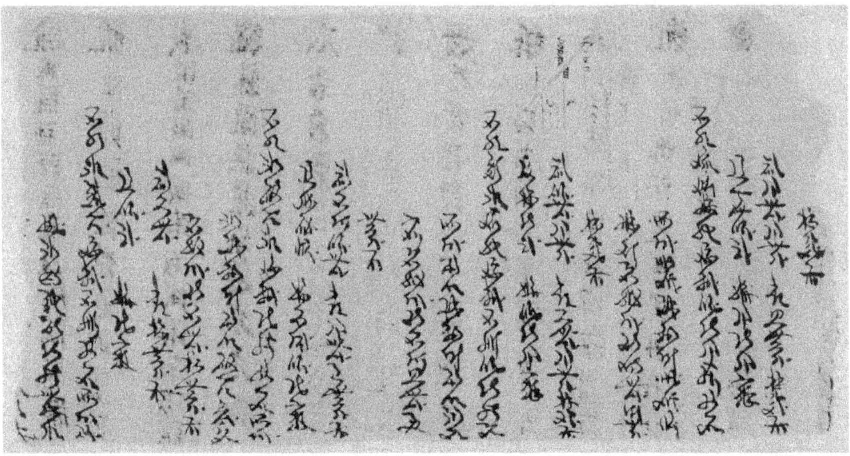

FIGURE 40 Инв. No. 5252: Household account of farmland, labour and hay taxes

In the above two cases, the amount of labour contribution at 35 days and 40 days, respectively, coincides expectedly with the legal requirement in the *Laws of Heavenly Prosperity* that "owners of anywhere between 100 *mu* and 1 *qing* and 20 *mu* of land are obliged to offer 35 days of service. As for owners of as much land as between 1 *qing* and 20 *mu* and 1 *qing* and 50 *mu*, they are required to contribute a full range of 40 days." Basically, the manuscripts convey the critical information that the 'labour service' as meant in the Khara-Khoto documents referred to the same tax obligation as the 'burden of labour' in the context of springtime canal construction around the imperial capital, as mentioned in the text of the *Laws of Heavenly Prosperity*. This type of tax payment in the form of manual labour was therefore not unique to the area in close proximity to the Tangut royal house; it was also present in peripheral, albeit important, territories like the city of Khara-Khoto.

As referenced repeatedly before, a critical portion of Tangut taxation consisted of 'forage,' which refers to the supply of hay used to feed horses both on domestic pastures over the harvestless wintry days of the year and in the cavalries and transport teams of a marching army. The importance of forage demands no redundant elaborations, given the important status of pasturing and animal husbandry in the economy of Western Xia. Besides, Tangut agriculture could not flourish without ample irrigation, which required a thick layer of hay underneath the canal pathways in the time of spring. For this variety of reasons, the *Laws of Heavenly Prosperity* mentions not only land, livestock and grains as household properties, but also 'bundles' (of hay), such as in the statement that "in cases of men who accidentally set on fire livestock, houses, persons, grains and foods, or bundles of hay, it is necessary to investigate and ascertain the actual amount of property losses."[23] It is not surprising, then, for the same law code to also require the payment of tax-in-kind not only in terms of rents and labour but also forage, in very specific units of bundles which are determined based on the size of land ownership:

> For each taxable household, apart from the winter reed clumps and summer herbs, all the other types of plants grown in its land are taxed at the rate of 5 *chi*/*mu* as a bundle; for 15 *mu*, 4 *chi* in pampas grass, willow branches and vines are all taxed by the amount of 1 bundle.[24]

Here is a list of the 10 households' land ownership and bundles of hays paid as tax:

23 *Revised Laws of Heavenly Prosperity* 8, "On Burning, Injuring, and Murdering," pp. 292–293.
24 *Revised Laws of Heavenly Prosperity* 15, "On Water Canals," p. 503.

Household #3, land: 75 *mu*, hay: 75 bundles;
Household #4, land: 10 *mu*, hay: 10 bundles;
Household #5, land: 10 *mu*, hay: 10 bundles;
Household #6, land: 38 *mu*, hay: 38 bundles;
Household #7, land: 10 *mu*, hay: 10 bundles;
Household #8, land: 35 *mu*, hay: 35 bundles;
Household #10, land: 73 *mu*, hay: 73 bundles;
Household #11, land: 63 *mu*, hay: 63 bundles;
Household # 13, land: 15 *mu*, hay: 50 bundles;
Household # 14, land: 40 *mu*, hay: 40 bundles.

With the exception of household #13, the 1:1 land-to-hay ratio remains consistent. As for the data on household #13, the 15 *mu* of land v. 50 bundles of hay: Could it be the land size or the hay data that are erroneous? Fortunately, we have the amount of grain taxes under the same household, which reads "1 *dou*, 8 *sheng*, 7 *ge* and a half." Given the tax rate of 1 *sheng*, 2.5 *ge*/*mu* in Khara-Khoto, the household's owned land is calculated to be exactly 15 *mu*. It is therefore safe to say that the land size is correct, whereas the hay data suffered some typological or statistical error. Again, this analytical exercise demonstrates that the Tangut laws on hay taxes were thoroughly enforced even in remote territories.

The *Laws of Heavenly Prosperity* also stipulates:

> For the heads of households to distribute the duties of ryegrass to the farmers, apart from the winter grass turfs and the rafters from their own land, for each *qing* and fifty *mu* of land, there is a duty of seven bundles of ryegrass and thirty bundles of millet grass. The rope bound to the bundles should be four *chi* and five *cun* in length. Additionally, they should place three *hu* of wheat Brans in the bag of each bundle.[25]

The Tangut classifier for 'bundle' (of grass, hay, forage, etc.) is 𗘂 [śja]. Originally a verb meaning 'to bind, or to fasten with a rope,' it evolved into a unit of measurement, signifying the result of the verbal action. This law specifies that for the 150 *mu* of land, in addition to the allocated amount of winter grass and beams, there were an additional 37 bundles of rye and millet grasses. It is quite likely that a 1:1 ratio, namely 1 bundle of hay per 1 *mu* of land, was the 'original' requirement as referenced here in the background, while the additional 37 bundles were amendments posterior to the era of Tiansheng. Tangut bureaucrats imposed fastidious requirements on the size of bundles by standardising

25 *Revised Laws of Heavenly Prosperity* 15, "On Urging the Payment of Taxes," p. 490.

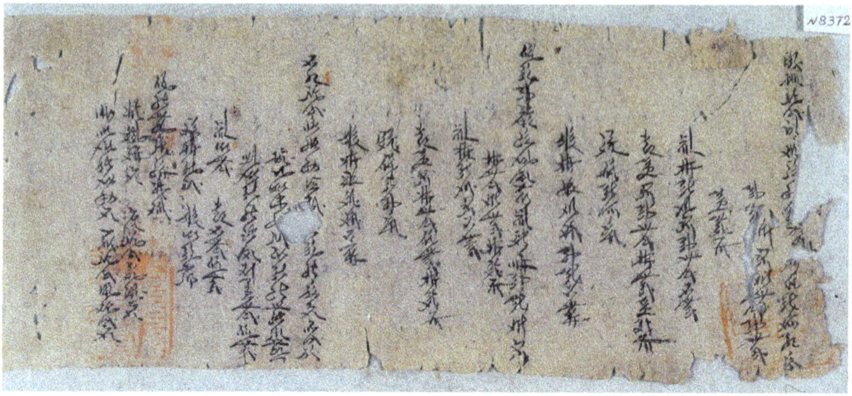

FIGURE 41 Инв. No. 8372: Household account of farmland, labour and hay taxes

the lengths of ropes used to bind them. Likewise, the Jurchens also required, in addition to the standard tax rate per *mu* of land, an additional string of stalk (left in the plant after threshing), whereby each 'string' had to weigh 15 *jin*. The stalks (Chinese: 秸) are the straws of the crops. In that sense, what the Tanguts referred to as ryegrass and millet grass were also 'stalks' or 'straws.' The only difference between Tangut and Jurchen legislations is that the former measured by the length of the attached rope, whereas the latter did so by weight.

The Khara-Khoto tax records also show that the accounts of land, labour and hay taxes were registered by units of farming households. The statistical registers are, in turn, organised by the spatial unit of *liliu*. The Инв. No. 8372 manuscript is a 19.5 × 49 cm tax account with 21 lines of Tangut in the cursive style. There is some damage at the front and missing parts near the end. Additionally, the document features three red stamps.[26]

The following is a translation:

Liliu 豩?? [tśhjiw zjwi.] a total of 54 households, taxes
16 *dan* 6 *dou* 3 *sheng*
7 *ge* and a half
Coarse, 29 *dan* 3 *dou* 1 *sheng*
Wheat 7 *dan* 3 *dou* 2 *sheng* 7 *ge* and a half
Labour 54 persons
Hay 2,931 bundles

26 *Russian Collection of Khara-Khoto Manuscripts* 14, p. 262.

53 farming families? Farmers have fine/coarse grains, in total 36 *dan*
2 *dou* 6 *sheng* 2 *ge* and a half
Coarse 29 *dan* 1 *dou*
Wheat 7 *dan* 2 *dou* 5 *sheng* 2 *ge* and a half
Labour 53 persons
Hay 2901 bundles
Household 𗤻? [tśhjiw zjwi. tśhjwor], registered 60 *mu* of land on records; with ?? all
??large or small size? 10 *mu* already
And 60 *mu* already retained, tax 7 *dou* 5 *sheng*
Coarse 6 *dou* wheat 1 *dou* 5 *sheng*
Labour 20 days hay 60 bundles
5 *mu* connected to the canals
To the east to "Bird"? (border) To the south, to …(border)
To the west, to "Prosperity of the Sixth Month" (𗏁𗼃𗤻) (border); To the north, to 𗤻? [tśhjiw zjwi. wa] (border)
……

This document registers 54 households within a unit of *liliu*. Unfortunately, the farmland (size and border), tax and hay statistics of only one household survives, leaving all other data missing. According to the *Laws of Heavenly Prosperity*, the administration of one *liliu* oversaw the management of 100 households. However, this manuscript shows that only 54 families fell into this *liliu*. In the case of the other document mentioned above, Инв. No. 6342, the *liliu* unit was comprised of 79 households. Therefore, more than one document seems to support the hypothesis that, notwithstanding the "100 households per *liliu*" requirement on government papers, the actual number of households within each *liliu* fluctuated from one area to another, depending on the realities of the area. But in any case, it was permissible for a *liliu* to have a smaller population than required in the law code.

Despite quite a few obstacles, including lost, blurred, and illegible characters and figures, it is possible to tell from the document that the 54 households turned in a total of 36 *dan*, 6 *dou*, 3 *sheng* and 7 *ge* and a half. Amongst them, coarse grains made up for 29 *dan*, 3 *dou* and 1 *sheng*, in addition to 7 *dan*, 3 *dou*, 2 *sheng* and 7 *ge* and a half of wheat. We also know that there was a total of 29 *qing* and 31 *mu* of farmland. 54 individuals paid taxes by physical labour—that is, most likely, 1 person per household. As for how many days they toiled, however, there are no details. The documents record a total payment of 2,931 bundles of hay, which is also the accurate number based on the size of the farmland in *mu*. If 54 households turn in 36 *dan*, 6 *dou*, 3 *sheng* and 7 *ge* and a half of grains, whereas 53 households are taxed 36 *dan*, 2 *dou*, 6 *sheng* and 2 *ge* and a half, the difference in tax of one-unit household is 3.75 *dou*. Given that the Khara-Khoto government levied 1.25 *sheng* of grains per *mu* of land, the household in question should have owned about 30 *mu* of farmland. Besides, we also know that the 54 households turned in 2931 bundles of hay or grass, which is 30 bundles more than the total amount levied on the 53 households (2901 bundles), for 1 more household. Therefore, the tax in hay also proves that the one household owned 30 *mu* of land. Unfortunately, because of damages to the manuscript fragment, it is impossible to identify what exactly set this one household apart from the other 53. One may conjecture many possibilities such as, for example, that this household was that of a lowlier family of *shijun* (semi-slaves).

Tax-in-kind was one of the main forms of tax levied on the agrarian populations of Western Xia. Not unlike in the Central Plains, tax-in-kind was the predominant regime of agricultural taxation. Another form of tax was physical labour. In Western Xia, corvée labour was used to build, renovate and manage canals. Given lower degrees of circularity in the Tangut currency, most of the taxes as referred to in the Khara-Khoto manuscripts were in terms of taxes-in-kinds. Very few of these documents record taxes in cash or in real currencies.

2.2 *Receipts of Grain Taxes*

Amongst the British manuscripts of Khara-Khoto, Or. 12380-2349 (k.k.), an 11 × 8.5 cm block-printed document with filled-in characters, is a fragment with few remaining words—some clear, others pale or blurred—on both sides of the paper.[27]

Close scrutiny reveals the following in the first line on the first page: "Now from …"; in the second line, (unclear characters in the block print) filled out in black ink, "interest due Barley …"; in the third line, the block-printed characters read, "Tiansheng," whilst the part handwritten in black ink states, "twenty," followed by what may be inferred as "year"; the third line also has the following block-printed content: "office agent (*sili*) Yehe …" Of course, the Tiansheng era falls into Emperor Renzong's reign, and Yehe is a Dangxiang Tangut family name. This government employee holds the office of an agent, or *sili*, with a seal of the characters [illegible] [rjijr njijr ɣu ka.] (the fourth character is blurred), which literally translates into "measure/calculate, aspect/dimension, head, monitor/supervise,"—that is, a "junior accounting magistrate." Undersigned

27 These two images are photographed by the author. See also, *British Collection of Khara-Khoto Manuscripts*, p. 80.

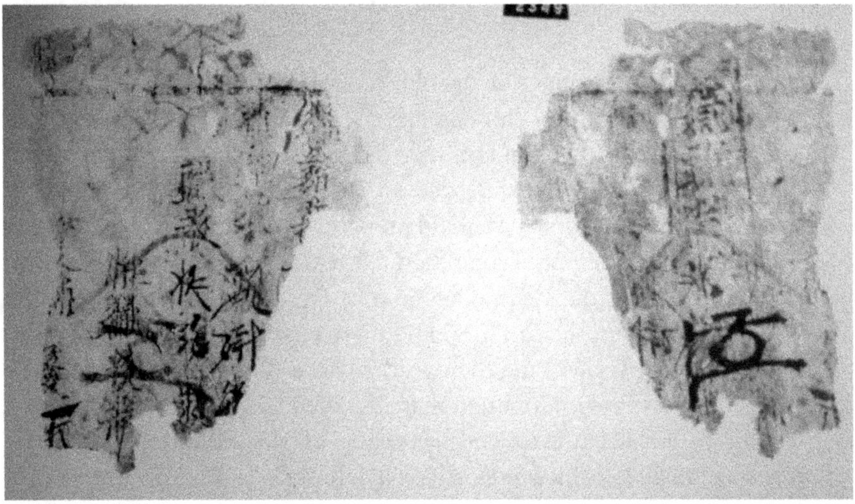

FIGURE 42 British Or. 12380-2349 (k.k.): twentieth year of Tiansheng (1168) grain tax receipt

is a printed sign. Concerning the "junior accounting magistrate," the *Laws of Heavenly Prosperity* states:

> When it is time for the collection of various taxes, the junior accounting magistrate should sit at the gate of the storage house. The patrolling magistrates should sit by the side of the junior accounting magistrate. They should call the names of those paying grains as taxes, in due order, and then measure what they offer before taking them over. They should also issue receipts to the taxpayers, which label the total sums in *hu* and *dou*, and the signatures of the junior accounting magistrate. Any adulteration or falsification in the payment of grains is strictly forbidden. If the junior accounting magistrate and the patrolling magistrate from higher or lower offices are unable to check the amounts with accuracy, the local prefects in charge should take over the responsibility of supervision. If there is any violation of law—for instance, if those who did not pay are listed as having paid—and if there is inflation or falsification of the numbers, let the sum of the unpaid amount of grains be calculated, and let the culprit be tried on the charge of theft. If officials commit bribery, then the gravity of this offence is to be compared to the charge of 'Violation of Law and Corruption,' and whichever is more severe is to be applied to the culprit. If the concerned personality is not bribed, but rather committed errors in examinations and calculations, he is to be punished by the confiscation of a horse if an official, and by thirteen strokes if a commoner.

And:

> In addition to and alongside the old register book, the junior accounting magistrate is responsible for compiling a new book of statistics, according to the amount of grains taxed. Upon completion, he is obliged to compare the new book to the old, to ensure there is no inaccuracy or discrepancy. At the end, he should prepare a volume of clean copy to be attached to the memorial submitted to the Central Secretariat. The staff members within the Central Secretariat are expected to examine the records for yet another time. Should there be any discrepancy, let them report it to the Crown, and then proceed according to what instructions they receive. If the information matches, then let the new and old registers be preserved at the Central Secretariat, and let the additional copy be returned to be informed and delivered to the relevant offices in charge.[28]

This "junior accounting magistrate" in the passages above was a kind of tax-collecting agent in offices of local governments. As he received grains from the farming families in the area, he issued receipts with the amount of grains taxed and his own handwritten signature.

The document features the expression "interest due," handwritten here in this text. It essentially refers to the taxes. This word also appears multiple times in the *Laws of Heavenly Prosperity*, especially in the table of contents in the sixteenth volume. All the more regrettable, then, that the main content of that volume has been lost. So, there is practically no easy access to the specific legal items related to "interest due." However, the table of contents provides some clues. The sixteenth volume refers specifically to the notion of "due interest" for as many as 17 times: "On the Interests Due by the Peasants" includes "'interest due' to holders of the plough in the ditches and in the field," "'interest due' to holders of the plough in the border lines," "Sums of 'interests due' for royal provision of rice," "'interests due' to holders of the plough," "'interest due' to farm owners affiliated with the Department of Construction etc. holding their ploughs," "'interests due' on hemp plantations, etc.," "Urging the payment of 'due interests,'" "Urging the examination of 'interests due' on the day of tax payment," "Urging the examination of 'due interests' in the border regions," "'due interests' unable to enter the account," "Commuted sentence after no longer being able to wear shackles on charges related to 'due interests,'" "Political promotion rewarded for competency in managing grains and 'due interests,'" "the

28 *Revised Laws of Heavenly Prosperity* 15, "On the Dispatchment of Junior Accounting Magistrate to Collect Taxes in the Form of Grains," pp. 513–514.

amount of 'interests due' to the farm owner," "The method of examining 'interest due' on ploughed fields," "failure to bring about the grains by the office in charge of collecting the 'due interests.'" From these terms and items, especially "Urging the payment of 'due interests,'" it is possible to surmise that "interest due" refers to the taxes that people pay to the government. Since the word for "barley" appears under the "interest due" in these texts, one could also infer and conclude that the taxes-in-kind are paid in terms of barley. Therefore, this manuscript is properly entitled "Receipt of grain tax payment in the twentieth year of Heavenly Prosperity (1168)."

The laws and regulations as they appear in the *Laws of Heavenly Prosperity* also match the content of these unearthed documents. The twenty or more characters on this manuscript, despite severe damages, once again testify to the efficiency, expediency and enforceability of the *Laws of Heavenly Prosperity*.[29] Moreover, the grain tax receipt itself is an invaluable piece of textual material. There are multiple reasons for this, but one, at least, is the format of the document. The receipt is block-printed en masse, to be filled out by hand at a later time. Ground-breaking for its own time, this method renders the structure of the document fixed in format, systematic in scaled production, and thus more convenient for use, operation and management, despite their large quantity. It represents a major development in the ancient and medieval history of economic documents.

2.3 *Receipts of Increased Taxes on Bundles of Hay*

Some manuscripts shed light on additional impositions of taxes in bundles of hay. Amongst the manuscripts unearthed from the Haimu Cave in Wuwei, Gansu, there are two copies of a record on additional hay taxes, dated to the You Year of Qianding Reign (1225). The G31.05[6730]–[6731] are single pages on hemp paper, which measure up to 17.5 × 13 cm and 19 × 13.5 cm in size, respectively.

Both pages of the two documents are both printed with Tangut characters. At the front left corner of the front page, there is a large Tangut character inked in the standard script [Tangut character] [kow], which translates into the Chinese 官, meaning political office. This may be seen as the symbol that marks the nature of a document, not unlike official letter heads in modern formats of

29 This document was published for the first time in 2010. See Shi, Jinbo. "Yingcang Heishuicheng Wenxian Dingming Chuyi ji Buzheng" [英藏黑水城文獻定名芻議及補正]: "A Preliminary Proposal for Naming and Amending the British collection of Khara-Khoto manuscripts" in *Xixiaxue* [西夏學]: *Tangut Studies*, No. 5, September 2010. Additional findings and insights on the nature and interpretation of the text are herein supplied.

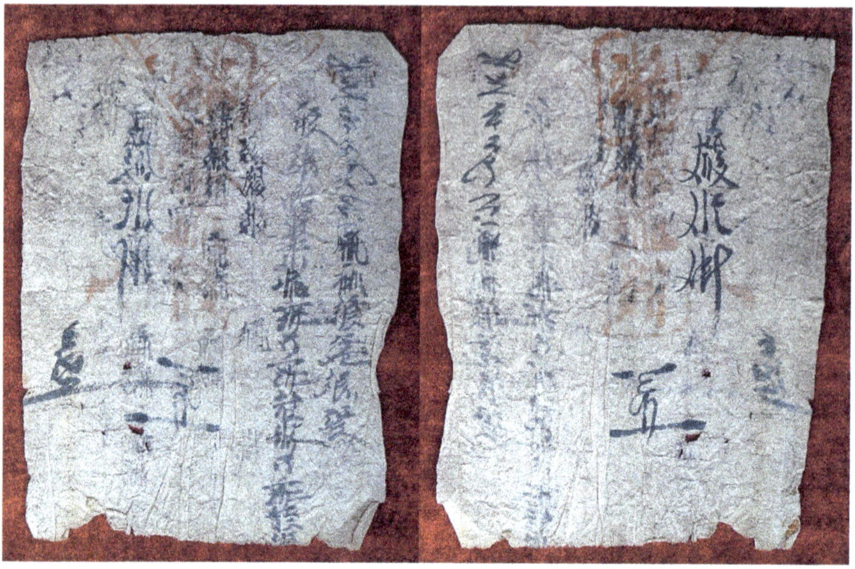

FIGURE 43 Wuwei manuscript G31.05[6730]: You year of Qianding, additional levies of hay in bundles, "government" document (front and back)

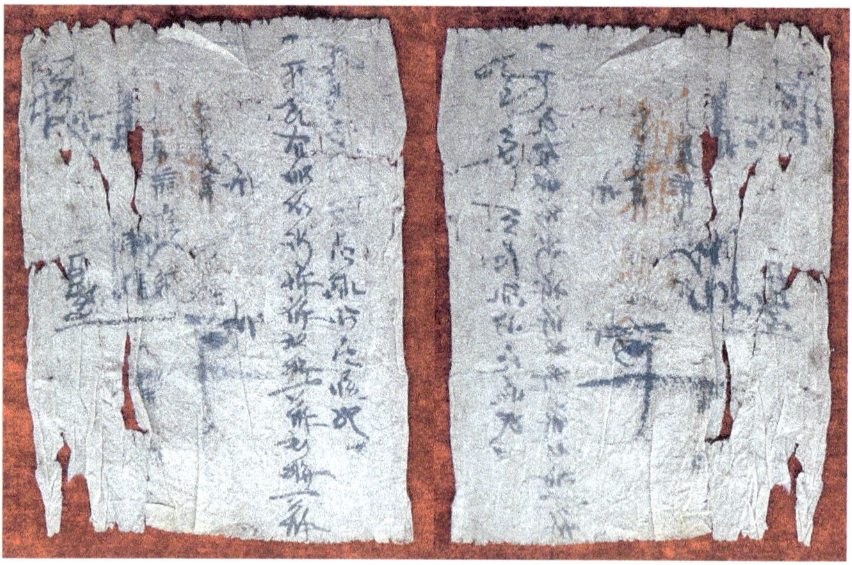

FIGURE 44 Wuwei manuscript G31.05[6731]: You year of Qianding, additional levies of hay in bundles, "household" document (front and back)

political documents. On the back, there is a large character [ɣa], also inked in standard script Tangut, which can be translated into the Chinese character 戶, meaning house, household or family.

The [kow] document begins with two lines of handwritten Tangut in the cursive script, which roughly translates as follows:

> The head of the *Liliu*, Moxi "Prosperous sprout"
> One household, [dźiew ɣiew u][30] added 2 bundles, 1 bundle of ryegrass, 1 bundle of millet grass.

Five lines of characters are printed at the end of this text:

> You Year of Qianding Reign month day
> The guardian of the storage, Hao, [31]
> The one who made the official book of registers, Zhong
> □□
> The guardian of the storage house,

The document is sealed in red with a stamp of carved-in characters. The shape resembles an inverted triangle, and the words are unfortunately illegible. But from the inklings of what remains, it is possible to tell that the seal was originally square in shape, its four sides about 5.7 cm in length each. The size and format of this seal comes very close to the standard for the seals of Tangut chiefs.

There are two lines of Tangut in the cursive style on the back of the document. The first line reads: [dźjwow kjiw xo], "You Year (the year of Chicken) of" followed by formal prints. The four standard-script Tangut characters in the 10.5 × 2.8 cm rectangular seal at the centre of the page are identified as [khju_·u. ɣu ka.], the main officer in charge of the storage house.

Another document, the manuscript G31.05[6731] features 5 lines of Tangut on the front, which also begins with two lines handwritten in the cursive script. Apart from the different names which appear under "One household" in the second line, the rest of the content is almost identical. There are an additional 5 printed lines, which are so light and blurred that they cannot be fully

30 These three characters seem to be the name of a person. The first character is the family name [dźiew]. The next two characters are cursive and illegible. One guess based on the shape is [ɣiew ·u].

31 TN: [thej śji] (Dashi).

identified. But again, from what remains, it seems quite similar to the 𗏁 document mentioned above.

Both documents record the officer in charge of this *liliu* district by the fine name of Moxi "the Prosperous Sprout." The record is a receipt that confirmed the types, quantities and payments of additional hay (in bundles) to the government by the farmers in the area for the You Year of Qianding Reign (1225). The printed content of the document was pre-inked onto the text so the individuals concerned could simply fill in the blanks—time of payment, the amount of taxes due and paid—during the tax registration process. This type of document was really a receipt issued at the submission of additional bundles of hays. It should be noted here that this format, whereby the pre-printed document with blanks to be filled out by hand, is of special cultural and material value in the history of books, history of printing and the history of economic institutions.

After all, the "official" (𗏁) documents were public records and archives of the government for future legal references. The "household" (𗒘) document, on the other hand, was the receipt issued to the taxpaying farmers for their own references. This tale of two documents in Western Xia—one for public office and the other for private household—is a testament to the rigorous enforcement of the institutional procedures of operation and supervision at multiple levels of the Tangut tax system. In accordance with the *Laws of Heavenly Prosperity*, governments could not further impose levies on the taxpaying households in addition to the taxes specified on the land registers. However, these two documents both impose the burden of 'additional' bundles of hay onto the households. Given the dating of these manuscripts to the You Year of Qianding Reign (1225), the reference to "added 2 bundles" refers to taxes beyond those specified in the laws. These extrajudicial acts of tax collection reveal the existence and the extent of economic exploitation of the local poor at the bottom of the Tangut society. In the context of their own time, these materials also portray the social realities in an era of chaos and decline, near the end of Western Xia's imperial glory.[32]

32 Liang, Jihong. "Wuwei cang Xixixawen Qianding Younian Zengna Caokun Wenshu Chutan" [武威藏西夏文乾定酉年增納草捆文書初探]: "A Preliminary Survey of the Documents on additional levies of hay in bundles, written in Tangut, dated to the You Year of Qianding, Preserved in Wuwei" in *Xixiaxue* [西夏學]: *Tangut Studies*, No. 10. Shanghai: Shanghai Ancient Works Publishing House, 2014. See also *Chinese Collection of Tangut Manuscripts* 16, pp. 390–393.

2.4 *Documents of Land Taxes and Land-Ownership of Peasant Households*

There are some revelations on the conditions of land ownership in Western Xia in the *shoushi* self-reports mentioned above. Additionally, there is a large quantity of sources on the farmers' ownership of land in tax records. Some of the tax documents do not register the size of owned lands in straightforward statistics. But it remains possible, in most cases, to infer the amount of land owned based on how much tax is paid (given our knowledge of the tax rate, of course). For example, the manuscript Инв. No. 1755-4, an account of grain paid as taxes by households, reveals the farmland tax rate at 1 *sheng* of coarse assorted grains and 0.25 *sheng* of wheat per *mu* of land.[33] The Khara-Khoto manuscript Инв. No. 4808 mentioned above, including an account of *liliu* grain taxes and another of household tax payments, gives us the quantity of barley and wheat paid by these farming families. With these statistics, it is possible to infer the land ownership of these households:

> One household, pays Barley 1 *dan* 1 *dou* 5 *sheng*, wheat 2 *dou* 8 *sheng* 7.5 *ge*; estimated land size: 115 *mu*.
> One household, pays Barley 4 *dou* 3 *sheng*, wheat 1 *dou* 7 *ge* and a half, estimated land size: 43 *mu*.
> One household, pays Barley 6 *dou* 7 *sheng*, wheat 1 *dou* 6 *sheng* 7.5 *ge*, estimated land size: 67 *mu*.
> One household, pays Barley 1 *dan* 5 *dou*, wheat 3 *dou* 7 *sheng* and a half, estimated land size 150 *mu*.
> One household, pays Barley 7 *dou* 5 *sheng*, wheat 1 *dou* 8 *sheng* 7 *ge* and a half, estimated land size 75 *mu*.

The fourth section in the same tax account features some slightly different types of foodstuff. The following are the ownership, conditions and use of land by the first five households on the list:

> One household, pays coarse grains 2 *dou*, wheat 5 *sheng*, estimated land size 20 *mu*.
> One household, pays coarse grains 1 *dou*, wheat 2.5 *sheng*, estimated land size 10 *mu*.
> One household, pays coarse grains 1 *dan* 5 *dou*, wheat 3 *dou* 7.5 *sheng*, estimated land size 150 *mu*,

33 Shi Jinbo, 2005 (a). For the original, see *Russian Collection of Khara-Khoto Manuscripts* 13, p. 293.

One household, pays coarse grains 7 *dou*, wheat 1 *dou* 7.5 *sheng*, estimated land size 70 *mu*.

One household, pays coarse grains 6 *dou*, wheat 1 *dou* 5 *sheng* 2 *ge*, estimated land size 60 *mu* (this family registers the payment of 2 *ge* more of wheat).

The manuscript fragments of the grain tax document 1755-4 records not only the amount of tax payment, but also the ownership of land by each household:

One household, owns land 150 *mu*, pays coarse grains 1 *dan* 5 *dou*, wheat 3 *dou* 7.5 *sheng*

One household, owns land 10 *mu*, tax 3 *dou* 7.5 *sheng*, coarse grains 4 *dou*, wheat 7.5 *sheng*.

One household, owns land 30 *mu*, tax 3 *dou* 7 *sheng* and a half, coarse grains 3 *dou*, wheat 7.5 *sheng*

One household, owns land 150 *mu*, tax 1 *dan* 8 *dou* 7.5 *sheng*, coarse grains 1 *dan* 5 *dou*, wheat 3 *dou* 7.5 *sheng*.

One household, owns land 70 *mu*, tax 8 *dou* 7 *sheng* and a half, coarse grains 7 *dou*, wheat 1 *dou* 7.5 *sheng*

One household, owns land 139 *mu*, tax 1 *dan* 7 *dou* 3 *sheng* 7.5 *ge* …[34]

The wealthier farming families owned more than 100 *mu* of land, the richest amongst whom boasted 150 *mu* of owned land. The less opulent owned dozens of *mu*, with the least propertied family owning only 10 *mu* of farmland. These numbers, once compared to those in land sale contracts, seem to match the sizes of land that were to be sold: 200, 150, 80, 100, 100, 50, 50 and 30 *mu*. It may thus be inferred that these farmers sold all the land they owned. The 4 pieces of single-page land sale contracts were the documents of widow Yehe "a guide to treasures" ([illegible]): 22 *mu*; Maze "the dog father and son" ([illegible]): 23 *mu*; Xiaoshi Tongpan ([illegible]): 100 *dan* of seeds, equivalent to about 1000 *mu*; and Liang Suyin ([illegible]??): 10 *dan* of seeds, or 70 *mu*. It does appear that other than Xiaoshi Tongpan, the majority of Tangut farmers in Khara-Khoto owned somewhere between dozens to a hundred *mu* of land.

There were also a number of households that owned large patches of farmland in the Khara-Khoto region of Western Xia. Some of them had more than one unit or stretch of land. The aforementioned Khara-Khoto manuscript Инв. No. 8203 refers to a family that owned four patches of land: the first bordered the new canal, where 7 *dan* of seeds were sowed; the second bordered the

34 *Russian Collection of Khara-Khoto Manuscripts* 12, p. 306.

Lüyi Canal, where 6 *dan* of seeds were sowed; the third bordered Xipan Canal, where 7 *dan* of sees were sowed; the fourth was a piece of assorted land at the opening of a field, where 7 *dan* of seeds were sowed. Holding constant the rate of 1 *dan* of seeds per 10 *mu* of land, this household owned 280 *mu* of farmland. Manuscript Инв. No. 7893-9, another *shoushi* (self-reporting) document, also registers a household that owned four patches of land: the first connected to the Yang canal and bordered the land of a man named Yehe "the Exuberant at Heart," where 20 *dan* of seeds were sowed; the second was connected to the Daoli Canal, bordering the land of Liang "the Happy Realm," where 15 *dan* of seeds were sowed; the third was connected to the Lüyi Canal, which bordered the land of Yihe "the prosperous lady," where 10 *dan* of seeds were sowed; the fourth was connected to the Qihu Canal, which bordered the land of Liang Nianniyou, where 7 *dan* of seeds were sowed. In sum, the size of all owned lands was 570 *mu* of land.[35] The first family herein concerned had 6 members with multiple livestock. The second household boasted some political status, with 18 members and also some livestock. They were not the standard, everyday Tangut family, but affluent landlords with bountiful cultivation and possession.

3 Poll Tax

The Tanguts paid poll taxes, in addition to land, labour and hay duties. This *tributum capitis*, as the name suggests, was levied on each head of a resident in an area jurisdiction. The Khara-Khoto corpus of documents has yielded a number of poll tax accounts, the most exemplary and focused of which is perhaps the manuscript Инв. No. 4991.

The five poll tax fragments, registered from Инв. No. 4991-5 to 4991-9, are manuscripts written in the Tangut running and cursive script on 18 cm-wide hemp papers. The length varies: 28.5 cm, 31.5 cm, 40.2 cm, 43.4 cm and 9.6 cm.[36] Amongst them, the manuscript fragment Инв. No. 4991-5 poll tax account registers numbers by the unit of households. Statistics on two and a half families are recorded in 16 lines of Tangut in the running and cursive script. The same expression, "one household," sets off the poll tax statement on each family, followed by the name of the head of the family, the demographic information of the household, and finally, the sum of taxes due and the distribution of this burden across individual men and women in the family.

35 Shi Jinbo, 2004 (a).
36 *Russian Collection of Khara-Khoto Manuscripts* 13, pp. 322–324.

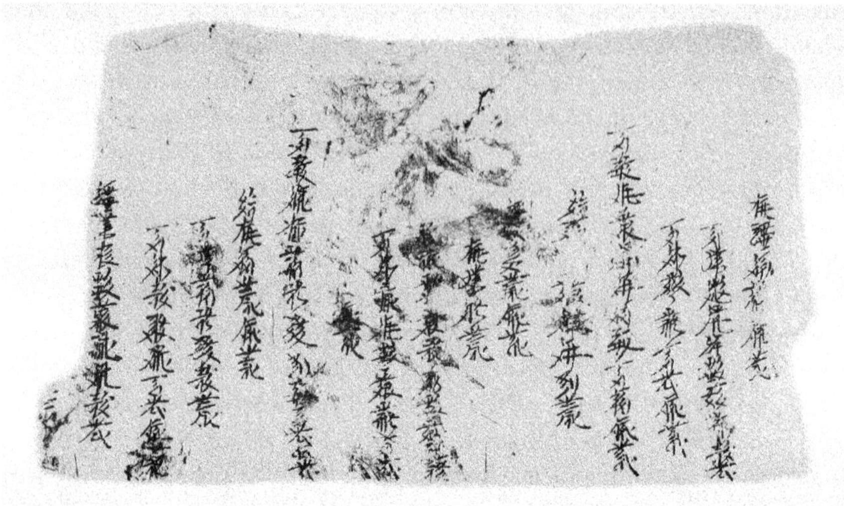

FIGURE 45 Инв. No. 4991-5: Poll tax account

Translation:

…

Women 2 …

One adult, wife, Liang “brothers’ gold” ([Tangut]) 3 *dou*

One junior, “maternal uncle’s gold” ([Tangut]) 1 *dou* 5 *sheng*

One household [Tangut]? [kew śjow low], 4 members, 1 *dan* 5 *dou*

Male 1, [Tangut]? 3 *dou*

Female 3, 7 *dou* 5 *sheng*

2 adults, 6 *dou*

[Tangut] [mə rar zji-. zji], Zhang “Iron son/man” ([Tangut]?)

1 junior, Gao “the iron gold” ([Tangut]), 1 *dou*
5 *sheng*

One household, [Tangut] [ŋwe zjwi. śji-j ·jiw wejr], 3 members, 7 *dou* 5 *sheng*

Male 2, 4 *dou* 5 *sheng*

1 adult, [Tangut] 3 *dou*

1 junior, “Dog of the Triratna” ([Tangut]) 1 *dou* 5 *sheng*

Female adult, [Tangut] [pu. zji-. śja phji] 3 *dou*

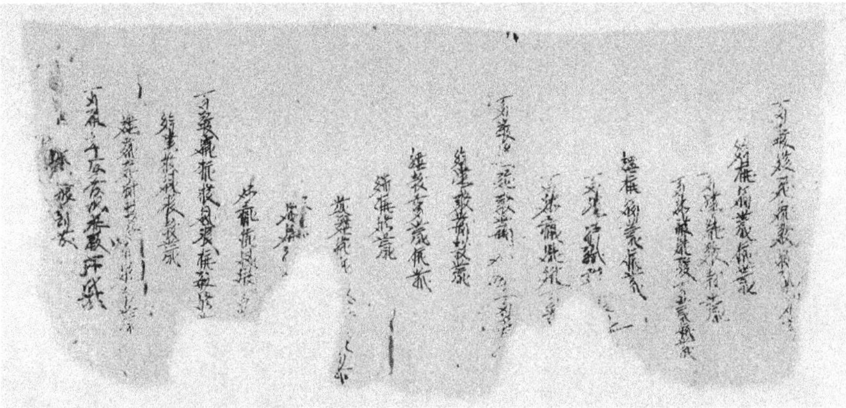

FIGURE 46 Инв. No. 4991-7: Poll tax account

Manuscript Инв. No. 4991-7 is also a poll tax account fragment on hemp paper, 18 × 40.2 cm, with 19 lines of Tangut—very much in the same format as Инв. No. 4991-5. Tax statistics on three out of four households have survived and remain legible.[37]

In spite of some missing and blurry parts, enough of this manuscript has survived for us to infer the tax records of the three families. The first household had four members. Of the two males, the adult paid 3 *dou* and the child 1 *dou* and 5 *sheng*. Of the two females, the adult and child paid taxes at the same rate. The second house also had four members, one adult male who paid 3 *dou*, three women, of whom two female adults paid 6 *dou*, and a girl paid 1 *dou* and 5 *sheng*. The third family had only two members, an adult couple who paid 6 *dou*.

It is easy to tell from the statistics in these two poll tax accounts that adults, regardless of gender, paid 3 *dou* per capita. Likewise, for the underage, in cases of both genders, the tax rate was 1 *dou* and a half.

Two other manuscript fragments, Инв. No. 4991-6 and Инв. No. 4991-8, are also poll tax accounts. The style of handwriting and quality of the paper suggest that the two pieces may have been connected as one manuscript. They are 18 × 31.5 cm and 18 × 43.4 cm in size with 16 and 19 lines of Tangut in the running script, respectively. These two poll tax accounts not only register the statistics by household, but also include a list of numbers on the poll taxes of an entire *liliu* district.[38]

37 *Russian Collection of Khara-Khoto Manuscripts* 13, p. 323.

38 *Russian Collection of Khara-Khoto Manuscripts* 13, pp. 323–324.

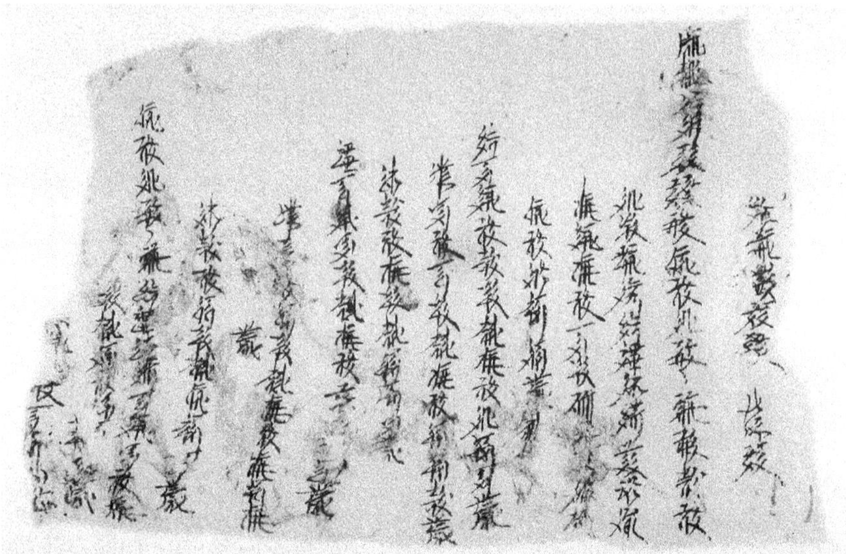

FIGURE 47 Инв. No. 4991-6: *Liliu* Poll tax account

The first line is probably the last bit of information left off from the previous *liliu* account. The following is a translation of the content of this manuscript, starting with the second line:

> *Liliu*: Liang Suji ([illegible])'s Bureau, 59 households, in entirety, and 3-9 single men and women, adult and underage, total sum: 221 individuals' ? taxed grains, 56 *dan* 4 *dou* in number,
>
> Males 113, grains 29 *dan* 1 *dou*
>
> Adults 81, grains 24 *dan* 3 *dou*
>
> Underage 32, grains 4 *dan* 8 *dou*
>
> Females 108, grains 27 [*dan* 3] *dou*
>
> Adults 74, grains 22 *dan* 2 *dou*
>
> underage 34, grains 5 *dan* [1] *dou*
>
> 59 households in entirety, men and women, adults and underage, 182 Individuals, grains 4[4 *dan* 7] *dou*
>
> Males adults and underage 87, grains 21 *dan* 3 *dou*
>
> …

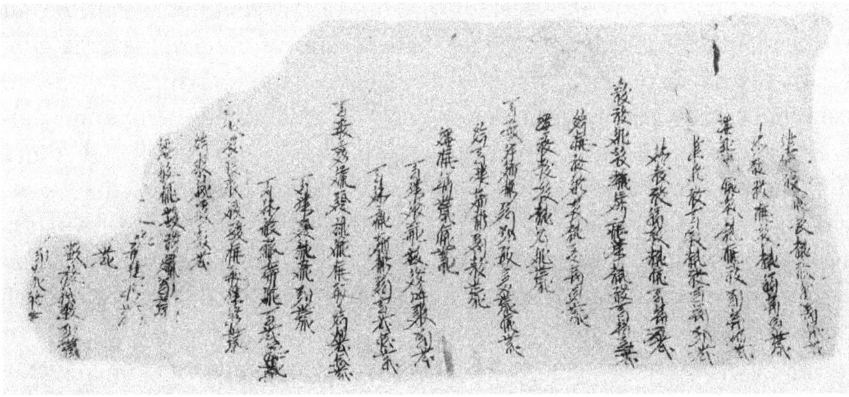

FIGURE 48 Инв. No. 4991-8: *Liliu* Poll tax account

Adults [55], grains 16 *dan* 5 *dou*
Underage 32, grains 4 *dan* 8 *dou*
Females 95, grains 23 *dan* 4 *dou*
Adults 61, grains 18 *dan* 3 *dou*
Underage 34, grains 51[39] *dan* 1 *dou*
39 singles, all adults, grains 11 *dan* 7 *dou*
Males 26, grains 7 *dan* 8 *dou*
Females, grains [3][40] *dan* 4 *dou*
One household Liang "the force of fortune" ([illegible]) 3 members, 7 *dou* 5 *sheng*
Male, 1 adult, "the force of fortune," 3 *dou*
Female, 24 *dou* 5 *sheng*
One adult, Maze "Treasure of the Old House" ([illegible]), 3 *dou*
One underage female, "the force of fortune" 1 *dou* 5 *sheng*
One household, Yi'e "Bird-Dog" ([illegible]), 2 members, males 4 *dou* 5 *sheng*
One adult, "Bird-Dog" 4 *dou*
One underage, son "Heavenly-King Dog" ([illegible]) 1 *dou* 5 *sheng*
[One household]?? "Prosperous Twelfth Month" ([illegible]) 2 members, adults 6 *dou*
Male, "Prosperous Twelfth Month" 3 *dou*
Female, ??name? 3 *dou*
…

39 Interpretive edit: [illegible] [lew] (one).
40 Resupply [illegible] [so.] (three).

The first part of the above text is the statistical account of the entire *liliu* residential district, including the person in charge of the *liliu* area, the total number of households, the number of single men and women, as well as the conditions of tax payments: the number of men and women, adults and children, and how much grain they paid. The account registered the adult and underage males and females in the 59 households, in addition to the 39 singles, as well as their due taxes. There was a total of 221 residents, who paid a sum of 56 *dan* and 4 *dou* grains as poll taxes. This information is followed by detailed accounts of demographics and tax payments by the units of households, including the concerned individuals' names, their relationships to the head of the family, their age—grown or underage—and the amount of grains they paid.

A comparison of the tax rate derived from the general account of the taxes paid by men and women, adults and children, and the rate generated from the statistics in the detailed household registers, points to the same conclusion on the standard of taxation: Distinction was based on age only, not gender. Each adult paid 3 *dou*, whereas a child paid 1 *dou* and a half. Armed with this tax rate, and holding it constant, it is possible to fill in the blanks for a lot of the other statistical charts generated from manuscript fragments, including information on missing tax numbers and demographics:

CHART 4 Инв. No. 4991-6 & 8: Liliu poll tax account

<table>
<tr><td>Categories</td><td colspan="4">59 households</td><td colspan="4">39 singles</td><td></td></tr>
<tr><td rowspan="3">Person count (per)</td><td colspan="2">Male, 87</td><td colspan="2">Female, 95</td><td colspan="2">Male, 26</td><td colspan="2">Female, 13</td><td rowspan="3">221 persons</td></tr>
<tr><td>Adult</td><td>Minor</td><td>Adult</td><td>Minor</td><td>Adult</td><td>Minor</td><td>Adult</td><td>Minor</td></tr>
<tr><td>55</td><td>32</td><td>61</td><td>34</td><td>26</td><td>0</td><td>13</td><td>0</td></tr>
<tr><td rowspan="3">Taxes paid (dou)</td><td>165</td><td>48</td><td>183</td><td>51</td><td>78</td><td></td><td>39</td><td></td><td rowspan="3">564 dou</td></tr>
<tr><td colspan="2">213</td><td colspan="2">234</td><td colspan="2">78</td><td colspan="2">39</td></tr>
<tr><td colspan="4">447</td><td colspan="4">117</td></tr>
</table>

It can be inferred from these records that the administrative unit of *liliu* was in charge of setting up poll tax accounts for its households. The account first lists the overall account of the total poll taxes in the *liliu*, including the numbers of men and women, adults and children, as well as their due taxes. It then proceeds to register the demographic and tax statistics of each household.

In addition, manuscript Инв. No. 4991-6 and others also belong to the same type of poll tax account. Инв. No. 5223-2 is a poll tax account fragment with ink for handwriting practice on its back.

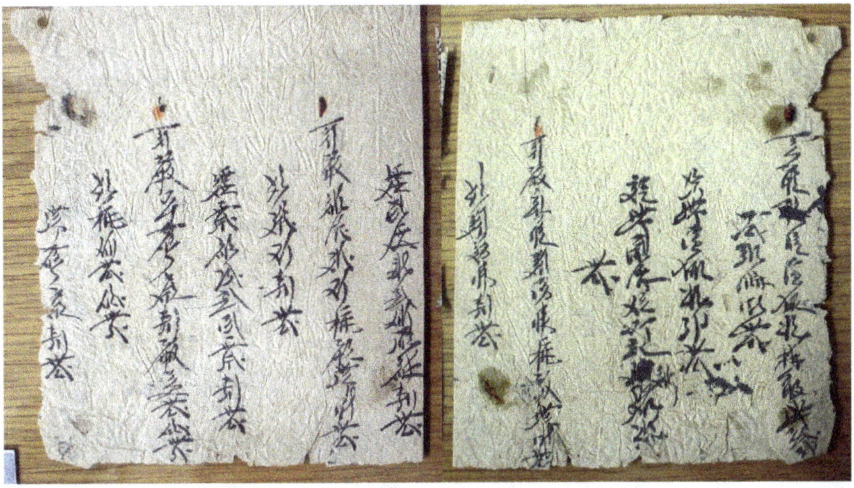

FIGURE 49 British 0324 (k.k.II.0285b): Poll tax account (front and back)

There are likewise poll tax accounts amongst the Khara-Khoto manuscripts housed at the British Library, such as Or. 12380-0324v (k.k.II.0285b): two handwritten, 176 × 145 cm remnant pages of a poll tax account, with 7 lines of Tangut in the cursive on each page.[41]

A literal translation as follows:

…

  Female, wife, Lang [illegible] [xo tshji-j phiow] 3 *dou*

One household, Langming "the lucky dog" ([illegible]), two adults, 6 *dou*

  Male, "lucky dog" 3 *dou*

  Female, [ka de_r] (Geyu) [illegible] [bie_j]? 3 *dou*

One household, [illegible] [ljow] (Liang) [illegible] [dju. dju. śjow], 3 members, 7 *dou* 5 *sheng*

  Male 2, 4 *dou* 5 *sheng*

    Adult, [illegible] 3 *dou*

…

…

One household, Yehe "the Sunk Treasure Mine" ([illegible]), two adults, each 3

    dou, sum total 6 *dou*

  Male adult, "Sunk Treasure Mine" 3 *dou*

41 *British Collection of Khara-Khoto Manuscripts*, p. 130. It was originally named "New Laws of Year Hai" but here retitled "Poll Tax Account."

> Female, adult, wife, Qianyu "the blessed" ([illegible]) 3 *dou*
>
> One household, Yehe "Force, Merit, Mount" ([illegible]) 2 adults, 6 *dou*
>
> Male adult, "Force, Merit, Mount" 3 *dou*
>
> ...

Likewise, gender was not a variable in the determination of tax rate. Each adult, male or female, paid 3 *dou* in poll tax, whereas the child always paid half of that sum. The tax rate was exactly the same as we have derived from the poll tax accounts in Инв. No. 4991.

There are also overall accounts of poll taxes in the *British Collection of Khara-Khoto Manuscripts*. For example, the Or. 12380-0344 (k.k.) poll tax account is a manuscript fragment written in the cursive, featuring total sums of poll taxes.[42]

FIGURE 50 British 0344 (k.k.): Poll tax account

42 This image was photographed by the author of this book. See also *British Collection of Khara-Khoto Manuscripts*, p. 135. The document was originally named "A cursively hand-written piece of manuscript" but is given the caption "Poll Tax Account" in the context of this book.

Translation:

...
... total: 140 *dan*
... total amount of grains: 40 *dan* 3 *dou*
5 *sheng*
Males: 79, total amount of grains, 22 *dan* 8
dou 5 *sheng*
Adults: 73, each about 3 *dou*; total
amount of grains, 21 *dan* 9 *dou*
Underage children 6, each around 1 *dou* 5 *sheng*, total
9 *dou*
Females: 63, total amount of grains, 17
dan 5 *dou* ? *sheng*
...

This document also provides summary statistics of all households within a *liliu*. Due to the damages at the start, the total population is missing—nor is the total tax payment information available. But given the parts that are still legible, we know there were 79 men and 63 women, for a total population of 142. In sum, the men paid 22 *dan* and 8 *dou*, and the women 17 *dan* and 5 *dou*. We know that there was a total of more than 40 *dan* of grains paid as poll tax. It is also clear that in this context, taxation maintained the rate of 3 *dou* per adult and 1 *dou* and 5 *sheng* per child.

The *Laws of Heavenly Prosperity* provides ample documentations on the payment of grains as land taxes, but no traces have been uncovered on poll taxes. What is revealed in the record above unveils the reality of Tangut poll tax for the first time. As for whether the poll tax levied in the Khara-Khoto region was a temporary tax that fell outside the domain of the tax regime under the mandate of written laws, or a new form of tax that emerged as a result of new legislations posterior to the "Heavenly Prosperity" era, it is impossible to settle on a conclusion without the aid of further investigation.

But from what is known about the poll tax, the burden on peasants was not light at all. The 9 *dou* of grains due for a family of two adults and a child was the equivalent of land taxes, in coarse grains, levied on 90 *mu* of farmland. A typical Tangut household of relatively small size did not own more than 90 *mu* of land. Therefore, this poll tax, many a times higher than the land tax, was obviously a heavy burden on the Tangut families.

4 Irrigation Tax

Vast stretches of Tangut territory fell within the arid and rainless northwest of modern China. Prior to the restoration of Tangut power in this area, there had been a tradition of diverting the Yellow River for irrigation, near what came to be the centre of Dangxiang rule, between the Xing and Ling Prefectures of Western Xia. The Tanguts built upon excellent existing water conservancy facilities by extending water canals. These infrastructures provided the pillars of the Tangut irrigation system and further consolidated the status of this area as the backbone of Tangut agriculture. Inland, continental waterways such as the 'Black Water'—part of the Ejin River—flow through the "Black Water City," the site of Khara-Khoto in the northwest of Western Xia. The availability of water sources made it possible to undertake water conservation projects for the purpose of irrigation. Historically, this area had witnessed settled peasants and garrisoned troops opening up wastelands to grow grains. The Tanguts erected and expanded the city of Khara-Khoto against the natural obstacle of its perennial drought, not least encouraged by the nourishing presence of the Black River as a sufficient condition for developments in farming and pasturing. In this way, Khara-Khoto emerged as an oasis in the middle of deserts, a prosperous metropolis in northern Xixia, a formidable military stronghold that hosted the base for the Khara-Khoto Military Supervisory Commission, and a stout and spirited shield at the empire's border against enemies from the north.

Documents unearthed in Khara-Khoto endorse the view that historically, this area witnessed agricultural prosperity thanks to an irrigation system that depended on water canals. Amongst the manuscripts found in the Black Water City are two pieces of texts that are identified as records of irrigation taxes. These are primary sources that speak directly to the payments of taxes for the irrigation of farmlands under Tangut administration.

One of the documents is the "Account of Farmland Irrigation Tax," Инв. No. 1454-2V, a 15.7 × 33.7 cm manuscript fragment with 14 lines in Tangut cursive.[43]

43 *Russian Collection of Khara-Khoto Manuscripts* 12, p. 247.

FIGURE 51 Инв. No. 1454-2V: Account of farmland irrigation tax

Translation:

One place, 14 (*dan*) place whither ......
Irrigation [yi] single ......
?? water tax 4 *dan*? *dou*
7 *sheng* and a half
Southeast Liang?? West
One place, Weiyi "dog, mountains and waters" ([Tangut]), irrigate 2 *dan* place whither
????? water tax? *dou*
2 *sheng* & a half
Southeast, Weiyi "the lucky dog" ([Tangut])
Northwest, Weiyi "the puppy?" ([Tangut]?)
One place, 4 *dan*, place whither, Weiyi "dog, mountains and waters" ...
Daily water tax 1 *dan* 2 *dou* ...
east ... west ...

Due to losses, damages, and some overlapping strokes of ink written on both the front and the back of the paper, quite a few words remain illegible and untranslated. But the words pertaining to farming and irrigation are still recognisable. The document refers to water taxes levied on three patches of farmland. The statement on each piece of land begins with the two characters, "go toward, place" (Tangut: [Tangut] [śji- tji.]). It has been mentioned earlier that the Tanguts measured sizes of land by the amount of seeds sowed. In that case, the quantities of seeds and grains are labelled by the reference, "place sowed." (Tangut: [Tangut] [lju tji.]). Likewise, the parallel expression "place whither/to which xxx goes" also refers to land where a certain quantity of seeds is sowed and a certain amount of grains grown. Records of irrigation taxes rely on this

CHART 5 Инв. No. 1454-2V: Account of farmland irrigation tax, chart

Location	Irrigation size	Irrigation tax	Irrigation tax/*dan* of seed
#1	14 *dan*	4 *dan* ?*dou* 7.5 *sheng*	Approx. 3 *dou*
#2	2 *dan*	?*dou* 2.5 *sheng*	?
#3	4 dan	1 *dan* 2 *dou* ?*sheng*	Approx. 3 *dou*

CHART 6 Инв. No. 1454-2V: Account of farmland irrigation tax, chart (2)

Location	Irrigation size	Irrigation tax	Irrigation tax/*dan* of seed
#1	14 *dan*	4 *dan* 3 *dou* 7.5 *sheng*	3.125 *dou*
#2	2 *dan*	6 *dou* 2.5 *sheng*	3.125 *dou*
#3	4 *dan*	1 *dan* 2 *dou* 5 *sheng*	3.125 *dou*

method to measure the amount of water used in irrigation and the corresponding quantity of tax to be paid. These documents also specify the locations of the land concerned.

Although some of the numbers in this statistical account of irrigation taxes are incomplete, it is possible to derive the missing figures from calculation, and even to determine the tax rate itself. From the statistics of location #3, it may be inferred that to water a piece of land where 1 *dan* of seeds are typically sowed, one has to pay irrigation taxes in the amount of roughly 3 *dou* of grains or above. Given the integers and remainders in the tax account, if we set the rate of water tax at 3.125 *dou* per patch of land wherein 1 *dan* of seeds are sowed, then location #1 would be taxed 4 *dan*, 3 *dou* and 7.5 *sheng*; location #2 would have to pay 6 *dou* and 2.5 *sheng*; and location #3 is liable for taxes in the amount of 1 *dan*, 2 *dou* and 5 *sheng*. These numbers would not only fit the integers and remainders of the water taxes in the three locations quite nicely, but also fill in the missing statistics to complete the chart.

It is possible to infer from these numbers that the water tax rate referenced in this record is 3.125 *dou* per unit of land for sowing 1 *dan* of seeds.

Another piece of document is the 12 × 33.5 cm manuscript fragment Инв. No. 1781-1, an "Account of Farmland Irrigation Tax" with 15 lines of Tangut writings in the running style.[44]

44 *Russian Collection of Khara-Khoto Manuscripts* 12, p. 313.

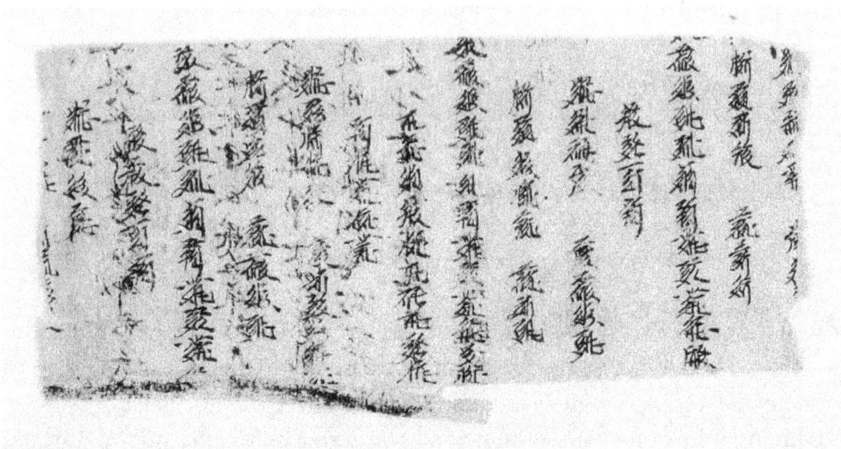

FIGURE 52 Инв. No. 1781-1: Account of farmland irrigation tax

Likewise, a number of factors have added obstacles to the interpretation of this text: damages at the beginning and the end, ink on both sides of the paper, and either light or blurred handwritings. A plausible translation is rendered as follows:

…
east ???? South? …
west slope, north, own land
One place Mount Cave Stream Irrigate 4 *dan* place whither [yi][six][green]
Water Tax 1 *dan*
East: [illegible] [phie dow dźjij] South: Stream from the Mountain Cave
West: [illegible] [tow ·ja mji] [yi] (*dan*) North: narrow canal
One place Mount Cave Stream Irrigate 9 *dan* place whither [yi][six]?
Half all day water to?? Half tax 2
dan 2 *dou* 5 *sheng*
East Nie Mount ?? South???
West many? (Temple) North Mount Cave Stream
One place mount cave stream irrigate 4 *dan* place whither [yi] …
Water tax 1 *dan*
East …

The document above also records three stretches of farmland with specified locations, the amount of water required for irrigation, and the tax levied on the water.

CHART 7 Инв. No. 1781-1: Account of farmland irrigation tax

Location	Irrigation size	Irrigation tax	Irrigation tax/*dan* of seed
#1	4 *dan*	1 *dan*	2 *dou* 5 *sheng*
#2	9 *dan*	2 *dan* 2 *dou* 5 *sheng*	2 *dou* 5 *sheng*
#3	4 dan	1 *dan*	2 *dou* 5 *sheng*

Fortunately, the statistics of the three instances of water tax payments are complete. Therefore, it is easy to calculate the standard tax rate on irrigation to be 2 *dou* and 5 *sheng* of grains per piece of land where 1 *dan* of seeds are sowed.

Although the entire agricultural zone of Khara-Khoto relies on water irrigation of farmlands, it seems that different tax rates apply across the area. In the manuscript Инв. No. 1454-2V, a grain tax of about 3 *dou* and 1 *sheng* is levied on each unit of land in which 1 *dan* of seeds are sowed, whereas in tax record Инв. No. 1781-1, irrigation taxes in the amount of 2 *dou* and 5 *sheng* are imposed on each unit of land where 1 *dan* of seeds are sowed. The variance may have to do with the variable quantity of water required across the terrains.

Information on water taxes has also been found in socio-economic documents that are not explicitly and entirely tax receipts or records. For example, in the long scrolls of land transaction contracts excavated at the site of Khara-Khoto, seven out of eight land sale contracts mention such information at the end, where two to three Tangut characters appear below the tax numbers. Some mention "daily water" whilst others refer to "narrow water" or "narrow water [in] half." These are records on the variable conditions of water supplies for irrigation of the land concerned. It is possible that the size and scale of irrigation, hence the tax rate of water, varies from 'daily water' to 'narrow water' and to 'narrow water in half.'[45]

The *Laws of Heavenly Prosperity* (15) stipulates rules and regulations on the "affairs of canal-construction in the spring," "supervision of water and pasture-maintenance," "water canals," and "Miscellaneous Guilts and Crimes Related to Irrigation of Land," which concern the use of canals to irrigate farmlands. Despite some loss of information due to manuscript damages, much information on Tangut water use and conservation projects survives and remains. These chapters bring to light how the Tangut imperial machine mobilised task forces to build canals in the spring, patrol and examine the state of canals, collect bundles of hays and rafters, maintain the conditions of bridges

45 Shi Jinbo, 2012 (a).

and roads above the canals, and plant and protect trees by the sides of the canals. However, the question of irrigation taxes is seldomly addressed directly. Rather, it is for the most part the specification of the procedural flow of official documents in the *Laws of Heavenly Prosperity* that mentions taxes levied on the "dispatchment/distribution of water" (Tangut: 𗼃𗿒 [zji-_r wji.j]) in the seven counties near the imperial capital. "Water tax" (Tangut: 𗼃𘍴 [zji-_r zji.j]) and "land tax" (𗏁𘍴 [lji-. zji.j]) are mentioned in connection and parallel.[46] Furthermore, according to the *Laws of Heavenly Prosperity*'s "Misbehaviours and Merits in Pressing for Payment":

> The following is the method of pressing for irrigation taxes: from Mingsha, the Jurisdiction over the district of the Commander in Chief, to the various counties and vicinities in the area of the Imperial Capital, concerning the senior officials and the order-bearers in the Bureau of Transfer and Transportation, one officer is to be dispatched each year □□.[47]

This "method" of levies on water for irrigation was applied in areas of the irrigable Hetao plains in the upper reaches of the Yellow River—the heart and veins of Tangut agriculture—on which the empire's populations depended. At the same time, agricultural taxation in these areas was the main source of government revenue for the state of Western Xia. In the *Laws of Heavenly Prosperity*, records and regulations on the taxes of land, labour, and hay abound, whereas specific items on taxing water are far less common. And yet, as a major and special category of agricultural tax, the levy of irrigation tax was widely practised in Western Xia. Accounts of farmland irrigation tax unearthed in Khara-Khoto provide us with detailed, authentic, and important primary sources on this type of tax in the Tangut Economy.

5 Land Tax Increase and Grain Storage

Thus far, Tangut documents found in the medieval city of Khara-Khoto have revealed records of farmland taxes and related taxes in labour and hay as well

46 *Revised Laws of Heavenly Prosperity* 9, "On Delays in Regulatory Duties," p. 319. The phrase was rendered 'case of family' in an earlier Chinese translation, but has since been revised to 'case of household.' In the original, little more than half of the character after 𗼃 [zji-_r] (water) remains legible. It has since been identified as 𘍴 [zji.j] (tax).

47 *Revised Laws of Heavenly Prosperity* 15, "On Guilt and Merit in Urging Tax Payments," p. 493.

as poll taxes and irrigation taxes. When it comes to levying taxes on agriculture, Western Xia followed a rigorous workflow procedure and system of operation.

5.1 *Procedure of Levying Agricultural Taxes*

Since Western Xia levies taxed in kinds, typically grains, according to the size of farmland, an important task of the government in Khara-Khoto was to determine the area of land owned by each household in order to calculate the amounts of grains and hay to be paid. In addition to requiring the households to report the size of their land (in the unit of *mu*) and, accordingly, quantity of grains and hay to be paid on official land registers, the *Laws of Heavenly Prosperity* also stated the following:

> The head of each household liable for taxation is obliged to report the time of farming, the number of oxen, and the amount of cultivation. The numbers in *hu, dou, sheng, ge* should be specified and written on a wooden board. Each household is to be given one piece of wooden board for this purpose.[48]

In other words, the Tangut government distributed wooden boards to households in order for families to report their land size, number of ploughing oxen, and amounts of grains and hay to be paid, with full publicity and transparency. The purpose of this law was not only to remind taxpayers of their own duties, but also to pre-empt both tax-evasion and abusive over-taxation.

China in the Central Plains had witnessed the maturation of a 'dual taxation' system since the mid-Tang period, whereby households were ranked and registered according to population and property, and taxed twice—once in the summer and then in the autumn. Instead, Western Xia collected taxes only once a year, according to the *Laws of Heavenly Prosperity*:

> All the many kinds of taxes for which the households are liable to pay are specified and stated in the 'land register' book. The officials in charge of this matter in all the counties should, in due order, closely monitor and press the households for their due amount, and see to it that all payments are made within time limits.[49]

48 *Revised Laws of Heavenly Prosperity* 15, "On the Dispatchment of Junior Accounting Magistrate to Collect Taxes in the Form of Grains," p. 514.

49 *Revised Laws of Heavenly Prosperity* 15, "On the Miscellaneous Taxes of Irrigation for Farmland," pp. 507–508.

The official book of registers, or 𗋽 [dźjij] in Tangut, is also translated as 'register,' 'registration documents,' or 'land registers.' This book of records was maintained by the government, in part, to also keep track of land tax payments. The passage above stipulates that farming families pay the due amount of taxes in time, according to their land ownership as recorded in the land registers. The 'many kinds' of tax records belong to the book of the registers, but this part does not mention the time of tax payment, which can be found in the following passage from the *Laws of Heavenly Prosperity*:

> If the officials in higher or lower bureaus of the counties do not report the statistics on the payments of various taxes in the areas of their jurisdiction to the Bureau of Transfer and Transportation, and submit the registers and receipts by the first day of November, they are to be tried on the charge of delay. If the submi ssion is overdue for one to five days, the punishment is thirteen strokes. If the submission is overdue for five to ten days, the punishment is imprisonment for three months. If the submissions are overdue for ten to twenty days, the imprisonment is 6 months long. If the delay is over twenty days, the guilty are to be imprisoned for one year.[50]

That is, county officials in Western Xia must submit the necessary books and receipts of taxes to the Department of Transfer and Transportation by the first day of the eleventh month, at the latest. Late submissions are subject to penalties. Therefore, the process of tax collection most likely took place and ended before November, or even October. It also means that the Tanguts paid their taxes in the autumn. Lying to the northwest of the Chinese Central Plains, most areas in Western Xia were colder than in territories of the Song Dynasty. Therefore, there was probably no more than one season for cultivation and for harvest. This would have especially been the case for Khara-Khoto, being further close to the north-western border of Western Xia, where the average temperature was lower than elsewhere in the country. Most of the grains were harvested once each year. What were 'summer grains' in the Central Plains, such as wheat, can only be harvested in Khara-Khoto in the seventh or eighth month in the lunar calendar. It is not surprising, then, that the Tanguts paid their taxes-in-kinds in the autumn.

Local magistrates had to issue receipts to the farmers and peasants who paid their taxes. According to the *Laws of Heavenly Prosperity*:

50 *Revised Laws of Heavenly Prosperity* 15, "On Urging the Payment of Taxes," p. 490.

> Let the magistrates in charge of urging payments of land taxes ride around the territories that fall under the jurisdiction of each Bureau of Transfer and Transportation, carrying white papers □□ stamped. The head of the household should claim the receipts and register on the white papers. The officer pressing for taxes should sign the papers in the presence of the owners of the receipts, in turn every fifteen days, to be examined by the staff in the Department of Transfer and Transportation. Any harassment against the heads of the household or solicitation of bribes from the families is strictly prohibited. Failure to register as required, in violation of the law, or failure to comply with the requirement of a signature by hand, will result in thirteen strokes. If the officers are bribed, then they are to be tried on the charge of corruption and contempt for law.[51]

It is no overstatement to say that the lawmakers of Western Xia designed a rather complete and comprehensive institutional system to pre-empt late payments, tax-evasions, and criminal activities on the part of magistrates susceptible to corruption or violation of law.

The Tangut government paid the highest regard and attention to agricultural taxes, which were the bloodline of the Tangut economy. Therefore, the imperial authority flexed its legal muscles and weaponised the laws to ensure a secure and smooth flow of the state's main source of revenue. To this end, the laws also specify the rewards and punishments for magistrates in charge of tax collection:

> The officials in charge of urging tax payments should discern how much is paid and how much still remains unpaid, within the time limit, of all the kinds of land taxes in the case of tax-paying households. They should then divide the total sum of owed taxes into ten equal parts. Those who manage to exact nine out of ten, and leave one unpaid, are not to be charged. Those who receive eight out of ten, with two unpaid, are jailed for six months. Those who obtain seven out of ten, with three unpaid, are jailed for a year. Those who obtain six out of ten, with four unpaid, are jailed for two years. Those who obtain five out of ten, with five unpaid, are jailed for three years. Those who obtain four out of ten, with six unpaid, are jailed for four years. Those who obtain three out of ten, with seven unpaid, are jailed for five years. Those who obtain two out of ten, with eight unpaid, are jailed for six years. Those who obtain only one out

51 *Revised Laws of Heavenly Prosperity* 15, "On the Miscellaneous Taxes of Irrigation for Farmland," p. 507.

> of ten, leaving nine unpaid, are jailed for eight years. Those who obtain none of the due taxes are jailed for ten years. Those who have collected all ten out of ten are rewarded the honour of a higher office, five *taels* in cash, and one *pi* of coloured cloth.[52]

Given this system of reward and punishment, the magistrate would not be exempt from penalties if he managed to secure 90% of the taxes that fall under his jurisdiction and supervision. Those who collected 80% or less of the full sum would be sentenced to six months to 10 years in prison, whereas savvy and dedicated magistrates who succeeded in procuring all due taxes for the government were rewarded cash, goods, and promotion. This institutional design, combining incentives with accountability, clearly promoted efficiency in tax collection.

Rare amongst all the law codes of dynastic empires in China, the *Tangut Laws of Heavenly Prosperity* is fastidious about the operational procedure of tax collection:

> When it is time for the collection of various taxes, the junior accounting magistrate should sit at the gate of the storage house. The patrolling magistrates should sit by the side of the junior accounting magistrate. They should call the names of those paying grains as taxes, in due order, and then measure what they offer before taking them over. They should also issue receipts to the taxpayers, which label the total sums in *hu* and *dou* and the signatures of the junior accounting magistrate. Any adulteration or falsification in the payment of grains is strictly forbidden. If the junior accounting magistrate and the patrolling magistrate from higher or lower offices are unable to check the amounts with accuracy, the local prefects in charge should take over the responsibility of supervision. If there is any violation of law—for instance, if those who did not pay are listed as having paid, or if there is inflation or falsification of the numbers—let the sum of the unpaid amount of grains be calculated, and let the culprit be tried on the charge of theft. If officials commit bribery, then the gravity of this offence is to be compared to the charge of 'Violation of Law and Corruption.' Whichever is more severe is to be applied to the culprit. If the concerned personality is not bribed, but rather committed errors in

52 *Revised Laws of Heavenly Prosperity* 15, "On Guilt and Merit in Urging Tax Payments," p. 493.

> examinations and calculations, he will be punished by the confiscation of a horse if an official, and by thirteen strokes if a commoner.[53]

More than an item of legislation, this passage contains a vivid portrayal of the actual and active scene of farmers paying their taxes. A junior accounting magistrate sits at the front gate of the government's storage house in the company of, but also under the watchful eyes of, a patrolling agent. The magistrate calls the heads or representatives of the households to come up to the front, in the order specified in the books of registers for grain tax payment. The taxpayers turn in their due taxes, which the magistrate then measures with tools, before receiving into the storage. Of course, the magistrate has to make sure there is no attempted misreporting or fraud throughout this process. The verbal description of this scenario furnishes us today with ample sources to reimagine the actual economic lives at the bottom end of a medieval society.

When local governments took in the grain taxes, magistrates prepared a new book. In Khara-Khoto, long documents running a hundred lines were quite common. These grain accounts such as the manuscripts Инв. No. 2568, Инв. No. 2851V2-6, and Инв. No. 2851V8-14 are, in fact, examples of such book registers for tax purposes. When these documents reached the Department of Transfer and Transportation, they were sent in turn to the Bureau of Review:

> The staff members of the Bureau of Transfer and Transportation are responsible for delivering the record files, receipts, and other documents to the Bureau of Review within a month, in the time window between the first day of the eleventh month and the end of that month. If this task is not finished, and the work is overdue, the senior officials, the order-bearers, administrators, clerks, and agents are all charged on the various levels of misconduct in procrastination according to the same standards that hold officers in the county bureaus accountable, as specified above.[54]

As the files arrived at the Bureau of Review from the Department of Transfer and Transportation, there was a lapse of one month for the inspection process:

53 *Revised Laws of Heavenly Prosperity* 15, "On the Dispatchment of Junior Accounting Magistrate to Collect Taxes in the Form of Grains," pp. 513–514.

54 *Revised Laws of Heavenly Prosperity* 15, "On Urging the Payment of Taxes," pp. 490–491.

> The staff at the Bureau of Review arrive on the first day of the twelfth month with official papers for registration and the receipts. There is a month of time to examine these records. If these tasks are not completed upon the due date, and if the work, the senior official, order-bearer, administrators, clerks, and all the other staff members in the bureau are transferred to the office of the Bureau of Transfer and Transportation to be judged by the gravity of their misconduct and, accordingly, to be charged guilty of procrastination.[55]

From local offices to the central government, the statistical compilation and analysis of taxes was not completed until the end of each year. Even after the process ended, magistrates across the board were responsible for seeking out and taking in the unpaid taxes, an additional labour which may as well extend into the next year.

5.2 *Burden of Tax on the Peasants*

Given the tax records of Western Xia that we have thus far considered in this chapter, it is possible to conclude that the Tanguts in the Khara-Khoto area paid three major types of taxes.

The first tax was in terms of grains, labour, and hay, according to the ownership of land (in units of *mu*). In most cases, the annual tax rate for farmland was 1 *sheng* of coarse grains and a quarter of wheat (0.25 *sheng*) per *mu* of land. Corvée labour was also measured by the size of owned lands, at the rate of 5 days of labour per 1 *mu*–10 *mu* of land; 15 days of labour per 11–40 *mu* of land; 20 days of labour per 41–75 *mu* of land; 30 days of labour per 75–100 *mu* of land; 35 days of labour per 100–120 *mu* of land; and 40 days of labour per 120–150 *mu* of land. In addition, 1 bundle of hay was levied annually on each *mu* of land.

In the Jurchen Empire of Jin, an ethnarchic economy contemporaneous to the later Western Xia, the state also levied taxes by land ownership, but twice: "in the summer, 3 *ge* of tax per *mu*; in the autumn, 5 *sheng* of tax per *mu*."[56] In sum, the Jin Dynasty imposed a tax of 5.3 *sheng* per *mu* of land. Tax rates in the Song Dynasty varied across landscapes. In the Liangzhe Circuits—the Eastern and Western Zhe districts of modern-day Zhejiang, Shanghai, and southern Jiangsu taxes were paid in silk (3 *chi* and 4 *cun*) and rice (1 *dou*, 5 *sheng* and 2 *ge*). The people of Fujian paid cash (between 3 and 4 *wen*) and rice (7–8 *sheng*). At a quick glance, it seems that in contrast, Western Xia set a rather low tax rate on agriculture. However, it should be noted that the Tangut *mu* is smaller than

---

55 Ibid.

56 *History of Jin* Bk. 47. Book of Food and Goods, II.

the Song *mu*. One unit of Song *mu* was roughly equivalent to 2.4 Tangut *mu*.[57] Besides, the Tanguts occupied some rough terrains in the northwest. The total size of arable lands and the per unit yield cannot be compared to the fertile plains of the Song Dynasty. Considering that the Tangut peasants bore additional burdens of other kinds of taxes, it should be said that the tax burden in Western Xia was not light at all.

The second type of tax was the poll tax account. As the name suggests, in line with the term's modern connotations, this '*tributum capitis*' was levied on each individual resident of the empire, regardless of gender, but with some variances between adults and juniors. An adult paid 3 *dou* of taxes, whereas a child paid half of that amount—1 *dou* and a half. But not unlike the land tax, the poll tax was levied on the household. Although no further details on the exaction of poll taxes are available in the *Laws of Heavenly Prosperity*, it suffices here to note that the burden of poll tax may not have been any lighter than that of land taxes.

The third category of tax was levied on the use of water for irrigation. Some land was taxed at the rate of 3 *dou* or more per *dan* of seeds; elsewhere, a different tax rate applied, at 2.5 *sheng* per *dan* of seeds sowed.

If a household of farmers was a family of four, with two adult parents and two children, and grew grains in a patch of land where they sowed 10 *dan* of seeds, then their precise burden of tax would amount to the following:

1. Given 10 *mu* of land for 1 *dan* of seeds, 10 *dan* of seeds would be sowed in 100 *mu* of land (roughly equivalent to 24 *mu* of land by the standard of Song Dynasty). This family would have to pay land taxes in the amount of 100 *sheng* (or 1 *dan*) of assorted coarse grains, and 2 *dou* and 5 *sheng* of wheat.
2. Moreover, this family must pay 6 *dou* of grains as poll taxes for the 2 adults, and 3 *dou* for the two children—9 *dou* in total. This sum of poll taxes was equivalent to taxes exacted on 90 *mu* of lands. Some of the smaller families in Western Xia owned less than 90 *mu* of lands. In such cases, poll taxes higher than land taxes imposed by the government would definitely prove a major financial burden on smaller and poorer families.
3. Finally, the family would need to pay water taxes in order to irrigate their farmland. At the rate of 2.5–3 + *dou* of grains as taxes for 1 *dan* of seeds, this family is required to pay 2.5–3 *dan* of grains as taxes for their land, measured by 10 *dan* of seeds.

A total sum of these three taxes is anything between 4.4 and 4.9 *dan* of assorted grains, plus 2 *dou* and 5 *sheng* of wheat. In comparison, the Song Dynasty levied

57 Shi Jinbo, 2002.

around 5 *dan* of grains on 24 (Song) *mu* of land each year. And there is, of course, the 100 bundles of hay, and the likelihood of being called upon to travel afar to conduct corvée labour. In light of this, it must be said that this Tangut family in our hypothetical scenario pays a heavy duty to their government.

5.3 *Agricultural Taxes and Grain Storage in Western Xia*

The many tax records enumerated and explained above point to the consensus that the Tanguts levied taxes-in-kinds, rather than in cash, on agricultural production. The taxes came down to foodstuff. Farmland taxes, poll taxes and irrigation taxes were all paid in grains—either coarse, assorted grains or finer wheat. Hay, another medium of taxation, was also a tax in the form of real goods. Of course, there was always the additional option of paying tributes through physical labour.

The grain levies not only furnished the dining tables of the royalties, but also provided for the diet and salaries of all officials within the entire imperial bureaucratic apparatus. Moreover, a large number of professional soldiers in the army lived on government provisions, which were taxpayers' grains. For the Tanguts, whose agricultural economy was less advanced than in the Central Plains due to geographic reasons, grains claimed even greater symbolic and practical importance. Even as a large levy came into the exchequer's hands, Western Xia officials had to plan its carefully calculated use to guarantee sustainability over time, for it would have been foolish to consume as it went. This made it all the more critical to maintain proper preservation of these provisions; therefore, the keeping and storing of grains was a crucial political task. Western Xia included rules and regulations on grain storage in its fundamental law code. The *Laws of Heavenly Prosperity* required that the grains be thoroughly checked before warehousing:

> When officials from local borders and from the district of the imperial capital arrive to collect all kinds of foodstuffs for the government, it is necessary to take care and caution to winnow the grains, in order that the finest foods and dry fruits enter the government's warehouses.[58]

There were also specific regulations on the construction of storage sites, where the foodstuffs exacted as taxes were held and preserved:

58 *Revised Laws of Heavenly Prosperity* 15, "On the Dispatchment of Junior Accounting Magistrate to Collect Taxes in the Form of Grains," p. 510.

> The Military Supervisory Commission and the bureaus of the other Commissions should prepare the statistical records of the grains collected from borders and from the regions. They should designate a warehouse where there is ample timber, but it is necessary to place tiles on the structure. Where there is no timber, it is fitting to dig a cellar into a dry and firm ground, and then bake it with fire, to let it dry. Grain piles and the layering hay should be dense. On the top, the officials should spill three *chi* of dust, so as to avoid any damages to the government-owned grains.[59]

We know therefore that the Tanguts relied on two types of warehouses: storage houses above the ground and cellars underground. The Tanguts accumulated rich experiences in building facilities for the storage of provisions. Zhuang Chuo of the Song Dynasty offered a detailed introduction to Tangut modes of food storage along the Song-Xia borders in Shaanxi:

> Given the high altitude of Shaanxi, and the vertical patterns of the earth, the government storage houses do not use other objects to store grains. Although wheat is the most difficult to endure, not a single granule is infected with pests throughout twenty years. Local residents would build a cellar within their land. These families would open up the ground, about the size of a well, and dig as deep as three to four *chi*. Given the limited capacity of the storage there, it is then expanded outward into its four borders. The earth is golden in colour, free of sand and stones. After burning, the twisted hay is nailed onto the four walls like ropes. A rich storage of grains reaches as much as several thousands of *dan*, and the quality is all the better in the progress of time. These people would use earth to firm up this opening. Right above the cellar, they still grow corns and cereals, and these grains would still be nourished as before. The only difference is that, now, once you knock on the ground, there is a sound. And once snow falls onto the earth, it is quick to melt. This is how you know that there is storage of grains underground. When enemies encroach upon the borders, this is how grain storages are discovered. And when our imperial armies reach the enemy camps, we also use this method to identify and seize these underground storages.[60]

59 Ibid., p. 513.

60 Zhuang, Chuo (Song Dynasty). *Ji Lei Pian* [雞肋篇]: *Essays: Chicken Ribs*. Beijing: Zhonghua Book Company, 1983.

The 'enemies' referred to in this rhetorical context refers obviously to the Tanguts. It is not difficult to see, based on Song narratives, that the Tanguts were perfectly aware of and versed in the art of underground storage popularly practised in the Shaanxi area. Rules and ordinances concerning the storage of foodstuff in the Tangut imperial law code shed similar light on this distinct method. All these materials point to the excellent standard and quality of Tangut storage and its local characteristics.

The arable lands of Western Xia yielded an abundance of grains, thus furnishing the empire with an opulence of taxes. The *Laws of Heavenly Prosperity* not only required that grains levied in various regions be turned over to the government, but also set the time limit according to the amounts of grains:

> Below 1,000 *hu* 10 days.
> 1,000 *hu*–2,000 *hu* 15 days.
> 2,000 *hu*–5,000 *hu* 1 month.
> 5,000 *hu*–10,000 *hu* 40 days.
> 10,000 *hu*–15,000 *hu* 50 days.
> 15,000 *hu*–20,000 *hu* 60 days.
> 20,000 *hu*–25,000 *hu* 70 days.
> 25,000 *hu*–30,000 *hu* 80 days.
> 30,000 *hu*–35,000 *hu* 90 days.
> 35,000 *hu*–40,000 *hu* 100 days.
> 40,000 *hu*–50,000 *hu* 115 days.
> 50,000 *hu*–60000 *hu* 130 days.
> 60,000 *hu*–70,000 *hu* 145 days.
> 70,000 *hu*–100,000 *hu* 160 days.
> Above 100,000 *hu*, 180 days.[61]

A district or area is required to turn over a maximum of 100,000 *hu* (*dan*) to the central government. The implication therein is the Tangut practice of amassing and concentrating grains from the vast expanse of the empire into particular locations. And for this purpose, the government had to build a great number of storage sites. Tangut granaries were of various sizes and capacities, ranging from small storehouses of a volume somewhere within 5,000 *hu* (*dan*) supervised by only two staff members, to large constructions with more than 100,000 *hu* of grains overseen by one *antou* official in charge of 6 *sili* clerks. Some of the storage sites mentioned in the *Laws of Heavenly Prosperity* include

61 *Revised Laws of Heavenly Prosperity* 15, "On the Dispatchment of Junior Accounting Magistrate to Collect Taxes in the Form of Grains," pp. 510–511.

the old and new Guanheishan granaries, the Central Commander's Land-Tax Granary, the Mingsha Military District Land-Tax Grain Storage, and the Woods and Nine Waters Land-Tax Grain Storage, etc.[62]

It is recorded in archives that in the midst of war, the Song army swiftly targeted Tangut granaries after occupying a new territory, sometimes capturing large sums of food supplies. In the seventh year of Da'an (1080), the Song general Li Xian conquered the Kangu area:

> The great army passed by the valley of Kangu, which Bingchang unduly refers to as the 'imperial manor.' It houses an exceedingly large storage … [I have] already dispatched my lieutenants to each lead a force to seize the grains, as well as bows and arrows for the defence of the city.[63]

Later, Song generals also seized a considerable amount of Tangut millet storages.[64]

As a counter-strategy to the Song seizure of granaries, the Tanguts resorted to relocating grain storages from areas about to fall to the enemies. For example, again in the seventh year of Da'an, (1080), Empress Liang "ordered that all civilians move the millet storages from the many districts" upon hearing news that the Song's Li Xian was about to breach the walls of Lanzhou.[65]

Western Xia boasted a mighty armed force in the hundreds of thousands, which rivalled the Song, Khitan and Jurchen soldieries for the duration of two centuries. Without a formidable economic engine, such a military machine would have been impossible to maintain. It is not difficult to see from the diverse documents mentioned above that the Tanguts had intention, the methods and ability to levy taxes and manage large storages, and in these ways, supported the operation of the government at home and the projection of power abroad.

62 *Revised Laws of Heavenly Prosperity* 17, "On Transfer and Transportation between Bureaus and Departments," pp. 529–534.

63 *Extended Edition of the Zizhi Tongjian*, Bk. 318, End of Tenth Year in the Winter of the Fourth Year of Yuanfeng, in Emperor Shenzong's reign (1081).

64 *Xixia Shushi*, Ch. 25. *History of Song*, Bk. 349, "Biography of Liu Changzuo"; *Extended Edition of the Zizhi Tongjian* Bk. 316. "Yiwei in the Ninth Month of the Fourth Year of Yuanfeng, in Shenzong Emperor's Reign. (1082)."

65 *Xixia Shushi*, Ch. 25.

6 Features of Agricultural Taxes in Western Xia

A thorough analysis of the Khara-Khoto tax records reveals several key characteristics of Western Xia's tax revenues in the agriculture-based territories.

First, the Tanguts enacted a taxation system based on the size of land ownership. In other words, it was an institution of fixed taxation. In the Khara-Khoto region, for example, the tax rate was 0.1 *dou* (or 1 *sheng*)/*mu* of assorted grains and 0.025 *dou* (or ¼ *sheng*) of wheat. Levying taxes based on land size was the most common tax system in the history of Chinese dynastic empires. The fact that the Tanguts inherited this system bears no small significance for our understanding of the agricultural economy in Western Xia.

Second, Tangut levies encompassed land, labour and forage (hay) taxes. That is to say, apart from paying the usual grain taxes by land size, it also fell on the landowners to contribute labour in days and hay in bundles. But the amounts of labour and forage were calculated in the same package as the grain taxes, by the standard of land size.

The social documents show that each year, based on the size of their owned lands, Tangut households contributed labour according to a scale of six levels: 5, 15, 20, 30, 35, and 40 days, respectively. The labour force was directed for the most part to the construction, maintenance and management of canals in the spring. The nature, purpose and amount of labour services specified in these socio-economic records basically coincided with the relevant requirements in the larger area around the imperial capital, as found in the Tangut legal codex, the *Laws of Heavenly Prosperity*. Scholars therefore draw the conclusion that such tax rates once applied to not only residents of the capital, but also to peripheral territories such as Khara-Khoto.

Forage played a critical role in the inner life of the Tangut Empire. The government ceaselessly collected taxes in the form of hay bundles, which it then constantly supplied to the imperial cavalries in the time of war or burden animals used for long-distance transportation of goods and provisions. Another use of forage was the application of layers of hay for canal constructions and irrigation. The Khara-Khoto documents confirm that the Tanguts paid an annual tax of 1 bundle of hay per *mu* of farmland. This was a peculiar form of taxation in Western Xia.

Third, tax-in-kind was the main form of agricultural taxation in Western Xia. Not unlike in the Central Plains, to submit taxes in the form of real goods or products remained the prevailing system of imperial tax collection at the time. It was supplemented, however, by tax in labour services. Because currency was not as well developed or commonly circulated in Western Xia as in the Central

Plains, monetary tax payment is quite rare in the Khara-Khoto documents, compared to taxes-in-kinds and in labours.

Fourth, the poll tax was another key characteristic of the Tangut tax system. The social documents show that each Tangut adult was required to pay 3 *dou* of tax and each underage child was to pay 1.5 *dou*, regardless of gender. Unmentioned in the *Laws of Heavenly Prosperity*, this tax is known to us solely through these economic documents—indeed a major breakthrough in historical research on Tangut taxation. Such a 'head tax' in addition to the normal taxes listed in the Tangut law code must have proved a source of heavy financial burden for large peasant households with very few lands.

Fifth, irrigation taxes as mentioned in the economic documents—levies on the use of water for farming purposes—constituted another special taxation in Western Xia. On the one hand, such a tax reflects the prosperity of agricultural-hydraulic projects and the heavy dependence on canals for irrigation in the Khara-Khoto area. On the other hand, these manuscripts document the details of the water tax rates at various levels. Given the different amounts of water used at various agricultural sites in Khara-Khoto, water taxes also varied to different degrees. Lands were taxed at rates ranging from 3 *dou* and 1 *sheng* to 2 *dou* and 5 *sheng* per *dan* of seeds sowed. As a special form of agricultural tax, irrigation and water taxes were widely collected throughout the vast expanse of Tangut territories. Tax records excavated from Khara-Khoto are the only known extant primary sources on Tangut irrigation taxation.

CHAPTER 5

Accounts of Grains and Properties

Apart from the land and grain taxes, accounts of grains and properties also constitute a part of the excavated corpus of Tangut documents. Although most are in fragments, there is still new information to be extracted from these primary sources, which add to our existing understanding of Tangut society and economy.

1 Accounts of Grains

Grain accounts include those kept by officials in military supervisory districts and those by the unit of *liliu*. The former, found mostly on the layering page of sutra covers, are rarely complete. However, the *liliu* accounts are kept as single pages, with the beginning and end more or less intact and the amounts of grains in large numbers.

1.1 *Grain Accounts of the Military Supervisory Districts*

Grain accounts at military supervisory districts survive mostly as page fragments in the inner layer of sutra covers, such as Russian manuscripts Инв. No. 438, Инв. No. 441 and Инв. No. 723 (year of *Si*). In these mostly incomplete accounts, the titles "military supervisory commission" or "imperial capital" are uniformly featured, suggesting that these grain accounts have to do with Tangut military affairs.

Grain account manuscript Инв. No. 438 is written in the cursive style on a 31.2 × 32 cm hemp cover paper, with the top and bottom pieces of paper stitched together into a single page. The Tangut writings are in lines 11 and 12.

Grain account manuscript Инв. No. 441 is written in the cursive style on a 31.6 × 32 cm hemp cover paper, with the top and bottom pieces stitched together into a single page. The Tangut writings are in lines 13 and 13.

Grain account manuscript Инв. No. 723 (year of *Si*) is written in the cursive style on a 31.6 × 30.8 cm hemp cover paper, likewise, with the top and bottom pieces stitched together into a single page. Each page features 12 lines of Tangut writings. While the top piece suffers more damages, written in lines 1 and 7 of the bottom piece are "Eleventh month in the Year of *Si*" and "last month in the Year of *Si*," respectively.[1]

1 *Russian Collection of Khara-Khoto Manuscripts* 12, pp. 117, 118, 136.

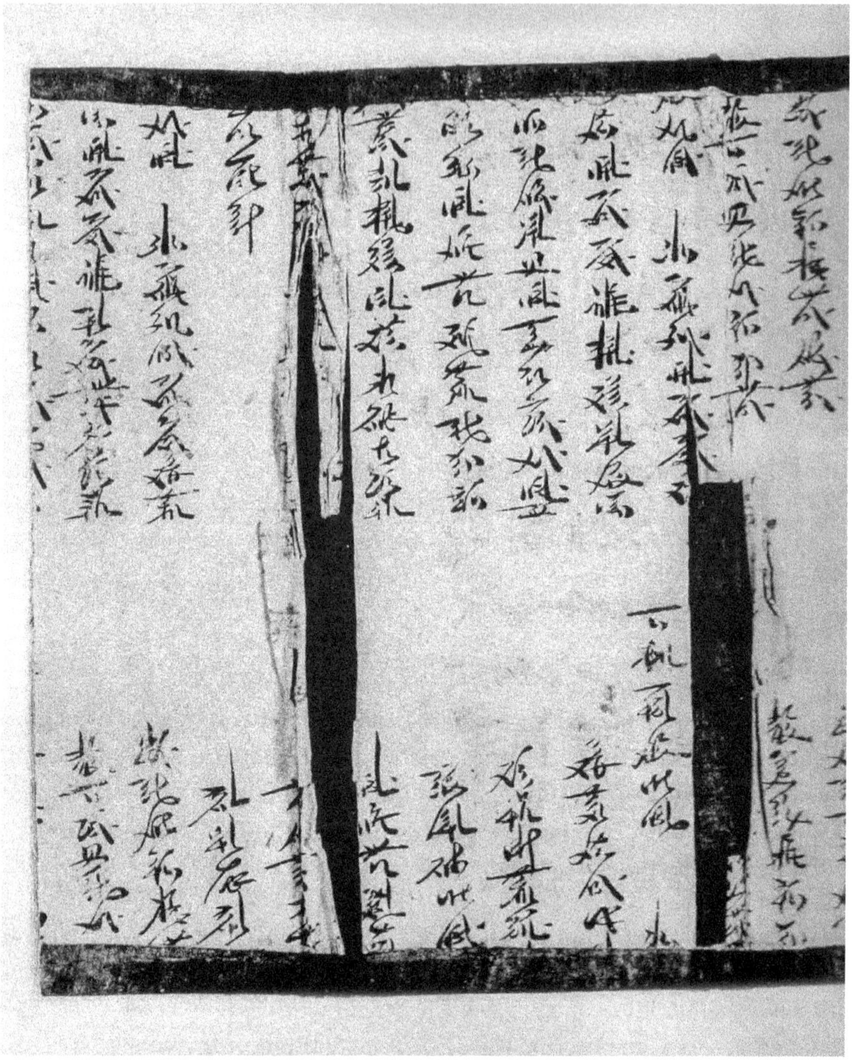

FIGURE 53 Инв. No. 438: Grain account

The content of the manuscript fragments is organised by itemised entries. Under the title of each item, the un-indented top begins with the Tangut characters [Tangut] (lit. one, *liu*). The numeral 'one' is straightforward and easy to understand. As for the second character, its generic meaning is 'item,' which extends to the use of the term 'military *liu*' as the basic unit of organization in the Tangut army. Since the latter is much more likely to be its meaning in this particular context, it is fair to assume that these grain accounts are kept by military divisions, with each *liu* as a single unit. Almost every entry features the titles [Tangut] (the military supervisory commission) and [Tangut] (imperial

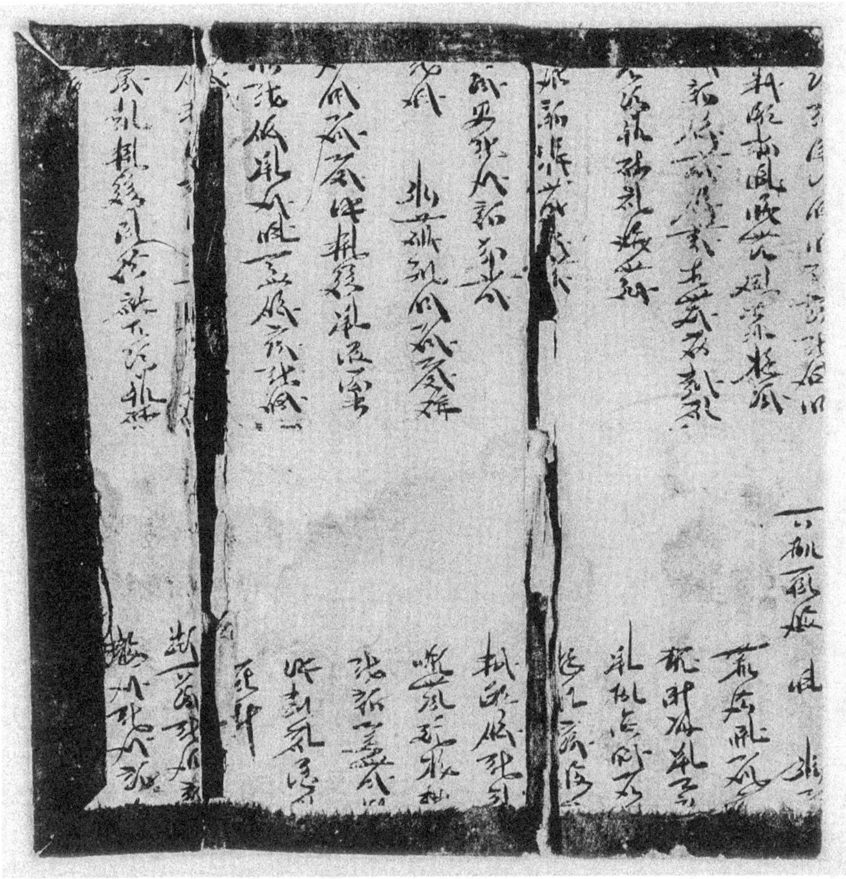

FIGURE 54 Инв. No. 441: Grain account

capital). They point to the possibility that these are records of the army's transportation of grains from the military supervisory district of Khara-Khoto to the imperial capital Zhongxing (present-day Yinchuan of Ningxia) by the unit of *liliu*. The amounts of grains recorded in these accounts are in large numbers, such as "189 *dan* and 3 *dou*" in Russian manuscript Инв. No. 438 (top page, line 3) and "296 *dan*, 2 *dou* and 5 *sheng*" in Инв. No. 723 (bottom page, lines 10–11). These numbers probably indicate the amounts of grains that the single *liliu* was put in charge of transporting to the capital.

The statistics in the grain accounts are compiled by months and years. For example, the notations "sixth month of Year *Si*" at the bottom and "ninth month" at the top of Russian manuscript Инв. No. 438 indicate that this is a grain account from the year *Si*. Similar notations of time include the lines "Year *Si* [ ] month" at the bottom and "[year], tenth month" at the top of Инв. No. 441, as well as "Year *Si*, eleventh month" and "Year *Si*, last month" in manuscript

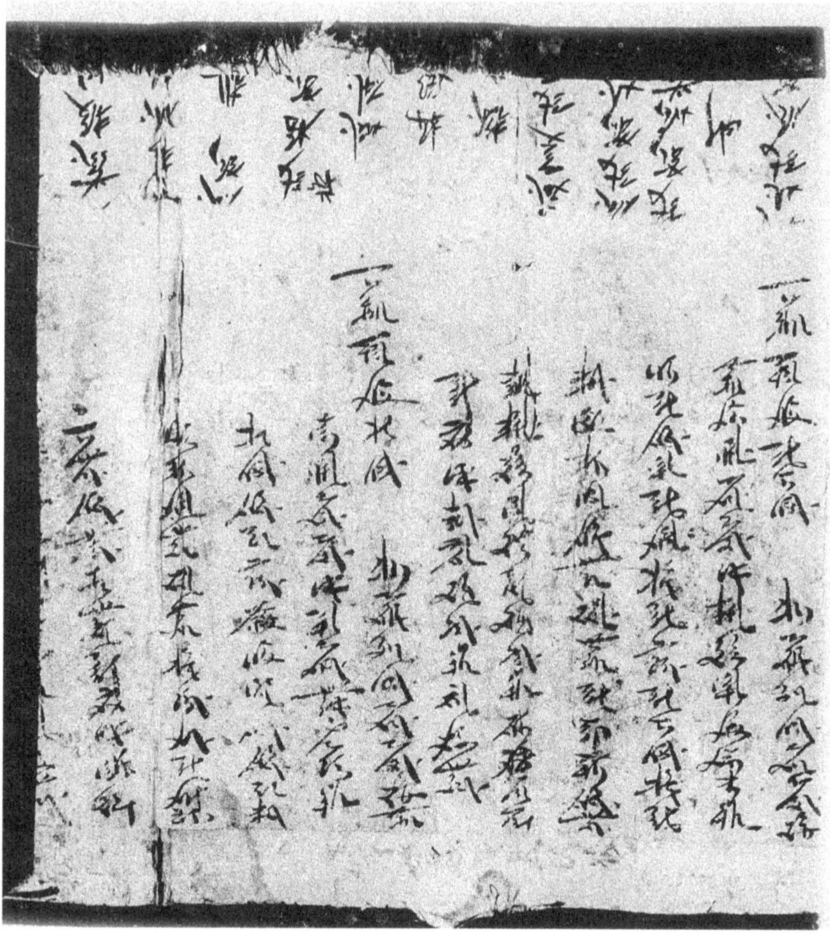

FIGURE 55 Инв. No. 723: Grain account

Инв. No. 723. There seems to be no doubt, then, that all these documents ought to be dated to the year of *Si*. The entries in these documents are sorted by months, which means that those beginning with 'June' are accounts for the June–July period, and entries that begin with 'September' are grain statistics for the September–October period. Likewise, entries beginning with the last month of year *Si* extend to January of the following year of *Wu*.

Despite general illegibility of the documents due to heavy damages and missing characters in almost every line, there remains valuable information in the more recognizable entries. For example, the records of "45 men in an entire month from Oct. 20th to Nov. 20th" and "13 *dan* & 5 *dou*" found at the bottom of manuscript Инв. No. 723 (lines 3–5) yield the result 3 *dou* of grains per person during this month. In another record, "45 men in the entire month from August 10th to September 10th" and "thirteen *dan* [?] *dou* of millet" in the upper section of manuscript Инв. No. 438 (lines 5–8) suffers from the loss of a missing word, likely the character for "five," based on information from adjacent documents. In this way, the daily provision per person also turns out to be 3 *dou* per person for the month (i.e., 1 *sheng* per day). This may be the grain subsidy provided to soldiers in a given *liliu*.

The *Laws of Heavenly Prosperity* offers detailed rules and regulations for the transportation of materials from local areas to the imperial capital:

> The many kinds of government-owned livestock, grains, cash and other properties that do not fall under the jurisdictions of Strategic Regulatory Commissioners (*Jinglueshi*), and which the staff of the bureaus in charge of storage have not,[2] based on their location, distributed to the relevant offices of local towns, districts, commandaries and military commissions for review, should be studied and dispatched all at once within fifteen days of their transfer. It is also necessary to clearly indicate the number of days required for their transportation based on their distance from the Imperial Capital and the time it requires for the bureaus in the Imperial Capital to review them.
>
> The two military supervisory commissions are obliged to transport goods to the jurisdiction of the imperial capital within forty days since the time of the dispatch; the political offices in the imperial capital are required to finish the review process in sixty days; the Bureau of Review conduct inspection for fifty days: Shazhou, Guazhou.
>
> The two military supervisory commissions are both obliged to transport goods to the imperial capital within thirty days since the time of the dispatch. The political offices of the Imperial capital are required to finish the review process within sixty days; the Bureau of Review conduct inspection for sixty days: Suzhou, Heishui (Khara-Khoto) …[3]

2 TN: This is a literal translation. According to Tangut laws, it is standard procedure for the local offices to review the goods and statistics, one level at a time, before referral to the office and the inspection bureau of the imperial office. Here, the text may refer to cash, goods and resources directly supplied to the capital. In general, finances of the military districts, the capital, and the empire as a whole are separated, not without overlaps.

3 *Revised Laws of Heavenly Prosperity* 17, "Rules concerning the departure of goods from the storage," p. 544.

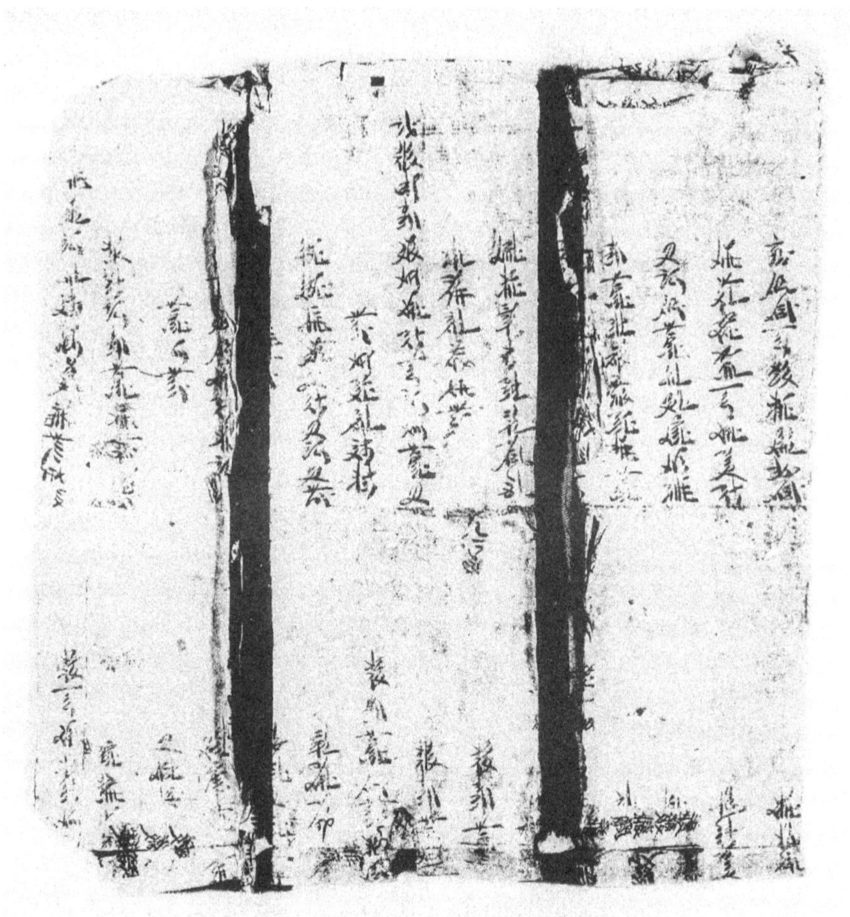

FIGURE 56 Инв. No. 2998: Grain account

This legislation concerns the time constraint on the transportation of goods from various local districts to the imperial capital. Sending goods and supplies from Shazhou and Guazhou, prefectures further from the destination, usually took about 40 days. For cities Suzhou and Khara-Khoto, time of transport was 30 days. This law coincides with and confirms the '30 days' recorded in the Khara-Khoto grain accounts.

Some grain accounts show unusually large numbers in the hundreds and even thousands of *dan*. For example, Russian manuscript Инв. No. 2998 records a total of 3611 *dan*. Manuscript Инв. No. 2998 is a grain account piece on a 33.3 × 32.3 hemp paper used as the layer of a book cover. The document is patched together with multiple broken pieces and divided into upper and lower parts, featuring 14 and 15 lines of Tangut cursive writings, respectively.[4]

According to lines 8–12 of the document, "Of the coarse and refined kinds of grains in the amount of 3611 *dan*, 4 *dou*, 8 *sheng*, 6 *ge*, there are: grains 2088 *dan*, 8 *dou*, 3 *sheng* and 6 *ge*; wheat 1512 *dan* 3 *dou* 4 *sheng*; millet 5 *dan*, 3 *dou*, 2.5 *sheng*." The first batch of (coarse) grain is in the large number of more than two thousand *dan*. The second type of grain, though officially unknown due to missing characters at the corner of the manuscript page, is judged to be 'wheat,' given that the third category is listed as 'millet.' The reason is simple: both 'grains' and 'millets' are considered to be 'coarse' ('assorted' or 'miscellaneous' grain types), so, without the refined 'wheat' listed in between, this document could not have claimed to cover both the 'coarse' and the 'refined.' The missing numeral '3' *dou* in 'wheat' can also be inferred by a simple subtraction of the numbers in the first and third categories from the total sum.

1.2 *Grain Accounts by* liliu

Grain accounts are sometimes registered by *liliu*, the basic unit of organization in Tangut communities, roughly equivalent to *li* (as in *lijia*) in the Central Plains. Grain accounts of similar types include manuscripts Инв. No. 4762-4 (*liliu* grain account, 20 × 40 cm hemp paper, 15 lines of Tangut cursive with signatures, edits and erasures) and Инв. No. 4762-5 (*liliu* grain account, hand-written manuscript, 19.3 × 89.2 cm hemp paper, 37 lines of Tangut cursive with signatures, edits and erasures).[5]

The first two well-preserved documents are similar in format and calligraphic style. The first line of the first *liliu* grain account reads, "[illegible][illegible][illegible][illegible][illegible][illegible][?]": the first and second characters may be literally translated as "soft grains," a general reference to grains and food. A similar word to the first character is [illegible], which combined with [illegible] forms the expression [illegible]. This noun is translated to the Chinese 斛㪷 (food and grain) in the Fan-Han *Pearl in the Palm*. The last character in the place of the question mark is illegible, but it should not prevent us from translating the whole phrase into the like of "transfer four kinds of grains (*liu*)." This is followed by the grain account of one unit of *liliu*. The second document contains the accounts of two *liliu* units. Overall, given the registration of four *liliu* accounts, there seems to be one more left undiscovered.

4 *Russian Collection of Khara-Khoto Manuscripts* 13, p. 163.

5 *Russian Collection of Khara-Khoto Manuscripts* 13, pp. 278, 279.

But in the surviving records of three *liliu* accounts, the first line begins with [illegible] (*liliu*), followed by the name of the chief in command of the unit, and ends with the two characters [illegible] (the local administrative bureau), signifying that the staff listed below are under the authority of the *liliu* chief. Thereafter, each line records the names, under which appear the statistics of grains. In general, each line contains information on the amounts of grains under two names.

For example, manuscript Инв. No. 4762-4 records the grain statistics under 23 names, which are, in order: 300, 200, 50, 50, 60, 30, 20, 30, 10, 20, 10, 20, 10, 5, 15, 5, 5, 5, 5, 10, 3, 3, 5 *dan*. The document records the amounts—as much as 300 and as little as 30 *dan*—but not the types of grains. The grain accounts of 2 *liliu* units, recorded in manuscript Инв. No. 4762-5, contain statistics under 33 and 31 men, respectively, each with cursive signatures and finger stamps at the end. Manuscript Инв. No. 4762-4 ends with the three characters [illegible] (twenty-nine); the account of the first *liliu* in Инв. No. 4762-5 also ends with the signature of "twenty-nine," whereas the record of the second *liliu* shows [illegible] (day one) instead. This is enough evidence to indicate that these are dates, signatures and finger stamps at the end of an official account, and that the first two documents were signed on the 29th—the last day of a 'short month' in the lunar calendar—whereas the latter was signed on the day after, on the first day of the following month.

An analysis of these grain accounts suggests that they do not concern household land taxes. The amounts of grains are in large numbers, from dozens to hundreds of *dan*, which greatly exceed the magnitude of even the severest rate of taxation. Moreover, we know that the grain versus wheat ratio in land taxes is about 4:1, which finds no echoes in these accounts. Nor do they resemble poll

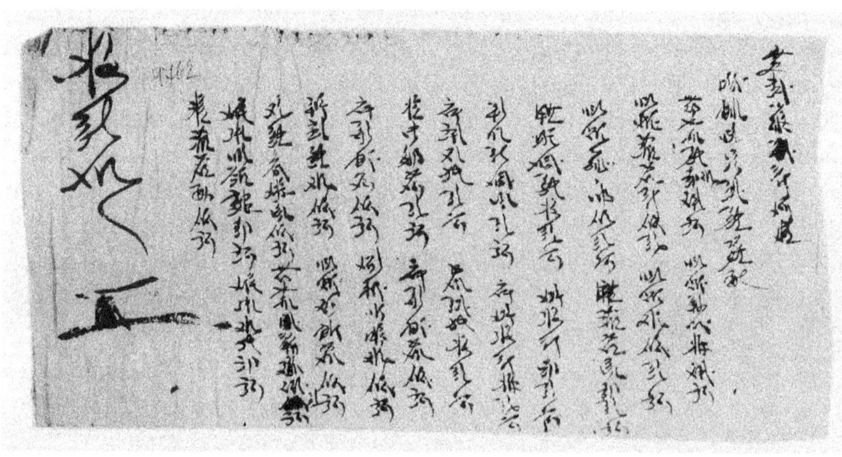

FIGURE 57 Инв. No. 4762-4: *Liliu* Grain account

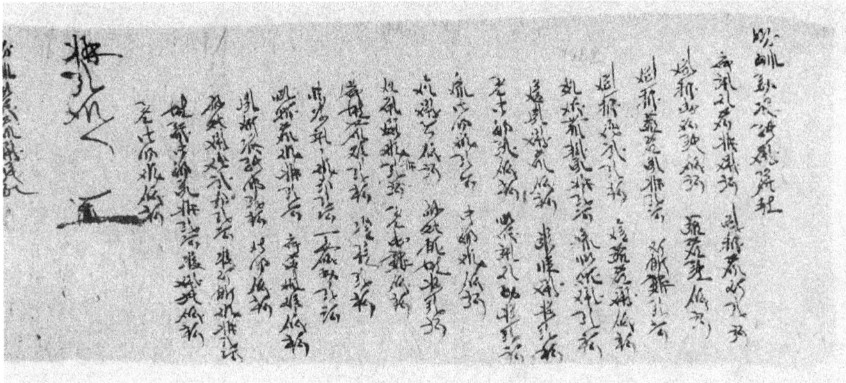

FIGURE 58 Инв. No. 4762-5 (1): *Liliu* Grain account

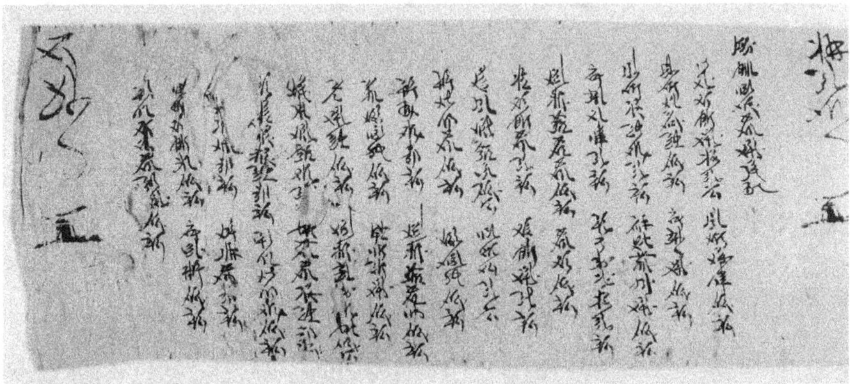

FIGURE 59 Инв. No. 4762-5 (2): *Liliu* Grain account

taxes, which are approximately 3 *dou* per adult and 1.5 *dou* per child. Given the large sums, and the fact that for records on so many households, the smallest unit of weight measurement in the first two documents is *dan*, rather than *dou* or *sheng*, they cannot be poll taxes, either. A quick comparison with the water and irrigation tax records also rules out this possible conjecture. So, what is the nature and purpose of these grain accounts?

Because of the large grain-per-household numbers, usually in the unit of *dan*, it is possible that they are accounts of grains distributed and transported to each household. Russian manuscript Инв. No. 4762-4 mentions the identity of *shijun* at the beginning, after which is recorded the amount of grains in 300 *dan*. We have mentioned that the *shijun* are semi-slaves, without personal freedom, at the bottom of Tangut society. They are least likely to be levied such large amounts of grains by the government, but they are the ones who

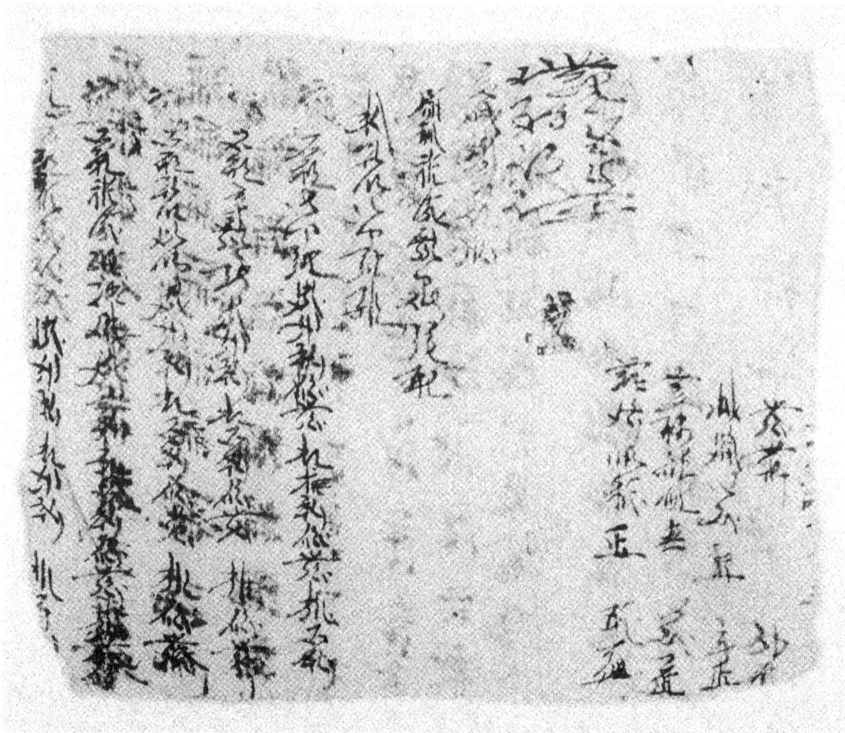

FIGURE 60 Инв. No. 4762-8: Grain account

provide labour service to transport the largest amounts of grains from one site to another. The grains are transported from the *liliu* to the individual households, which is an accurate portrayal of the socio-economic reality at the time. In particular, manuscript Инв. No. 4762-4 lists the "the transferor of grains" in the first line, the title of which further implies and corroborates the purpose of these grain accounts. It is likely that they are accounts of various sums of grains transferred and transported by staff in the organization of *liliu*.

The following Russian manuscript Инв. No. 4762-8 is another grain account on 18.7 × 23.5 cm hemp paper featuring 13 lines of Tangut cursive and signatures.[6]

This piece of document lost some of the first and last portions of its content, but given the signature and finger stamp, it is possible to categorise it as an account of grain statistics. Given that it also features the first half of a second *liliu* account, the manuscript seems to contain at least the accounts of two *liliu* units. The second account begins with the words [illegible][?][illegible],

6 *Russian Collection of Khara-Khoto Manuscripts* 13, p. 281.

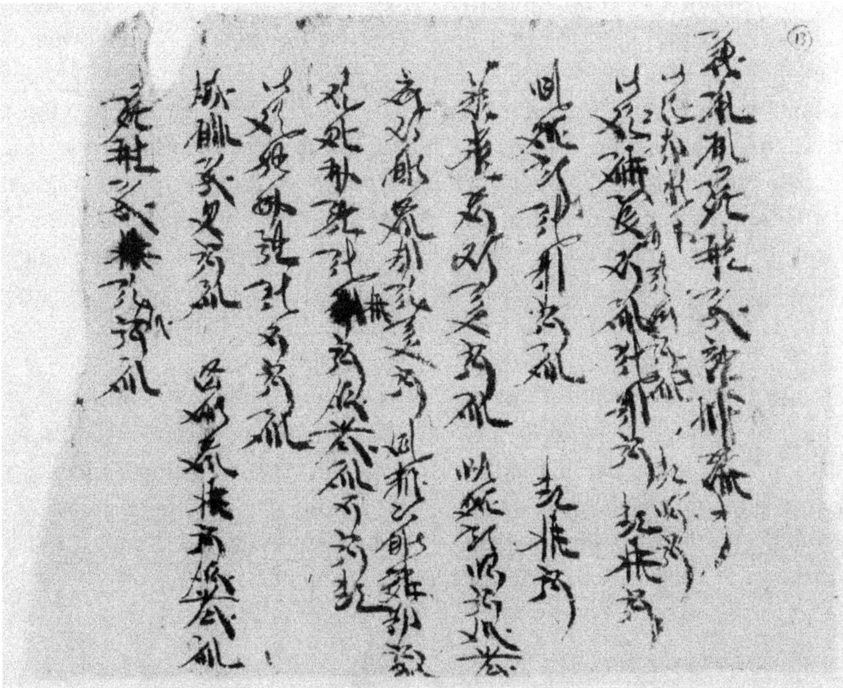

FIGURE 61 Инв. No. 6377-12: *Liliu* Grain account

meaning "*liliu* Luopujiu [?] bureau staff." As already mentioned, the characters for "Luopujiu[?]" are the name of the leader of the *liliu* concerned, whereas the "bureau" refers to the staff under his administrative authority.

The document shares some similarities with the grain accounts mentioned above, but remains different in several aspects of its format:

1. The unit of *jia* is found under *liliu*, with the surname of the *jia* chief recorded as Yehe;
2. Indication of two characters 𘂆𗣼 (one household) before the lines;
3. Grains are recorded separately under each type: barley, wheat, millet, etc.;
4. The smallest unit is no longer *dan*, as in the three aforementioned accounts, but in both *dan* and *dou*.

There are a few additional accounts of a similar kind. One example is manuscript Инв. No. 6377-12, a handwritten *liliu* grain account on a 19.5 × 24.8 cm hemp fragment paper, with ten lines of Tangut cursive as well as signs of erasures and edits.[7]

7 *Russian Collection of Khara-Khoto Manuscripts* 14, p. 143.

The first line of the document reads, "[illegible] …" (under the managerial authority of the transferors and the bureau staff …), followed by the kinds and amounts of food by persons: "Meiqi Nazhengji, assorted grains 13 *dan*, wheat 2 *dan*." The difference lies in the details of the last two lines: "8 *dan* of assorted grains in the *liliu*," "Jianli[?] 2 *dan* 5 *dou* of assorted grains," "bureau staff, 19 *dan* of assorted grains," etc. These three accounts concern the basic organisational unit of *liliu*. To ascertain whether the grains hereby concerned are supply reserves requires further archival and archaeological research.

1.3 *Deficit Supply Accounts*

Among the numerous and diverse Tangut social documents, manuscript Инв. No. 6569-1 stands out as a curious fragment page. Handwritten on an 18.7 × 37.5 cm hemp paper, the 18 lines of Tangut cursive writings (with edits and emendations) record many dates, under which are found grain statistics in relatively small numbers. In light of certain decrees in the *Laws of Heavenly Prosperity*, it appears to be a 'deficit supply account.'[8]

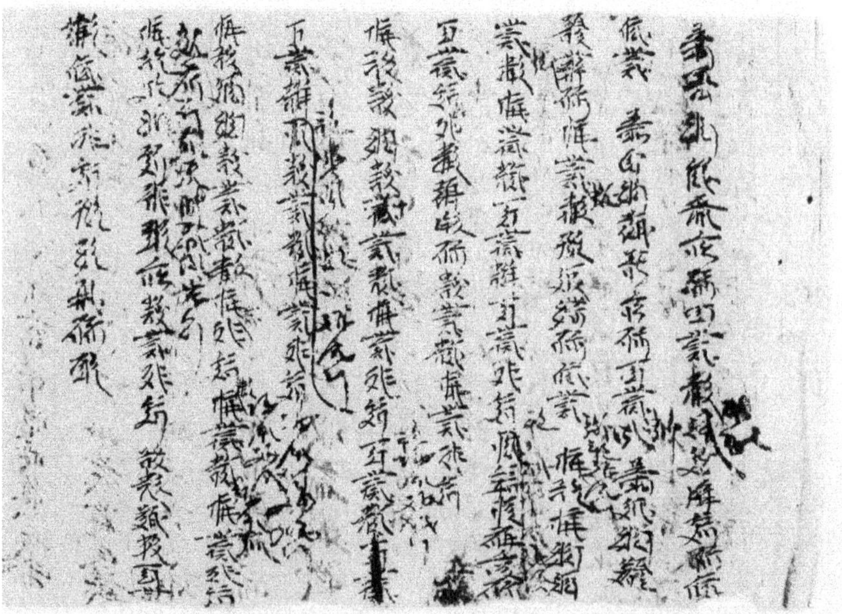

FIGURE 62 Инв. No. 6569-1: Deficit supply account

8 *Russian Collection of Khara-Khoto Manuscripts* 14, p. 157.

Translation:

> On the seventeenth day, to supply the [official] in charge of burden-transport, 1 *sheng*; and to [?] 厽𗊶𗁅 [da kia gju_] Five[?]
> 5 *sheng*. On the eighteenth day, to the one in charge of the task 1 *dou* of millet; on the nineteenth day, to supply the one
> responsible for the birds 2 *sheng* of flour, and to supply the high official 5 *sheng* of flour; On the twenty-second day;
> *sheng* and 2 *dou* of flour; 1 *dou* of rice, 1 *dou* of grinded grains; and to supply 𗍫𗗟𗊱𗅋 [mjij pu. dow dźjij]
> 1 *dou* of grinded grains, and to supply the envoy 3 *sheng* of flour; 2 *dou* of grinded grains.
> On the twenty-third, to supply 3 *sheng* of flour, 2 *sheng* of grinded grains, 1 *dou* of flour
> 1 *dou* of rice, and 3 *sheng* of flour, 2 *sheng* of grinded grains
> On the twenty-fourth, 3 *sheng* of flour and 2 *sheng* of grinded grains, 2 *dou* of flour, 2 *dou* of grinded grains
> On the twenty-sixth, to supply [?] 𗗙𗓱𗔃? 3 *sheng* of grinded grains. Ten scrolls [bureau] Price 1 (*dou* or *sheng*) and 5 *dou* of grinded grains, to supply 5 *jin*.

From the incomplete translation above, it is easy to see that these are provisions supplied to government staff. Some of them are referred to by titles, as in "the one in charge of transporting the burden [?]," the one "holding the birds," and a higher-ranking official in the capital. Others are personal names, such as "[?] the Auspicious Old House" (厽𗊶𗁅 [da kia gju_]) and 𗍫𗗟𗊱𗅋 [mjij pu. dow dźjij]. From day 17 to day 26, there are accounts for 7 days. Some of them do, whilst others don't specify the recipient. If no recipient is named, then it is presumed that it is the same recipient as in the previous document. Overall, this records the daily provision of grains that a given department supplies to its employees. The *Laws of Heavenly Prosperity* stipulates the rules concerning the salaries of regulators in both larger and smaller 'Bureaus of Review,' in charge of checking the statistics of military-owned livestock.

The following are the amounts of provisions provided to the staff in the Bureaus of Review and Inspection, according to their ranks:

> A Senior Official enjoys a slaughter every 10 days, 4 *sheng* of rice or grains per day; of the 2 horses, each one is allocated 7 *sheng*, the other 5 *sheng*; a Junior is allotted 1 *sheng* of rice.

> □ An official, such as a Secretary in the Bureau of Review and Inspection, enjoys a slaughter every 15 days, 1 *sheng* of rice per day; 5 *sheng* for the horse; a Junior is allotted 1 *sheng* of rice per day.
>
> Government employees: *Antou* (Clerk at the Desk) and *Sili* (Staff in the Office) both enjoy one slaughter every 20 days; each of them is allotted 1 *sheng* of rice per day; a Junior and a Keeper of the Rod each has 1 *sheng* of rice.

Provisions granted to the employees in the higher and lower bureaus of Livestock Review and Inspection, according to ranks:

> A senior official enjoys a slaughter every 7 days, 4 *sheng* of rice or grains per day, of which there is 1 *sheng* of rice; food for 4 horses, 7 *sheng* for one horse, 5 *sheng* in case of the 3 horses; for the three children, there is 1 *sheng* of rice per day.
>
> □ All serving agents in the Bureau of Review and Inspection and others enjoy a slaughter every 15 days, 1 *sheng* of rice per day, 5 *sheng* of food supply to the horse, as well as 1 *sheng* of rice to a single child.
>
> The two lower-level *Antou* and *Sili* officials enjoy a slaughter every 15 days; to each of them, there is a supply of horse food in 5 *sheng*; to each of them there is 1 *sheng* of rice per day; to the one child, there is 1 *sheng* of rice.
>
> Each of the two men receive an allocation of 1 *sheng* of rice per day:
> One in charge of the sticks.
> One in charge of equipment.[9]

A comparison of the document above to the stipulations of provisions in the *Laws of Heavenly Prosperity* suggests that the document records salary-provisions to government officials on active duty. There exist, however, some differences between the two. Whereas in the *Laws of Heavenly Prosperity*, government staff receive not only grains, but also meat as well as food for their horses, the two documents here mention only grains, not meat. This is perhaps the case for lower-ranked staff members.

9 *Revised Laws of Heavenly Prosperity* 20, "On the Different Degrees of Crimes and Liabilities," pp. 613–614.

2 Accounts of Properties

There is a large quantity and wide array of property accounts in the corpus of Tangut social documents. They furnish us with abundant information on goods and materials, cash and properties, as well as livestock and miscellaneous possessions. However, many of them remain uninterpreted, due to the illegibility of some cursive writings coupled with damages and fragmentation.

2.1 *Accounts of Cash and Valuables*

Manuscript fragment Инв. No. 4761-11, an account of cash and properties with prints and signatures in large characters, is a formal record registered by the government. This is a handwritten manuscript roll on an 18 cm × 42.4 cm hemp paper with 28 lines of Tangut characters in the cursive style. It features signs of edits and erasures, and prints and signatures, despite some damages in the beginning and lower sections on the right.[10]

Despite the damages to this manuscript, the names are still preserved. In this context, the document appears to be a property account for a transaction by a certain Shi Ashan ([illegible], see lines 2 and 15) and another with the surname of Zhao. In addition, an official named Xipan Aduo ([illegible], see lines 11, 16, and 25) takes part as a witness on behalf of the government.

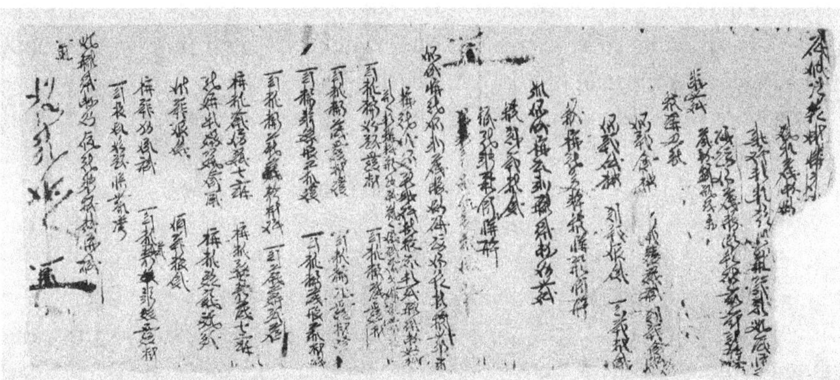

FIGURE 63 Инв. No. 4761-11: Account of cash and properties

10 *Russian Collection of Khara-Khoto Manuscripts* 13, p. 271.

There are several names of properties in this document. From lines 6–8, there are:

> Properties of eight kinds:
> 4 *pi* of silk: 1 *pi* of rouge-dyed silk, 3 *pi* of silk [??]
> 4 *pi* of cloth: 3 *pi* of Fan cloth, 1 *pi* of Han cloth

The so-called rouge-dyed silk (Chinese: 胭脂纈, *yanzhixie*; Tangut: 𗽀𗼇𗧽, [tśji ·ja~ xjij]) is a phonetic transliteration from Chinese. The first two characters are used specifically to represent the Chinese sounds for "rouge" and "blush" cosmetics in the *Pearl in the Palm*. The third character [xjij], which corresponds to a range of modern sounds from *xie*, *xing* to *xian*, sometimes appears as a last name. But here, it refers to a kind of refined silk with floral decorative patterns (Chinese: 纈). This type of silk is also mentioned in Khara-Khoto manuscripts of Chinese trade records.[11]

More property names are mentioned in line 11:

> Properties: 3 *pi* of Han cloth

17 items are mentioned in the 9 lines from 18–26: two in each of 8 lines, and one in the last line. Most of them are textile products, such as "6 *pi* of Fan cloth" and "4 *pi* of Han cloth," but many others have not yet been accurately interpreted.

Various amounts of cash are also mentioned: 27 *guan* (line 10), 10 *guan* (line 12), and the 50 *guan* of Xipan Aduo (line 25).

Specific dates are indicated in the manuscript: 2nd April (line 11, Xipan Aduo[?]), 24th April (line 15), etc. The large characters "twenty-four" signed at the end of the document may also refer to the date.

Overall, this is a social document with a large number of preserved characters, and therefore a great deal of information. It is also worth noting that the manuscript mentions both "Fan cloths" and "Han cloths." The first character of the "Fan cloth" (Tangut: 𗼇𗧽) refers to the Dangxiang Tangut identity, the ruling ethnic group in Western Xia. The expression is clear in distinguishing Tangut textiles from Han Chinese products (Tangut: 𗴂𗧽). The fact that Fan and Han cloths were traded in markets and used by local households at the same time also points to the possible existence of a Tangut textile industry before the Dangxiang integrated into the Han Chinese economy after the great

11 Du, Jianlu; Shi, Jinbo. *Xixia Shehui Wenshu Yanjiu* [西夏社會文書研究]: *A Study of Tangut Social Documents*. Shanghai: Shanghai Ancient Works Publishing House, 2012, pp. 257, 258.

northern migration. It seems that after entering into north-western China, the Tanguts did not replace their own cloths with Chinese merchandise, but continued to produce cloths with ethnic characteristics, and used them along with the finer Chinese products. If this is true, then the prevalent thesis that no Dangxiang Tangut textile industry existed surely requires modification. As to whether and how much of the Fan and Han cloths are made of hemp or cotton, we do not yet have sufficient sources to make the right conclusions. But this manuscript, rich in content and full of information, is to be further studied and interpreted as new data emerge.

2.2 *Accounts of Livestock*

It has been mentioned that many households' self-reports (*shoushi*) contain information on not only population but also the ownership of livestock. But many manuscript fragments only feature the types and statistics of livestock. Whether or not these records belong to the category of 'household register' requires further investigation. For example, manuscript No. 4761-15 is a livestock account handwritten on an 18.5 × 37 cm hemp paper, which contains 14 lines of Tangut cursive writings.[12]

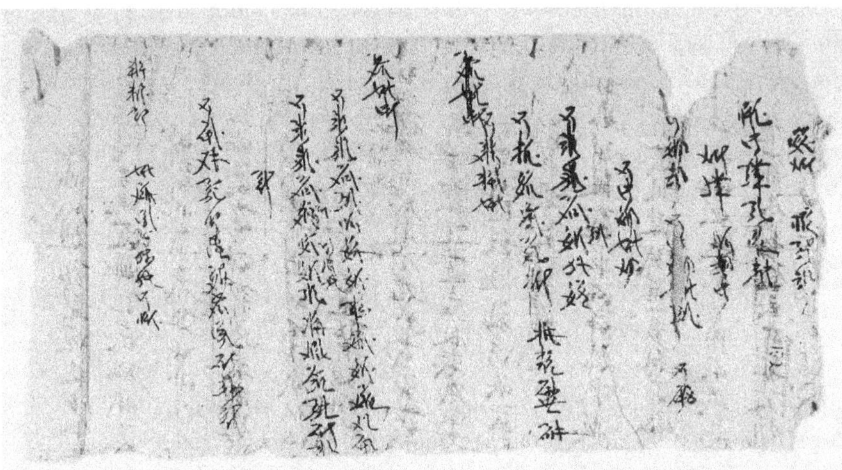

FIGURE 64 Инв. No. 4761-15V: Livestock account

12 *Russian Collection of Khara-Khoto Manuscripts* 13, p. 273.

This document is a rather detailed account of livestock statistics. It regrettably suffers some damages at the beginning, and many words remain blurry and ineligible. But the following is a tentative translation:

……
sheep six sheep (another kind) thirteen
cattle large/small, tens [?] kinds
six adults, four small
Donkeys 3 one small black mother donkey one mule
one small female donkey
one camel …… belongs; two fur carpets white
one [?][?] mother
……
one camel ……
one camel ……
One horse white ……
……

This is possibly a detailed statistical record of the livestock owned by a single household, including the types, numbers, sizes, fur-colours and even ages of the animals. The exhaustive and extensive nature of the record demonstrates the great attention paid by the government to the herding and pasturing industry. According to the *Laws of Heavenly Prosperity*, livestock is divided into private and public ownerships. The government owns animals on public pasturelands, whereas individual households keep their own livestock on private lands.[13] The small numbers indicated in this particular manuscript seem to suggest that they are private possessions.

Sometimes, livestock statistics of more than one household are compiled together. One example is manuscript Инв. No. 345, a handwritten account of livestock and properties on a 32.3 cm × 13.2 cm hemp paper (two fragments stitched and pasted together), which served as the layering paper to a book cover. The two pages feature 7 and 5 lines of Tangut, respectively.[14]

13 *Revised Laws of Heavenly Prosperity* 13, p. 467.
14 *Russian Collection of Khara-Khoto Manuscripts* 12, p. 103.

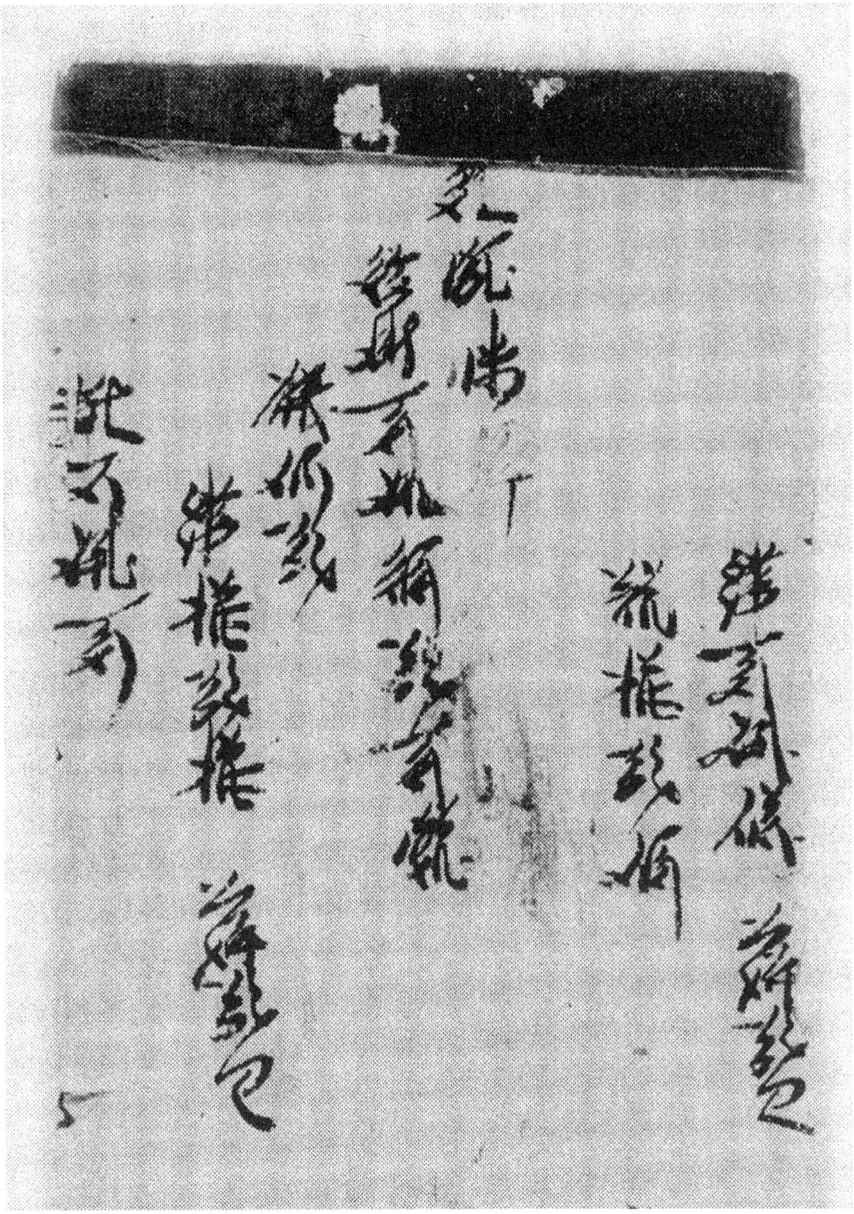

FIGURE 65 Инв. No. 345: Livestock account

The following is a literal translation:

……
adult 105, small 18
sheep 24,
Qianpu Shan[?] (a person's name)
private possession 141 sheep
livestock 40
adult 22, small 18
[?]101
……

Obviously, this fragment contains the livestock statistics of at least two households. It is possible to speculate thence that the Tanguts kept a special form of document on livestock statistics by individual households.

2.3 *Accounts of Miscellaneous Properties*

Some of the manuscripts unearthed at the site of Khara-Khoto contain information on a wide array of miscellaneous objects. For example, manuscript Инв. No. 7892-9 is a property account in the year of *You*. It is a hand-written manuscript on two pages of hemp paper (20 cm × 10.8 cm and 20 cm × 14 cm, respectively). There are 6 lines of Tangut writing in each document, and the second page features a signature and finger stamp. In line 2 on the left page-fragment, there is a date of "year of You, first (month), day twenty-five." In the original text, "five" comes after "day," but the hand-writer uses the √ sign to correct the typo. Furthermore, it is unclear which year of You it is.[15]

There remain 6 lines on the right page-fragment, among which are listed the following properties:

……
Thin clothes 6 stacks, 2 axes, 1[?]
[?] [?] vinegar 3, 3 Spider (skimmer),[16] millet [?] pearl
2 axes[?] 50[?] 1 iron[?]

15 *Russian Collection of Khara-Khoto Manuscripts* 14, p. 207.

16 Tangut: 𘞵𘟣 [tśiow lji], may be tentatively translated as the Chinese 笊篱 (the utensil, Spider). In the *Pearl in the Palm*, however, the Tangut phrase for 笊篱 is different.

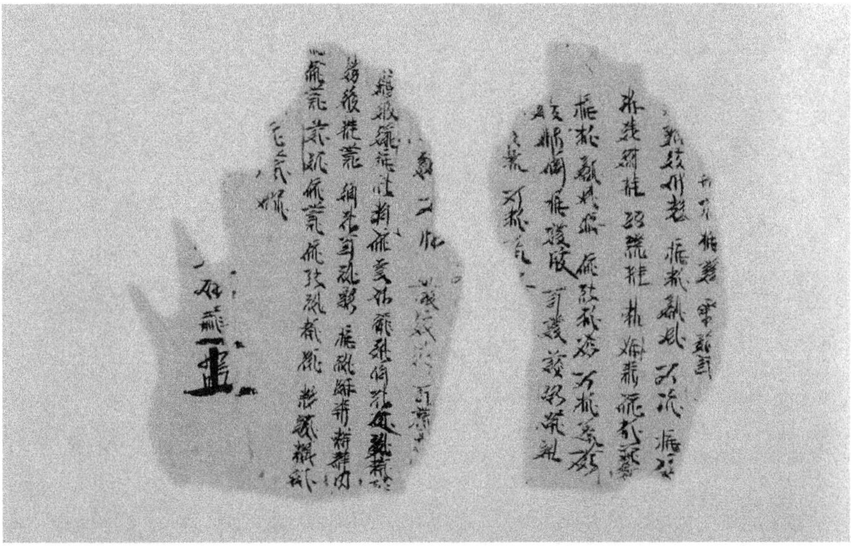

FIGURE 66 Инв. No. 7892-9: Property account in the year of You

On the left page-fragment, there are a number of properties listed under the name of a certain Li, which may be roughly translated as below:

> ……
> …… Year of *You*, first month, day 25, Li [?] [?] [?] 45 *jin* of glutinous rice
> …… [?] [?] 3 *sheng*, 41 *jin* of butter, 2 *jin* of *dou zuo*[17] white rice 8 ……
> …… 5 *sheng*, *geng* [?] 5 *sheng*; 50 *jin* black glutinous grain (sorghum) 3 [?] black grains
> ……
> (Signature in large characters with finger stamp)

The properties recorded here are rather miscellaneous: clothes, tools, butter, grains, etc. The scope of 'properties' in the more common household records mentioned earlier in the book is limited to land, livestock and larger possessions. But the level of detailedness in this manuscript suggests that it must have some special purposes.

Amongst the grain accounts excavated in Khara-Khoto, there is a special manuscript fragment, labelled Инв. No. 4761-10. It is written in cursive

17 TN: Tangut: [illegible] [tsow], could be a transliteration of the Chinese 胙, meat for sacrificial rituals, or 酢, vinegar.

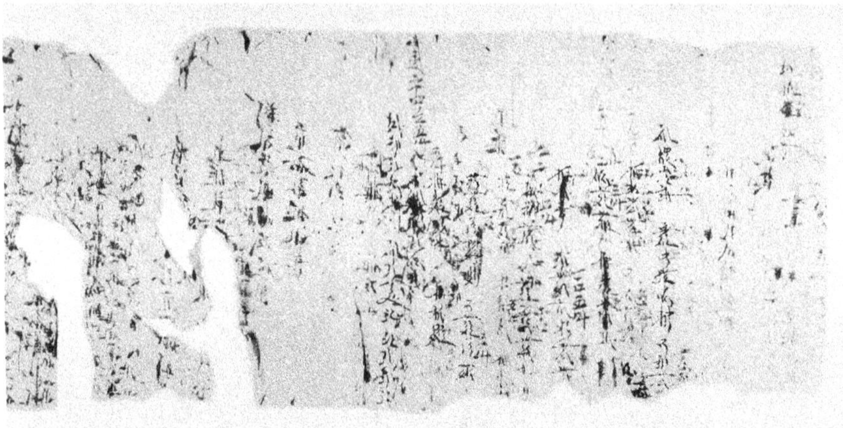

FIGURE 67 Инв. No. 4761-10: Tangut-Chinese bilingual grain account (1)

FIGURE 68 Инв. No. 4761-10: Tangut-Chinese bilingual grain account (2)

Tangut (56 lines, with edits and erasures), with Chinese notations by the side or on top of important numbers. The manuscript itself is handwritten on a 19 cm × 70.8 cm piece of hemp paper.[18]

This blurry and fragmented manuscript is difficult to read and interpret, but not without bits of writings still eligible. For example, one finds some Chinese

18 *Russian Collection of Khara-Khoto Manuscripts* 13, p. 270.

FIGURE 69 Инв. No. 4761-7V: Tangut-Chinese bilingual account

characters added to the side of Tangut text such as "3 *dou*," "1 *dan* 5 *dou*," "5 *dou*" and "wheat 24 *dan* 5 *dou*," etc.

In addition, there is a very special bilingual grain account, Russian manuscript Инв. No. 4761-7V. Written on the back page of a livestock account, the hemp-paper manuscript (17.8 cm × 39.5 cm) suffers damages at both of its ends.[19] The first of its 5 lines reads, "Ajian (a person's name) 3 *dan*." Lines 2, 4 and 5 indicate the names and quantities of the goods. The numbers are rendered in Han Chinese characters; for example, "three *dou*," "one *dou* & two *sheng*," "[?] *dou*," and "one *dou*" in line 1; "two *dou* & five *sheng*," "three *dou*," "three *dou*," "six *sheng*," and "three *sheng*" in line 4; and "one *dou*" in line 5. The types of goods and materials are written in Tangut characters, but most remain unclear in their meaning. One character in the last line appears to mean 'liquor.' In line 3, there are Chinese notes in smaller font for "day eighteen."

These accounts of goods and materials provide us with an invaluable source whence to learn the names of commodities in Tangut social life. With the excavation of these manuscripts, the long-time constraints on our glimpse into the private lives of the Tanguts now give way to a much more promising outlook on the productions and consumptions in the ordinary lives of the Tanguts. This is the first step toward reconstructing a holistic picture of the Tangut social experience.

In brief, the Khara-Khoto accounts of grains and goods compiled by local governments and agencies are large in sum and diverse in kind. They reveal much information on aspects of the Tangut economy that have seldom entered the historiographical conversation in Tangutology before they were

19 *Russian Collection of Khara-Khoto Manuscripts* 13, p. 267.

discovered and deciphered. Some of these records have been identified as statistics on grain provisions supplied to soldiers by the unit of *liu* in the army. Others document the duties of grain transportation assigned to the local populace. All of them add new materials to our analysis of the Tangut society by providing new angles to consider the Tangut economy.

The statistical accounts also reveal the nomenclatures of goods, products and commodities in common use in Western Xia—iconic and typical but hitherto unknown to historians. Such examples include the technical distinction between 'Fan cloths' and 'Han cloths,' terminology which implies the existence of a Tangut textile industry prior to Dangxiang entry to the Central Plains. It also shows that after the Tanguts established paramountcy in what is today the north-western region of China, Tangut cloths remained unreplaced and continued to be in use alongside the finer Chinese products. This evidence completely changes the once prevalent speculation that the Tanguts boasted no textile industry of their own.

CHAPTER 6

Records of Trade and Transaction

Economic records of Western Xia include not only transaction and loan contracts, which contain direct information on Tangut trade, but also a batch of statistical accounts that provide us with larger data on Tangut trade. Such a record is not of each single sale and purchase but rather of numerous interwoven commercial activities. Therefore, they offer us a historical lens through which it is now possible to take a fuller and broader glance at Tangut trade and transactions on the ground.

1 Transaction Accounts and Commodity Prices

Commodity prices are an important economic factor in the stability and prosperity of an imperial economy. Market prices of common merchandise are central to civic livelihood. It is, therefore, no exaggeration to say that price is an integral step to studying the economic lives of past societies. In general, Chinese archives lack information on commodity prices in Western Xia. In the Khara-Khoto manuscripts, however, Tangutologists have found a sizable corpus of trade records that include the types, quantities, and prices of the goods transacted. These precious manuscripts provide us with the primary sources with which we are now able to touch the vital pulses of Tangut economy.

1.1 *Accounts of Grain Sales and the Prices of Grain*

Grains are the most important supply of nutrition in the agricultural societies of medieval Inner and East Asia; hence, they are also the most indispensable commodity in Tangut markets. Therefore, although most of the accounts of grain prices excavated in Khara-Khoto have only survived as incomplete fragments, these manuscripts have remained precious primary sources, which provide us with the data necessary to analyse and calculate the market prices of grains at the time. It is, of course, unnecessary to elaborate at length the significance of data on food prices for historians trying to understand the history of agriculture, commerce, and other aspects of economic lives in Western Xia.

The Russian Manuscript Инв. No. 1167 contains multiple pieces of documents, the first three of which reflect the grain prices in Western Xia. The manuscript Инв. No. 1167-1, (21.5 × 31.9 cm, handwritten on hemp-paper and with damages at the beginning and the end) features six lines of cursive Tangut.

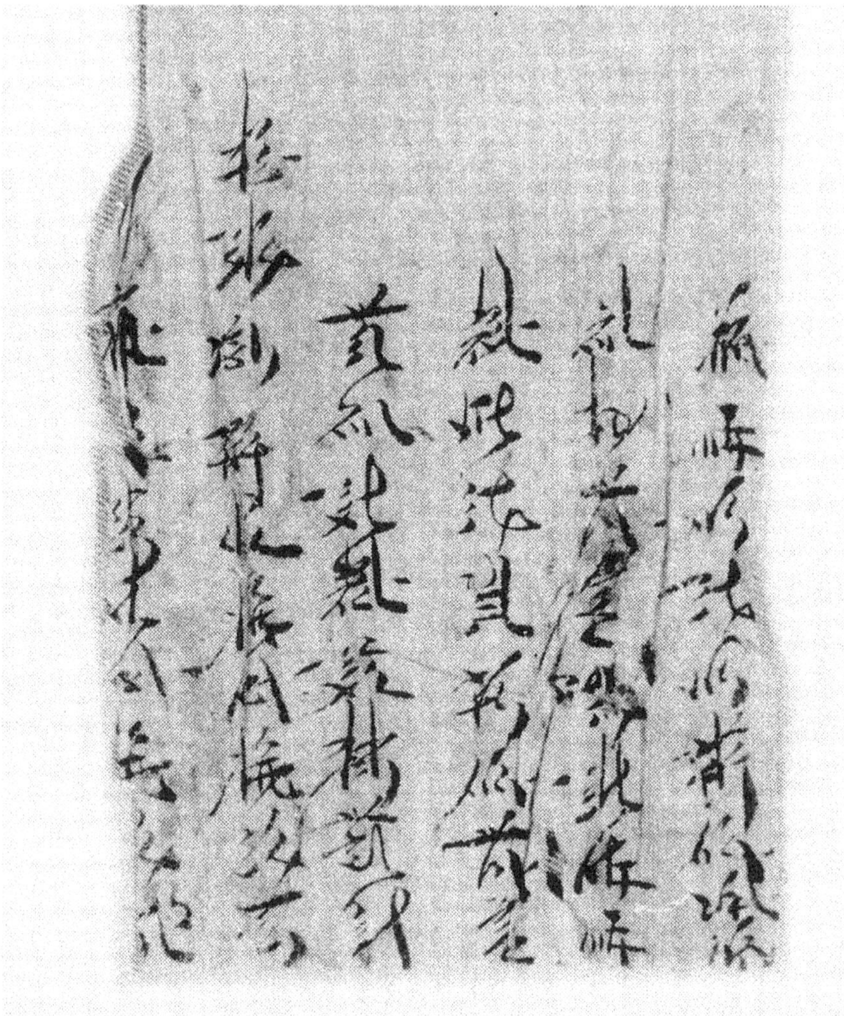

FIGURE 70 Инв. No. 1167-1: Account of grain sales

The fifth line indicates the year as [Tangut characters] [nej le kjiw nji-_ lhji. nji-_ ɣa. lew] "Ren-yin Year, second month, twenty (two ten)-first." The manuscript Инв. No. 1167-3 (likewise, hemp-paper fragment, 21.5 × 13.6 cm) features seven lines of cursive Tangut. Finally, the Инв. No. 1167-2 (hemp-paper fragment, 21.5 × 8.1 cm) has four lines of Tangut cursive. The first line begins with the two characters [Tangut characters] [du_ tser] "Gui Mao," a year apart from 1167-1.[1]
Russian Manuscript Инв. No. 1167-1, an account of grain prices, lists transactions in order and by items. Line 5, for example, switches to a new line with

1 *Russian Collection of Khara-Khoto Manuscripts* 12, pp. 193–194.

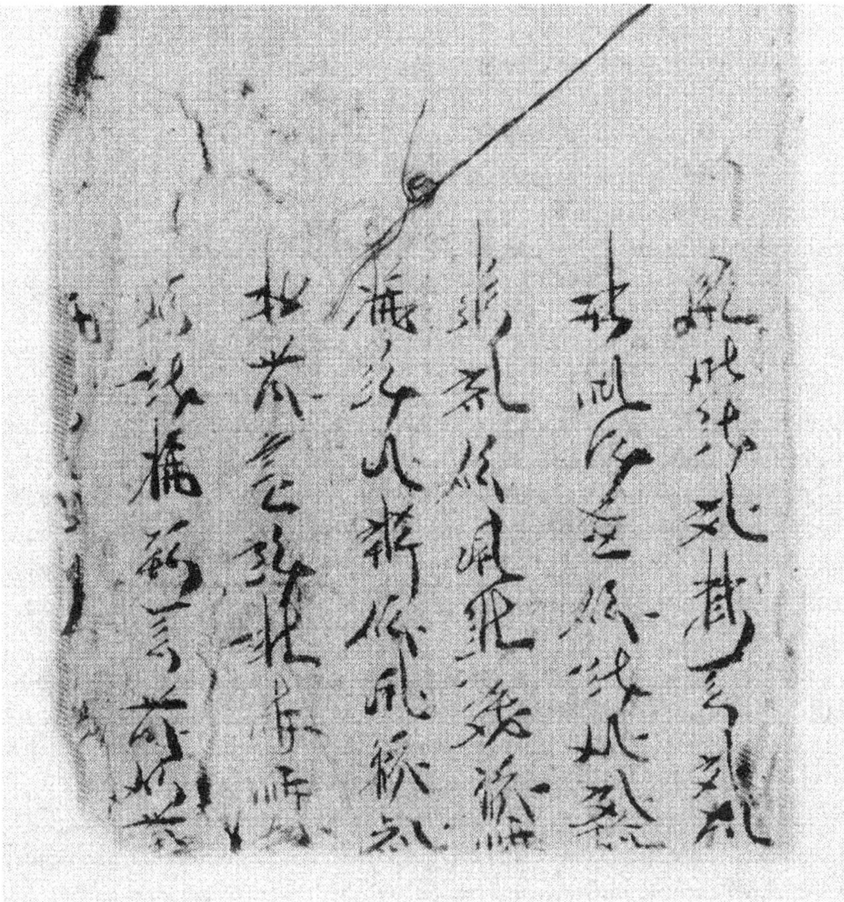

FIGURE 71 Инв. No. 1167-3: Account of grain sales

the two characters: 𘈩[illegible], "one item," i.e. the start of a new item on the list. Lines 1–4 make up the content of the previous item:

> ……
> Cash in total: 44 *guan* 500 *qian*,
> Assorted Grains 1 *dou*/70 counts (*qian*), total
> Grains 63 *dan* 5 *dou* 7
> *sheng* of assorted grains, placed in the grain storage.

The above content concerns the calculation of grain prices. 'Assorted grains' (again, general reference to coarse cereals and miscellaneous grain crops) are priced at 70 *qian*/*dou*. Based on this unit price, a total of 63 *dan*, 5 *dou*, and 7 *sheng* of grains are supposed to cost 44 *guan* and 499 *qian* in total sum of money, which show up in the manuscript as 44 *guan* and 500 *qian*, with 499 rounded to 500 in customary practice. A similar type of manuscript is Инв. No. 1167-3, which records the following information:

> ...
> The sixty days, with one day taken
> out, amount to an actual number of 59 days,
> each day 500 counts of copper coins (*qian*), total
> 29 *guan* 500 *qian*, assorted (grains)
> 1 *dou* 70 price, actual total?
> 42 *dan* 1 *dou* 4 *sheng*.

With the sum of 29 *guan* and 500 *qian*, and at the price of 70 *qian* per *dou*, one could have purchased exactly a total of 42 *dan*, 7 *dou*, and 4 *sheng* of grains. The Russian manuscript Инв. No. 1167-2 is another account of grain prices. Despite even more damages, its fourth line gives the same price: "assorted (grains), one *dou*, 70 counts (*qian*)." These several manuscripts suffice to show that the general market price of miscellaneous grains in the Khara-Khoto area at the time was 70 *qian* per *dou*.

The Инв. No. 1167-3 seems to calculate the price in the period of two months, with one of them subtracted by one day, probably because it was a leap month, which leaves us with 59 days left, at the price of 500 *qian* per day. It still remains difficult to determine what type of payment it is referring to, though it might be the wage of a worker. The manuscript is all the more precious because it gives away the grain price of the day and has thus become one of our most invaluable economic-historical sources.

The manuscript Инв. No. 1167-1 marks the "Ren-yin Year," whilst Инв. No. 1167-2 mentions both the "Gui-mao" and the "Jia-chen." Considering that most of the Khara-Khoto documents date to the late period of Western Xia, it makes a certain amount of sense to suppose these years to be the final three occurrences of "Ren-yin," "Gui-mao," and "Jia-chen" in the history of Western Xia: the thirteen (1182), the fourteenth (1183), and fifteenth (1184) years of Renzong's reign Qianyou, respectively. Given this time frame, it is possible that the price of 70 *qian* per *dou* of assorted grains reflected the market price of grains in Khara-Khoto during Renzong's reign.

There are also other types of cash and grain accounts in the corpus of Khara-Khoto manuscripts. The manuscript Инв. No. 2042-2 (handwritten on 10.8 × 30.5 cm fragment hemp-paper as a book-cover page, with 11 lines of

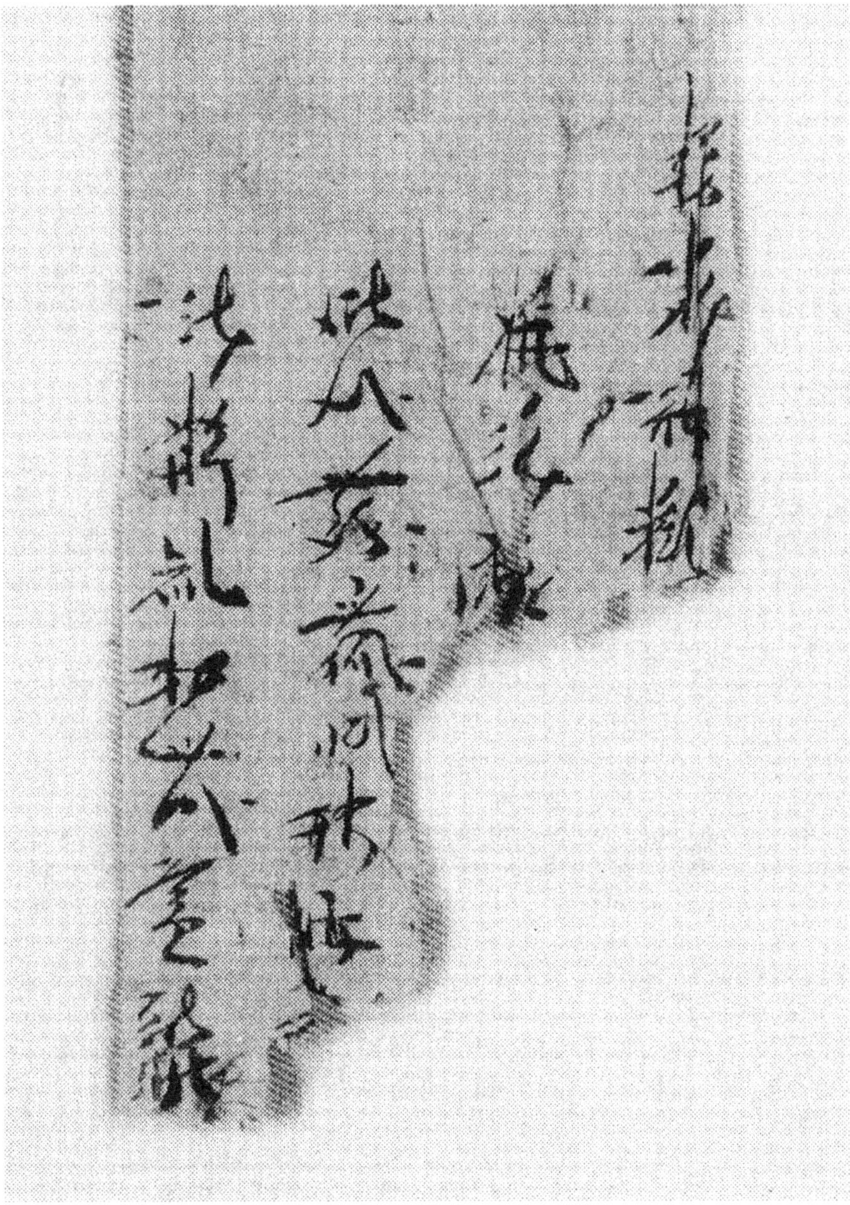

FIGURE 72 Инв. No. 1167-2: Account of grain sales

FIGURE 73 Инв. No. 2042-2: Account of cash and grains

Tangut cursive writings mixed with some Chinese characters) provides such an example.[2]

Line 2 reads, "5 *dou* of millet, 1 *guan*"; lines 3–4: "2 *dan* 2 *dou*? 5 *guan* to retrieve"; lines 4–5: "800 & 50 *qian*, 4 *dou* 5 *sheng*." Millet is considered one of the coarse or miscellaneous grains. However, according to the calculations in this manuscript, the unit price of millet grains was set at around 200 *qian*, far from the 70 *qian* derived from previous documents. But it is worth noting that the manuscripts we have looked at so far mostly label the cash unit *qian* as copper coins (*tongqian*), which were at the time worth more than iron coins in Western Xia. The copper-to-iron ratio in value was roughly 2.8:1.[3] The concerned document we have at hand does not specify what type of coin is in reference. But suppose the *qian* really are iron coins, then 70 copper coins *qian* × 2.8 = 196 iron coins *qian*, which falls more or less in line with the 200 *qian* derived from the present manuscript. One possible explanation for the variance in price units is that the previous manuscripts date to the Renzong era, when the Tangut society was relatively stable, whereas the later manuscripts reflect the economic instability of Western Xia. It is possible that social unrest towards the final years of the Empire affected the commodity prices and availability of cash.

On the layering paper of a text's cover page in the National Library of China collection of Khara-Khoto manuscripts, scholars have found a piece of Tangut account of grain sale, No. 010 (7.04X-1).[4] There are 13 lines of Tangut cursive

2 *Russian Collection of Khara-Khoto Manuscripts* 13, p. 17.
3 See later discussion on the price of horses.
4 No. 010 and 7.04X-1 are registered numbers for Khara-Khoto manuscript fragments at the National Library of China.

written on a yellowish hemp paper, despite damages both on the top and at the bottom. The document records the date of the grain sale, the names of the personalities involved in the transaction, the types of grains, and the price. The lines are mostly incomplete, with some lacking data on the quantity of grains while others missing the price numbers.

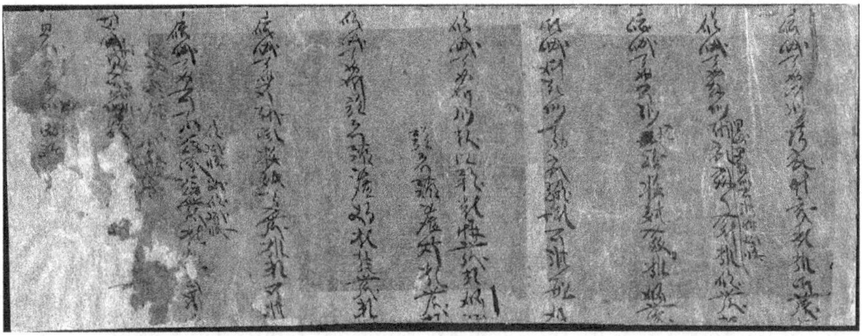

FIGURE 74 National Library of China, No. 010 (7.04X-1): Account of grain sales

The following is a rough translation:

...
May 16th, Lady Hao □□ wheat, millet, 4 *dou* ...
    August 8th, 1 *guan* 200
May 10th, Lady Qi, "maternal uncle's gold" ([illegible]) millet 5 *dou* ...
May 11th, Xipu "the puppy" ([illegible]?), millet 4 *dou* ...
June 4th, Zhang "the joyful dog" 1 *guan*, borrows 9 ...
May 16th, Jia?jiu ([illegible]?[illegible]), wheat 2 *dou*, price 400 ...
    Babe "the Bore treasure" ([illegible]), wheat *dou* price ...
May 16th, Babe "the Bore treasure," wheat 3 *dou* price ...
May 11th, □□ "Puppy" 7 *dou* millet price 1 *guan* ...
    500, once again 500,
May 11th, Zhang Jingle, *dou* wheat millet 1 *dan* ...
August 8th ...
August ...

Information on the prices are preserved to the most extent in lines 6 and 9. Line 6, for example, lists "wheat 2 *dou* price 4 ..."—the half of the character that follows 4 should be the character for 'hundred.' The price for 2 *dou* of wheat equals or exceeds 400 *qian*, but below 500 *qian*. We know, therefore, that the unit price of wheat in that local area ranged from 200 to 250 per *dou*, or 20–25 *qian* per *sheng*. From line 9, "7 *dou* of millet, price 1 *guan* …" we learn that the price of millet falls in the range of 100–200 *qian* per *dou*, or that the price of millet per *dan* is somewhere between 1 and 2 *guan*. In general, millet is cheaper than wheat. So, although the price of 7 *dou* of millet equals or exceeds 1 *guan*, it could hardly reach 1 *guan* and 750 *qian*, which would be the highest price of wheat (250 *qian* per *dou*). It is possible to infer the unit price per *dou* of millet to be around 150–200 *qian*, or 15–20 *qian* per *sheng*.[5] Despite all the missing information due to manuscript damages, this document provides scholars with the price of the most important commodity in the Tangut market: the price of refined and coarse grains in Tangut-controlled Khara-Khoto. Furthermore, these prices appear to be in line with the figures derived from the aforementioned manuscript Инв. No. 2042.

Chinese historical archives also make some sparse mentions of Tangut grain prices, but mostly in abnormal times of emergency. In the most painful years of Yuanhao's reign, ceaseless wars of combat and attrition wore out the economies of Western Xia. With the Tangut populations reduced and impoverished, armies drained of manpower, and commodity prices soaring out of control, the Tanguts ultimately asked for and accepted the Peace Treaty of Qingli. In September of the third year of Daqing in Western Xia (1142), "with Western Xia suffering a famine, the price of rice in the civil market soars by a hundred *qian*."[6] Due to the shortage of grains, food prices rose to unprecedented heights, almost four to five times of the normal price.

When the Song Emperor Renzong reigned, (mid-11th century), the price of rice per *dan* was 600–700 *qian*, subsequently increased to 1 *guan* 250 *wen* (*qian*), roughly 12.5 *wen* (*qian*) per *sheng*. In the era of Southern Song, price of rice per *dan* was 1 *guan* 500 *wen*, which at times rose to about 2 *guan*, roughly 20 *wen* per *sheng*. In the fourth year of Jiaxi, under Southern Song's Lizong Emperor (1240), the city of Lin'an suffered a severe famine.[7] At the time, the price of rice per *dan* reached 10 *guan*, or 100 *qian* per *sheng*. From this comparative perspective, it seems that grain prices in Song and Xia were quite similar, and in both cases, as was elsewhere, harvests, natural catastrophes, and political events affect the rise and fall of grain prices.

5 Shi, Jinbo. "Guojia Tushuguan Cang Xixiawen Shehui Wenshu Canye Kao" [國家圖書館藏西夏文社會文書殘頁考]: "A Study of Manuscript Fragments of Tangut Social Documents at the National Library of China" in *Wenxian* [文獻] *Documents*, issue 2, 2004.

6 *Xixia Shushi*, Ch. 35.

7 TN: Jiaxi (嘉熙; 1237–1240 AD), which lasted for four years, is the fourth era name of Emperor Lizong's reign.

1.2 *Accounts of Livestock Sales and the Prices of Livestock*

Livestock husbandry and pasturing is the traditional economic industry of the Dangxiang Tanguts, the ruling majority ethnic group of Western Xia. In the Tangut livestock economy, sheep, horses, cattle, and camels were the four main species of animals. The raising, loaning, and selling of livestock, the main produce of Western Xia, is the characteristic productive and commercial activity of the Tanguts. A careful reading of the manuscripts that document these exchanges also reveals the rituals and prices of animal transactions in Western Xia.

1.2.1 Price of Sheep

The price of sheep may be derived from several Khara-Khoto manuscripts that feature accounts of sheep transactions. For example, the Инв. No. 1219 is such a manuscript fragment that features an account of transaction prices. The manuscript Инв. No. 1219-1 and Инв. No. 1219-3 are supposed to be two parts of a connected account of transaction prices. Handwritten on hemp-papers and 36.9 × 9.2 cm and 36.9 × 13.4 cm in size, they feature five and seven lines of cursive Tangut, respectively, and contain some marks of edits and erasures.[8]

The following is a literal translation of the manuscript Инв. No. 1219-1 (lines 2–4):

> black goat (羊曆 = 羳, *li*)[9] and sheep 100, total price 109 *dan*
> black goat (*li*) 70, price: 64 *dan*
> adult 50, all female, each 1 *dan* 5 *dou*[10]
> total 50 *dan*

Russian Manuscript Инв. No. 1219-3 (lines 1–4, following the previous text). The following is a literal translation:

> Lamb 20, all male, each 7 *dou*, total
> 2(1)4[11] *dan*
> Sheep 30, all adult female, each 1 *dan* 5
> *dou*, total 45 *dan*.

8 *Russian Collection of Khara-Khoto Manuscripts* 12, pp. 222–223.

9 TN: the original text has only two characters. It is the translator's choice to add the composed character, 羳 *li*, which is roughly a synonym of 羖 *gu*: male goat, sometimes black, usually fierce, occasionally castrated, depending on the time and context.

10 TN: The corresponding shaded characters are first written on the manuscript and then erased/deleted by the author, probably in order to correct the typo.

11 TN: likewise, the correct figure is 14. The author corrected the typo.

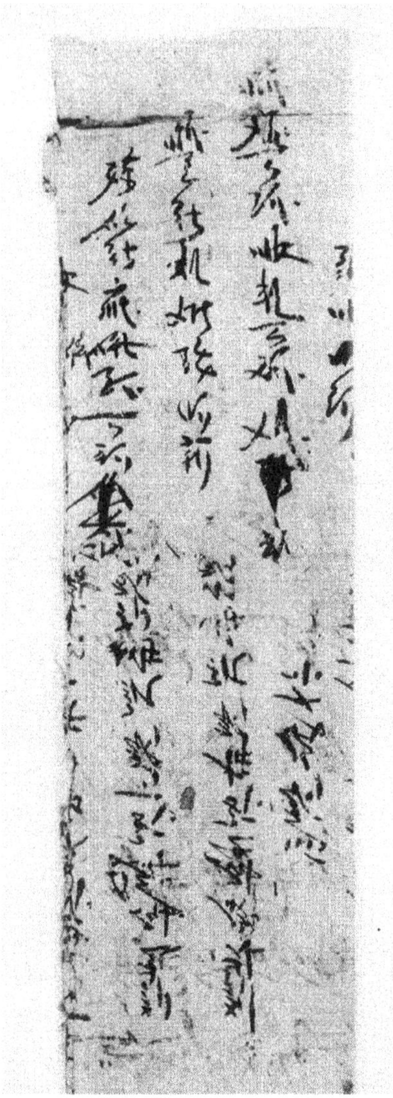

FIGURE 75 Инв. No. 1219-1: Account of transaction prices

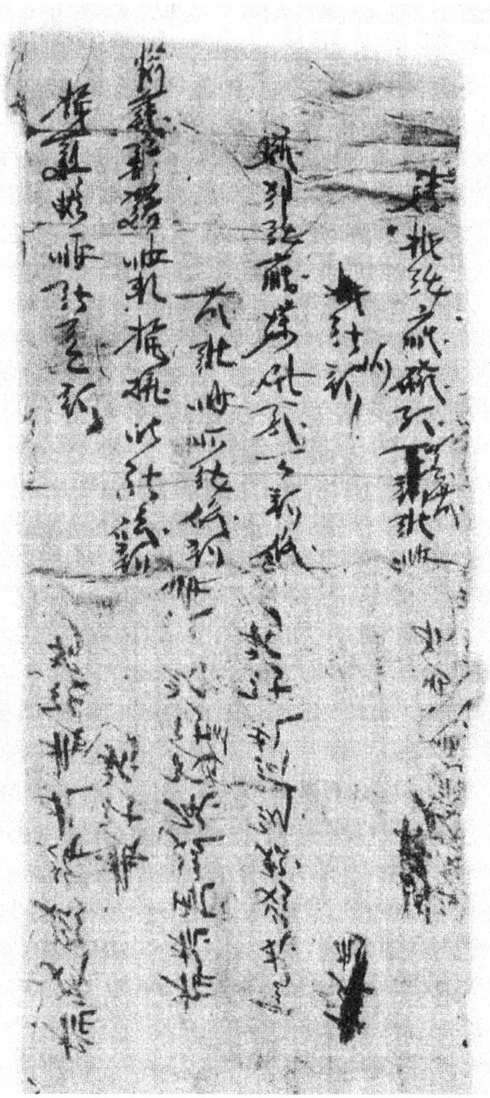

FIGURE 76 Инв. No. 1219-3: Account of transaction prices

The sale and purchase recorded in this manuscript involve 100 black goat and sheep, written in two transactions. The Tanguts raised both [illegible] [tshji-]: black goat (equivalent to the Chinese [illegible] *li*) and [illegible] [·jij] sheep (simply 羊), with the *Capra* and the *Ovis* clearly distinguished in the terms set by the *Fan-Han Timely Pearl in the Palm*.[12] The document begins with the first transaction of 70 black

12 *Russian Collection of Khara-Khoto Manuscripts* 10, p. 9.

goats: 50 adults and 20 smalls. Understandably, sexually mature rams and juvenile lambs were priced differently. Each of the 50 adult rams was worth 1 *dan* of grains, which makes a total of 50 *dan*. Every one of the 20 small black goats were priced at 7 *dou*, which amounts to a total of 14 *dan*. Combined, the rams are sold at the price of 64 *dan*. The other transaction was much simpler. All 30 sheep sold were female adults, which were the highest-priced: 1 *dan* 5 *dou*, making the total cost of purchase 45 *dan* of grains. The combined volume of the two transactions was 109 *dan*, which accords exactly with the figure given in the manuscript.

Evidently, the price of livestock depended on the species and sex of the animals in question. The unit price of black goats, 1 *dan*, was ⅔ that of a female sheep, 1 *dan* 5 *dou*. The manuscript 1219-1 seems to have first recorded the price of black goat at 1 *dan* and 5 *dou*. Apparently, a typo, the 5 *dou* was then crossed out from the manuscript. Likewise, adult goats and small lambs were priced differently. The price of a lamb, 7 *dou*, was 70% that of the same goat when it grew into maturity, 1 *dan*.

So far, the price of sheep is expressed in terms of another commodity: the grains. Given the 200 *qian* per *dou* price of miscellaneous grains, we may now calculate the unit monetary price of each small black goat (lamb) to be 1 *guan*–1 *guan* 400 *wen*/*qian*. The price of each adult black goat was 1 *guan* 500 *wen*/*qian*–2 *guan*. Each adult female sheep was worth 2 *guan* 250 *wen*/*qian*–3 *guan*.

1.2.2 Price of Horses

Historically known for pasturing, the Dangxiang people continued to raise excellent horses after their migration to what is today northwest China. Indeed, Dangxiang horses were the main source of steeds in the Chinese Central Plains. The reputation of Tangut horses dates back further to the Tang Dynasty, when the celebrated poet Yuan Zhen sang of "Procuring Dangxiang horses from the North, and fetching Tibetan parrots from the West."[13] Since the Five Dynasties, Dangxiang had sold horses en masse to empires in the Central Plains. During the reign of Mingzong Emperor of the Later-Tang:

> When the Imperial Majesty issues an edict to establish posts along the frontiers in order to trade horses, the many barbarians all entered

13 Guo, Maoqian (郭茂倩, Song Dynasty). *Yuefu Shiji* [樂府詩集] *Anthology of Yuefu Poetry*. Sibu Congkan Edition (四部叢刊) edited by Zhang, Yuanji et al. Shanghai: Commercial Press, 1922. Book 48, Lyrics for Songs in the Pure Shang Mode (清商曲辭五), Western Songs (西曲歌), Music of Traveling Merchants (估客樂), Yuanzhen (元稹).

> the markets of the Middle Kingdom. There were the Uyghurs, but the Dangxiang boasted the greatest number of horses.[14]

The Song Dynasty, which suffered chronic shortages of horses, sought horses from many lands and territories, which of course include the pasture lands under Tangut rule.

> In the early period of the Song Dynasty, horses were traded only in the three districts of Hedong, Shaanxi and Chuanxia. Horses were only imported from the Tibetans, Uyghurs, Dangxiang … and the many barbarian peoples.[15]

In Western Xia, horses not only constituted the regime's main export but also provided for agricultural and military use within its territories. For these reasons, the price of horses was extremely sensitive. When the *Laws of Heavenly Prosperity* mentions the confiscation of horses as a penalty, it indirectly provided us with some information on horse prices:

> Those who on account of their criminal guilt are punished with the confiscation of horses, are required to turn over their excellent, family-trained horses of sound teeth. If it is true that they cannot suffer the burden of losing these horses, then they should at least find the appropriate guarantors, and pay instead 20 *guan* in cash as the converted price of each horse.[16]

From the text above, we know that a Tangut horse was worth roughly 20 *guan*. In most cases, the converted price of an otherwise confiscated horse was slightly above the market price of a new horse.

There is an account of horse prices in the midst of the Khara-Khoto manuscripts: the document No. 1763, which has great value as a primary source on horse prices in Tangut markets. Handwritten on a 32.8 × 27.5 cm hemp-paper found within a book cover and patched together out of separate fragments, the manuscript features nine lines of Tangut in the cursive.[17]

---

14 *Old History of the Five Dynasties*, Bk. 138, "On Foreign States II."

15 *History of Song*, Bk. 198, "On Military Institutions."

16 *Revised Laws of Heavenly Prosperity* 20, "On the Various Levels of Criminal Responsibility," p. 602.

17 *Russian Collection of Khara-Khoto Manuscripts* 12, p. 311.

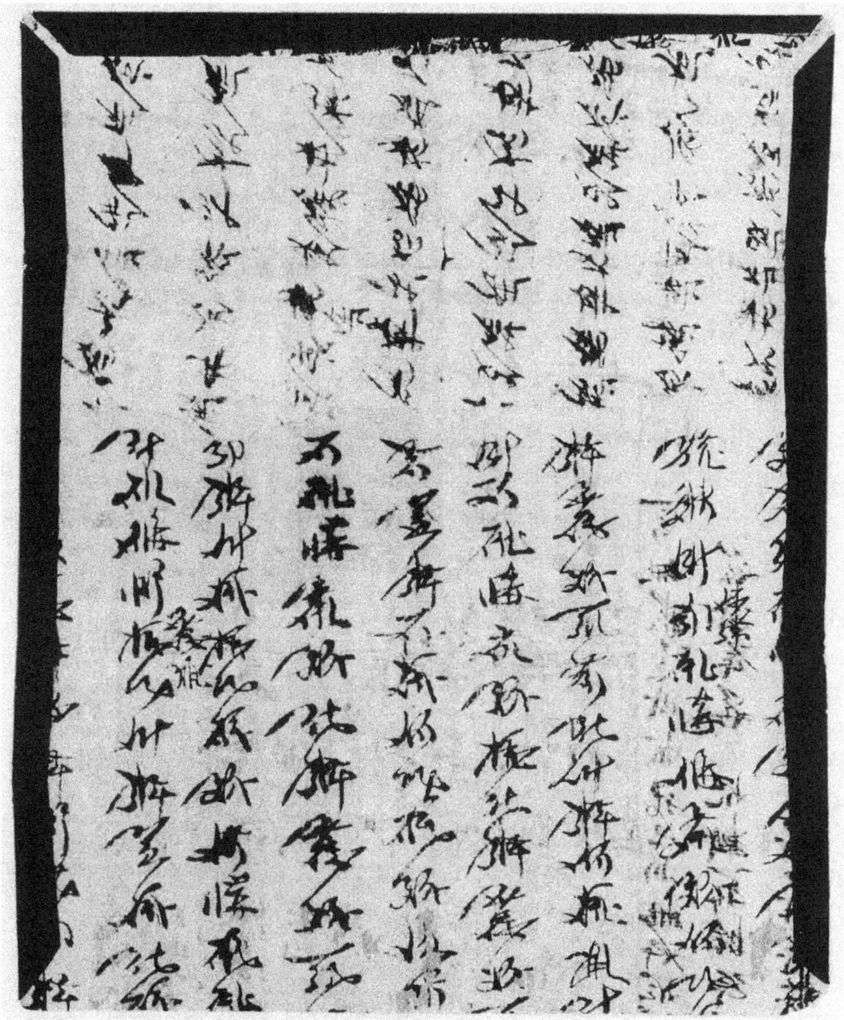

FIGURE 77 No. 1763: Account of horse prices

In the manuscript, lines 1–2 mention "of the three horses large and small, the total sum is 40 iron *qian* ? *guan*, copper coins 16 *guan*"; lines 3–4 read, "one horse counts iron coins 20 *guan*, or in copper coins, 7 *guan* 145 *qian*"; lines 5–6, "one horse counts iron coins 10 *guan*, in copper coins 3 *guan* 625 *qian*"; lines 6–7 contains the total statistics of three horse transactions: "five horses ... copper coins 26 *guan* 710 *qian*."

First of all, the document records the unit price of a horse: three horses were worth 40+ guan of iron coins, one other horse was worth 20 guan of iron coins, and yet another one was worth only 10 *guan*. Of course, prices differed given the ages and strengths of particular horses, but it is still possible to infer from the text above that the unit price of a horse in the market was roughly 10–20 guan in (iron) cash.

This document is curious for another reason: it not only lists the various prices of horses, but it also renders the statistics both in copper and in the converted currency of iron coins. In this period, Western Xia suffered a shortage of copper so severe that the empire had no other recourse than to mint iron coins en masse. Trading with both currencies, the Tanguts circled out special zones for the use of copper and iron, respectively. According to the *Laws of Heavenly Prosperity*,

> The many are not allowed to transport the black iron coins from the Southern Realm to the Imperial Capital, or to relocate the copper coins from the Imperial Capital to the Southern Realm, etc. In case the law is violated, whether by a few or many, all perpetrators are sentenced to two years of imprisonment.[18]

The so-called "Southern Realm" refers to the area around Liangzhou, which includes iron-circulated Khara-Khoto. The two currencies were swapped at the market rate, which has been unknown until recently. This document, for example, records the iron to copper ratio in the context of labelling the horse prices in different types of coins. In the first transaction, the digit after 40 *guan* is missing. So, although the sum should be between 40 and 50 *guan*, we do not know yet how to make the conversion. The second and third transactions, however, provide full data in the iron and copper cash, which makes it possible to calculate the currency rate:

CHART 8 Инв. No. 1763: Account of horse prices, statistics

	Number of horses	**Iron coins (*qian*)**	**Converted to copper coins (*qian*)**	**Copper: Iron**
Transaction 1	3	4? *guan*	16 *guan* 400 *qian*	
Transaction 2	1	20 *guan*	7 *guan* 145 *qian*	2.799
Transaction 3	1	10 *guan*	3 *guan* 625 *qian*	2.758

18 *Revised Laws of Heavenly Prosperity* 7, "Imperial Prohibitions," p. 287.

If we take the conversion rate that every 1 *guan* in copper was worth about 2.8 or 2.75 *guan* in iron, it is possible to calculate the price in the first transaction of iron coins. At the ratio of 2.8, the 16 *guan* 400 *qian* in copper coins amounts to 45.92 *guan* in iron coins, or approximately 46 *guan*. At a ratio of 2.75, the result of the conversion is about 45.1 *guan* in iron, or around 45 *guan*. The total sum of the three transactions is 7.145 + 3.625 + 16.4 = 27.17 in copper coins, which is 460 *qian* more than the sum as stated in the manuscript: 26 *guan* 710 *qian*. Therefore, it is fitting to fill in the missing digit in the first column to make it 46 *guan*. The following chart shows why 46 *guan* is the reasonable guess:

CHART 9 Инв. No. 1763: Account of horse prices, appendix to transaction 1

	Iron coins (*qian*)	**Converted to copper coins (*qian*)**	**Copper: Iron**
Transaction 1	46 *guan*	16 guan 400 *qian*	2.804 ≈ 2.8
Total	76 *guan*	27 guan 17 *qian*	2.797 ≈ 2.8

This manuscript fragment confirms the market price of horses in the Khara-Khoto area to be between 10 and 20 *guan* in iron coins, which is approximately 3.5–7 guan in copper coins. Moreover, it sets iron-to-copper ratio at about 2.8:1. Both horse prices and the copper-to-iron conversion rate are critical economic information.

In general, it is possible to derive precise commodity prices from records of particular transactions that took place in Western Xia, such as Tangut transaction contracts found in Khara-Khoto that list the prices of livestock directly on the document. The Russian Manuscript Инв. No. 5404-10, dated to the Zi year of Tianqing (1204), is such a livestock-transaction contract, with 12 lines of Tangut in the cursive.[19]

Lines 3–4 list the prices of livestock: a horse of five teeth was worth 4 *dan* miscellaneous coarse grains, roughly equivalent to 6–8 *guan*.

Compared to prices in Tangut markets, prices of horses in the Song Dynasty were usually exorbitantly high. In the Northern Song era, a horse was regularly priced at 30–50 *guan*, while the more famous were worth up to 70, 80, and even 100 *guan*. In Southern Song, a 300–400 *guan* per horse was the norm. Given

19 *Russian Collection of Khara-Khoto Manuscripts* 14, p. 35.

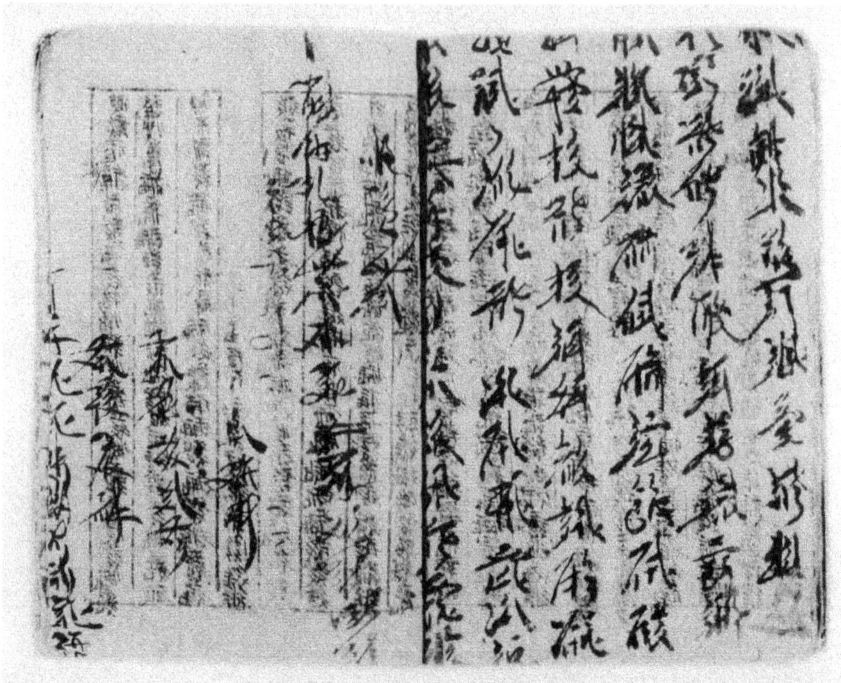

FIGURE 78 Инв. No. 5404-10: Contract of livestock sale in the Zi year of Tianqing

these prices, it is easy to tell how lucrative the trade was to export horses to the Song Dynasty.

The *Laws of Heavenly Prosperity* requires also that after a government-owned horse dies, the flesh is priced at 1 *guan* for cooked meat or 500 *qian* for raw meat.[20] From this law, we learn the prices of not only the horse but also the horse meat.

There are also Tangut contracts of livestock transactions that list the prices of cattle and camels.[21] It is impossible to underestimate the value of knowing the market prices of the four main livestock, horses, camels, cattle, and sheep, to the study of the Tangut economy.

1.3 *Accounts of Alcohol Sales and the Prices of Alcohol*

Alcohol production was a major pillar of Tangut manufacturing, partly because there was a base and tradition for brewing in the territories controlled by the

20 *Revised Laws of Heavenly Prosperity* 19, "On the Sickness of Livestock," p. 583.

21 See further discussions on the transaction of livestock in the section on livestock sale contracts in Chapter 7.

Tangut Empire. Of all ethnic groups and tribes living within the bounds of Western Xia, not a single of them lived without alcohol. Making alcohol was not only a matter of satiating the appetite of men, but it also added an alcohol tax to the government's income. Alcohol's importance as a commodity to both the quotidian lives of the Tanguts and in the inter-state trade of the empire is testified by the establishment of a governmental bureau for the management of alcohol production in Western Xia. The Chinese edition of the Tangut *Assorted Words* also mentions the departments related to liquor and fermentation.[22] Although the *Laws of Heavenly Prosperity* does not specify the departments of alcohol management in the chapter on the five order of bureaus and commissions, it is possible to discern this from the list of staff dispatched to government offices and the several organisations devoted to alcohol-related issues, such as Storage of Liquor Ferment (*qu*), Bureau of Qu Sales Tax, Storage of Liquor, etc.

Yulin Cave No. 3, which dates to the Tangut period, features a realistic and vivid fresco that depicts the process of fermentation and the production of liquor in a Tangut household. Two women sit aside a flagon, an alcohol-container, and a wooden pot. One of them fans the fire from the stove whilst the other holds the ceramic bowl to let the liquor ferment.[23] Experts have studied the device as portrayed in the fresco and determined that it represents a type of highly-advanced liquor distiller of the time.

It is also possible to infer liquor prices from Khara-Khoto manuscript fragments of alcohol transaction accounts. The Russian Manuscript Инв. No. 4696-8, a long scroll of 163 lines of Tangut cursive writings (with crossings) handwritten on 19.4 × 278.8 cm hemp-paper, is such an account of alcohol prices. It mentions a certain "account of the quantities of rice wine from Ganzhou already sold," stating clearly that the rice-distilled alcoholic beverage concerned here came from the nearby metropolis of Ganzhou, not too far from Khara-Khoto. Each transaction is recorded in about two lines, with some exceptions occupying one line or multiple lines. Each item of transaction usually begins with the two characters 𗍫𘈩 [lew dzjwo] "one person," followed by

22 Shi Jinbo. "Xixia Hanwenben Zazi Chutan" (西夏漢文本雜字初探): "Initial Thoughts on the Chinese *Miscellaneous Characters* in Western Xia" in *Zhongguo Minzushi Yanjiu* (中國民族史研究): *Studies in Chinese Ethnic History*, issue 2. Beijing: Minzu College (University) of China Press, 1989.

23 Bai, Bin; Shi, Jinbo. "Mogaoku Yulinku Xixia Ziliao Gaishu" [莫高窟榆林窟西夏資料概述]: "A Summary of Tangut Materials in the Yulin Cave of Mogao Grottoes" in *Lanzhou Daxue Xuebao* [蘭州大學學報]: *Bulletin of Lanzhou University*, issue 2, 1980.

FIGURE 79 Yulin Cave No. 3: Tangut fresco depicting liquor distillation

the name of the individual(s) who purchased the liquor, then the quantities and prices of wine, usually paid in the form of grains.[24]

The manuscript, almost three meters in length, suffers some damages at the end. But amongst the more than 80 transactions of liquor it documents, each provides information on the persons involved, as well as the quantities and prices at which the alcohol was traded. In the account, the volume of alcohol

24 *Russian Collection of Khara-Khoto Manuscripts* 13, pp. 248–251. The title was confused for the previous register, "Grain Loan Contract in the Shen Year of Guangding Reign" but has since been corrected. It should instead be an account of alcohol prices.

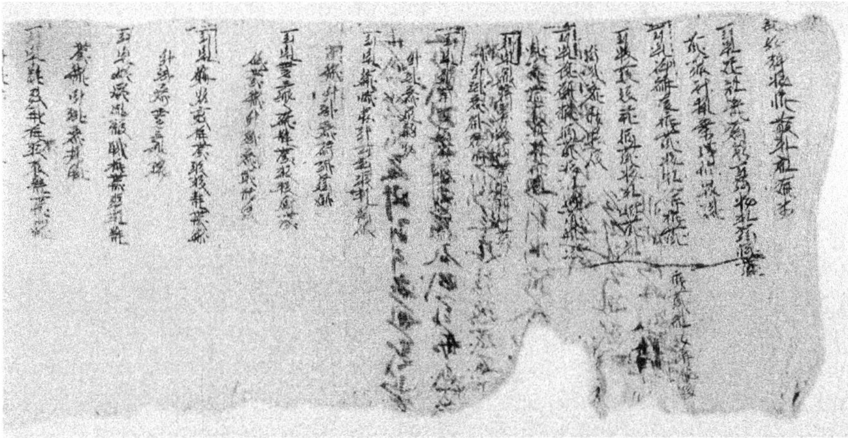

FIGURE 80 Инв. No. 4696-8: Account of alcohol prices (1)

is measured in the unit of *dou*. As for how many *jin* there is in a unit of *dou*, the document does not state clearly. The value of alcohol is not given in monetary terms but rather in the amounts of barley, which belongs to the category of assorted coarse grains, for which reason it is sometimes simply referred to as 'assorted' or 'miscellaneous.' However, it is true also that barley is an ideal material for the production of liquor.

Transactions of liquor sales could be divided into two groups. The first includes the following:

> Transaction 1 records that one purchases "1 *dan* liquor, at the price of 1 *dan* 5 *dou*," two guarantors;
> Transaction 3: one purchased "4 *dou* of liquor, at the price of 6 *dou* miscellaneous grains," 1 guarantor;
> Transaction 4: one purchased "4 *dou* of liquor, at the price of 6 *dou* of barley" 1 guarantor;
> Transaction 5: one purchased "4 *dou* of liquor, at the price of 6 *dou* of barley" 1 guarantor;
> Transaction 6: one purchased "4 *dou* of liquor, at the price of 6 *dou* of barley" 1 guarantor;
> Transaction 7: one purchased "1 *dan* of liquor, at the price of 1 *dan* 5 *dou* of barley" 1 guarantor;
> Transaction 8: one purchased "3 *dou* of liquor, at the price of 4 *dou* 5 *sheng* of barley" 1 guarantor;

> Transaction 9: one purchased "2 *dou* of liquor, at the price of 3 *dou* of barley" 1 guarantor;
>
> Transaction 10: one purchased "2 *dou* of liquor, at the price of 3 *dou* of barley" 1 guarantor;
>
> …

This kind of transaction is the majority, where the price is generally 1 *dou* 5 *sheng* of miscellaneous grains per *dou* of liquor. Each transaction ends with a 'the connector/receiver of the document,' i.e. a 'guarantor' who shares the legal responsibility with the contractor. It seems that the greater the volume of the transaction, the more guarantors that were needed. For example, in transaction 19, Gequan and others sold 1 *dan* 6 *dou* of liquor, at the price of 2 *dan* 4 *dou* of barley, which required 4 guarantors in total.

Another kind of transaction looks like the following:

> Transaction 2: one purchased "2 *dou* of liquor, paid in 2 *dou* of miscellaneous grains at present" below: "2 *dou* of miscellaneous grains presently paid";
>
> Transaction 22: one purchased "2 *dou* of liquor, paid in 2 *dou* at present" below: "2 *dou* of barley presently paid";
>
> Transaction 23: one purchased "3 *dou* of liquor, paid in 3 *dou* at present" below: "3 *dou* of barley presently paid."

The price of liquor calculated from these data points is 1 *dou* of grains per *dou* of liquor, which is "paid presently" in grains. The contrast between the two types of transactions is self-evident: it turns out that if the buyer of liquor chooses to pay the liquor in full at once, then the lower price of 1 *dan* of grains per *dou* of liquor applies. If the buyer opts to buy on credit, the higher price of 1 *dou* 5 *sheng* of grains per *dou* of alcohol applies. In addition, the debtor would have to register for guarantors in case of default. If we look at the actual commodity prices in Western Xia at the time, the latter price came closer to the actual price of alcohol, i.e. 1 *dou* of grains for 1 *dou* of liquor. We know from before that the price of miscellaneous grains in Khara-Khoto was about 15–20 *qian* per sheng, from which it is possible to calculate the monetary price of alcohol to be 150–200 *qian* per *dou* of liquor.

The manuscript records a large number of names of liquor-buyers, which include not only Dangxiang Tangut names, such as Eyi, Weiming, Weiyi, Nünü, and Mazu/Maze, but also Han Chinese family names such as Zhao, Duan, Liu, Jia, Zhang, Cao, Li, etc. Of course, both the Tanguts and the Han Chinese delighted in drinking. The fact that many men exchanged grains for liquor right on the spot, and on large credits, testifies to the pervasive drinking culture in Western Xia at the time.

In addition, four pages of alcohol accounts have been found in Manuscript Инв. No. 1366-6 to 9. All of them are fragments handwritten on hemp paper in the cursive style, not without edits and erasures. The 13.6 × 12.5 cm manuscript Инв. No. 1366-6 contains five lines of Tangut and an additional seven lines in a smaller font. The 13.6 × 12.5 cm Инв. No. 1366-7 has eight lines of large Tangut characters and 5 lines of smaller characters. The 18.7 × 29.3 cm Инв. No. 1366-8 features 14 lines of Tangut. Finally, the 25.4 × 25.2 cm Инв. No. 1366-9 has 15 and 16 lines of Tangut, with prints and signatures. At the beginning of each transaction is the name of the liquor buyer, though some of these names in the fragments are missing.[25]

FIGURE 81 Инв. No. 1366-6: Account of alcohol prices

25 *Russian Collection of Khara-Khoto Manuscripts* 12, pp. 241–243.

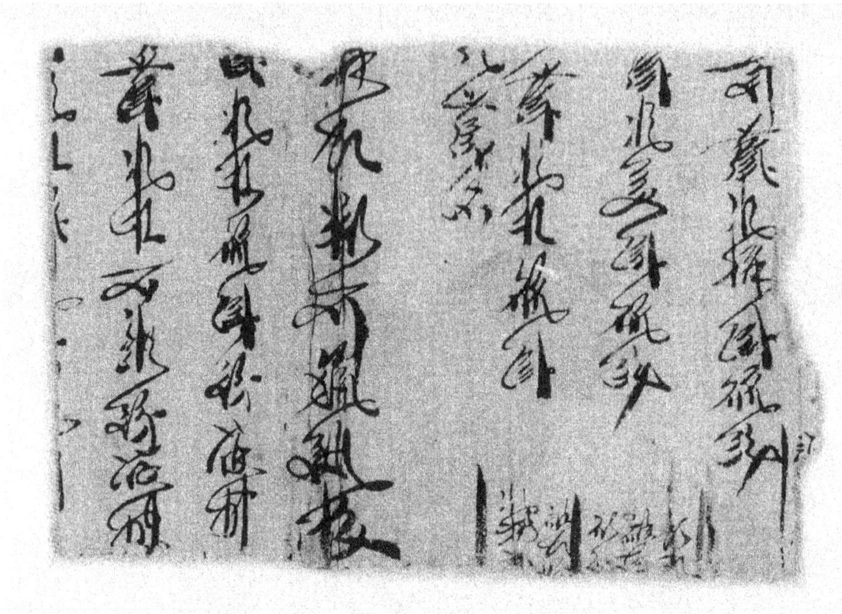

FIGURE 82 Инв. No. 1366-7: Account of alcohol prices

FIGURE 83 Инв. No. 1366-8: Account of alcohol prices

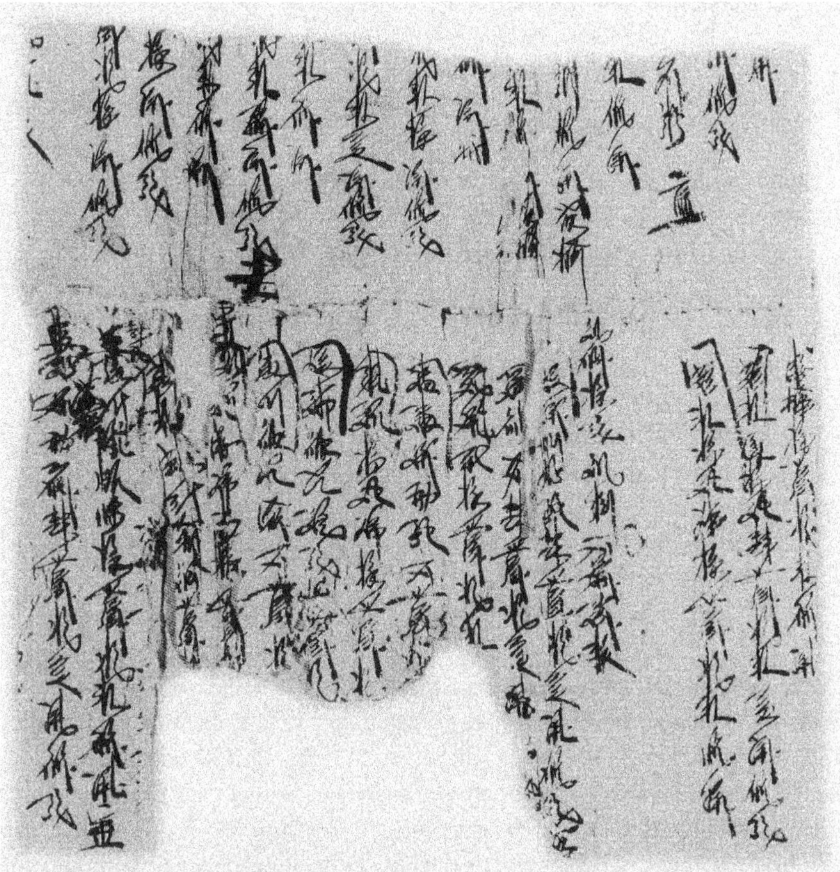

FIGURE 84 Инв. No. 1366-9: Account of alcohol prices

The following is a literal translation of the first three lines in the Russian Manuscript Инв. No. 1366-6 (account of alcohol prices):

> … One *dou* of liquor, two hundred fifty
> … four *dou* of liquor, one *guan*
> … "Dog? Mount" et al. Four *dou* at the liquor price of one *guan*

The following is a literal translation of the Russian Manuscript Инв. No. 1366-7 (account of alcohol prices):

> … one *dou* of liquor, two hundred fifty
> … three *dou* of liquor, seven hundred fifty
> … two *dou* of liquor, price five hundred

... second day, one pot sold
... *dou* liquor, price 500 *qian* presently paid
... *dou* liquor, price 1 *guan* presently paid
...

On the Russian Manuscript Инв. No. 1366-8 (account of alcohol prices), the top sections of lines 3–8 remain only in fragments. The following is a literal translation of lines 1, 2, 9 and afterwards:

... zi aba ([illegible]) et al., 3 *dou* of liquor, 750
... 2 *dou* of liquor, price 500 *qian*
...
... "mount" (... [illegible]), 12 *dou* of liquor, price 3 *guan*
... "the lucky one" (... [illegible]), 7 *dou* of liquor, price 1 *guan* 750 *qian* paid
... "joy, you" (... [illegible]), 2 *dou* of liquor, price 500 *qian*
... "prosperous" ([illegible]), 5 *dou* of liquor, 1 *guan* 250 *qian* paid
... "manure, mount" ([illegible]), 6 *dou* of liquor, price 1 *guan* 500
...

The two fragment pages of the Russian Manuscript Инв. No. 1366-9 (account of alcohol prices) feature some similar transactions. Line 4 of the second section also mentions "Sep. 29th, a pot of liquor sold." It is not difficult to see that all such aforementioned purchases are transacted in cash at the price of 250 *qian* per *dou*, slightly higher than the retail price of alcohol in terms of grains. The unit price of liquor per *dou* exceeds the unit price of miscellaneous grains (per *dou*) and reaches the price of wheat (per *dou*). It speaks to the profitability of the alcohol industries.

Consistent with Tangut economic policies elsewhere, the Western Xia imperial government imposed special regulations on the sale of alcohol, especially liquor ferment (*qu*, or *jiuqu*), a material essential to the fermentation and manufacture of alcohol. The production of liquor ferment, or liquor-starter, is subject to total control and comprehensive supervision of state agencies. The *Laws of Heavenly Prosperity* has a special chapter "On miscellaneous affairs related to the Liquor Ferment" which stipulates for the management of *qu* and alcohol in multiple statements, ruling above all that no private enterprise be allowed to produce liquor ferment:

> The many are not allowed to produce liquor ferments. In case this law is violated, it is necessary for officials to measure the weight of privately-made *qu* throughout this period in terms of *jin*. If the illegally-made liquor

> ferment is within one string, let those with criminal intention be punished with thirteen strokes, and all accomplices, ten strokes ... between eight and ten strings, let those with criminal intention be imprisoned for four years, and all accomplices, three years ... above twenty strings, let those with criminal intentions be sentenced to life imprisonment, and all accomplices, imprisonment for twelve years; in case the buyers of these liquor ferments are aware of their illegality, they should suffer penalty at one level below the accomplices; if they are not aware of the crimes, let them not suffer punishment.[26]

The sale of liquor ferments is an exclusive business of the government. By purchasing them from official sources, owners of alcohol factories contributed taxes to the finances of the empire. As expected, the *Laws of Heavenly Prosperity* regulated the price of liquor starters: "Where liquor starters are sold, 2 *dou* of barley and wheat count toward 15 *jin*, and each *jin* [of *qu*] should be sold at the price of 300 *qian*."[27] We know therefore the extortionate price of liquor starters at the time to be 4 *guan* 500 *qian* per *dou*/15 *jin* of qu.

1.4 *Accounts of Other Commodities and Their Prices*

1.4.1 Account of Silk Sales and Silk Prices

The early phase of Western Xia's path to imperial glory is marked by frequent wars with the Song empire. According to the narrative of Chinese archives, "the enemies (TN: refers to the Tanguts) are likewise exhausted, then deprived of resting time for farming and pasturing, with the result that amongst the barbarians (TN: again, the Tanguts, in particular), the cost of cloth reaches exorbitant prices in the tens of thousands."[28] It credibly shows that in the most difficult time of war in early Tangut history, when cash was destitute and resource was scarce, the unit price of cloth per *pi* was as high as more than ten *guan*.

Amongst the Khara-Khoto manuscripts in Russia is the Инв. No. 3858-1, a fragment account of commodity prices, handwritten on a 33.8 × 31 cm pasted hemp paper used originally as a layering page to a book cover, with 14 lines of prices and other information written in the Tangut cursive.[29]

---

26 *Revised Laws of Heavenly Prosperity* 18, "On the Miscellaneous Qu," pp. 565–566.

27 *Revised Laws of Heavenly Prosperity* 18, "On the Opening and Closing of Salt Pond," p. 566.

28 Su Shi, *Complete Works of Su Dongpo*, Bk. 88, Inscription for Sir Zhang Wending (張文定公墓志銘).

29 *Russian Collection of Khara-Khoto Manuscripts* 13, p. 173.

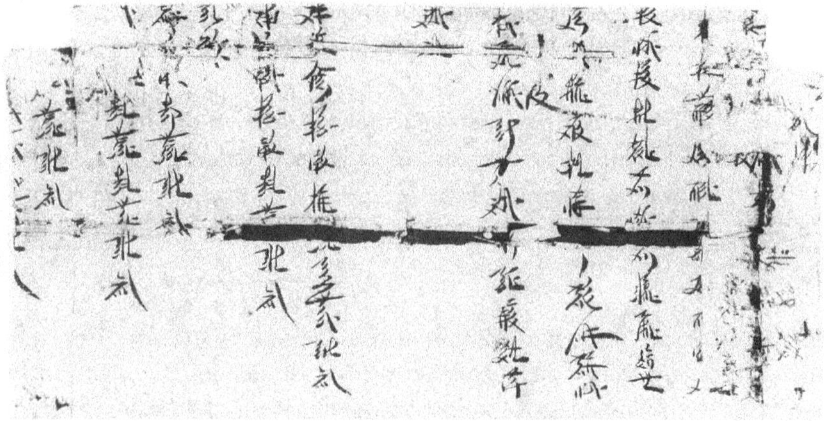

FIGURE 85 Инв. No. 3858-1 (top section): Account of commodity prices

In this manuscript, line 6 documents "silk, 1 *chi* 2 *dou* 7 *sheng*, several miscellaneous" followed by the account of silk and cloth prices, despite missing characters in the names of the goods and materials. At the price of assorted grains at 150–200 *qian* per *dou*, it is possible to narrow down the price of silk per *chi* at around 400–540 *qian*. At the time, each pi of silk was measured at about 4 *zhang*, or 40 *chi*. If so, it is possible to infer the price of silk per *pi* to be somewhere around 16–21 *guan*, which is obviously too expensive for the impoverished plebeian families of Western Xia.

The price of silk in the Song Dynasty varied greatly from the early to later periods. In Northern Song, silk was relatively affordable, being around 500 *wen*/*qian* to 1 *guan* per *pi*. In Southern Song, however, silk prices soared higher to 2–8 *guan* per *pi*.[30] By comparison, however, the price of silk in Tangut markets far exceeded that in the Central Plains even at the time of Southern Song.

Another relevant document in the Khara-Khoto corpus of economic records is the fragment manuscript Инв. No. 625, account of transaction prices. The text records time and dates, as well as the titles and prices of silk. However, due to non-ideal conditions of preservation, too few legible data remain for us to calculate the actual prices.

1.4.2 Account of Butter Sales

The Khara-Khoto Russian Manuscript Инв. No. 5808 is a rare bilingual account of butter sales, in both Tangut and Chinese. It is likewise handwritten on an

30 Qi, Xia. *Zhongguo Jingji Tongshi* [中國經濟通史]: *Complete History of the Chinese Economy*, vol. II, Economic Daily Press (經濟日報社), 1999, pp. 1242–1243.

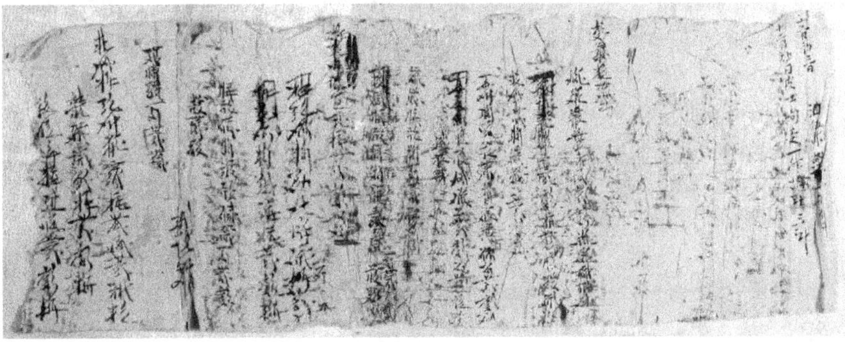

FIGURE 86 Инв. No. 5808: Account of butter sales

18.5 × 51.6 cm fragment hemp paper, which begins with two lines of Chinese and 19 lines of Tangut in cursive, featuring also prints, signatures, and crossings.[31]

On the right are shown the following two vertical lines in Chinese characters:

> Twelfth month, the third day, oil (butter) five *jin*
> Twelfth month, first day ... one *sheng* ... three *dou*.[32]

In the distance of about five to six lines, there are 19 lines in Tangut characters, which are not altogether perfectly legible. The following is a selective translation of whatever still remains identifiable.

The first line provides the title, which literally translates as "oil, milk (TN: butter), sale, list" i.e. "account of butter sales." As for the identities of the parties and departments involved, there is little to no information. The document then proceeds to list the sales of butter by individual transactions, some of which begin with time, while others with the names of the customers. The first line, for example, records that "Weiyi Bore? ([illegible]?) 5 *sheng* of butter, Weiyi 'the auspicious' ([illegible]) ..." Obviously, whereas a certain person named Weiyi Bore? purchased 5 *sheng* of butter, we are not fortunate enough to know how much the other Weiyi bought from the same shop. Line 4 features a curious expression, "Twelfth month, on the fifteenth day, the 'many burdens' one *sheng* of butter, distributed"—it does not appear that the "many burdens" sounds like a typical Tangut name, but rather that a group of merchants with a team of burden-bearing camels came to purchase butter together. This hypothesis is further corroborated by the reappearance of butter-buying 'burdens' in

31 *Russian Collection of Khara-Khoto Manuscripts* 14, p. 52.

32 TN: Chinese characters as shown on the manuscript: "十二月初三日 油伍斤" and "十二月初日皮士 ?? 一升，胡 ? 三斗."

line 8. Lines 11 and 12 narrate: "on the twenty-fourth day, Zhang Laofangquan ([illegible]), one and a half sheng of butter" and "on the twenty-fourth day, Shi Jiao, two *sheng* of butter, purchased," respectively.

Especially worthy of notice are lines 13 and 14: "On the twenty-fifth day, Cao Shiyuequan ([illegible]), one *sheng* of butter, 3 *dou* of miscellaneous [grains]." It is uncertain if Cao paid for 1 *sheng* of butter with 3 *dou* of miscellaneous grains. Should this be the case, the butter-to-grain price ratio would appear higher than expected.

Line 16 narrates that "Eshansheng one *sheng* holds," that is, he retrieves, or supposedly purchases 1 *sheng* of butter.

Line 17 tells the story that "in the final month, on the twenty-sixth day, the quantity of 2 *dou* 5 *sheng* is sold." This statement is written unindented, at a position on the page higher than other lines. The format signifies that the number hereby indicated is the total sum of the multiple transactions in the several following lines, hence the relatively large number of 2 *dou* and 5 *sheng*. The next line writes, "the House of Dog-posting Craft Station, two *sheng* of butter, purchased." It is decidedly unclear what sort of institution this dog-relaying station could have been. Finally, the person named Yehe "the overjoyed at heart" ([illegible]) who "purchased two *sheng* of butter" as recorded in line 19, is evidently a man of Tangut ethnicity.

In general, Tangut accounts of butter sales are rare manuscripts. Despite the evident incompleteness of information, the texts related and translated above do provide scholars with valuable sources on the economic lives and activities of the Tangut communities in Khara-Khoto. The fact that a merchant daily preoccupied with selling butter records his transactions so formally and meticulously testifies to the detail-oriented character of the sales management of common commodities, as well as the systematic documentation, if not regulation, of commercial activities at the local level.

1.4.3 Other Accounts of Transactions

With pasturing and livestock-raising being the most developed sector of the Tangut economy, it is no surprise that the warmth-keeping and humidity-checking fur products constituted both a major daily necessity and a key source of export for the Tanguts. Camels, horses, cattle, sheep, jade, fur carpets, and liquorice (glycyrrhiza uralensis) were the local specialties in Tangut trade with the Song Dynasty.[33] There is, for example, an account of fur carpet prices in the Russian collection of Khara-Khoto manuscripts. The Инв. No. 1219-2 "account of transaction prices" are two fragments patched as one document,

33 *History of Song*, Book 186.

FIGURE 87 Инв. No. 1219-2: Account of prices

handwritten on a 36.9 × 13.4 piece of hemp paper, with seven lines of Tangut in the cursive style.[34]

The prices of fur carpets can be found in the first and second lines of the text. The Tangut character for fur carpet is 𗾞 [lju]. The following is a translation of the twelfth line of the document: "Fan carpet, 2 *dan* each, total count 12 *dan*"; "6 white fur carpet, 1 *dan* 5 *dou* each, total count 9 *dan*." Note with care that the 'Fan' in "Fan fur carpet" is not the character that refers to the Dangxiang Tangut 𗴂 [mji], but the Tangut character 𗿧 [xiwa~] that is often borrowed to translate Sanskrit. It is possible that it may be referring to 'Tangut' in this case, after all. Either way, we know the prices of the two types of carpet: a roll of Fan carpet costs 2 *dan* of grains each and a roll of the white fur carpet is 1 *dan* 5 *dou* each.

Some transaction accounts miss the critical information on the very types of goods that are being traded. Nonetheless, it is possible to calculate the prices of these unidentified goods. One example is the 23.5 × 55.8 cm manuscript fragment Инв. No. 7885, an account of transaction prices handwritten on a piece of hemp paper, with 20 lines of Tangut in cursive and formal prints.[35]

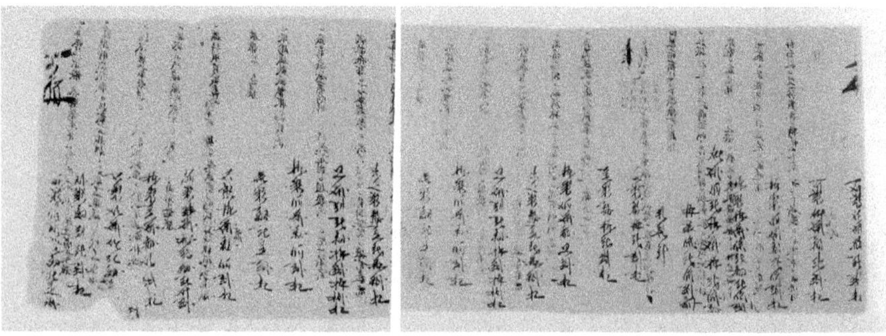

FIGURE 88 Инв. No. 7885: Account of transaction prices

The following is a literal translation:

> …
> 1 *guan* 600 mace, 10 *jin* price
> 1 *guan* 600 mace, 10 *jin* price
> 2 *guan* 400 mace 15 *jin* price

34 *Russian Collection of Khara-Khoto Manuscripts* 14, p. 52.

35 *Russian Collection of Khara-Khoto Manuscripts* 14, pp. 199, 200.

2 *guan* 215 mace 15 *jin* price
642 (*guan*) 125 mace
  2055 *jin*?
  price? is
7 *guan* 20 *jin* price
7 *guan* 20 *jin* price
2 *guan* 400 mace 8 *jin* price
18 *guan* mace 72 *jin* price
830 mace 2 *jin* 2 *liang* price
2 *guan* 400 mace 4 *jin* price
5 *guan* mace 17 *jin* price
...

Some of the items above are single transaction accounts. Others, such as lines 5, 6, and 7, are summary accounts. The following is a statistical analysis of the price (per *jin*) in these transactions:

CHART 10 Инв. No. 7885: Account of transaction prices (statistics on the first 4 transactions)

	Purchase Prices	Quantity (*jin*)	Price (per *jin*)
Transaction 1	1 *guan* 600 *qian*	10	160
Transaction 2	1 *guan* 600 *qian*	10	160
Transaction 3	2 *guan* 400 *qian*	15	160
Transaction 4	2 *guan* 250 *qian*	15	150

The unit price is easily derived from the division of purchase prices by the quantity purchased. The first four listings seem to fit together in one section. The last seven may be grouped together, separately. Lamentably, the condition of the manuscript leaves us no viable evidence to infer what type of good these transactions concern. The unit price of the first four transactions ranges between 150 and 160 mace per *jin*. The price is higher in the last seven transactions, around 300 mace per *jin*. Only in the sixth transaction is the price as high as 600 mace per *jin*. Between the two accounts, there is a line of summary statistics. Readers may resupply the currency unit "guan" after the first number: total sum 642 (*guan*) and 125 mace, for 2055 *jin*, whereby the unit price is 316 mace per *jin*, not too far off from the price derived from the last seven transactions. It is possible, therefore, that this number records the sum of the next seven transactions.

It is evident from the transactions of alcohol, livestock, and silk, that at least in some regions, the Tanguts exchanged more often than not in kinds, rather than in cash. One might think that it speaks to the underdeveloped nature of the Tangut commodity economy. Still, another factor to consider is the scarcity of copper and iron mines in Western Xia, aggravated by the policy of iron and copper embargo from the Song and Jin Dynasties. Therefore, in the tumultuous times toward the end of Tangut power, exchange in kinds prevailed in the market.

The Tangut text, *Golden Fragments* states that "whilst the mixed conditions bemuse, the prices clearly vary."[36] In other words, the prices vary according to the qualities of the goods traded in Tangut markets.

The commodity prices presented and analysed above are generally equivalent to contemporaneous prices in the Song Dynasty. The closeness of their prices has a lot to do with their neighbouring status, similarity in both modes of production and living conditions, and the circulation of Song cash across imperial boundaries.

Tangut commodities are plentiful and diverse. The prices analysed in this chapter are only the tip of an iceberg. From the prices of these important goods and critical commodities, it is possible to understand the actual living conditions of the Tangut people.

2 Accounts of Transaction Taxes

Western Xia relies on taxation to support the operation of its political machine and bureaucratic offices, pay government employees, build its army and feed the soldiers, and sustain cultural and religious developments. Apart from agricultural taxes, commercial tax is a large source of income. The *Golden Fragments* refers to the [illegible] [rjur we źji. zji.j dźji-.]: "all the cities raise transaction tax." The "commercial tax" or "transaction tax" literally refers to "sales tax," the levy on the selling of a commodity. This reference speaks to the fact that the Tanguts raised transaction taxes in the commercial markets of major cities.[37]

36 Nie Hongyin and Shi Jinbo, 1995.

37 Ibid.

The *Laws of Heavenly Prosperity* (18) features a section on "Raising transaction tax." Literally "sales and purchase tax," the 𗆧𗏹𗒁 [lwə źji. zji.j] contains the following 19 items:[38]

> Hiding transaction tax
> Method of tax payment in order when opening a new business
> Opening business on tax exemption
> Tax across various regions
> Requested tax on litigation
> Rules on government purchase of certain goods
> Tax on livestock on ships
> Omission of tax at certain selling prices.
> Extraterritorial tax exemption
> Trade with enemy envoys
> Merchants from the borders visit the Capital
> Tax exemption for reselling
> Forced exchange of livestock
> Obtaining the goods when the money equals the value of the pawned goods
> Omission of tax concerning a matchmaker and an abandoned wife
> Inaccurate reporting to seek tax exemption
> Coordination when the authority over tax is not explicitly mentioned
> Receiving tax document at specified times
> Government review of transactions[39]

These legislations testify to the historical presence of shops and markets in Western Xia. Opening a new business is taxable, but the tax rates vary from one region to another. Occasionally, it is possible to file for tax exemption.

Both sales and purchases are taxed in Western Xia. The rates and amounts of taxes are not recorded in traditional historical sources, either in Tangut or in Chinese. Due to missing information in legislations on transaction taxes in the *Laws of Heavenly Prosperity*, little evidence is there for historians to work out the tax rate. Some special statements in the *Laws of Heavenly Prosperity* offer us a glimpse at certain types of taxes, such as the tax on salt sales:

---

38 TN: The following is a list of headings in the table of contents. The actual content is missing, so wherever the meaning of the title itself is unclear, I have taken the liberty to either frame the translation intentionally in a broad way, or to interpret as seems most sensible.

39 *Revised Laws of Heavenly Prosperity*, "Part II of the Titles," pp. 96–97.

> Concerning all salt dealers, the salt from the *Wu* Pond should be sold at the price of a hundred and fifty maces per *dou*; for salt extracted from other salt ponds, the price is a hundred maces per *dou*. Let all taxes be levied and leave no tax evaded. In case of a violation of law, the amount of taxes evaded is to be calculated, and the concerned individuals will be prosecuted on the charge of theft.[40]

Here, the tax is calculated in terms of cash currency rather than grains. The salt reservoir is overseen by the House of Salt Tax. The head of this political office and the "Patrolling Supervisory Officer" are both in charge of guarding the salt resources of Western Xia.[41]

A large quantity of transaction tax accounts has been discovered in the city of Khara-Khoto. Although most are disjointed leaves and manuscript fragments, these documents show that practically all transactions in Western Xia were liable for taxation. The amounts of taxes vary according to the quantity sold or purchased as well as the types of commodities being traded. These primary materials add significantly to the historians' understanding of general Tangut commerce and transaction taxes, in particular.

Although largely incomplete, these accounts of transaction taxes reveal the basic format of transaction tax records in Khara-Khoto. In most cases, each line is devoted to one transaction. In special cases where the volume is large and the information convoluted, one transaction may be written in two lines. Each transaction record begins with the name of the seller, followed by the goods concerned, sometimes also the quantity of the products sold, and finally the sum of taxes to be paid. In all existing cases known to Tangutologists today, the payments are in kinds—mostly grains—rather than in cash. Oftentimes, buyers purchase a good by either barley or wheat. Of course, the transaction tax rate varies according to the different types of goods.

The commodities traded in these transaction accounts are quite diverse, from cloth to sheep, horse, and cattle. Others purchase gold and even human beings. Some of the goods remain unidentified. For example, in the manuscript Инв. No. 4790-2, it is unclear what is being purchased here. All we know is the relatively low tax rate: 1 *sheng* of wheat. Some documents only record the taxes but then leave the types and quantities of commodities unmentioned.

---

40 *Revised Laws of Heavenly Prosperity* 18, "On the Opening and Closing of Salt Reservoirs," p. 566.

41 *Revised Laws of Heavenly Prosperity* 17, "On the Transfer and Transportation between Bureaus," p. 535.

The manuscript Инв. No. 4790 is an account of transaction taxes composed of four leaf fragments, all of which are handwritten on hemp papers in cursive. The manuscripts Инв. No. 4790-2 and Инв. No. 4790-3 are both 19.3 × 11.2 cm in size, with five lines of Tangut each. The Инв. No. 4790-4, likewise 19.3 × 11.2 cm in size with five lines of Tangut, features a red seal. The manuscript Инв. No. 4790-5 of the same size has four lines of Tangut, and a red seal.[42]

The four manuscript fragments follow the same format of recording a transaction on each line. In spite of missing information on the quantity of commodities sold and purchased and on many goods that remain unidentifiable and untranslated, it is possible to survey the bits and pieces of these transaction tax records that can be deciphered and interpreted.

The five lines in the manuscript Инв. No. 4790-3, an account of transaction taxes, record the taxes paid for the purchase of commodities. The identity of the goods remains impenetrable and mysterious, but the amounts of taxes in the first four lines are clearly legible: wheat 1 *sheng*, 1 *dou* 5 *sheng*, wheat 1 *dou*, wheat 1 *sheng*.

Lines 2–3 in the manuscript Инв. No. 4790-3, an account of transaction taxes, mentions that "Gao 'the Lucky Dog' for the purchase of human being(s), taxes 1 *dan* 3 *dou* and … white cloth, paid"; line 4 in the same text speaks of "Gao??Mount purchases camel(s), tax wheat 3 *dou*." Line 2 in the manuscript Инв. No. 4790-4, also an account of transaction taxes, refers to a certain "??Kind Mount, purchases cloth, tax 1 *sheng*." There is no doubt that the socio economic phenomenon of human transaction took place in Western Xia, wherein a buyer has to shoulder the burden of transaction taxes.[43] From the records of many transactions that remain legible and have been studied, it is also clear that human transactions are the most taxed. The camels come next, followed by fine silk.

The manuscript Инв. No. 4790-4 account of transaction taxes features a square seal in the middle, with four Tangut characters in the seal script. Judging on the basis of their shape and content, it is possible that the four characters are 𗼑𘅫𗥃𗏁 [lwə źji. zji.j io.] (lit. purchase, sell, tax, house; i.e. The Office of Transaction Tax). A larger and rectangular seal of the Office of Transaction has been identified in a land sale contract. The right half of the same seal is found in the manuscript Инв. No. 4790-5, another account of transaction taxes.

The account of transaction taxes Инв. No. 5943 is also composed of four fragment leaves, all written in the cursive style. The 20.5 × 11.3 cm manuscript Инв.

42 *Russian Collection of Khara-Khoto Manuscripts* 14, pp. 288–289.

43 For more discussions on human transactions, see later sections on human transaction contracts.

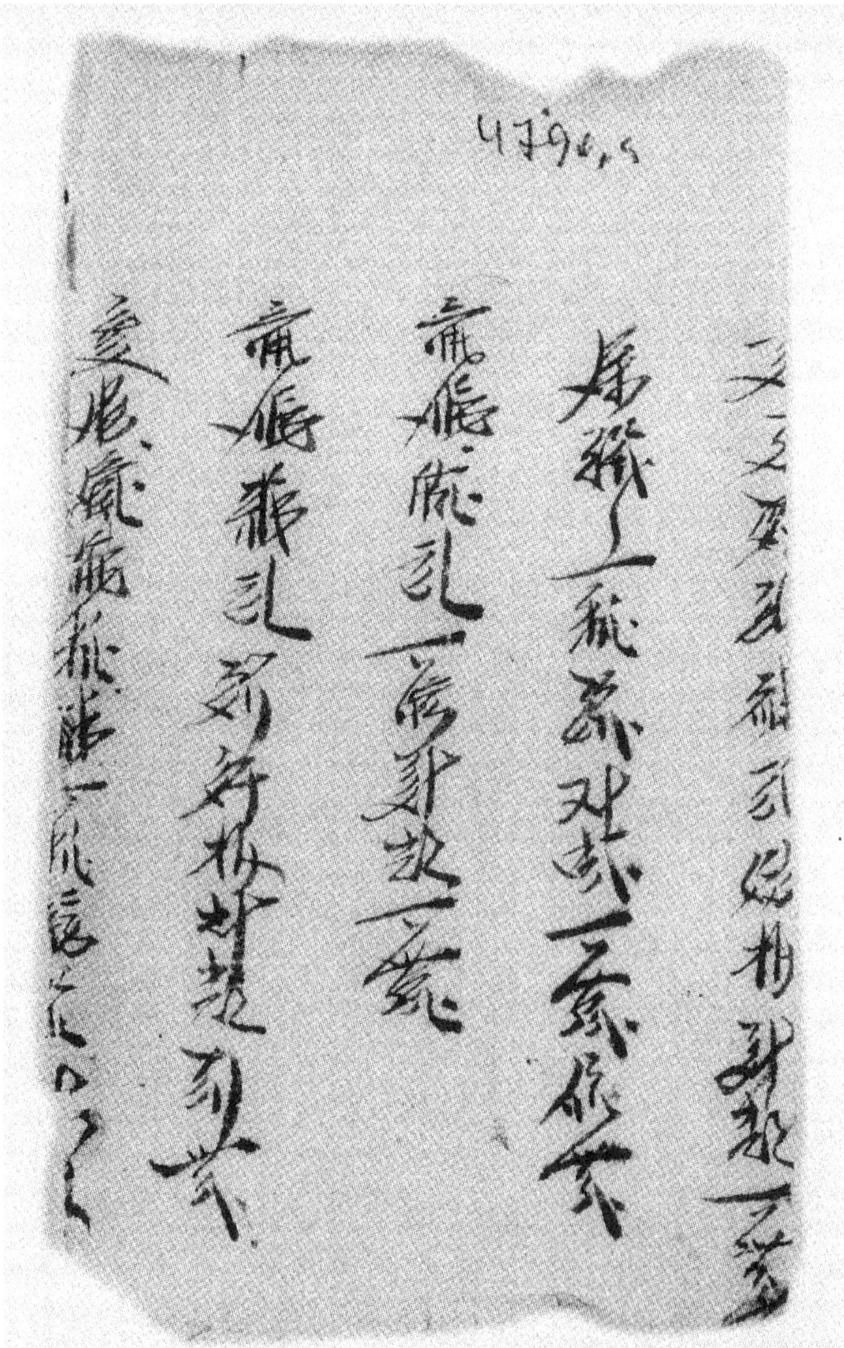

FIGURE 89 Инв. No. 4790-2: Account of transaction taxes

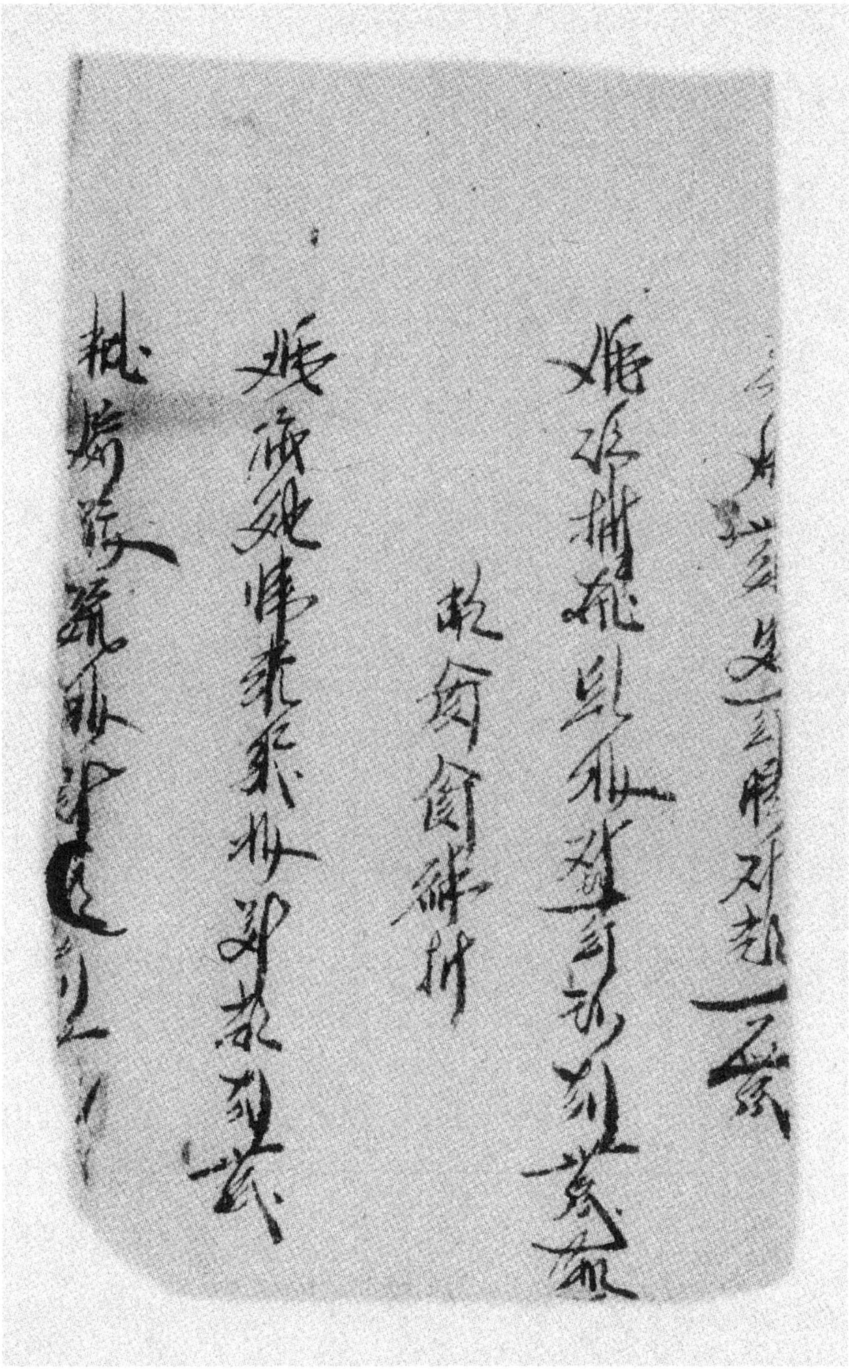

FIGURE 90 Инв. No. 4790-3: Account of transaction taxes

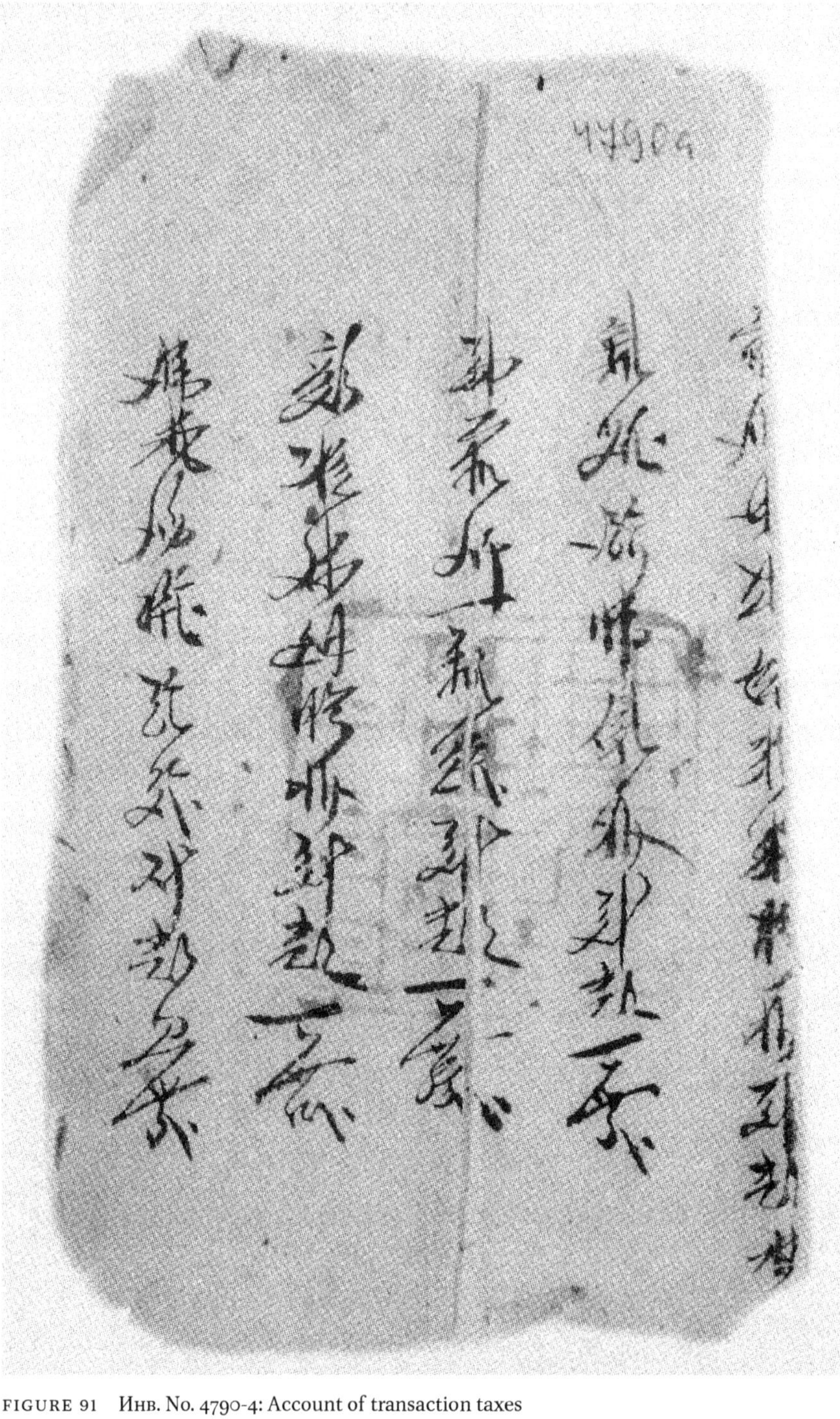

FIGURE 91 Инв. No. 4790-4: Account of transaction taxes

FIGURE 92 Инв. No. 4790-5: Account of transaction taxes

No. 5943-1 contains six lines of Tangut; the Инв. No. 5943-2 and Инв. No. 5943-3 are of the same size and each has five lines. The manuscript Инв. No. 5943-4, also 20.5 × 11.3 cm, has four lines of Tangut, a seal, stamp, and signature.[44]

In line 4 of the manuscript Инв. No. 5943-1, it is mentioned that "Langluo Xian?nu pays the land purchase tax in the amount of barley 2 *dan* 4 *dou*"; Line 2 of the manuscript Инв. No. 5943-3 records that "Weiming Lijiade pays wheat 2 *dou* 4 *sheng* in tax for the purchase of gold"; Near the end of manuscript Инв. No. 5943-4, an account of transaction taxes, there are three large characters: 𗍱 [kju], 𗧓 [khio] (skilful, adept), and 𗴺 [kwa~]. The first and third are common words used for transliteration purposes. Altogether, they may be translated to "tax-collector."[45]

The documents Инв. No. 6377-13 and 14, both manuscript fragments written in the Tangut cursive, are important accounts of transaction taxes. The Инв. No. 6377-13 is 19.8 × 36.5 cm in size, with 21 lines of Tangut, the red seal of the Tangut House of Purchase and Sell Taxes, print, and signature; the 19.8 × 23.2 cm manuscript Инв. No. 6377-14 features 14 lines of Tangut with print and signature.[46]

The manuscript Инв. No. 6377-13 suffers a range of damages and losses of characters, including at the beginning and the end, and with the first characters of a few lines; lines 1 and 2 are also not clear and barely legible. What remains of lines 3–21 suggests that for each transaction, the document lists the name of the buyer, the type and quantity of commodity being purchased, and finally the amount of taxes to be paid in terms of grains (rather than in cash). Lines 3–6 are tax records from the previous day. Lines 7–8 are names of parties of transaction on the present day. The 10th line features prints and signatures. The 11th records the total sum of taxes raised on the sixth day of a certain month: 3 *dan* 4 *dou* 1 *sheng*. Lines 12–21 are an account of purchase and sell taxes by single transactions. The following is a literal translation:

> …
> ??? purchases 2 pi cloth tax 1 *dou* 2 *sheng*
> "Prosperous Old House" (𗗙𗢳𗷝) purchases 3 sheep tax 2 *dou* 8 *sheng*
> "Old House?" (𗗙𗢳?) purchases 1 sheep 4 black goats tax 3 *dou* 2 *sheng*
> Mingbu "? Force, mount" (𗹬𗤋?) purchases 1 sheep tax 1 *dou* 2 *sheng*
> The main keeper of the document: Weiyi

44 *Russian Collection of Khara-Khoto Manuscripts* 15, p. 65.

45 TN: That is, to take 𗍱 [kju] as the Chinese 繳 (raise, levy), and 𗴺 [kwa~] as 官 (office, officer).

46 *Russian Collection of Khara-Khoto Manuscripts* 14, p. 144.

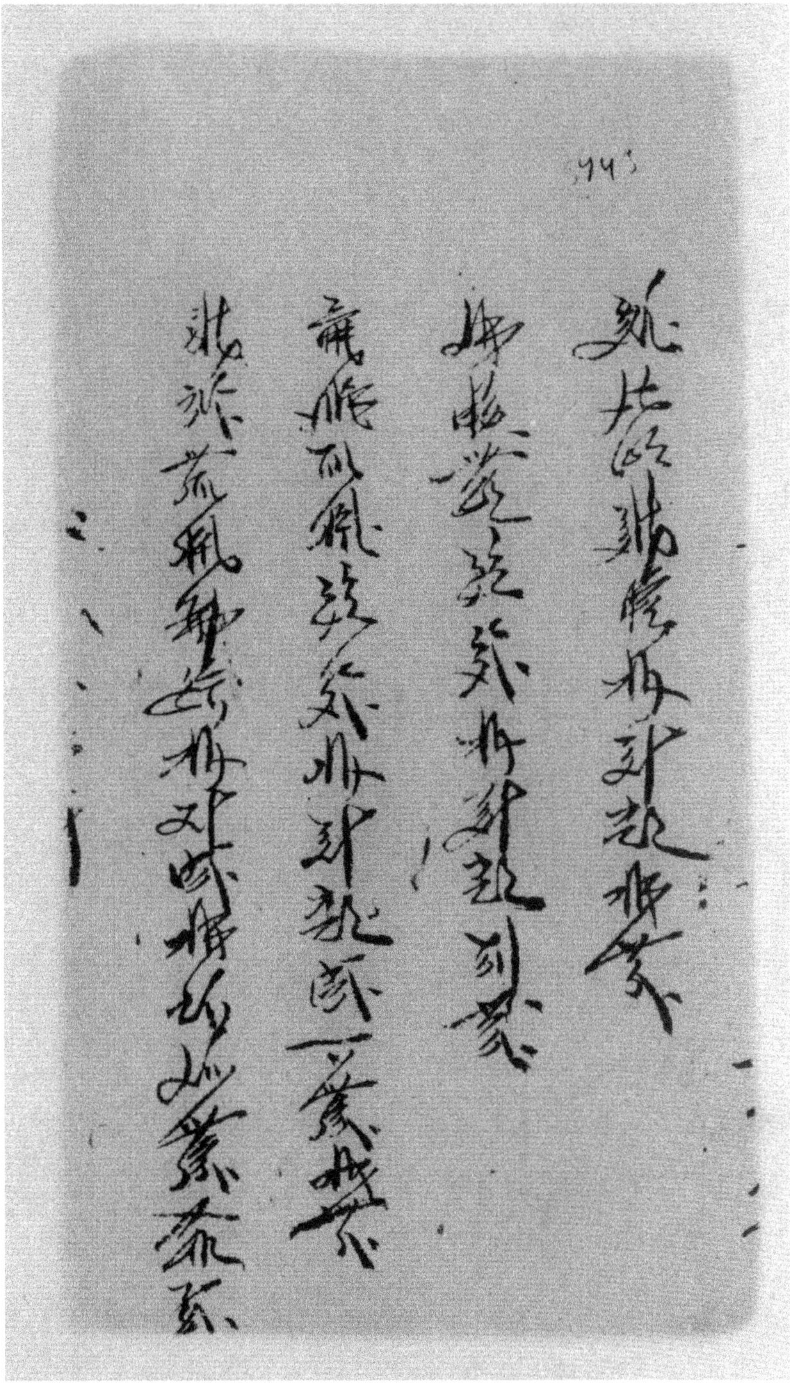

FIGURE 93 Инв. No. 5943-1: Account of transaction taxes

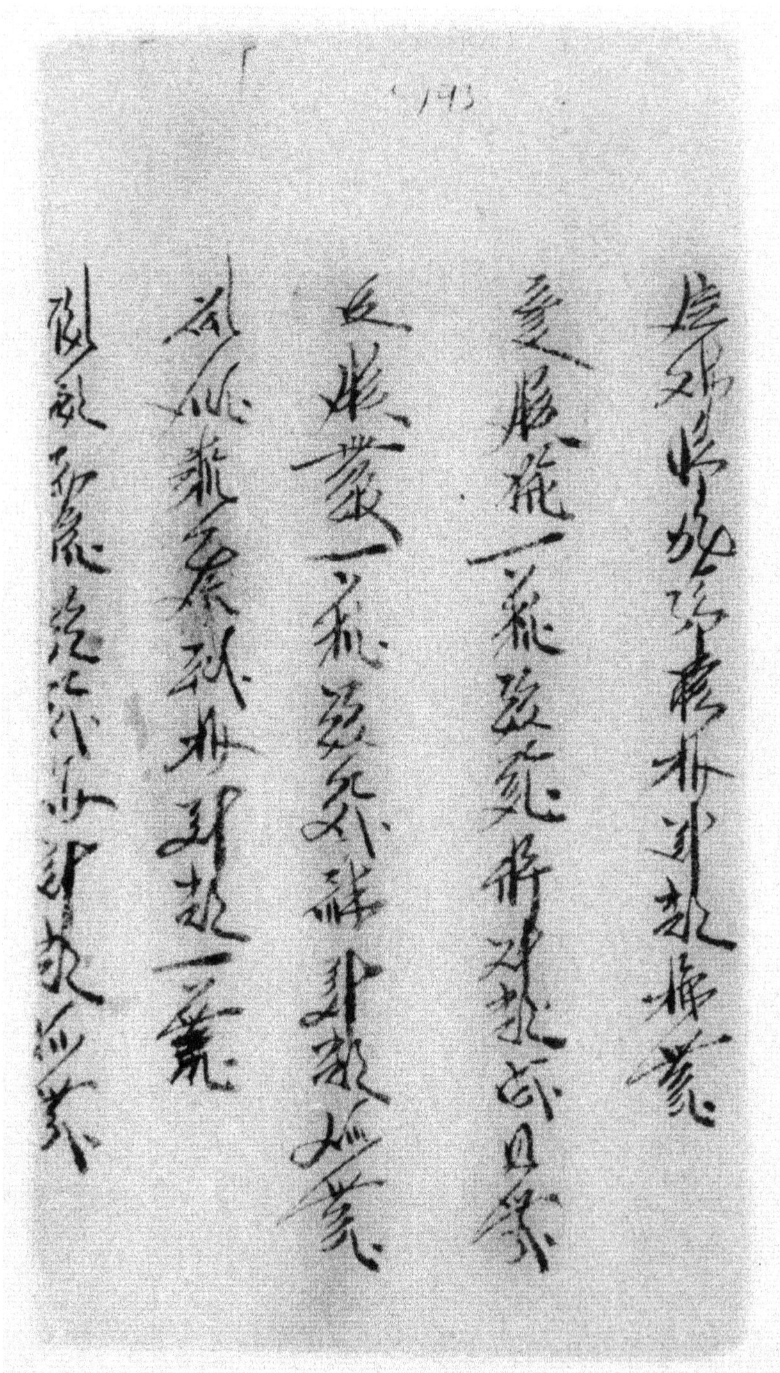

FIGURE 94 Инв. No. 5943-2: Account of transaction taxes

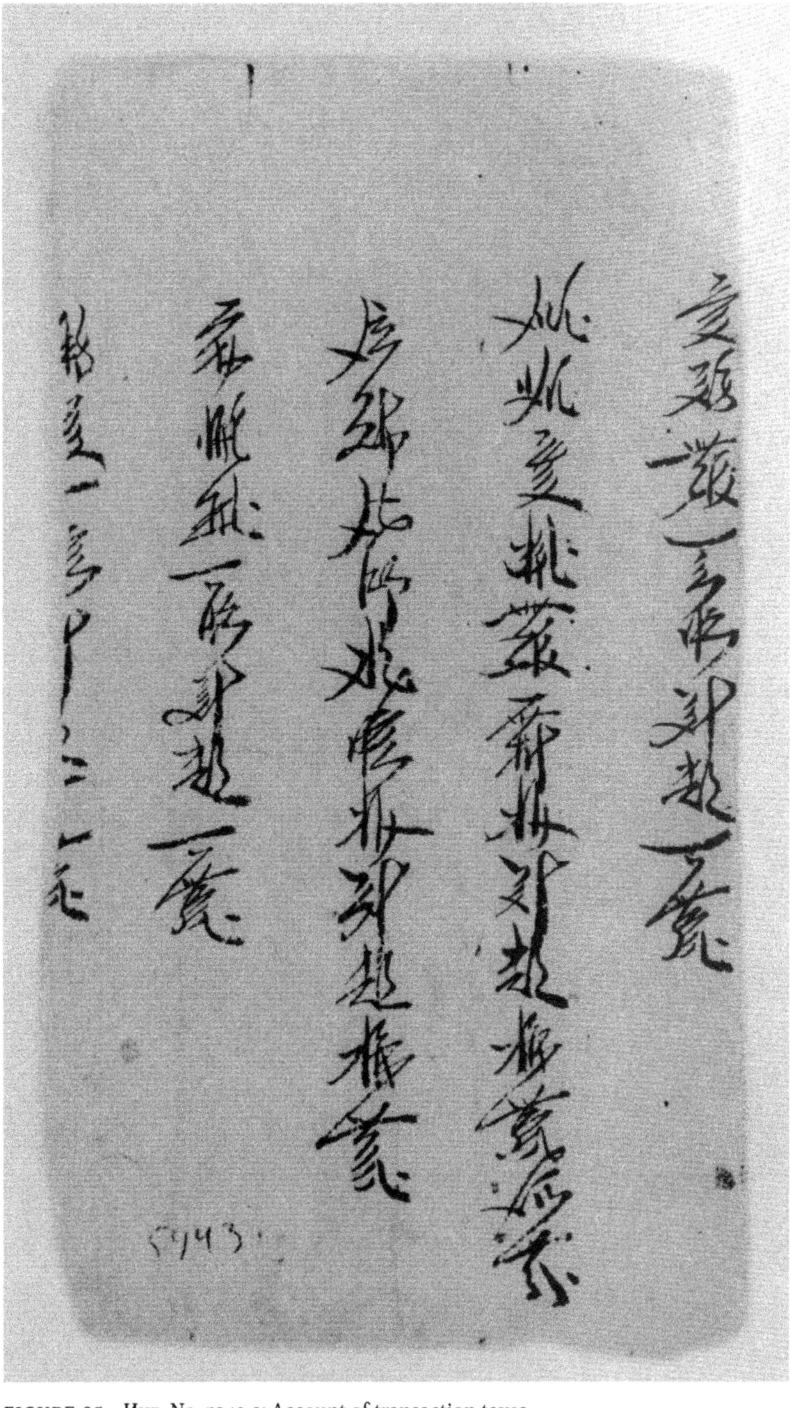

FIGURE 95 Инв. No. 5943-3: Account of transaction taxes

FIGURE 96 Инв. No. 5943-4: Account of transaction taxes

FIGURE 97 Инв. No. 6377-13: Account of transaction taxes

? borrow ??

Warehouse Supervisor: Weiming ??

... Senior Official (large characters) (prints)

... sixth day, 3 *dan* 4 *dou* 1 *sheng*

...??? purchases black goat tax 4 *dou*

... nu ([illegible])? Purchases cattle 3 *dou* 2 *sheng* Zhu? Sheep tax 2 *dou*

Zhang Nuzi ([illegible]) sheep tax 2 *dou*

Khitan "Vajra" ([illegible]) purchases 7 sheep 4 black goat 8 *dou* 2 *sheng*

??? 2 'turned' 1 sheep 1 *dou* 2 *sheng*

Li Fanmao ([illegible]) purchases 3 sheep turned 2 *dou* 8 *sheng*

Zhang Nuzi purchases 2 black goat 1 *dou* 2 *sheng*

Dashi??? ([illegible]???) purchases 2 'turned' tax 8 *sheng*

Weiyi?ling ([illegible]?[illegible]) 4 female sheep 2 *dou* 2 *sheng*

Shijun "the Joyful Iron" ([illegible]) 3 black goat, baby lamb 2 *dou*

...

The taxes "turned" may refer to paying taxes for the purchase of dead sheep. One could tell from this piece of record that to purchase one *pi* of cloth, one has to pay 1 *dou* 6 *sheng* of tax. The purchase of one sheep is taxed 6–9 *sheng*. It is mentioned earlier that the price of each adult female sheep is 1 *dan* 5 *dou*, an adult sheep costs 1 *dan*, and a lamb costs 7 *dou*. The transaction tax falls in the range of 5%–10% of the price of sheep. As for cattle, the purchase of each animal is taxed 3 *dou* 2 *sheng*. If the unit price of cattle is indeed 4 *dan* of assorted coarse grains, then the transaction tax rate seems to have been set around 8%. To purchase one black goat, one has to pay 4–6 *sheng* of tax. The transaction tax for buying a dead sheep is 4 *sheng*. All evidence seems to suggest that Western Xia raises high transaction taxes from its markets. The manuscript Инв. No. 6377-13 features a red seal of the House of Sell and Purchase Taxes, with prints and signatures, as well as those of the warehouse supervisors. The format of the text suggests that the record of transaction taxes is an official government document. All taxes are received and deposited in the government's designated warehouses.

The following is a summary chart of those accounts of transaction taxes that are legible enough for interpretation: (All registered numbers in the first column begin with "*Russian Collection of Khara-Khoto Manuscripts* Инв. No.").

These are merely a small fraction of the entire body of transaction tax accounts found and identified in Khara-Khoto, and yet, this morsel of information is enough to shed light on the diversity of goods traded in Western Xia. Apart from cloth and sheep, commodities also include land, gold, and even human beings.

CHART 11 Account of transaction taxes

No. #	Goods purchased	Quantity	Tax levied	Tax per unit
4790-3	human beings		1 *dan* 3 *dou* ? & white cloth	
4790-3	camels		wheat 3 *dou*	
4790-4	cloth		wheat 1 *dou*	
5943-1	land		barley 2 *dan* 4 *dou*	
5943-3	gold		wheat 2 *dou* 4 *sheng*	
6377-13	cloth	2 *pi*	1 *dou* 2 *sheng*	6 *sheng*
6377-13	sheep	3 sheep	2 *dou* 8 *sheng*	9 *sheng* +
6377-13	sheep	1 sheep, 4 black goats	3 *dou* 2 *sheng*	
6377-13	sheep	3 black goats	1 *dou* 2 *sheng*	4 *sheng*
6377-13	sheep	1	1 *dou* 2 *sheng*	
6377-13	sheep	7 sheep, 4 black goat	8 *dou* 2 *sheng*	
6377-13	sheep	3 lamb	2 *dou* 8 *sheng*	
6377-13	sheep	4 sheep	2 *dou* 2 *sheng*	
6377-13	sheep	3 sheep & black goats	2 *dou*	

In addition, three pieces of tax account fragments have been identified in the midst of Khara-Khoto documents at the National Library of China. The tax information is written on top of yellow hemp papers originally used as covers or layers of books. Written in the Tangut cursive script, some of the content is still legible despite damages at the beginning and the end.

Amongst these manuscripts, No. 125 (7.17X-43) records the "purchase of one cattle? Tax 2 *dou* 4 (*sheng*)," "added one camel, tax 3 *dou*." No. 127 (7.17X-45) speaks of "one person Jin?wan beef tax 1 *dou* 8 *sheng* coarse [grains]; one person Hongluo 'Gold and Iron' purchases cattle and camel skin, tax 1 *dou* 2 *sheng* coarse [grains]." This document reveals that the Tangut government levied taxes on trades of livestock, meat, and animal skins.

No. 126 (7.17X-44) shows that the transaction of human beings is also liable for tax. "purchase of servants, tax 6 *dou*." This statement reflects the dire reality of Tangut trade of human beings (*nupu*: serfs, servants) and the taxes raised therein. Upon the completion of the transaction, the parties involved had to pay taxes as if they were trading livestock. The only difference lied in the

FIGURE 98 National Library of China No. 125 (7.17X-43): Tax account

FIGURE 99 National Library of China No. 126 (7.17X-44): Tax account

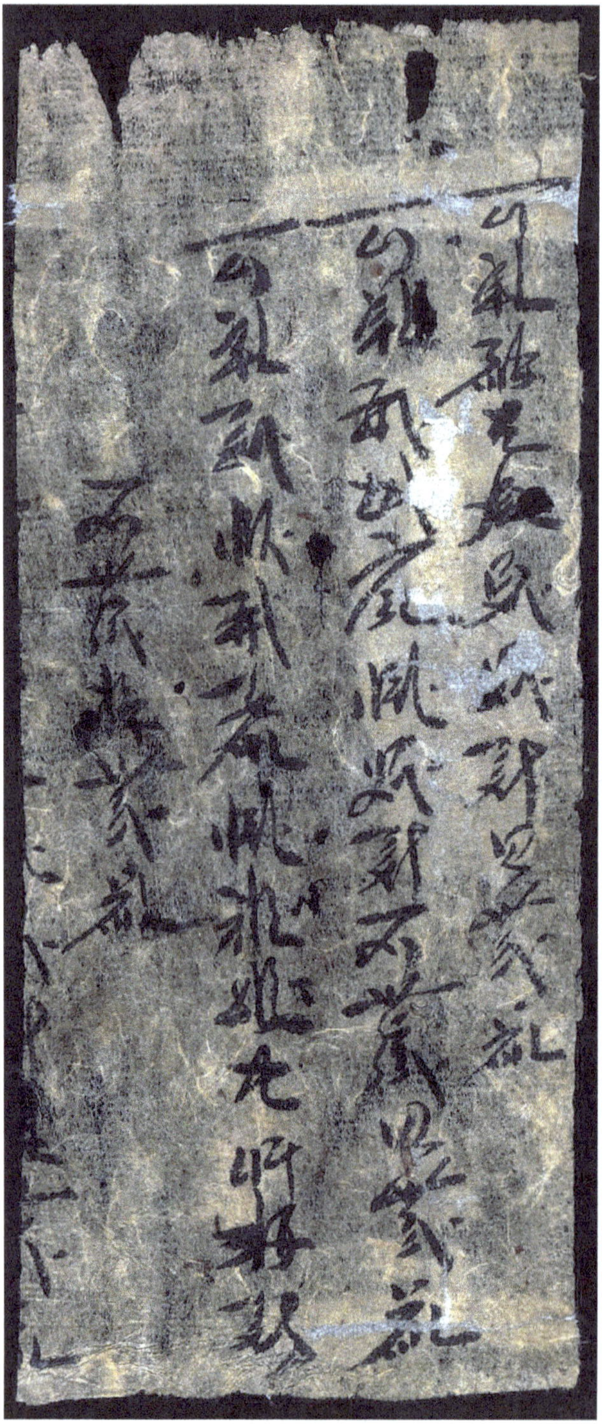

FIGURE 100
National Library of China No. 127 (7.17X-45): Tax account

higher tax rate for trading humans. The reason is none other than the generally higher prices of human beings than those of animals in Western Xia.[47]

The sources analysed above give rise to the following conclusions:

1. The goods most frequently subject to transaction taxes are commodities for daily consumption such as cloth, and livestock such as sheep, camel, cattle, and horse. Valuables such as gold are also traded and taxed.
2. As a type of fixed asset, land is taxed when the ownership concerned is traded and transferred. As a very special kind of commodity, human beings are also sold and purchased. The transaction of live human beings is limited to *shijun* (semi-slaves of military origins) and *nupu* (serfs and servants), and is subject to taxation. High tax rates are applied to the trade of land and human beings.
3. Concerning the same type of livestock, the transaction tax rate depends on the age, size, and condition of the animal.
4. Most of the transaction taxes are paid in kinds, in terms of grains. The Tanguts minted and circulated their own currency, in addition to Song coins. However, the prevalence of selling and purchasing tax payments in grains speaks to the smaller scope and stricter limitations of trading with cash in Western Xia. The Khara-Khoto materials, especially at the local level, testifies to this.
5. A holistic view of the transaction tax documents yields the conclusion that the Tanguts adjusted their transaction tax rate according to the turnover and trade volume.

In addition to the Three Bureaus of fiscal and financial policies on the Chinese model,[48] the Tangut Empire tasked the Bureau of Transfer and Transportation with the duties of adjusting and evening tax rates to balance the government's budget. These institutions borrowed more or less from the political organisation in the Central Plains. But the Tanguts also established an institution of its own design, the Bureau of Revenue and Repository, which was in charge of maintaining storage, income, and expenses. First founded in the early Tangut period, the institution lasted through the final years of the empire. The Bureau of Revenue and Repository was a mid-level governmental agency, run by four

47 Shi Jinbo, 2004 (b).

48 TN: The author refers to the Tangut fiscal and financial institution as the equivalent of the Three Bureaus (三司) of late Tang and Song Dynasty, not those from Han to mid-Tang dynasties, or after the Song Dynasty. The Three Bureaus of Western Xia would have fulfilled the same bureaucratic functions of the Bureau of Salt and Iron (鹽鐵司), the Fiscal and Tax Bureau (度支司) and the Census Bureau (戶部司) of the Song Empire.

main officers, four 'Order-Bearers' (*Chengzhi*), three 'Administrators' (*Du'an*), and four assisting Clerks (*Antou*).[49]

The two main offices overseeing taxation were the House of Taxation in Capital Zhongxing and the House of Taxation in the Central Commander's Region. The office in the capital was run by one Clerk (*antou*), four agents (*sili*), two junior supervisors, and two accountants. In the Central Commander's office in Lingwu County, there were two agents, two junior supervisors, and two accountants. There were, in addition, 18 offices affiliated with the House of Taxation on the Sales of Alcohol Distiller's Yeast, all of whom were equipped with the expertise of two junior supervisors and two accountants.[50] The Tangut government obviously placed great emphasis on taxing alcohol fermentation as a source of revenue.

3 Accounts of Monetary Loans and Interests

The discovery of a distinct type of documents amongst the Khara-Khoto manuscripts: accounts of monetary, property loans and their interests, testify to the professional practice of loaning money and physical properties in the economic history of Western Xia. These accounts, for a long time unknown and thus unexamined, provide exhaustive information on how the Tanguts loaned money and properties.

A class of monetary and property loan accounts, such as the manuscript Инв. No. 23-10 and the Инв. No. 23-11, are all page fragments hand-written in the cursive style. The Инв. No. 23-10 is 15 cm × 32 cm in size, with 19 lines of Tangut writings, as well as some crossing and markings. Near the end, there are also traces of some broken pieces that look like an account of the military *chao*. Then, the manuscript Инв. No. 23-11 is 15 cm × 32 cm in size, also featuring 19 lines of Tangut. The formats of these two accounts are similar, in that each transaction is recorded in a total of two lines. The first line, written in large font, documents the date of the monetary or property loan, names of the borrowers, the principle value and amount of the money or property in the loan. On the right, there is a line of writings in a smaller font that details the interests applied. In the manuscript Инв. No. 23-10, for example, shows the second transaction as: "... 18th day ?wang" "Iron of the Old House: principle money 2 guan ..." on the left, and "interest 400 mace to be returned" on

49 *Revised Laws of Heavenly Prosperity* 10, "On the Order of Political Offices," p. 368.

50 *Revised Laws of Heavenly Prosperity* 17, "On the Transfer and Transportation between Bureaus," pp. 529, 532.

FIGURE 101 Инв. No. 23-10: Account of loan interests

FIGURE 102 Инв. No. 23-11: Account of loan interests

the right. Another example is the manuscript Инв. No. 23-11. Its fourth listed transaction reads, "… 21st day, Duluo 'with Prosperity': principle money 500 …" on the left, and "interest 100 mace to be returned" on the right. The character after "500" should be the unit of currency, "mace." The interest rate across these contracts is approximately 20%.[51]

Interest rates in cash or property loans can also exceed 20%. Such is the case in the fifth transaction documented in the manuscript Инв. No. 23-11, where the principle is over 3 *guan* of cash, and the interest 850 mace—in other

51 *Russian Collection of Khara-Khoto Manuscripts* 12, pp. 6–7.

words, a 35% interest rate. Others are below 20%: in the third transaction in the manuscript Инв. No. 23-10, the principle is around 1 *guan* of cash, but the interest is only 100 mace, at the rate of about 10%.

So far, these manuscripts do not seem to indicate the time and duration of the loans. Therefore, it is technically unknown whether these interests are monthly or annual dues. But in the light of the 50%, or 20%–100% range of interest rates in multiple grain loan contracts found in Khara-Khoto, and given that most daily interest rates are around 1%, only rising up to 20% in a month, it is possible that the interest rates listed in these cash and property accounts are on a monthly basis.

What are the identities of the borrowers? Some are Dangxiang Tangut ethnics: Maze and Duluo, whilst are Han Chinese, such as the Zhangs. The diversity of surnames testifies to the broad and inclusive participation in the financial activity of monetary loans.

Apart from cash, a type of property recorded in these loan contracts is cloth. But the interest is paid in terms of cash. In both the 8th and 9th transactions in the manuscript Инв. No. 23-10, for example, the loan consists in a piece of cloth. The interest rates applied are 150 and 30 mace, respectively.

There is yet another type of loan and interest account that is by far the richest in detail. An example is the Инв. No. 1576-2, a 24.8 cm × 31.8 cm manuscript in two patched fragments handwritten in the cursive style on a piece of layering paper in the cover of a Buddhist sutra. The two pieces, both suffering some damages and losses, contain 13 and 10 lines of Tangut, respectively, and some checkmarks and crossings. The upper page is larger and more informative, including up to 10 transactions.[52] Due to the small font and the casual handwriting, some of the characters are extremely hard to identify and interpret. It is clear, however, that each transaction begins with the date. Due to the damages on the upper side, most of the years are lost. But the months are there in order, and very much legible: second, eleventh, fourth, fourth, first, second, fourth, second, seventh, third months. It is probably not the account of the same year. In the 8th transaction, there is an entry for a loan in the second month, which is repaid in the eleventh year of Year Hai. So, the other transactions probably also took place in or around the year Hai, but as for which year of Hai, it remains a mystery.

In the entry for each transaction, the data on the quantity of cash or grain loans is registered under each name, followed by the amounts of interests or the total cash or grains to be repaid at the end. The following is a tentative analysis based on the more complete, legible, and deployable of the data in these manuscripts.

52 *Russian Collection of Khara-Khoto Manuscripts* 12, p. 273.

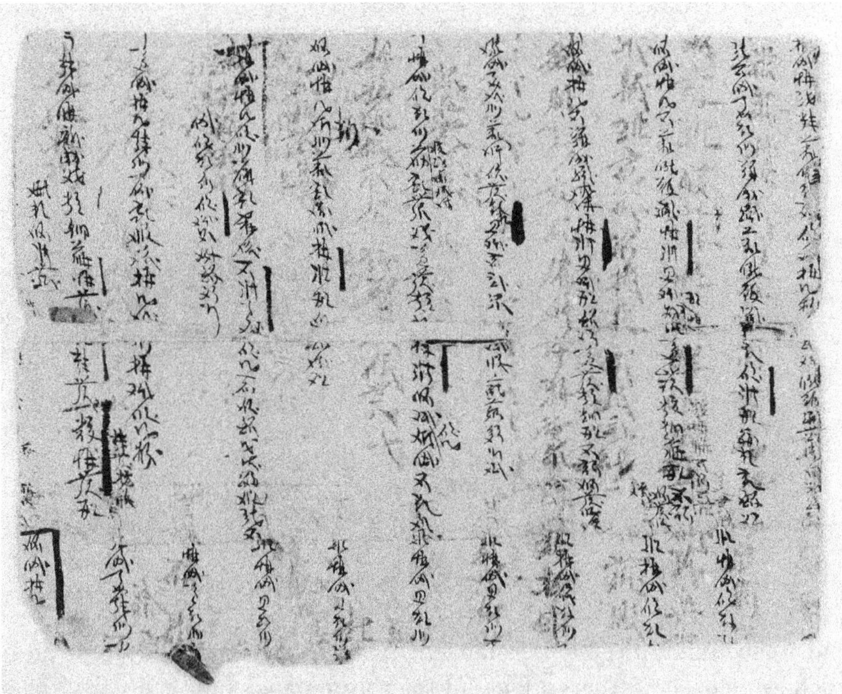

FIGURE 103 Инв. No. 1576-2: Account of loan interests

Both borrowers in the third and fourth transactions takes out "a loan of cash in 2 *guan* 800 mace, interest: 7 *dou* of beans; let the total repayment be 1 *dan* 4 *dou*." Here, the principle and the interest are 7 *dou* each, at the interest rate of 100%. The seventh transaction is fairly simple: A lady named Luo takes a loan of 2 *guan* of cash, and pays back 3 *guan*, at the interest rate of 50%. And in the light of all we know about Tangut food prices, if 7 *dou* of grains is worth 2 *guan* 800 mace, then the price of beans is around 400 mace per *dou*. And since grains are usually purchased at 200 mace per *dou*, and wheat at the price of 250 mace per *dou*, the 400 mace here is much higher than the common prices of grains elsewhere.

Another type of monetary loan document is best described as somewhere between a loan contract and a proper account. Such is the case in the manuscript Инв. No. 1523-24, a 20.8 × 33.7 cm document of monetary loan with 17 lines of Tangut writings, that suffers some damages both at the front and at the end.[53]

The format of this document is clear and distinct: each transaction begins un-indented, aligned at the top of the paper. From the second line on, till the

53 *Russian Collection of Khara-Khoto Manuscripts* 12, p. 265.

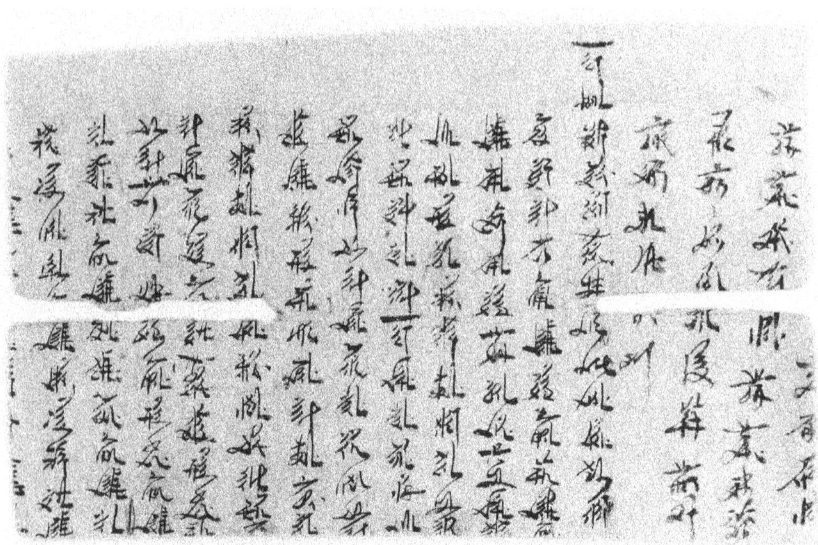

FIGURE 104 Инв. No. 1523-24: Document of monetary loan

end of the same entry, there is an indentation of 2 characters' space. The present document shows the last four lines of a given transaction, and starts a new transaction record in the 5th line. This entry begins with "One entry: in the Third Renchen Year of the Qianyou Era, on the fifth day of the sixth month, the contract set by Dashi ??" The third Renchen Year of Qianyou is the third year of Qianyou (1172 AD). The contractor is a certain "Dashi" (Dayi) which, given that "Khitan" is also a Khitan surname, and "Xianbei" a Xianbei surname, could actually be the name of a person of Arabic lineage. But whoever he is, there is no question that he borrowed 700 *guan* of cash, at the daily interest rate of 8 mace per guan; the total sum of both the principle and the interests is due to be repaid in 100 days. At this rate of 0.8% per day, in a hundred days he would have paid 800 mace per *guan* of his cash loan. This amounts to an 80% cumulative interest rate, not a low rate at all. Since the principle loan is 700 *guan*, in a hundred days, the total interests due are 700 × 0.8% = 560 *guan*. So, the borrower has to repay 700 (principle) + 560 (interest) = 1260 *guan*, in total.

The document also specifies that, in case of an overdue repayment, an additional daily interest of 5 mace or less per *guan* is applied to the accumulated debt, starting from the first day past the due date. The 5% is no small burden upon the borrower. A delay of 10 days would result in 35 *guan* of cash as a penalty fee.

We have seen in the manuscript fragments the references to at least two Khitans, whose surnames are none other than 'Khitan.' In this entry, the

FIGURE 105 Инв. No. 7893-15: Statistical account

borrower's surname is Dashi (Dayi). The loan is a large one, and at a high interest rate. Rather than an ordinary personal loan, it could as well be a business loan. It is no secret to historians that the Arabs were active in trans-Eurasian trade. Perhaps this document provides us with a glimpse at the commercial activities of the Arabs in the era of the Tangut empire.

In rare occasions, Tangut contracts officiate loan transactions in silver. The manuscript Инв. No. 7893-15 is a 19 cm × 22.2 cm fragment with 5 lines of Tangut handwritings and some edits and erasures.[54]

The first 3 lines are detailed accounts of 6 transactions by different individuals. The last 2 lines are summary statistics. The following is a simplified translation:

> "Joy and Fortune" (蘢祕繖): 40; "Gold of the Last Month" (㭸繊𦽳): 30
> "Joyful Puppy" (㑰殲繖): 13; "Fortune Realised" (蘢祕䔯): 40

54 *Russian Collection of Khara-Khoto Manuscripts* 14, p. 216.

"Joy and Fortune" ([illegible]): 20; "Flourishing Treasure" ([illegible]): 20
Assorted things:[55] 150 *liang* silver
Earlier:[56] all the 10 *liang* [of silver]

The total sum of the six transactions is 163 *liang* in silver. The first line of the summary statistics reads 150 *liang*; the second line, however, notes that there was a previous entry for 10 *liang*. Still, there is a 3 *liang* gap unaccounted for in the fragment we have. This rare document, possibly a cash loan account, is a record of statistics in in the currency of silver. Although very few Khara-Khoto documents refer to silver at all, this account shows that silver cash was, after all, in circulation in the Khara-Khoto region.

4 Accounts of Grain Loans and Debt

The Khara-Khoto economic records include not only a great amount of grain loan contracts, but also accounts of grain debt and loans. Most of these grain loan accounts are fragments of the original, handwritten on layering papers or cover pages of Buddhist sutras. Expectedly, the single-paged accounts are easier to survive in full length. Most of these grain accounts are summary statistical accounts of grain loans over a period of time. Although they are not contracts in the legal and the technical sense, the grain loan and debt accounts are by their nature interlinked with grain loan contracts. The accounts can be regarded as cumulative, concentrated, and comprehensive overviews of multiple contracts.

4.1 *Grain Loans*

Some of the grain loan documents discovered in Khara-Khoto are not separate contracts of specific transactions, but summary accounts of individual loans. One example is the manuscript Инв. No. 2176, in two page-fragments. Инв. No. 2176-1 is an account of grain loan in the Renyin year of Qianyou era, handwritten on a piece of protective layering paper from another printed text. of grain loan. The two pages are patched together 18.9 × 16.4 cm, with 10 and 8 lines of Tangut cursive writings, respectively. The first line marks the date and year: "Renyin Year of Qianyou, first day of the third month"—that is, 1182 AD. The manuscript Инв. No. 2176-2 is a similar handwritten copy, also on a protective layering paper. It is 19.4 × 15.7 cm, with 11 and 9 lines of Tangut writings

55 TN: I am not entirely clear what these two characters are doing in this context.
56 These two characters look like [illegible] [də_ no], lit. earlier in the past; before.

on each of its pages.[57] In terms of the period, it is a rather early account of grain loan.

The Russian manuscript Инв. No. 2176 is an account of grain loan that is relatively well-preserved at the top and the bottom, but suffers some damages and loss of information on the left. The first line begins at the top, without indentation, with the title of the account: "Renyin year of Qianyou, first day of the third month, Grains." The two-character word for "grains" or "foodstuff" is

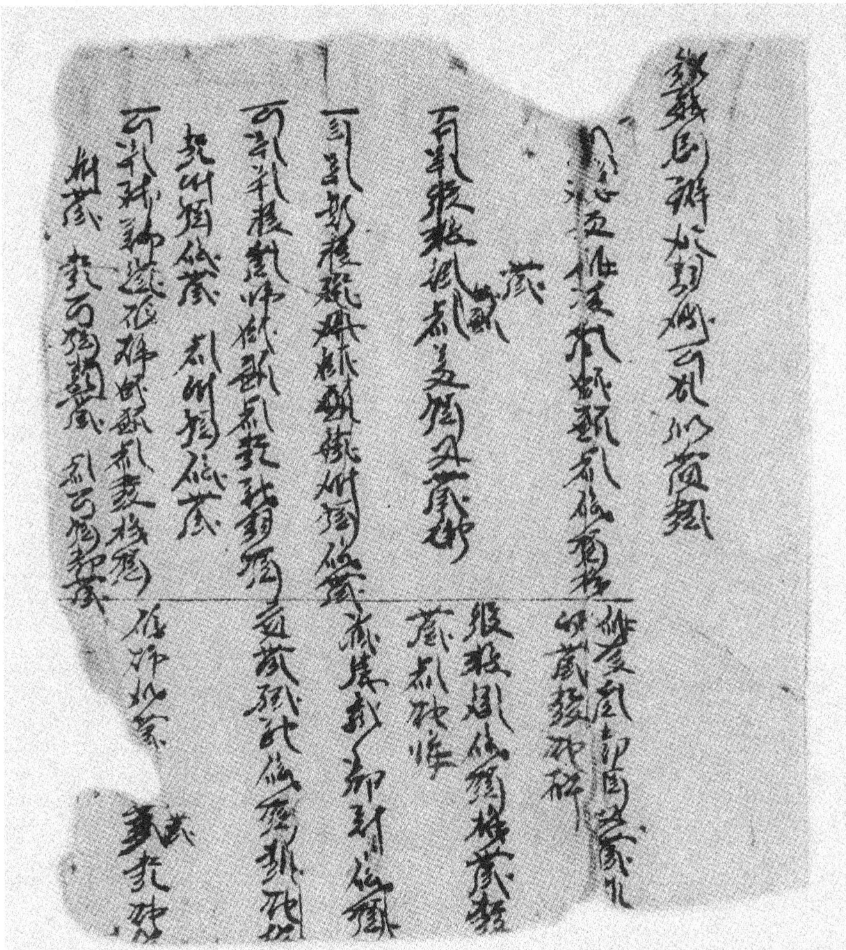

FIGURE 106 Инв. No. 2176-1: Renyin year of Qianyou, account of grain loan

57 *Russian Collection of Khara-Khoto Manuscripts* 13, p. 64.

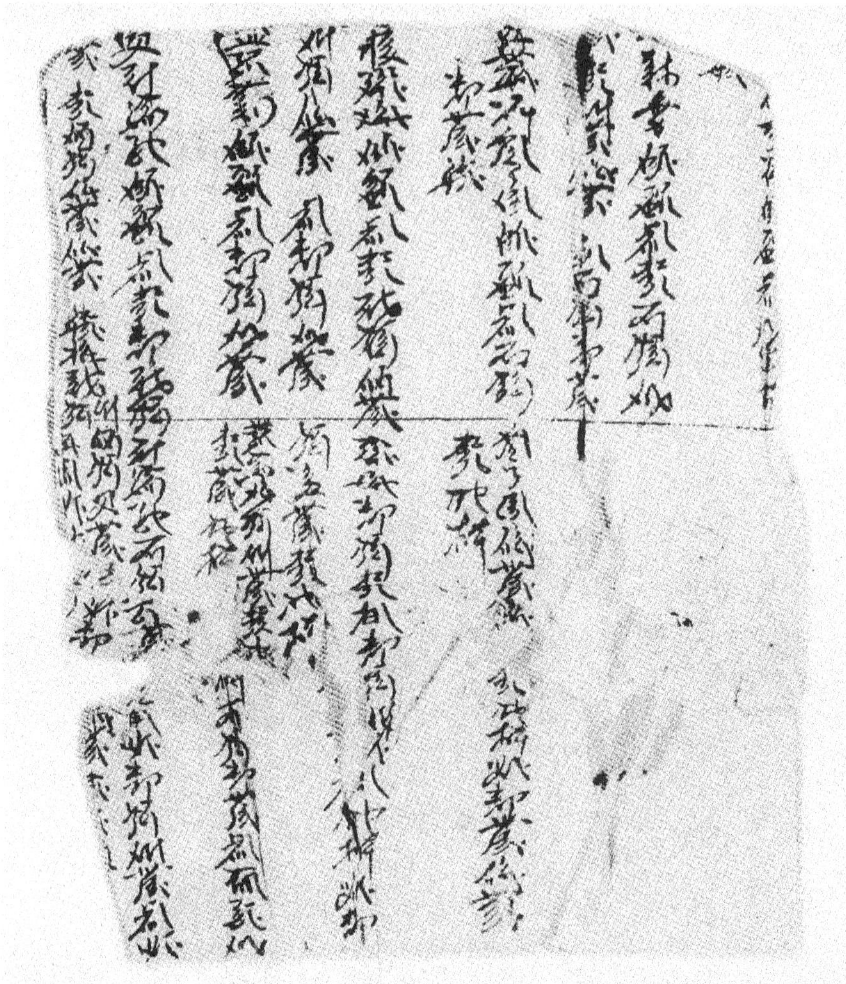

FIGURE 107 Инв. No. 2176-2: Account of grain loan

𗡶𗗙 [śio_w śji]. In the *Fan-Han Pearl in the Palm*, the expression is translated as "斛豆"—a generic reference to grain, foodstuff, and agricultural produce.[58] This account of grain loans in the thirteenth Renyin year of Qianyou in Tangut Emperor Renzong's reign (1182) documents the principle and interests of each

58 Huang, Zhenhua; Nie, Hongyin; Shi, Jinbo (eds.). *Fan Han Heshi Zhangzhongzhu* [番漢合時掌中珠]: *Fan-Han Pearl in the Palm*. Yinchuan: Ningxia People's Press, 1989, p. 15. See also, *Russian Collection of Khara-Khoto Manuscripts* 10.

loan. Each transaction begins with the same legal formula: "one person …" referring to the abstract moral persona of the debtor, under which is the actual name of each borrower, and further below, records of the types and quantities of grains in the loan. The following are 5 transactions listed at the top of the account:

> Renyin Year of Qianyou, First Day of the Third Month: Grains
>
> One person: [Tangut] [Tangut] [wa gu_ dow zji-r bie_j] principle and interest: coarse grains 5 *dan* 2
>
> *dou*
>
> One person: Cao Ale ([Tangut]), coarse grains 7 *dou* 8 *sheng*?
>
> One person: ?pu "Mother Dog" ([Tangut]) principle and interest: barley 6 *dan* 5 *dou*
>
> One person: Yehe "Joyful Mount" ([Tangut]) principle & interest: coarse & wheat 13 *dan*[59]
>
> Wheat 6 *dan* 5 *dou*; coarse grains 6 *dan* 5 *dou*
>
> One person? 6 ?? "Luck and Joy" ([Tangut]) principle & interest coarse & wheat 2 *dan*
>
> 6 *dou* wheat, 1 *dan* 3 *dou* coarse 1 *dan* 3 *dou*
>
> …

There are, likewise, 5 transactions listed at the bottom of the grain loan account, with damages at the front and at the end. The manuscript Инв. No. 2176-2 is a similar kind of grain loan account, patched together with two page-fragments. The two-track system of both singing contracts and keeping accounts suggests that, historically, the Tanguts would compile the data in a number of their signed contracts into an account.

Another such account is the Инв. No. 7892-2V, a 22.3 cm × 12 cm fragment with 4 lines of cursive handwritings in Tangut. This piece is hard to read, partly because the ink on the front and back pages intersect and overlap, mixing up the shapes and strokes of a number of characters.[60]

59 TN: It would have to be "coarse grains and wheat" because barley would have been included in "coarse grains," so "coarse grains and barley" is redundant.

60 *Russian Collection of Khara-Khoto Manuscripts* 14, p. 204. The title of the document is listed as "submission of political report" in the book format, whereas it is actually an account of grain loans.

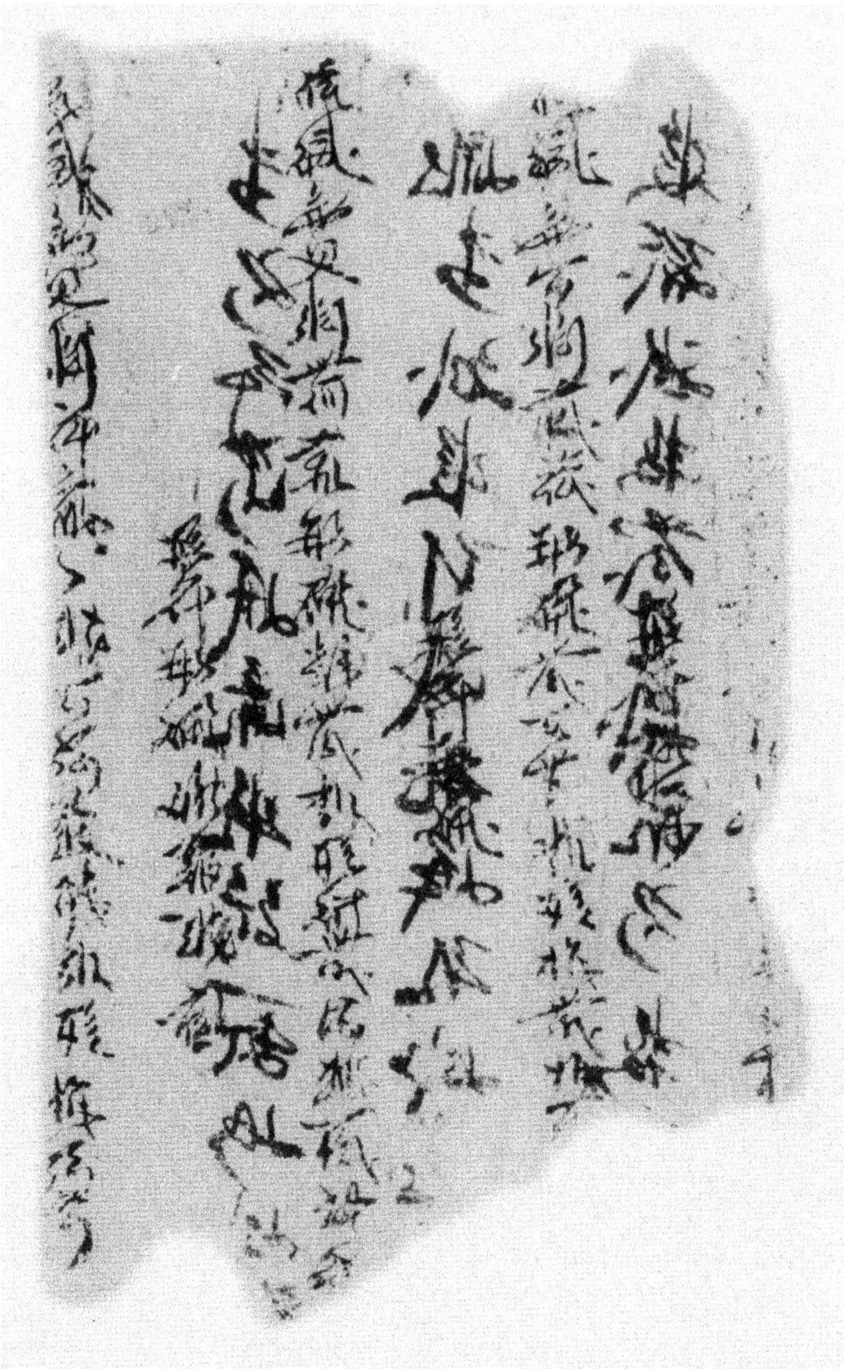

FIGURE 108 Инв. No. 7892-2V: Account of grain loan

The following is a literal translation:

> 5th month 11th day: Maluo "the slave dog" ([illegible]): 5 *dou* 1 *sheng* proso millet loaned 2 *dou* 2 *sheng* ...
>
> Borrower: "the slave dog"
>
> 5th month 18th day: *shijun* "the slave dog" 3 *dou* proso millet, loaned 6 *dou*?? up??
>
> Borrower: "slave dog"????
>
> 5th month 18th day: Liang?? "treasure" 1 *dan*???, loan 2 *dan* ...

This particular account resembles a simple format of grain loan contracts: there is the time, the name of the borrower(s), the types and quantities of the grain loan(s), and the sum of debt repayment. But there is another line that repeats the name of the borrower. What is missing, however, is the signature and stamp of the borrower. Without notarising and sanctioning, the document is probably an account of grain loans rather than a proper legal contract.

In recent years, thanks to the superb organising and coordinating initiatives on the part of the Rare Books staff at the National Library of China, there has been a sustained effort to restore and compile the Tangut manuscripts at the Library. In that process, a number of new fragments of Tangut social documents have emerged, likewise from the front covers, back covers, and layering papers of Khara-Khoto Buddhist sutras. There is a total of 170 piece of papers, where more than 10 grain loan accounts have been identified. Most of these documents are individual pages that came off an entire account. Written in the Tangut cursive, these pages record the names of the loaners (creditors), the types and quantities of the grains, the amounts of the principle and the interests, etc. They are most likely to have been kept by the 'banks'—more precisely, the loaning or pawning shops—as a back-up copy, or security copy. In all likelihood, rich Tanguts would hoard their surplus grains in these pawnshops or loan-shops. The financiers who run these shops would then coordinate the release of these loans and serve as an intermediary in paying back the creditors' interests. These accounts show that, whichever type of grains are concerned: wheat, barley, beans, and peas, and whatever the quantity of the loan, the interest is stabilised at around 50%.[61]

It is worth generalising the legal distinctions between a grain loan contract and a loan account. Crucially, the focus of the grain loan contracts is on the borrowers, the proper 'contractors' in whose name, stamp, and signature the contract obtains its legal force. In other words, the contract reflects the legal

61 Shi Jinbo, 2004 (a).

relationship between the lender and the borrower, that is, the creditor and the debtor. In contrast, an account of grain loan is creditor-centred, for it is recorded by, for, or on behalf of the lender, in order to keep track of all the loans that have been released, and are expected to generate revenues in due time. It reflects the legal relationship between the creditor and the intermediaries. These intermediary agents or representatives, in particular the pawnshop 'bankers,' would add their own interests on top of the 50% expected by the creditors, in order to also extract some profits out of the loan arrangements. They profit from the loans without even pledging any principle in the first term.

These grain loan accounts are found in more than ten morsels of papers, which are probably taken out of the same booklet of accounts. The materiality of the paper is best described as thin hemp paper, and the handwritings are mostly cursive Tangut, written on both pages of the papers. Some suffer more damages at the bottom, whereas others are broken near the top. Below are some rough translations of some of the more legible and better-preserved manuscripts.

FIGURE 109 National Library of China No. 042 (7.10X-8): Account of grain loan

National Library Register No. 042 (7.10X-8): 7 lines remain legible. Translation:

Weiming "The Old Home" barley principle 5 (*dan*) ...
  Interest 2 *dan* ...
Wheat principle 2 (*dan*) ...
  Interest 1 *dan* ...

Liu "the mountain dog" barley principle 3 (*dan*) ...
Interest 1 *dan*
wheat ...

No. 043 (7.10X-8): 6 lines have survived. The following is a literal translation:

Interest 5 *dou*
Wheat principle 5 *dou* ...
Interest 2 *dou* 5
Weiming (née) "the double treasure" barley principle 1 *dan* 5 ...
Wheat principle 1 *dan* 5 *dou*
Interest, coarse grains 1 *dan* ...

Register 045 (7.13X-1): 2 lines have survived. Here is a literal translation:

Dong "dog of the first month" wheat principle 5 *dou*
Interest 2 *dou* 5 *sheng*

Register No. 051 (7.13X-2): 5 lines have survived. Here is a literal translation:

Liu "a little pair" wheat principle 7
Interest 3 *dou* 5 *sheng dou*
Zhu "Joy of the last month" wheat principle 5 *dou*
Interest 2 *dou* 5 *sheng*
Moshang "deer-catcher" wheat 5 *dou*
...

FIGURE 110 National Library of China No. 061 (7.13X-8): Account of grain loan

Register No. 061 (7.13X-8): 7 lines have survived. Translation:

Interest 3 *dou* ...
Xichan Dingji (𗐱𗦻𗢭𗆧): wheat 1 *dou*
Interest 5 *sheng*
Bonian "dog of the first month" (𗗙𗕥𗖍𗂧𗏵): proso millet, principle 1 *dan* 5 *dou*
Interest 7 *dou* 5 *sheng*
Wheat principle 1 *dan*
Interest 5 *dou*

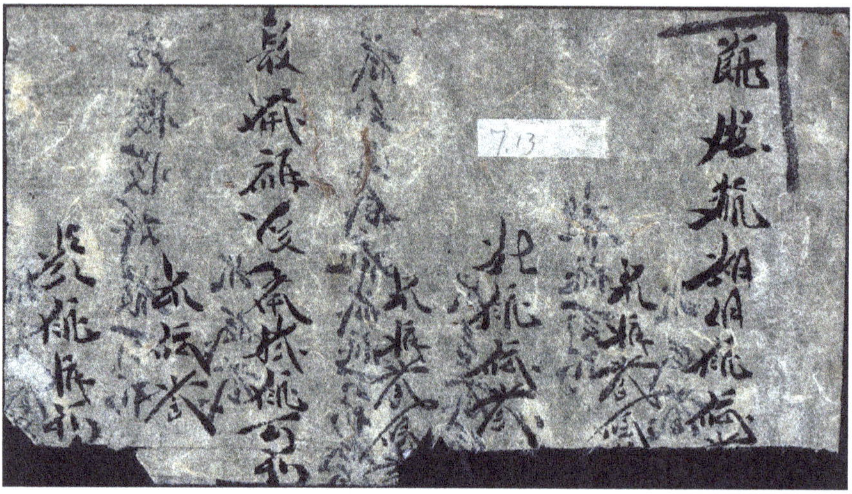

FIGURE 111 National Library of China No. 062 (7.13X-8B): Account of grain loan

Register No. 062 (7.13X-8B): 7 lines have survived. The following is a literal translation:

Zhao Afu (𗘂𗉔𗗙), peas, principle 5 *dou*
Interest 2 *dou* 5 *sheng*
Wheat principle 5 *dou*
Interest 2 *dou* 5 *sheng*
𗏁𗏵𗗚𗔫𗀔 [bji_j khjwi- dow dźjij śjow], barley principle 1 *dan*
Interest 5 *dou*
Wheat principle 2 *dan*

Register No. 055 (7.13X-4): 5 lines have survived. The following is a literal translation:

... ?city ??
... barley principle 1 *dan* 5 *dou*
Interest 7 *dou* 5 sheng
Wheat 3 *dan* 5 *dou*
Beans 1 *dan* 1 *dou*; beans 1 *dan* 4 *dou*

Register No. 056 (7.13X-4B): 6 lines have survived. The following is a literal translation:

... black barley 1 *dan* 5 *dou*; wheat 1 *dan*
Interest 7 *dou* 5 *sheng*
Wheat principle 1 *dan*; wheat 1 *dan* 3 *dou*
Interest 5 *dou*
Barley principle 2 *dan*; barley 2 *dan* 2 *dou*
interest ...

Register No. 039 (7.10X-5): 5 lines have survived. The following is a literal translation:

Principle ... principle 350
... wheat and beans, in total, 5 *dou* proso millet, 2 *dou* wheat loaned
... month, first day, 15 bundles of hay
... interest there is 3 *dou*? Barley principle loaned, 4 *dou* 5 ...
...... cash? 150

Similar registers include No. 48, 49, 50, 51, 52, 53, 54, 57, 58, 59, and so forth. An overview of these documents reveals some commonality: they accentuate the identity of the creditor, record the types of grains involved in the loan concerned, the quantity of the principle, as well as the interest rate therein applied. These are neither proper contracts, nor simply compiled statistics and summaries of contracts. Instead, they seem to be accounts that keep track of 'which creditor retains how many loans,' etc. In this case, then, it is most sensible to speculate that these are accounts of creditors and their loans, kept not by the creditors themselves but by the pawnshops or other financial institutions, for their own information. These agents, in order to manage the assets of multiple creditors, keep these accounts to keep track of the whereabouts of the loans and interests.

A quick glance at the names of the creditors finds quite a number of Dangxiang Tanguts, some of whom are from illustrious families: the royal Weimings, the Yelis who are close kins to the emperors; the glorious Gule, as well as ethnic Tangut families such as the 𗄊𗎫 [ba be] (Babe/Bobei), 𗒹𘉒 [bji_j khjwi-] (Mingqu), 𘟀𗈪 [bə njij] (Bonian), and others. Amongst Han Chinese names are Zhao, Liu, Zhu, Dong, and so on. These are all wealthy households in possessions of surplus grains.

But perhaps more importantly, these accounts provide us with the data, so badly needed, in order to derive the interest rates of grain loans during this period of the Tangut economy. The rather full account in Register No. 043 reads, "wheat principle 5 *dou*, interest 2 *dou* & 5"; No. 045: "Dong 'dog of the first month' wheat principle 5 *dou*, interest 2 *dou* 5 *sheng*"; No. 055: "barley principle 1 *dan* 5 *dou*, interest 7 *dou* 5 *sheng*"; No. 051 "Liu Ache wheat principle 7 *dou*, interest 3 *dou* 5 sheng"; No. 051 "Zhu 'Joy of the last month' wheat principle 5 *dou*, interest 2 *dou* 5 *sheng*"; No. 061 "Xichan Dingji (𗼃𗱱𗧊𗁅): wheat 1 *dou*, interest 5 *sheng*"; No. 061 "Bonian 'dog of the first month' (𘟀𗈪𗹙𗺋𘉒) proso millet principle 1 *dan* 5 *dou*, interest 7 *dou* 5 *sheng*; wheat principle 1 *dan*, interest 5 *dou*"; No. 062: "Zhao Afu: peas principle 5 *dou*, interest 2 *dou* 5 *sheng*; wheat principle 5 *dou*, interest 2 *dou* 5 *sheng*"; "𗒹𘉒𗗙𗤁𗦲 [bji_j khjwi- dow dźjij śjow] proso millet principle 1 *dan*, interest 5 *dou*"; No. 056: "barley 1 *dan* 5 *dou*, interest 7 *dou* 5 *sheng*; wheat principle 1 *dan*, interest 5 *dou*."

Obviously, regardless of the grain type—whether it is wheat, barley, beans, peas—or the quantity of the loan, the interest rate stabilises at 50%. Most of these documents, however, do not reveal the time or duration of these loans. But we know from extensive readings of Khara-Khoto grain loan contracts preserved in Russia, that most of the contracts are signed in the second month of the year, in the difficult intervening time between two harvests. The debt is due to be repaid by the eighth month, when a new harvest materialises. So, the duration of the loan would encompass the first half of the year. An interest rate of 50% for a loan that lasts for a half a year is a usurious loan by dictionary definition. Tangut peasants depend on one harvest to pay the land lease, cover the land and irrigation taxes, feed their family in the next six months, and to pay back all that they owe to their exploitative creditors. Such is the degree of poverty and hardship they must have faced.

A rather curious document is the No. 43: "wheat principle 1 *dan* 5 *dou*, interest: coarse grains 1 *dan* …" So, it does seem that a loan in fine grains can be repaid in coarse grains, but of course at a larger quantity to compensate for the price difference. At the common interest rate, 1 *dan* 5 *dou* of principle in wheat would correspond to an interest payment of 7 *dou* 5 *sheng* of wheat. But since the borrower repays not in wheat but in coarse grains, in the amount of 1 *dan* or more, it turns out that there is a surge of ⅓ in the interest rate, when coarse grains are repaid to cover debt in fine grains.

4.2 *Grain Debts*

There is also a type of 'grain debt account' that, in addition to the parties directly involved in the loan, records the name of a guarantor, and requires the notarisation of a stamp. Therefore, it is also referred to as the "guarantor's account of grain debt," a special, if not unique kind of Tangut legal document. The peasants deeply in debt would have to find guarantors in order to take out loans. This is probably a measure by which the Tanguts tried to manage their taxes and grains. One such example is the Khara-Khoto document Инв. No. 866 "guarantor's account of grain debt," a 21.7 cm × 61.4 cm manuscript with 26 lines of Tangut cursive writings and the validation of a stamp.[62]

This is an incomplete manuscript fragment of 26 lines, that contain the statistical account of grain debts owed by 4 households in a given *liliu* district. Lines 1 and 2 start off with the name of the leader in charge of the *liliu* (*lizheng*): [illegible] [khji-_dow dźjij] and the name of the *liliu* under his supervision, followed with a stamp. The account proceeds to the record the statistics by individual households, including the amounts of grains owed, the names of the borrowers (with stamps) and the guarantors (with stamps). For example, in the household No. 1, lines 1–2 state that [illegible] [zjwi. ·o tśhjwor bie_j] has a patch of 'wet land' (Tangut: [illegible] [lji-. tsji]), where 10 *dan* of seeds can be sowed, and which borders a certain canal. Line 3 details the types of grains, barley, and wheat. Line 4 states the following: "One debtor: [illegible]"—that is, the

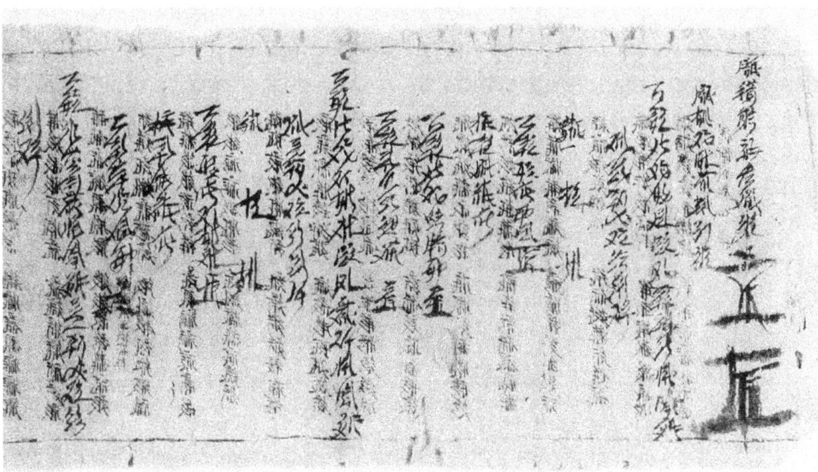

FIGURE 112 Инв. No. 866: Guarantor's account of grain debt (1)

62 *Russian Collection of Khara-Khoto Manuscripts* 12, p. 145.

FIGURE 113 Инв. No. 866: Guarantor's account of grain debt (2)

name of the head of the first household, followed by his stamp. Line 5 refers to "two guarantors"; then in lines 6 and 7 are the names and stamps of the two guarantors. The same format is applied to the three following households, all of which owe various amounts of debt. The only variables are the heads of the families (the legal persona owing the debt), the size of their lands, and the identities of the guarantors.

There is, in addition, a similar manuscript Инв. No. 4760, a scroll of 'guarantor's account of grain debt' fragments more than 3 meters long. It contains an incomplete statistical account of the debts owed by 20 households. The 19.7 cm × 303.5 cm manuscript scroll features 138 lines of cursive Tangut handwritings, with stamps and signatures.[63]

The debtor and the guarantor each provide a signature and a stamp. What is strange about this document is that the loan is written as, "coarse [and] fine [grains] in total [...] *dan* [...] *dou*," where the numbers are mysteriously missing. Perhaps the amount of debt in this particular context is simply the total amount of grain dues, which may be a fixed number that does not have to be spelled out in the document. In any case, both the debtor and the guarantor would still have to provide a stamp.

63 *Russian Collection of Khara-Khoto Manuscripts* 13, pp. 258–262.

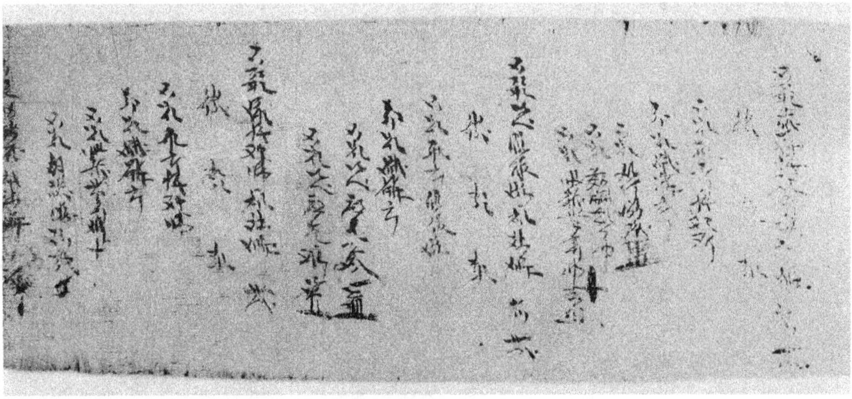

FIGURE 114 Инв. No. 4760: Guarantor's account of grain debt

5 Accounts of Land Sales

A batch of Khara-Khoto land sale contracts in the Tangut language have unveiled the colourful practices of land sales in Western Xia. These contracts will be the subject of analysis in the next chapter. But aside from these legal documents, there are also non-contractual documents of land sales that, from a different perspective, offer just as much information on land transactions in Tangut Khara-Khoto.

The manuscript No. 2156-2 is an incomplete account of land sale in the Tianqing era, handwritten on a piece of layering paper in a sutra cover. The manuscript is 23.1 cm × 30 cm in size, with 11 lines of Tangut cursive writings.[64]

In spite of the incompleteness, and sometimes the illegibility of the manuscript, there is much valuable information on land transactions to be extracted from the document. The following is a selective translation of the first 4 lines of a more important section of the manuscript:

> ... Tianqing year ... all/each year ...
> ?length: 165 *chi*; width: 100 *chi*? patch ...
> 265 *chi* of land, sold as, price 140?[65]
> cash [in] guan already paid ... contract done ... money, land ...
> ...

64 *Russian Collection of Khara-Khoto Manuscripts* 13, p. 30. The title as it appears in the book format is "submission of political report," whereas it is actually a land sales account.

65 TN: It may be the single digit here that is missing.

FIGURE 115 Инв. No. 2156-2: Account of land sale in the year of Tianqing

Here, we find the size (length and width) and price of the land, both key data on land sales. The *Tangut Sea of Characters* offers a precise definition of the unit 'mu': "a land that has each of its sides 50 *chi* along, and all four sides 200 *chi* in total, that counts as 1 *mu*."[66] Therefore, a Tangut 'mu' corresponds to the size of 2500 square *chi*, or 25 square *zhang*, or yet, 100 square *bu*. Given this data, one could derive that, if 1 Tangut *cun* is 3.12 cm, a Tangut *mu* is about 243 square meters. In the Tang and Song system of measurement, 1 *mu* equals 240 square *bu*, or roughly 600 square meters. In other words, 1 Song *mu* is about 2.4 Tangut *mu*. With this in mind, we know that in the manuscript referred to above, the area of the land sold is 165 chi × 100 *chi* = 16,500 square chi, or 6.6 Tangut *mu*. But the document also mentions that a "265 *chi* of land" is sold. This number is obviously the sum of the length and the width: 165 + 100 = 265. It is unclear what this addition really amounts to. But since the document also gives the total payment as 140 *guan*, then the unit price per *mu* of land is around 21 *guan*. The price is so high that it does not seem to be a normal patch of farmland.

66 Shi Jinbo; Bai Bin; Huang Zhenhua. *Wenhai Yanjiu* [文海研究]: *A Study on the Sea of Characters*. Beijing: China Social Sciences Press, 1983, pp. 316, 534.

A similar type of manuscript is the Инв. No. 2156-4, also a fragment written on a layering paper of a book, that is 11.3 cm × 28.8 cm in size, with 10 lines of Tangut cursive writings.[67]

FIGURE 116 Инв. No. 2156-4: Account of land sale

Translation:

...
... Tiansheng Gengyin twenty ...
... month, twenty-five upon ...
...
... land, large, *dan*, xx and[68]
... place, already purchased land, four ...
... 310 *guan* in cash
...

It is unlikely that any extensive further analysis can come about with this little data and this much damage. But it definitely looks like the same type of document as the account of land sale discussed above. Furthermore, we know at least the year in which the contract is signed: "Tiansheng *Gengyin* twenty ..." It is most likely to be the 22nd Geng-yin year of Tiansheng (1170).

67 *Russian Collection of Khara-Khoto Manuscripts* 13, p. 31. The title appears as "submission of a political report," whereas it is actually a land sales account.

68 TN: This line is difficult to crack without more characters.

6 Features of Tangut Trade and Transaction Records

A large quantity of commercial documents of Western Xia have survived to this day. In spite of their general state of scars, wears, and tears, they offer a wealth and wide range of information encompassing various sectors of the economy.

(1) The goods featured in the survived commercial documents of Western Xia cover a broad range of daily goods for consumption, such as cloth, silk, and grains. These necessities, the Tanguts could not do away with for a single second in their quotidian lives. There are also goods that bear the marks of ethnic cultures, from alcohol that was popular across ethnic communities, to large and small livestock, which are both factors of production and means of subsistence, as well as the main factors of economic production such as land and human labour.

(2) These commercial records connect the dots between production and consumption. They not only accurately portray the realities of trade and transaction in Western Xia, but also offer the statistics from which a subtler picture of the medieval Tangut economy seems to emerge. Data in transaction accounts, in particular, we now have the market prices of numerous important Tangut commodities, including the prices of grains, livestock, and alcohol. Only when armed with these and such economic data could a historian penetrate into the socio-economic eco-system of the Western Xia.

(3) An inquiry into the Tangut tax documents in previous chapters reveals a great deal about the Tangut taxation on agriculture. The commercial documents, on the other hand, expand the scope of Tangut taxes to other sectors and industries beyond the farmland. The accounts of transaction taxes, in particular, show how the Tangut government tried to intervene with a 'visible hand' and impose taxes upon the circulation of goods in the realm of the market. When it comes to the purchase and sell of cloth, livestock, gold, land, and even human beings, the Tanguts had to pay sales taxes. Land and population are the most heavily taxed. Commercial taxes are a key source of fiscal income for the Tangut local and imperial governments.

(4) The Tangut accounts of loans, interests, and debt document the historically popular practice of loans—cash, grains, and properties—in the Tangut economy. These loans are reflected not only in legally-binding contracts, but also in accounts. In most cases, a single contract is prepared for one particular transaction. The accounts, however, compile the records of multiple loans. In virtue of such a format, the accounts of loans, interests, and debts reveal more general patterns of Tangut loans

through a macroscopic lens, such as the comparative rates of loan interests. Once compiled and concentrated, economic data can turn into a richer historical narrative.

(5) Most of the taxes referred to in the commercial documents such as the accounts of sales taxes are levied in terms of grains, rather than cash. But other documents, such as accounts of grain sales and accounts of cash and grains, testify to the use of cash currency in real transactions. In alcohol sales, there is a mixed use of cash and grains as methods of payment. In most cases, however, the Tanguts purchased livestock, cloth, and other key commodities by means of grains as a form of currency. The Tanguts minted their own coins, no doubt, but they also circulated Song currencies. But at least the Khara-Khoto region witnessed a mixed currency regime of both cash and grains.

CHAPTER 7

Tangut Contracts

Contracts are the legal records of bilateral or multilateral agreements on transactions, mortgage, leases, and loans, according to the spirit and formality of laws. Therefore, contracts are private documents that specify the rights and profits, status and obligations, and the legal relationships between persons in society. It is generally the case that in ancient China, contracts dominated the sphere of private law, hence the dual track of laws as captured in the saying, "Political (public) laws to the government, private contracts to the populace." It is also true that throughout the dynastic eras of ancient China, the vast number of legal documents were produced and popularised in the economically advanced areas of the Central Plains, especially in the Han Chinese commercial communities. By contrast, the ethnic regimes and ethnic-minority areas in the medieval period have left sparse and scattered records of private contracts. Even rarer are manuscripts of legal documents written in ethnic-minority languages.

The imperial law code of Western Xia, the *Laws of Heavenly Prosperity*, not only recognises the juridical force of privately-signed contracts but also requires that all especially important contracts, such as the records of large-scale land, livestock, and human sales, be approved with the red stamp of the government's Bureau of Transaction Tax. Such a requirement speaks to the solemnity of contract-signing as a legal ritual in the Tangut Empire.

The corpus of Tangut contracts, therefore, offers a realistic lens through which scholars are now able to reflect on the commerce, transactions, and concrete economic activities that took place under Tangut rule. These contracts, themselves invaluable manuscripts, constitute a critical and indispensable primary source on Tangut society and economy.

Each of the contracts comes with a meticulous documentation of time, personalities, events, and scenarios, which form a distinct narrative of a historical story. Looking closely into these sources, it is no longer impossible to imagine the vivid scenes of the Tanguts borrowing and lending, buying and mortgaging, selling and employing, and at times pledging mutual support. The rich historical data in the contracts enable us to restore the plots and settings of the Tanguts transacting amongst themselves in villages, towns, and cities. For these reasons, the discovery and survey of Tangut contracts make great progress in the historical research of Tangut economy, deepening our inquiry into the foundation of Tangut society.

 | DOI:10.1163/9789004461321_009

1 Types and Formats of Tangut Contracts

Amongst the manuscripts excavated in Khara-Khoto, Tangut contracts are by far the most numerous and diverse, with a total of more than 150 registered numbers and about 400 pieces of contracts. They also constitute the largest portion of all contracts dated to the Tang and Song period (including the corpus of contracts found in the Dunhuang cave).

1.1 *Types*

Not unlike other medieval legal documents, Tangut contracts in the Russsian collection of Khara-Khto manuscripts are relatively easy to identify, thanks to the evidence of prints and signatures as required by legal formality. Not all social documents with the print (of finger-length) or with the label of a name, however, are necessarily contracts. One exception is the genre of 'military document' unique to the Tangut textual tradition, which also conventionally ends with similar prints and signatures but obviously does not fall into the category of private legal contracts. From a different perspective, the literal identification and statistical compilation of Tangut contract is, after all, far from a simple task. Only a small fraction of Tangut contracts was written and preserved on a single page of paper for the exclusive purpose of legal documentation. Far more frequently, the content of the contract was scribed on a manuscript-roll fragment, or even a broken piece of paper. It oftentimes happens that even the prints and signatures are lost, when the main paper loosens from its certain parts. Many other contracts were written on the back pages of books, usually Buddhist sutras. Sometimes, a fragmented manuscript roll contains multiple different contracts. However, based on available statistics, manuscripts that contain contracts within exceed the number of 200 registers, and given that some texts include more than one contract, the total number of different contracts reach up to more than 400 pieces, on a wide spectrum of preservation-quality.

1.1.1 Loan Contracts

Most loan contracts are in fact accounts of grain loan, which total a number of more than 110 registers and 320 items, indeed the largest in quantity and in diversity of all Tangut documents. In terms of materiality, some are long scrolls while others are book volumes, single pages, and fragmented pieces. There are quite a number of single-page contracts complete in content and rich in information; others are scrolls that contain anywhere between four or five to eight or ten documents, and sometimes even more. The largest single register is the Инв. No. 4696-6, "Grain loan account in the Shen Year of Guangding," 288 cm in length and with a total of 24 distinct contracts in 190 lines of Tangut text. At the same time, legal documents tend to be as short as a single line, when, for example, the amount of grain loaned was quite small. There are, in addition, one contract of loan-repayment and two others of monetary loans.

1.1.2 Transaction Contracts

Transaction contracts documented the legal exchanges of land, livestock, and human beings. Amongst the 13 pieces of land sale contracts, some are single pages and with damages, but overall, they remain thorough and well-preserved. Livestock sales have been identified in more than 20 documents, whereas contracts of human transactions are much rarer, with only three pieces discovered thus far. A long scroll of contracts, the Инв. No. 5124, contains 23 contracts dated to late first or second months in the Yin Year of Tianqing (1194), ranging from land sales (eight items), land leases, livestock transactions, employments, and grain loans. Because most of the Tangut transaction contracts involve agreements on foreclosure, the trading volume is usually quite large, and the texts of the contracts are complex and comprehensive.

1.1.3 Lease Contracts

Contracts of both land-lease and livestock-lease have been excavated in Khara-Khoto. There are three registers and eight pieces of such lease contracts. In both Dunhuang and Turfan social documents, farming lands on lease is referred to as 'to till a land rented from the landlord' (Chinese: 夏田 or 佃田). Land leases are therefore called "contracts of land rent" (Chinese: 夏田券, 夏田契 or 佃田契).[1] Khara-Khoto leases refer to the cultivation of rented land as 𗉘 [phio], which derives phonetically from the Chinese character 包 [pau], the character for "charter," "farmland rent," and "to place a lease under contract."

Besides, there are eight registers and 14 pieces of grain-loan and livestock-mortgage contracts. There are several other contracts whereby the exchange of

1 Han, Guopan. "Cong Tulufan Chutu Wenshu zhong Xiatian Quanqi lai Tan Gaochang Zudian de Jige Wenti" [從吐魯番出土文書中夏田券契來談高昌租佃的幾個問題]: "A Discussion on Several Issues about Tenancy in Gaochang, based on Farmland Lease Contracts in the Unearthed Turfan Documents" Han, Guopan (eds.). *Dunhuang Tulufan Chutu Jingji Wenshu Yanjiu* [敦煌吐魯番出土經濟文書研究]: *Studies on the Economic Documents Excavated in Turfan and Dunhuang*. Xiamen: Xiamen University Press, 1986, pp. 199–224; Yang, Jiping. "Qushi Gaochang yu Tangdai Xizhou Shazhou Zudianzhi Yanjiu" [麴氏高昌與唐代西州沙洲租佃制研究]: "A Study of Land Lease Contracts in Gaochang of the Qu Family, and Xizhou and Shazhou of Tang Dynasty" in Han, 1986, pp. 225–292.

livestocks is guaranteed under the condition that it is to be supplemented by an additional form of compensation.

1.1.4 Employment Contracts

Legal documents of employment include contracts of either labour or livestock employment. Only one piece of labour contract, an extremely rare and precious find, has been identified. One other contract, however, is a 'labour mortgage' deed, whereby the signer of the contract willingly conveyed his labour to the creditor as security on a loan. The numerous livestock-employment contracts were signed, more often than not, when a household had already sold its livestock but had to secure a loan of the same animals from the current owner who purchased them. There are, besides two items of grain-loans, livestock-employment and land-mortgage contracts.

1.1.5 Communal Contracts

Communal contracts are statements of rules and requirements of civilian societies. Only two such documents have survived to date, both of which are Tangut-era contracts of social groups founded by the pledge of 'mutual support' of inducted members. They add new materials to 12th–13th century sources on Chinese social communities, which demonstrate the existence of self-organised communal organisations at the bottom of the civil society in Western Xia.

Other contracts are more difficult to identify and categorise due to higher levels of damage and the paucity of eligible traces of words in the texts. In some cases, contracts are preliminarily identified as official documentation of either loans or transactions, but information on the goods concerned are either missing or unclear.

An additional batch of contracts has been found in the pile of Tangut manuscripts which Sir Marc Aurel Stein seized from Kara-Khoto and stored in the British Library. Amongst the smaller number of Tangut texts that remain at the National Library of China, a few manuscripts have also been identified as contracts. Archeologists in Gansu and Inner Mongolia in recent years have made new discoveries of contracts in the midst of other documents. Especially worth noting is a particular piece of Tangut loan document found in a hoard of Tangut materials in Chanshan village, Wuwei, Gansu in the 1980s.[2] Of course,

2 Sun, Shouling. "Xixia Qianding Shennian Dianmi Qiyue" [西夏乾定申年典糜契約]: "Proso Millet Loan Contract in the Shen Year of Qianding in Western Xia" in *Zhongguo Wenwu Bao* [中國文物報]: *China Cultural Relics News*, issue 5, 1993.

contracts dated to Western Xia written in Chinese characters are also of great value and have been the subject of fruitful research in recent years.

1.2 *Formats*

Tangut contracts are often written on slightly yellowish white hemp papers. With a contract that was fully written out on one piece of paper, the manuscript is usually 20 cm × 30 cm. The Инв. No. 5227 “Contract of Grain loan on mortgage in the Chou Year of Tianqing,” 19.3 cm × 30.5 cm, is about exactly this size; others are slightly narrower in length, such as the 18.7 cm × 13.4 cm Инв. No. 2996-3, a contract of livestock mortgage. A considerable number of Tangut contracts appear in clusters, with multiple documents written on the same piece of paper. It often happens that one long scroll contains dozens of contracts at the same time, which form a chain of legal documents that looks like a series of accounts. One example is the 19.5 cm × 152 cm Russian manuscript-scroll Инв. No. 4596, “Account of grain loans in the Chou Year of Guangding” with eight contracts; the Инв. No. 4696 “Account of grain loans in the Shen Year of Guangding” is broken into a few segments that patched together form a long scroll as long as 500 cm and with more than 50 contracts. Despite the large quantity, contracts such as these are usually written on papers of lower quality and are subject to further damage and deterioration at the fronts and ends.

Each contract begins with an unindented line, always written in ink and mostly rendered in cursive, though occasionally in the running or standard script. The Contract Parties follow a relatively set format, which starts with the exact time of the contract, including the reign era, *jiazi* (the period of sixty years in the sexagenary cycle), year, month, and day. Usually under the character for ‘day’ (date, the temporal unit) [illegible] [djij], there may be found a smaller Tangut character for ‘day’ (as in daylight, as opposed to night) [illegible] [nji-_]. It is only in particular contexts that the complete indication of time may be abbreviated. For example, where there is already a specific reference to a certain year, the Contract Party may only sign “Yin Year” or names of other years that only include the “Earthly Branches.” When, of course, a contract immediately follows a preceding one, a “same day” (ibid.) suffices. After the year and date of the contract come naturally the identities of the Contract Parties themselves, which are referred to in Tangut as the [illegible] [·jwi-r dźiow wji mjijr] lit. “text/document, plea/plaint, conduct/compose, person/party” i.e. “the Contract Parties who compose the documents.” This is then followed by the main content of the contract—the terms, conditions, and agreements of loans and transactions. Information such as quantities, prices, interests, payments, and compensations are recorded in great detail. As a rule, the contract also clearly lays out the forms and amounts of penalties in the sorry case of default. The Contract Parties have to make clear of their consent, typically in the expression that their "heart willingly submits" to the terms. In the last and usually indented line, the Contract Parties sign their own names and print the required figures, along with the 'co-signer' of the contract: [illegible] [dźiow dźjwi- sa mjijr] lit. "plea/plaint, reciprocal/additional, link/associate, person/party" i.e. "the party associated with the contract." A separate line or space is reserved for the same formality of the witness: [illegible] [nwə dzjwo] lit. "know, person" i.e. "the person who bears witness to this transaction." With the names and prints of the signing parties indented, these final lines usually align with the main text at the bottom. Sometimes, the types and quantities of goods traded or loaned are labelled again, either in words or notations, above the Contract Parties' signatures.

The more important ones of the unearthed documents, especially the large-volume foreclosure contracts, are stamped in red by the Bureau of Transaction Tax. The rectangle-shaped red stamp is large in size, supported from below by the shape of a lotus flower and decorated from above with the figure of lotus leaves. On the top of the stamp is a line of four Tangut characters, which read from right to left, [illegible] [phə źji. zji.j io.] lit. "price, market, tax, office" i.e. "The Bureau of Transaction Tax." Contracts with such a red stamp were approved by the government. Those who paid transaction taxes were entitled to the so-called 'red contracts.'

A considerable number of Tangut contracts, however, are short in length and simple in content. These are records of small and non-foreclosure loans or transactions, such as borrowing a small quantity of grains. Some of these legal documents feature no more than one line, which notes the name of the borrower, the amount of the loan, the promised repayment, and the signatures of other relevant parties.

Communal contracts are a distinct category of Tangut legal documents. Such contracts begin with a prolegomenon-like general statement, the indication of time, day, and year, followed by the rules and regulations of the [illegible] (communal organisations). Each rule begins with the phrase [illegible] [·ja tjij] lit. "one, item/chapter/order" i.e. "the one item of rule." The common activity of the community is referred to in the rules as [illegible] [ljwu dzji-.], lit. "meeting/alliance, gather/congregate" and members of the community are [illegible] [tha ·ji], lit. "large many/majority" i.e. the greater public, the many, or the masses. The contracts end with the signatures and prints of all constituent members.

Overall, it may be said that Tangut contracts inherited the format and formalities of Chinese traditions in the Central Plains. Contracts in Western Xia contain all of the most basic elements of traditional contracts in this era, but they also exhibit special features, either in content or in terminology, that are unique to Tangut economic culture.

2 Loan Contracts

The largest number of Tangut contracts are loan records, with accounts of grain loans as the majority. Lending and loaning grains is an economic activity that took place at a massive scale and on a frequent basis at the bottom level of Tangut society. And although it is only food concerned, such loans in fact concern many aspects of Tangut society.

Among the social documents discovered in Dunhuang, about 70 pieces are grain loan contracts, commonly referred to by scholars as "wheat loan contracts" or "millet loan contracts."[3] The significantly larger corpus of Khara-Khoto grain loan contracts are several times the quantity of Dunhuang documents. Indeed, Western Xia is by far identified as the dynasty with the greatest number of survived contracts prior to Ming and Qing.

In the past, scholarship on Tangut contracts was sparse and limited. About 15 remnant pawn and mortgage contracts have been studied and published by Chen Guocan.[4] Towards the end of 1980s, a batch of Tangut archives and artifacts were discovered in the Chanshan village, which is located in the rural outskirts of Wuwei city of Gansu province. Among the discoveries, one piece of Tangut grain loan contract has been interpreted and introduced by Sun Shouling.[5]

2.1 *Grain Loans*

2.1.1 Rules and Institutions for Making Grain Loan Contracts

The Tangut *Laws of Heavenly Prosperity* incorporates the rules on lending and loaning into the imperial law code, especially the 15 items of legislation in Book III on "pressing and requesting debt and interest" which provide a concentrated and comprehensive set of regulations on debt. Indeed, the fact that a separate section in the imperial dynastic law is devoted to the question of debt shows the level of attention that the Tangut bureaucracy paid to the protection

3 Tang, Geng'ou; Lu, Hongji (eds.). *Dunhuang Shehui Jingji Wenxian Zhenji Shilu* [敦煌社會經濟文獻真跡釋錄]: *An Interpretive Transcription of the Original Dunhuang Economic Documents* (hereafter *Dunhuang Economic Documents*). Beijing: National Library of China, Quanguo Tushuguan Wenxian Suowei Fuzhi Zhongxin [全國圖書館文獻縮微複製中心], 1990, pp. 76–147.

4 Chen Guocan, 1980, pp. 143–150.

5 Sun Shouling, 1993.

of the creditors' proper rights. It also reveals the government's stance on using written and codified laws as an instrument to press the poor to yield to the debt solicitations of the wealthy.

The following are specific regulations concerning the establishment and sanctions of contracts, according to legislations on the solicitation of debt in the *Laws of Heavenly Prosperity*:

> Individuals who sell or purchase, lend or loan, or conduct a variety of other businesses that involve multiple parties, who thus voluntarily associate with one another, may establish a written document, on which are written the relevant words that indicate the prices of purchase, the amounts of money, the contexts of equal measurement, as well as single and collective numbers, all of which the public and private transactors are supposed to command in clear language on the written document. In case of any parting regretting or defaulting on the contract in the future, penalties under official terms are to be delivered in the government, whereas under private names, to private individuals. Those who change their pledge, who enjoy an official title, are penalised with the confiscation of a horse; those who change their heart, who are commoners in status, are sentenced to 13 lashes.[6]

Tangut laws promoted the use of "written records"—or contracts—to document loans, transactions, and other civil affairs, in order to protect the interests and rights of the creditors. They also regulated and normalised economic affairs in the private social space of civil life, thus avoiding potential escalations and proliferations of civil disputes into larger causes of social unrests. Moreover, the laws set specific requirements on the main content of the contracts and penalise those who breached them. Penalties in the form of cash, grains, and properties were sometimes turned over to the government, and other times to the private individuals who own the debt.

Once again, the discovery of such a large amount of Khara-Khoto loan contracts suggests that the enforcement of Tangut laws on the making of contracts extended to the peripheral territories of Western Xia, such as the rural areas of Khara-Khoto near the northwestern borders of the empire.

Most of the known Tangut loan contracts were documented in clusters of several documents on single pages. Some long scrolls contain several dozens of contracts, which are connected in serial accounts of contracts. In most cases of such long scrolls, although the borrowers appear to be different, the

6 *Revised Laws of Heavenly Prosperity* 3, "Urging the Repayment of Interests," pp. 189–190.

creditors are sometimes the same. These turn out to be accounts kept by a single creditor, whose lending contracts with multiple debtors were compiled together for the sake of convenience. The aforementioned Инв. No. 4696 is such an account of more than 50 grain loan contracts patched together into a long scroll.

Contracts were not only records of proof and evidence but also documents of legal force that occupied a critical role in the socio-economic lives of individuals and communities. A Tangut grain loan account was, therefore, both a written agreement that facilitated the making of loans and transactions as well as a proper contract with all its legal force and implications.

2.1.2 Categories, Translations and Interpretations of Grain Loan Accounts

Although most of the grain loan accounts found in Khara-Khoto were bound as long scrolls of multiple contracts, rather than single-page documents, many contracts of land, livestock, and human transactions (including animal loans) were in fact recorded on single pages. In most cases, single-page contracts were used in larger transactions of valuable goods. By contrast, the serial accounts of grain loans were devoted to regular lendings of common commodities, which were conveniently written or kept together.

There is a great variety of Tangut grain loan accounts. For a fuller understanding of the diverse formats and contents of Tangut grain loan contracts, below is a selected list of translated Tangut contracts of various degrees of simplicity and complexity:

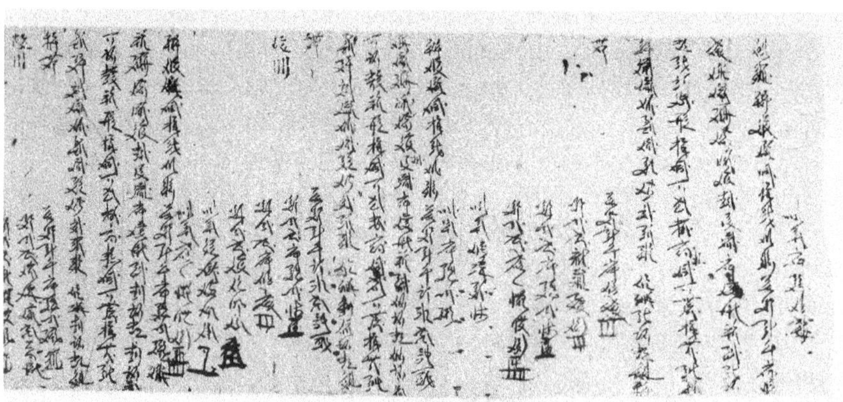

FIGURE 117 Инв. No. 4762-6(1) (front of manuscript): Yin year of Tianqing (1194) grain loan account

1. Инв. No. 4762-6(1) Yin Year of Tianqing (1194): serial account of multiple grain loan contracts, a 20.6 × 52 cm handwritten manuscript on hemp-paper scroll, with 31 lines in Tangut cursive.[7]

Translation:[8]

> Yin Year of Tianqing, 29th Day of 1st Month, Contract Party[9] [illegible] [ljow mjijr]
> [illegible] [śjow] presently from the Pudu Temple's[10] grain-agents[11] [illegible] [ljow lja mja][12] et al. loans[13] 10 *dan*
> of wheat, 10 *dan* of barley; since the first day of February, 1 *dou* 2 *sheng* of interest per month,
> Repaid till capital and interest are equal; overdue fines by official law[14] is 10 *dan* of wheat, willingly agreed.
> Contract Party [illegible] [mjijr śjow] (stamp)
> Co-Contract Party[15] son, [illegible] [parya ne_w][16] (stamp)
> Co-Contract Party [illegible] [ljow phə tśhja śia~] (stamp)
> Co-Contract Party [illegible] [dju. dju. śja~ dji-j ne_w] (print)[17]

---

7 TN: see *Russian Collection of Khara-Khoto Manuscripts*, vol. 13, 279–280. Numbers in smaller fonts reflect the order of the contracts in the long scroll. In the main text of the translation, I have used brackets, (1), (2) … instead of circles, ①, ②… as in the Chinese edition.

8 The first line is left off from the previous contract, and is therefore left untranslated.

9 The borrowing party in a Tangut contract is known as 'the one who sets up the contract': "[illegible]" (lit. word, document, make, person). The "word document" is the "contract." To "make" is to do, to set up, and to establish.

10 The Tangut is "[illegible]": given the strong resemblance between [illegible] and [illegible], [illegible] might as well be [illegible] (Pudu, 'universal salvation'); "[illegible]" (the many palaces) are in fact "the many temples." "[illegible]" [tśjow] also means 'temple.' This temple is commonly translated as "Pudu Temple," one of the Buddhist temples in Khara-Khoto in the Tangut period.

11 Tangut: "[illegible]" [śji la. tśhju], lit. "grain, hand, have" i.e. "the one who holds the grains." These are persons in charge of managing the grains in the temples.

12 TN: Liang Lama is the primary agent in charge of handling the properties of the Pudu Temple, an asset manager who takes care of loans, sales, and leases.

13 Tangut: "[illegible]" [lhjwi], lit. "to take," here "to borrow."

14 Tangut: "[illegible]" [kow bju], lit. "office/government, accord" i.e. "according to the government authority." This is a way of saying "according to the laws and regulations established by the political authority."

15 The Tangut "[illegible]" [dźiow sa dźjwi-], lit. "document, receive, to" i.e. "the one who receives the contract." In most cases, it refers to a co-Contract Party, who agrees to take over the financial liability in case the principle Contract Party can no longer fulfil the terms therein. The co-contractors are in most cases the family relatives or close friends of the main Contract Party.

16 TN: [illegible] [pa rya] = प्रज्ञा = 般若 = wisdom; [illegible] [ne_w] = kindness, benevolence.

17 TN: the smaller-font character □ on the side is purposefully neglected in order to render a sensible name.

Witness[18] [illegible] [phjij śjo wa śia~] (stamp)
Witness: [illegible]? [ljow phə ? khjwi-] (stamp)

2. Инв. No. 6377-16(1) in the Mao Year of Guangding (1219), handwritten manuscript of Grain loan account on a 20.6 × 53.7 hemp-paper fragment, with 28 lines of writings in the Tangut cursive.[19]

Translation:

Mao Year of Guangding, sixth day of March, Contract set by [illegible] [ljow śja lhji.]
[illegible] [khjwi-], (who) presently from [illegible] [tśhji-j śjow parya śia~] the owner of capital[20] Laofangshi's place, loans
1 *dan* 5 *dou* of wheat, with an interest of 5 *dou* per *dan* loaned, which in total amount to 2
dan 2 *dou* 5 *sheng*, with the due date being the first day of August in the same year
(at which time the debtor) should come with amount of grains prepared. After that date, there will be a charge of 2 *dan* (penalty fee) per dan of loan.

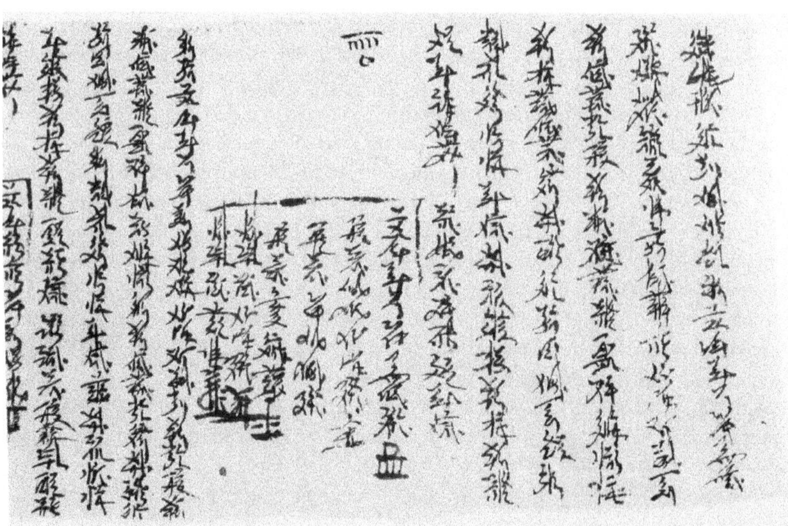

FIGURE 118 Инв. No. 6377-16: Mao year of Guangding (1219) grain loan account

18 Tangut: "[illegible]" [nwə dzjwo], lit. "the person who knows," is translated into "witness" throughout this book.

19 *Russian Collection of Khara-Khoto Manuscripts* 14, pp. 145–146.

20 Tangut: "[illegible]" [tśhji zow mjijr], lit. "principle-holder," i.e. the creditor who legally owns the loan.

Willing: the amount recorded on the document[21] is to be repaid.
Contract Party: [illegible] [ljow śja lhji. khjwi-] (stamp)
Co-loaner:[22] [illegible] [tśhji-j śjow da kia khjwi-] (stamp)
Co-loaner: [illegible] [ljow gji-_ lhji. khjwi-]
Co-loaner: [illegible] [lji ɣə. bju] (stamp)
Witness: [illegible] [·jow da kia khjwi-] (stamp)
Witness: [illegible] [·jow śja. śia~] (stamp)

The two manuscripts above are fairly standard examples of Tangut loan contracts. Grain loan accounts of the same type include the Инв. No. 7741, 4762-6–7, 5870, and 8005.[23] It seems that in format, Tangut contracts were for the most part similar to documents used by the Han Chinese populations in the Central Plains, especially with respect to the key information covered: the date when the contract was signed, the name(s) of the main 'Contract Party' (here it refers to the borrower or debtor), the name of the lender or creditor, the types and quantities of the grain loan, the time limit of the loan and due dates of repayment, the interest rate, and finally the overdue penalty fees in case of default. The document ends with the signatures and prints of the witnesses.

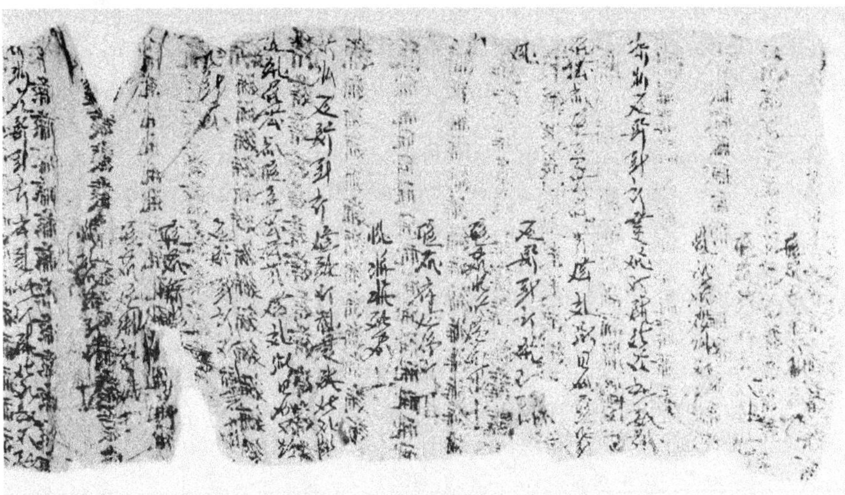

FIGURE 119 Инв. No. 4526: Serial account of grain loans

21 Tangut: "[illegible]" [lji. lu. ɣa ·o], lit. "enter, stick/stem/handle, on, there is" i.e. "there are [recorded/found] on the document."

22 Tangut: "[illegible]" [lhjwi dźjwi-], lit. "borrow, with" i.e. co-borrower.

23 *Russian Collection of Khara-Khoto Manuscripts* 14, pp. 188–191; 13, pp. 279–280; 14, pp. 57–61; 14, pp. 250–252.

3. Инв. No. 4526 (2) serial accounts of five grain loans, handwritten on an 18.6 × 65 cm hemp-paper remnant manuscript, with 27 lines of Tangut in the cursive.[24]

This piece of manuscript continues as the end of the previous contract. Lines 4–9 are translated as follows:

> On the same day, contract set by [Tangut] [lji khjwi- gju_], first from [Tangut]? [zjwi. ·o ? wejr] borrows
> 5 *dan* of assorted grains, which is turned into[25] 7 *dan* 5 *sheng*, due on the first day of August, to be
> repaid.
> Contract set by [Tangut] [khjwi- gju_] (stamp)
> To borrow □□□□□ (stamp)
> Lender [Tangut] [ljow] (Liang)□ [Tangut] [gju_] (stamp)
> Witness:[26] Hun [Tangut] [kə ta śjow] (print)

Although there are six lines in this contract, the main content concerning the terms of the agreements is written out in only two lines plus one character with key information including the date, identities of the Contract Party (debtor) and lender (creditor), the amount of grain loaned, interest rate, and the terms of repayment. Although the penalty fees seem to have been omitted, the contract does end with the signatures and prints of the Contract Party and the witness.

4. Инв. No. 7892-7 account of grain loans, handwritten on a 20.7 × 21.4 cm hemp-paper remnant manuscript with 15 lines of Tangut writings in the cursive.[27] The contracts contained in this manuscript are even simpler legal records of loans, as short as three or two lines.
The content of the first three contracts is translated as follows:

> One person named Liang?? and his son [Tangut] [dźjij wejr], et al., borrow 5 *sheng* of wheat; amounts to 1 *dou*.
> (calculative notation) 5 *sheng* of wheat, borrower Liang??
> Co-borrower, son (of Liang) [Tangut]
> One person, a *shijun* named [Tangut] [khjwi- wejr], borrows 5 *dou* of wheat; amounts to 1 *dan*.
> Borrower: [Tangut] [khjwi- wejr]

24 *Russian Collection of Khara-Khoto Manuscripts* 13, pp. 217–218.
25 Tangut: "[Tangut]" [we], "to become," "to turn into."
26 Tangut: "[Tangut]" [nwə], "to know," "the one who knows," i.e. witness.
27 *Russian Collection of Khara-Khoto Manuscripts* 14, p. 206.

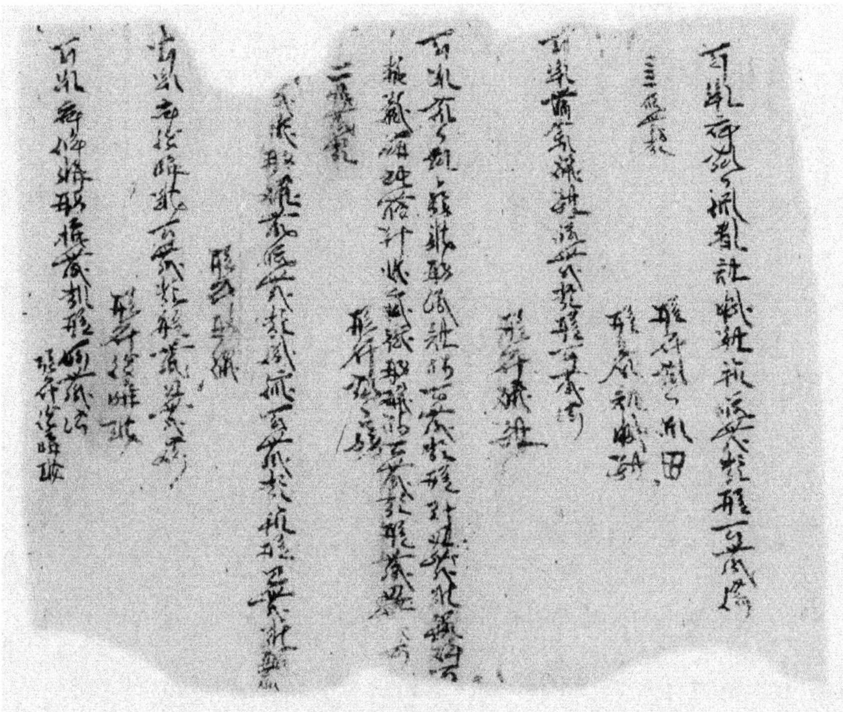

FIGURE 120 Инв. No. 7892-7: Account of grain loan contracts

> One person, [illegible] [dju. dju. ɣji- ɣji- kjir], from [illegible] [lhowr tśh-jwor bie_j] borrows 1 *dou* of wheat; interest of more than 8 *sheng*, 1 sword is now mortgaged as security; then from Qingluo borrows 1 *dou* of wheat; turns into 1 *dou* 8 *sheng*.
> (numerical notation) 2 *dou* of wheat; lender: [illegible] [ɣji- ɣji-]

Despite the simplicity of the two documents above, neither actually lacks the key information of a contract. The first piece contains three lines, including the name of the Contract Party and the co-borrower, the amount of grain to be loaned, interest rate, and the names of both the lender and the witness, followed by their prints. The only elements missing are the date and terms of penalties in case of default. The second contract is even simpler: two lines in total, the 'main text' is compressed into only one line, which nonetheless provides the name of the Contract Party, the types and amounts of grains loaned, and the amount of capital and interest. Usually, the smaller the amount loaned, the simpler the contract is. In these two cases, the first contract involves a mere 5 *sheng* of wheat, and the slightly more capacious deal in the second contract concerns only 5 *dou* of wheat.

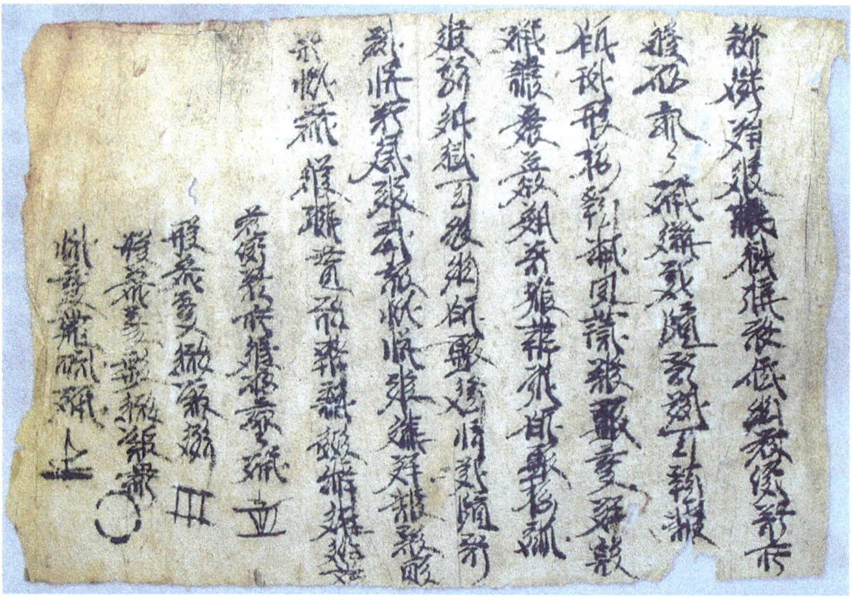

FIGURE 121 Wuwei G31.004 [6728]: Shen year of Qianding (1224) grain loan contract

5. Wuwei G31.004 [6728] Shen Year of Qianding Reign (1224) grain loan account, handwritten on an 18 × 27 cm white (with light yellowish taints) hemp-paper manuscript, with 11 lines of Tangut writings in the cursive.[28] It is a complete, detailed, and rare single-page grain loan.

Translation:

Shen Year of Qianding Reign, 25th day of February, contract set by
[Tangut] [mə śjwi wa wa khjwi-], presently from Master E, borrowed 1
dan of millet (capital), at the interest rate of 8 *dou* per *dan*,[29] arranged to be
retrieved from [Tangut] [parya śjow]. The combined loan and interest are to be
prepared by the 1st day of September in the same year, and repaid to master E
in case[30] the sum is not paid after the due date, besides the payment of the millet,

28 *Chinese Collection of Tangut Manuscripts* 16, p. 389.

29 Some erasing, etc. seems to have been applied to the original Tangut character for "interest"; below is the character for the Tangut surname "Li."

30 The original character is "[Tangut]" [tjij], "quality," "rank," etc. By its position, and by comparative analysis with other contracts, it is possibly intended to be "[Tangut]" [tjij], meaning "if."

there will be a penalty fee of 70 *guan* of cash according to the official law; (each's) own[31] heart is willing.

Contract Party: [Tangut characters] [mə śjwi wa wa khjwi-] (stamp)
Lender: [Tangut characters] [lji ɣa. wa. ne_w] (stamp)
Lender: [Tangut characters] [lji zji-. ɣa. wa. kie.] (print)[32]
Witness: [Tangut characters] [lji śja phji khjwi-] (print)

The total of more than 250 characters in this contract introduces the precise date (era-title, earthly branch, month, and day), names of the Contract Party and lenders, types of grains loaned, interest rate, the due date of repayment, where to retrieve and to whom to repay, and the terms of penalty fees, concluded with the signatures and prints of all contracting parties and the witness. The grains loaned thereby is not a large sum, but the content of the contract is comprehensive and rendered in a standardised format. It may therefore be treated as a classic example of Tangut grain loan accounts.

The Institute of Cultural Relics and Archaeology in Inner Mongolia houses an additional piece of Khara-Khoto grain loan account. Registered as M21.003[F135: W75/2026], the 27 × 20 cm wheat-loan contract manuscript is dated to Year Yihai (1215?).[33] It is similar in format to regular grain loan accounts, with the exception of a notation added to the contract at the end of the document [Tangut characters]: "the Contract Party who hereby borrows wheat," a title which specifies the nature and type of borrowing behaviour involved in the legal-commercial relationship.

2.1.3 Time of the Contract

Each Tangut grain loan contract begins by indicating the time when the agreement is reached and the document signed. The better-preserved contracts provide extensive details with respect to time: the title of era and reign, the sexagenary cycle, the calendar year, month, and day. Most contracts provide not only the time when the contract officially went into legal force but also the time when the agreement was expected to be fulfilled. Needless to say, this is

---

The two characters are close in resemblance. The first character is the bottom part of the second.

31 The original character is "[Tangut character]" [·jij]: surname. Given its position, and by comparative analysis in the light of parallel formats in similar contracts, it is possibly a miswritten "[Tangut character]" [mər], meaning "principle." The two characters look similar, since their right parts are almost identical.

32 The stamp here is a circle, unlikely to have been hand-drawn, but rather the print of an object with a circle-shaped cross-section. This type of stamping is quite rare, and probably one of the primitive and preliminary forms of stamping in the modern sense.

33 *Chinese Collection of Tangut Manuscripts* 17, p. 153.

especially the case when the interests were calculated based on the temporal duration of the loan.

Despite the large quantity of Tangut grain loan contracts, they tend to come from the latest 50 years of the Western Xia dynasty. One of the earliest manuscripts, the Инв. No. 4079, for example, is dated to "Ren-chen Year of Qianyou Reign" (information on month and day missing), which was the Third Year of Qianyou (1172) under the reign of the Renzong Emperor of Xia, Weiming Renxiao. Инв. No. 1570 is dated to "(Qian)you, Xu year, day 12 of May," a formulation that refers to the 'earthly branch' only but omits the 'heavenly stem.' Given that Renzong emperor Qianyou's reign lasted for 24 years, there were not one but two Xu years in between: the Wuxu, ninth year of Qianyou (1178), and the Gengxu, twenty-first Year of Qianyou (1190). The first Xu year was perhaps the more likely, for the simple thought that had it been the second Xu year, when the Contract Parties would have had more reason to specify the complete 'stem and branch' in order to differentiate this date from the first. Another example is the Инв. No. 5949-28,[34] which mentions its date as "Qianyou, Zi year, twenty-fifth day of the tenth month." But it soon becomes clear that there were also two Zi years within the Qianyou era: the Gengzi, eleventh Year of Qianyou (1180), and the Renzi, twenty-third year of Qianyou (1192). For the same reason, it may be speculated that the first Zi year was slightly more likely than the second.

A certain number of loan contracts are simple in their recording, or are, in fact, incomplete manuscripts. It requires some rigorous analysis to ascertain the time of such documents. For example, Инв. No. 5949-22 contains four pieces of contracts, none of which provides information on date or time. The third piece mentions "the first day of leap-year March in the Mao Year." Based on this evidence, an investigation into all possible instances of "March in the leap-year of Mao" in Tangut history points to the lone possibility: the Jimao ninth year of Guangding (1219). Scholars may then date not only this one contract, in particular, but also the other three pieces recorded in the same manuscript to the same year. Likewise, although the five contracts contained in the Инв. No. 5949-27 are without precise dates, given the reference to "the second day of the leap-year March in the same year," it is possible to also date these five documents to 1219.

It is difficult to date contracts which only document the 'earthly-branches' but not the 'heavenly stems,' especially when there were two identical earthly-branch years within the same reign era. In some cases, however, rigorous

34 Shi Jinbo, 2005 (b). The registers of the documents were later readjusted in the publication of the *Russian Collection of Khara-Khoto Manuscripts*.

textual scholarship may overcome the challenge of incomplete information. For example, the Инв. No. 5949-18 reads, "Wei Year of Guangding, day 29 of the third month." Within the Guangding era of Western Xia, however, there were thirteen years (1211–1223), long enough to encompass two Wei years, namely the Xinwei first year of Guangding (1211) and the Guiwei thirteenth year of Guangding (1223). It should be noted, however, that the Shenzong emperor Zunxu forced Xiangzong emperor Anquan out of the throne in the seventh month of the Xinwei year, which was then renamed the first year of Guangding.[35] Therefore, since there was not yet a proper reign of Guangding in the previous sixth months of the Xinwei year, it is safe to conclude that this contract signed in "The Third Month, in the Wei Year of Guangding" is from the second Wei year, namely the Guiwei thirteenth year of Guangding (1223). And once this time is established, it is now possible to date the two other contracts from the same page to the same year of 1223.

As mentioned above, the vast majority of Tangut grain loan accounts surviving to this day are dated to the late period of Western Xia. Even Renzong-era manuscripts are quite rare, by comparison to the more numerous examples of documents from the time of Huanzong and Shenzong. The largest number of these contracts were signed during the reign of Huanzong's Tianqing and Shenzong's Guangding years. In fact, Huanzong emperor Weiming Chunyou enjoyed only one reign-era in the name of Tianqing, which lasted for 12 years (1194–1205). Likewise, the only reign-era under the rule of Shenzong emperor Weiming Zunxu was the span of 13 years known as Guangding (1211–1224). Below are some of the contracts that mention the eras of Tianqing and Guangding in their main texts:

- Jiayin Year of Tianqing (1194): Инв. No. 3586, 4384-7, 4762-6, 5870, 7741
- Mao Year of Tianqing (1195): Инв. No. 4696-1
- Wei Year of Tianqing (1199): Инв. No. 7892-3
- Guihai Year of Tianqing (1203): Инв. No. 7889, 7892-4, 7892-5
- Jiazi Year of Tianqing (1204): Инв. No. 4978-1
- Chou Year of Tianqing (1205): Инв. No. 5227, 7910-3
- Wei Year of Guangding (1211): Инв. No. 5949-18
- Shen Year of Guangding (1212): Инв. No. 4696-2, 4696-3, 4696-4, 4696-5, 4696-6, 4696-7,[36] 5949-19–21
- Chou Year of Guangding (1217): Инв. No. 4596
- Wuyin year of Guangding (1218): Инв. No. 8005-1, 8005-2

35 *History of Song*, Bk. 486, "Western Xia" Part II.

36 *Russian Collection of Khara-Khoto Manuscripts* 13, pp. 237–247. The title "Grain Loan Contract in the Shen year of Guangding" in Инв. No. 4696-6 has been confused with the "Account of Alcohol Prices" in Инв. No. 4696-8.

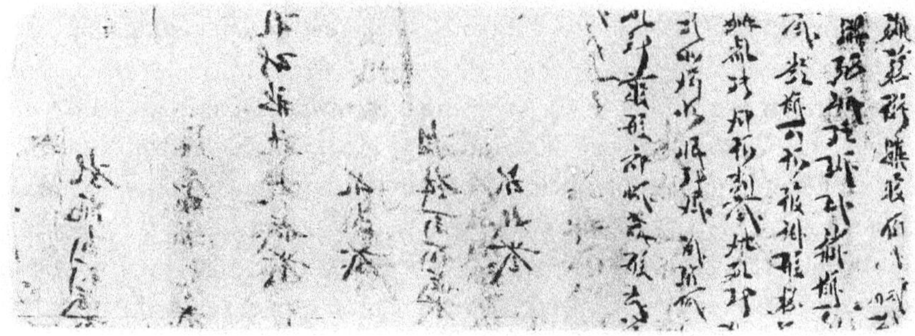

FIGURE 122 Инв. No. 3586: Jiayin First Year of Tianqing (1194) Account of grain loan fragment

- Mao Year of Guangding (1219): Инв. No. 5949-22, 6377-16
- Gengchen and Si Year of Guangding (1220, 1221): Инв. No. 986-1
- Si Year of Guangding (1221): Инв. No. 2955, 5949-23
- Wu Year of Guangding (1222): Инв. No. 4783-6, 5147-1, 5147-2, 5147-3, 5147-4, 5949-23, 6377-17
- Wei Year of Guangding (1223): Инв. No. 5223-3, 5949-18, 7893-5

The latest existing Tangut contract is dated to the Wei Year of Guangding (1223), a mere space of four years before the fall of the Tangut Empire and only two years before the Mongol army captured the city of Khara-Khoto.

If information such as the date and time of a given contract is referred to in previous contracts within the same batch, the Contract Parties customarily omitted a few words in order to avoid redundancy. If, for example, the contract was signed in the same year but in different months and days, then the signing parties had the option to omit the precise year and sexagenary cycle, thus simply noting down "same year, x month x day." If the contract was written both in the same month and in the same year, then the signatories would typically shorten it to "same month, x day." If multiple contracts were signed into effect on the exact same date, most would simply write, "same day." For this reason, there sometimes existed a series of contracts that begin with the same reference: "same day," suggesting that multiple parties took out grain loans at the same location, probably from the same creditor. One could imagine the many visitations by an endless stream of borrowers at the doorsteps of the rich, and the scene of multiple debtors going to and from, lining up, lingering, and departing the site. The omission or abbreviation of references to date and time has its pros and cons. It lends more convenience, but once the string of contracts is damaged, resulting in the loss of previous contracts, then there would be no way to ascertain the precise time as listed in a given contract.

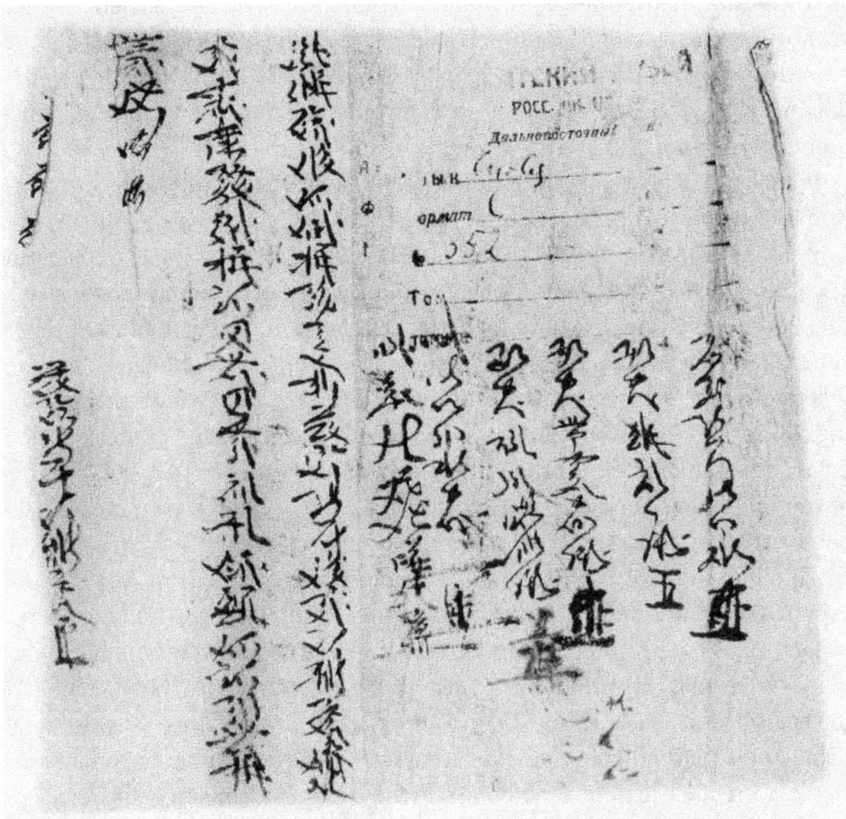

FIGURE 123 Инв. No. 5223-3: Wei Year of Guangding (1223) Account of grain loan fragment
Note: TN: Not manuscript 3586.

Occasionally, however, contracts that come later may fill in some badly needed information. In general, the Tanguts take out grain loans in the spring and the summer. Thanks to the higher altitude of Khara-Khoto and the cooler temperature of its continental climate, the Tanguts here sowed in the spring and harvested in the autumn. The interlude between spring and autumn was the time of shortage in supply, depletions in the granary, and lack of income. Whilst some loan contracts were signed in the last month of the previous year, at the earliest, most were negotiated from the second to the fifth month of the year.

2.1.4 The Identity of the Borrowers

In the Tangut tradition, the contracting parties in a financial loan or transaction were referred to as "the ones who set up the document," i.e. the signatories to a legal contract. In a monetary loan contract written in Chinese characters, in the Khara-Khoto document Инв. No. 7779A from the Fifteenth year of Tiansheng, a signatory by the name of Langna refers to himself as "the one who sets up the words." It is safe to assume that "the one who sets up the document" and "the one who set up the words" are interchangeable and customary translations.

In the technical legal language of Tangut grain loan accounts and contracts, "the one who sets up the document" refers to the party which initiates the contractual transaction, i.e. the Tangut poor who actively sought to take out a loan to alleviate hunger and poverty, the lack of seeds for the sowing season, and literally the dearth of foodstuff for subsistence. The names of these contract-initiators appear twice in a standard contract. The borrower's name first appears at the beginning of the contract, immediately after the time of the contract. Then again, it is featured a second time at the end of the contract, below the main content of the document and where the borrower signed his or her own name, in addition to a stamp. At the second appearance of the debtor's name, it was acceptable, if not customary, to omit the family name.

Although most of the documented debtors were Dangxiang Tanguts, the overall demographics of Tangut borrowers were anything but homogeneous. In fact, the Khara-Khoto economic records exhibit a robust ethnic heterogeneity. As the majority ethnicity in Western Xia, the Dangxiang Tanguts refered to themselves as 𗼇𗟲 (Minyak), or Fan (番) in Chinese. Most Tangut family names were bisyllabic 'compound surnames.'[37] A large number of Tangut borrowers were identified by their names in the contracts: Zhiyi in Инв. No. 4079-6(2); Mingni in Инв. No. 4384-7(2); Mingbu in Инв. No. 4762-6(2); Qiluo in Инв. No. 5147-1(1);[38] Jili in Инв. No. 5870(1); Pingshang in Инв. No. 5870(13); Weili in Инв. No. 5870(16); Xiyu in Инв. No. 5870(17); Yepu in Инв. No. 5949-27(2); Yehe Инв. No. 5949-28(2); Luopu in Инв. No. 5949-23(1); Weiyi in Инв. No. 7741-1(3); Jili "The Benevolent Dog" in Инв. No. 7741-2(1); Guding in Инв. No. 8005/1(2), etc. The "Moshui" that appears in the Wuwei loan contract G31.004[6728] is also a Dangxiang Tangut name.

---

37 *Russian Collection of Khara-Khoto Manuscripts* 6, pp. 137–138; 10, pp. 39–69; Shi Jinbo, 1989; Nie, Hongyin; Shi, Jinbo. "Xixiawen Sancai Zazi Kao" [西夏文三才雜字考]: "A Study of the Assorted Characters of the Three Realms" in *Zhongyang Minzu Daxue Xuebao* [中央民族大學學報]: *Bulletin of the Minzu University of China*, issue 6, 1995, pp. 81–88; Li, Fanwen, and Nakajima, Motoki, "Computational Analysis of Tangut Literature Zazi," Research Institute for Languages and Cultures of Asia and Africa (ILCAA) at the Tokyo University of Foreign Studies, 1997, pp. 82–83 and 117–125.

38 *Russian Collection of Khara-Khoto Manuscripts* 14, p. 22. Only a part of the image, Инв. No. 5147–1 "Grain Loan Contract in the Wu Year of Guangding" is printed in that collection. A full image is supplied here.

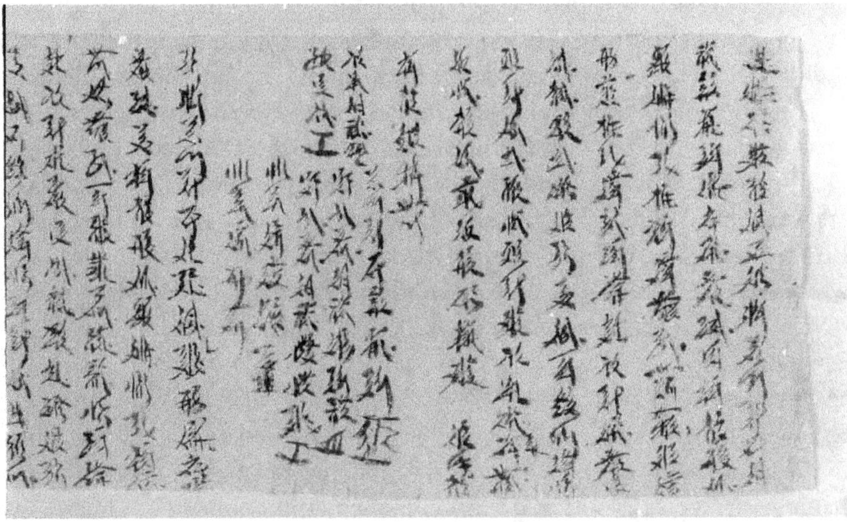

FIGURE 124 Инв. No. 5147-1: Wu year of Guangding (1222) account of grain loan

Some borrowers are easily identified as Han Chinese: Li Baiji in Инв. No. 4526(2); Yang "Qianqianquan" in Инв. No. 4696-3(2); Cao Suzhou in Инв. No. 4696-3–5; Wu Xianling in Инв. No. 5820(1); Hun "Shiyuesheng" in Инв. No. 5949-18(1); Luo "Wuyuebao" in Инв. No. 6377-20(2); Xu Wujin in Инв. No. 7893-20V, etc. Li, Yang, Cao, Wu, Hun, and Luo are all Han Chinese surnames. Certainly, the area that came under Tangut domination was inhabited by Han Chinese prior to the migration of the Dangxiang Tanguts. Throughout the imperial era of Western Xia, large Han Chinese populations subsisted on Tangut territories and for the most part engaged in agriculture. Some Han Chinese even held government offices. Both the Tangut and the Chinese editions of the *Assorted Words*, edited and published in Western Xia, feature long lists of Fan and Han surnames. The only difference lies in the order; whereas the Tangut *Assorted Words* places Fan names before Han names, the Chinese edition reverses that order. It is also evident and curious from the examples above that, under Tangut cultural influences, some Chinese parents resorted to multiple-character given names, beyond the convention of adhering to one or two characters. Qianqianquan (謙謙犬), Nazhengma (那征麻) and Wuyuebao (五月寶) are Chinese names given in the Tangut style. Typical Tangut given names include "The force of Helan [mountains]," "The Fortunate Mountain," "The Joy of the River," and so forth.

It often happens that both Fan and Han names appear across several contracts within the same batch of documents. The fact that ethnic Tanguts and the Han Chinese loaned from the same creditor shows that the ethnic groups dwelled in the same area, and even cohabited the same communities and neighbourhoods. The contracts, therefore, offer one more testimony to the tight and interlinked socio-economic exchanges between the Fan and Han populations.

The name of a borrower in the contract Инв. No. 7741-3(2) appears to be [Tangut] [ɣwej ɣwə ku.]. [Tangut] (Huihu, Uyghur) is, of course, the name of an ethnic group. A sizeable population of the Huihus lived in Western Xia, whilst others were close neighbours of the Tanguts. In the Tangut *Assorted Characters*, Huihu is also listed as one of the Fan surnames. This particular borrower, whose surname is Huihu, is probably also a medieval Uyghur ethnic. It shows that the Huihus also lived in the Khara-Khoto region towards the end of the Tangut era.

Инв. No. 8005-2(2), a contract with a missing first line, identifies the name of another interesting borrower. Despite the omission of his surname, the contract features his given name at the end of the document: [Tangut] [tśhji-ta~tśjow]. [Tangut] was also the name of an ethnic group: the Khitans. So, in all likelihood, this [Tangut] was also an ethnic Khitan, or at least related to the Khitans in family kinships. This contract therefore shows that the Khitans lived in Khara-Khoto under Tangut rule. Overall, it is easy to tell from Tangut contracts that the demographic in Khara-Khoto was multi-ethnic and diverse.

Some contracts also testify to the historical practice of inter-ethnic marriage. When the borrowers and co-borrowers appear to be spouses, one Dangxiang Tangut and the other Han Chinese, the evidence seems quite convincing. In the Инв. No. 4696-3(5), for exmaple, the main Contract Party is a Han Chinese by the name of Cao Suzhou, whilst the accompanying borrower (or the contract-receiver/co-Contract Party) is listed as his wife, Eqi (née) Youbao ("Treasure of the You year"). Eqi is obviously a Tangut surname. It often occurs that the Tanguts inserted the character for 'name' (née) into their compound surname in order to indicate the lineage of a woman, which she inherited from her family. The matrimonial bond of a Han Chinese husband and a Tangut wife, as shown on this contract, is evidence of inter-ethnic marriages in the Khara-Khoto area, or, indeed, throughout Western Xia.

The Liangs were a large presence amongst the major creditors in Khara-Khoto: [Tangut]? in Инв. No. 4596-1(2); [Tangut] [ljow mjijr śjow] in Инв. No. 4762-6(1); Liang "Force of Fortune" in Инв. No. 5147-1(3); Liang "Treasure of ?th Month" in Инв. No. 5870-2(2) and Liang [Tangut] [khjwi- wejr]; Liang (née) "the Puppet's Mother" in Инв. No. 5870-2(3); Liang "The Prosperous Tenth Month" in Инв. No. 5870-4(2); [Tangut] [ljow śja lhji. khjwi-] in Инв. No. 6377-6(1); Liang "the Treasure of Force and Merit" in Инв. No. 6377-16(2), amongst many others. No doubt, Liang is a major Han surname. But of course, two successive generations of matriarchal regency spearheaded by two Empresses Liang, an aunt and a niece, dominated Tangut politics during the reigns of Emperors Huizong and Yizong. Moreover, the Liang clans, especially the brothers and nephews of the empresses in the Liang family, occupied key positions of power in the imperial court. The Liangs advocated "Fan Customs" and sought to undermine "Han Customs," suggesting that they might not have had an inkling of sympathy for the Han Chinese cause.[39] Besides, the Tangut *Golden Fragments* lists Liang as a Tangut "Fan name."[40] Therefore, at least the Liang family at the epicentre of Tangut ethnarchism was ethnically Dangxiang Tangut. The only logical conclusion is that both Han Liangs and Tangut Liangs coexisted in Western Xia.[41]

With regard to gender identities of the borrowers, it should be said, first of all, that most of the Contract Parties were men, since a typical Tangut household was patrilineal and patriarchal. Some borrowers, however, were women. In the Инв. No. 4762-6(2), the borrower is [illegible] [mjij pu. zji-. zji śio] Mingbu (née) "Guide for the Son"; in Инв. No. 5870-2(3), [illegible] [ljow zji-. kə ta mja], Liang (née) "The Puppy's Mother"; in Инв. No. 7889(1) [illegible]? [tśjow zji-. mja ? zji]: Zhang (née) "Mother? Son." A considerable number of Tangut households were managed by and centred around women. Three families in Khara-Khoto household registers mentioned earlier (household 2, 5 and 13 in Инв. No. 6342) were all single-parent families without paterfamilias and run by an adult woman. Two of the female heads of the households were clearly labeled as child-rearing widows.[42] Mingbu the "Guide for the Son" and Liang the "Puppy's Mother" were both female heads of households in charge of their families. They could have also been adult widows left with heavy burdens of and authority over their families.

Most Contract Parties signed their names, without reference to their social status nor identity. There were a few, however, who revealed their identities in their signatures, oftentimes in a few characters preceding their own names. For example, in Инв. No. 4079-13(2), we have 'the one who sets up the contract' as [illegible] [phji_ gia kia xiwa~ khjwi- nja_] (Shijun: Jia "the ordinary black dog"); in No. 7892-2V(2), the borrower is listed as [illegible] [phji_ gia so. khjwi-] (Shijun: The Three Dogs); finally, the borrower in Инв. No. 7892-8(1) is [illegible] [njijr njij dzju. kie.] (Nupu, "The Gold Rain").

39 *History of Song*, Bk. 486, "Western Xia" Part II.

40 Nie Hongyin and Shi Jinbo, 1995 (a).

41 TN: Throughout the book (chapters 1, 4) 'ethnarch,' 'ethnarchy,' and 'ethnarchism' are my own coinages. With regard to the ethnic ambiguity of Liang, it can be said that towards the mid- and late-Tang periods, Dangxiang Tanguts who took up certain transliterated Chinese surnames share the same characters with ethnic Han Chinese names.

42 Shi Jinbo, 2004 (a).

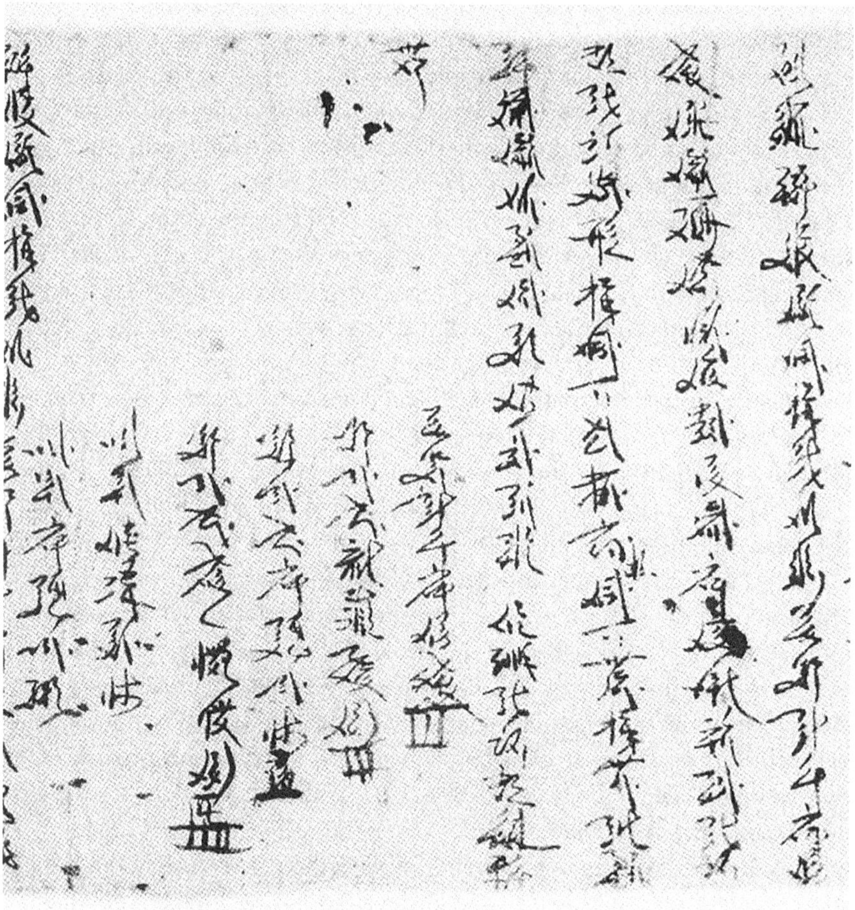

FIGURE 125 Инв. No. 4762-6 (1) (2): Yin year of Tianqing (1294) account of grain loan by Lady named Mingbu Zidao

Shijuns and *Nupus* formed a very special class of men and women struggling at the very bottom of Tangut social hierarchy. They were much lower in status than even ordinary commoners. *Shijuns* may have owned a bit of property, enough to establish and sustain a household, but they also relied on and orbited around their masters. Therefore, the Shijuns did not have 'personal freedom' in any strict sense of the term. They were more accurately described as serfs or semi-slaves.

Dunhuang contracts from the 8th to the 10th century often list the reasons, causes, and motivations for borrowers to take loans: "for consumable grains in a year without seeds" "for use, due to the shortage of grains," "for the lack of

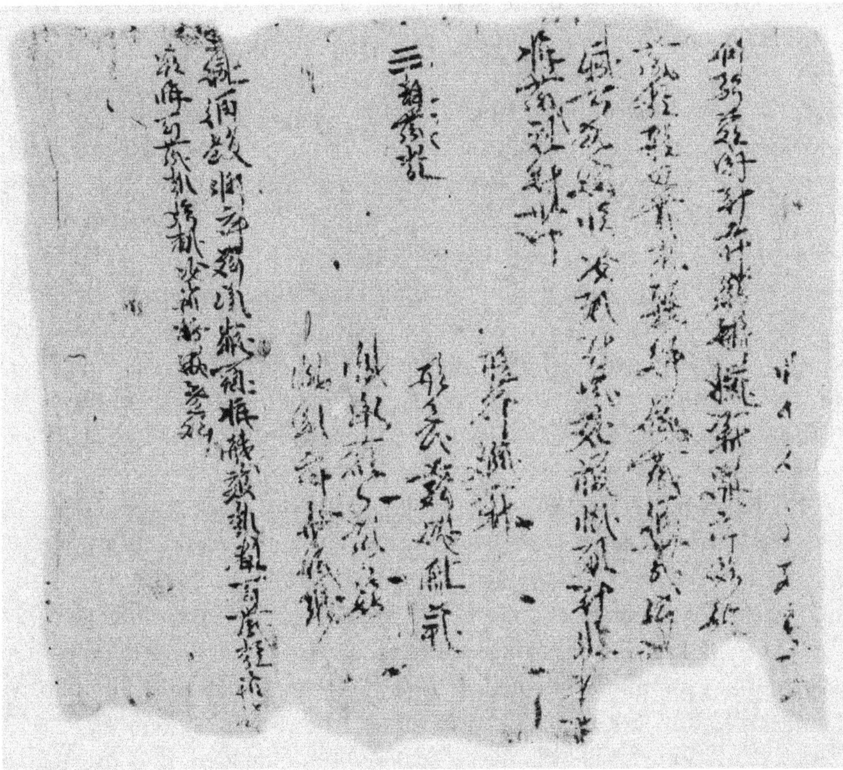

FIGURE 126 Инв. No. 7892-8: Account of grain loan by Nupu named Yujin

hu/dou"[43] "because of debt," etc. Khara-Khoto contracts in the 12th–13th centuries, however, recorded only the names of borrowers, not the reasons for the borrowing. Needless to say, most borrowers took out loans because they ran short of their food supply. It does seem, therefore, that an additional line of reference to their shortage of grains is simply redundant or serves as a mere matter of formulaic language in legal rituals. So, it is likely that in the progression of time, the self-evident reasons for taking loans became an increasingly less important part of the contract, up to a point of going almost defunct. The substance of the contract are the facts and terms of the loan. However, at any rate, the precise reasons for the loans are not difficult to infer, provided the time and season of the year. Each year, the Tanguts took out loans between the last month of the previous year and the first three months of the new year to sow seeds in their fields. Sometimes, they were also hard pressed by a shortage

43 TN: "without hu/dou" i.e. without grains.

of food. Whereas those who borrowed grains in the fourth and fifth months, in all likelihood, had daily consumption on their minds.

2.1.5 Identities of the Loaners

Needless to say, the creditors who owned enough to loan grains en masse in the barren months between two harvests came from some of the richest Tangut families in the area. In many loan contracts, the names of the contractors are followed by this line of reference to the loaner: "presently (from) xxx's place, borrow." Most of the creditors seem to be Dangxiang Tanguts: [Tangut characters] [zjwi. ·o ɣji-. njij wejr] in Инв. No. 5223-3; [Tangut characters] [zjwi. ·o śji-j lji-.] in Инв. No. 1570-2; [Tangut characters] [zjwi. ·o] ? [Tangut character] [wejr] in Инв. No. 4526(2); [Tangut characters] [·jaxwa] in Инв. No. 5949-18(1); [Tangut characters] [tśhji-j śjow parya śia~] in Инв. No. 6377-16(1); and [Tangut characters] [ŋwe mji tha ·wejr śji-j] in Инв. No. 8005-1(2) and Инв. No. 8005-2(2).

[Tangut characters] [zjwi. ·o], [Tangut characters] [·jaxwa], [Tangut characters] [tśhji-j śjow], and [Tangut characters] [ŋwe mji] are all Dangxiang Tangut names. [Tangut characters] (Weiming), in particular, was the royal name of the rulers of Western Xia. Dangxiang Tangut names have been identified in the signatures of both loaners and borrowers. It is manifestly the case that whereas some Tanguts kept on pasturing and herding, others settled—literally—for agriculture. A prominent example of an ethnic Dangxiang-Tangut creditor is "State Preceptor E," whose name appears on a loan contract in Wuwei.

The Liangs were a major family of loaners. The nine loans documented in Инв. No. 4696-1 and dozens of grain loan accounts in Инв. No. 4696-2, 3, 4, 5, 6, as well as contracts in 7892-4, 5, all feature the signature of a certain [Tangut characters] [ljow ne_w wejr], Liang "The Greatly Benevolent"; the three contracts in Инв. No. 5147-1, another three in Инв. No. 5147-2, 1 in Инв. No. 5147-3, and two in Инв. No. 5147-4 all list the loaner as Liang "The Iron Dog." These two figures were the most prominent creditors who offered loans on a frequent basis. They also penned contracts to lend grains to other Liangs, often at fairly high interest rates even though the borrowing parties were from the same extended family. One strange thing is that, whilst Liang "the Greatly Benevolent" loaned out grains in dozens of *dan* in the Mao Year of Tianqing (1195), in the Wei Year of Tianqing (1199), and in the Hai Year of Tianqing (1203), a "Liang 'the Greatly Benevolent'" seemed to have borrowed 4 *dan* of grains in the contract 7741(19), dated to the Yin Year of Tianqing (1194). There is no way to ascertain whether the borrower "Liang 'the Greatly Benevolent'" was the same as the loaner. If it was the same person throughout, then the next question is: how did he turn it all around in a year, from someone who took out loans to a creditor of grains?

The contracts also reveal eye-catching commercial activities of Buddhist temples. It turns out that these religious establishments were some of the

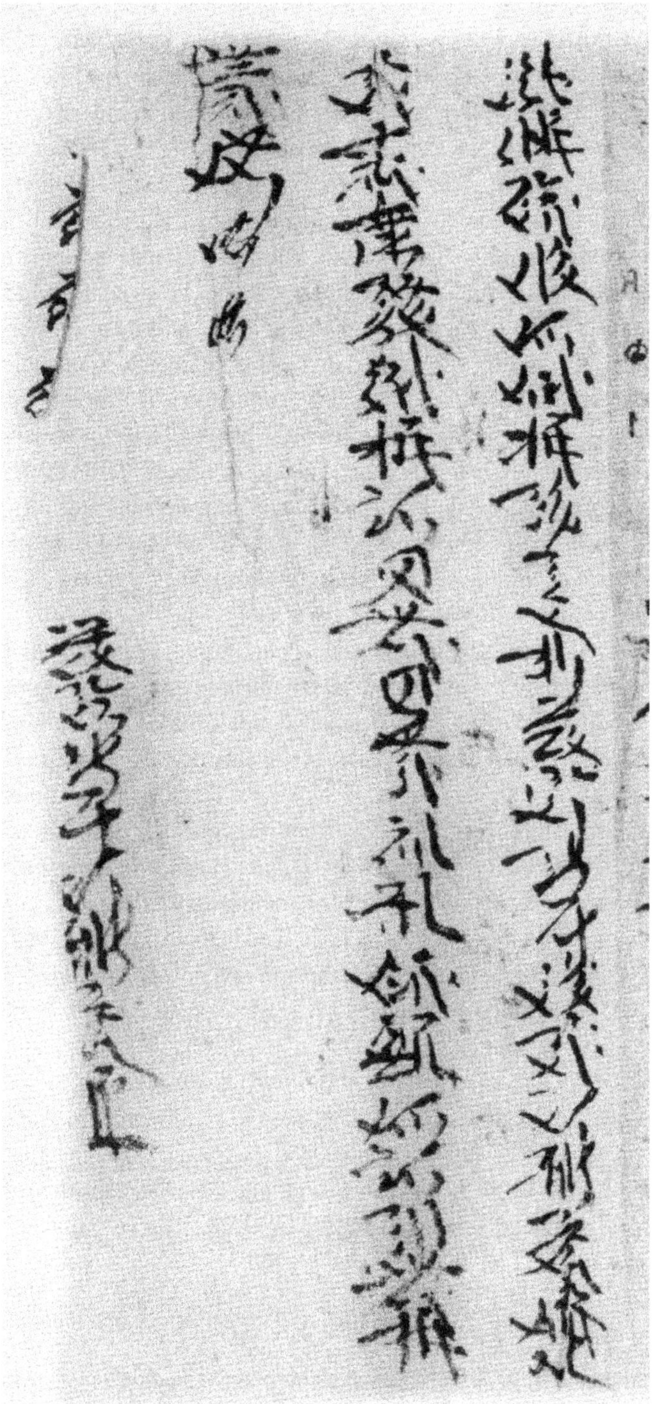

FIGURE 127
Инв. No. 5223-3: Wei year of Guangding (1223) account of grain loan (usurer: [illegible] the prosperous Vajra King)

largest loaners and usurers in Western Xia. Scores of accounts in Инв. No. 4384-7, 4762-6, 5870-1–9 feature two Liang-surnamed lamas from the Pudu Temple as the creditors. Both Liangs are referred to as "'hand-havers' of grains." In the technical legal terminology of the *Laws of Heavenly Prosperity*, "hand-having" is repeatedly referred to in the sense of 'taking by hand,' i.e. the right of laying one's hands on a piece of property. Therefore, both monks were either owners of the grains or authorised personnels delegated to manage the property. But since the contracts do make sure to mention the Buddhist Temple before the loaners' signatures, it is safer to bet that the temple was the actual legal owner of the grains. In fact, there was a long-standing tradition for Buddhist temples to warehouse grains. Many creditors identified in the Dunhuang loan contracts are temples, such as Yongshou Temple, Yongkang Temple, Lingtu Temple, etc. There is a "State preceptor E" in a Wuwei contract. A "state preceptor" was a high-ranking Buddhist monastic, oftentimes also given an honorary title of the "Department of Merit" in the state apparatus.[44] "State preceptor E" not only profited from usuries but charged extremely high interest rates. The exploitative economic activities of the monks form a sharp contrast to the Buddhist teachings of universal charity and benevolence.

At any rate, Buddhism was the most popular religious faith in Western Xia. It was championed by the Tangut royalties and greatly promulgated throughout the empire. Everywhere, a vast number of monks occupied a plethora of temples and pagodas. Monasteries benefited from tax exemptions, and temples occupied lands otherwise suited for cultivation by Tangut farmers. Since many Tanguts chose to enter monastic life, the government eventually resorted to setting a quota on Buddhist conversions in order to curb the growth in monastic population.[45] A statistical analysis of the contracts shows that the Buddhis temples were the main and largest force in the army of creditors. The vast presence of Khara-Khoto temples in usurious loans reveals how the monastics exploited famines and other economic crises to extract surplus profits from the local poor.

Surprisingly, a number of creditors are identified as *Shijun*, or Tangut semi-slaves. In several contracts, such as the 38 pieces of contracts in Инв. No. 4696-3, grains were loaned out by "*Shijun* Wu Heicheng." And in Инв. No. 6377-20(2), despite the suboptimal legibility, the same *Shijun* seems to also be the loaner in this contract. How could a *Shijun*, himself at the very bottom

44 Shi, Jinbo. *Xixia Fojiao Shilue* [西夏佛教史略]: *A Brief History of Tangut Buddhism*. Ningxia People's Press, 1988, pp. 143–146.

45 *Revised Laws of Heavenly Prosperity* 11, "Constructions and Renovations of Temples for Buddhist and Taoist Monastics," pp. 407–410.

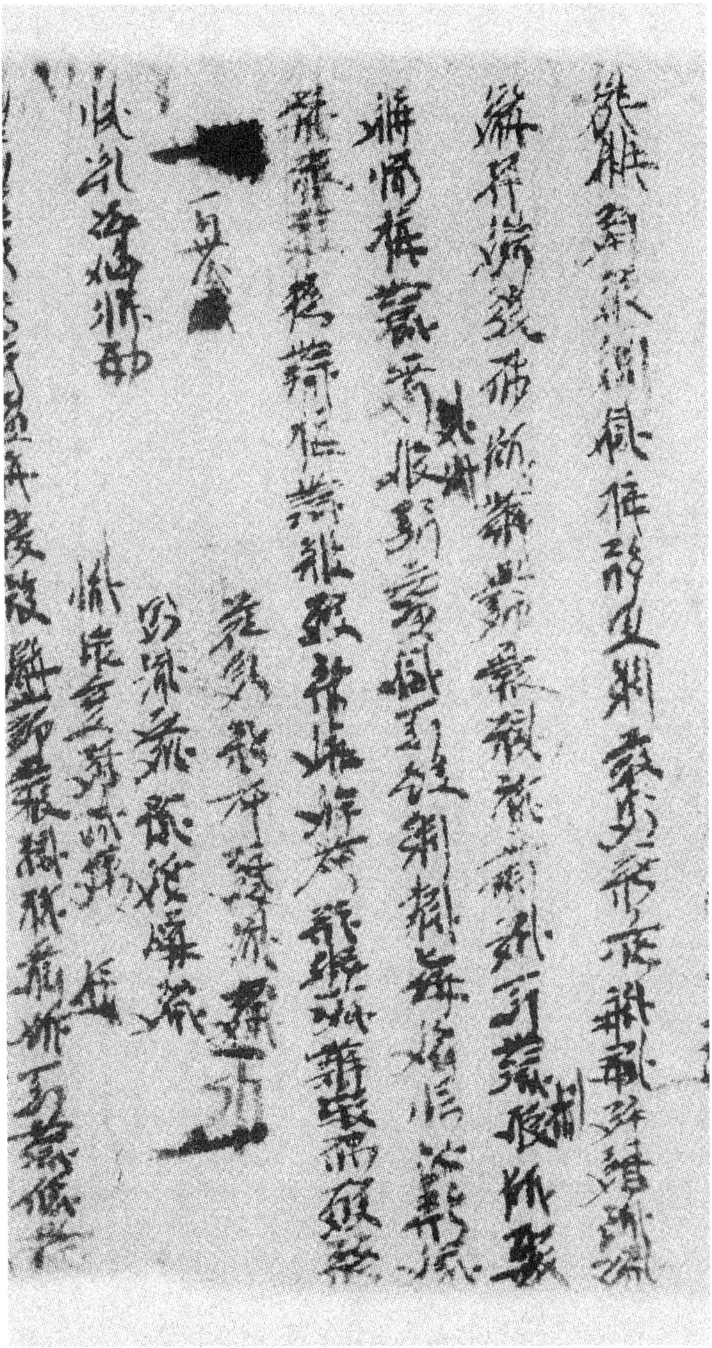

FIGURE 128 Инв. No. 4696-6: Shen year of Guangding (1212) account of grain loan (creditor: [illegible]; Shijun: Wu Heicheng)

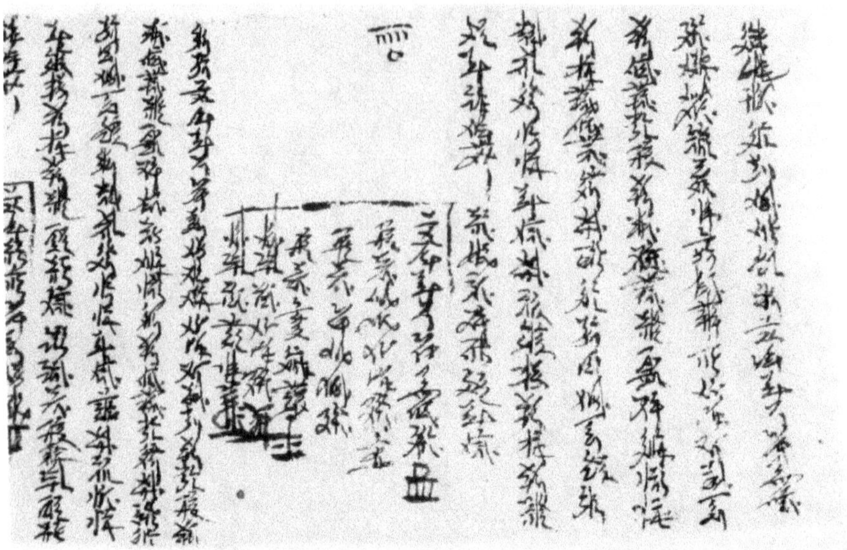

FIGURE 129 Инв. No. 6377-16: Mao year of Guangding (1218) account of grain loan (usurer: [Tangut], dealer: [Tangut])

level of social hierarchy, offer loans to others? An answer lies in Инв. No. 4696-6, a grain loan account in the Shen Year of Guangding (1212). It turns out that, one piece of contract in the long scroll records the full title of the loaner: "the 'holder' of the granary of Liang 'the Greatly Benevolent': *Shijun*, Wu Heicheng." That is, Wu was the keeper of Liang's granary. So, it is unsurprising that the grain loans were offered under his names, even though the property was owned by Liang. In other words, the Shijun acted as an agent or representative, on behalf of his master and the owner of the grains.

Throughout the nine pieces of loan contracts in Инв. No. 4696-1, Liang 'the Greatly Benevolent' released the loans by signing his own name. Similarly, Инв. No. 6377-16(1) records that "At the [Tangut] [tśhji-j śjow parya śia~]'s, from the actual owner, from the [Tangut] [da kia ɣwie] loaned 1 *dan* 5 *dou* of wheat." In other words, the grains were owned by [Tangut] [tśhji-j śjow parya śia~] but loaned at the hands of [Tangut] [da kia śji-j]. The manuscript Инв. No. 6377-16(3), a grain loan contract in the Mao Year of Guangding (1218) states that "from *Shijun* [Tangut] loaned 2 *dan* of wheat," leaving no doubt that the agent who handled the loan is a semi-slave, *Shijun*. Likewise, the one said to have 'held' the grains in the Wuwei loan contract [Tangut] [parya śjow] was also such an agent, rather than the owner of the property.

Simpler contracts only recorded the names of the borrowers but not those of the loaners. These 'unilateral contracts' are signed by one party but preserved at the hands of the opposite party. The creditors in contracts Инв. No. 5949-22, Инв. No. 5949-27-1, Инв. No. 5949-27-2, and other contracts all chose not to sign their own names.

2.1.6 Types and Quantities of Grains in the Loans

Most of the grains referred to in the Khara-Khoto grain loan contracts are either "𗐱" [lhji.] (wheat) or "𗍥" [dza] (assorted, coarse grains). Tangut diet included wheat, barley, grains, millet, beans, and some rice. The residents of Khara-Khoto could not really enjoy rice. But apart from that, all other types of crops grew in the area. Most of the Khara-Khoto agricultural tax accounts referred to either fine wheat and coarse grains, or 𗐱 [lhji.] (wheat) and 𗏁 [śjij] (barley), such as in Инв. No. 4808. The contracts show that most borrowers took loans of coarse grains. Others borrowed barley, proso (Инв. No. 7741-2(3), Инв. No. 7741-6(2), Инв. No. 7741-7(1)), or foxtail millet (Инв. No. 5870-2(1), Инв. No. 7741-2(2), Инв. No. 7741-6(3)). The loan in Инв. No. 4762-6(4) is 3 *dan* of wheat, 3 *dan* of coarse grains, and 1 *dan* of foxtail millet. The contract in Инв. No. 5870-2(1) refers to 6 *dan* of coarse grains, 1 *dan* of wheat, and 1 *dan* of foxtail millet; Инв. No. 7741-2(3) refers to 4 *dan* of wheat, 4 *dan* of coarse grains, and 2 *dan* of foxtail millet. The fact that coarse grains and foxtail millet are mentioned separately and side-by-side in these contracts shows that the Tanguts did not count foxtail millet as coarse grains.

In the Инв. No. 7741-1(3), a borrower took out "a loan of 3 *dan* of wheat, 7 *dan* of coarse grains," but at the end, the numerical notations show 6 *dan* of barley, 1 *dan* of proso millet, and 3 *dan* of wheat. This shows, in the contrary, that the Tanguts considered both barley and proso millet as a type of coarse grain. Given existing knowledge of Tangut contracts, the Tanguts never referred to loans of either barley or proso millet along with "coarse grains" within the same contract. It points to the high probability that the "coarse grains" as a collective term refers to both types of crops, or a mixture of the two. But the Tanguts listed both barley and proso millet separately within the same contract, instead of a collective reference to "coarse grains." In (3) and (4) of Инв. No. 4762-6, for example, the loans are "4 *dan* of wheat, 4 *dan* of barley, 1 *dan* of proso millet" and "3 *dan* of wheat, 3 *dan* of barley, 1 *dan* of proso millet." The contract fragment in Инв. No. 3586 specifies that the loan of "cereals and wheat" was to be repaid in the amount of "coarse and refined grains, 6 *dan* 3 *dou*." Since the Tanguts considered wheat as 'refined,' the reference suggests that cereals might have been counted as "coarse."

The grain loan contract in Инв. No. 5949-22(1) notes "grain principle [of the loan]: 3 *dan* of coarse grains, 2 *dan* of wheat; [repayment of] principle and interests: altogether 7 *dan* 5 *dou*." With regard to the total sum of 7 *dan* 5 *dou*,

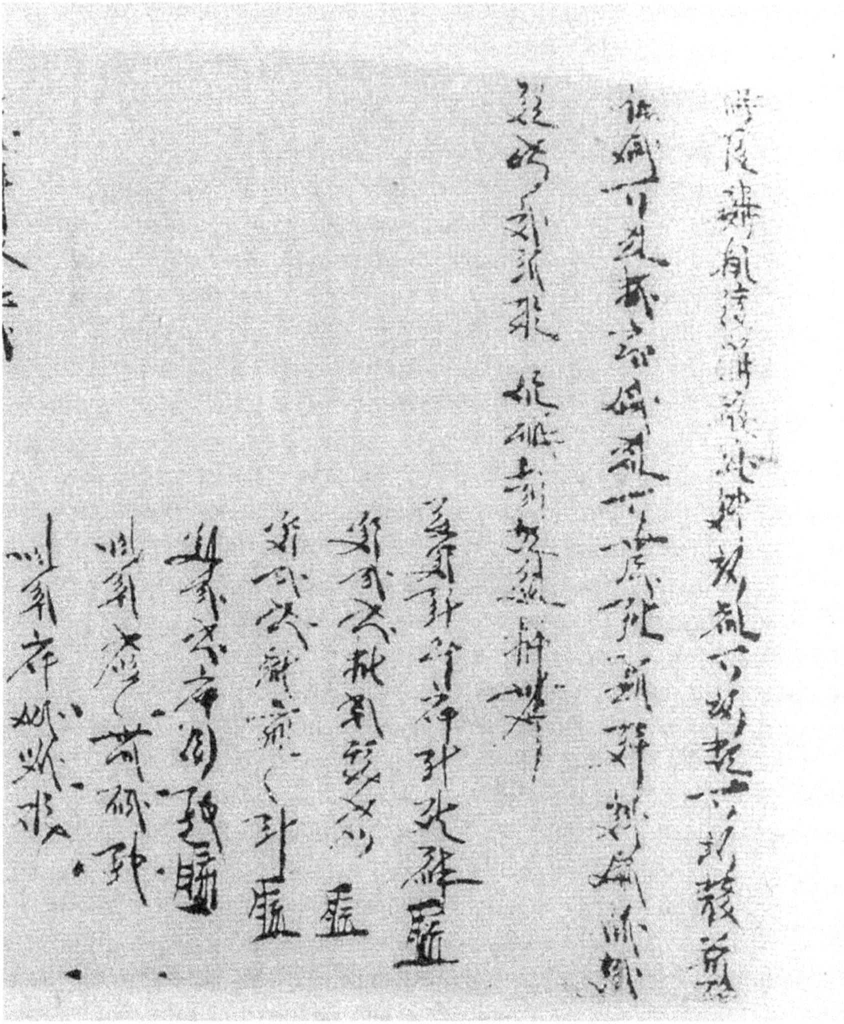

FIGURE 130 Инв. No. 5870-2: Yin year of Tianqing (1194) account of grain loan

the contract does not record the fine vs. coarse grains separately. But it is assumed that the actual repayment would be delivered in terms of both coarse grains and wheat, given the different prices of the two crops.

The grain loans recorded in Tangut contracts vary greatly in size, from a few *sheng* or 1 *dou* to several or a dozen *dan*. The amounts of grains loaned in the 5 pieces of contracts in Инв. No. 4696-5 are 3 *dou*, 2 *dou*, 3 *dou*, 5 *dou* 5 *sheng*, 5 *dou* 5 *sheng* of coarse grains; in a total of 23 contracts in Инв. No. 4696-6: 3 *dou* 5 *sheng*, 1 *dou*, 1 *dou* 5 *sheng*, 1 *dou* 5 *sheng*, 1 *dan* 5 *dou*, 3 *dou*, 1 *dan* 5 *dou*, 1 *dou* 5 *sheng*, 2 *dou* 5 *sheng*, 7 *dou* 5 *sheng*, 3 *dou* 5 *sheng*, 7 *dou*, 3 *dou*

5 *sheng*, 3 *dou*, 5 *dou*, 1 *dou* 5 *sheng*, 2 *dou* 5 *sheng*, 4 *dou* 5 *sheng*, 3 *dou* 5 *sheng*, 1 *dou* 5 *sheng*, 1 *dou*, 5 *dou* 5 *sheng*, 4 *dou* 5 *sheng* of coarse grains. For the most part, a smaller loan was less than 1 *dou*, and the largest was no more than 6 *dou*. Only 2 loans exceeded 1 *dan*. Therefore, most Tangut loans were, on the whole, 'micro-loans.'

In rare occasions, however, the loans were in great quantities. The total amount of 8 grain loans by Lüzini in Инв. No. 4596 reached 29 *dan* 7 *dou*. Инв. No. 4696(1–5) likewise contains 8 loans by 𗼃𘋩𗥤 [ljow ne_w wejr], which number up to 43 *dan* 5 *dou*. In Инв. No. 4696(6–7), there are 24 loans, in the amount of 15 *dan* 6 *dou* 3 *sheng*. And in Инв. No. 7892-7(1)–(6), 21 contracts, loaned out by Liang and mostly written in simple formats (19 loans with clear indications of the loan size), recorded up to 8 *dan* 6 *dou* 8 *sheng* of grains. The smallest loan was 1 *dou* or 5 *sheng*, such as in Инв. No. 7892/7 & 8. In 48 times, 𗼃𘋩𗥤 [ljow ne_w wejr] loaned out a total of 67 *dan* 8 *dou* 1 *sheng*. The average loan was the size of 1 *dan* 4 *dou*. As of now, it is impossible to ascertain without further research whether 𗼃𘋩𗥤 "the Greatly Benevolent," was monastic or not.

The contracts make it clear to historians that in Western Xia, most grain loans were offered by temples. In Инв. No. 5870(1), for example, Pudu Temple loaned out 10 *dan* of wheat and 4 *dan* of barley. In 19 pieces of contracts, the temple offered a loan of 129 *dan*, 9 *dou*, and 5 *sheng* in total. On average, each borrower owed a bit more than 6 *dan* and 8 *dou*. The largest loan was 15 *dan* of wheat and 16 *dan* of coarse grains, totaling to 31 *dan* of grains. The smallest was merely 1 *dan* of grains. The one who took out the largest loan was called 𗼃𗪘𗹦, who signed the contract on the first day of the second month. He was either in grave shortage of subsistence at home or in desperate need of a large quantity of seeds for the sowing season. He probably took the loan out on behalf of a large farming family, which would have had a large household and sizeable ownership of land. The 20 loans documented in the Инв. No. 7741 contracts, also offered by the Pudu Temple, amount to a total of 147 *dan* of grains. Pudu Temple is also the listed creditor in the seven contracts in Инв. No. 4384-7. Only two pieces survive, which show a loan of 6 *dan*. All the 41 pieces of contracts in three registers were signed by Pudu Temple within the span of the Yin Year of Tianqing (1194). In total, the temple loaned out 282 *dan* 9 *dou* 5 *sheng* of grains. This is only a scratch of the surface because these are only the contracts that happened to have survived. As for how much loans the monks at the Pudu Temple offered in total within that year, there is no way to ever know. But here, it is telling that each single loan is considerable in size: an average of 6 *dan* and 9 *sheng* per loan, up to five times more than the average loan offered by 𗼃𘋩𗥤 [ljow ne_w wejr], "the Greatly Benevolent."

For a minority of rich temples and families to persist in the lucrative business of offering usurious loans, there must have been a majority of the Tangut poor in a perennial shortage of grains. Song chronicles made sure to mention the plight of food shortage in Western Xia:

> The northwest suffers a shortage of the five grains. Whenever wars break out, the provision of grains is limited to barley, the *bi* beans,[46] abutilon,[47] and the sort. The people in that area consume the stems of *guzi* flowers[48] and *jianpeng* seepweeds[49] in the spring; seedings of Cistanche herbs[50] and little *wuyi*[51] in the summer; *xijizi*,[52] *dihuang* leaves,[53] *dengxiang* grass[54] in the autumn; 'sandy onions',[55] wild chives,[56] *jushuang*,[57] grey *tiao* grass,[58] white mugwort,[59] *jiansongzi*[60] in the winter, as a means of subsistence at the turn of the year.[61]

The image of Tangut commoners feeding on assorted wild herbs all year long is probably a slight exaggeration. However, given the rates, terms, and amounts of grain loans in Khara-Khoto contracts, it is obviously true that a significant

46 TN: 蓽豆 is different from *piper longtum*.

47 TN: for the lack of a better translation for 青麻.

48 TN: 鼓子蔓 most probably refers to the tenderer seedlings or stems of 鼓子花 or a close relative of it, within the Convolvulaceae ('morning-glory') family. Some botanical and medical journals list it as *Calystegia silvatica subsp. orientalis*. Historically, the plant was common in northwestern China. Nowadays, it is very rarely consumed as vegetables.

49 TN: These days, 碱蓬 (*Suaeda glauca*) weeds are still consumed as vegetables in China.

50 TN: 苁蓉 (Cistanche deserticola) a type of Cistanche in the family of Orobanchaceae, still a medicine and delicacy, known as a specialty of Hotan and the Alxa League.

51 TN: There are two types of Wuyi (蕪荑), large and small. It is processed from the seeds of *Ulmus macrocarpa* (*fructus ulmi macrocarpae preparatus*).

52 TN: It is unclear what 席雞子 is, other than a type of egg or a herb, probably halophyte.

53 TN: 地黃葉: leaves of *Rehmannia glutinosa* (Gaetn.) Libosch., a key herbal medicine.

54 TN: 登厢 is a type of grass that grow in sandy areas of nothwestern China. Both the grass and the seeds are edible.

55 TN: 沙蔥 (*Allium mongolicum*), also known as 蒙古韭, is a type of wild onion that grows in northwestern China, Inner and Central Asia.

56 TN: Chinese chives (*Allium tuberosum*).

57 TN: 拒霜, or 木芙蓉 (*Hibiscus mutabilis Linn.*).

58 TN: I take 灰莜子 to be, instead of a type of mildly poisonous medical herb known otherwise as 龍葵草, an edible herbal grass: 莜, that is pronounced *tiao* or *diao*.

59 TN: 白蒿 (*Herba Artimisiae Sieversianae*) is edible and commonly used as medicine. It is similar to *Artemisia argyi* (silvery wormwood).

60 TN: 碱松子 is most probably a halophyte plant.

61 Zeng Gong, *Long Ping Ji*, Bk. 20, "The Barbarians [夷狄傳]: The State of Xia [夏國]."

proportion of the population suffered constant shortage of food and the general hardship of life.

2.1.7 Interests and Interest Rates in Grain Loans

All Tangut loan contracts thus far identified were contracts of personal loans with interests, which detail the amounts of the principle and interests, sometimes even the total sum to be repaid by a certain date. In comparison and contrast, most of the Dunhuang grain loan accounts and contracts only emphasise the repayment deadline and specify that an overdue payment would result in the principle multiplying beyond the due date. Whereas 7th-century contracts found in the Western Region document the interest rates in detail, they have a close resemblance to the Khara-Khoto contracts.[62]

The Khara-Khoto loans not only generated interests, but the interest rates were, for the most part, exorbitant. All the principles appear to be the basic amounts of grains taken out as a loan. But with regard to the interests, there seems to be three main ways of calculating the rate.

2.1.7.1 *Total Interest Rate, Based on the Principle*

For a grain loan that bears interests for three to four months, the interests in sum amounts to half of the principle. Some of the contracts refer to "change by a half," that is, to increase the repayment by 50% of the principle. Thus, the final repayment would be 1.5 times of the principle. In this case, a given contract would clearly document the principle amount and the interest rate as well as specify the due date by which the total sum was to be repaid, typically in the seventh or eighth month of the lunar calendar. This interest rate at 50% is found in Инв. No. 4596-1(1), a contract of 2 *dan* wheat that yielded a total repayment of 3 *dan*; in (3), the loan of 1 *dan* wheat and 1 *dan* coarse grains (2 *dan* in total) demanded a total repayment of 3 *dan*; in Инв. No. 4526(2), the borrower took out a loan of 5 *dan* coarse grains, with a promise to pay back 7 *dan* and 5 *sheng*; in Инв. No. 5147/1(3), the 1 *dan* of wheat yielded a total of principle and interests in the amount of 1 *dan* and 5 *dou* (1.5 *dan*); the contract Инв. No. 5223-4(2) documented a loan of coarse grains in the amount of 2 *dan* 8 *sheng*, whereby the debtor was under obligation to repay 4 *dan* 3 *dou* 2 *sheng*, as a total sum of both the principle and the interests. The Инв. No. 5949-41(1) effectuated a loan of coarse grains in 8 *dou*, which resulted in a repayment of

62 Trombert, Éric. *Le crédit à Dunhuang—Vie matérielle et société en Chine médiévale*. Paris: Collège de France (*Institut des hautes études chinoises*), 1995.

1 *dan* and 2 *dou* in total; the Инв. No. 8005-3(2) documented a loan of 1 *dan* 5 *dou* of wheat that required a repayment of 2 *dan* 2 *dou* 5 *sheng*. All the examples above belong in the category of 50% interest rate. This rate was extremely high for a short-term loan of three to four months.

And yet, even higher interest rates have been identified. According to a piece of contract fragment in Инв. No. 2158, a borrower took out a loan of wheat in 2 *dan*, bearing an interest of 6 *dou* per *dan*. By the time the total repayment was due, he had to pay back 3 *dan* and 2 *dou* of wheat, that is, at an interest rate of 60%. What is more, in Инв. No. 7889(1), the wheat loan in the amount of 6 *dou* was taken at the interest rate of 8 *sheng* per *dou*. A total repayment reached up to 1 *dan* and 8 *sheng*, at an interest rate of 80%. Likewise, the state preceptor E of Wuwei released a loan of 1 *dan* that charged an interest of 8 *dou*, which was also at a rate of 80%.

That, however, is not the end of the story. Interest rates reached up to 100% in Western Xia, similar to what is known as "doubling interest" (倍稱之息) in the Song Dynasty. In the Инв. No. 4696-1(1), a grain loan contract in the Mao Year of Tianqing (1195), the debtor borrowed a loan of wheat in 8 *dan* and was due to return precisely 16 *dan* of wheat, which was twice the amount of the principle and at an interest rate of 100%. Another example is the contract Инв. No. 4696-3(8), signed on the 25th day of the 4th month, whereby 1 *dan* of coarse grain was repaid in 2 *dan*; an additional 2 *dou* of coarse grains was due to be repaid with 4 *dou*. More astonishingly, these repayments, at the exorbitant interest rate of 100%, were due by the 1st day of the 7th month in the lunar calendar, a mere space of 2 months and a few days from the signing date of the contract. And in the Инв. No. 5949-19(3), whilst the principle was listed as 4 *dan*, 2 *dou*, and 5 *sheng* of wheat along with 10 *dan* and 4 *dou* of coarse grains, the due amount was 29 *dan*, 2 *dou*, and 2 *sheng*. This amount was very close again to an interest rate at 100%, which would have been 29 *dan* 3 *dou*. This discrepancy of 8 *sheng* was due either to miscalculation or to certain norms governing the conversion of fine grains to coarse grains.

It is also worth considering that although some loans were offered at the interest rate of 50%, the charge was much higher when taking into account the shorter time frame of the loan. For instance, in Инв. No. 5949/16(1), a loan of 8 *dou* coarse grains was offered on the 29th day of the 5th month. By the 1st day of the 7th month, a total of 1 *dan* and 2 *dou*, including both the principle and the interests, was due. If the interest rate for 1 month was 50%, then if the borrower had been in debt for just another month, he would have effectively been subjected to a 100% interest rate.

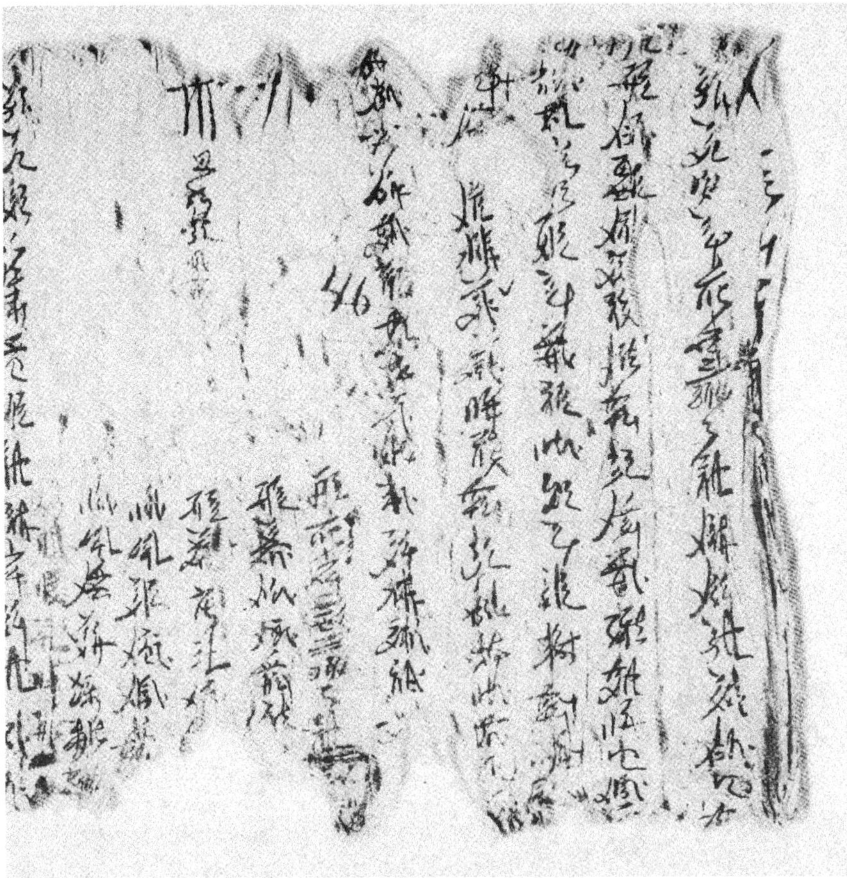

FIGURE 131 Инв. No. 4696-1: Mao year of Tianqing (1195) account of grain loan

2.1.7.2 *Monthly Interest Rate*

An interest rate charged on top of the principle grains on a monthly basis could also reach the 100% rate. Indeed, this was another way of imposing a 'doubling interest rate.' In the contract Инв. No. 4762-6(1), for example, the borrower took out a loan of wheat and barley, each in the amount of 10 *dan*, on the 29th Day of the 1st Month. The loan officially began on the 1st day of the 2nd month. Every month, the loan generated 2 *sheng* of interests per *dou* of principle, at a monthly interest rate of 20%. The contract notes that this arrangement would remain in force "until the interest equals the principle." Although the document does not supply a precise due date by which this was to be achieved, it is easy to derive from the terms that, at least in the progress

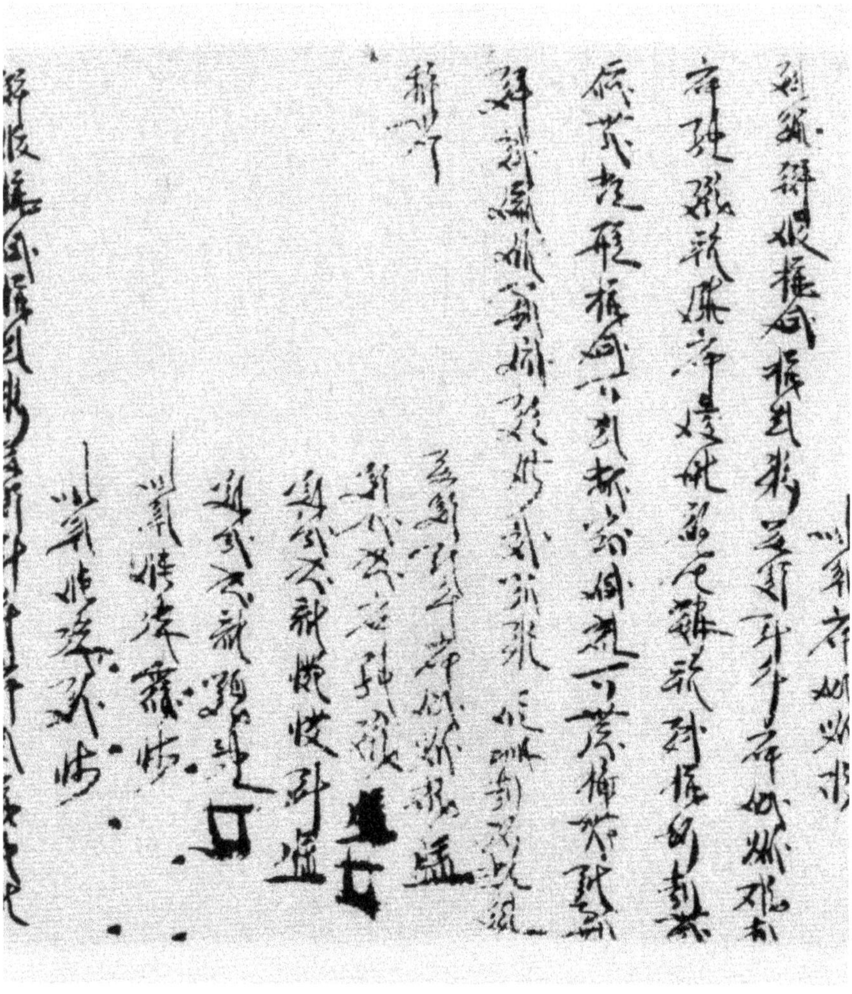

FIGURE 132 Инв. No. 5870-2(2): Yin year of Tianqing (1194) account of grain loan

of five months—that is, till the 1st day of July—the total interest rate would virtually become 100%. By July, the debtor would have to turn in 20 *dan* of wheat and barley each. Likewise, in Инв. No. 5870-2(2), a contract signed into effect on the 2nd day of the 2nd month, the borrower took out a loan of 2 *dan* 3 *dou* 5 *sheng* of wheat. From the 1st day of the 2nd month to the 1st day of the 7th month, a monthly interest of 2 *sheng* was applied per *dou* of the principle, at an interest rate of 20%. By July, the total interest reached 100% of the principle in the original loan.

Another example is a piece of loan contract unearthed in Khara-Khoto by the Institute of Archaeology of Inner Mongolia. The register "84H.F135:

W75/2026" is a grain loan contract signed on the 5th day of the 2nd month in the Year Yihai. The contract required the debtor to repay a monthly interest of 1.5 *dou* per *dan* borrowed., i.e. a monthly interest rate of 15%. If the loan bore interest for half a year, the rate would reach up to 90%. A full repayment by August would entail 2 *dan* 8 *dou* 5 *sheng*, effectively doubling the principle. This is an obvious example of a usurious loan.

A certain [illegible] was the borrower of 31 *dan* of grains, as listed in the contract Инв. No. 5870. The loan started in the 2nd month of the year, at a monthly interest rate of 20%. Both the interest and the principle—62 *dan* in total—were due back in the 7th month. With this arrangement, the interest rate also reached up to 100%.

2.1.7.3 *Daily Interest Rate*

Some loans bore daily interests out of the principle. In Инв. No. 5812-3(1), for example, the 1 *dan* and 5 *dou* of grains were to be repaid on the basis of "[illegible]" [dźja_ ɣa nji-_ ŋewr ·ja śji-j]—"1 *sheng* of interest per *dan* on a daily basis," in other words a daily interest rate of 1%. But in a progression of 100 days, the interest rate also reached 100%. Similarly, with a loan of 1 *dan* of coarse grains in Инв. No. 5812(2), the contract required "half a *sheng* of interest in five days," i.e. a daily interest of 1% (0.5 *sheng* of interest per 1 *dou* of grains in 5 days). In 100 days, the interest rate also reached 100%.

In some rare occasions, the interest rates surpassed 100%. The contract in Инв. No. 7892/8(3) recorded that "8 *dou* of interest for 7 *dou* of

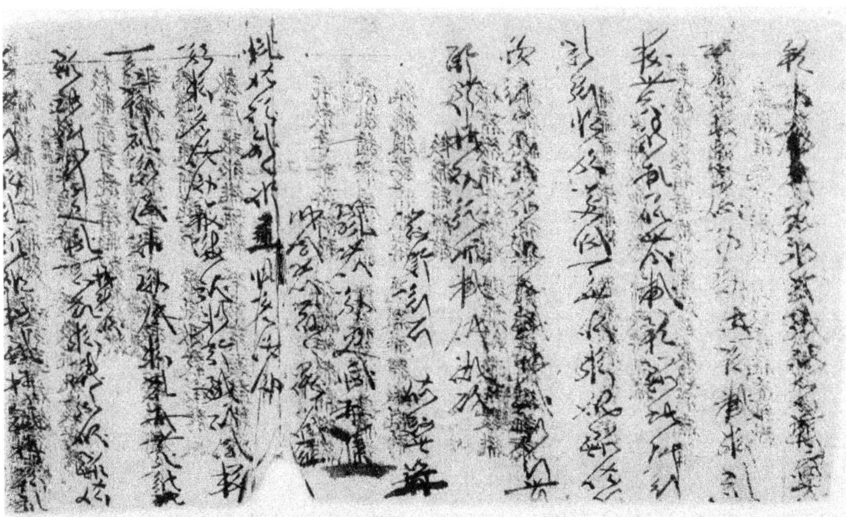

FIGURE 133 Инв. No. 5812-3(1): Account of grain loan

wheat," which suggests an interest rate of 114%. But according to the *Laws of Heavenly Prosperity*:

> Where the many release public or private wealth in the country as loans, with the principle in terms of grains, for each string(*min*) of cash, there may be an amount of interest under 5 mace; for each *hu* (*dan*) [of grains], there may be an interest under 1 *hu*; in such cases, interests may be charged on a voluntary basis, and should not exceed these limits.[63]

This law set the limits to both monetary and grain loans: A daily interest of 5 mace or less for each string/*min* of cash coins (daily interest rate: 0.5%; monthly interest rate: 15%); a total interest of 1 *hu* (i.e. 1 *dan*) or less for each *hu*/*dan* of grains, regardless of time. Such legislations put a cap on usuries, to the benefit of the borrowers. The Tangut laws also required that:

> With regard to the aforementioned terms of loans, aside from rendering clear the laws of generating interests from the principle taken out as the principle, it is necessary that with daily, monthly, and annual payments, or payments over the years whilst the principle is held in possession, as soon as the interest equals the principle, no one is permitted to exceed this amount. If a party receives more interest than this maximum according to the law, let a guilty office-holder be punished by the confiscation of a horse, and let a guilty commoner be punished by thirteen strokes. The extra amount of interest unlawfully charged should be duly returned to its lawful owner.[64]

This law underscored the due procedure of loans and interests. It stated that a grain loan may bear interests over days, months, and years, in a variety of rituals and formats. However, the creditor may not charge any surplus interest as soon as the cumulative interest equaled the principle—that is, as soon as the cumulative interest rate reached 100%. This regulation is, in fact, reflected in contracts of various types that circulated amongst the Tanguts. However, actual contracts were much more complicated than the straightforward demands of the law. In some contracts, the virtual interest rate charged had effectually soared beyond 100%. These contracts showed, on the one hand, that violation of the laws did occur, and on the other, that the laws were enacted for a reason. The Tangut laws went to great lengths to spell out the limits on

63 *Revised Laws of Heavenly Prosperity* 3, "Urging the Payment of Debt," pp. 188–189.

64 *Revised Laws of Heavenly Prosperity* 3, "Urging the Payment of Debt," p. 189.

usurious loan interests, the terms of redistribution of excessive interests back to the exploited borrower, and the penalties for an overly greedy creditor. All of these were legal measures that shield the debtors from undue interference and excessive economic domination by the creditors. Still, many of the helplessly impoverished opted for usurious loans for their own survival and at their own risks. High-interest usurious loans may have alleviated the plight of hunger and even death, but often times, the ahead-of-time consumption multiplied in the autumn. Most of the meager harvest went into the pocket of the creditors, leaving the peasants with little grains for subsistence. This vicious circle of poverty was often exacerbated by natural disasters, such as fire and famine, pests and pestilence, and other myriad causes of a bad harvest. If whatever surplus amount was not enough for seeding and consuming, the debtor would be further indebted in the following spring and summer. They once again took out loans in order to sow and eat. Therefore, for the Tangut poor, to take out a high-interest usurious loan was to 'drink the Zhen bird's poison to quench one's thirst' as the Chinese idiom goes. These loans often led to nothing but bankruptcy. To pay back the loans, peasants sold off their land and houses. These transfers of property further aggravated the wealth inequality of Tangut society and even caused social instabilities. The Tangut proverb, "In the second and third month, do not eat food on a loan; in the eleventh and last month, do not wear clothes on a loan," was a vivid testimony to the fear of exploitation at the hands of usurious loans.[65]

2.1.8 Terms of Payment and Default Penalties

There was only one growing season in the Khara-Khoto area, and the annual harvest was timed around the seventh and eighth months of the year. Therefore, most of the grain loan contracts also set a due date between these two months. Contracts were specific about the terms of repayment, and most loaners asked the debtors to return the principle and interests by the first day of either the seventh or the eighth month. The contract Инв. No. 5820-2, for example, required that "due date be the first day of the eighth month in the same year, when the debtor is obliged to gather and repay all the owned grains." The contract Инв. No. 5949-16 specified that "due date is set at the first day of the seventh month, when all the grains are to be gathered and repaid." The lines on due dates were usually followed by the terms of penalties in terms of delay or failure of repayment. There were two modes of punishment.

65 Chen Bingying. *Xixia Yanyu* [西夏諺語]: *Tangut Proverbs*. Taiyuan: Shanxi People's Press, 1993, pp. 13–14.

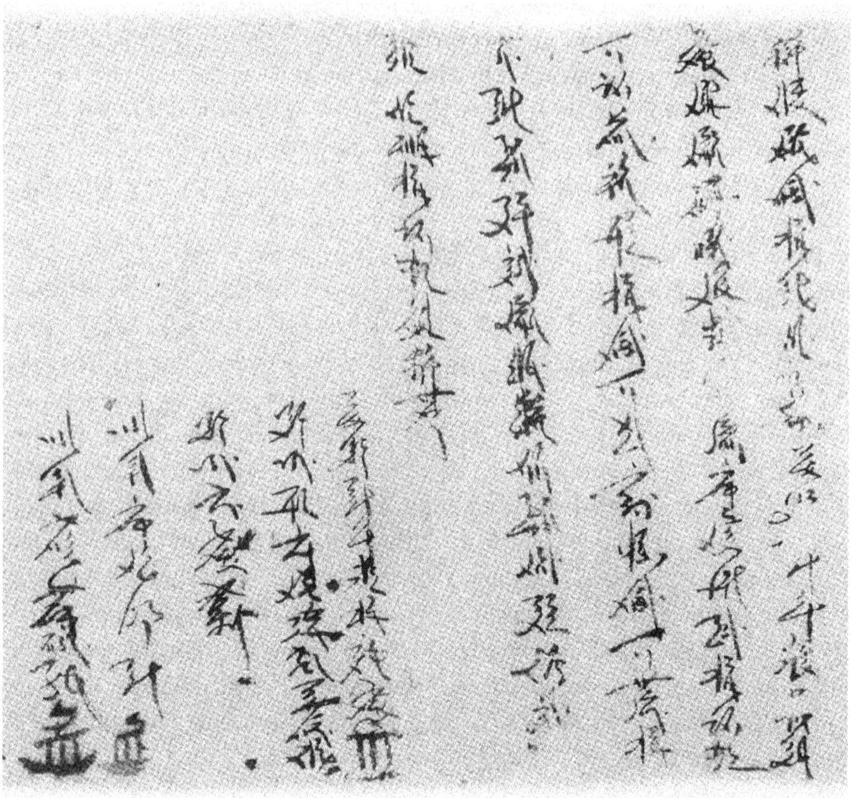

FIGURE 134 Инв. No. 4384-7(1): Yin year of Tianqing (1194) account of grain loan

The first was to penalise the borrower with extra grains, according to the size of the loan in question. The loan concerned in the document Инв. No. 4384-7(1) involved 2 *dan* of wheat and 1 *dan* of coarse grains. The contract required that "when the repayment is overdue, the penalty is 2 *dan* of wheat according to the laws; willing." That is, the borrower was willing to be subject to the penalty fee in accordance with laws.

In fact, the terms of penalties were set by the loaners, who took advantage of their ownership of grain surpluses protected by the laws. So there would be no other option for the debtor than to note down "willing" in the contract, regardless of their actual willingness and despite their reluctance. Likewise, in Инв. No. 4384-9(2), the debtor borrowed 2 *dan* of barley and 1 *dan* of coarse grains. By the contract, he had to pay "1 *dan* of wheat according to laws, in case of overdue repayment; willing." And in Инв. No. 5870(1), whereby the borrower took out a loan of 10 *dan* of wheat and 4 *dan* of barley, the contract stipulated that "in case of overdue repayment, the penalty is 10 *dan* of wheat according to the laws; willing." All these references, and many others, fall into the same category of penalty, which is set at a particular quantity.

Another approach to penalising overdue or unmaterialised repayment was to set a particular ratio, rather than a fixed amount. The contract Инв. No. 4596-4(3) states, for example, that "if the borrower does not show up past the due date, 2 *dan* of penalty fee is to be applied to each *dan* of unrepaid loan; if the debtor is incapable of furnishing this much, he is responsible for enlisting his own people to repay the sum; (debtor's) own mind is willing." In other words, overdue payment would result in 2 *dan* of penalty fee per 1 *dan* of loan. A thoroughly impoverished debtor would have had to divide the surcharge into chunks and implore others to repay on his behalf. Needless to say, the debtor's 'own heart' submitted to the rule. Similar terms of requirements were found in Инв. No. 5949-18 and other contracts.

The section on "Urging the Repayment of Debt" in the *Laws of Heavenly Prosperity* protected the interests of loaner and the rights of the creditor. The chapter opens with a straightforward call for coercion in urging for repayments:

> All the concerned parties are to press the debtors for the return of the principle and interests; in case of failure to repay, it is necessary to report the incident to the relevant bureau, in order that coercive search and investigation be adopted to materialise the repayment. In case of failed repayment of debt in the amount under 10 strings of cash, an office-holder is to be punished 5 strings; a commoner is to receive 10 strokes; for an amount of debt above 10 strings of cash, an office-holder is to be punished by the confiscation of a horse; a commoner is to suffer 13 strokes. In all cases, the debt is to be repaid in accordance with the requirement of law. Any attempt to deny an existing debt is strictly prohibited. Any violation of law in this regard is to be treated in the same category as the failure to repay. The principle is to be returned, and the debt to be repaid according to the laws.[66]

Terms of penalty are different for officeholders with social and political status and for commoners without privileges.[67] Whereas the elites were penalised by cash and horses, the commoners suffered the ferocity of lashes. After the 10 or 13 strokes, the criminalised remain obliged to repay the debt in full. The *Laws*

---

66 *Revised Laws of Heavenly Prosperity* 3, "Urging the Payment of Debt," pp. 189–190.

67 Shi, Jinbo. "Xixia de Zhiguan Zhidu" [西夏的職官制度]: "The Bureaucratic System of Western Xia" in *Lishi Yanjiu* [歷史研究]: *Historical Research*, issue 2, 1994, pp. 62–71.

of Heavenly Prosperity also made it clear that the party defaulting on the terms of a contract would be duly prosecuted:

> A party that thereafter reneged on the terms of the contract are to fulfil the obligations either to the public authority or to a private party; the repudiator of the terms, if an office-holder, is penalised by the confiscation of a horse; and if a commoner, by thirteen strokes.[68]

The second item in the laws of "Pressing the Repayment of Debt" offered some leniency to the debtor incapable of repayment:

> All the relevant parties who fail to repay their debt, and remain incapable of returning the sum after admission of their guilt, are to be given another 2 or 3 extensions of the deadline, according to their distance, so that they may procure more means of repayment, such as to repay by labour. But in case of repeated defaults, the debtors are to receive strokes of a certain number, calculated based on the size of the debt. In case of persistent default after three granted extensions, let the laws be strictly applied with no more leniency.[69]

The law was open to the possibility of repaying debt by labour. Yet, repeated defaults resulted in physical penalties. The maximum application of leniency was capped at three times. These measures of leniency were put in place, ostensibly out of a spirit of compassion but ultimately for the expediency of the creditors. They preferred fulfilling their economic interests to unleashing brute force for the pleasure of vengeance. Without some flexibility, it would be extremely difficult to receive the principle and interests at all. At any rate, it is not difficult to see that the reference to "overdue repayment penalised according to the laws" in the contracts was not a technical formality or empty words of deterrence. Rather, it was backed up by robust institutions of imperial criminal laws.

It is also worth noting that although the laws offer the option to repay debt by labour, this practice was not confirmed in the grain loan contracts found in Khara-Khoto. So, there is a slight mismatch between the law code and the contracts, in this wise.

Another point of interest is a comparison with the loan contracts in Dunhuang. The Dunhuang contracts deterred financial defaults by the threat

68 *Revised Laws of Heavenly Prosperity* 3, "Urging the Payment of Debt," pp. 189–190.

69 Ibid., p. 188.

of penalty fees multiple times greater than the principle: "to suffer the confiscation of familial properties, to repay the debt in terms of grains"; "to bear the confiscation of household properties and miscellaneous goods to repay the debt accrued in wheat"; "to suffer the confiscation of family properties, miscellaneous goods, and the cattle, etc."[70] These contracts warned the debtors of the prospect of suffering the coercive confiscation of their properties in cases of default. These documents even made specific arrangements on how properties were to be converted to cash and grains as well as how much was to be confiscated. These measures easily gave rise to disputes and conflicts. Moreover, it is not clear where the juridical power resided in judging, overseeing, and enforcing these procedures. Without thorough stipulations on these terms, it was difficult to enforce the contract by simply letting the process unfold between the creditor and the debtor, without giving rise to even graver conflicts. In general, Tangut contracts differed from Dunhuang contracts in that the former did not contain such challenging requirements. The *Laws of Heavenly Prosperity* also did not make reference to the forceful confiscation of properties in cases of default. But there is no doubt that the Tanguts mortgaged their livestock and even human beings in their contracts. Some of these legal documents provide detailed accounts of the items pawned and mortgaged: type and outlook, quality and quantity. Certainly, in cases of overdue payment or default, the creditor had every right to receive the transfer of these properties according to the terms set out in the contract. These preventive measures that involved the practice of pawning and mortgaging will be discussed later. But at least the reasonable anticipation of a property transfer into the hands of the creditor in lieu of debt repayment was more normative and easier to imagine than an opaque reference to a "confiscation of household properties." Perhaps this difference also speaks to the refinement of legal loopholes of earlier laws, from Tang to Tangut periods. Along with or as a result of the socioeconomic developments, medieval contract laws did evolve and improve over time. It is also found in the *Laws of Heavenly Prosperity* that:

> If the co-borrower cannot repay the sum either, it is still not permitted to pay the debt with these two parties' wives, daughters-in-law, or unmarried daughters. It is permitted, however, to pay the debt by their physical labour.[71]

70 *Dunhuang Economic Documents*, pp. 76–147.

71 *Revised Laws of Heavenly Prosperity* 3, "Urging the Payment of Debt," p. 189.

This stark prohibition of repaying debt by the borrower's and the co-borrower's female kins speaks to the historical practices of either selling women, or at least selling their labour for debt payment. Of course, the transaction of women was not absent in these historical periods and in societies where women occupied the lower status of social hierarchies. However, the Tangut law code explicitly prohibited the transaction of women, either for profit or for debt payment. It shows at once the existence of such commercial activities, and the strong measures adopted by the empire to stamp out this crime.

2.1.9 Signatures and Stamps of Concerned and Relevant Parties at the End of the Contract

The signatures and stamps of the principle and relevant parties at the end of a contract are critically important components of the legal procedure. Signatures and stamps endowed an effectual legal force to the contract as a document, thus guaranteeing the enforcement of the terms. Contracts without signatures and stamps were deemed ineffective. As for a certain number of Khara-Khoto contracts that do not show stamps and signatures, it is likely that they are drafts rather than official documents.

2.1.9.1 *The First to Sign and Stamp Is the Borrower*

Grain loan contracts usually begin and end with the stamps and signatures of the borrower, with the expression, "Contract Party ×××". The names could appear in full or only in the given name, thus omitting the family name. Elsewhere, the reference to 'Contract Party' is missing, replaced by "the one who repays the grains," i.e. the borrower. For example, this is evident in the manuscript Инв. No. 162-12, an account of grain loan fragment. There are also contracts that refer to the 'borrower,' such as in Инв. No. 4696/1(1)(2), etc. In Инв. No. 1570-2 and Инв. No. 7977-7, however, the borrower is listed as a 'formal borrower,' whereas his son was *de facto* the principle party in the loan.

2.1.9.2 *Signatures and Stamps of Borrower(s) and Other Liable Parties at the End of the Contract*

In order to doubly ensure the proper and prompt return of the principle and interest, the loaner sometimes also required, in addition to the stamp and signature of the debtor and family relatives, the name of "the borrower who receives the contract," "receiver of the contract," "the borrowing party" "hand-receiver of the loan contract," etc. These 'co-contracting parties' were quasi-guarantors, warrantors, or referees affiliated with the borrower. In cases where the debtor defaulted, died prematurely, escaped, or goes into exile, these co-contracting

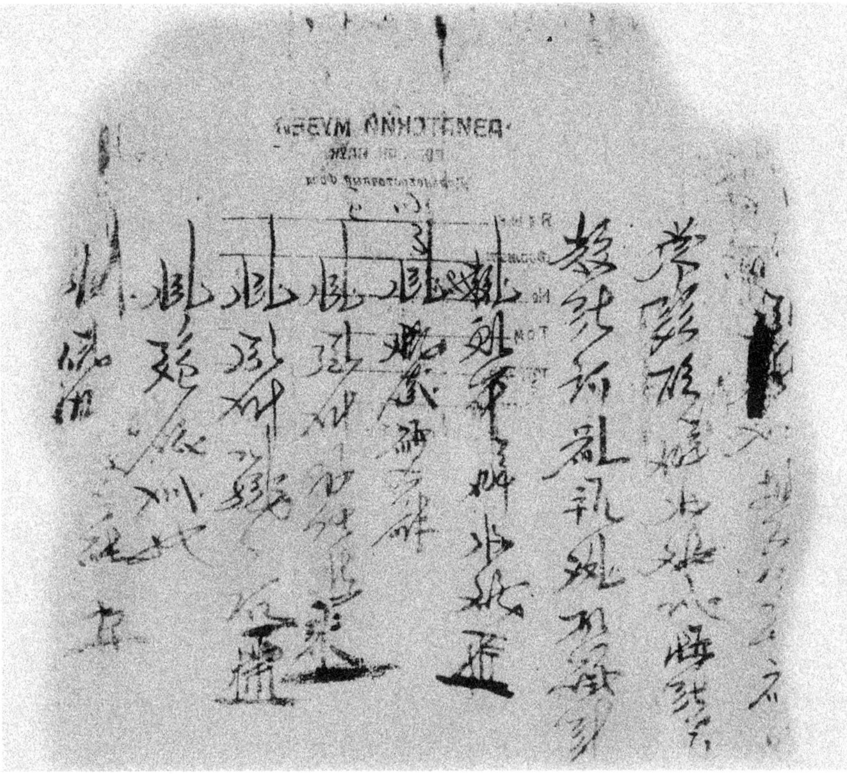

FIGURE 135 Инв. No. 162-12: Account of grain loan

personalities would shoulder joint and several liabilities in the context of the concerned contract.

There may be one or multiple co-Contract Parties. They were either wives, sons, or other kinsmen and relatives. In the manuscript Инв. No. 4596(1), an account of grain loan dated to the Chou Year of Guangding (1217), the name of the Contract Party is followed by [illegible] □□ [lhjwi dźjwi- gji bjij zjwi. ·o zji-. □□]: "co-borrower, wife: [illegible] [zjwi. ·o] □□." At the end of the contract Инв. No. 5870(13), the name of the Contract Party is followed by that of his wife, "co-receiver of the contract, wife: Liang the Joyful and Benevolent Treasure," a proof of the couple's joint liability. The Инв. No. 7741 (4) (6) (8) (9) (10) (11) (12) (13) (14) (15) (16) all feature the stamps and signatures of the Contract Parties' wives as co-Contract Parties at the end of the contracts.

Sometimes, the account of grain loan does not specify 'wife' as an affiliation at the end of the contract, but the spousal identity is surmised with some ease and safety. For example, the manuscript Инв. No. 954 features at the end of the contract a reference to "hand-receiver of the loan, Liang the Treasure

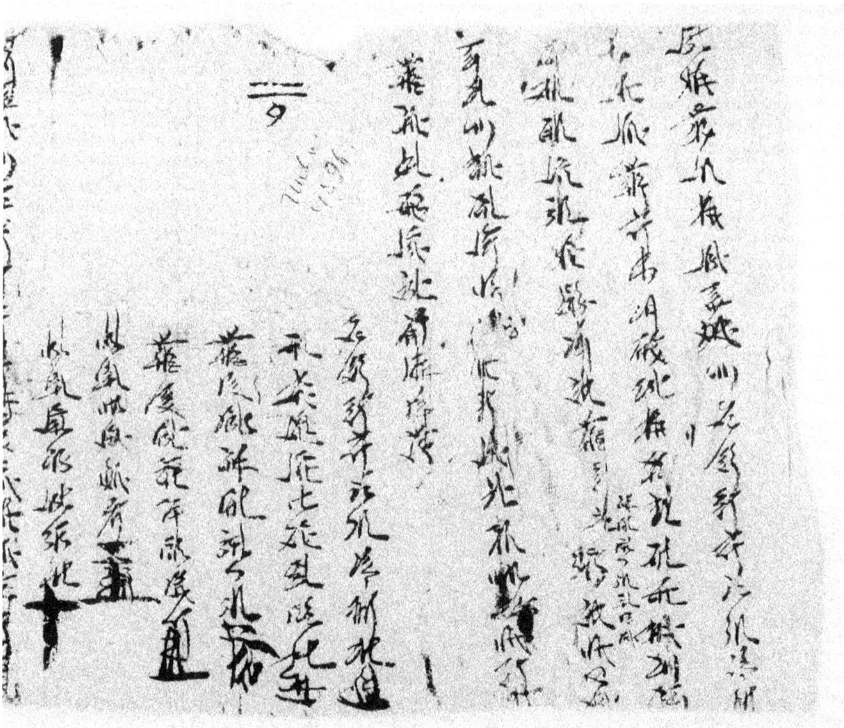

FIGURE 136 Инв. No. 4596(1): Chou year of Guangding (1217) account of grain loan

of the Benevolent Moon," who is most probably the wife of the principle Contract Party "Eyi the Puppet Mount." Similarly, the "borrower who receives the contract: Xishang Treasure of the Seventh Month" in Инв. No. 4384-7, the "Meina the Treasure?" in the Инв. No. 7741(18), the "receiver of the contract Ming? Brother's Guidance" in the Инв. No. 7741(1), may all be the spouses of the debtors. Dunhuang loan contracts feature fathers and sons, elder and younger brothers as guarantors, but curiously, not wives. The fact that the Tanguts relied on their wives as warrantors in formal contracts speaks to a relatively higher socio-economic-legal status of women within and beyond the domestic spheres of the household. Indeed, the prevalent practice of having professional housewives bear the legal burden of financial debt formed a sharp contrast to the Central Plains during the same period and to the diverse and dynamic Dunhuang area in the Tang Dynasty. But of course, this phenomenon could as well be an extended effect, if not a natural consequence of the historically higher status of women within the Tangut society.

In Инв. No. 5949-23(1), an account of grain loan dated to the Si Year of Guangding (1221), a reference to [illegible] [dźiow dźjwi- tji- gji rar mə lji-.]: "(co-receiver) of the contract: son Luo the Accomplished Treasure" is found after name of the principle Contract Party at the end of the contract. It clearly points out that the co-borrower with joint liability was the son of the principle Contract Party. The son's family name, however, is listed as "Luo" in abbreviation, rather than the fuller "Luoming" in his father's name. Naturally, when the father was no longer capable of full repayment, the son inherited the debt. This arrangement belongs with the historical legal tradition that is best summarised in the saying, "the son pays his father's debt."

The abbreviation, or even omission of the son's family name on the assumption that he shared the same name as his father, finds additional evidence and testimony in Инв. No. 4762-6(1). The stamps and signatures of the Contract Party is followed by the "co-receiver of the contract [Tangut] [parya ne_w]," whose relationship to the debtor is noted as "son." Because the son inherited the same family name as his father, and [Tangut] (Bore-benevolence) was the son of [Tangut] [ljow mjijr śjow] it is assumed that the full name of the co-borrower was "Liang Bore-Benevolence." Likewise, the co-borrower [Tangut] [śja~ dji-j lji-.] "Dhyāna-samādhi (*Chan-ding*) Treasure" in the contract Инв. No. 4762-6(3) probably sharesd the same last name as the principle Contract Party [Tangut]? [ljow phə khjwi-] because the relationship of the former to the latter is noted to be "son." But more curious and striking is the appearance of the stamps and signatures of another figure between the father and the son: the "co-receiver of the contract, wife: Su the Five Joys." In the light of this peculiar order, it does seem that in some families in rural Tangut communities, the spouse of the male figure claimed a higher economic status than the son.[72]

Some "co-receivers of the contract" were not necessarily kinsmen and family members of the debtor, but more distant family relations or even close friends. The Инв. No. 5147-1-3(1) was co-signed by "co-receive of the contract Qiluo 'the one with the force'" and "Liquo the Dhyāna-samādhi Treasure"; the chief borrow was Liang "The force of Longevity." The Liang and the Qiluos don't seem like they were from the same household, at least on the paternal side; and the Qiluos were most probably not the spouse(s) of the debtor.

Another point worth noting and calling our attention is the Инв. No. 7741 account of grain loan from the Yin Year of Tianqing (1194). The borrower who signed at the end of one contract turns out to be the warrantor, or-borrower, in another contract. The principle Contract Party in 7741(10) was [Tangut] [ljow dow zji-r khjwi-], who appears in the same register (11) as [Tangut] Bore's

72 TN: That is, in contrast to common understandings of situations in the Central Plains, whereby the son of the patriarch is for the most part the second highest on the socio-economic ladder.

FIGURE 137 Инв. No. 5949-23: Si year of Guangding (1221) account of grain loan

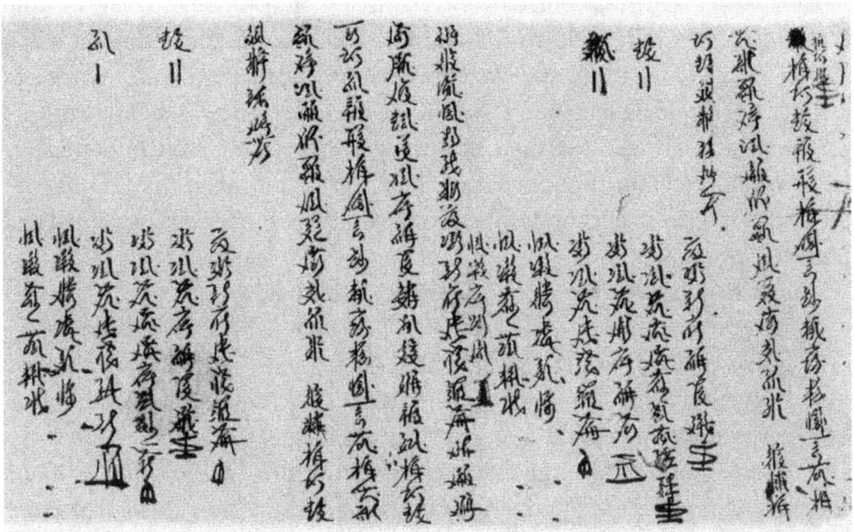

FIGURE 138 Инв. No. 7741(4) (11–12): Yin year of Tianqing (1194) account of grain loan

guarantor, as well as the co-borrower of [Tangut] in (12), of [Tangut] "The Benign Dog" in (13), and of [Tangut] in (16) all within the same register. Likewise, the principle borrower [Tangut] Bore in 7741(11) co-signed the contracts of others in (10) (12) (13) and (16) of the same register; The borrower [Tangut] in 7741(12) served as guarantors in contracts (10) (11) (13) in the same register. Obviously, these three figures served as each other's guarantors across contracts. Their loans are dated to the 30th day of the first month and the 1st day of the second month on the lunar calendar. It can be conjectured that these three people warranted for each other's grain loans, based on their acquaintance, collective need, and mutual trust. They might have been distant relatives, close friends, or neighbours.

In most of the loan contracts found in Dunhuang, the debtor and co-borrowers were required to provide information on their age in addition to their signatures. In the Khara-Khoto contracts, however, Contract Parties did not note down their age.

Upon the successful signing of a contract, the creditor was left with the one and only hope that the principle and interests would be returned promptly and properly. The rights of the creditors were well protected by the legal regime founded upon the *Laws of Heavenly Prosperity*. The laws provided several means of enforcement, measures that were not only coercive in cases of default, but also procedural, so "when the debtor is no longer capable of repayment, press the co-borrower."[73] The laws confirm our impression from the contracts that the co-borrowers were *de facto* warrantors with joint liability. According to the terms specified in the contracts, they would take over and assume the financial-legal responsibility of repayments in case the principle Contract Party(s) defaulted, died, escaped, went into exile, or encountered any unexpected accidents that prevented them from repaying in full. In this way, the rights, interests, and profits of the creditors were further strengthened and protected under law.

The *Laws of Heavenly Prosperity* also stipulates that,

> If the sons, daughters, daughters-in-law, grandchildren, and brothers invite themselves to take out loans of livestocks, grains, cash, and properties, either government-owned or from the private sector, without the proper knowledge and acknowledgement of their parents and brothers who dwell and dine in the same household, and if they thus incur interests, and act in an inopportune and inappropriate time, with the consequence that their properties evaporate into nothingness, the parents may repay the debt if they do agree to bear the financial burdens, but are not legally obliged to repay the sum if they do not agree to do so. In the latter case, the borrower, or debtor, would have to shoulder the responsibility alone.[74]

In other words, family members were provided a shield of financial security in cases of major defaults by their kins. Under such circumstances, the family relatives, especially the parents who were legally responsible for the financial arrangement of the household, had the option of either extending a helpful hand to their families who took out loans without having notified the family, or leaving the audacious adventurists to their own financial ruins. In this case, certainly without the legal force that came with the ritual and record of co-signing the contract, there is a possibility that joint financial liability was not necessary. On the other hand, the co-borrowers had no choice but to share liability in case of default. What accounts for the different levels of legal obligations between the unaware parents and the fully cognizant co-signers was, of course, their respective lack of information. Thus, legal obligation was not immediately implied in degree of familiarity and affiliation but defined in the strict terms of the contract as a legally effectual and enforceable document.

73 *Revised Laws of Heavenly Prosperity* 3, "Urging the Payment of Debt," p. 189.

74 Ibid., pp. 190–191.

2.1.9.3 *The Third Undersigned Party Is the Witness to the Transaction*

The legal terminology for the "witness" to a financial loan or transaction is usually expressed in the two-character phrase, [illegible] [nwə dzjwo], literally "the knowing person," or "the cognizant person," i.e. a "witness." There were usually two or more "witnesses," sometimes numbering up to six of them as a group of witnesses. Some served as the witness to multiple loan contracts. For example, in Инв. No. 4696-3(5)-1, the witness is a certain [illegible] [ljow da kia lji-.]

FIGURE 139 Инв. No. 4696-3(1): Shen year of Guangding (1212) account of grain loan (witness: Liang Laofangbao)

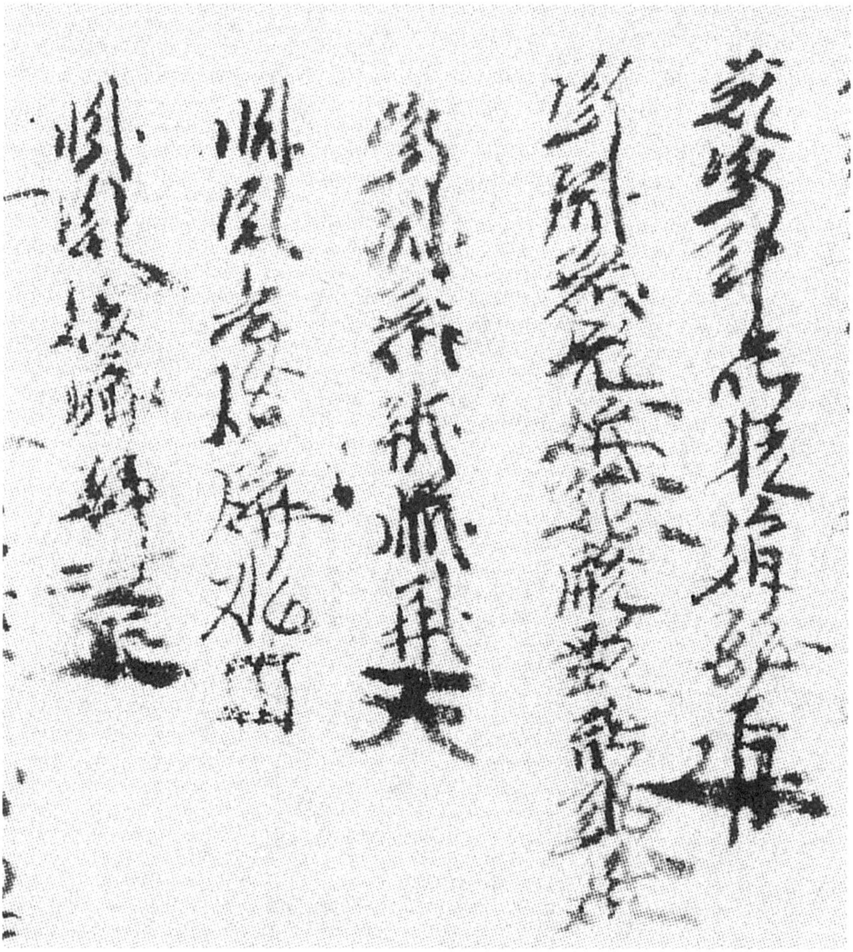

FIGURE 140 Инв. No. 4696-3(5): Shen year of Guangding (1212) account of grain loan (witness: Liang Laofangbao)

Liang "Treasure of the Old House" served as a witness to (2) (6) (7) (8) (9) (16) (17) (18) (19) (35) and altogether more than a dozen contracts of grain loans. Likewise, the witness Pingshang "Force of the Mountain" in Инв. No. 4696-7-33(1) served as a witness to three grain loans, contracts (2) (6) and (15). There was a significant legal distinction between the stamps and signatures of a witness and those of the co-borrowers. The witnesses served no more than to bear witness to the existence of such a legal arrangement, and therefore, they assume no joint liability at all. Whereas a co-Contract Party by all means also witnessed the transaction between the creditor and the debtor, but he had to guarantee the enforcement of terms therein contained by his own financial resources, if needed be.

2.1.9.4 *Signing and Stamping*

The signatures and stamps of relevant parties of a contract were required for the document to obtain legal force by the acknowledgement of concerned parties in a given loan or transaction. Stamping and signing a contract has a long cultural and economic history that precedes Western Xia, and the Tanguts readily took over the legal format and ritual. Conventionally, the concerned parties either noted down certain characters or drew special symbols underneath their signatures in a given contract in order to certify their solemn approval of the terms. Signing and stamping were correlated, and in most cases, they co-existed. Given that, considering the vastly divergent levels of literacy in the use of contracts across times and territories, the signature part was often completed not by the party directly concerned in the transaction but by an agent or representative. The stamping of symbols was in many cases the only possible way to verify the credit and acknowledgement of the Contract Party. Oftentimes, the calligraphic styles of the handwriting in the signatures, as well as in them main text of the contract, of both the concerned and the related parties, appear nearly identical, suggesting that the same agent or representative might have not only issued the signatures on behalf of multiple persons, but also drafted the contract itself. This phenomenon speaks to the possible existence of a class of professional handwriters who were paid to process the entire contracting process for the parties involved. It is possible that in the local area, those capable of fluent and fluid use of Tangut drafted legal documents or even just signed their own names. They are, after all, in the minority.

There are two main ways to stamp: to draw symbols or to print the shape and length of one's own finger segments. Both types of stamps were found in the Khara-Khoto grain loan contracts.

The concerned parties may draw a special symbol of their own liking and marking below their signatures. To follow this practice with consistency, one would have to make a maximum effort to maintain the same shape and style in drawing the symbol over long stretches of time. Individuals designed their own symbols. All four Contract Parties and co-Contract Parties who signed the Инв. No. 4762-6(1), a grain loan contract officiated in Yin Year of Tianqing, signalled their approval of the legal document with symbolic stamps. The Tanguts designed symbolic stamps of various degrees of complexity on their contracts, ranging from simple strokes that resemble the Chinese characters '一,' '工,' '天,' etc., to extremely composite and complex symbols that are difficult to replicate. But others did not bother to exercise their artistic ingenuity, resorting instead to a simple ink dot by their names. The stamp of the aforementioned Liang "Treasure of the Old Home" looks like a square, with a cross or a vertical stroke in the middle. The Инв. No. 4696-3(1)–(1) features something like the Chinese character "田" (see image), and the stamps in (6) (8) (16) (17) and (18) resemble a horizontal version of the Chinese character "日." The symbol in contract No. (9) looks similar to a "井." No symbolic stamp is found, however, in contract (7).

"Finger-painting," also referred to as "finger-modelling," is the practice of fitting one's finger to the space next to the signature on the contract, to mark the positions of one's fingertips and finger segments with ink. The resulted horizontal strokes mark the pledge of personal trust, approval, and acknowledgement of the signatory. In the Chinese tradition, men usually mark their left finger, whereas women often use their right hand. The most popular finger for this purpose is either the middle finger or the index finger. Either two or three segments are marked on the contract. Most Tangut contracts feature three segments of a finger in four strokes. Two witnesses provide an example of this type of finger-stamping in Инв. No. 4762-6(1), an account of grain loan in Yin Year of Tianqing.

It is worth noting that nearly all Khara-Khoto loan contracts lack the prints and signatures of the loaners—the creditors offering the loans—at the end of the contracts. This format, which may be referred to in modern legal terminology as a 'unilateral contract,' shows the superior socio-legal status of the lender in financial transactions. This is due to the fact that the contract was preserved under the dominion of the creditor. It is therefore assumed that he was under no necessary obligation to sign the document for it to maintain legal force. It was as recent as in the late imperial era of Tang Dynasty that creditors were legally obliged to sign their names at the end of contracts for them to obtain force. And with greater geographical and ethnographical proximity, it should be pointed out that contracts in 8th–9th century Western Regions do mention the creditors, which appear more often in the abstract *persona moralis* as "owner of wheat," "owner of millet," "owner of beans," and "cash owner" rather than by their personal names. Moving toward the 10th century, however, the creditors seemed to no longer sign their titles or names. The lack of signature by the creditors in Tangut contracts reflects one outcome of this historical development in the medieval history of contracts.[75]

75 See *Dunhuang Economic Documents*, pp. 76–147; see also Trombert, 1995.

FIGURE 141 Инв. No. 4762-6(1): Yin year of Tianqing (1194) account of grain loan (first four: printed; last two: finger-stamped)

2.1.10 Numerical Notation

There existed parallel systems of numbers and numerical notations in ancient China. Numerical notations signify numbers by the special, spatial arrangement of tallies and tokens. Originally, these tallies were little sticks made of bamboo, wood, and bones, to denote a limited range of numbers. When tokens are rearranged to signify certain numbers, they may be placed horizontally or vertically. When the horizontal is the default, unit digits, hundreds, and tens of thousands are denoted by horizontal strokes; tens, thousands, and hundred-thousands are expressed in terms of vertical lines. When, however, the vertical is the default, the unit digits, hundreds, and tens of thousands are denoted by vertical strokes, whereas tens, thousands, and hundred-thousands are expressed in terms of horizontal strokes. Zero is always signified with the help of a blank space. The application of tokens to numerical denotations and calculations in a textual format is referred to as numerical notation.

Numerical notations use to specify the quantity of grain loans in Tangut contracts usually appear right above the signatures, near the end of the document. Numerical notations are applied to a document that already makes explicit reference to the types and quantities of the grains in prose, for the purpose of accuracy and security—that is, in order to forestall errors and confusions in the main text. This practice may come to better illumination when considered in the contexts of medieval Tangut palaeography. Given the prevalent use of the Tangut cursive script in drafting contracts, it often occurs that the simplified, interlinked, and free-flying strokes may challenge the eagle eyes of the Tanguts themselves. It is therefore much more expedient to adopt a different system of notation in order to check the numbers. Moreover, the numerical notations are symbolic, expressive, and intuitive. Even those inadequately versed in the Tangut scripts, of which there were many who resided in Tangut territories, would be able to grasp the numbers without much difficulties, and without entering into confusions and conflicts with the other parties.

Numerical notations in Xixia largely retained the logic of the system that prevailed in the Central Plains. Both rely on the combined use of horizontal and vertical strokes to denote certain numbers across different digits. A broad survey of Khara-Khoto contracts shows that the use of numerical notations is wide-ranging but not omnipresent, popular but not absolutely necessary. Furthermore, the symbolic and mathematical meanings of the horizontal and vertical strokes are not always consistent. The formula could even vary according to the habits of the loaners themselves.

One horizontal stroke "—" may signify 1 *dan*, and 2 strokes 2 *dan*, then one vertical stroke " | " meaning 1 *dou* and 2 strokes 2 *dou*; 10 *dan* may be denoted by the symbol "+". In the manuscript Инв. No. 4783-7(2), for example, 6 horizontal lines "—" are found under a cross, "+"—that is, 16 *dan*. Then next to it we see 7 lines under 1 cross, which would be 17 *dan*. In Инв. No. 4596(5), two vertical strokes " | " are found under three "—" in the amount of 3 *dan* 2 *dou*.

Some contracts have 10 *dan* denoted by a large horizontal stroke, whereas a simple vertical stroke signifies 1 *dan*. A short horizontal stroke? That would be 1 *dou*. This is the case in the manuscript Инв. No. 5949-27 (1) (2), where "— |" means 11 dan. A vertical line on the left and 5 short horizontal strokes on the right would add up to 1 *dan* and 5 *dou*.

Likewise, there are two distinct ways of denoting the number 5. Some prefer simplifying 5 or more with one horizontal and one vertical strokes, rather

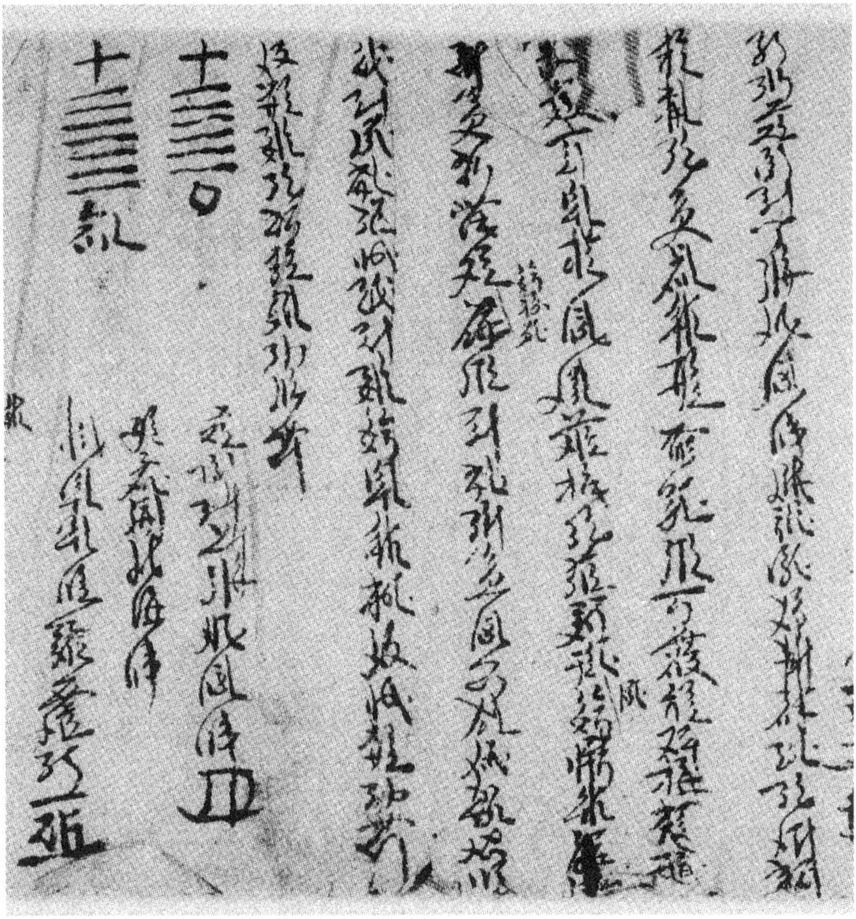

FIGURE 142 Инв. No. 4783-7(2): Account of grain loan (upper left corner: numerical notation)

than 5 consecutive strokes, horizontal or vertical. So, to indicate 6 with this 'quinary' system of horizontal strokes, one would draw 5 1 = 6: "丅". In like manner, 7 would be "╥". Here, it is critical and necessary that the horizontal and vertical strokes are connected. Otherwise, 丅 and ╥ would be confused with "1 *dan* and 1 *dou*" and "1 *dan* and 2 *dou*." For example, the parties in the contract Инв. No. 4696-1(1) negotiate for the loan of 8 *dan*, which is notated by 1 horizontal and 3 vertical strokes. In the Инв. No. 4696-1 (1) (2), there is a large horizontal line above 4 vertical strokes, signifying 9 *dan*; to the left are 3 short horizontal strokes, meaning 3 *dou*; further to the left are 5 even tinier vertical strokes, signifying 5 *sheng*. Altogether, the notation says 9 *dan* 3 *dou* 5 *sheng*. A line of Tangut notes in small font reads, "9 *dan* 3 *dou* 5 *sheng* wheat" confirms the accuracy of our reading.

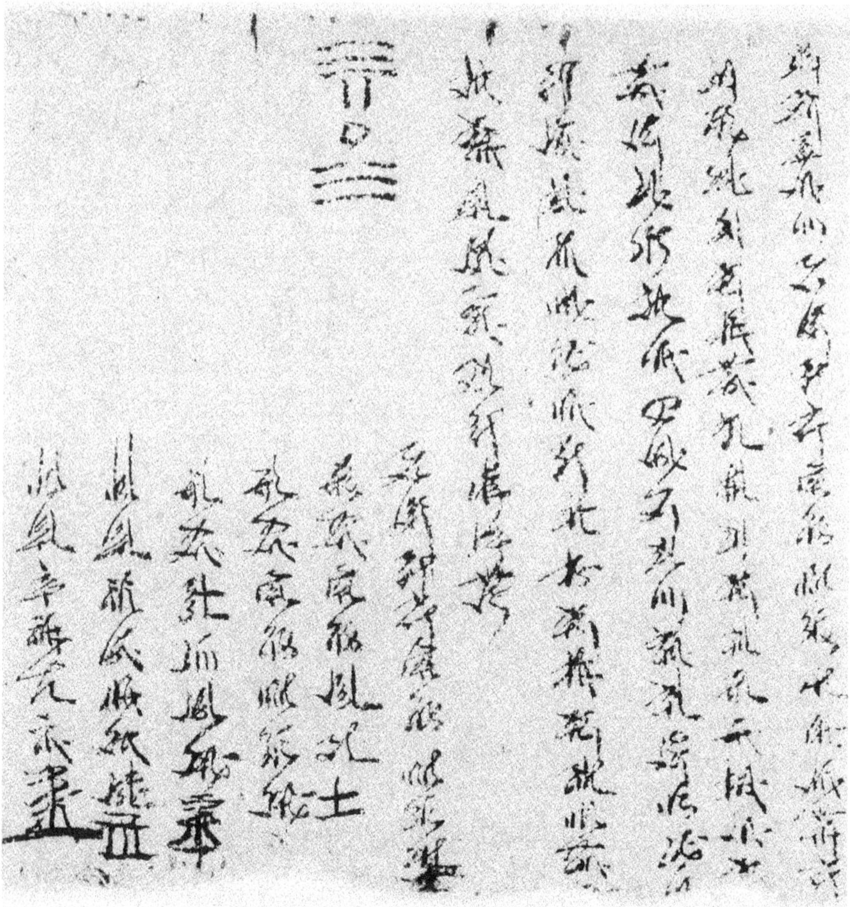

FIGURE 143 Инв. No. 4596(5): Chou year of Guangding (1217) account of grain loan (above: numerical notation)

The loan concerned in the document Инв. No. 5949-22 (2) (4) is in the amount of 27 *dan* of coarse grains: two large horizontal lines, and a compound symbol of one stroke with two connected vertical strokes (5 + 2 = 7): "═ ╥".

Another 'quinary' notation is based on the use of a vertical stroke. So, a vertical plus a horizontal at its bottom: "⊥" signifies 6. To make it 7, add one more horizontal stroke to the base of 5: "╧". One such example is the contract Инв. No. 4696-2(1), where by the borrower takes out a loan of coarse grains in the amount of 6 *dou*: "⊥"; In 7892-6(3), the loan is 7 *dou* of wheat: "╧". So, in both of these cases, the vertical line is used to signal a set of 5 *dou*. Yet, some others prefer the old way: drawing 5 strokes one piled upon another. In Инв. No. 7741(3)-9, for example, the 7 *dan* of wheat appear as 7 vertical lines; in Инв. No. 5949-23(1), the 8 *dou* of coarse grains is notated by 8 vertical strokes; finally, in Инв. No. 5949-19(1), the 8 *dan* 5 *dou* are take the form of 8 horizontal over 5 vertical strokes.

Oftentimes, the notations are supplied with footnotes in Tangut characters that specify the types of grains concerned: wheat, assorted (coarse), barley, proso millet, and foxtail millet. Elsewhere, symbols are used to denote the types of grains: "o" is wheat/barley; where there is no symbol, coarse grains are implied. Toward the end of Инв. No. 4596-1(1), there is a marking of two horizontal strokes above a small circle—that is, a loan of 2 *dan* of wheat. In Инв. No. 4596-1(5), also near the end, there are 2 horizontal strokes at the top and 5 vertical strokes below; further down is also a small circle. This would be a loan of wheat in the amount of 2 *dan* and 5 *dou*. The additional two horizontal strokes indicate another 2 *dan* of coarse grains. Sometimes, instead of leaving no symbol to imply coarse grains, there would be a Tangut character for 'assorted.' In Инв. No. 4783-6(2), whereas the notation for 1 *dan* of wheat is a horizontal stroke above a small circle, that for 1 *dan* of coarse grains is a horizontal stroke above a Tangtu character 𗪚 [dza]. Likewise, in Инв. No. 4783-7(2), there is a cross above, 6 horizontal lines in the middle, and a small circle at the bottom (16 *dan* of wheat), and a cross at the top, 7 horizontal strokes in the middle, and a Tangut character 𗪚 [dza] at the bottom: a loan of coarse grains in the amount of 17 *dan*.

Some of the contract fragments have lost the main content altogether, but it is still possible to take a peek at the ending. In these cases, the numerical notation reveals the quantity of the grain loan, even if the number indicated in the main text is missing. For example, in the manuscript Инв. No. 5949/31, a remnant end-page of the original contract, we find the following numerical notation: four horizontal lines above 2 vertical strokes, and right to the two vertical lines, there is a small horizontal stroke; below which is found a tiny circle; further below is a cross +, followed by 4 vertical strokes. From these symbols we know that this particular loan consists of 4 *dan* 2 *dou* 1 *sheng* wheat, and 10 *dan* 4 *dou* coarse grains.

The above discussions in multiple parts reveal the richness, diversity, and various levels of complexity in the corpus of Khara-Khoto grain loan contracts. Accounts of large-quantity loans, or those that involve complex terms of loans and relationships, are usually written in a complete and thorough format.

Several relevant legislations in the *Laws of Heavenly Prosperity* provide the juridical principles and legal basis for contract-making under Tangut laws. The excavation of these contracts provides original historical sources that are never known to historians before. These varied materials are also remarkable for their stark level of details in the procedures of offering and taking grain loans in Western Xia. With these invaluable and irreplaceable sources, it is altogether possible to repaint a colourful and blow-by-blow canvas of grain-loaning

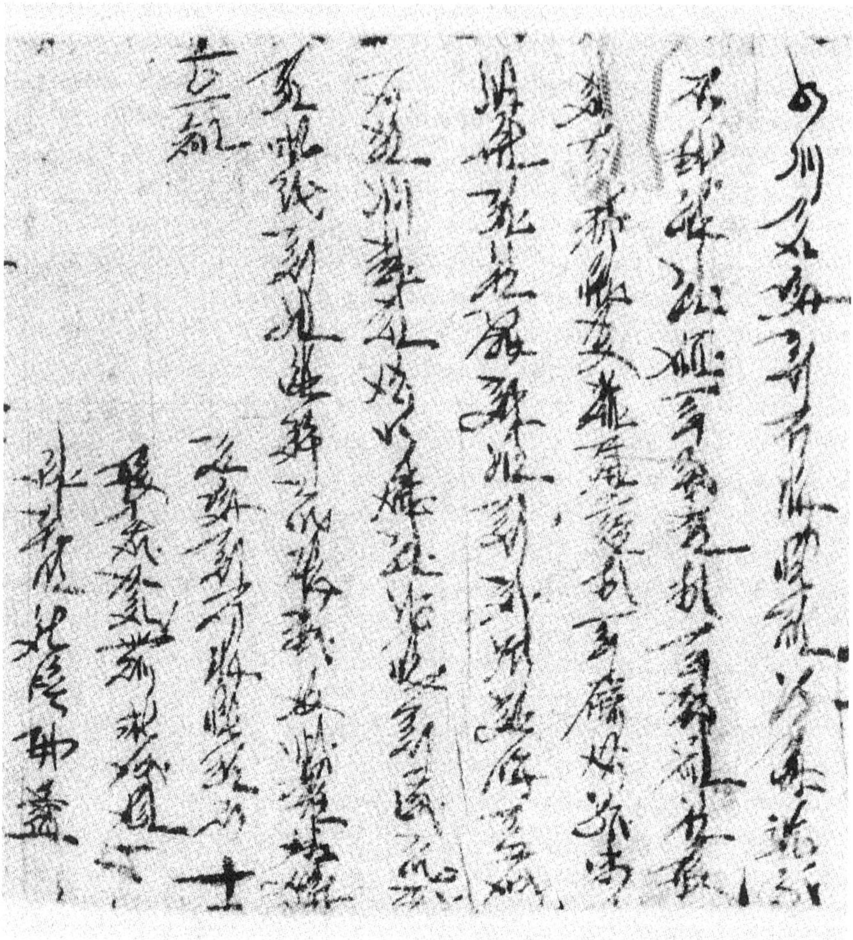

FIGURE 144 Инв. No. 4783-6(2): Wu year of Guangding (1222) account of grain loan

scenes at the base level of the Tangut society. A comparative and connective reading of the contracts and the law code would gain a deeply penetrating insight into the residential life, economic conditions, agricultural productions, living standards, and wealth inequality in Tangut households, neighborhoods, and communities.

2.1.11 Conclusive Remarks on Tangut Grain Loan Contracts

A comprehensive survey of the Tangut accounts of grain loan unearthed in Khara-Khoto yields the following conclusions:

1. The vast plurality of Khara-Khoto contracts are grain loan accounts, numbering up to more than 110 registers and 300 pieces, about ⅔ of the total

corpus of Tangut contracts. These documents are as diverse as numerous, more so than grain loan contracts found in the Dunhuang.

2. Most Tangut loan contracts are written in a set format. Oftentimes, multiple contracts are written on the same piece of paper. Longer scrolls contain as many as dozens of contracts, which form a chain of interlinked accounts. Single-page accounts of grain loan are, in contrast, much fewer and rarer.
3. Grain loan accounts do not record the reasons for loaning. Most of the loaning takes place in the spring, a gap period between two harvests. Those who apply for loans are Dangxiang Tanguts, but also Han Chinese, as well as serfs and semi-slaves such as *shijun* and *nupu*. Those who offer the loans are either landlords with a huge surplus or, indeed, religious establishments at Buddhist temples.
4. The Tanguts loaned grains with interests, and the rate is oftentimes exorbitant. The loan arrangement and the setting of interest rates are based on the 'principle'—the base number of grains. There are roughly three types of loans: daily interest, monthly interest, and interest on total sum. Whichever type it might be, the interest rate usually reaches 50%, and even 80% and 100% in the matter of 3–4 months. Some even cross the ceiling of 'multiple-times interest' set by the regulatory agencies of the Tangut government. These contracts are living testimonies to the many and grave financial exploitations of the Tangut poor at the hands of 'loan sharks.'
5. Nearly all contracts set out terms of penalties for borrowers unable to return the principle and interests in due time. These terms are secured and guaranteed by prints of finger lengths and personal signatures. These materials provide evidence on the guarantee of loaner's legal rights.
6. A certain number of grain loan contracts employ not only verbal language to denote the types and quantities of the grains, but also a system of numeral notation at the end of the contract. From a lateral, case-study perspective, this evidence points to the fact that the contracts written in Tangut, by an ethnic people, inherit the system of numerical calculation and notation. It again speaks to the cultural transfer and influence of the Central Plains on Western Xia.

2.2 *Monetary Loans*

Monetary loans are rare finds amongst Tangut loan accounts and contracts. But the Khara-Khoto manuscript Инв. No. 986-1 contains a set of two contracts of this type. Dated to the Gengchen, Tenth Year of Guangding (1220) and the Si year (1221), it is a Tangut monetary loan document handwritten on

FIGURE 145 Инв. No. 986-1: Gengchen 10th year of Guangding (1220) contract of monetary loan

a 22.2 × 31.2 cm hemp paper fragment, with 11 lines of Tangut in the cursive script. It begins with the year: Gengchen, Tenth Year of Guangding (1220); then in line 8, "7th day of the 1st month in the Si Year" (1221).[76]

Two contracts are found in the page fragments. The lower sections are damaged and some words are lost. The contracts are written in the cursive, some of which are blurry and illegible. But from the words that do lend themselves to interpretation, we know that in the first contract, someone obtains a cash loan in the amount of 7 *guan* and 10 rolls of materials, on a mortgage of 200 pieces of some other goods, in the Gengchen Tenth Year of Guangding. Repayment is due on the 10th day of the 10th month. Any party which reneges on the agreement is punished according to the terms set in the contract. The document ends with signatures and stamps. The second contract is simpler. It records a loan of ?*guan* and 500 mace on the 10th day of the 1st month in the Si Year (the following year since the previous contract). Although both contracts are short of key information and much remains unknown, they more than suffice to show that the Tanguts in Khara-Khoto did practice monetary loans.

76 *Russian Collection of Khara-Khoto Manuscripts* 12, p. 156.

FIGURE 146 Инв. No. 1523-23: Chen year of Qianyou. Document of monetary loan

Another document of monetary loan is the manuscript Инв. No. 1523-23, handwritten in 5 lines of cursive Tangut on a 23.1 × 25.8 cm cover-layering paper, which is patched together from two pieces of papers. In line 4, the text indicates the time of the contract as "the last month in the Chen Year of Qianyou" (1172, or 1973, or 1185).[77] There are stamps and signatures.

This document is probably not a contract in the strict sense, but it surely testifies to the practice of monetary loans. For although much information is lost, we still find this line: "overdue payment doubles, each 1 *guan* will be repaid in 2 *guan*." So, the Tanguts must have loaned and borrowed cash, not just goods and grains.

In the Инв. No. 1523-24 cash loan account, there is a reference to "One item: on the 5th day of the 6th month in the Renchen Third Year of Qianyou (1172), Contract Party Dashi?? First himself borrows 700 *guan* of cash, at the interest rate of 8 wen per string of cash per day. The loan is due in 100 days, upon which

77 *Russian Collection of Khara-Khoto Manuscripts* 12, p. 265.

time both the principle and the interests are to be repaid in full." This, too, is evidence that the Tanguts practiced monetary loans in cash.

2.3 *Material Loans*

Loans of objects and materials are also rare amongst Khara-Khoto documents. There is the manuscript Инв. No. 955, a material loan contract dated to the Si Year of Guangding (1221). It is a single-page contract fragment with 9 lines of cursive Tangut handwritten on a 19.9 × 23.3 cm hemp paper. It begins with the year, and ends with stamps and signatures.[78]

FIGURE 147 Инв. No. 955: Si year of Guangding (1221) contract of loaning goods

Translation:

> On the 5th day of the 7th month, in the Si Year of Guangding, Contract Party Li??, ??? et al., presently from [illegible] [ljow ne_w lji-.]
> Borrow 7700 rolls [kji], due in the same month

78 *Russian Collection of Khara-Khoto Manuscripts* 12, p. 146.

By the 15th day, to be repaid. If overdue, the [kji]
Has to be doubled in repayment, i.e. 15400 rolls. Own
Hearts Willing.
Contract Party: ?? (stamp)
Co-Contract Party: ?? (stamp)
Witness: ??? (stamp)

The goods concerned in this loan are [Tangut] [śja. tu. śja. ·jir piej kji] (7700 rolls of [Tangut]). As for what [Tangut] is, we remain still in the dark. But we know that the character pronounces as [kji], and it is a type of good counted by the unit of [Tangut] [piej] (roll). The contract does not make mention of any interest, only insists on timely return of the goods. A possible reason is that this type of good is not consumable or easily liable to loss or damage. Still, overdue return is severely punished: the borrower will have to return twice the quantity in the loan.

3 Transaction Contracts

As a form of economic activity, sell and purchase is central to commerce. Therefore, sale contracts are crucial to private law, past and present. As a basic type of contract, it is often also the most formal, detailed, and well-crafted. For these and other reasons, Khara-Khoto sell and purchase contracts are crucial primary sources to studies of the Tangut economy.

3.1 *Land Sales*

In an agriculture-based economy, it is no surprise that the selling and buying of farmland is the single most important economic activity in medieval Western Xia. A batch of Tangut land sale contracts found in Khara-Khoto have furnished us with the necessary primary sources to understand the way farmland was exchanged in the historical Tangut economy.

Back in 1972, Soviet Tangutologist Evgenij Ivanovich Kychanov identified and translated amongst the Khara-Khoto manuscripts in Russia a piece of land sale contract written in the running style, dated to the Gengyin, 22nd Year of Heavenly Prosperity (1170 AD).[79] This is the first time ever a Tangut social document is openly published, an event of great significance to the study of Tangut commerce and agriculture, and even to answering geological question

79 Кычанов, Е.И. Тангутский документ 1170г. о продаже земли, “Письменные памятника Востока.Ежгодник. 1971,” М., 1974, pp. 196–203.

of land and soil in the area. This contract is complete, with full information on the date, main parties of the transaction, size of the land and the fixtures that come with it, the seller, price (in terms of livestocks), terms of guarantee, penalties for the breach of the contract, the four boundaries of the land, and finally, the stamps and signatures of the seller, guarantor, and the witness. As the only known piece of land sale contract at the time, its publication caught the attention of Tangutologists worldwide. Given the difficulty of the running script, experts have continued to probe into the document.[80]

In preparation for the publication of the Russian Collection of Khara-Khoto Manuscripts, we have found another 11 pieces of farmland sale contracts in the pile of newly discovered Khara-Khoto social documents. Along with the one studied by Kychanov, there are now a total of 12 Tangut land sale contracts. These contracts from 700–800 years ago are authentic primary sources on land exchange in Tangut Khara-Khoto. There are only a very few incomplete land sale contracts from the Song, Liao, and Jin Dynasties. Whereas Western Xia alone supplies a whole batch of contracts rich in data and information. These documents are the best materials to rely on in the historical study of the Tangut economy.

3.1.1 Translation and Interpretation of Land Sale Contracts

Some Khara-Khoto land sale contracts are single-page documents, others are found in multi-document series. The Gengyin, 22nd year of Tiansheng land sale contract Инв. No. 5010 mentioned just now is an example of a single-page document. 19 lines of Tangut in the cursive script are handwritten on a 22.5 × 49.6 hemp paper.[81] Other single contracts include the Инв. No. 4199: Liang's land and house sale contract on the 16th day of the 6th month in the Bingchen Year (1196); Инв. No. 4193: Maze's land sale contract on the 5th day of the 1st month in Wuwu, the 5th year of Tianqing (1198); Инв. No. 4194: 𘞗𗄡𗍊𗍑 [lew śji thow pha~]'s land and house sale contract in the Gengshen Year of Heavenly Celebration (1200). These three contracts are, in the same order,

80 Huang, Zhenhua. "Xixia Tiansheng Ershiernian Maidi Wenqi Kaoshi" [西夏天盛二十二年賣地文契考釋]: "A study of the land sale contract in the 22nd year of Tiansheng" in *Xixiashi Lunwenji* [西夏史論文集]: *Collection of Essays on Tangut History*. Yinchuan: Ningxia People's Press, 1984, pp. 313–319; Chen Bingying.

Xixia Wenwu Yanjiu [西夏文物研究]: *A Study of Tangut Cultural Relics*. Yinchuan: Ningxia People's Press, 1985, pp. 275–279. Shi Jinbo, 2007, pp. 72–73; Nomura, Hiroshi (松泽博, 野村博). "Wuwei Xixia Bowuguan cang Haimudong Chutu Xixiawen Qiyue Wenshu" [武威西夏博物館藏亥母洞出土西夏文契約文書] in Dongyang Shiyuan [東洋史苑] Issue 75, July 2010, pp. 21–64.

81 *Russian Collection of Khara-Khoto Manuscripts*, vol. 14, see images 1 and No. 2.

handwritten in cursive Tangut on a 23.5 × 45 cm hemp paper; handwritten in the cursive style on a 23.2 × 43.1 cm hemp paper; handwritten in the cursive on a 22.9 × 57.1 cm hemp paper.[82] Later, a new batch of contracts has been discovered: the Инв. No. 5124 long scroll of contracts, wherein are found 23 contracts dated from the end of the 1st month to the early 2nd month in the Yin year of Heavenly Celebration (1194). Amongst them are contracts of not only land sale, but also land lease, livestock sale, livestock loan, as well as grain loan accounts. The long scroll is patched horizontally from multiple pages, in a total of three segments. The scroll is 20.5 cm in length, and 55, 175, 260 cm wide, respectively. So, if we count the 8 land sale contracts in the long scroll,[83] adding it to the 4 enumerated above, we could say that so far, there are a total of 12 Tangut land sale contracts. Except for the earliest-found contract, which is written in the running script, all other contracts are written in the even less decipherable cursive style. In the light of the equal scarcity and significance of Tangut land sale contracts, I shall present a translation of each of the 12 contracts below, in the order of time.

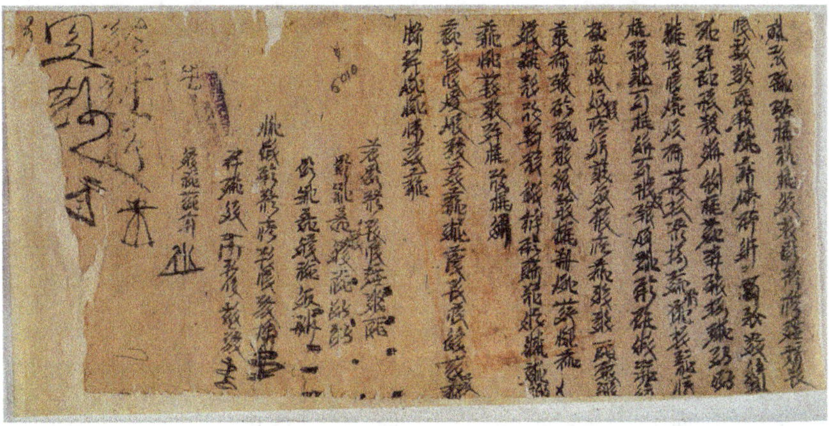

FIGURE 148 Инв. No. 5010: 22nd year of Tiansheng (1170) widow [illegible] et al., contract of land sale

82 *Russian Collection of Khara-Khoto Manuscripts* 13, pp. 199, 194.

83 *Russian Collection of Khara-Khoto Manuscripts* 14, pp. 13–22. The contract scroll is patched horizontally into one manuscript from multiple pieces of paper. As the scroll ages over time, the parts begin to fall off. A total of 18 photographs were taken on this set of manuscripts, which are reorganised into three sections, in the order of content and chronology. Part I: 2 and 3; Part II (loss of content at the beginning): 1, 6 left, 7, 8, 9, 10, 11 left; Part III: 4, 5, 6 right, 11 right, 12, 15, 13, 14, 16, 17, 18.

1. Инв. No. 5010: contract of land sale by Widow 𗼃𗄈𗫂𗽇𗯴 [·jaxwa zji-. lji-.śio] in the 22nd year of Heavenly Celebration (1170), a single-page contract with 19 lines of cursive Tangut on a 22 × 48.5 cm hemp paper, with stamp, signature, and red seal.[84]

Translation:

> In the Gengyin, 22nd year of Heavenly Prosperity,[85] Contract Party Widow 𗼃 [·ja]-
> 𗼃𗽇𗯴 [xwa zji-. lji-.śio] et al., presently has her own ripe/unripe land for 2 *dan* of seeds, 1-
> patch,[86] along with a yard & 3 thatched cottages, 2 trees altogether
> voluntarily sold to 𗼃𗄈𗏁𗗙 [·jaxwa mji-_tshja] at the price hereupon agreed: 2 full-teethed camels,
> 1 two-teethed,[87] 1 old ox—4 in total.[88] Hereafter, on this land[89]
> Let there be no dispute.[90] In case of a dispute, let Baoyin be responsible.[91]
> Let any reneging party[92] not only[93] be punished according to the *Laws and Orders*,[94]

84 *Russian Collection of Khara-Khoto Manuscripts*, vol. 14.

85 Tiansheng (Heavenly Prosperity) is an era name of the Renzong Emperor of Western Xia. It lasted for 21 years (1149–1169). In the Gengyin, 22nd year of Heavenly Prosperity (1170), the title is changed to Qianyou (Heavenly Blessing). In the 8th month of that year, Renzong emperor arrests and executes the powerful court official Ren Dejing (任得敬), upon which occasion he changed the era name. If so, then the contract should have been drafted and signed before the eighth month of that year.

86 In the manuscript, there are two vertical dots before 𗦗 [dźja_] (*dan*). The character preceding *dan* is likely to be a number, i.e. two. Land fit to sow 2 *dan* of seeds also matches the "22 *mu*" that comes later in the text.

87 𗍫𗗙 [nji-_ dzjiw] lit. two there are (vertical existence), i.e. a livestock is at a certain age when it has vertically grown two teeth.

88 The full price is the total of the four large livestocks.

89 𗐱𗾈𗧓 [thja lji-. ɣa] lit. that land upon, i.e. concerning/on this land.

90 𗖵𗆮 [lja_ bej] lit. mouth entangled, i.e. dispute, controversy.

91 𗯿 [kwa~], a loanword from the Chinese 管, to manage and oversee, to bear the responsibility.

92 𗹙𗕑 [da. lhej] lit. speech change, i.e. to eat one's words, to alter opinions, to renege on promises.

93 𗅋𗗚 [mji dźjij] lit. not purely, not only, esp. at the conjunction of two clauses.

94 𗗙𗖻 [kie dzji-_] lit. rules and orders; laws and orders. It refers to Tangut laws in general, including the *Revised Laws of Heavenly Prosperity*, etc.

But also, according to the laws,[95] pay a penalty fee of 30 *dan* of wheat, according to the circumstances[96] and the document.[97]

Down the administrative hall there are 22 mu of land.

To the north it borders the land of Yehe 'the prosperous Huihu'; to the east and south, it borders with [illegible] [·jaxwa]??

To the west it borders Liang 'Mount Weiming'

Contract Party: [illegible] [·jaxwa zji-. lji-.śio] (finger-segment)

Co-Contract Party:[98] son [illegible] [mə rar ko tśjow] (finger-segment)

Co-Contract Party: [illegible] [mə rar lja_ bju] (finger-segment)

Witness: Introducer[99] [illegible] [·jaxwa śjow wejr] (?) (stamp)

[illegible] [ljow khjwi- tshja] (stamp) [illegible] [·jaxwa ɣji- wejr] (stamp) [illegible] [mə rar sji thjij] (stamp)

Tax paid (stamp)

8? (stamp)[100]

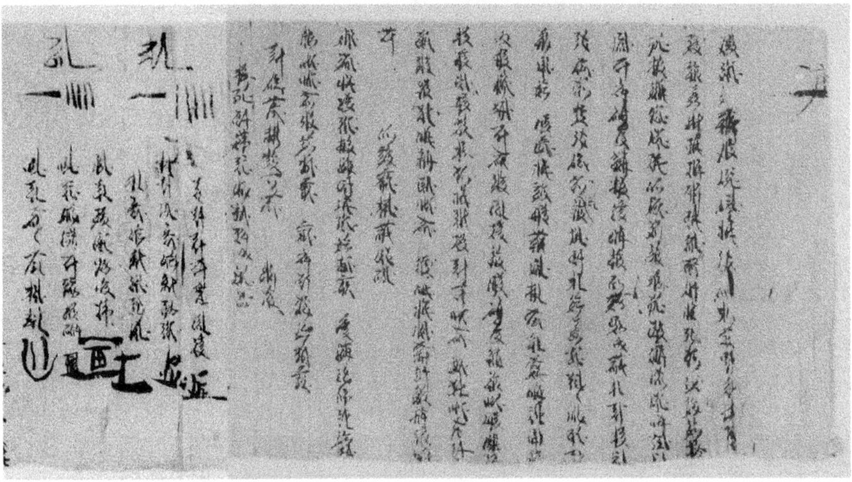

FIGURE 149 Инв. No. 5124-2: 24th day of 1st month in Yin year of Tianqing (1194) contract of land sale by [illegible]

95 [illegible] [know bju] lit. office/government accord, i.e. in accordance with the rules and laws set by the government.

96 [illegible] [da. kwər] lit. a body of speech, i.e. conditions and circumstances.

97 [illegible] [lji. lu.] lit. to fall into the rod/stick, i.e. to formulate a text: a textual receipt, a contract.

98 [illegible] [dźiow sa dźjwi-] lit. the document receiving-one, i.e. a co-seller of the land, a co-Contract Party who also partake in the transaction and shares liability.

99 [illegible] [da. wji mjijr] lit. speech-making one, i.e. an agent, introducer, negotiator between the selling and purchasing parties, who also serves as a witness to the signing of the contract.

100 Cursive, large-character [illegible] [zji.j kji- tśjwow] lit. tax, self/have offered/submitted, i.e. tax already paid.

2. Инв. No. 5124-2: Contract of land sale by [khjiw bie_j ta] on the 24th day of the 1st month in the Yin Year Heavenly Celebration (1194), found in the Contract scroll Инв. No. 5124-2, in 20 lines of cursive Tangut, signatures, and stamps.[101]

Translation:

> On the 24th day of the 1st month in the jia[102]yin year of Heavenly Prosperity, Contract Party [khjiw bie_j]—
>
> [ta] (et al.) has his own ripe/unripe land fit to sow 20 *dan* of seeds, which borders the left canal at the end of the canal,
>
> one patch, along with a full set of house and yard, including a 4-cabin house, etc. altogether voluntarily sold to Pudu Temple's
>
> agent for grain transactions, [ljow dow dźjij phu_],[103] [lja mja] et al., at the sale price, in coarse grains,
>
> 15 *dan*, wheat 15 *dan*. The payment and land are exchanged, with no debt incurred.[104]
>
> In case of any other attempts to mortgage or transfer the title, either publicly or privately,[105] or if members of the same *chao*[106]
>
> Launch a dispute,[107] let [bie_j ta] et al. take responsibility; let no liability fall on [dow dźjij phu_] et al. Not only

101 *Russian Collection of Khara-Khoto Manuscripts* 14, pp. 13–14.

102 The character [de.j] (Jia) is resupplied to form the sexagenary combination, Jiayin, in the era of Tianqing. There are two years of Yin in the Tianqing era: Jiayin the first year, and renyin the thirteenth year. What remains of the illegible character suggests that it could only be Jia, as opposed to Ren.

103 TN: The name of this man has been transliterated into Chinese. Here, I present it in the Tangut original with a phonetic notation. A possible literal meaning of the name could be: "Liang the lush, evil god," which very much befits his profession.

104 [phə lji-. do do wji- lji-j], lit. "price, land, difference, aligned" i.e. the payment and the land are aligned in their values, and there remains no discrepancy. A comparison to the Chinese text of the same content yields a smoother translation: there is no debt incurred in either payment or land. That is, the payment is made, and the land is transferred, at the price that both sides have agreed upon.

105 [kow dzej nji-_ tśjow nur rar], lit. "government, private, two kinds of loan transfer," i.e. to transfer the title as a loan either through/to the government, or in private transactions. In Western Xia, loans, pawning, and mortgaging could be done either through the government or privately. The contract specifies that upon the completion of the contract, no other transfer either publicly or privately will be permitted.

106 [tśhiew gu], lit. "sharing a *chao*," i.e. members of the same *chao*. Chao is not only a basic military unit in Western Xia, but also a socio-economic one. Those who belong to the same chao have intimate social ties and extensive economic associations.

107 [lja_ bej dźjiw dze_j], lit. "pursuit and contest in rhetorical entanglements," i.e. legal disputes.

Will the penalty double the sale price of the land, upon willing agreement, but also let the party reneging on its promise

bear any responsibility in accordance with the *Laws and Orders*, and pay 2 *liang* of gold according to the government regulations. Own hearts

Willing. 4 boundaries[108] are now specified,

To the east it borders the land of [illegible] [kə ta nja_] (the black little puppy) and [illegible] [ko dji-nja ?] (Su black?); To the South, that of [illegible] [da kia wejr]

To the west, the land of [illegible] [ŋwe mji dju lji-. ɣa]; to the north, the land of [illegible] [ljow ɣwie]?

Tax: 1 out of 5 *dou* of wheat; water for irrigation

All terms are to be enforced according to the terms set in this document.

Contract Party: [illegible] [khjiw bie_j ta] (stamp)

Co-Contract Party: son, [illegible] [tśhjwor nja_], 'the black slave' (stamp)

Co-seller[109] son, [illegible] [khjwi- njij], 'the red dog' (stamp)

Witness: [illegible]? [tow zjwi. tśjow zji-_r gju_] (stamp)

Witness and scriber:[110] [illegible] [tśhiə lji-. wejr] (stamp)

Witness: [illegible] [dju. dju. śja rjar sjwi] (stamp)

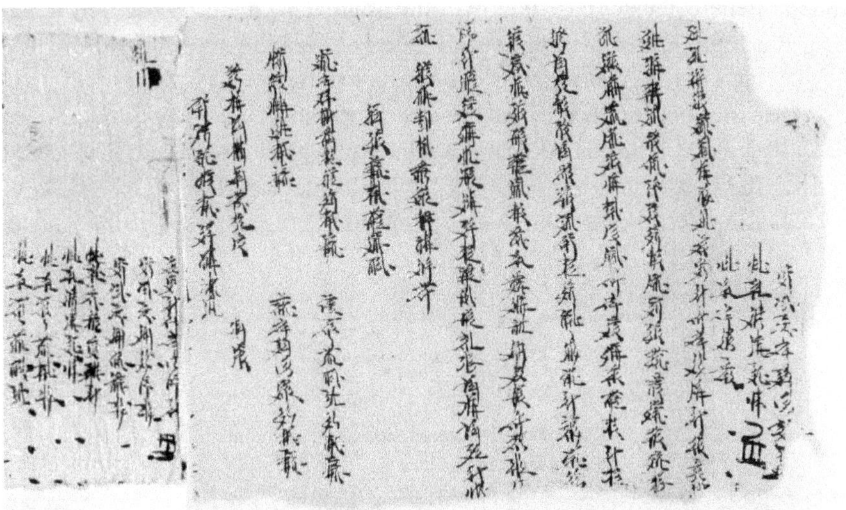

FIGURE 150 Инв. No. 5124-1, 5124-3(3): 29th day of 1st month in Yin year of Tianqing (1194) contract of land and house sale by [illegible] et al.

108 [illegible] [lji-r we], the four enclosures, i.e. the four ends, borders.

109 [illegible] [źji. dźjwi-], lit. to sell with, i.e. co-seller.

110 [illegible] [lji. lu. rjar], lit. "to enter the rod for writing," i.e. the one who undertakes to write; the professional transcriber who handwrites the entire contract, and also acts as a witness to the agreement.

3. Инв. No. 5124-1, 5124-3 (3): contract of land and house sale by [Tangut] [ljow da kia ·jiw] on the 29th Day of 1st Month in the Yin Year of Heavenly Prosperity (1194), reassembled from the contract scroll Инв. No. 5124-1 and lines 7–13 in the third part of 5124-3. There are 20 lines of Tangut in the cursive, followed by stamps and signatures.[111]

Translation:

> On the 29th Day of 1st Month in the Yin Year of Heavenly Celebration,[112] Contract Party [Tangut] [ljow da kia ·jiw] et al., has his own
>
> Land fit to sow 15 *dan*[113] of seeds, irrigated by water from the end of the left canal, along with the house and yard, trees and stone graves? etc. altogether
>
> Sold to the grain-agent of the Pudu Temple, [Tangut] [ljow lja mja] et al., at the agreed-upon[114] price
>
> of 6 *dan* of wheat and 10 *dan* of coarse grains. Debt incurred in neither the payment nor the land. If other
>
> parties attempt to transfer or loan the title, either publicly or privately, or if members of the same *chao* initiate a dispute, let [Tangut] [da kia ·jiw] take responsibility, not [Tangut] [lja mja]. In that case, not only is the penalty fee double the sum of the original payment,
>
> But there is an additional fee of 3 *liang* of gold in accordance with the laws of the government. Own hearts willing.
>
> The four borders of the land are clearly specified.
>
> To the east it borders the land of Liang "the lucky and accomplished"; to the south it borders [Tangut] [dju. dju. śja phji wejr]
>
> To the west it borders the Pudao canal; to the north it borders the land of [Tangut] [ljow ɣwie ·o bie_j][115]

---

111 *Russian Collection of Khara-Khoto Manuscripts*, vol. 14, pp. 13 and 15.

112 A missing [Tangut] [nji-_] "day" is resupplied.

113 A missing [Tangut] [dźja_] "dan" is resupplied.

114 [Tangut] [rji-r da.], lit. has already been said, i.e. negotiated and agreed upon.

115 TN: In some of the contracts, the third character of the name appears as [Tangut] [gia_], which means the same as [Tangut] [·o]. Not being able to consult the man himself, for the sake of expediency and clarity (to differentiate between this man and [Tangut], whose second character for "force" and "power," by the way, was mis-transcribed as [Tangut] in many texts, including, unfortunately, the Chinese edition of this book), and in order to maintain consistency, I have translated the name as [Tangut] throughout the book. But note that readers may see [Tangut] in the images and transcriptions.

Tax is 2 *dan*, including 4 *dou* of wheat; there is water for irrigation
The terms are to be enforced according to the items listed in this document
Contract Party: [illegible] [ljow da kia ·jiw] (stamp)
Co-Contract Party: younger brother [illegible] [da kia lji-.], treasure of the old house (finger-segment)
Co-Contract Party: younger brother: [illegible] [ŋwə dji.j lji-.], treasure of the five realms (finger-segment)
Co-witness: son, [illegible] ? [zji-r ? ·jiw] (finger-segment)
Witness: [illegible] [phjij śjo wa śia~] (finger-segment)
Witness: [illegible] [dju. dju. śja rjar lji-.] (finger-segment)
Witness: [illegible] (finger-segment)

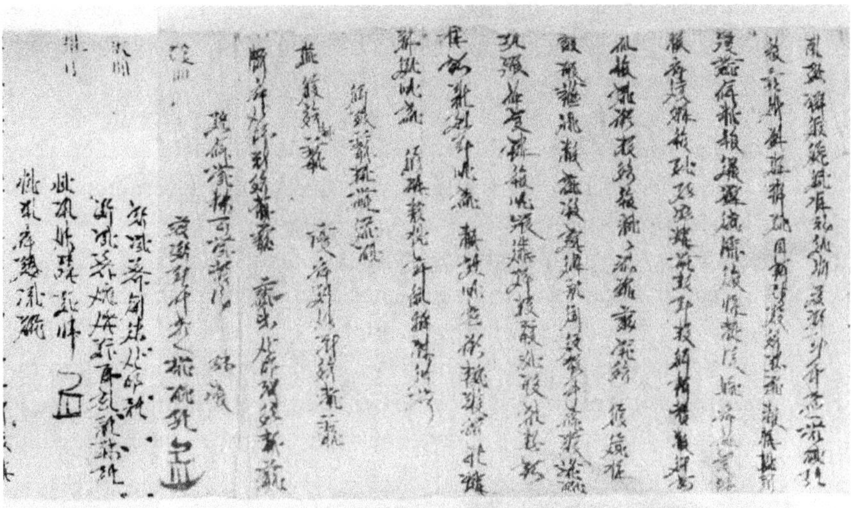

FIGURE 151 Инв. No. 5124-3(4, 5): 29th day of the 1st month in Yin year of Tianqing (1194) contract of land sale by [illegible]

4. Инв. No. 5124-3(4, 5): "contract of land sale by [illegible] [dju. dju. śja phji wejr] and prosperous" on the 29th Day of 1st Month in the Yin Year of Tianqing (1194). The contract begins with line 4 in part 4 of the long scroll Инв. No. 5124-3 and ends with the beginning of part 5. The 18 lines of Tangut in the cursive are followed by stamps and signatures.[116]

116 *Russian Collection of Khara-Khoto Manuscripts*, vol. 14, p. 16.

Translation:

On the 29th Day of 1st Month in the Yin Year of Heavenly Celebration, Contract Party [Tangut] [dju. dju. śja phji]

Et al., has her own land fit to sow 8 *dan* of seeds irrigated by water from the end of the left canal, along with a two-cabin

House, 5 live trees, etc., voluntarily sold to the grain-agents from the Pudu Temple, [Tangut]

[Tangut] [ljow dow dźjij phu_], [Tangut] [ljow lja mja] et al., at the agreed price of 4 *dan* of wheat & 6 *dan* of coarse grains,

No debt incurred in payment or in land. If other parties attempt to transfer or mortgage the title, either publicly or privately,

Or if the members of the same *chao* should initiate any dispute, let Xianling be responsible,

Not [Tangut] [dow dźjij phu_] et al. In such cases, let not only the penalty double the sale price,

But the regretting or reneging party be prosecuted in accordance with the *Laws and Orders*,

And pay a fee of 1 *liang* of gold, as required by the government. Own Hearts are willing.

The four borders of the land are hereby specified:

To the east it borders government-owned land; to the south it borders the land of [Tangut] [ljow ɣwie gia_ ·jiw]

To the west, it borders the land of [Tangut] [ljow da kia ·jiw]; to the north, it borders the land of "little old house of Year You"

Tax is 5 *dan*, including 1 *dou* of wheat narrow water [canal for irrigation]

Contract Party: [Tangut] [dju. dju. śja phji wejr] (stamp)

Co-Contract Party: brother, [Tangut] [ŋwu da kia zji] (finger-segment)

Co-Contract Party: wife, [Tangut] [·o gu_]? [Tangut] [zji tja wejr] (finger-segment)

Witness: [Tangut] [phjij śjo wa śia~] (stamp)

Witness: [Tangut] ?? [ljow? sa ?]

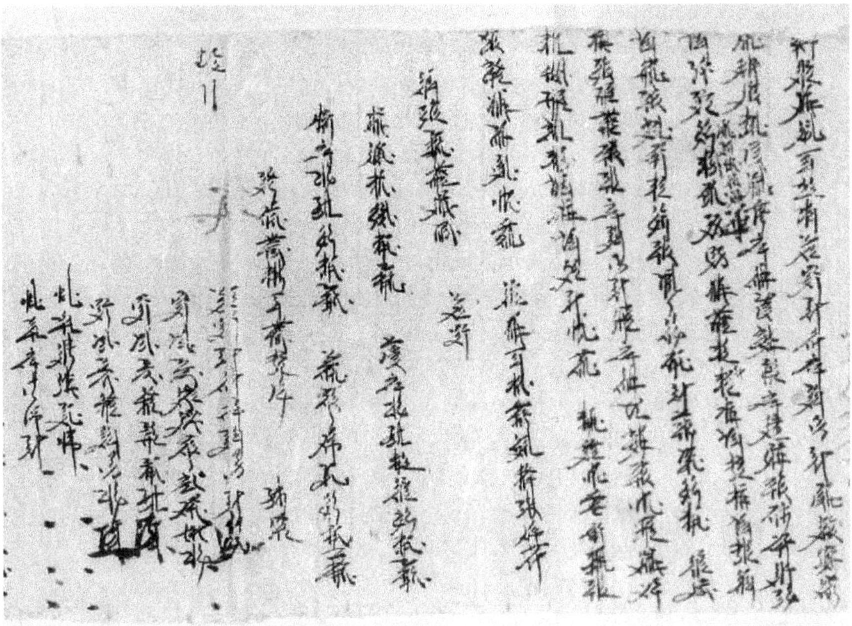

FIGURE 152 Инв. No. 5124-3(6, 7): 1st day of 2nd month in Yin year of Tianqing (1194) contract of land sale by [illegible]

5. Инв. No. 5124-3(6, 7): Contract of Land sale by [illegible] [ljow ɣwie gia_ ·jiw] on the 1st day of the 2nd month in the Yin Year of Heavenly Celebration (1194). The main text of the document is found in the long scroll Инв. No. 5124-3 and patched together from the end of image 6 and the beginning of image 7. There is a total of 18 lines of cursive Tangut, ending with signatures and stamps.[117]

Translation:

> On the 1st day of the 2nd month in the Yin Year, Contract Party [illegible] [ljow ɣwie gia_ ·jiw] presently to Pudu Temple's
> Grain-agents [illegible] [ljow dow dźjij phu_], [illegible] [ljow lja mja] etc. has a ripe/unripe
> Land fit to sow 10 *dan* of seeds, houses and walls included, voluntarily sold, at the agreed price of 2 *dan* of wheat, 2 *dan* of millet,
> And 4 *dan* of grains. There is no discrepancy in either land or payment. If there ever arise any attempt to either publicly or private
> Transfer or loan the properties on this land, let [illegible] [ljow ɣwie gia_ ·jiw], not Liang Nahzengmao et al., bear the responsibility. Not only

117 *Russian Collection of Khara-Khoto Manuscripts*, vol. 14, p. 17.

Let the recompensation be double the sum of the original sale price, but whichever party reneges on the promise,
Let it be prosecuted according to the laws and orders and suffer the penalty of *liang* of gold by the government. Own hearts are willing.
The four borders are hereby specified: [contract][118]
To the east, it borders Weiyi River; to the south, the land of [ljow lji-. wejr] and government-owned land,
To the west it borders sthe land of [ljow lji-. wejr]; to the north it borders the land of [dju. dju. gju_ ·o].
Tax is 5 *dou*, including 1 *dou* of wheat. Narrow water for irrigation
Contract Party: [ljow ɣwie gia_ ·jiw] (stamp)
Co-Contract Party: wife, [dju. dju. zji-. khjwi- mja lji-.] (finger segment)
Co-Contract Party: son, [zjo. dźjo wejr] (stamp)
Co-Contract Party: son, [ɣwie gia_ lji-.] (stamp)
Witness: [phjij śjo wa śia~] (finger segment)
Witness: [ljow da kia ·jiw] (finger segment)

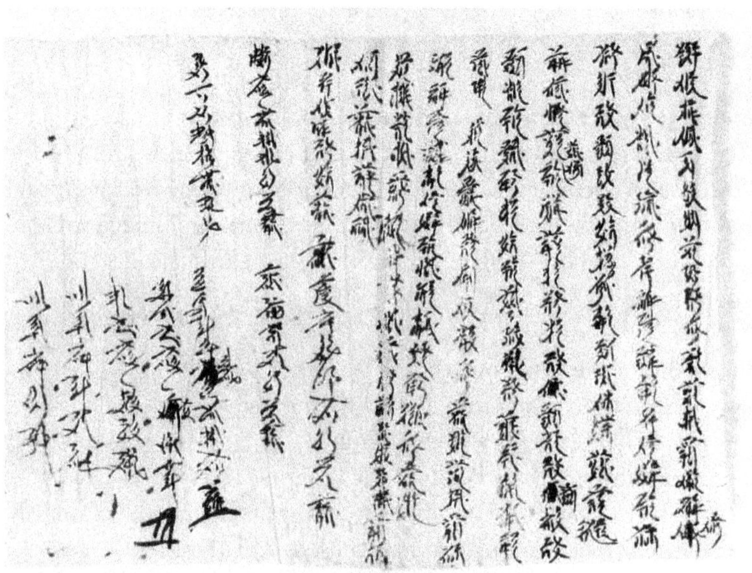

FIGURE 153 Инв. No. 5124-3(1-1): 1st day of 2nd month in Yin year of Tianqing (1194) contract of land sale by

118 These two characters are superfluous, and probably misplaced. Possibly, the transcriber intended to start recording the identities and names of the contracting parties, but switched gears upon realising that he has not yet produced information on the four borders and the taxes.

6. Инв. No. 5124-3(1-1) Contract of land sale by [Tangut] [khjij śja rjar śji-j] on the 1st day of the 2nd month in the Yin Year of Heavenly Celebration (1194), identified in image 1 in Инв. No. 5124-3, the long scroll of contracts. The text of 17 lines in cursive Tangut ends with signatures and stamps.[119]

Translation:

> On the 1st day of the 2nd month in the Yin Year, Contract Party [Tangut] [khjij śja rjar śji-j], to Pudu Temple's
>
> Grain agents, [Tangut] [ljow dow dźjij phu_], [Tangut] [ljow lja mja], et al.,
>
> Sell a patch of ripe/unripe land fit to sow 10 *dan* of seeds, along with cottages large and small, farming tools for the oxen,
>
> Stone gate with fence, pentamerous yokes, tree yard, etc. at the agreed-upon price of 10 *dan* of wheat, 10 *dan* of coarse grains,
>
> 10 *dan* of millet. Neither payment nor land falls short. If other parties,
>
> Such as members of the same *chao*, either publicly or private initiate a dispute, let Luocheng be responsible,
>
> Not [Tangut] [dow dźjij phu_], nor [Tangut] [lja mja]. Whichever party wishes to change these terms, let there be
>
> Not only a penalty fee of 3 *liang* of gold according to the laws, with their hearts willing, but also let the terms of the contract be enforced according to document and given the requirements of the circumstances.
>
> The four borders of the land are clearly delineated:
>
> To the east, it borders the land of [Tangut] [ljow da kia ·jiw]; to the south, the land of [Tangut] [ljow da kia dju]
>
> To the west, the land of [Tangut] [dju. dju. śja rjar lji-.]; to the north, the land of [Tangut] [tśhiə dzji_j ta]
>
> The tax is 10 *dan* of grains,[120] 2 *dou* of wheat
>
> Contract Party: [Tangut] (stamp)
> Co-Contract Party: [Tangut]??[Tangut] [dju. dju. rji-r mja kie.] (stamp)
> Co-seller: [Tangut] [dju. dju. wja. śjwo khjwi-] (finger-segment)
> Witness: [Tangut] [ljow ·jiw ta phiow] (finger segment)
> Witness: [Tangut] [ljow ne_w wejr] (finger segment)

119 *Russian Collection of Khara-Khoto Manuscripts*, vol. 14, p. 14.

120 The Tangut character for 'grain' here refers to foodstuff in general.

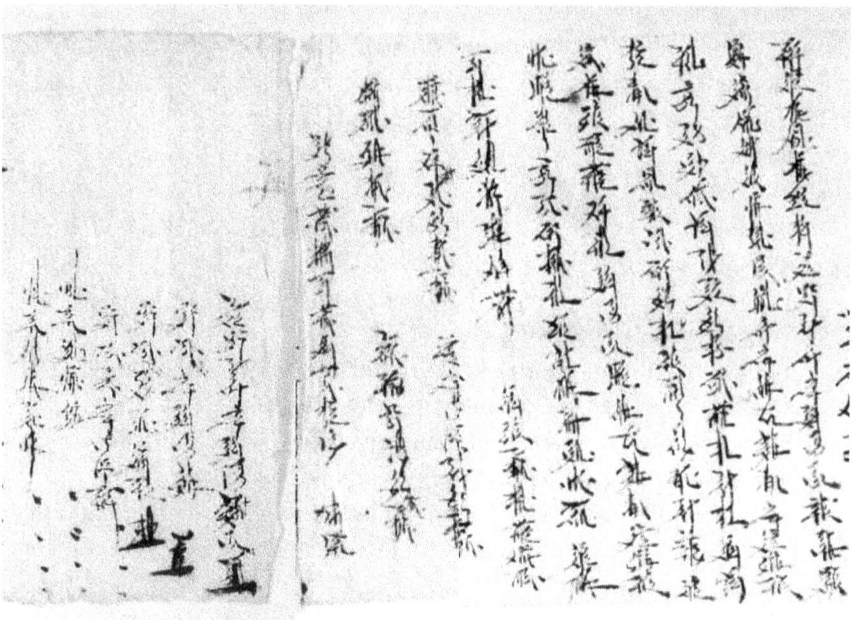

FIGURE 154 Инв. No. 5124-3(2, 3), 5124-4(1): 2nd day of 2nd month in Yin year of Tianqing (1194) contract of land sale by [illegible]

7. Инв. No. 5124-3(2, 3) and 5124-4(1): Contract of land sale by [illegible] [ljow ɣwie ·o bie_j] on the 2nd day of the 2nd month in the Yin Year of Heavenly Celebration (1194) is found in the long scroll of contracts, reprinted in volume 14 of the *Russian Collection of Khara-Khoto Manuscripts*. The main text is reassembled from the end of part 2 in Инв. No. 5124-3, and the beginning of part 3, as well as the first 6 lines in part 1 of 5124-4. There is a total of 16 lines in cursive Tangut, followed by stamps and signatures.[121]

Translation:

> On the 2nd day of the 2nd month in the Yin Year, Contract Party [illegible] [ljow ɣwie ·o bie_j] et al., presently out of their own will, to Pu-
> du Temple's grain agents [illegible] [ljow dow dźjij phu_], [illegible] [ljow lja mja], et al.
> sells his patch of land fit to sow 5 *dan* of seeds at the agreed price of 4 *dan*
> of wheat and 9 *dan* of coarse grains. There is no discrepancy in either land or payment. If either publicly
> or privately, there should ever arise any attempt to transfer or mortgage this title, let [illegible]

121 *Russian Collection of Khara-Khoto Manuscripts*, vol. 14, pp. 15 and 18.

[Tangut] [ɣwie ·o bie_j] bear all responsibility; let [Tangut] [dow dźjij phu_] or [Tangut] [lja mja] share no liability. Whichever party should violate the agreement, let it not only be prosecuted by the laws, but also, according to the government's rules, pay 1 *liang* of gold as a penalty fee. Own hearts willing. The four borders of the land are clearly demarcated:

To the east it borders the land of [Tangut] [dju. dju. gju_ ·o]; to the south it borders the land of [Tangut] [ljow da kia ·jiw]

To the west it borders the canals for irrigation; to the north it borders the land of [Tangut] [tśhiə dzji_j ta]

The tax is 7 *dou*, including 1 *dou* 4 *sheng* of wheat. Narrow water is used for irrigation.

Contract Party: [Tangut] [ljow ɣwie ·o bie_j] (stamp)

Co-Contract Party: [Tangut] [ljow ɣwie gia_ phu_] (stamp)

Co-Contract Party: [Tangut] [me_ nja_ dźjwow thja] (stamp)

Co-Contract Party: [Tangut] [ljow da kia kie.] (finger-segment)

Witness: Chen Yanshuang (finger-segment)

Witness: [Tangut] [phjij śjo wa śia~] (finger-segment)

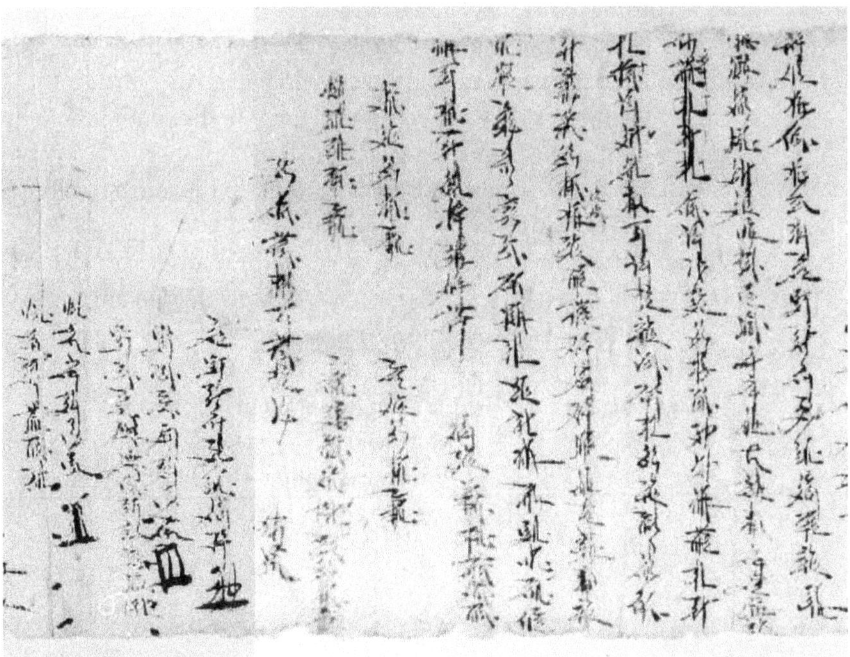

FIGURE 155 Инв. No. 5124-4(2, 3): 2nd day of 2nd month in Yin year of Tianqing (1194) contract of land sale by [Tangut]

8. Инв. No. 5124-4(2, 3): Contract of land sale by [Tangut] on the 2nd day of the 2nd month in the Yin Year of Heavenly Celebration (1194 AD). The manuscript is a part of the long scroll of contracts, reprinted in Volume 14 of the *Russian Collection of Khara-Khoto Manuscripts*. It is reassembled from the later section of image 2 and the first part of image 3 in Инв. No. 5124-4. There is a total of 16 lines of cursive Tangut. The contract ends with signatures and stamps.[122]

Translation:

> On the 2nd day of the 2nd month in the Yin Year, Contract Party [Tangut] [me_ nja_ dźjwow thja] et al., presently
> To the grain-agents at the Pudu Temple, [Tangut] [ljow dow dźjij phu_] and Liang La-
> ma, etc. voluntarily sells a patch of land large enough to sow 5 *dan* of seeds, at the agreed price of
> 6 *dan* of coarse grains and 1 *dan* of wheat. There is no discrepancy in payment or in land.
> In case of any attempt to transfer or mortgage the titlte of this land, let Xuanzhu et al., not [Tangut] [dow dźjij phu_] et al., be responsible.
> Whichever party violates these terms, let it not only bear legal responsibility according to the *Laws and Orders*,
> But also pay 1 *liang* of gold as a penalty fee. Own Hearts willing. The four borders of the land concerned are clearly demarcated:
> To the east it borders government-owned land. To the south it borders government-owned land.
> To the west it borders the canals for irrigation. To the north it borders the land of Lu?? Matie.
> The tax is 5 *dou*, including 1 *dou* of wheat. Narrow water for irrigation.
> Contract Party: [Tangut] [me_ nja_ dźjwow thja] (stamp)
> Co-Contract Party: younger brother [Tangut] [ɣwie gia_śjow] (stamp)
> Co-Contract Party: wife, ?? (finger-segment)
> Witness: [Tangut] [ljow ɣwie ·o bie_j] (stamp)
> Witness: [Tangut] [dju. dju. śja phji wejr] (finger-segment)

122 *Russian Collection of Khara-Khoto Manuscripts*, vol. 14, p. 19.

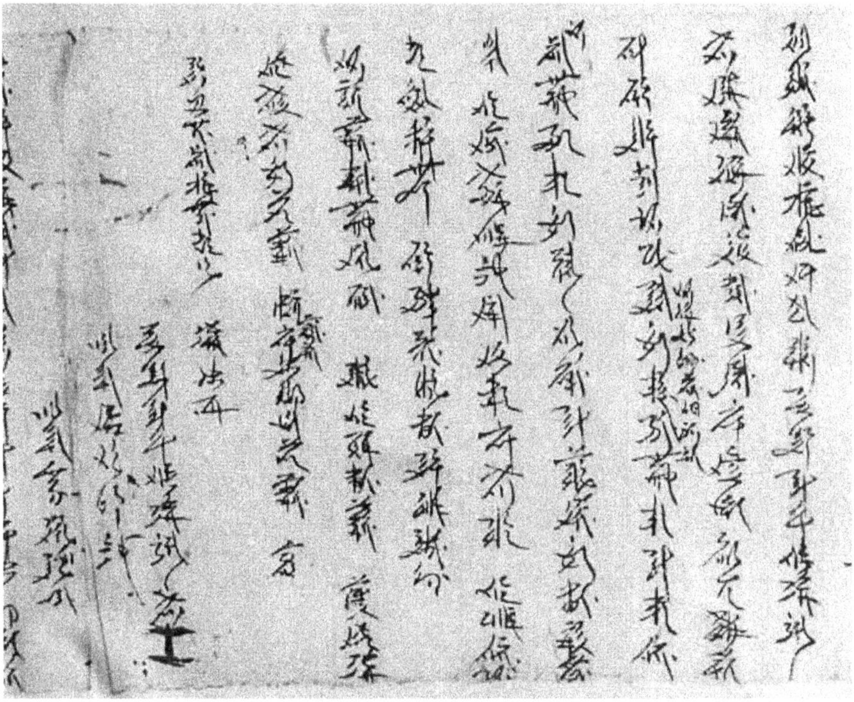

FIGURE 156 Инв. No. 5124-4(6): 6th day of 2nd month in Yin year of Tianqing (1194) contract of land sale by [Tangut]

9. Инв. No. 5124-4(6): Contract of land sale by [Tangut] [phjij śjo sjwi sjwi dju] on the 6th day of the 2nd month in the Yin Year of Heavenly Celebration (1194). It consists of 14 lines of cursive Tangut in the long scroll of contracts, ending with signatures and stamps.[123]

Translation:

> On the 6th day of the 2nd month in the Yin Year of Heavenly Celebration,
> Contract Party [Tangut] [phjij śjo sjwi sjwi]—
> [Tangut] [dju] to the grain-agents at the Pudu Temple, [Tangut] [ljow lja mja], [Tangut] [dow dźjij phu_] et al., sells a patch of ripe/unripe land fit to sow 3 *dan* of seeds, along with an old four-cabin house, etc. at the price of 5
> *dan* of coarse grains, which is already paid. There is no discrepancy in either the payment or the land. If on this land any other party,

123 The image of the original manuscript should have been included in the *Russian Collection of Khara-Khoto Manuscripts*, vol. 14, p. 21. However, for some reason that page is blank. But the image is resupplied below.

such as members of the same *chao*, should either publicly or privately dispute the property ownership, let the penalty be, in accordance with the laws established by the government, 5 *dan* of

wheat. Hearts willing. Let the contract be enforced according to the circumstances and to the terms set herein.

The four borders are clearly demarcated: to the east it borders government-owned canals; to the south it borders the land of Xishang

Nüyou; to the northwest it borders the land of Liang "the donkey's mother" to the north[124]

The tax is 8 *dou* of coarse grains and 2 *dou* of wheat; half a narrow stream of water suffices to irrigate the land.

Contract Party: [illegible] [phjij śjo sjwi sjwi dju] (stamp)[125]

Witness: [illegible] [sji śjo da kia zji] (finger-segment)

Witness: [illegible] [khjiw khjwi- phə bie_j] (finger-segment)

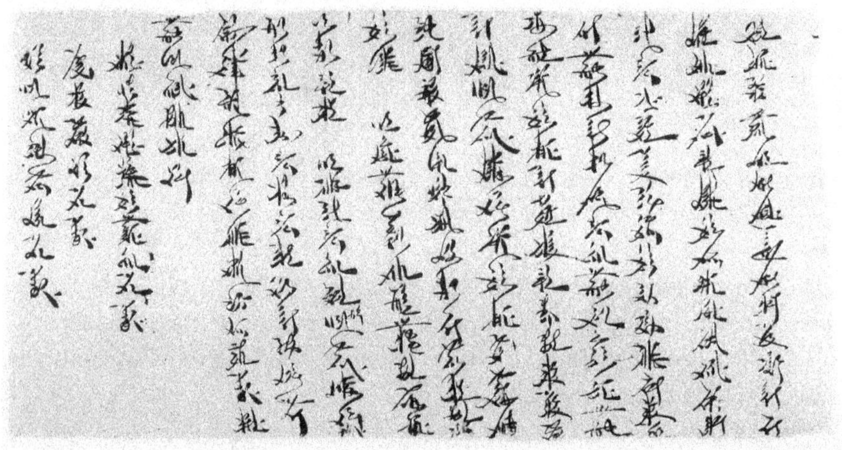

FIGURE 157 Инв. No. 4199: 16th day of 6th month in Bingchen year of Tianqing (1196) contract of land sale by [illegible]??

124 The character is incomplete. It could have been the character for expanse/border.

125 TN: Note that the name often appears as [illegible], with three [illegible] rather than two. The reduplicated [illegible] is often translated into the Chinese character 歳, hence the best wishes for having a bit of wealth each and every year. The character itself also means fortune and luck. So, it amounts to the same meaning, more or less.

10. Инв. No. 4199: Contract of land sale by 𗏹𗼇𗾈?? [ljow śiə nio_w ??][126] on the 16th day of the 6th month in the Bingchen year of Heavenly Celebration (1196 AD). It is a single-page manuscript with 15 lines of cursive Tangut hand-written on a 23.5 × 45 cm hemp paper.[127]

Translation:

> On the 16th day of the 6th month in the Bingchen year of Heavenly Celebration, Contract Party [ljow][128]
> 𗼇𗾈?? [śiə nio_w ??] et al., presently has his own ripe/unripe land, watered by the canal at the hillside of four wells,
> Which is 70 *mu* large and fit to sow 10 *dan* of seeds, voluntarily sold to 𗏹𗍫𗹨𗰭 [ljow tśju. ·wejr śjow]
> At the price of 5 *dan* of coarse grains. Each ?? bought,
> Three items, including the hay tax on the land,[129] 𗍫𗹨𗰭 [tśju. ·wejr śjow]
> Bears the costs; other than that, first?, on this land, if
> Other members of the same *chao* strive to dispute the property ownership, ?
> Attempt to either publicly or privately transfer? Or loan the land, and who??
> Let the relevant party not only pay 10 *dan* of grains as a penalty fee, according to the laws set by the government, but also
> Recompensate double the sum of the original purchase price. Own hearts willing.
> Let the agreement be enforced according to what is written in the contract and required by circumstances. The four borders [of the land]
> Are clearly demarcated. ?:
> To the east it borders the land of 𗣼𗏁𗴿𗤶 [phjij śjo mja tsə.]
> To the south it borders the land of Cao "Iron"?
> To the west it borders the land of Weiming "the prosperous and entertained"
> ......[130]

---

126 TN: The name is barely legible. The author's guess is that it is a four-character name: "Liang, benevolence, cause, bear, sound." Here, I've given only the first three characters.

127 *Russian Collection of Khara-Khoto Manuscripts*, vol. 13, p. 199.

128 The lower section of the contract suffers damages. There are missing characters in some lines. However, it is possible to resupply certain information in context, and based on common legal formulas in Tangut contracts.

129 Shi Jinbo, 2005 (a).

130 The contract is damaged near the end. Information on the northern border, along with the signatures and stamps of the main parties to the contract are missing.

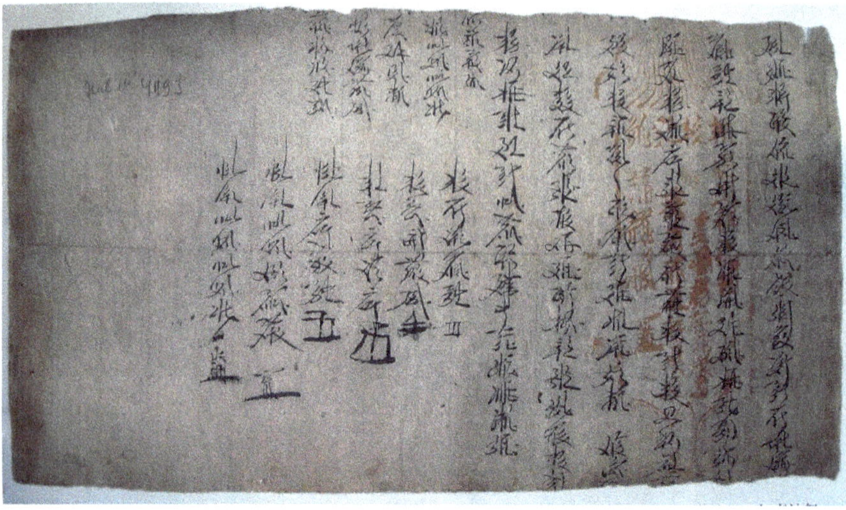

FIGURE 158 Инв. No. 4193: 5th day of 1st month, Wuwu fifth year of Tianqing (1198) contract of land and house sale by [illegible]

11. Инв. No. 4193: Contract of Land and House sale by [illegible] [mjadzjwi-khjwi-wjazji] on the 5th day of the 1st month in Wuwu, the fifth year of Heavenly Celebration (1198 AD). It is a single-page contract with 12 lines of cursive Tangut written on a 23.2 × 43.1 cm hemp paper. The first line begins with the date, proceeds to the main content of the contract, and ends with the signatures and stamps, where the four borders of the land are demarcated. There are a lotus sign and a 22 × 7 cm red seal.[131]

Translation:

> On the 5th day of the 1st month in Wuwu, the fifth year of Heavenly Celebration, Contract Party: Maze "old
>
> Father and son" et al., presently have their own 23 mu of land irrigated by the water from the Mingbu Hillside Canal[132]
>
> Along with a yard, altogether sold to [illegible] [ljow tśju. ·wejr śjow]; the price, in 8 *dan* of coarse grains, has been paid.
>
> There is no discrepancy in either the payment or the land. Hereafter, should any party either publicly or private

131 *Russian Collection of Khara-Khoto Manuscripts*, vol. 13, p. 194.

132 The Tangut character for *qing* ([illegible]) looks quite similar to *mu* ([illegible]). The two are especially easily confused in cursive writings. Given the ratio of land prices, it is more likely that the intended character is *mu*.

Launch a dispute or renege on the agreement, let the recompensation be double the sum of the sale price,

Each 1 *dan* is repaid 2 *dan*,[133] and let the terms be enforced according to what is written in the document and required by the circumstances.

(Upper section)

The four borders of the land are clearly demarcated

To the east [it borders the land of]???? "the treasure"

To the south, the hillside where the canal is found.

To the west, [the land of] [Tangut] [mja dzjwi- śja phji]

To the north, [the land of] Hun? "the black dog" ([Tangut])

(Lower section)

Seller: [Tangut] [mjadzjwi- khjwi-wjazji] (stamp)

Co-seller: younger brother, [Tangut] [śja phji] (stamp)

Co-seller Liang?? (stamp)

Witness: Liang [Tangut] [la~ wejr] (stamp)

Witness: ??[Tangut] [??·ji. tsji_r śjow] (stamp)

Witness: ???? [Tangut] [???? lji-.] (stamp)

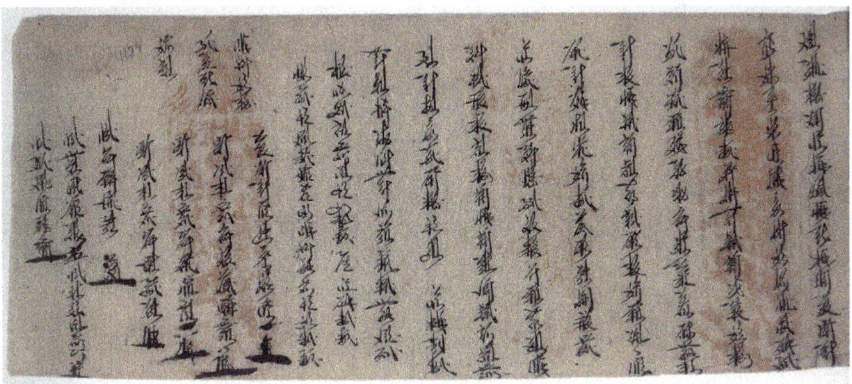

FIGURE 159 Инв. No. 4194: Gengshen year of Tianqing (1200) contract of land and house sale by [Tangut]

12. Инв. No. 4194: Contract of land and house sale by [Tangut] [lew śji thow pha~] in the Gengshen Year of Heavenly Celebration (1200). It is a single-page manuscript with 19 lines of cursive Tangut handwritten on a 22.9 × 57.1 cm hemp paper. It begins with the date and ends with the signatures and stamps. Above the stamps are the demarcations of the four borders of the land. There

133 The character for *dan* is missing.

is also a lotus figure, and three prints of the official red seal of the 22 × 7 cm House of Trade and Taxes.[134]

Translation:

On the 22nd day of the 2nd month in the Gengshen Year of Heavenly Celebration, Contract—

or [Tangut] [lew śji thow pha~] presently has his own land, irrigated by the canal of the Four-well hillside,

by the side of [Tangut] ? [Tangut] [xwe~ dźju_(?) bo_ śji-j]'s land, a patch of ripe/unripe land fit to sow 100 *dan* of seeds,

along with a full set of yard and houses, voluntarily sold to [Tangut] [ljow tśju. ·wejr śjow] at the agreed

price of 200 *dan* of coarse grains. There is no discrepancy in either the payment or the land

hereafter, if on this land any affiliates of these parties

attempt to transfer or mortgage the title, either publicly or privately, and fall into a state of chaos as they dispute over the property, let it be recompensated in twice the sum of the original sell & purchase price.

Let the repayment be 400

dan, and any party which reneges on these terms should be penalised according to the laws by 3 *liang*

Of gold. Own hearts willing. The four borders of the land are demarcated:

To the east, it borders ???; to the south it borders the government-owned canal

To the northwest it borders the land of Lüyi [Tangut] [parya ne_w] et al.

(Upper Part)

There was one

Patch of land that is 75

mu

(Lower Part)

Contract Party: [Tangut] [lew śji thow pha~] (stamp)

Co-Contract Party and seller: [Tangut] [ljow tshja wja ku. śju_] (stamp)

Co-Contract Party and seller: [Tangut] [ljow khjwi- tshjij ɣji-] (stamp)

Co-Contract Party and seller: [Tangut] [ljow mja dzow wej] (stamp)

Witness: [Tangut] [ljow le bo zji] (stamp)

134 *Russian Collection of Khara-Khoto Manuscripts*, vol. 13, p. 194.

Witness: 蕠㵖㵗㵘 [tsew ɣa. ·ji- lji-.] (stamp) witness: 㵙㵚 [zjwi. ·o] 㵛?㵜 [wja. ? ɣwie] (stamp)
Witness: 㵝? [tśhji? kjir] (stamp)

The 12 contracts presented and translated above show some general patterns. Overall, Tangut contracts of land sale inherit the same format from contracts in the Central Plains tradition. These Tangut manuscripts contain nearly all the essential elements of sell and purchase contracts. A thorough analysis of these legal documents open the door to a deeper understanding of land and transaction in Western Xia, as well as the Tangut society in general.

3.1.2 The Reasons behind Land Sales and the Identities of the Buyers and Sellers

3.1.2.1 *Time and Causes of Land Sales*

The Tangut city of Khara-Khoto is located to the north of the Badain Jaran Desert, on the northern bank of the downstream inland waterways of the Ejin River, or the Black River. Indeed, Khara-Khoto's agriculture prospered in the Tangut era, thanks to the nourishment of the Black River. There is no better way to probe the conditions of farmland in this region than to survey this batch of Tangut land sale contracts.

The earliest amongst the 12 contracts is dated to the 22nd year of Heavenly Prosperity. Then come the 8 contracts in the Инв. No. 5124 scroll, all of which are signed in the first year of Heavenly Celebration (1194 AD). The remaining 3 documents are from the 3rd, 5th, and 7th years of Heavenly Celebration (Tianqing), respectively.

Tangut power endured for a span of 190 years (1038–1227 AD) since the foundation of the Xixia dynasty. Given this time frame, it is obvious that these land sale contracts fall into the late period of Tangut history, across 31 years. Except for the earliest, which dates to the reign of Renzong Emperor, the other 11 all hail from the first 7 years of Huanzong Emperor's rule. The latest one was signed just 28 years before the fall of the Tangut Empire. Therefore, it should be said that this specific sample of Tangut land records, which happens to have survived to the present day, is only representative of the Khara-Khoto economy in the late Tangut period.

None of these land sale contracts openly states the reason for the sale. But the motives are not difficult to infer, given the dates and months recorded in these documents. All 8 contracts found in the long scroll provide precise dates, and all fall into either the first or the second months of the lunar calendar. Amongst the 4 individual contracts, one only documents the year but leaves the month and date unmentioned, which is quite rare and abnormal. All the other three begin with precise dates, two of which are also drafted in the first and second months of the new year, whereas one is written in the sixth month. To summarise, of the 11 clearly dated contracts, 10 are signed in the first and second months, right in the middle of the interim between two autumn harvests. Since land is the one fundamental factor of production on which entire households and extended families depend in rural Khara-Khoto, peasants never easily bring themselves to sell land. Although no direct evidence is available, it is safe to assume that the protagonists in these contracts are selling their land out of dire necessity, that is, shortage of grains at home. Under the duress and difficulty of poverty and starvation, the peasants are left no other option than to give up their land in exchange for foodstuff to feed on for the next six months or so.

The particular contract dating to the sixth month is signed on the 16th day of the 6th month in the Bingchen Year of Tianqing (1196). Liang, who sells 70 *mu* of land at this strange time, must have been motivated by some personal reasons, rather than the hardship of life.

The limited number of Tangut contracts of land sale known to modern scholars are only a small fraction of this type of legal documents. Even the long scroll, where contracts are systematically compiled and densely concentrated, is only the temple's record for less than a single month—from the 24th day of the 1st month to the 20th day of the 2nd month in the first year of Tianqing. It is remarkable how much land is sold within such a short span of time and within such a limited geographical scope—a single Buddhist temple. One could only imagine the plight of poverty faced by the local poor. Despite the abundance of farmland and the convenience of irrigation from the Black River, the contracts show that peasant families suffered grain deficits in the first and second months of the year. One possible cause was a natural disaster that might have befallen the area the year before, which would have sharply reduced the yield in the last harvest, thus cut the peasants off halfway through the tilling season, and forced them to sell land in exchange for food. In fact, many of the Tangut grain loan accounts also date to the years between Tianqing and Guangding, particularly the first year of Tianqing, suggesting that Tangut agriculture suffered a blow at the time.[135] Social, legal, and economic documents such as these point to the possibility of a famine. However, since Western Xia is not represented in official imperial chronicles, there is scant historical source on natural disasters in Western Xia. No one is known to have recorded anything on natural calamities in Khara-Khoto.

135 Shi Jinbo, 2005 (b), pp. 186–204.

3.1.2.2 *The Seller and the Size of Land Sold*

The earliest known Tanguts were experts in pasturing and livestock-raising, who knew little about tilling and sowing. As a result, there was a perennial shortage of grains amongst the Dangxiang tribes. But when Dangxiang power morphed into a stronger and stabler regime, and before the Tanguts founded the Xiazhou regime and proclaimed the status of an empire, a batch of husbandry-minded Tanguts turned to agriculture as they resettled on arable lands that recently fell under Tangut dominion. For an *ethnos*, this transition marked a historical transformation. It made entire populations of Tangut peasants, which never existed before. Most of the land-sellers we identify in Khara-Khoto contracts are descendants of this first generation of Tangut farmers. Nearly all the Contract Parties and witnesses are local, ethnic-Fan (Dangxiang Tangut) peasants: [illegible] [·jaxwa], [illegible] [mə rar], [illegible] [dju.dju.], [illegible] [·o gu_], [illegible] [phjij śjo], [illegible] [me_nja_], [illegible] [sji śjo], [illegible] [mjadzjwi-], etc. There are also a handful of Han Chinese, such as the Qiu, Cao, and Chen. Liang is much more complicated: although it is originally a Han surname, we also know of ethnic Tangut Liangs, most notably the Liang empresses who championed the cause of Fan customs against sinicisation and Confucianisation in their nearly 30 years of rule and regency. So, there is no way to attest the ethnic make-up of the Liangs we see in Khara-Khoto land sale contracts. Historically, when the first Dangxiang Tanguts switched from pasturing to farming, they acquired and owned land allotted or approved by the government. These free farmers cultivated their own land and harvested their own grains, so long as they paid taxes to the state. But the late-Tangut contracts we have show that many of their descendants could no longer make ends meet, without selling their ancestral land.

The name of the seller, size of land, and quantity of assets as recorded in the 8 contracts in the Инв. No. 5124 scroll are, in respective order, (1) [illegible] [khjiw bie_j ta] sells a patch of land fit to sow 20 *dan* of seeds along with the houses; (2) [illegible] [ljow da kia ·jiw] sells his land fit to sow 15 *dan* of seeds along with the houses, (3) [illegible] [dju. dju. śja phji wejr] sells land fit to sow 8 *dan* of seeds along with houses and trees; (4) [illegible] [ljow ɣwie gia_ ·jiw] sells land fit to sow 10 *dan* of seeds along with the houses; (5) [illegible] [khjij śja rjar śji-j] sells land fit to sow 10 *dan* of seeds, houses, tilling tools and equipment, and a tree yard; (6) [illegible] [ljow ɣwie ·o bie_j] sells land fit to sow 5 *dan* of seeds; (7) [illegible] [me_ nja_ dźjwow thja] sells land fit to sow 5 *dan* of seeds; (8) [illegible] [phjij śjo sjwi sjwi dju] sells land fit to sow 3 *dan* of seeds, along with the houses. The same information in the 4 single-page contracts are: (9) widow [illegible] [·jaxwa zji-. lji-.śio] sells land fit to sow 2 *dan* of seeds along with the yard and three thatched cottages, as well as 2 trees; (10) ??[ljow śiə nio_w ??] sells 70 *mu* of land fit to sow 10 *dan* of seeds, watered by the canals from the Hillside of Four Wells; (11) [mjadzjwi- khjwi-wjazji] sells 23 *mu* of land along with the house and yard; (12) [lew śji thow pha~] sells land large enough to sow 100 *dan* of seeds. All the sellers are the original owners of the title concerned. In most cases, they are the patriarchs of peasant households and male heads of the family. There is, however, one example of a matriarch and female head of the household, the widow [·jaxwa].

The data in the contracts show a certain degree of disparity in land size across households. Most contracts do not indicate the precise size of the land in standard measurements, such as *qing* or *mu*, but in the amount of seeds (*dan*) to be sowed in a patch of land. But wherever both measurements are given, it is possible to find a rough conversion rate. For example, the widow [·jaxwa] sold 22 *mu* of land, where 2 *dan* of seeds can be sowed. That is, each *dan* of seeds is sowed on a little more than 10 *mu* of land. The land sold by ?? [ljow śiə nio_w ??] is 70 *mu* in size, large enough to sow 10 *dan* of seeds. There, the unit of land for 1 *dan* of seeds is less than 10 *mu*. Therefore, it should be noted that to measure land size by *dan* of seeds sowed is only an approximate measure. However, it may be assumed for the purpose of simplification and generalisation that a unit of land for 1 *dan* of seeds is more or less the equivalent of 10 *mu*.

The land sizes as recorded in the 8 contracts of the long scroll are, in the amounts of seeds to be sowed, 20 *dan*, 15 *dan*, 8 *dan*, 10 *dan*, 10 *dan*, 5 *dan*, 5 *dan*, 3 *dan*; or, once converted to the measurement of area: 200, 150, 80, 100, 100, 50, 50, 30 Tangut *mu*. The land ranges between 7.5 to 50 Song *mu*. One could tell that an average Tangut household owns a large amount of farmland. This is unsurprising, given the far northwestern location of Khara-Khoto, the wide space and sparse populations in the area. Land size varies more sharply in the four individual contracts. [·jaxwa zji-. lji-. śio] sells 22 *mu* of land, whilst [lew śji thow pha~] sells land large enough to sow 100 *dan* of seeds, roughly a thousand *mu* (or 250 Song *mu*) of land. This is an outlying datapoint, statistically, and a very special case of land sale, historically.

3.1.2.3 *Buyers and the Quantity of Property Purchased*

The buyers in all the 8 contracts across the manuscript scroll are the same two figures, [ljow dow zji-r phu_] and [ljow lja mja], who are referred to as 'the ones who handle the grains,' i.e. agents employed by the Pudu Temple to manage the temple's assets and properties. They could as well be monks based at the temple. [lja mja] is obviously the a for a follower of the Dharma in Tantric Buddhism. Originally, it is reserved for the *thera*,[136] a learned elder, a *bhadanta*.[137] But over time, the term proliferated to more common usage, and came to mean any Buddhist monk. Given the prevalence and popularity of Tantric Buddhism in Western Xia, the Pudu Temple is likely to have been a Tantric monastery. Moreover, this particular temple in Khara-Khoto is unmentioned in Chinese sources. The contracts tell us that by this time, monks in charge of pragmatic affairs, such as managing grains and land, were called Lama. It could be the case that "Lama" already turned into a generic title for any monk in the Tangut period.

The long scroll of contracts shows that within less than a month in the spring of the first year of Heavenly Celebration, the Pudu Temple bought in a startling 760 *mu* of land, or approximately 190 in Song *mu*.

Of the four single-page contract manuscripts, the first was signed by widow [Tangut] [·jaxwa zji-. lji-.śio], who sold her 22 *mu* of land to a Tangut man by the name of [Tangut] [·jaxwa mji-_tshja]. The buyer in the other three contracts is the same man, called [Tangut] [ljow tśju. ·wejr śjow]: 70 *mu* of land for sowing 10 *dan* of seeds, 23 *mu*, and land fit to sow 100 *dan* of seeds; in total, around 1000 *mu* of land. This is an enormous amount of land to purchase. The seller [Tangut] [lew śji thow pha~] does not sound like an everyday peasant, but rather a landlord of some wealth and capacity. For the buyer [Tangut] [ljow tśju. ·wejr śjow] to acquire so many properties within the span of 5 years, he would have been an even more powerful landlord and grain-owner. Curiously, the Инв. No. 5949-2 Khara-Khoto military *liu* report is signed by a certain "[Tangut]," who must have been a commander of the military *liu*. It is possible that this may be our landlord [Tangut].[138]

3.1.3 Farmland and Irrigation

3.1.3.1 *Farmland and Yard*

There is a noteworthy phenomenon in Tangut land transfers: the fixed asset is included in the sale. When a previous landowner sells the title of his or her property, more often than not, the farmland comes with yards, buildings, and plants. Say, when [Tangut] [·jaxwa zji-. lji-.śio] charges a price for her farmland, she sells the fixed assets attached to the land, in the same deal: a yard, 3 thatched cottages, and 2 trees. Likewise, [Tangut] [khjiw bie_j ta] sells a yard and a house along with his land. [Tangut] [da kia ·jiw] sells not only the house

136 TN: Sanskrit: स्थवरि.

137 TN: Sanskrit: भदन्त, or आर्य; Tibetan: འཕགས་པ་; Chinese: 大德, 尊者.

138 *Russian Collection of Khara-Khoto Manuscripts*, vol. 14, p. 72.

and yard, but also the trees. [illegible] [dju. dju. śja phji wejr] vends the 2 cottages and 5 live trees on her land. [illegible] [ljow ɣwie gia_ ·jiw]'s land also comes with houses and walls. [illegible] [khjij śja rjar śji-j] offers houses both large and small, as well as a tree yard. On [illegible] [phjij śjo sjwi sjwi dju]'s land there are four old cabins. [illegible] [mjadzjwi- khjwi-wjazji] sells his yard on the land. Finally, [illegible] [lew śji thow pha~] sells both the yard and the house along with the farmland. In 9 out of the 12 contracts, land comes with houses and yards. In 2 of the remaining 3 documents, the land to be sold is not as large. Both [illegible] [ljow ɣwie ·o bie_j] and [illegible] [me_ nja_ dźjwow thja] sell a patch of land only just enough to sow 5 *dan* of seeds. The last patch of land is about 70 *mu* in size.

It seems that the actual abodes of Khara-Khoto peasant families are scattered around the farmland of the households. With this rather odd picture, one cannot but imagine the legacy of herding as factor of influence on the practice of building lodgings across pastures. Clearly, the structure and architecture of the quarters in rural Khara-Khoto is different from farming villages in the Central Plains. In most times, peasant families in a Chinese village cluster around a common residential quarter, whence they venture out into their respective farmlands during the day, which scatter onto the outskirt of the settlement. In contrast, Khara-Khoto residences are found scattered right on the family farmlands, like stars in a constellation or pieces on a chessboard. This curious phenomenon is extremely helpful when it comes to studying the farming community and farmland management in the agricultural hub of historical Khara-Khoto.

The first generations of the Dangxiang Tanguts were herdsmen who chose their dwelling places whither their herds roamed, and wherever pasture and water there were for cattles to graze. Since herding took place across vast grassland, individual households lived in felt tents as a mobile, single unit, at a large distance from other families. Although the peasants in Khara-Khoto had adapted to the settled economic life of agriculture, they still preserved some degree of the scattered settlement, with its roots in hunting and herding. At any rate, it must be noted that the Tanguts' conversion to agriculturalism was never to the point of totality. Most Tangut peasants engaged in tilling and pasturing at the same time, and maintained interests in animal-husbandry despite their reduced mobility. Families owned various numbers of livestocks. The family in the household record Инв. No. 8203 manuscript, for example, owns as many as three camels, 10 cattles, and 80 sheep. In the Инв. No. 7893-9 record, the household keeps an impressive 3 horses and 32 camels. In one of our land sales contracts, [illegible] [·jaxwa zji-. lji-. śio] sells land in exchange for none other than more livestocks. It shows that agriculture and animal-husbandry were intertwined and integrated. Scattered settlement is especially suited to an industrial structure of integrated agriculture and livestock-raising, and to the economic life of simultaneous farming and pasturing. Finally, given the spacious farmland in the relatively sparsely-populated Khara-Khoto, it was much easier for the families to manage their properties if they lived right on their own land.

As a matter of either strategy or practicality, to sell the fixtures along with the land clears the sale and cuts out complications at the single stroke of a deal. It is also much easier if the new landowner takes over the management of the properties immediately. It would be troublesome, for example, for the new landlord to lease the land out without the houses and yards.

3.1.3.2 *Four Borders and Neighbouring Farmland*

All Tangut land sale contracts hitherto found demarcate the four borders of the land near the end of the document, in order to specify the locations and direction of the land with precision. The common expression for demarcation is [Tangut script] [lji-r we kiew ɣa dja mjijr phji] or [Tangut script] [lji-r njijr kiew ɣa dja mjijr phji]: the four borders are clearly specified. The short sentence is followed by the neighbouring lands or locations to the east, south, west, and north of the patch of land to be sold. It could either be a private land of a neighbour, or a certain canal.

FIGURE 160 Инв. No. 4193: Wuwu fifth year of Tianqing (1198) four boundaries of the land specified in the contract of land sale

It is remarkable that given the information on land demarcation near the end of the contracts, it is possible to map out the neighbouring lands along their borders, their direction and location relative to the canals and government-owned land. With 5 interrelated contracts, it is possible to sketch the following diagram:

CHART 12 Reconstructed diagram representing the location of farmland in Khara-Khoto

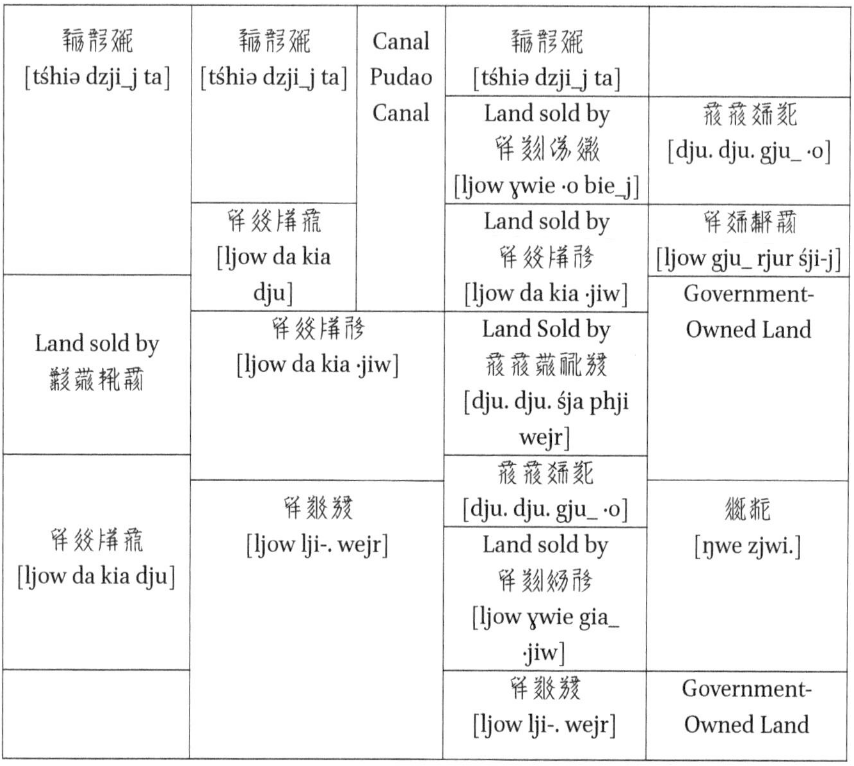

The diagram should by no means be taken literally at its face value. For a historically accurate demarcation of farmland, forever irrecoverable, could not have been made of neat squares and rectangulars. But for now, the graphical representation serves our purpose and aids our understanding of where the families are, and what land they sell. Apart from private farmland, there is also government-owned land. In addition, there is also land owned by Buddhist temples. It should be said that individual historical land sale contracts surviving to this day are precious finds. But a series of contracts where multiple patches of neighbouring lands are sold, wherewith it is possible for historians to reconstruct the landscape of historical farmlands, canals, and government-owned land, is even more valuable.

3.1.3.3 *Canals and Water Supply*

Names of local canals are mentioned in Tangut land sale contracts, especially in the demarcation of the land. These references provide key sources on Tangut irrigation system in Khara-Khoto area. The contracts mention a number of canals: the End of the Left Canal ([illegible] [gju mji_j tsow gju]),[139] Pudao Canal ([illegible] [pu tew gju]), Canal for Irrigation ([illegible] [zer gju]), Government-owned Canal ([illegible] [kow gju]), Canal from the Hillside of Four Wells ([illegible] [lji-r khja wjor gju]), Canal from the Hillside of Mingbu Wells ([illegible] [mjij pu. khja wjor gju]), and the Southern Canal ([illegible] [zji-r gju]). One could see the complexity of the Khara-Khoto irrigation system. Some of the canals are owned and managed by the government. Others, such as Pudao and Mingbu, are named after Tangut tribes and families. As for whether they are privately owned, there is no settled conclusion without further evidence. Still, other canal names contain geographical references, such as the Southern or the Left Canals. There is much to be researched about these directions, and about the names of localities such as the Hillside of Four Wells. But we are reminded of canal names in Khara-Khoto Household Registers, such as the New Canal ([illegible] [gju sjiw]), Lüyi Canal ([illegible] [lwərze gju]), Xipan Canal ([illegible] [·ji-r dzji-j gju]), Yang Canal ([illegible] [so sjiw]), and Daoli Canals ([illegible] [tśja low gju]). Some of these names are more intuitive than others. But again, much research remains to be done.

In 7 of the 8 land sale contracts, there is a concise, two-character or three-character expression right underneath the land tax, which is easy to overlook. The phrase has little to do with the text that comes immediately before or after, and therefore seems even a bit out of place. For example, in the contract of [illegible] [khjiw bie_j ta] and [illegible] [ljow da kia ·jiw], there is a reference to [illegible] [nji-_ zji-_r] (day, water); in the contracts of [illegible] [dju. dju. śja phji wejr], [illegible] [ljow ɣwie gia_ ·jiw], [illegible] [ljow ɣwie ·o bie_j], and [illegible] [me_ nja_ dźjwow thja], we find instead the characters [illegible] [tshji-j zji-_r] (narrow water). Finally, in the document of [illegible] [phjij śjo sjwi sjwi dju], there are three characters: [illegible] [zji-_r tshji-j khwɔ] (narrow water, half).

139 TN: The third character transliterates a number of loan words. It could be "left" or another name.

FIGURE 161 Инв. No. 5124: 'daily water' 'slim water' 'half slim water' under tax information in different land sale contracts

These are references to the amount of water supply required to irrigate a given patch of farmland. A comparative survey of the water supply data across multiple contracts shows a strong correlation between the land size (hence value) and the water supply for irrigation. For instance, the land of [khjiw bie_j ta] fit to sow 20 *dan* of seeds, and that of [ljow da kia ·jiw] fit for 15 *dan* of seeds, both require a "daily" dose of water irrigation. By comparison, the patch of land sold by [dju. dju. śja phji wejr], fit to sow 8 *dan* of seeds, by [ljow ɣwie gia_ ·jiw] for 10 *dan* of seeds, by [ljow ɣwie ·o bie_j] for 5 *dan* of seeds, and by [me_ nja_ dźjwow thja] for 15 *dan* of seeds, all use "narrow" water for irrigation. [phjij śjo sjwi sjwi dju] states in his contract that a a "half-narrow" supply suffices for his land, where only 5 *dan* of seeds are sowed in a typical farming season. So, the general rule is exactly what anyone would expect, a positive correlation between farmland size and the amount of water supply. But there is a certain degree of variability within a certain range of land size, perhaps due to other factors of influence. In the macroscope, these references reveal the open secret that Khara-Khoto farmland relied almost exclusively on canals for irrigation, and that water is distributed largely according to the size of land owned by local households.

In Book 15 of the *Laws of Heavenly Prosperity*, there are laws on "opening canals in the spring," "raising pastures and monitoring the waters," "canal waters," "various crimes related to land and water." All 5 items in the section on "raising pastures and monitoring the waters" are lost. The surviving content on canals and water are mostly to do with the management of irrigation systems. There is no explicit reference to the various levels of water supplies in the laws, nor definitions of such terms as "daily," "narrow," and "half-narrow." How exactly was water quantified, classified, and supplied to farmland, are first seen, and only to be reconstructed from land sale contracts.

3.1.3.4 *Government-Owned Land vs. Private Land*

There are both privately-owned and government-owned lands in Western Xia. Government-owned land, either farmland or pasture-land, is the property of the royalty, or assets under the proprietorship of the Department of Farmland (Agriculture). Government-owned farmland is still cultivated by peasant households. They turn in a portion of their yields after each harvest. Private land is owned legally by private households. These lands are managed by individuals and their families, or leased out to others. Those who tend to their own land pay taxes to the state, whereas those who survive on land lease pay rents to the landlords, who in turn pay taxes to the government. More than a few times, the *Laws of Heavenly Prosperity* refers to "government and private land," emphasising that "government and private lands should be separated"; "let government and private lands not be confused and mixed up" or exchanged at will.[140]

The government-private distinction is also apparent in land sale contracts. The contracts stipulate that the seller, rather than the buyer, assume full liability, should any transfer or lease of title occur, "either publicly or privately." This provision is intended to warn individuals against selling land illegally appropriated from private or government properties, which typically leads to a legal dispute. In addition, "government land" is frequently referenced in the demarcation of lands with respect to their four borders. The properties of [Tangut] [ljow da kia ·jiw], [Tangut] [dju. dju. śja phji wejr], [Tangut] [ljow ɣwie gia_ ·jiw], and [Tangut] [me_ nja_ dźjwow thja], for example, all border government-owned lands.

All land sold in these private contracts must have been privately owned. The previous owners are the sellers, and upon the signing of the contract, the

140 *Revised Laws of Heavenly Prosperity* 15, "Opening Canals in the Spring"; "Raising the Pasture and Supervising Irrigation"; "Canals and Waters"; "Miscellaneous Crimes Related to Land and Water," pp. 496–509.

buyers become the new landlords: 𘟣𘀴𘟙𘗽 [·jaxwa mji-_tshja] (1 patch of land), Pudu Temple (8 patches of land), 𘝦𘐨𘄿𘒾 [ljow tśju. ·wejr śjow] (3 patches of land). Naturally, with the transfer of titles, the new owners take over tax obligations, as well.

3.1.3.5 *Ripe vs. Unripe Land*

The Tanguts also distinguished between 'ripe' and 'unripe' land. 'Ripe' land refers to land already tilted and cultivated. The *Laws of Heavenly Prosperity*, for example, warns workers in canal projects against impairing ripe farmlands.[141] 'Unripe' land refers to untitled or unfertile land that falls under neither private nor government proprietorship. The Tangut government encourages the cultivation of unripe land, and incentives peasants to reclaim wasteland with three years of tax exemption. The *Laws of Heavenly Prosperity* states that:

> Where the many are not capable of cultivating a patch of land, and for this reason abandon it for three years without generating any tax, labour, or hay, whereupon the land is considered neither privately-owned nor government-owned; if then, the many wish to hold and cultivate it, let them report their intention to the Bureau of Transfer and Transportation. Let the staff consult the neighbouring heads of households who own properties that border the land concerned, and thereupon, after extensive and exhaustive examinations, let the staff inform the previous owner of the abandoned land of the present state of affairs. If all are true as they are alleged, let the staff issue a statement of cultivation to the concerned party, permitting it to farm the land, and record this in the official files. In three years' time, let the bureau dispatch another round of staff and officers to inspect and measure the outcome and output. Given the state of the seedlings and the measurements of tax in neighbouring lands, let the staff determine to which of the five levels of quality this farmland belongs. Then, let the land be taxed at the appropriate level. Within the same year, let this also enter the record of the files, as previously mentioned. Let the quantity of tax, labour, and hay be determined according to the laws along the frontiers, etc.[142]

There is a similar distinction between 'ripe land' and 'grassland' in the Song Dynasty. The *Extended Zizhi Tongjian* records that "reports from Youzhou: within 10 *li* outside the city walls, there are ripe lands. In another 10 *li* further

141 *Revised Laws of Heavenly Prosperity* 15, "Canals and Water," p. 502.
142 *Revised Laws of Heavenly Prosperity* 15, "On Taking Unused Land," p. 492.

on the outskirt, there is uncultivated grassland."[143] At that time, Youzhou was a border city between Song and Xia.

The land is labeled as 'ripe or unripe' in 6 of the 12 Khara-Khoto land sale contracts. The expression is 𗂧𗈪 [ślo_w śiəj] in Tangut, which may be a loan word from the Chinese 熟生. Since the Dangxiang Tanguts for a long time knew little about agriculture, there is no reason to have the word for "ripe/unripe" land in the native tongue. Only when a part of the Tangut population embarked on agriculture, did they borrow the concepts of the ripe and the unripe from Chinese peasants. Then the question is how ripe or unripe is 'ripe/unripe'? Given that the landowners are paying taxes as recorded in these contracts, the land must have been yielding grains past three years of tax-exemption. This would have been impossible had they been untitled or barely cultivated. 'Ripe or unripe' may refer to unfertile land that is nonetheless yielding harvests and taxes.[144] It is possible that over time, the expression congealed and morphed into a term, wherewith the buyers expressed their personal likings and dislikings of the land. In that case, it would not have necessarily been an evaluation of the land's fertility.

3.1.4 Price of Farmland

In a society of private property, land price is one of the most important commodity prices in the economy, for it interlinks with various aspects of the society. In Western Xia, especially, land tax is the main source of government revenue. Therefore, land price has to do with national income and the peasants' livelihood. In Chinese sources, however, there is barely any record on Tangut land price or land tax. For this and many other reasons, Tangut land price and tax data in sell and purchase documents are of real significance to the study of the Tangut society.

At least in the surviving land sale contracts, land is traded not in cash, but in kinds. Apart from one contract (widow 𗆧𗗚𗤁𗰛𗷅 [·jaxwa zji-. lji-.śio]'s land sale contract), where the land is exchanged for livestocks, all other buyers purchase their land by grains. The contract lists the size of the land and the quantity of grains, so it is no difficult task to calculate the land price in terms of grains (usually in *dan*) per *mu*. But because the land comes with a variety of fixtures ranging from houses to trees and tools, the task is much more complex

143 *Zi Zhi Tong Jian*, Bk. 436, 4th year of Yuanyou in Zhezong Emperor's Reign (1089), Jiazi, 12th month of the year.

144 TN: That is to say, 'ripe and unripe' is more 'unripe' than 'ripe.' I think this could have been a derogatory term that the buyer leverages as a rhetorical instrument to deflate the value of the land in the negotiation process.

if it were to render the calculation accurate. Furthermore, the quality and fertility of land varies widely. Lands also differ in terms of whence and how much water is required for irrigation. Yet another factor of complication is a difficulty with which we are not unfamiliar, that land size is often given in terms of the amounts of seeds to be sowed in it. The conversion from seeds needed to the actual size in mu turns out to be rather elastic. For all these reasons, accuracy cannot be fully achieved.

Since land sales without additional asset involved are much simpler and more straightforward, let us first try to derive some land prices from contracts of land sale without fixtures. Of the eight in total, there are two such simple contracts, which could provide the basis for our analysis. On the second day of the second month in the Year of Yin, [illegible] [ljow ɣwie ·o bie_j] sells a patch of land where 5 *dan* of seeds may be sowed in the farming season (approximately 50 *mu* in size) at the price of 4 *dan* of wheat and 9 *dan* of coarse grains. On the same day, [illegible] [me_ nja_ dźjwow thja] sells land where 5 *dan* of seeds may be sowed, (likewise, around 50 *mu*) for 6 *dan* of coarse grains and 1 *dan* of wheat. Earlier in the book, we have derived the price of wheat in Khara-Khoto as somewhere between 200–250 mace, and the price of millet (a type of coarse grain) as 150–200 mace, both from fragments of Tangut grain sale accounts.[145] That is to say, the unit price of coarse grains falls within 75%–80% that of wheat. If we convert the 4 *dan* of wheat in the first contract to about 5 *dan* of coarse grains, we then have the price at which the land was sold: 14 *dan* of coarse grains in total, or 2.8 *dou* of coarse grains per *mu*. The same could be done to in the case of the second contract. Convert the 1 *dan* of wheat to 1 *dan* 3 *dou* of coarse grains. This way, the total price turns out to be 7 *dan* 3 *dou* of coarse grains, or 1.46 *dou* of coarse grains per *mu*.

So far, we have derived two unit-prices of Khara-Khoto land: 2.8 *dou* of coarse grains per *mu* versus 1.46 *dou* of coarse grains per *mu*. The land size in both cases are identical, and yet the prices are so far apart: a whopping 50% in difference. Perhaps the difference lies in their locations. The land of [illegible] [ljow ɣwie ·o bie_j] borders the land of [illegible] [dju. dju. gju_ ·o] to the east, the land of [illegible] [ljow da kia ·jiw] to the south, the canals to the west, the land of [illegible] [tśhiə dzji_j ta] to the north. The land of [illegible] [me_ nja_ dźjwow thja] borders government-owned land to the east and the south, the canal to the west, and the land of a certain [illegible]??[illegible] [rar ?? mja śjow] to the north. Both lands face the canal to the west. The key difference seems to be that the cheaper land borders government-owned land to the east and south.

And of the four separate, single-page contracts, two record the sales of land and houses only, without more complex assets. In the Bingchen Year of

145 Shi Jinbo, 2008.

Heavenly Celebration, [illegible]?? [ljow śiə nio_w ??] sells his 70 *mu* of land and house for 5 *dan* of coarse grains—that is a mere 0.7 *dou* per *mu*. This is the lowest unit price recorded in any of the surviving contracts. In the Gengshen year of Heavenly Celebration, [illegible] [lew śji thow pha~] sells land fit to sow 100 *dan* of seeds, about 1000 *mu* in size, at the price of 200 *dan* of coarse grains, or the unit price of 2 *dou* per *mu*.

Four of the contracts in the long scroll record transactions of land along with houses, yards, and additional assets. Because it is not easy to pin down the specific values of these properties, there is no reliable way to calculate the land price. If we simply ignore these assets, and focus only on the land, we derive the following prices: On the 24th day of the 1st month in the Yin Year of Heavenly Celebration, [illegible] [khjiw bie_j ta] sells his land fit to sow 20 *dan* of seeds, along with his yard, house, and cabins, altogether for 15 *dan* of coarse grains and 15 *dan* of wheat = 34 *dan* of coarse grains, at the unit price of 1.7 *dou* per *mu*; On the 29th Day of 1st Month in the Yin Year of Heavenly Celebration, [illegible] [ljow da kia ·jiw] sells land fit for 15 *dan* of seeds, along with houses, trees, and stone graves, for 6 *dan* of wheat and 10 *dan* of coarse grains = 18 *dan* of coarse grains in total, at the unit price of 1.2 *dou* per *mu*; On the same day, [illegible] [dju. dju. śja phji wejr] sells land fit for 8 *dan* of seeds, along with 2 houses and 5 live trees, for 4 *dan* of wheat and 6 *dan* of coarse grains = 11 *dan* of coarse grains, at the unit price of 1.37 *dou* per *mu*; on the 1st day of the 2nd month in the Yin year, [illegible] [ljow ɣwie gia_ ·jiw] sells ripe/unripe land fit for 10 *dan* seeds, along with houses and walls, at the price of 2 *dan* of wheat, 2 *dan* of millet, and 4 *dan* of grains = 8.6 *dan* of coarse grains, at the unit price of 0.86 *dou* per *mu*. There is an additional contract of land transaction where large assets are involved. So, at least there, it is easy to explain the high price in the light of this confounding factor. On the 1st day of the 2nd month in the Yin Year of Heavenly Celebration, [illegible] [khjij śja rjar śji-j] sells land fit to sow 10 *dan* of seeds, along with infrastructures, tools, and trees, all for 15 *dan* of wheat, 10 *dan* of coarse grains, and 10 *dan* of millet = 40 *dan* of coarse grains in total. It does seem that the additional assets weigh heavily in land pricing.

A case stands out in the contract of land sale by [illegible] [·jaxwa zji-. lji-.śio] in the 22nd year of Heavenly Prosperity, where the widow sold her land for neither cash nor grains, but livestocks, rather than cash or grains. So, at least at the first glance, we cannot derive a price that is comparative to the other transactions. However, we have the general price of Tangut livestocks from a comparative analysis of the *Laws of Heavenly Prosperity* and data in the Khara-Khoto Livestock Sale contracts: a camel is worth about 6 *dan* of coarse grains; 1 ox is worth around 4 *dan* of coarse grains.[146] Now, [illegible]

146 Ibid.

[·jaxwa zji-. lji-.śio] sells land for 2 full-teethed camels, 1 two-teethed livestock, 2 old ox. First, the two camels are worth 12 *dan* of coarse grains. If we take the two-teethed animal to be some bovine, then the cattles are worth altogether 8 *dan* of coarse grains. In this way, we convert the value of the 4 livestocks to approximately 20 *dan* of coarse grains. This number could be verified based on the penalty fee for breaching the contracts. Khara-Khoto contracts usually specify that the party reneges on the transaction be punished twice the amount of the sell & purchase price. In this contract, the penalty fee is 30 *dan* of wheat, which means the transaction price must have been around 15 *dan* of wheat, or 20 *dan* of coarse grains, which is precisely the number derived from livestock prices. If we suppose for a moment that the assets are evenly distributed across the land to which they are attached, we could say that the price per *mu* of land is around 1 *dan* of coarse grains. Now, the exorbitant price is possibly due to the assets that come with it, or because land price in the era of Heavenly Prosperity—about 20 years prior to the other contracts—was simply much higher. Another separate contract was signed in the fifth year of Heavenly Celebration (1198), where [illegible] [mjadzjwi- khjwi-wjazji] sold 23 *mu* of land along with his yard and houses, all for 8 *dan* of coarse grains. The unit price is at 3.5 *dou* per *mu* of land, which is rather high, as well. Likewise, we could pinpoint the properties as the causal variable. Below is a chart that compiles the data from all 12 contracts of land sales (all register numbers are in Инв. No.).[147]

CHART 13 Statistics on size and value of land in land sale contracts

No.	Register	Date	Seller	Land size (seeds/*mu*)	Value/Price	Assets and Fixtures included
1	5010	Gengyin, 22nd year of Tiansheng	[illegible] [·jaxwa zji-. lji-.śio]	Ripe/ unripe land for 2 *dan* of seeds	2 full-teethed camels, 1 two-teethed,[a] 1 old ox	Yard, 3 thatched cottages, 2 trees, etc.
2	5124-2	24th day of 1st month, Year Yin of Tianqing	[illegible] [khjiw bie_j ta]	Ripe/ unripe land for 20 *dan* of seeds	Coarse grains 15 *dan*, wheat 15 *dan*	House and yard, full set of 4 cabins

a The expression in the original text is: “there exist two [vertical things],” which might refer to a livestock that has grown two vertical teeth. It is a way of indicating the age of the animal.

147 TN: No. 1–12 correspond to Figures 148–159.

CHART 13 Statistics on size and value of land in land sale contracts (*cont.*)

No.	Register	Date	Seller	Land size (seeds/*mu*)	Value/Price	Assets and Fixtures included
3	5124-1, 5124-3 (4)	29th Day of 1st Month, Year Yin of Tianqing	[illegible] [ljow da kia ·jiw]	Land for 15 *dan* of seeds	6 *dan* of wheat, 10 *dan* of coarse grains	Yard, house, trees, stone grave, etc.
4	5124-3 (5)	29th Day of 1st Month	[illegible] [dju. dju. śja phji wejr]	Land for 8 *dan* of seeds	4 *dan* of wheat, 6 *dan* of coarse grains[b]	2 houses, 5 live trees
5	5124-3 (10)	1st day of 2nd month, Yin Year	[illegible] [ljow ɣwie gia_ ·jiw]	Land for 10 *dan* of seeds	2 *dan* of wheat, 2 *dan* of millet, 4 *dan* of grains	House, wall
6	5124-3 (1)	1st day of 2nd month, Yin Year	[illegible] [khjij śja rjar śji-j]	Ripe/unripe land for 10 *dan* of seeds	10 *dan* of wheat, 10 *dan* of coarse grains, 10 *dan* of millet	Cabins large and small, tilling tools for oxen, stone gate with bamboo fence, pentamerous yokes, tree yard
7	5124-3 (3), 5124-4 (1)	2nd day of 2nd month, Yin Year	[illegible] [ljow ɣwie ·o bie_j]	Land for 5 *dan* of seeds	4 *dan* of wheat, 9 *dan* of coarse grains	
8	5124-4 (3)	2nd day of 2nd month, Yin Year	[illegible] [me_ nja_ dźjwow thja]	Land for 5 *dan* of seeds	6 *dan* of coarse grains, 1 *dan* of wheat	
9	5124-4 (10)	6th day of 2nd month, Year Yin of Tianqing	[illegible] [phjij śjo sjwi sjwi dju]	Ripe/unripe land for 3 *dan* of seeds	5 *dan* of coarse grains	Four old cabins

b TN: Due to a typological or typesetting error, the input for price here erroneously shows assets (houses & trees) in the Chinese edition of the book, p. 278.

CHART 13 Statistics on size and value of land in land sale contracts (*cont.*)

No.	Register	Date	Seller	Land size (seeds/*mu*)	Value/Price	Assets and Fixtures included
10	4199	16th day of 6th month, Bingchenyear of Tianqing	[illegible]?? [ljow śiə nio_w ??]	Ripe/unripe land for 10 *dan* of seeds, (70 mu)	5 *dan* of coarse grains	
11	4193	5th day of 1st month, Wuwu, 5th Year of Tianqing	[illegible] [mjadzjwi-khjwi-wjazji]	23 *mu*	8 *dan* of coarse grains	Yard
12	4194	22nd day of 2nd month, Gengshen Year of Tianqing	[illegible] [lew śji thow pha~]	Ripe/unripe land for 100 *dan* of seeds	200 *dan* of coarse grains	Yard and abode, full set

The prices above suggest that toward the late Tangut period, land price in Khara-Khoto remained as low as 2 *dou* of coarse grains per *mu*. The contracts are signed at times of great urgency and necessity. The buyers exploit of the sellers' shortage of grains to force the price down, in order to extract maximum surplus value.

3.1.5 Farmland Tax

3.1.5.1 *Farmland Taxes in the Contracts*

All holders of land titles in Western Xia have to pay land taxes to the government according to the laws. All the 8 land sale contracts of the long scroll record the amounts of taxes levied on the given patch of land. The typical formula is: "there are taxes in the amounts of × *dou*, of which there is wheat × *dou* × *sheng*." In Tangut, verbs are postpositional. So, the existential verb "there is" is found at the end, following the object. There are various kinds of existential verbs in Tangut, which serve to denote the different modes of existence of various kinds of entities. There are, for example, different existential verbs that denote the existences of things precious, internal, attached, parallel, belonging, or vertical.[148] The existential verb used in land sale contracts to denote

148 TN: Shi, Jinbo and Li, Hansong. *Tangut Language and Manuscripts: An Introduction*. Leiden: Brill, 2020, pp. 317–354.

the existence of farmland taxes is the verb of 'fixed existence': [illegible] [wjij]. The diction suggests that the tax rate here is fixed, or at least that it is fixed by the state, impermeable to changes of proprietorship.[149]

The amounts of taxes in the 8 contracts are as follows: [illegible] [khjiw bie_j ta]: 1 *dou* of wheat and 4 *dou* of coarse grains = 5 *dou*; [illegible] [ljow da kia ·jiw]: 2 *dan*, including 4 *dou* of wheat; [illegible] [dju. dju. śja phji wejr]: 5 *dou*, including 1 *dou* of wheat; [illegible] [ljow ɣwie gia_ ·jiw]: 5 *dou*, including 1 *dou* of wheat; [illegible] [khjij śja rjar śji-j]: 1 *dan*, 2 *dou* of wheat; [illegible] [ljow ɣwie ·o bie_j]: 7 *dou*, including 1 *dou* 4 *sheng* of wheat; [illegible] [me_ nja_ dźjwow thja]: 5 *dou*, including 1 *dou* of wheat; [illegible] [phjij śjo sjwi sjwi dju]: 8 *dou* of coarse grains, 2 *dou* of wheat.

None of the four separate contracts outside the long scroll document the land taxes in their precise quantities. But of them, the contract dated to the 16th day of the 6th month in the Bingchen Year of Heavenly Celebration states that "The burdens of obligations in all three forms of levies: tax, labour, and hay, fall on [illegible] [·wejr tśju. śjow]." This is a clear indication that upon completion of the transaction, the tax obligations are transferred along with the property to the new landlord.

At length, the *Laws of Heavenly Prosperity* elaborates on the procedures and practices of taxation. Laws on farmland taxes seem to concentrate in Book 15: "On Urging the Payments of Taxes," "Merits and Misdemeanors in Urging Tax Payments" etc. The laws set forth household obligations to pay various kinds of taxes, to turn in always the right amount, and to register tax payments with the government.[150]

The government rolls out extensive and exhaustive rules and regulations, primarily to ensure tax revenues. Whether the land is farmed, transacted, or leased, the rock of certainty and security, in the eyes of the empire, is the uninterrupted income from agricultural taxation. Therefore, it is imperative that contracts specify whether and how much taxes are levied on each patch of land. As the titles transfer from peasant households to the ownership of the Pudu Temple in Khara-Khoto, the tax obligations attached to the land are also transferred onto the new owner. It is a matter of great importance for both parties to specify this obligation in the contract.

The *Laws of Heavenly Prosperity* also stipulates the following:

> Buddhist and Taoist monks, all the many officials of higher or lower ranks, if for public purposes seek farmland under the proprietorship of

149 TN: Ibid., pp. 330–334, 345, 347, 350–351.

150 *Revised Laws of Heavenly Prosperity* 15, p. 508.

> either the Department of Farmland, Monasteries, or the Royalties, let the transacting parties inform the Bureau of Transfer and Transportation within a year of the purchase's completion, so that the transaction may enter into government files and land records, and that affairs of tax, hay, and labour may proceed according to the laws.[151]

Western Xia installs Bureau of Transfer and Transportation offices across its territory, especially along the frontiers, to supervise farming and canal projects, to collect taxes, and to transport grains from one area to another. One such office is located in the city of Khara-Khoto.[152]

Tangut laws do not enumerate or elaborate on farmland tax rates. However, given the data on the size of land owned and the amount of tax paid by individual households in Khara-Khoto tax accounts, we arrive at a tax rate of 0.1 *dou* (or 1 *sheng*) of coarse grains, and 0.025 *dou* (1/4 *sheng*) of wheat per *mu*.[153] Obviously, the Tanguts pay taxes at fixed rates, based on their farmland sizes. The rulers of Western Xia could have borrowed the tax system from medieval Central Plains, where it had been a standard practice. But it is in the Khara-Khoto contracts, more than anywhere else, that we see farmland tax at work.

3.1.5.2 *Land Taxes in Contracts versus Tax Documents*

The farmland tax rates derived from the 8 contracts in the long scroll may be tested against the tax rates available in Khara-Khoto tax accounts. For example, at the farmland tax rate derived from the accounts, [khjiw bie_j ta] should have paid 5 *dou* of grains for a land at least 50 *mu* in size. In reality, the actual land size as recorded in the contracts is enough for 20 *dan* of seeds, or around 200 *mu*. One could not but wonder what accounts for such huge discrepancies. To take another example, [ljow da kia ·jiw] is supposed to have paid 2 *dan* of coarse grains for 200 *mu* of land. The contract gives the actual land size as 15 *dan* of seeds, or 150 *mu*. Here, the numbers are much closer, but the discrepancy is there, nonetheless. Likewise, discprenacies are found in the cases of [dju. dju. śja phji wejr] (5 *dou* of tax ↔ 50 *mu* of land, versus 80 *mu* of land = 8 *dan* of seeds), [ljow ɣwie gia_ ·jiw] (5 *dou* of tax ↔ 50 *mu* of land, versus 100 *mu* of land = 10 *dan* of seeds), [ljow ɣwie ·o bie_j] (7 *dou* of tax ↔ 70 *mu* of land, versus 50 *mu* of land = 5 *dan* of seeds), and [phjij śjo sjwi sjwi dju] (8 *dou* of coarse grains +

151 Ibid., p. 496.

152 *Revised Laws of Heavenly Prosperity* 10, pp. 368–375.

153 Shi Jinbo, 2005 (a).

2 *dou* of wheat = 1 *dan* of grains ↔ 100 *mu* of land, versus 30 *mu* of land = 3 *dan* of seeds). Only in the contracts of [illegible] [khjij śja rjar śji-j] (1 *dan* of tax ↔ 100 *mu* of land = 100 *mu* of land = 10 *dan* of seeds) and [illegible] [me_ nja_ dźjwow thja] (5 *dou* of tax ↔ 50 *mu* of land = 50 *mu* of land = 5 *dan* of seeds) are the expected and the actual land size found to be equal.

Only 2 of the 8 contracts match the tax rate derived from Khara-Khoto tax accounts. Several factors may account for the large and small discrepancies. First of all, given the greater abundance of farmland in Khara-Khoto, measurement is sometimes loose. After all, to measure land size by the amounts of seeds to be sowed there is in approximate terms. The idea that Khara-Khoto residents even thought it necessary to measure land in precise terms could be an anachronistic, or outright false assumption to begin with. After all, land size is registered in terms of seeds even in *shoushi* household reports. In the 8 contracts where land size is measured by seeds, the unit of measurement begins with *dan*, rather than *dou*. That means we are approximating land size in the units of 10 *mu* at a time. Precision is basically out of the question. But imprecise data cannot serve as the basis of tax calculation. Furthermore, variable land quality, relative 'ripeness' or 'unripeness,' or supplies of water and states of irrigation, could all lead to significant variations in the seeds vs. yields ratio. Therefore, tax on a given farmland is determined regardless of the amounts of seeds. Rather, tax depends solely on the expected yield. We already know from the afore-quoted passage in the *Laws of Heavenly Prosperity* that, upon three years of cultivation, officers would inspect the land, and assign it one of the five levels of fertility, whereby the tax rate in the future shall be determined.[154] It turns out that the Tangut government cared not only about land size but also land productivity. Along this line of thinking, we find ourselves in a better position to unveil the mystery of tax rate discrepancies. Some farmland in Khara-Khoto are large in size, but are not particularly fertile. Therefore, farmers are granted the leniency of a lighter tax burden. And vice versa. This is why we should not have been calculating 'expected land size' based on the standard tax rate. In the *Laws of Heavenly Prosperity*, we also find the stipulation that "Heads of farming households in the seven counties in the vicinities of the imperial capital are to pay taxes according to five levels of land quality: highest: 1 *dou* per *mu*; secondary: 8 *sheng*; middle: 6 *sheng*; lower: 5 *sheng*; lowest: 3 *sheng*."[155] Even within nearby vicinities, land taxes could vary as much as

154 *Revised Laws of Heavenly Prosperity* 15, "Miscellaneous Crimes Related to Land and Water," 492.

155 *Russian Collection of Khara-Khoto Manuscripts*, vol. 8, pp. 300, 307, 301; see also, Pan Jie, 2012.

three times, depending on perceived fertility and expected yield. Overall, land fertility in Khara-Khoto doesn't compare to the Hetao area near the capital. But one could easily see that large and diverse landscapes in Khara-Khoto cause tax variations.

There is also great consistency in Khara-Khoto tax accounts and land sale contracts. For example, in the document Инв. No. 1178, a land 1 *qing* 50 *mu* large is taxed 1 *dan* 8 *dou* and 7.5 *sheng*, including 1 *dan* 5 *dou* of coarse grains, and 3 *dou* 7.5 *sheng* of wheat; another patch of land 1 *qing* 43 *mu* large is taxed 1 *dan* 7 *dou* 8 *sheng* 7.5 *ge*.[156] It could be that these farmlands classified into the same level of quality. At least in Khara-Khoto tax accounts, the coarse grain to wheat ratio is 4:1, the same ratio as in land sale contracts.

3.1.6 Guarantee of the Contracts

3.1.6.1 *The Force of Law in the Contracts*

Sell and purchase contracts acquire the force of law, as both parties voluntarily recognise and agree to enforce the terms set therein. Of all transactions, land transfer is an economic and legal activity of vital importance. Therefore, the terms of penalty against breach of contract are harsher, and written in greater details than in loan contracts. For this reason, all Khara-Khoto land sale contracts, without exception, specify penalty fees after recording the price.

The earliest of the surviving land sale contracts (widow [illegible] [·jaxwa zji-. lji-.śio], 22nd Year of Heavenly Prosperity) states that, should any dispute over the title arise, the seller [illegible] bears all responsibility. If a party reneges on the contract, it will be prosecuted according to the *Laws and Orders*, as well as pay 30 *dan* of wheat according to the laws.

The long scroll goes to greater lengths. The contract of [illegible] [khjiw bie_j ta] (24th day of the 1st month in the Yin Year of Heavenly Celebration) states that, upon signing the contract, neither the land nor the payment is overdue. Should any be any (illegal) transfer of land, either from the government or from a private individual, or should any dispute arise amongst members of the same *chao*, it is the seller [illegible], not [illegible] [dow dźjij phu_], responsible for the consequences. In cases such as these, recompensation is twice the purchase price. The reneging party bears all legal costs, and pays 2 liang of gold as a penalty fee, according to the laws. In other words, if the seller attempts to transfer a title that is not legally in his dominion—say, if he loaned it from the real proprietor, or appropriated it from the government—he would be punished for the criminal conduct. As for disputes, they are usually initiated by "members of the same *chao*"—these are family relatives, friends and comrades who may

---

156 Shi Jinbo, 2005 (a).

lay a claim to common proprietorship or partial inheritance rights. Needless to say, should such a quarrel ever happen, the responsibility falls solely on the seller. He or she would be punished twice. First, it is necessary to repay twice the sum of the price. Sellers, mostly needy peasants desperate to refill their fast emptying granaries, are pressured into declaring that their "own hearts are willing," that is, they voluntarily agree to the term. But such a penalty would be unbearable to anyone, lest a peasant household. So, the whole purpose of adding this clause in the contract is to ensure the categorical prevention of the remotest chance that legal troubles might ensue. Then comes the penalty against the 'reneging party' for breaching the contract. On the surface of things, this clause applies to both the selling and the buying parties. However, given that the price is forced down to the minimum, the only party that would ever possibly regret is the seller. So, this clause is also better understood as a restraint on the seller. It is also worth noting that the penalty against unilateral withdrawal from the contract by a reneging party is in gold, rather than grains or a less valuable cash.

Penalty terms are more or less similar from one contract to another. Some note only that in disputes, the recompensation is double the sum of the price, but not penalty fees for a reneging party. 7 of the 8 land sale contracts in the long scroll specify penalty fees. The one exception is where the land is also the smallest. The penalty fee has to do with the volume of transaction, but without a uniform ratio or percentage. For example, [Tangut] [khjij śja rjar śji-j] sells for a higher price: 15 *dan* of wheat, 10 *dan* of coarse grains, and 10 *dan* of millet. In this case, the penalty fee is a whopping 3 *liang* of gold. [Tangut] [khjiw bie_j ta] is paid 15 *dan* of coarse grains and 15 *dan* of wheat. His penalty fee would be a considerable 2 *liang* of gold. [Tangut] [ljow ɣwie gia_ ·jiw] sells for only 2 *dan* of wheat, 2 *dan* of millet, and 4 *dan* of grains. The penalty is 1 *liang* of gold. Further down the scale of trade volume, [Tangut] [me_ nja_ dźjwow thja] earns only 6 dan of coarse grains and 1 dan of wheat. His penalty fee is also 1 liang of gold. However, it is curious to note that even though [Tangut] [ljow da kia ·jiw] sells his land and houses for a medium 6 *dan* of wheat and 10 *dan* of coarse grains, the penalty fee in his contracts is as high as 3 *liang* of gold.

In one of the individual land sale contracts, the volume of transaction by [Tangut] [lew śji thow pha~] reaches 200 *dan* of coarse grains, but the penalty fee remains at 3 *liang* of gold. It could be that 3 *liang* is the maximum penalty fee under the law. In another individual contract, [Tangut]?? [ljow śiə nio_w ??] sells his land and houses for 5 *dan* of coarse grains. But his penalty fee is listed not in gold, but 10 *dan* of coarse grains. We could do the gold-to-grain the conversion here. A transaction of 7–8 *dan* of grains corresponds to 1 *liang* of gold as penalty fee. We know that the Tanguts customarily penalise demeanors by doubling the initial value. If that is true, then 1 *liang* of gold is worth 15–30 *dan* of grains. To set the penalty fee in gold is not a unique practice of the Tanguts. Penalty fees paid in gold are found in Dunhuang sell and purchase contracts. It is also worth noting that no corporal punishment, such as strokes, are seen in these Tangut contracts.

CHART 14 Terms of penalty for breaching the contract

No.	Seller	Land size (*dan* of seeds)	Value/Price	Penalty in case of a dispute	Penalty for the reneging party
1	[illegible] [·jaxwa zji-. lji-. śio]	Land for 2 *dan* of seeds	2 full-teethed camels, 1 two-teethed, 1 old ox	2 *dan* of penalty per 1 *dan* of payment	Penalty: 30 *dan* of wheat
2	[illegible] [lhju da kia gji]	Land for 20 *dan* of seeds	15 *dan* of coarse grains, 15 *dan* of wheat	2 *dan* of penalty per 1 *dan* of payment	Penalty: 2 *liang* of gold
3	[illegible] [ljow da kia śji-j]	Land for 15 *dan* of seeds	6 *dan* of wheat, 10 *dan* of coarse grains	2 *dan* of penalty per 1 *dan* of payment	Penalty: 3 *liang* of gold
4[a]	[illegible] [ljow da kia ·jiw]	Land for 8 *dan* of seeds	4 *dan* of wheat, 6 *dan* of coarse grains[b]	2 *dan* of penalty per 1 *dan* of payment	Penalty: 1 *liang* of gold
5	[illegible] [ljow da kia phu_]	Land for 10 *dan* of seeds	2 *dan* of wheat, 2 *dan* of millet, 4 *dan* of grains	2 *dan* of penalty per 1 *dan* of payment	Penalty: 1 *liang* of gold
6	[illegible] [mjadzow pji. phə tśhja wejr]	Land for 10 *dan* of seeds	10 *dan* of wheat, 10 *dan* of coarse grains, 10 *dan* of millet	n/a	Penalty: 3 *liang* of gold
7	[illegible] [ljow da kia phu_]	Land for 5 *dan* of seeds	4 *dan* of wheat, 9 *dan* of coarse grains	n/a	Penalty: 1 *liang* of gold
8	[illegible] [ljow ɣwie gia_ phu_]	Land for 5 *dan* of seeds	6 *dan* of coarse grains, 1 *dan* of wheat	n/a	Penalty: 1 *liang* of gold

a TN: Erroneous numbering in the Chinese edition, p. 283.
b TN: Erroneous input in the Chinese edition, ibid.

CHART 14 Terms of penalty for breaching the contract (*cont.*)

No.	Seller	Land size (*dan* of seeds)	Value/Price	Penalty in case of a dispute	Penalty for the reneging party
9	[Tangut characters] [ljow ŋwu ne_w mja]	Land for 5 *dan* of seeds	5 *dan* of coarse grains	Penalty fee: 5 *dan* of wheat	
10	[Tangut characters]?? [ljow śiə nio_w ??]	Land for 10 *dan* of seeds, 70 *mu*	5 *dan* of coarse grains	Penalty: 10 *dan* of coarse grains + 2 *dan* of compensation per 1 *dan* of payment	
11	[Tangut characters] [mjadzjwi-khjwi-wjazji]	23 *mu*	8 *dan* of coarse grains	2 *dan* of penalty per 1 *dan* of payment	
12	[Tangut characters] [lew śji thow pha~]	Land for 100 *dan* of seeds	200 *dan* of coarse grains	2 *dan* of penalty per 1 *dan* of payment	Penalty: 3 *liang* of gold

Besides, the *Laws of Heavenly Prosperity* is unequivocal on punishing the acts of reneging on promises and defaulting on debt:

> When the many lend or sell their own *shijun* serfs, *nupu* servants, farmland, and houses to other parties, let them make contracts. When the pawned or mortgaged properties are not retrieved and the debt not yet covered, if the pawning party changes his mind, let the reneging party be punished a horse if he holds a title, or thirteen strokes if he is a commoner. If the pawned properties have been retrieved, but the pawning party claims otherwise, and in this way change his mind, let the case be judged, given the value of the properties retrieved, and in accordance with the laws on change of conduct in debt payment. If the pawn is not yet covered, but the party claims otherwise, out of the intention to claim it, or if the pawning price is accepted, but the accepting party claims otherwise, let him be tried on the same charges as in the change of conduct in debt payment.[157]

157 *Revised Laws of Heavenly Prosperity* 11, "On Hired Labour," p. 390.

The imperial laws guarantee the enforcement of all the terms set forth in Tangut sell and purchase contracts.

3.1.6.2 *Signature and Stamp*

Stamps and signatures are crucial to ensuring the accuracy and the reliability of the contracts. It is also a necessary procedural step in the legal formalism of the contract, symbolising the moment the text acquires its effectual legal force. An unsigned and unstamped contract is deemed as null.

As in Chinese contracts, signatures and stamps are found near the end of Tangut contracts. Typically, each signatory takes up a line. In rare cases, two witnesses could share a single line. In all surviving land sale contracts, the seller signs first, then the co-liable, followed by the witnesses. There could be up to two or more co-liable parties and witnesses. One easily notices that the fluent cursive style of Tangut calligraphy is consistent throughout the text, with no variation even between the signatures of Contract Parties and witnesses. In fact, not unlike grain loan accounts, land sale accounts are written not by the one of the principle parties, but by a professional transcriber. In the contract belonging to [illegible] [khjiw bie_j ta], there is a reference to a certain [illegible]: "the knowing party who scribed the document, [illegible] [tśhiə lji-. wejr]." Evidently, he is one of the witnesses to the contract, but also the one who wrote out the entire text. This is the first contract in the long scroll. Other contracts exhibit a nearly identical calligraphic style. So, it does seem that the entire scroll is handwritten by this [illegible] [tśhiə lji-. wejr]. The identity of the man is impenetrable but not impervious to inference. Since long scroll is prepared by the Pudu Temple, and concerns land lease and purchase by the monastery, the main transcriber must have been arranged for by the temple, as well. The most accessible transcriber is one of the monks, who must have been trained to recite and transcribe the sutras in Tangut. [illegible] [tśhiə lji-. wejr] may well have been one of the literate monastics. The name [illegible] (the prosperous maṅgala) itself also invokes Buddhist imageries.

Tangut contracts are signed in the collective presence of all involved parties: the seller, buyer, co-seller, transcriber, and witnesses. In general, the more land is sold, the more co-sellers and witnesses there are. The one selling the most land is [illegible] [lew śji thow pha~], who summoned 3 co-sellers, 4 witnesses. A total of 8 names appear on the contract. The one selling the least is [illegible] [phjij śjo sjwi sjwi dju], with only 2 witnesses and no Co-contract Party.

A majority of Tangut contracts are unilateral: there is only one copy, held by one of the two principal parties involved in the transaction. The contract is drafted in the voice of the party requesting or initiating the transaction, usually the seller or the borrower. The party that keeps the contract in possession

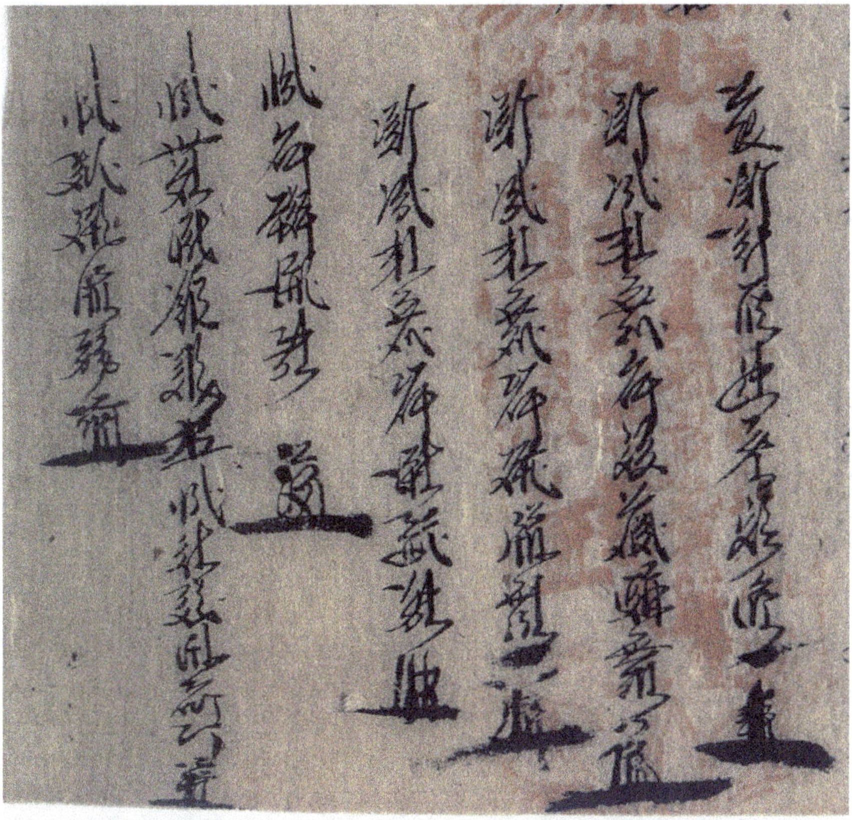

FIGURE 162 Инв. No. 4194: Gengshen year of Tianqing (1200) contract of land sale by [illegible][illegible] [illegible][illegible], signed and stamped

is the creditor or the buyer, whose name does not have to appear on the contract. Unilateral contracts are used for not only absolute sales, but also pawning, mortgaging, leasing, and loaning. They showcase the position of economic advantage of the buyer or the creditor. They are the side with privileges, whose rights are better secured. The seller or the debtors claim fewer rights, given their position of economic disadvantage. They are the party expected to fulfil a set of obligations. Or, it should be said that unilateral contracts is characterised by the system of partial obligation.

A unilateral contract cannot be authenticated by examination against a second original copy. For this reason, the signatures and stamps are the only way to ensure its authenticity. The signature of the seller begins with the title [illegible][illegible] [illegible][illegible] [·jwi-r dźiow wji mjijr]: "the one making the contract," i.e. the principle party to contract initiating the agreement. Sometimes, it is written as [illegible][illegible] [źji.

mjijr], "the seller," followed by the person's name, e.g. [Tangut] [·jaxwa zji-. lji-.śio]. The signature is not supposed to omit the surname, as in the main text.

Co-liable parties to the contract are referred to as [Tangut] [dźiow sa dźjwi-], lit. "contract receiver," i.e. a co-contracting party. In sell and purchase contracts, the title is sometimes rendered [Tangut] [dźiow sa źji. dźjwi-], lit. "contract receiver-seller," i.e. the co-contracting seller. In fact, it could be further shortened to [Tangut] [źji. dźjwi-], the "co-seller." In some contracts of land and house sales, a co-liable party called [Tangut] [nwə dzjwo dźjwi-]: "co-witness" is added to the signatures of main and co-liable contracting parties. In most cases, liability-sharing parties to a contract are the family relatives of the main contract party: sons, wives, and brothers. This is to confirm that the sale is not an individual decision, but one made jointly or in consultation with the family. The presence of co-contracting parties ensures the restraining and authenticating power of the contract, thus rendering it more effective and enforceable. Precedents of this practice are found in some of the Dunhuang sell and purchase contracts.[158]

Should disputes arise, co-contracting parties share liability with the main party to contract. If the seller dies, escapes, or enters into exiles, the co-liable parties assume full or main responsibility. With the exception of 1 contract with a missing end, 10 of the other 11 contracts feature 2 or more co-contractors. The one contract without is [Tangut] [phjij śjo sjwi sjwi dju], who sells the least amount of land. The contracts make sure to indicate the relationship of the co-contractor to the main contract party. For example, [Tangut] [·jaxwa zji-. lji-.śio]'s co-contractors are his "son, [Tangut] [mə rar ko tśjow]." [Tangut] [mə rar] is a Dangxiang Tangut family name. So, the widow [Tangut] [·jaxwa zji-. lji-.śio]'s deceased husband must have been an Dangxiang ethnic and a [Tangut] [mə rar]. The second co-contractor is [Tangut] [mə rar lja_ bju], who could have been the son's brother, paternal uncle, or another member of the extended [Tangut] [mə rar] family. In the contract of [Tangut] [mjadzjwi-khjwi-wjazji], the first co-seller is referred to as "younger brother, [Tangut] [śja phji]," that is [Tangut] [mjadzjwi- khjwi-wjazji]'s younger brother [Tangut] [mja dzjwi- śja phji]. Because a younge brother is supposed to share the same surname, only his given name appears on the contract. The second co-seller to this contract appears to be [Tangut] ? [ljow ? ljow], whose relationship to the main party to contract is unclear. He certainly does not share the same family name, but could have been an in-law. Similar patterns are found in other contracts. [Tangut] [khjiw bie_j ta]'s co-sellers are his two sons, the

158 TN: Gernet, Jacques. "La vente en Chine d'après les contrats de Touen-houang (IXe–Xe siècles)" *T'oung pao*, 1957-01-01, Vol. 45 (4/5), pp. 295–391.

'black slave' and the 'red dog'; [illegible] [ljow da kia ·jiw]'s co-contractors are his two younger brothers, [illegible] [da kia lji-.] and [illegible] [ŋwə dji.j lji-.]; [illegible] [dju. dju. śja phji wejr]'s co-contractors are his younger brother [illegible] [ŋwu da kia zji] and wife [illegible] ?[illegible] [·o gu_? zji-. zji tja wejr]; [illegible] [ljow ɣwie gia_ ·jiw]'s co-sellers are his wife [illegible] [dju. dju. zji-. khjwi- mja lji-.] and their two sons, [illegible] [zjo. dźjo wejr] "the long-living and prosperous," and [illegible] [ɣwie], "a treasure with great joy."[159]

Witnesses are addressed as [illegible] [nwə dzjwo], "the ones who know," i.e. the witnesses. It is sometimes abbreviated as [illegible] [nwə] (to know, the knower). Usually, the main party to contract and the co-contractors are signed in parallel, whereas the the names of witnesses are a half or one space above, without indention. This is to show that the witnesses, as legal functionaries, do not share liability with the main signatories. There are between 2 and 4 witnesses. Sometimes, a man acts as a witness to multiple contracts signed around the same time. [illegible] [phjij śjo wa śia~], for example, is a witness to the land sale contracts of [illegible] [ljow da kia ·jiw], [illegible] [dju. dju. śja phji wejr], [illegible] [ljow ɣwie gia_ ·jiw], and [illegible] [ljow ɣwie ·o bie_j]. The same man acts thrice as witness to land lease contracts. What is more, he also helped authenticate a grain loan account.[160] It also happens that seller, a main party to one contract, serves as witness to other contracts. [illegible] [ljow da kia ·jiw], for instance, is a seller in his own contract, but a witness in that of [illegible] [ljow ɣwie gia_ ·jiw].

Signatures and stamps are conjoined and complementary. Stamping, either a print of the shape and length of the signatory's finger, or a symbolic icon that represents the signatory's legal persona, come after the signatures in the typical format of a contract. Stamping is an act of credit and commitment. Whether in sell and purchase, lease and loan contracts, stamping is necessary. In this case, the stamps are in the same order as the signatures: first the seller, then the co-contractors, followed by the witnesses. Since the 'signatures' are in fact written by a professional transcriber, these icons and symbols are the only way to authenticate the credibility of the parties to the contract.

As we have noted before, individual icons are considered to be more solemn than the print of finger segments. Given the significance of land sale contracts, the signatories are many and the stamps tend to be more formal. The signatories try their best to maintain consistency in their way of drawing their trademark icons. For example, [illegible] [phjij śjo wa śia~]'s stamp is . Otherwise,

159 TN: the first character should be [illegible] [ɣwie] rather than [illegible] [lji-r], as appears in the Chinese edition of the book.

160 Shi Jinbo, 2005 (b), pp. 201–202.

the signatories draw three segments of their fingers in four strokes. Sometimes, both icons and finger-segments are featured in the same contract. In the earliest land sale contract, dated to the Gengyin, 22nd year of Heavenly Prosperity, the seller and the co-sellers print their finger segments, whereas the witnesses drew their icons.

Over time, fewer sellers resorted to printing finger segments. In later contracts, only witnesses, and sometimes co-sellers, printed finger-segments. It seemed that there was an emerging consensus that the printed shapes of finger-segments were less reliable than iconic symbols. In most of these contracts, the principle seller draws his icon, whereas other parties, sometimes co-sellers included, printed their finger-segments. It is worth noting, for instance, that [Tangut] [dju. dju. śja phji wejr] draws an icon as a seller, but prints finger-segments as a witness in [Tangut] [ljow da kia ·jiw]'s contract.

In rare cases, some parties involved in the contract fail to produce any stamp. This duty might have eluded [Tangut]?? [ljow?sa?], the last witness to [Tangut]'s contract.

The Tanguts did use stamps in a more modern and literal sense, with the icons inscribed into a seal. Seal stamps are found in Инв. No. 2157-4 and Инв. No. 5522-3 accounts, amongst others. Seals are much more formal and reliable than the spontaneous artistic stimulus of the signatory. Only a consistent icon signals credibility.

A considerable number of Chinese social documents found in Khara-Khoto date to the Yuan Dynasty. Contracts in the Yuan era feature not only icons and finger-segments, but also black-ink stamps. During this period, both the "signature + icon" formula and increasingly formalised seal stamps were in use. Finger-segments in the Tangut era had by then all but disappeared.[161]

3.1.6.3 *White vs. Red Contracts*

The overarching policy on land sale in the *Laws of Heavenly Prosperity* is that of non-intervention: the imperial government recognises the validity of contracts made privately by consenting parties, so long as the flow of tax revenues remains uninterrupted. The contract dated to the 22nd year of Heavenly Prosperity, for example, states unequivocally that "taxes are paid," followed by what looks like the stamp of a tax-collector.

161 See Tala; Du, Jianlu; Gao Guoxiang (eds.). *Zhongguo cang Heishuicheng Hanwen Wenxian* [中國藏黑水城漢文文獻]: *Han Chinese Documents in the Chinese Collection of Khara-Khoto Manuscripts*, vol. 6. Beijing: National Library of China Press, 2008, pp. 1237–1263.

In the Chinese legal tradition, there is a distinction between the "red" and "white" contracts. White contracts are the more common contracts, not stamped by the red seal of the government. Red contracts, on the other hand, are recognised by the government. Such a distinction also exists in Western Xia. The Инв. No. 5010 contract of [Tangut] [·jaxwa zji-. lji-. śio] and the Инв. No. 4193 contract of [Tangut] [mjadzjwi- khjwi-wjazji] are "red contracts" that feature red seals.

The seals that produce these red stamps are not local govenrments, but the local offices of the Department of Transaction Taxes. These are large, usually 23.2 × 7.3 cm rectangular seals, with lotus flowers and leaves below and above. When stamped on a regular piece of paper, the seal almost takes up the entire width. The red stamp reads, from right to left, [Tangut] [phə źji. zji.j io.], "Department of Transaction (Sell and Purchase) Taxes." Further down, there are four vertical lines of characters. The first three are in small font and barely legible. In the fourth line, three characters are large enough for us to read: [Tangut] [kju khio kwa~]. The first character may be here for the purpose of phonetic notation. The second character means "well," "adept," or "artful." The third character means could also be a notation of some sort, but it also means "to fill" or "to water" in other contexts. The precise meaning of the three-character expression remains so far impenetrable. This line is followed by the iconic stamps, which are also found below the second line. With the red seal, the contract is certified by the government. It also proves beyond doubt that all taxes have been paid.

The seal of transaction taxes is used beyond the context of sell and purchase contracts, in a wide array of legal documents. Both the Инв. No. 6377-13 account of transaction taxes, and the Инв. No. 7630-2 Livestock Sale Contract dated to the You year of Guangding, for example, feature the official seal of the Department of Transaction Taxes.

Generally, "white contracts" are technically illegal contracts, for they allow room for tax evasion. The question then is: are all the formal contracts prepared and kept by the Pudu Temple illegal, despite all the signatures, stamps, and other formalisms? It should be noted that these "white contracts" do specify that any breach of contract would be prosecuted by the laws of the empire, and that the penalised party has to pay gold to the government. Therefore, these are not informal agreements outside the orbit of the government. Quite the contrary, they invoke and invite heavy involvement by the government. Perhaps it is best to consider them as contracts established by customary laws, in coordination with the imperial laws.

The key practical purpose of red contracts is to ensure tax payment, and to stem out tax evasion. In later periods, to preempt any corruption on the part of government officials, tax laws require that the receipts be attached to the end of the contract. These are referred to as the "tails" of contracts. But this practice did not yet gain currency in the Tangut era.

3.1.7 Land Acquisition, Monopoly, and Aggravation of Wealth Inequality

The imperial court of Western Xia placed an equal emphasis on farming and pasturing. Agricuture in fertile farmlands was essential to filling the granaries, providing for the armies, and ensuring stability for the empire. Although Khara-Khoto lies at the northwestern frontier, and suffers constant drought, the area boasts ample arable land nourished by the meltwater in the Qilian mountains. Therefore, Khara-Khoto claims both economic and strategic importance in the Tangut Empire.

Given the general shortage of arable land within its borders, the Tangut rulers were especially keen to maximise efficiency by sound management tactics. They borrowed heavily from Chinese land governance, but also built on them and developed a rigorous institution of land use and management. The *Laws of Heavenly Prosperity* requires that all peasant households register their land in details.[162]

Land was traded freely in Western Xia. Book 16 of the Laws of Heavenly Prosperity contains extensive rules and regulations on land transaction, but unfortunately this chapter is entirely lost. Therefore, we are deprived of the opportunity to see more details. But there are inklings of these laws in other chapters, such as the rules on measurement and registration in Book 15:

> When the many undertake to transact land, let the name of the seller be cancelled out in the files. Let the buyer proclaim, "I wish to register the land under my name" to the Bureau of Transfer and Transportation. Let the buyer follow the laws on tax, labour, and hay levies. If the seller's name is cancelled, but the buyer does not register his name in a timely manner, then let the evasion of taxes in the interim time be tried as if in a case of theft.[163]

Poorer peasant households end up losing their means of subsistence after the sale. Even a seller who owns multiple patches of land is worse off after selling one of them. In most cases, peasants are left landless after selling their land for grains. They would have to rent a patch of land to farm from wealthy landlords. The long scroll of land sale and lease contracts shows that it is oftentimes the same buyer who loans out the land to a needy seller. For example, on the

162 *Revised Laws of Heavenly Prosperity* 15, p. 514.
163 *Revised Laws of Heavenly Prosperity* 15, p. 509.

same day [illegible] [ljow da kia ·jiw] sells his land where 15 *dan* of seeds are sowed, he rents a land slightly smaller, where 8 *dan* of seeds are sowed, from his buyer, the monks at the Pudu Temple. The leased land seems to have been purchased by the Pudu Temple from [illegible] [dju. dju. śja phji wejr], also on the same day. As for the land sold by [illegible] [ljow da kia ·jiw], it was also leased out on the same day.

The landless peasants, doubly exploited in the process of selling and renting, become tenant farmers. The price at which they sold their own land is forced down to the minimum, given their neediness and desperation. For the same neediness and desperation, the rent is pushed to the maximum by the landlords.

The long scroll of land sale and lease contracts shows that the Pudu Temple exploited the poverty of peasant families in the interim months between two harvests. The monks acquired land on a massive scale. The scroll that survives to the present day is a manuscript fragment, so we do not know how long the original contract scroll was. What we see could have been the tip of an iceberg. We also do not know how much more land the Pudu Temple might have acquired in times before or after the first year of Heavenly Celebration, whereto all our surviving contracts are dated. But one could imagine that these predatory economic activities could have been enduring legacy of the Pudu Temple. As early as in the Dunhuang contracts, we see that temples were buying land. In Khara-Khoto, both temples and landlords leveraged their resources to amass land and concentrate wealth, turning countless land-owning farmers into tenant peasants, and exacerbating preexisting inequalities. As the tenant peasants struggled to pay their rents and enter into a vicious cycle of impoverishment, their social status spirals down, further destabilising the base of the Tangut society. One practical consequence is on defence. The Dangxiang Tanguts provided the main force of the Tangut army. We know that despite all the impressive resistance that Western Xia put up against Mongol invaders, the performance of the military was suboptimal by earlier standards. In particular, Khara-Khoto was taken without fierce counterattacks. It seems that as the society and its economy further destabilised in the late Tangut period, the centripetal force of Tangut power weakened steadily and significantly. Therefore, the Tanguts could not have effectively defended a government whereto they no longer entrusted, and on which they could not depend.

3.1.8 Features of Tangut Land Sale Contracts

3.1.8.1 *New Historical Sources for the History of Contracts*

The discovery of Khara-Khoto land sale contracts adds new materials to the historical study of Tangut society and economy, in particular, but also to the historiography of contracts, in general. A comparative and connective survey of these 12 contracts opens up new ways to understand the idea and the use of contracts in historical contexts.

3.1.8.2 *Reflection on Land Transaction and Social Lives*

The contracts paint a picture of poverty and hardship in Khara-Khoto toward the end of the Tangut era. The peasants suffer a grave shortage of grains in the first two months of the year, and cannot maintain subsistence without selling their ancestral land. Their impoverishment feeds into the monopolistic and acquisitive ventures of large landlords and temples. Such phenomena usually occur in the declining years of Chinese dynasties. Western Xia is no exception.

3.1.8.3 *Insights on Land Conditions and Management*

The contracts shed new light on the conditions of government-owned or privately owned land, changing dynamics and states of peasant ownership of farmland, modes of land management, land transactions, land prices, and so forth. With a series of interrelated contracts, in particular, we are able to paint a picture of land locations, their directions to canals and water supplies, their neighbouring lands, size, and distribution.

3.1.8.4 *Characteristics of Local Settlements*

The contracts show that Khara-Khoto peasants built their abodes on their own land. The scattered pattern of residential quarters may be explained either by the pasturing tradition of the Dangxiang people, or in the light of local realities: sparse populations across spacious lands.

3.1.8.5 *Irrigation System*

Given the draught and the dearth of natural rain, the bloodline of Khara-Khoto farmlands relied on artificial irrigation through manmade canals, and the supply of the Black River. Extensive references to various canals in the land sale contracts confirms what we know from the *Laws of Heavenly Prosperity*, and greatly enriches and visualises our understanding of how water was used and managed in Khara-Khoto.

3.1.8.6 *Data on Tangut Land Prices*

For the first time, the contracts reveal en masse the prices of Tangut farmlands. The rigorous documentation of land taxes in the land sale contracts shows the level of importance the Tangut bureaucracy attaches to agriculture and the revenue it generates. Tax data in these contracts also verify the tax rate, clarify the complexities of tax payments in Western Xia, and fill in the details that are nowhere to be found in a law code such as the *Laws of Heavenly Prosperity*.

3.1.8.7 *Inter-Ethnic Influences on the Structure of Economic Sectors*

The contracts tell the story of the Dangxiang Tanguts whose ancestors acquired farming skills from Han Chinese peasants, and are now more land-based than pasture-roaming. Historically, inter-ethnic exchanges and contacts have shaped the economic lives of populations across spatial frontiers.

3.1.8.8 *Heritage and Innovation in Tangut Sell and Purchase Contracts*

Tangut land sale contracts inherit the basic legal format from the Chinese tradition. But on top of it, the Tanguts developed their own styles and formulas. The contract begins with the date but omits the reasons for the transaction. It severely penalises any breach of the contract, records the tax rate, demarcates the four borders of the land concerned, permits two forms of stamping (symbols and finger-segments), as well as both "red contracts" and "white contracts." Some of the formats and formalities can be seen as intermediate forms in transition from Tang and Song to Yuan-Dynasty styles of contracts.

3.2 *Livestock Sales*

More than 20 Khara-Khoto social documents are contracts of livestock sale. They make up a large proportion of the entire corpus of medieval livestock sale and loan contracts. Additional Tangut livestock sale contracts have been excavated in the Haimu Cave, in Wuwei, Gansu. These contracts are critically informative primary sources that shed light on livestock-raising and trading in Western Xia.

3.2.1 Translations of Tangut Contracts of Livestock Sale

Khara-Khoto livestock sale contracts are either individual, single-page contracts, or documents within a large scroll of papers, or still, recycled to bind Buddhist sutras. In the last case, the contracts are usually incomplete, left with only half of its original content, or with its upper and lower sections cut out and cast away. All these contracts are written in the Tangut cursive. Below, I present, in chronological order, the translations of 11 surviving Khara-Khoto livestock sale contracts, where key information and data, such as price, quantity, and types of commodities, remain legible and identifiable. They are followed by the two pieces of livestock sale contracts found in Wuwei.

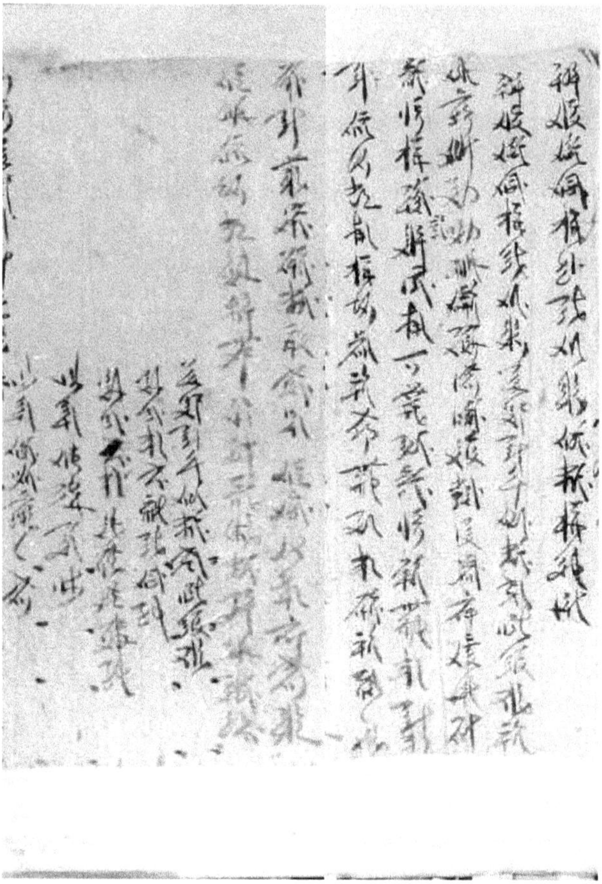

FIGURE 163 Инв. No. 5124-3(5, 6): Yin year of Tianqing (1194) contract of livestock sale

1. Инв. No. 5124-3(5, 6) Contract of Livestock Sale in the Yin Year of Heavenly Celebration (1194), found in the long scroll of manuscript Инв. No. 5124-3. There are 12 lines of Tangut in the cursive. Perhaps due to errors in the first line, the second restarts the main text of the contract. The contract features signatures and stamps (all finger-segments) near the end.[164]

Translation:

> On the 29th Day of 1st Month of the Yin Year, the contract party [illegible] [ŋwe ze zji-.ɣa. wa. lji-.]

164 *Russian Collection of Khara-Khoto Manuscripts*, vol. 14, pp. 16 and 17.

Presently to the grain managers at the Pudu Temple [illegible] [ljow lja mja], voluntarily sells his
Two full-teethed cattles, 1 full-teethed black ox et al., at the price of
5 *dan* of wheat and 2 *dan* of coarse grains, already paid. Neither the payment nor the livestocks are overdue. Should any dispute arise either from the government or privately,
let the penalty be 5 *dan* of wheat, according to the laws. Willing. Let the terms be enforced according to the contract.

Contract Party: [illegible] [ŋwe ze ɣa. wa. lji-.] (stamp)
Co-contractor and seller: son, [illegible] [ɣa. lhji wejr] (stamp)
Co-contractor and seller: [illegible] [dzji. rjir sji gju wejr] (stamp)
Witness: [illegible] [phjij śjo wa śia~] (stamp)
Witness: [illegible] [ŋwe mji wa wa dju] (stamp)

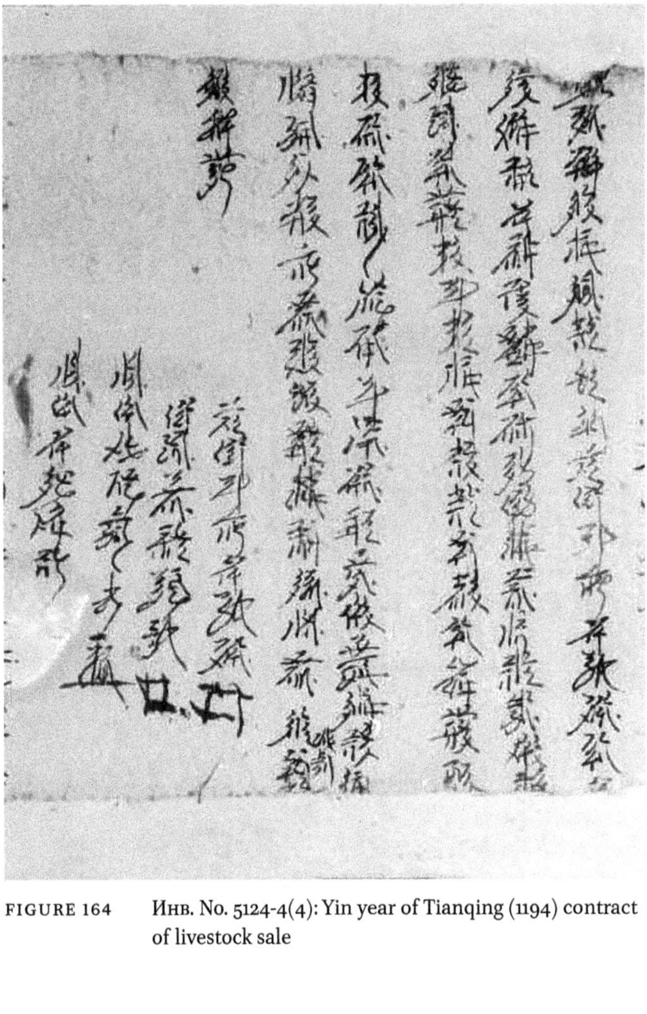

FIGURE 164 Инв. No. 5124-4(4): Yin year of Tianqing (1194) contract of livestock sale

2. Инв. No. 5124-4(4): Contract of Livestock Sale in the Yin Year of Heavenly Celebration (1194), from the contract scroll Инв. No. 5124-4. There are 9 lines of Tangut in the cursive style, ending with signatures and stamps.[165]

Translation:

> On the 3rd day of the 2nd month in the Yin Year of Heavenly Celebration, the contract party [Tangut] [ljow wejr khjwi-] et al., to [Tangut] [ljow]
> [Tangut] [lja mja] and [Tangut] [ljow dow dźjij phu_] et al., voluntarily sell a full-teethed female camel and
> A horse, at the price of 2 *dan* of wheat and 3 *dan* of coarse grains, already paid.
> Neither the payment nor the livestocks are overdue. If third parties, such as members of the same *chao*,
> initiate a dispute over the livestocks, let the guilty party be prosectued according to the *Laws and Orders*, and pay the penalty fee, according to the laws, of 3
> *dan* of wheat. Willing.
> Contract Party: [Tangut] [ljow wejr khjwi-] (stamp)
> Co-contractor: son, [Tangut] [dźjwo wejr][166] (stamp)
> Witness: [Tangut] [dzji. rjir wa wa tsji-] (stamp)
> Witness: [Tangut] [ljow da kia ·jiw] (stamp)

165 *Russian Collection of Khara-Khoto Manuscripts*, vol. 14, p. 20.

166 TN: I read the name as 擲盛. They appear as 打子 in the Chinese edition.

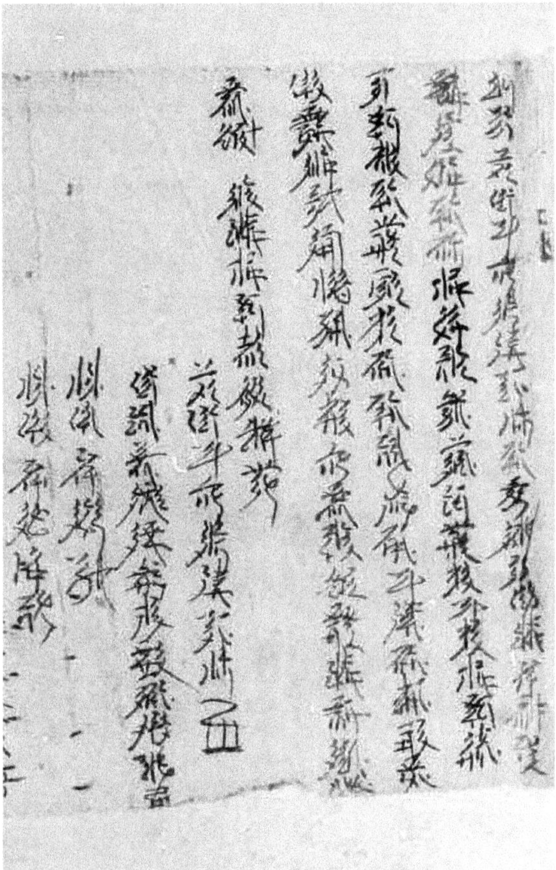

FIGURE 165 Инв. No. 5124-4(5): Yin year of Tianqing (1194) contract of livestock sale

3. Инв. No. 5124-4(5): Contract of Livestock Sale in the Yin Year of Heavenly Celebration (1194), from the long scroll Инв. No. 5124-4. There are 9 lines of Tangut in the cursive script. The contract ends with signatures and stamps.[167]

Translation:

> On the same day,[168] contract party [illegible] [phjij śjo wa śia~] et al., voluntarily to [illegible] [ljow dow dźjij phu_]
>
> [illegible] [lja mja] et al., sell their own 2-teethed male camel, at the price of 2 *dan* of barley

167 *Russian Collection of Khara-Khoto Manuscripts*, vol. 14, p. 20.

168 The precise date is the third day of the second month in the Yin Year of Tianqing.

and 1 *dan* of millet, already paid. Neither the payment nor the livestock is overdue. If third

Parties, such as members of the same *chao*, should initiate disputes, let the culpable party not only be prosecuted according to the *Laws and Orders*,

But also pay the government a penalty fee of 2 *dan* of coarse grains.

Contract party: [illegible] [phjij śjo wa śia~] (stamp)

Co-contractor: wife, [illegible] [mjij pu. zji-. khjwi- mja lji-.] (stamp)

Witness: [illegible] [ljow ne_w wejr] (stamp)

Witness: [illegible] [ljow da kia ·jiw] (stamp)

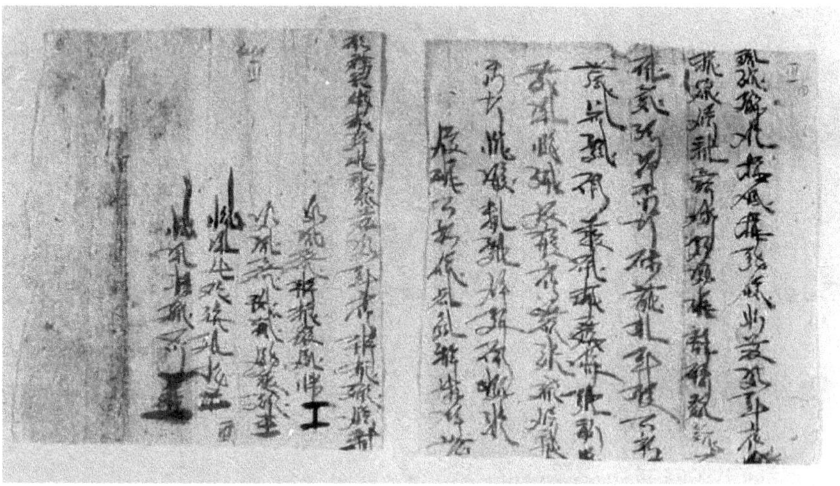

FIGURE 166 Инв. No. 2546-2, 3: Hai year of Tianqing (1203) contract of livestock sale

4. Инв. No. 2546-2, 3: Contract of Livestock Sale in the Hai Year of Heavenly Celebration (1203). The contract features 12 lines of cursive Tangut handwritten on a 19.6 × 34.5 cm hemp paper. The materiality of the paper and the identity of the contracting parties seemt to suggest that the two papers belong in the same document.[169]

Translation:

On the 25th day of the 2nd month in the Hai Year of Heavenly Celebration, the contract party [illegible] [tsow]

[illegible] [ze khjwi- tji-. gji] voluntarily sells his own three-teethed, short?

169 *Russian Collection of Khara-Khoto Manuscripts*, vol. 13, p. 84.

red horse to [illegible] [ljow lhew gju_] at the price of 1 *dan* ?
dou of coarse grains, hereby agreed upon. Should members of the same *chao* ever raise a dispute over the horse,
let [illegible] bear the responsibility,
not [illegible]. Let the party that reneges on its promise
be punished 1 *dan* 5 *dou* of coarse grains according to the laws. Own hearts willing.
Let the terms be enforced according to the contract and the actual circumstances.
Contract party: [illegible] [tsow ze khjwi- tji-. gji] (stamp)
Co-contractor: [illegible]? [tsow ze lhji.j śia~] (stamp)
Co-contractor: ?[illegible] [do ɣa. wa. khjwi-][170] (stamp)
Witness: [illegible] [zjwi. ·o kə ta lji-.] (stamp)
Witness: [illegible] [pu. khjwi- dju] (stamp)

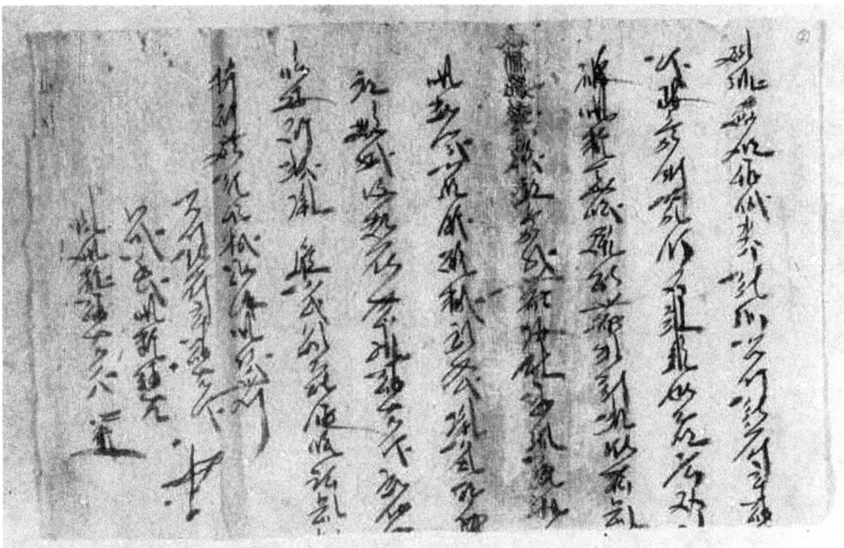

FIGURE 167 Инв. No. 2546-1: Hai year of Tianqing (1203) contract of livestock sale

5. Инв. No. 2546-1: Contract of Livestock Sale in the Hai Year of Heavenly Celebration (1203), is an individual contract, with 11 lines of cursive Tangut handwritten on a 20 × 31.2 cm hemp paper. The contract begins with the year, and ends with signatures and stamps.[171]

170 TN: I am quite certain that at least the four characters listed here (difference, marriage, dog) all form a part of the name.

171 *Russian Collection of Khara-Khoto Manuscripts*, vol. 13, p. 84.

Translation:

On the 30th day of the 2nd month in the Hai Year of Heavenly Celebration, contract party [illegible]

[illegible] [ljow dow dźjij wa] presently sells his own full-teethed femal camel ? voluntarily

to [illegible] [ŋwe ze śja lhji khjwi-] at the price of 6 *dan* of coarse grains.

Now ? that the livestock is <> purchased and transferred ? ? and ? ?

[illegible] [ŋwe ze wa], if other parties such as members of the same *chao* should ever raise

a dispute over the property right of the livestock, let [illegible] be liable. If

any party regrets and reneges on the promise, let it be punished 5 *dan* of coarse grains according to the laws.

Let the above terms be enforced according to the contract and the actual circumstances.

Contract Party: [illegible] [ljow dow dźjij wa] (stamp)

Co-contractor: [illegible]? [ŋwe ze] (stamp)

Witness: [illegible] [ŋwe ze dow dźjij wa] (stamp)

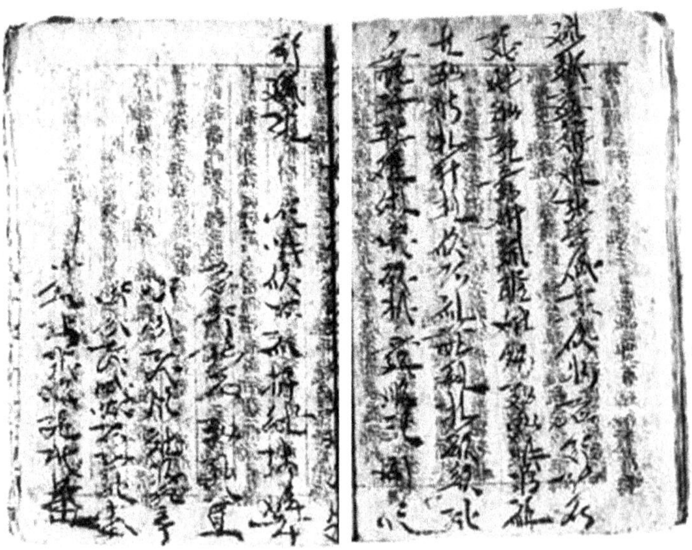

FIGURE 168 Инв. No. 5404-8, 9: Jiazi year of Tianqing (1204) contract of livestock sale

6. Инв. No. 5404-8, 9: Contract of Livestock Sale in the Jiazi Year of Heavenly Celebration (1204), a handwritten manuscript on a 19.6 × 27 cm hemp paper, found inside a Buddhist sutra of sewn binding. Some sutras are written on the back of used papers and sewn back into a text. Given available information on the main contract party, the font, character-spacing, line spacing, along with other clues from either content or format on the two pages of the paper, it seems that the 4 lines on the first page and 5 lines on the second page are the upper and lower sections of different contracts. The text on the first page begins with the date, month, and year: the 15th day of the 11th month in the Jiazi Year of Heavenly Celebration (1204). On the second page there are signatures and the stamps. In fact, the first page and the second page of manuscript No. 5404-9 should have formed the same contract. There is a total of 10 lines of Tangut in the cursive script. The second page here should have been in the same document as the first page of manuscript No. 5404-9. The contract ends with signatures and stamps.[172]

Translation:

On the 15th day of the 11th month in the Jiaiz Year of Heavenly Celebration, the contracting party
[illegible][illegible]? [·o tshji-j ? wejr] voluntarily sells his mare with bridle to [illegible][illegible] [xa dow]
[illegible][illegible] [dźjij tśhjwor], at the price of 5 *dan* of coarse grains, paid. There is no discrepancy in payment or livestock,
Thereafter, if members of the same *chao* either publicly or privately raise a dispute
…
A reneging party is punished 5 *dan* of coarse grains according to the laws.
Own hearts willing.
Contract Party: ?[illegible] [wejr] (stamp)
Co-contractor: …… (stamp)
Co-contractor: …… (stamp)
Witness: [illegible][illegible][illegible] [ljow ne_w wejr] (stamp)

172 *Russian Collection of Khara-Khoto Manuscripts*, vol. 14, pp. 34–35.

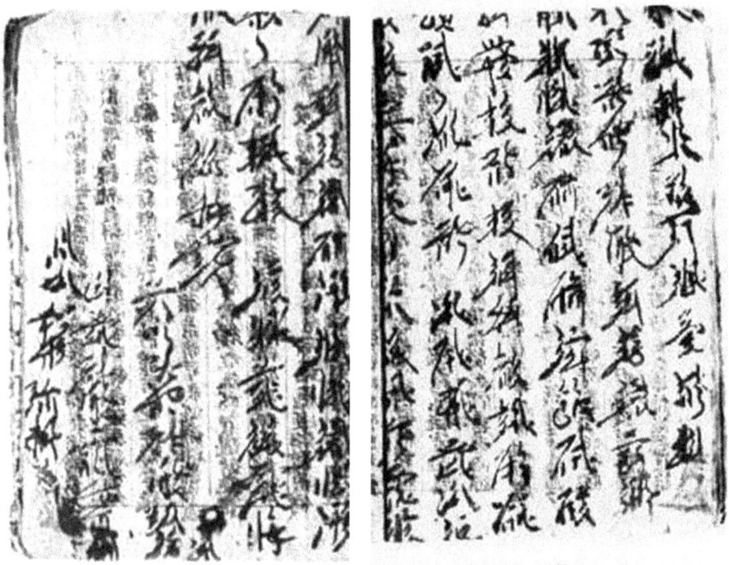

FIGURE 169 Инв. No. 5404-10, 5404-7: Zi year of Tianqing (1204) contract of livestock sale

7. Инв. No. 5404-10, 5404-7: Contract of Livestock Sale in the Zi Year of Heavenly Celebration (1204) is a contract reassembled from the right page of manuscript Инв. No. 5404-10 and the left page of manuscript Инв. No. 5404-7. There are 12 lines of Tangut in the cursive script, ending with signatures and stamps.[173]

Translation:

> On the 16th day of the 11th month in the Zi Year of Heavenly Celebration,
> The Contracting Party [illegible] [phiow tshji-j ɣwie rjijr njo_r] has his own
> Livestock sold to [illegible] [ŋwe mji njo_r], a five-teethed, usable maroon horse,
> At the agreed price of 4 *dan* of coarse grains. Payment for the livestock
> Is not amiss. Over the horse, if any third party initiates
> A dispute … When ? is overdue,
> Let [illegible], not [illegible] be liable.
> Let any reneging party, according to the laws on embezzlement,
> Pay a penalty fee of 5 *dan* of coarse grains. Own hearts willing.

173 *Russian Collection of Khara-Khoto Manuscripts*, vol. 14, pp. 34–35.

Contract Party: [illegible] [phiow tshji-j ɣwie rjijr njo_r] (stamp)
Co-contractor: ?[illegible] [ɣji-. njij] (stamp)
Witness: [illegible] [bji gju_ rjur] (stamp)

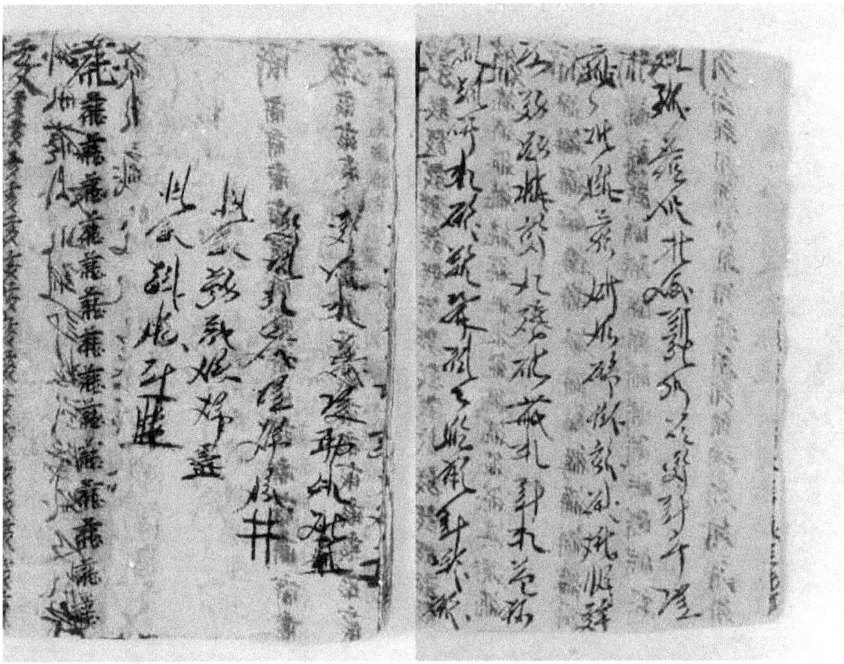

FIGURE 170 Инв. No. 2858-1: Chou year of Tianqing (1205) contract of livestock sale

8. Инв. No. 2858-1 Contract of Livestock Sale in the Chou Year of Heavenly Celebration (1205), is handwritten on a 19.8 × 25.7 hemp paper found in a sewn-bound Buddhist sutra. The 4 lines on the right are the livestock sale contract. There is another piece on the right page of the manuscript Инв. No. 2858-12. The 4 lines seem to be the second end section of a contract. The renaming first lines links it to the left of the contracting party's name in No. 2858-1. These two pieces are parts of the same contract.[174]

Translation:

On the 30th day of the last month in the Chou Year of Heavenly Celebration, the Contracting Party [illegible] [xa]
[illegible] [wa wa lji-.] presently has his own four-teethed usable red mare
Voluntarily sold to [illegible] [thu tshja ta] for 7 *dan*

174 *Russian Collection of Khara-Khoto Manuscripts*, vol. 13, p. 119.

Of coarse grains. The price is agreed upon and is not amiss. The livestock …

Contract Party: [wa wa lji-.]
Co-contractor: [xa gju_ bie_j]
witness? [zji dźji_j gju_]
witness? [·ja ·jiw]

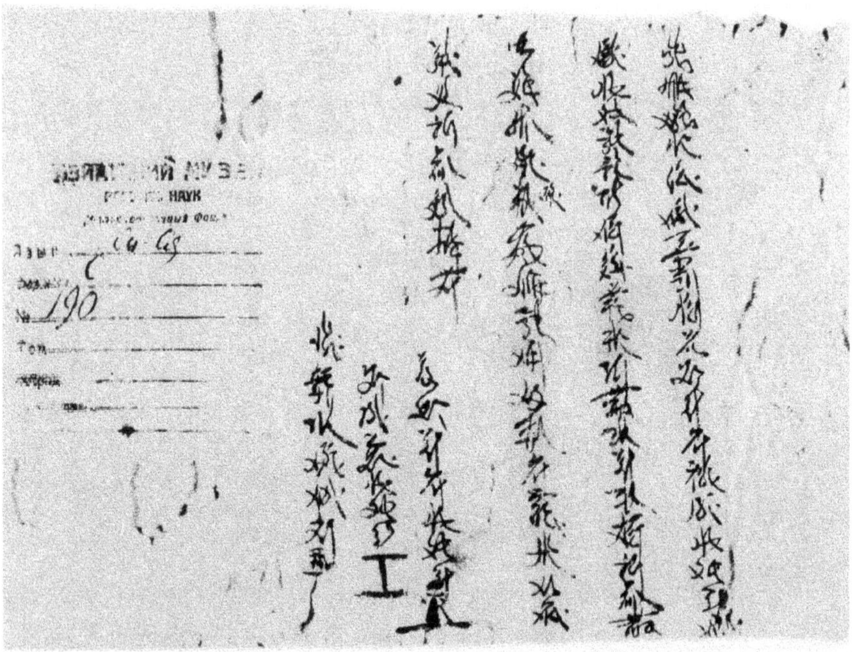

FIGURE 171 Инв. No. 7630-2: You year of Guangding (1213) contract of livestock sale

9. Инв. No. 7630-2: Contract of Livestock Sale in the You Year of Guangding (1213), is an individual contract with 7 lines of Tangut in the cursive script handwritten on a 19.7 × 39.5 cm hemp paper. The contract begins with the date, ends with signatures and stamps, and features the red seal of the Department of Transaction Taxes.[175]

Translation:

On the 30th day of the 5th month in the You Year of Guangding, the contracting party [rar bju kə ta ·jiw] to

175 *Russian Collection of Khara-Khoto Manuscripts*, vol. 14, p. 187.

[illegible] [ŋwe zjwi. kə ta zji] et al. sells a 4 vertical(-teethed) live ox, at the agreed-upon price of 4 *dan* of coarse grains.
Hereupon should any member of the same *chao* dispute the property ownership, let the seller assume responsibility.
And pay the penalty fee of 8 *dan* of coarse grains. Willing.
Contract Party: [illegible] [kə ta ·jiw] (stamp)
Co-contractor: [illegible] [kə ta zji][176] (stamp)
Witness: [illegible] [mjij pu. tśjow lhji. gju_] (stamp)

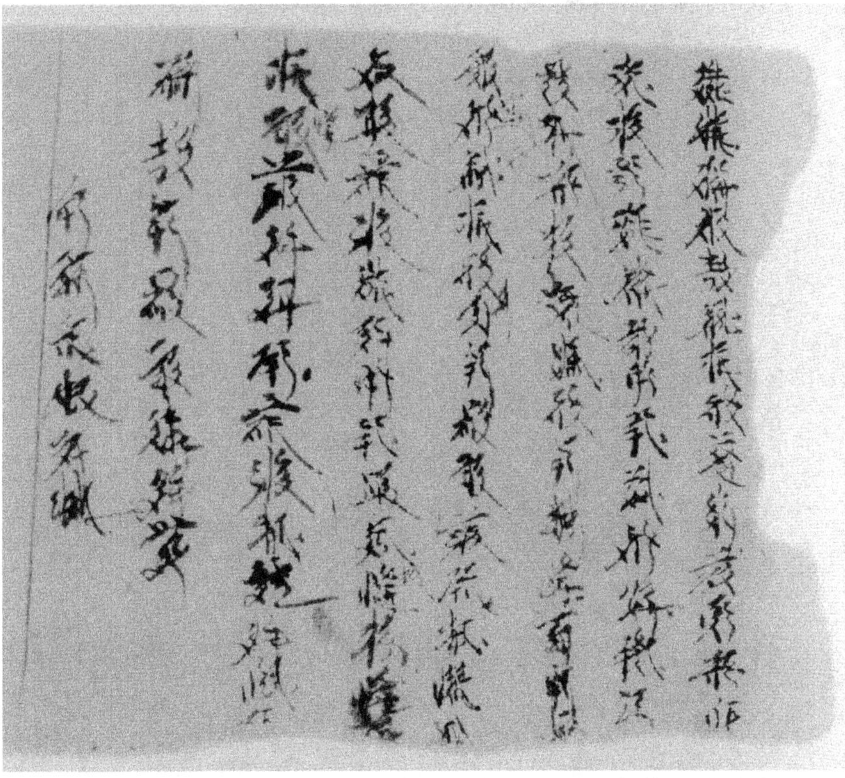

FIGURE 172 Инв. No. 7994-14: Hai year of Guangding (1215) contract of livestock sale

10. Инв. No. 7994-14: Contract of Livestock Sale in the Hai Year of Guangding (1215) is features 8 lines of cursive Tangut handwritten on a 17.7 × 37.9 cm hemp paper. The text begins with the date, 27th day of the 3rd month, but it lacks signatures and stamps. There are also traces of erasures in the text.[177]

176 TN: This is another "little puppy," not the buyer referred to in the main text.
177 *Russian Collection of Khara-Khoto Manuscripts*, vol. 14, p. 243.

Translation:

On the 27th day of the 3rd month in the Hai Year of Guangding, the Contract Party
[illegible] [rar pu. dzji_j no] presently purchases from Zhang Shunli[178] a six-
Vertical(-teethed) ox, at the price of 10 *dan*, 1 *dan* of which has been paid.
Another 8 *dan* has to be paid by the 20th day of the 6th month. If over the livestock there
Ever arises a dispute, let the aforementioned Shunli take responsibility. And let the penalty
Be double the sum of the price. Let any party that regrets over this arrangement pay the unregretting party
3 *dan* of coarse grains. Own hearts willing.

FIGURE 173 Инв. No. 6377-15: Zi year of Guangding (1216) contract of livestock sale

178 TN: The Tangut is [illegible] [tśjow śjwa~ kjiw].

11. Инв. No. 6377-15: Contract of Livestock Sale in the Zi year of Guangding (1216) is a single contract that consists of 11 lines of cursive Tangut handwritten on a 19.5 × 21.1 cm hemp paper. The contract begins with the date: 16th day of 5th month in the Zi Year of Guangding, and ends with signatures and stamps.[179]

Translation:

On the 16th day of the 5th month in the Zi year of Guangding, the contracting party [Tangut] (?)[180] [ljow khjwi- ɣwie]

Sells his own 2 vertical(-teethed), 6 female camels, 1 vertical(?), 1 maroon horse,

Voluntarily to [Tangut]? [tśhjiw zjwi.][181] [Tangut] [ŋwe zjwi.]?? [śia~], at the total value

Of 90 *liang* in silver, a price hereby agreed upon. Neither the livestock nor the payment is amiss.

Should any dispute over the horses, let the seller be responsible. If?

Regrets and reneges on the promise, let the party pay a penalty fee of 10 guan of cash, according to the laws. Own hearts willing.

Let the terms be enforced according to the contract and the circumstances.

Contract Party: [Tangut] [ljow khjwi- ɣwie] (stamp)

Co-contractor: [Tangut] ?? [Tangut] [ljow ?? khjwi-] (stamp)

Co-contractor: ??[Tangut] [?? wa wa śia~] (stamp)

Witness: [Tangut] ?[182] [·jiw dji.j ?] (stamp)

---

179 *Russian Collection of Khara-Khoto Manuscripts*, vol. 14, p. 145.

180 TN: I replaced [Tangut] with [Tangut].

181 TN: I do not think the [Tangut] [bju] is part of the name, as suggested in the Chinese edition. It's a preposition that goes with the verb of "selling volutnarily to" or "let someone have" ([Tangut]). For the name, I start with [Tangut].

182 TN: The [Tangut] seems to be a typo in the Chinese edition.

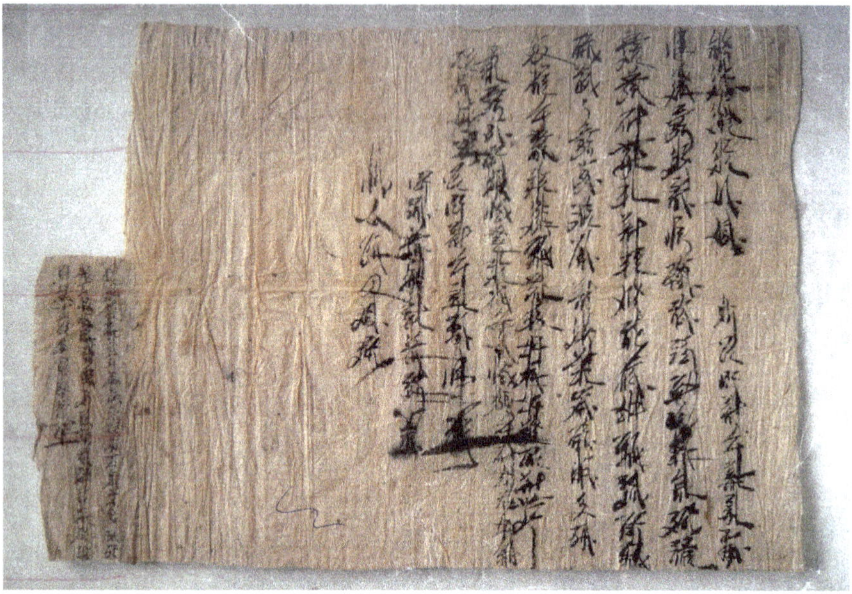

FIGURE 174 Wuwei G31·003[6727]1–2: You year of Qianding (1225) contract of cattle sale

12. Haimu Cave, Wuwei G31·003[6727]1–2 (1225): Contract of Cattle Sale in the You year of Qianding, now curated in the Wuwei Museum. The contract consists of 9 lines in cursive Tangut handwritten on a 30 × 44 cm hemp paper. The text begins with the month and year, 9th month in the You Year of Qianding (1225). There is a small piece of paper attached to its lower left corner, where there are 3 lines of Tangut cursive writings, most of which are not legible.[183]

Translation:

On the ?day of the 9th month in the You Year of Qianding, Contract Party: [illegible]
[illegible] [dzow zjo. dźjo śia~], presently out of his own will sells a full-teethed black ox to [bji_j khjwi-]
[pa rja śjow] at the price of 65 *guan* in cash, hereby agreed upon. Neither the payment
Nor the livestock is amiss. If over the livestock a dispute ever arises,
Let the penalty be double the sum of the price. Willing.
If an individual is dishonest, let the reneging party pay 30 *guan* of cash to the unregretting party.
Contract Party: [illegible] [zjo. dźjo śia~] (stamp)

183 *Chinese Collection of Tangut Manuscripts*, vol. 16, pp. 387–388.

Co-Contractor: [illegible] (Wu Mao) [gu_ phu_] (stamp)
Witness: [illegible] (Zhao Bayuequan) [tśhjiw ·jar lhji. khjwi-] (stamp)

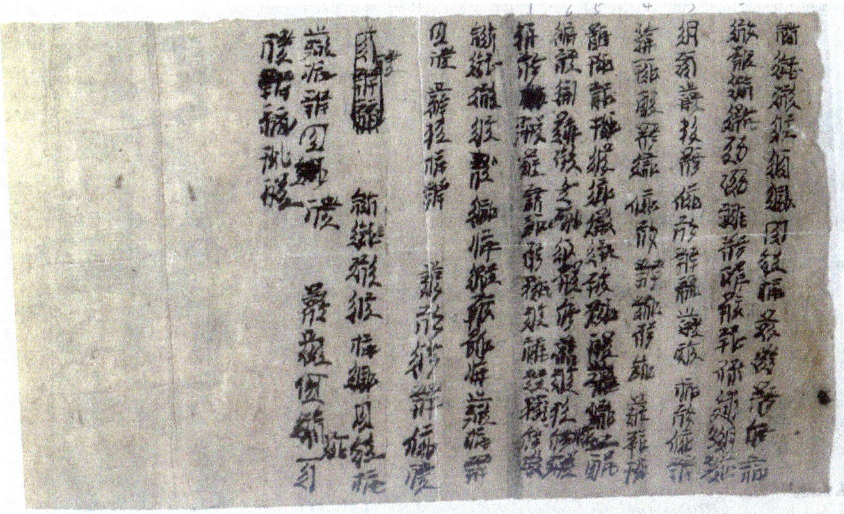

FIGURE 175 Wuwei G31·002[6726]: Xu year of Qianding (1226) contract of donkey sale

13. Haimu Cave, Wuwei G31·002[6726]: Contract of Donkey Sale in the Xu Year of Qianding (1226) consists of 12 lines of Tangut in the cursive script handwritten on a 17 × 55 cm paper. The contract has not properly ended, and lacks both signatures and stamps. Furthermore, there are miscellaneous characters on the page that do not belong to the contract. They could be scribblings on the scrap paper by someone practicing handwriting.[184]

Translation:

On the 8th day of the 4th month in Xu Year of Qianding, contracting party [illegible] [śjwo]
[illegible] [ɣa. wa. ne_w] now voluntarily sells [illegible] [thji xjwi- kjiw]
A yellow donkey for 50 *guan* in cash, of which 25 is paid
Immediately. The price of 50 *guan* is negotiated and agreed upon. If any party is deceitful
Such as transferring the commodity as a loan privately or publicly, or if members of the same *chao*
Dispute the ownership of the property, let the seller be fully responsible,
Not the buyer. Let a party that regrets and reneges on the promise …

184 *Chinese Collection of Tangut Manuscripts*, vol. 16, p. 386.

In addition, the Инв. No. 5404-9, 5404-8 manuscript is a Contract of Livestock Sale on the 25th day in the 10th month of the Wei Year of Tianqing (1199). It is reassembled from the right section of Инв. No. 5404-9 and the left section of 5404-8. The 9 lines of Tangut are handwritten in the cursive style on hemp paper. The text begins with the date and ends with signatures and stamps. The extraordinary cursiveness of the handwriting, exacerbated by the fact that it has a Buddhist sutra written on the back, and by extra ink and soaking, leaves the text less than legible for our purposes.[185]

3.2.2 The Format and Content of Livestock Sale Contracts

Livestock sale contracts follow the general format of most Tangut contracts. Each contract begins with the date, and proceeds to state the name of the main contracting party, the type, quantity, and price of the livestock sold, as well as penalties against any breach of contract. The document ends with signatures and stamps of the contracting and co-contracting parties, as well as the witnesses.

3.2.2.1 *Time, Contract Party, and Buyer*

The earliest of the 11 Khara-Khoto livestock sale contracts is dated to the 29th day of 1st month in the Yin Year of Tianqing (1194). The latest is signed on the 16th day of the 5th month in the Zi year of Guangding. The entire range falls within the late Tangut period. The selling takes place mostly in the winter months, from the last month of the previous year to the third month of the new year. But unlike grain loan accounts and land sale contracts, livestock contracts are not exclusively concentrated in these months. There are, for instance, 2 livestock contracts in the fifth month and 2 in the eleventh. Dates are customarily simplified in long scrolls. Here, by "Yin Year" is meant the Jiayin Year of the Tianqing era (1194). As in grain loan accounts, livestock sale contracts may indicate "on the same day" to refer to the precise dates in preceding documents. The two livestock sale contracts from Wuwei are dated to the You and the Xu Years of Qianding, only a year or two before the fall of the empire.

The Инв. No. 7994-14 document stands out amongst all livstock sale contracts, for the main contracting party is not the seller, but the buyer. It is all the more a source of regret that the end of the contract is missing. So, we do not know what the signatures might have looked like. But in this case, the buyer initiates the contract.

Amongst all the names featured in the 13 contracts, there is some ethnic diversity in both the buyers and the sellers. Most are Dangxiang Tanguts. Some names, such as Lu, Hao, and Tu, seem to be of Chinese origins. As usual, we

185 *Russian Collection of Khara-Khoto Manuscripts*, vol. 14, pp. 34–35.

cannot say with full confidence if the Liangs fall into the Fan or Han camps. It could be one way or the other.

It should perhaps be mentioned that our familiar friends, 𗍳𗓾𗘂𗎘 [ljow dow dźjij phu_] and 𗍳𗏁𗒘 [ljow lja mja], who act as 'grain agents' on behalf of the Pudu Temple in land sale contracts, appear in contracts of livestock sale as authorised managers of livestock for the same temple. As agents, or asset managers, these two fellows acquire properties and then lease them out to make profit for the monastic establishment.

3.2.2.2 *Reasons for Selling Large Livestocks*

In medieval Western Xia, livestocks are both means of consumption and means of production. Large livestocks are employed to tilt the land, bear burdens, and to carry soldiers and provisions in land warfare across large swaps of complex landscapes. Although Western Xia was renowned for its livestocks as a Tangu specialty, the empire forbids arbitrary slaughter of large livestocks, given their important status in the economy and the military. In fact, the Tangut government applies stringent rules and regulations on the slaughtering of large livestocks. The *Laws of Heavenly Prosperity* states that,

> The many who slaughter their own cattles, camels, and horses, let each be tried and sentenced to four years of imprisonment for each animal killed, regardless of size. Let the sentence be five years for two animals killed. Let the sentence be six years for killing three or more large livestocks.[186]

Tangut farmers and herdsmen raised livestock primarily for domestic use. But surplus animals were also sold for cash and grains. Therefore, there is a subtle difference between the socioeconomic reasons underlying land and livestock sales. Most peasants sell the land on which their livelihood depends only as a last resort, when they are hard pressed by dire necessities of subsistence. In contrast, motivations for selling livestocks are more complex. There are two main reasons. A family sells its livestocks either out of poverty, especially in the inter-harvest months of the early spring, or to expand its income when there are extra animals on the farm, especially during and after their breeding seasons. Both motives are present in the livestock sale contracts studied in this chapter.

In the cases of Инв. No. 5404-8, 9 and Инв. No. 5404-10, mares and horses are sold in the 11th month of the year, a short while after the autumn harvest. The sellers could not have been out of grains so quickly. And although the Инв.

186 *Revised Laws of Heavenly Prosperity* 2, "On Stealing and Killing Cattles, Camels, and Horses," p. 154.

No. 6377-15 contract was signed in the 5th month, it does not seem that someone who could afford to sell 9 horses and camels for as much as 90 *liang* of silver—and not in grains—is doing it for subsistence. Chances are, in all these three cases, the sellers are selling surplus livestocks for extra income.

Of course, it is undeniable that most other livestock sales take place during the hard-pressing, inter-harvest months of the late winters and early springs. Such is the case in the three contracts found in the Инв. No. 5124 manuscript, and the two contracts found in the Инв. No. 2546 manuscript, the Инв. No. 2858 and the Инв. No. 7994 livestock sale contracts. In particular, the three contracts in the Инв. No. 5124 manuscript testify to the acquisitive and exploitative ventures of the Pudu Temple. They show that the asset managers of the monastery purchased large livestocks and leased then immediately leased them out to peasants deprived of their means of production.

3.2.2.3 *Types and Quantities of Livestocks Sold*

The animals sold in the 13 surviving livestock sale contracts are camels, horses, and cattles. The *Laws of Heavenly Prosperity* categories Tangut livestocks into four major categories: camels, horses, cattles, and sheep.[187] What we see in the contracts are the first three, but not sheep. Perhaps the sheep are small enough to be traded without a formal contract.

Western Xia boasts a highly advanced pasturing industry. It is, after all, the ancestral legacy and traditional industry of the Dangxiang Tanguts. It is worth pointing out that, located in northwestern Western Xia, Khara-Khoto was a highly developed centre of the Tangut camel industry. Even to the present day, the area is known for its famed camels. By normal standards, Khara-Khoto shows all the undesirable natural conditions: sandy winds, scarce water, and freezing winters. However, the camels are uniquely suited withstand strong winds, sandy deserts, extraordinary temperature differences, and constant lack of water. Camels survived, reproduced, and prospered in the Khara-Khoto area. They were not only superb burden animals and excellent mounts, but also capable of tilling the soil, dragging carts and carriages, as well as moving mills and lifting up water. Needless to say, alas, camel fur and meat are of tremendous economic value.

But the Tangut livestock sale contracts document not only the species of the animal but their particular features, whether it is a full-teethed female camel, a two-teethed male camel, a camel usable for three years, a red mare, a five-teethed, usable maroon horse, six-vertical(-teethed) ox, etc. The number of teeth is used as a proxy for the approximate age of the animal concerned. It is equivalent to the notion of *Suikou* in the livestock industry of the Central

187 *Revised Laws of Heavenly Prosperity* 19, p. 599.

Plains.[188] It is also important to know the number of teeth to assess the animal's chewing and labouring ability. All things considered, the number of teeth is a simple way to represent the quality of the animal. An average Tangut would have known, for example, that a foal begins to shed its desiduous teeth and to grow a permanent set after two and a half years. By the age of five, the permanent incisors, pre-molars and molars should be in place. By this time, a male horse's canine teeth should also have emerged.[189] To inspect a horse, one usually takes a glimpse at the lower incisors. An animal is 'two-teethed' if it grows the two lower incisors. It is 'four-teethed' if it has the pre-molars, as well. Once all the lower molars are properly in place, the horse is said to be "full-teethed" (*qikou*).[190] The cattles do not have upper incisors, but four pairs of lower incisors. The middle pair is called the 'pincer teeth.' Permanent 'pincer' incisors are grown between 1.5 and 2 years of age. The next pair is the inner intermediate teeth. The permanent inner intermediate teeth are grown between years 2–2.5. The neighbouring set of teeth is the outer intermediate teeth, which are grown when the calve reaches 3–3.5 years old. The outermost pair of teeth are the molars, which emerge in years 4–4.5. The bovines are tically five years old when their molars reach up to the incisors. This is the prime age of the cattle.

Pasturing is the forte of the Tanguts. For the same reason, the Tanguts used an elaborate language to describe and differentiate livestocks. Some terms and expressions may have regional, local, or ethnic origins and characteristics, which are obstacles to identification and translation. The meanings and applications of some of them remain obscure. But with other basic terms, scholars are more confident. For example, the Tanguts signal the age of the livestock by the state of their teeth. As for the term "vertical," it is possible that the verb of vertical existence here refers to the existence of teeth grown in a vertical direction. This term is used to describe the teeth of the cattle that have grown two, four, or six vertical teeth. Whether these correspond to the 'pincer,' 'middle' and 'molar' teeth of the lower incisors remains a question to be asked in future research. As for "usable for three years" camels and "usable, five-teethed maroon" horses, the descriptions there seem to underscore the features, values, and practical utilities of the animals. Some contracts indicate the colours of the livestocks to avoid confusions.

There is an additional livestock sale contract fragment, in the manuscript Инв. No. 840-3, a layering paper in a Buddhist sutra. There are two paper fragments, and the livestock sale contract is found in the upper section. There is

188 TN: Chinese: 歲口.

189 TN: Although minimally trained in equine studies, I suspect that not all mares lack canine teeth.

190 TN: Chinese: 齊口.

a diverse range of livestocks recorded in the text, from sheep and donkeys to horses, cattles, and camels. The total price is 98 *dan* 6 *dou* 5 *sheng* of coarse grains. Regrettably, both the beginning and end of the document are lost, so we literally couldn't make heads or tails of the larger context in which it was drafted.[191]

3.2.2.4 *Livestock Prices*

Price is the key data point in any livestock sale contract. In 10 of the 11 surviving contracts, the method of payment is grain. Only in one large-volume transaction, the payment is made in cash. In grain payments, the buyer may pay a mixture of fine and coarse grains. For the sake of convenience and consistency, I have converted all grain payments to coarse grains, based on rates derived from other Khara-Khoto documents studied in this book.[192] The following is a chart that presents the data extracted from the livestock sale contracts, in chronological order.

CHART 15 Data in Khara-Khoto livestock sale contracts

Register	Date	Livestock	Price	Price in coarse grains
Инв. No. 5124-3 (5, 6)	Yin Year of Tianqing (1194) 29th Day of 1st Month	2 live, usable, full-teethed, red cattle, 1 full-teethed black cattle	5 *dan* of wheat, 2 *dan* of coarse grains	≈ 8.6 *dan* of coarse grains
Инв. No. 5124-4 (4)	Yin Year of Tianqing (1194) 3rd Day of the 2nd Month	Full-teethed female camel, 1 horse	2 *dan* of wheat, 3 *dan* of coarse grains	≈ 5.7 *dan* of coarse grains
Инв. No. 5124-4 (5)	Yin Year of Tianqing (1194) 3rd Day of the 2nd Month	1 two-teethed male camel	2 *dan* of wheat, 1 *dan* of millet	3 *dan* of coarse grains
Инв. No. 2546-2, 3	Hai Year of Tianqing (1203) 25th Day of the 2nd Month	1 three-teethed red, short horse	1 *dan*? *dou* of coarse grains	1 *dan* ? *dou* of coarse grains

191 *Russian Collection of Khara-Khoto Manuscripts*, vol. 12, p. 141.
192 Shi Jinbo, 2008.

CHART 15 Data in Khara-Khoto livestock sale contracts (*cont.*)

Register	Date	Livestock	Price	Price in coarse grains
Инв. No. 2546-1	Hai Year of Tianqing (1203) 30th Day of the 2nd Month	1 full-teethed female camel	6 *dan* of coarse grains	6 *dan* of coarse grains
Инв. No. 5404-8, 9	Jiazi Year of Tianqing (1204) 15th Day of the 11th Month	A mare with bridle	5 *dan* of coarse grains	5 *dan* of coarse grains
Инв. No. 5404-10	Zi Year of Tianqing (1204) 16th Day of the 11th Month	1 five-teethed usable maroon horse	4 *dan* of coarse grains	4 *dan* of coarse grains
Инв. No. 2858-1	Chou Year of Tianqing (1206) 30th Day of the 12th Month	Four-teethed, usable, red mare	7 *dan* of coarse grains	7 *dan* of coarse grains
Инв. No. 7630-2	You Year of Guangding (1213) 30th Day of the 5th Month	1 four-teethed live cattle	4 *dan* of coarse grains	4 *dan* of coarse grains
Инв. No. 7994-14	Hai Year of Guangding (1215) 27th Day of the 3rd Month	1 six-teethed cattle	10 *dan* (1 *dan* paid, 8 *dan* due by the 6th month)	10 *dan*
Инв. No. 6377-15	Zi Year of Guangding (1216) 16th Day of the 5th Month	1 two-vertical (teethed) female camel, 6 female camels, 1 vertical (cattle?), 1 maroon horse	90 *liang* of silver	10 *guan* of cash

In both livestock sale contracts found in Wuwei, the livestocks are paid for in cash.

CHART 16 A list of livestock sale contracts unearthed in Wuwei

Register	Date	Livestock	Price
G31·003[6727]1–2	?th day of 9th month in the You Year of Qianding (1225)	1 full-teethed black cattle	65 *guan* in cash
G31·002[6726]	8th day in the 4th month, Xu Year of Qianding (1226)	1 yellow donkey	50 *guan* in cash

Livestock sale contracts are the most direct access to the actual market prices of livestocks. There is price variation not only between different commodities, but also based on the age, gender, strength, and other qualities of the livestocks in question. Therefore, pricing is much more complex in the case of livestocks than in grains. Besides, different timing and location also affect the transaction prices. At times, the livestocks are sold in bundles and packages. Therefore, the contracts only record the total price, rather than the unit price. These scenarios further add to the difficulty of recovering market prices. As always, it is easier to at least convert all grains into coarse grains, to make it easier to calculate and analyse pricing where livestocks are exchanged for grains.

Livestock sale contracts that deal with only one kind of animal are the easiest to analyse. Manuscript Инв. No. 5124-4(5), for example, gives the price of a two-teethed male camel as 3 *dan* of coarse grains; Инв. No. 2546-1 reveals the price of a full-teethed female camel as 6 *dan*; in Инв. No. 5404-8, 9, a mare is sold for 5 *dan*; from Инв. No. 5404-10, we know that the unit price of a five-teethed, usable, maroon horse is 4 *dan*; Инв. No. 2858-1 tells us that a four-teethed, usable, red mare is worth 7 *dan*; Инв. No. 7630-2 indicates the price of a four-teethed cattle as 4 *dan*; whereas in Инв. No. 7994-14, a six-teethed cattle is sold for 10 *dan*. A preliminary analysis of the data gives us the basic price ranges: the price of a camel is between 3 and 6 *dan* of coarse grains, with a female often slightly more expensive than a male. A horse is worth 4–7 *dan*, and the mare also costs more than a stallion. Cattle price is trickier. A cattle sale contract shows that a cattle costs 4 *dan* of coarse grains, whereas in Инв. No. 7994-14, where the buyer, rather than the seller is the main contracting party, the six-teethed cattle is transacted for 10 *dan* in installment. At the signing of the contract, the seller receives a down payment of 1 *dan*, and expects another 8 *dan* by the sixth month. It is also strange that the sum of the two payments is 9, rather than 10 *dan* in total. It looks like the contract misses content near the end. Nor does it feature the signatures and stamps of the main parties to contract. Therefore, it could be seen as an incomplete and invalid contract.

The price it lists, therefore, is less than reliable. The typical unit price of cattle is slightly less than that of camels and horses, around 3–5 *dan*.

With the unit prices at hand, it is now possible to study the wholesale prices of livestocks sold in a bundle or package. In the Инв. No. 5124-3(5, 6) manuscripts, 2 full-teethed cattles, and one that is full-teethed and black, are sold altogether for 5 *dan* of wheat and 2 *dan* of coarse grains = 8.6 *dan* of coarse grains. Holding traits such as colours constant, each cattle is worth 3 *dan* of coarse grains, on average. In the Инв. No. 5124-4(4) contract, a full-teethed female camel and a horse are sold for 2 *dan* of wheat and 3 *dan* of coarse grains = 5.7 *dan* of coarse grains, where the average price of each livestock is within 3 *dan*. We see that the average wholesale prices here are lower than the unit prices of the animals. In fact, these two wholesale contracts are not market transactions but the acquisitions of livestocks by the Pudu Temple. The temple's agents bargained for a discount, taking advantage over livestock-owners desperate to sell livestocks for grains.

Livestocks are also paid for in cash. In contract No. 6377-15, for instance, a total of 9 livestocks: a 2-vertical(-teethed) female camel, 6 female camels, 1 vertical(-teethed ?), a maroon horse, are sold for 90 *liang* in silver. The average price of each animals is 10 *liang*. If we allow that the average price of any large livestock is around 5 *dan* of coarse grains, then 1 *dan* of coarse grains ≈ 2 liang of silver.

Payments are in cash in both Wuwei livestock contracts. In G31·003[6727]1–2, an ox/cow is sold for 65 *guan*; in G31·002[6726], a donkey is sold for 50 *guan*. Transactions in Khara-Khoto contracts, however, are generally done in grains—that is, in kinds rather than in cash. There, we see a difference in the economic lives of Wuwei and Khara-Khoto. Wuwei counts as the 'second best city' after the imperial capital Zhongxing. Wuwei boasts a commerce-based cash economy that is more advanced than Khara-Khoto. Statements in IOU debt bills found in Xiaoxigouxian, Wuwei: "Li Banchu owes 3 strings and 500 *wen*"; "Liu Dede owes 2 strings and 250 *wen*" show that "cash was in circulation."[193] It should not be assumed, however, that there was no cash flow in Khara-Khoto. Three contracts of human sales in Khara-Khoto, Инв. No. 5949-29, 4597 and 7903, are all transacted in cash.

Another way to make sense of livestocks sale is to compare prices in cash and in kinds. We have established, in the chapters on grain prices, that each

193 Museum of Gansu. "Gansu Wuwei Faxian Yipi Xixia Yiwu" [甘肅武威發現一批西夏遺物]: "A Batch of Tangut Materials has been Discovered in Wuwei, Gansu" in Kaogu [考古]: *Archaeology*, issue 3, 1974.

dou of coarse grains costs 150–200 mace, or 1.5–2 *guan*.[194] In the first contract, an ox/cow costs 65 guan in cash, that is an unreasonably high 32–43 *dan* in coarse grains. It could only be explained in contexts of high inflation caused by socioeconomic instabilities. In the third year of Daqing (1142), in the ninth month, "there is a famine in Western Xia, where the grain price rose to a hundred mace per *sheng*."[195] The price of grain is 1 *guan*/*dou*, or 10 *guan*/*dan*, soaring past 4–5 times the normal price. Grain price during the reign of Renzong Emperor of Northern Song is 600–700 mace per *dan*. Later, it rose to the level of 1 *guan* and 250 *wen*. In Southern Song, it increased to around 2 *guan*, and at times, even 10 *guan* per *dan*.

The Wuwei contracts are dated to the You (1225) and Xu (1226) Years of Qianding, both in the late Tangut period, only a year or two before the empire fell to the Mongols (1227). By this time, the Hexi Corridor was under constant threat from the Mongol army. The twilight of Tangut power witnessed incessant wars with the Mongols and the Jurchens. In 1225, the year G31·003[6727]1–2 contract was signed, the Mongol army once again invaded Western Xia. In the second month of the following year, Genghis Khan led an army 100,000 strong into Tangut territories, taking Khara-Khoto, Wulahai (Uraqai), and then Shazhou.[196] The Mongols breached the walls of Suzhou in the fifth month, and entered Ganzhou in the following month. In the seventh month, they stormed Xiliang (present-day city of Wuwei, Gansu). Terrorised by the unstoppable force of Genghis Khan, Xianzong Emperor of Western Xia passed away in fright. The Wuwei contract G31·002[6726] is dated to that year, when Khara-Khoto and Dunhuang were under siege, a mere 3 months before Wuwei would fall. It was, in short, a time of turmoil along the Hexi Corridor, and of the utmost insecurity in the Tangut society. Inflation of commodity prices and devaluation of currency value are the natural consequence of these historical episodes. Whether it is the grains or the livestocks, all prices soared. Under such circumstances, it was much easier to maintain the price ratio by trading in kinds rather than in cash. So, one would understand why the cattle is sold for 65 *guan* in cash. If it were priced 3–5 *dan*, then at the rate of 13–20 *guan* per *dan*, the cost would have exceeded the grain prices during the Lin'an famine.

194 Shi Jinbo, 2008.

195 *Xixia Shushi*, Ch. 35.

196 TN: See Dunnell, Ruth. "Locating the Tangut Military Establishment: Uraqai (Wulahai) and the Heishui Zhenyan Army" *Monumenta Serica*, 1992, pp. 219–234.

3.2.3 Guarantee of the Contract

3.2.3.1 *Penalty for Breach of Contract*

Most livestock sale contracts specify the procedures and penalties in case any financial dispute should arise. Since large livestocks are key assets in the Tangut economy, there may be legal challenges to their ownership from family relatives, or members in the same military *chao* as the legal or putative owner. To preempt the chaos and complexities of legal disputes, the contracts stipulate where liability falls: it is always the seller, rather than the buyer, who bears the responsibility. In addition, some contracts require that the seller pay a penalty fee in either grains or cash. The sum usually falls below the sale price. Another arrangement is to double the sum of the sell & purchase price. Some contracts include both kinds of penalties, while others adopt only one of the two stipulations. Besides, if a party regrets over the transaction and reneges on its promises, there would also be a penalty. It seems as if this last requirement is the result of bipartisan negotiations and mutual consensus. However, it often turns out to be a way for the buyer to restrain the seller. Below is a chart that compiles all data on penalties from the 13 Khara-Khoto livestock sale contracts. Given the connection between sale price and penalty fee, it also lists the prices as a point of comparison.

CHART 17 Penalty fees in contracts of livestock sale

Register	Livestock price	Price in coarse grains	Penalty for seller in case of dispute	Penalty for the reneging party
Инв. No. 5124-3 (5, 6)	5 *dan* of wheat & 2 *dan* of coarse grains	≈ 8.6 *dan* of coarse grains	Penalty Fee: 5 *dan* of wheat	
Инв. No. 5124-4 (4)	2 *dan* of wheat, 3 *dan* of coarse grains	≈ 5.7 *dan* of coarse grains	Criminal Liability in accordance with the *Laws and Orders*, plus penalty fee of 3 *dan* of wheat	
Инв. No. 5124-4 (5)	2 *dan* of barley, 1 *dan* of millet	3 *dan* of coarse grains	Criminal Liability in accordance with the *Laws and Orders*, plus penalty fee of 2 *dan* of coarse grains	

CHART 17 Penalty fees in contracts of livestock sale (*cont.*)

Register	**Livestock price**	**Price in coarse grains**	**Penalty for seller in case of dispute**	**Penalty for the reneging party**
Инв. No. 2546-2, 3	1 *dan*? of coarse grains	1 *dan* ? *dou* of coarse grains	Seller liable	Penalty Fee: 5 *dan* of coarse grains
Инв. No. 2546-1	6 *dan* of coarse grains	6 *dan* of coarse grains	Seller liable	Penalty Fee: 1 *dan* 5 *dou* of coarse grains
Инв. No. 5404-8, 9	5 *dan* of coarse grains	5 *dan* of coarse grains	(Missing?)	Penalty Fee: 5 *dan* of coarse grains
Инв. No. 5404-10	4 *dan* of coarse grains	4 *dan* of coarse grains	(Missing)	Missing
Инв. No. 2858-1	7 *dan* of coarse grains	7 *dan* of coarse grains	Seller liable	Missing
Инв. No. 7630-2	4 *dan* of coarse grains	4 *dan* of coarse grains	Seller liable, penalty fee: 8 *dan* of coarse grains	
Инв. No. 7994-14	10 *dan* (1 *dan* paid, 8 *dan* to be paid in the 6th month)	10 *dan*	Seller liable, penalty fee: 2 *dan* per 1 *dan* of sale price	3 *dan* of coarse grains
Инв. No. 6377-15	90 *liang* of silver		Seller liable	Penalty Fee: 10 *guan* of cash
Wuwei G31·003[6727]1–2	65 *guan* of cash		Penalty Fee: 1 *guan* per 2 *guan* of sale price	Penalty Fee: 30 *guan* of cash
Wuwei G31·002[6726]	50 *guan* of cash		Seller liable	n/a

Most contracts are unequivocal on the point of seller liability. Others, which do not state in explicit terms that the seller is the sole liable party, nonetheless stipulate that the seller pay penalty fees under certain circumstances. The implication is the same, that the seller is responsible should any dispute arise. Some penalty fees are set below the sale price. In the long scroll Инв. No. 5124, penalty fees are lower than the sale prices. In manuscripts Инв. No. 7630-2, 7994-14, and G31·003[6727]1–2, however, the penalty is twice as much as the sale price. Whilst some contracts such as No. 5124 do not specify any penalty against reneging on the terms of the contract, other contracts indicate the penalty fee in precise numbers, which are typically less or equal to the sale price. In Инв. No. 2546-2, 3, where the sale price is very low, the penalty fee is much higher.

As always, the expression "willing" or "own heart willing" refers to the seller's acknowledgement of the terms set in the contract, especially the terms of penalties.

Terms of penalties in livestock sale contracts are more complex than in grain loan accounts, and less so than in land sale contracts. The force and amount of penalty is greater than in grain loans and less than in land sales. Of course, these patterns of difference have everything to do with the nature of the contract, the value of the commodity, and the volume of transaction in question. Grain loan documents are records of borrowing and lending, whereas land and livestock transactions are 'absolute sales'—the transfer of titles from one property-owner to another. Within the scope of absolute sales, land is worth more than livestocks. Therefore, the penalties in one are more severe than in the other. Penalty fees in gold are found only in land sale contracts, and nowhere else.

3.2.3.2 *Signature, Stamp, and Seal*

Tangut livestock sale contracts are unilateral legal documents. In other words, they are kept in the possession of one party—usually the buyer—rather than by both parties. To signal the seller's approval and acknowledgement, the name of the main contracting party has to appear at the end of the contract. The seller also has to produce a stamp, either an icon or the shape of his finger segments, along with the co-contractors and the witnesses. As in land sale and lease contracts, each signature or stamp takes up a separate line near the end of the contract. The order is also the same: firs the main contracting party, then the co-liable associates, followed by the witnesses. Stamping conveys the solemn pledge of faith and knowledge to the agreement. Since the signatures are often written by a professional transcriber, the stamps are the only way to authenticate a contract.

The Инв. No. 7630-2 contract of cattle sale dated to the You Year of Guangding (1213) features the red seal of the Department of Transaction Taxes. "Red contracts" are rare amongst Tangut contracts. Of all 12 land sale contracts, only Инв. No. 5010 dated to the 22nd year of Heavenly Prosperity is a "red seal." The seal of the Department of Transaction Taxes produces a 23.2 × 7.3 cm rectangular stamp with images of lotus leaves and flowers. The stamp reads [illegible] (lit. Department of Sell and Purchase Taxes). The stamp shows that this one-time transaction is approved and taxed by the government.

3.2.4 Features of Livestock Sale Contracts

The impressive corpus of Khara-Khoto livestock contracts reveals a wealth of details on how livestocks are exchanged in Western Xia. First, these contracts give us the market prices of large livestocks such as horses, camels, and cattles. They shed some light on the causes of price variations. A comparison of the Khara-Khoto and Wuwei contracts, where animals are paid for in grains and in cash, respectively, also confirms our prior understanding of the differences between the Khara-Khoto and the Wuwei economies. Secondly, the livestock sale contracts provide a perspective on the soaring commodity prices and hyper inflation in the late Tangut period, as the Mongol army invaded and the Tangut imperium crumbled. Thirdly, whereas some transactions are normal exchanges at market prices, others are acquisitions by large property-owners at the expense of peasant farmers who have to sell their livestocks for foodstuff. Finally, a comparison between livestock loan and livestock sale contracts shows that the Pudu Temple not only amassed assets, but also issued lucrative loans to impoverished peasants in hardship. In a year or two, the temple could have acquired the livestocks for free. The monastery's acquisitive and exploitative ventures further exacerbated wealth inequality, driving propertyless peasants to the path of deprivation and desperation.

3.3 *Transaction of Humans*

Three rare Khara-Khoto contracts of human sales reveal the peculiar phenomenon of human transactions in Western Xia, an important primary source on the nature and the lived experiences of the Tangut society.

3.3.1 Translation and Interpretation of the Human Sale Contracts

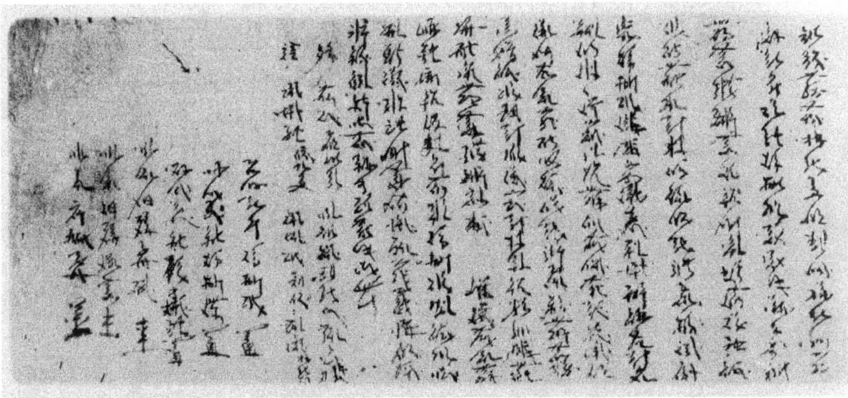

FIGURE 176 Инв. No. 5949-29: Jiachen 27th year of Qianyou. Contract of Shijun/Nupu sale
Note: TN: There are only 24 years in the Qianyou Reign.

1. Инв. No. 5949-29: Contract of Shijun/Nupu Sale in the Jiachen, 27th year of Qianyou is an individual contract of 20 lines in cursive Tangut written on a 20.3 × 55.2 cm hemp paper. It is a fragment with some parts missing. The text begins with the date, 20th day of the 3rd month, and ends with signatures and stamps.[197]

Translation:

> On the 24th day of the 3rd month in the Jiachen, 27th year of Qianyou,
> Contract party [illegible] [·o da][198] [illegible] [gju_ rjur lji-.] now volutnarily sells his own
> six persons, *shijun*, *nupu*, and *jun'e*,[199] to [illegible] [·o zji tsji_r]
> [illegible] [lji-.][200] at the price of 450 *guan* of iron coins,[201] hereby agreed upon.

197 *Russian Collection of Khara-Khoto Manuscripts*, vol. 14, p. 91.

198 [illegible] [·o da], a Dangxiang Tangut surname. There is a series of Tangut surnames formed by adding numbers, from one to eight, onto the character [illegible]. See Shi, Jinbo. *Xixia Wenhua* [西夏文化]. Changchun: Jilin Education Press, 1986, p. 185.

199 [illegible] [phji_ gia] (shijun) [illegible] [njijr njij] (nupu) [illegible] [gia wa]. The precise meaning of the third and last category remains unclear, but it is a social class, status, and identity parallel to the semi-slaves and servants.

200 [illegible] is a Dangxiang Tangut surname, and [illegible] [·o zji tsji_r lji-.] sounds like the Dharma name of a monk.

201 [illegible] [śjow dzji-j] iron coins. Both copper and iron coins were circulated in Western Xia. Copper coins were worth more than iron coins.

[illegible] originally from lord? [illegible] [mja dow dźjij ·jiw][202]
not? clothes, hands ?? only? in?[203]
? ? holds 450 *guan* iron coins, ??
Inspected by ?? Both the payment and the persons have by this day
been transferred. In case a dispute erupts over these shijun and nupu, either by the government or by private individuals, such as members of the same *chao*
Let [illegible], not [illegible], be responsible.
Let any party that breaches the contract be judged by the Bureau of Military Supervision to which he belongs; let him not only be fined
500 *guan* in cash, but also tried in accordance with the *Laws and Orders*. Hearts willing.

Male: [illegible] [śji-j wa], age 60; [illegible]? [ŋwe ? khjwi-], 39; ??, 28.

Female: [illegible] [khjwi- mja wejr], 57; [illegible] [khjwi- mja lji-.], 35; ? [illegible] [khjwi-], 23.

Contract Party: [illegible] [gju_ rjur lji-.] (stamp)
Co-contractor: son, [illegible] [gju_ rjur khwej] (stamp)
Co-contractor: son, ??[illegible] [wejr] (stamp)
Witness: [illegible] [me dji. źji-r bju] (stamp)
Witness: [illegible]? [me dji. bie_j ?] (stamp)
Witness: [illegible] [ljow wjo. źji-r] (stamp)

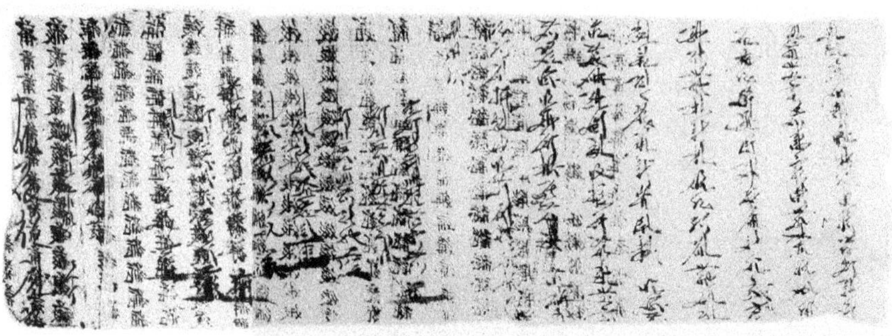

FIGURE 177 Инв. No. 4597: Wei year of Tianqing (1199) contract of Shijun sale

2. Инв. No. 4597: Contract of Shijun Sale in the Wei Year of Tianqing (1199) is an individual contract with 19 lines of cursive Tangut written on a 20.4 × 57.8 cm hemp paper. The ink is light and blurry, further muddled and riddled by the

202 [illegible] [mja le] is likely to have been the family name here.
203 TN: most of this line is illegible.

sutra text written on the back of the paper. The contract begins with the date, 29th day of the 3rd month in the Wei Year of Tianqing, and ends with signatures and stamps.[204]

Translation:

> On the 24th day of the 3rd month in the Wei Year of Tianqing, the Contract Party
> 𗌗𗖋𗏁𗟲𗌬 [ŋwe ze lhji_ śji-j dju] now sells his own *shijun* 𘂤𗗙𗤋 [ŋwə lhji. khjwi-]
> et al., two persons young and old, volutnarily sold to ?? 𗓁𗟻𗶷 [?? ɣji-. njij wejr] according to the terms of this contract,
> At the price of 50 *dan* of coarse grains, already paid. Neither the persons
> Nor the grains are amiss. If external parties initiate public or private disputes,
> Such as members of the same *chao*, let ?𗟲𗌬
> Be responsible. Let any party that reneges on its promises pay a penalty, according to the laws of the government,
> In the amount of 30 *dan* of coarse grains. Heart willing.[205] Let the terms be enforced according to the contract and the circumstances.
> Contract Party: 𗌗𗖋𗏁𗟲𗌬 [ŋwe ze lhji_ śji-j dju] (stamp)
> Co-contractor: 𗌗 ?? [ŋwe ze lhji_ ??]
> Co-contractor: 𗌗𗖋𗌬𗗚? [ŋwe ze dju zji wejr] (stamp)
> Witness: 𗂸𗋃??𗏵 [·jiw dji.j ?? bie_j] (stamp)
> Witness: ???? (stamp)
> Contract written by 𗢯𗍫𗶷 [tśhiə lji-. wejr] (stamp)
> Co-contractor: 𗌗𗖋𗃮𗴮 [ŋwe ze sji lu.] (stamp)
> Witness: ???? (stamp)

204 *Russian Collection of Khara-Khoto Manuscripts*, vol. 13, p. 223.

205 𗼃𗣼𗓦 [nji_j lja_ wə_], lit. "heart, mouth, submit" i.e. the party is willing, at heart or in his mind.

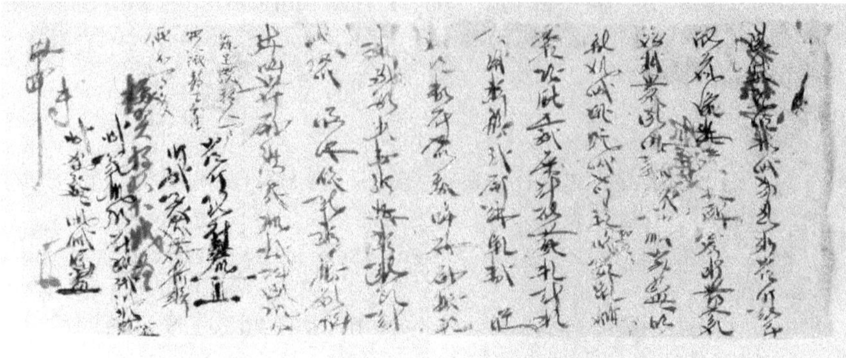

FIGURE 178 Инв. No. 7903: Wu year of Huangjian (1210) Su [??] contract of Shijun sale

3. Инв. No. 7903: Contract of Shijun Sale in the Wu Year of Huangjian (1210). The manuscript fragment features of 16 lines of cursive Tangut handwritten on a 18 × 44.8 cm hemp paper. The ink on the page are soaked from the other side of paper. The contract begins with the date, 3rd day of the 2nd month in the Wu Year of Huangjian (1210), and ends with signatures and stamps. There are traces of erasures, as well as three lines of Chinese characters in a smaller font.[206]

Translation:

> On the 3rd day of the 2nd month in the Wu Year of Huangjian, Contract Party
> Su ??? presently sells his own *shijun*
> [illegible] [kjij kia dźjo. phəj ·wio.] ???? [illegible] [thji]
> sons [illegible] [gji-_ lhji. bie_j], [tśjow lhji. śji-j] et al., four persons in total, sold
> to ?[illegible] [? ɣji-. njij ·jiw] of the same *chao*, at the price of
> the agreed price of 100 *guan*. If either party initiates a public
> or private dispute, or reneges on the agreement,
> let not only the penalty be double the sale price,
> but let the relevant party pay 50 *guan* according ot the laws.
> Own hearts willing. Terms to be enforced according to the contract and the circumstances.
> (*3 lines of Chinese characters in a small font above, 1 line in a larger font*)[207]
> (*Signatures in Tangut, stamps*)

206 See *Russian Collection of Khara-Khoto Manuscripts*, vol. 14, pp. 221–222.

207 TN: The Chinese text is as follows: 蘇足說?私人一戶/四人?轉王?和由/價錢一百貫/楊賀好????

Contract Party: 𘄀 [su] (Su) ?? (stamp)
Co-contractor: wife, 𘂤𘊐 [kow wju_]
Witness, transcriber of the contract, ???? (𘃡?) (stamp)
Witness: ?? 𘄐𘃞 [ŋwe mji]? (stamp)

3.3.2 Format and Content of Human Transaction Contracts

Contracts of human transactions follow the same general format of Tangut contracts. Each line begins without indentation, first with the date, month, and year, then the names of the main contract party, followed by the names, number, and prices of the human beings being sold. The contract lays out the terms on which to transfer the persons from one owner to another, to address the rights of families and neighbours, and to allocate liability. The contract ends with the signatures and stamps of the principle parties and the guarantors.

3.3.2.1 *Time*

The date recorded in the Инв. No. 5949-29 manuscript, "24th day of the 3rd month in Jiachen, the 27th year of Qianyou" is erroneous, for there are only 24 years in the Qianyou era of Western Xia. The Jiachen year of Qianyou is, in fact, the 15th year of Qianyou (1184). But if we were to extend the years from the 24th year of Qianyou onward, for three additional years, we arrive at a fictional '27th year of Qianyou,' which is in fact the Bingchen, 3rd year of Tianqing (1196). The second contract in the Инв. No. 4597 manuscript is dated to the 24th day of the 3rd month in the Wei Year of Tianqing, or Jiwei, the 6th year of Tianqing (1199). The contract in manuscript Инв. No. 7903 is signed on the 3rd day of the 2nd month, in the Wu Year of Huangjian, or Gengwu, the first year of Huangjian (1210). All three contracts are dated to the late Tangut period, only 17 years before the dynasty came to its end. And all three contracts are signed in the second and third months, which is also the inter-harvest period when the Tanguts tend to take out grain loans, and to sell their land, livestocks, as well as other properties.

3.3.2.2 *Sellers and Buyers of Human Beings*

By the *Laws of Heavenly Prosperity*, it is necessary to make contracts in order to transact human beings such as *shijun* and *nupu*:

> Let the many who loan or sell their own *shijun*, *nupu*, farmland, and houses to other parties make contracts.[208]

208 *Revised Laws of Heavenly Prosperity* 11, "On Hired Labour," no. 390.

The *Laws of Heavenly Prosperity* categorises the serfs, servants, and semi-slaves such as *shijun* and *nupu* into the same class of private property as farmland and houses. As usual, the contracting parties named and signed in the contracts are the sellers, or the previous owner of the persons to be sold. Of the three sellers in the contracts above, [illegible] and [illegible] are Dangxiang Tanguts. The third has a Chinese name, Su ([illegible] = 蘇).

All three buyers seem to be ethnic Dangxiang Tanguts. [illegible] is a classic Dangxiang surname. [illegible] (Vajra) which appears in the two other names ("the prosperous Vajra" and "the Vajra of the You Year"), along with [illegible], (Dharma-ratna) invokes Buddhist ideas and imageries.

3.3.2.3 *Identities, Quantities, and Prices of the Humans Sold*

The commodities transacted in these contracts are humans, rather than inanimate properties. The Khara-Khoto contracts of human transactions records the numbers and conditions of the persons being traded, but not the reasons for them to be bought and sold. Some, though not all of the Dunhuang contracts of human transactions, however, do state the reasons. For example, in the Bingzi year (916), Awu sells her son, "because the husband dies early, all the males, females, and children, are deep in debt, unprovided for food and clothing."[209]

The Khara-Khoto contracts of human transaction are written in cursive and damaged writings that are by no means easy to identify. As a result, many names remain illegible. A total of 6 persons, 3 men and 3 women, are sold by the Инв. No. 5949-29 document. They seem to be either one and the same family, three separate couples, or six unrelated individuals. In Инв. No. 4597, there could be 2 *shijun* being sold. One of the two names is unidentifiable. Nor do we know their gender as a matter of fact. In Инв. No. 7903, there seems to be a couple with their two sons. We know they belong to the same family from the Chinese characters near the end of the contract. Due to his low social status, the *shijun* is registered in files and documents with his first name only, without a last name.

In the first contract, the 6 persons are sold for 450 *guan* in iron coins; in the second, the two persons are sold for 50 *dan* of coarse grains; in the third, the four persons are sold for 100 *guan* in cash.

---

209 Tang and Lu (eds.). *Dunhuang Economic Documents* II, pp. 47–49.

3.3.3 The Guarantee of Contracts

3.3.3.1 *Penalty Fee*

The *Laws of Heavenly Prosperity* issue penalties against the renegation of contract at different levels, in various stages of the process:

> If the seller or lender changes his words at a time when the loan is not taken or the payment not yet made, let an office-holder be fined a horse, and let a commoner suffer 13 strokes; if the loan is taken or the payment made, and yet a party claims the contrary, and whereby reneges on its promise, let the case by tried in accordance with the laws on renegation in the case of debt payment; if the transaction is not completed, but a party claims that the loan or good has been purchased, and in this way seeks to acquire it, or if the loan or good is purchased, but a party claims that it has not, let the case be tried in accordance with the laws on renegations in debt payment, as well.[210]

All the three contracts of human transaction make clear that in cases of any dispute, the seller bears full liability. If a party reneges on the agreement, the penalty fee is 500 *guan* in the first contract (and a trial in accordance with the *Laws and Orders*), 30 *dan* of coarse grains (and criminal liability according to the circumstances) in the second contract, and double the sell & purchase price, plus 50 *guan* of penalty fee, in the third contract.

3.3.3.2 *Signatures and Stamps*

Contracts of human transactions are important legal records of absolute sales. Therefore, there tend to be more co-contractors and witnesses. There are 2 co-sellers and 3 witnesses in the first contract; 3 co-sellers and 3 witnesses in the second contract; 1 co-seller and 2 witnesses in the third contract. As usual, the signatures are written by a professional, rather than by the signatories themselves. So, the stamps are the only source of identification, legitimation, and authentification. In all three contracts, the signatories produced their icons. Only the main contracting party's wife does not produce any stamp in the third contract. The use of icons, instead of finger segments, shows the formality of these contracts.

3.3.4 Human Transactions in Western Xia

In general, the historical practice of trading and transacting persons takes place in slave societies where human beings are owned by slave-owners. The

210 *Revised Laws of Heavenly Prosperity* 11, p. 390.

slave-owner exercises property rights and imposes supra-economic power over the enslaved. Therefore, the slaves are private properties without persona liberty. In feudal societies of China, the personal attachment of the yeomen, tenant farmers, and semi-independent peasants to the landlord is rather weak. Therefore, for long periods of time, the laws forbid the transaction of human beings. However, this type of feudal society remains a society of caste. Human transaction persists as a marginal phenomenon under the regime of class and status.

The premise of human transaction is full ownership and property right over human beings. There have always existed small groups of human beings who do not entirely own their own legal persons. The unfree, such as the *buqu* (部曲) and *nubi* (奴婢) have always been exchanged as commodities. Moreover, in times of chaos and poverty, the struggling poor often sold their wives, children, and even themselves for survival. Both the *Tang Laws* and the *Song Compendium* forbid the sale of human beings by deceitful or violent means.[211] But neither prohibits human transaction, per se. And even with the laws in place, violations occurred on a regular basis.[212]

3.3.4.1 *Tangut Laws on Human Transactions*

The *Laws of Heavenly Prosperity* prohibits any transaction of one's own kins, for families are the likeliest to exercise dominations over their relatives.

> Junior members of the family who sell their senior kins, such as grandfather, grandmother, father, mother, etc., are to be executed by sword if intention is established; accomplices are to be sentenced to imprisonment for life.[213]

211 Zhangsun Wuji [Tang Dynasty] et al.; Liu Junwen (ed.). *Tanglü Shuyi* [唐律疏議]: *Commentary on the Tang Code*. Beijing: Law Press, China, 1999, pp. 399–406; Dou, Yi [Song Dynasty] et al.; Xue, Meiqing (ed.). *Song Xingtong* [宋刑統]: *Compendium of Song Laws*. Beijing: Law Press of China, 1998, pp. 356–362.

212 Yu, Guilin. "Songdai Maimai Funü Xianxiang Chutan" [宋代買賣婦女現象初探]: "A Preliminary Study of the Phenomenon of Selling and Purchasing Women in the Song Dynasty" *Zhongguoshi Yanjiu* [中國史研究]: *Journal of Chinese Historical Studies*, issue 3, 2000, pp. 102–112.

213 *Revised Laws of Heavenly Prosperity* 1, "On Disharmony," p. 128. The 'segment' is a Tangut term for "generation"; so 'higher segment above' refers to senior members of the older generation, and 'lower segment below' are the younger generations, or junior members of the family.

The *Laws* also penalise the sale of other kins,

> Junior members of the family who sell their senior kins, such as their own grandparents and parents, in addition to judging their crimes, let anyone who attempts to sell kins who fall within the mourning period be hanged; let any accomplice be sentenced to 12 years in jail.
>
> For senior members of the family accused of selling their younger kins,
> who ought to perform mourning for 3 months, let him be sentenced to 12 years of imprisonment if there is intention; let the accomplice be sentenced to ten years;
> who ought to perform mourning for 5 months, let him be sentenced to 10 years of imprisonment if there is intention; let the accomplice be sentenced to eight years;
> who ought to perform mourning for 9 months, let him be sentenced to 8 years of imprisonment if there is intention; let the accomplice be sentenced to 6 years;
> who ought to perform mourning for 1 year, let him be sentenced to 6 years if there is intention; let the accomplice be sentenced to 5 years;
> who ought to perform mourning for 3 years, let him be sentenced to 5 years of imprisonment if there is intention; let the accomplice be sentenced to 4 years.[214]
>
> In all the aforementioned cases of a senior member of the family selling his junior kins, if the sold person is willing to oblige, let the seller's sentence be commuted to one level below.
>
> If a man attempts to sell his own wife, and the wife is unwilling to be sold, let the man be sentenced to six years of imprisonment. If the wife is willing, let the man be sentenced to five years, instead. If the wife, or the father, brother, and other third parties report the sale, first let the woman go whither she wishes. Then, let the one who reported be rewarded in accordance with the laws on rewarding reports on miscellaneous crimes. If the husband regrets and reports himself, let him be acquitted, and let the wife and the payment be returned.[215]

---

214 TN: The point is that, the longer the mourning period is required of the junior kin, the lower his or her status must be within the family; the lower his or her status is, the lighter the crime it is to sell him or her, hence the shorter the sentence.

215 *Revised Laws of Heavenly Prosperity* 6, pp. 258–259.

However, Tangut laws do not prohibit the sale of *shijun* and *nupu*, who are treated as tradable commodities, along with farmland and houses. These semi-slaves constituted a special class within the Tangut society. The *shijun* is the equivalent to the *buqu* in the Tang Dynasty. They could have been criminals exiled to the frontiers, or captured in the wars, spared their lives, and turned into serfs and servants by their conquerors.[216] The *Laws of Heavenly Prosperity* state that,

> If our party has captured çertain individuals by force, and enslaved them as shijun and nupu; whereas their family kins and relatives cross over and surrender to the Fan state; thereupon, if it is determined that they are indeed the kinsmen of the ones captured by force, let them be voluntarily reunited ...[217]

Some *shijun* might also have been bankrupt peasants and serfs.

Owners of *shijun* and *nupu* are referred to in the *Laws of Heavenly Prosperity* as 𘘄𘛼 [ɣu dzju], which literally translate to "head supervisers," or simply owners. It is an extraordinarily capacious term in the *Laws of Heavenly Prosperity*. In Western Xia, there are 'head supervisers' in almost every aspect of society, let alone branch of government: in the offices, the military, and even in hierarchical monastic establishments. A large number of references to the 'head supervisers' in the *Laws of Heavenly Prosperity* are, in fact, those who supervise their own servants, serfs, and semi-slaves. In other words, these 'head supervisers' are, simply put, de facto slave owners who exercise special power over the individuals in their dominion. The social status of the owned persons is such that they cannot make decisions over their private affairs without the intervention of the masters. The *Laws of Heavenly Prosperity* is clear that,

> If the *shijun* in possession do not consult their head supervisers, and do not obtain the necessary documents, they are not allowed to sell their own children, daughters-in-law, aunts, and sisters to others out of their own will. If they thus violate the laws, let them be indicted of the crime that is one level above theft of cash and property. If the buyers are aware of the illegality of the trade, and yet proceed to the transaction, let them be tried as accomplices; if they are not aware, let them not be indicted. If

216 TN: As in the case of Roman slaves. See Shi, Jinbo and Li, Hansong. *Tangut Language and Manuscripts: An Introduction*. Leiden: Brill, 2020, pp. 445, 472–473.

217 *Revised Laws of Heavenly Prosperity* 7, "To Resettle Those Who Cross over to our Side and Surrender," pp. 273–274.

> the seller does not initiate the discussion on the sale, and yet the buyer is makes explicit his intention to purchase, and raises the price to obtain the purchase, then let the buyer be tried for the same crime as the seller. If the sold women bear children, let all of them be returned to the lawful owner. As for the payment already made, let the seller cover it if he is able to; if he isn't, then let the seller be penalised for the sum. Let the intermediary agents who go between the seller and the buyer be sentenced to 6 months of imprisonment. Let them not be indicted, if they are unaware of the illegal nature of the transaction.
>
> If the shijun in possession do not consult their head supervisers, and do not obtain the necessary documents, they are not permitted to marry their daughters, sisters, aunts, et al. to others. Let those who violate this law be sentenced to four years of imprisonment. The children born out of these wedlocks should be returned to the lawful owners. As for any payment maid for the marriage, let the shijun who arranged for the marriage cover it if he is able; if he is not, let the owner bear the costs.
>
> If the aforementioned shijun have consulted their head supervisers, who are willing to grant the legal papers, then let them be permitted to sell or marry their children, daughters-in-law, aunts, and sisters to others.[218]

In other words, not only could the masters sell their *shijun*, but the *shijun* also have the right to sell the women in his own household, provided that the obtains consent from his master. It is also found in the *Laws of Heavenly Prosperity* that,

> If the daughters, sons, wives, daughters-in-law, *shijun*, and *nupu* enter into a verbal quarrel, and which escalates into a physical altercation with the parents, husband, and supervisers, in the midst of which the former are accidentally wounded in the eyes, ears, and noses, injured in their hands and feet, or have their muscles and bones broken, let the culprit be fined a horse if he has official status, or suffer 13 lashes if he is a commoner. If the person is not wounded but dead, let the individual concerned be sentenced to 6 months of imprisonment. If the injury is afflicted by a sword or knife upon the eyes, ears, noses, feet, hands, and muscles, to the

218 *Revised Laws of Heavenly Prosperity* 12, p. 417.

> point that it causes the death of the person, then let the case be judged in accordance with the laws as follows.[219]

The *Laws of Heavenly Prosperity* enumerates several severe crimes in parallel, "the murder of great (great) grandparents, grandparents, parents, and father's concubines; the murder of parents-in-law by the daughter-in-law; the murder of husband by wife; the murder of the head superviser by the *shijun* …"[220] It suggests that the Tanguts saw the relationship between the master and the *shijun* or *nupu* as equivalent to that between parents and children, husband and wife.

In the three Tangut contracts of human transaction, all the persons to be sold are either *shijun* or *nupu*. Near the end of the third contract, there is an additional line written in Chinese, which makes clear that the "the private persons are a household of four" which "cost 100 *guan*." The "private men" refer to the persons held in private possession. The same expression in found in the *Laws of Heavenly Prosperity*, for instance:

> The higher and lower officials are not permitted to demand government-owned persons to be their privately-owned persons. Nor are they allowed to turn those who are indicted for severe crimes, exempted from capital punishment, and instead commuted into an exile in the frontiers as persons bound to a farmland or a pasture, into their own privately-owned persons.[221]

The so-called government-owned persons are quasi-'palace slaves,' legally owned by the court or by a government office. They are also deprived of personal freedom, but they differ from quasi-'household slaves,' persons owned by private individuals and their families. The laws demand that private ownership not interfere and conflict with government ownership. There are also criminals who end up exiled to the remote areas of the empire, after their death or life sentence is communited, and work as indentured labourers on farms or pastures. These men, too, are not eligible to be turned into 'private men.' Tangut masters also counted on the laws to safeguard their rights, should their 'private men' seek to escape.[222]

Three years after the Renzong Emperor passed away, in the third year of Tianqing (1196), Empress Luo released the 'private men' at large or to the

219 *Revised Laws of Heavenly Prosperity* 8, pp. 296–297.
220 *Revised Laws of Heavenly Prosperity* 13, p. 447.
221 *Revised Laws of Heavenly Prosperity* 6, pp. 254–255.
222 *Revised Laws of Heavenly Prosperity* 7, "On the Defection and Escape of the Fan," pp. 275–281.

government, released prisoners 52 times, assisted the poor 65 times, released 70,790 sheep, and granted a universal amnesty.[223]

3.3.4.2 *Price Analysis*

The primary purpose of human transactions is to optimise labour value. Unsurprisingly, younger and stronger men are worth more than the elderly, and women in their fertile ages are especially valuable, since they are able to give birth to new labour. In the first contract, 6 persons are sold for 450 *guan*, at an average price of 75 *guan* in iron coins. Each of the 4 younger ones may have been worth about 80 *guan*. In the second contract, 2 persons are sold for 50 *dan* of coarse grains. We have inferred from Khara-Khoto grain accounts that the price of coarse grains is at approximately 150–200 mace per *dou*. The cash value of 50 *dan* of coarse grains falls in the 75–100 *guan* range, which gives the average price as 35–50 *guan*. In the third contract, 4 persons are sold for 100 *guan*, at the average of 25 *guan*.

All three contracts are found in Khara-Khoto. They are, above all, representative of human sale and purchase in that area. Nonetheless, we see a considerable discrepancy in the prices across the three contracts. Perhaps the timing of the contract is an important explanatory variable.

There is an error in the dating of the first contract. But whether it is signed in the fifteenth year of Qianyou (1184) or Bingchen, the third year of Tianqing (1196, allegedly, the 27th year of Qianyou), this contract is the earliest of all three documents. The second contract is dated to the Yiwei, Sixth year of Tianqing (1199), 15 years after the Jiachen year of Qianyou. The third contract is written in the Gengwu, First Year of Huangjian (1210) near the very end of the Western Xia Dynasty, and another 11 years apart from the second contract.

CHART 18 Statistics on human sales

Register	**Date**	**Persons sold**	**Total price**	**Average price per person**
Инв. No. 15949-29	Jiachen, 27th year of Qianyou	6	450 *guan* iron coins	75 *guan* +
Инв. No. 4597	Jiwei, 6th year of Tianqing (1199)	2	50 *dan* of coarse grains	35–50 *guan*
Инв. No. 7903	Gengwu, 1st year of Huangjian (1210)	4	100 *guan* coins	25 *guan*

223 *Russian Collection of Khara-Khoto Manuscripts*, vol. 2, TK98, pp. 372–373.

The chart above shows that over the progress of time, the later it is, the lower the price is. Usually, the more stable a society is, the higher the labour cost, and vice versa. Under the reign of Emperor Renzong, Western Xia in the Qianyou era witnessed impressive cultural prosperity, considerable economic development, and relative social stability. After Emperor Renzong passed away, Huanzong succeeded to the throne. Over time, Tangut power went downhill, but managed the decline with some ability and stability. In the final 22 years, however, external threats compounded the anxieties at home. The Tangut society suffered a stream of upheavals, whereby the lived experiences of populations in the empire quickly deteriorated. Under these circumstances, it is no surprise that the market price in human transactions should have fallen. As a result, we see the trend of tumbling prices over time, as reflected in the three contracts.

Another detail of interest and import is the use of iron coins in the first contract: 450 *guan* in iron coins. Whether it is in the Central Plains or in Western Xia, iron coins are worth less than copper coins. Western Xia always suffered a scarcity of copper. Worse still, the Jurchens placed an embargo on copper, forcing the Tanguts to adopt Song coins. In fact, the Song Dynasty began to co-circulate iron and copper coins much earlier. To avoid the flow of copper into Western Xia, the Song Dynasty minted iron coins in its border zones in Shaanxi and Hedong. The Tanguts, on their part, sought to trade their iron coins *en masse* for the Song copper coins, a venture that greatly troubled the Zhezong Emperor of Song,

> The Shaan region is the border zone where copper and iron coins are exchanged. When the westerners visit, they must exchange for copper coins in order to go further east. To the point where today, in the private market, as much as 1700 iron coins are exchanged for 1000 copper coins. As a result, the iron coin devalues, whilst the copper coin appreciates even more. All the commodity prices are inflated. This causes the gravest harm.[224]

The 'westerners' are of course the travellers and merchants from Western Xia. The Tanguts' massive currency exchange devalues the Song iron coins, and thus affects the commodity prices in the Song market. Policy-makers in the Song court enacted counter-measures to solve this problem. They enacted legislations that set a quota on how much a Tangut is allowed to exchange for,

224 *Extended Zizhi Tongjian* [續資治通鑒長編] Book 457, Sixth Year of Yuanyou in Zhezong Emperor's Reign (1091), fourth month, Jiawu.

at the rate of 2/10 of their tax, with a cap of 5000 copper coins, at the maximum. In addition, those who exchange iron for copper coins at relay stations in Shaanzhou and Xiashi, have no choice but to exchange 1000 iron coins for 800 copper coins.

The use of iron versus copper coins within Western Xia varies across its geography. The *Laws of Heavenly Prosperity* state that,

> The many are prohibited from transporting the black iron coins from the domain of the Southern Realm etc. to the Imperial Capital, or the copper coins in the Imperial Capital to the domain of the Southern Realm etc. Any violation of law results in two years of imprisonment, regardless of the amount of cash involved. Anyone who reports such misconduct is rewarded in accordance with the laws on rewarding reporters of miscellaneous crimes.[225]

We know from the inscription of the Liangzhou stele that the administrative region of the "Southern Realm" corresponds to the Chinese geographical term, Youxiang (右厢).[226] The region concerned is the larger area of Liangzhou. In fact, iron coins circulated widely across Western Xia. "Southern Realm, etc." encompasses almost the entire northwestern region of the Tangut Empire, including, of course, Khara-Khoto. But iron coins appear in only one of the three contracts of human transactions. The third contract does not specify what coins are used. But given the context, it is more likely to be iron, rather than copper. But even if it isn't iron, we know for certain that at the conversion rate of 4:5, the average price in the first contract remains the highest.

The transaction of human beings is not rare in history. However, original and authentic contracts of human transactions are as rare and precious as the feather of phoenix and the horns of unicorns. There are three Dunhuang contracts of human transactions, all from the 10th century: in the Bingzi year of 916, Awu sells a 7-year-old son for 30 *dan*; in the 9th year of Zhenming (923), Cao Liuzhu sells a 10-year-old son for ?.5 *pi* of raw silk; in the 2nd year of Chunhua (991), a 28-year-old girl is sold for 3 *pi* of raw silk and 2 *pi* of processed silk.[227] We could peform a simple and quick comparative analysis of the Dunhuang and Khara-Khoto contracts.

---

225 *Revised Laws of Heavenly Prosperity* 7, p. 287.

226 Shi, Jinbo. *Xixia Fojiao Shilüe* [西夏佛教史略]: *A Brief History of Tangut Buddhism*, pp. 249, 253.

227 *Dunhuang Economic Documents* II, pp. 47–49.

In the first Khara-Khoto contract, the average price is 75 *guan*, or 37–50 *dan*, given the price of coarse grains at about 150–200 mace per *dou*; In the second Khara-Khoto contract, the average price is 25 *dan*; in the third contract, the average price ranges between 13 and 17 *dan*. In the first Dunhuang contract, the price is 30 *dan*; the second contract is incomplete and may therefore be set aside for the time being; in the third contract, the girl is sold for 5 *pi* of raw and processed silk. Assuming that silk price in Dunhuang at the time comes close to the standard silk price in Western Xia, that is, 16–21 *guan* per *pi*, or 8–10 *dan* per *pi*, then the girl was sold for about 40–50 *dan* of coarse grains (again, assuming that the price difference between raw and processed silk could be evened out). Despite the lapse of two to three centuries, and the variations of conditions and contexts across different cases, we could see that when it comes to the grain-to-price ratio in human sales, there is a remarkable degree of consistency.

3.3.4.3 *Social Issues in Western Xia, as Reflected in Human Transactions*

The land-owning and pasture-owning Tangut aristocracy, with the royal house at its core, is the cetnre of power in the feudal society of Western Xia. The vast majority of the Xixia population consisted of ordinary peasants, herdsmen, and craftsmen. However, there are still classes of slave-like men and women, such as the *shijun* and *nupu*, at the very base of the social order. They suffered serious economic exploitation, without basic freedoms and human dignity, as they were traded as commodities. And yet, such a cruel conduct was legitimated in the imperial code of laws.

To be sure, there existed a more conspicuous vestigial class of slaves in the early history of the Dangxiang Tanguts. At the time, there were four sources of enslavement: those captured in war, purchased in sale, unable to pay debt, and punished for crimes.[228] The *History of Song* notes that "in the Gengyin year, there is an imperial interdict against selling off live human beings in the many prefectures along the Shaanxi frontier"; "In the autumn, the seventh month of the Yihai year, there is an imperial command issued to the many prefectures along the Shaanxi frontier, that their governments should random any famine refugees who fled to neighbouring tribes."[229]

Amongst all hitherto discovered Tangut contracts, the vast majority are records of grain loan. Very few are purchase and sell contracts. We have mentioned that there are only 12 land sale contracts. The fact that 3 contracts of

228 Wu, Tianchi. *Xixia Shigao* [西夏史稿]. Beijing: Commercial Press, 2010, pp. 136–137.
229 *History of Song*, Bk. 2. Taizong Ji'er [太宗紀二].

human transaction have survived to this day suggests that the selling and purchasing of human beings was anything but exceptions in Western Xia.

4 Lease Contracts

Renting and leasing is a common form of economic activity in Western Xia. The standard story in most of ancient Chinese history is that the state owns the land, whereto all peasants paid their taxes. Another form of land-use is where the major land-owners lease out their land to those with little or no land to farm. Tangut lease contracts belong to the latter case.

4.1 *Land Lease*

There is a large number of farmland lease contracts in the corpus of Khara-Khoto social documents. In the Инв. No. 5124 scroll of contracts, there are 8 Tangut land lease contracts, which are of vital importance to anyone who wishes to study the social lives and agricultural economy of this area, during this time.

There are 23 pieces of contracts in that long scroll mentioned above. Apart from the contracts of land and livestock sale, and accounts of livestock and grain loans, there are an additional 8 contracts of land lease.[230] In the following pages, let me present a translation, interpretation, and survey of these documents.

4.1.1 Translation and Interpretation of Land Lease Contracts

Khara-Khoto land lease contracts are scattered across long scrolls of other contracts, oftentimes attached to contracts of land sales. So, land is sometimes sold and immediately leased out. Like the land sale contracts, land lease documents are usually written in nearly inscrutable cursive styles. In the next few pages, I translate a series of Tangut contracts of land lease at fixed prices.

230 *Russian Collection of Khara-Khoto Manuscripts*, vol. 14, pp. 13–22.

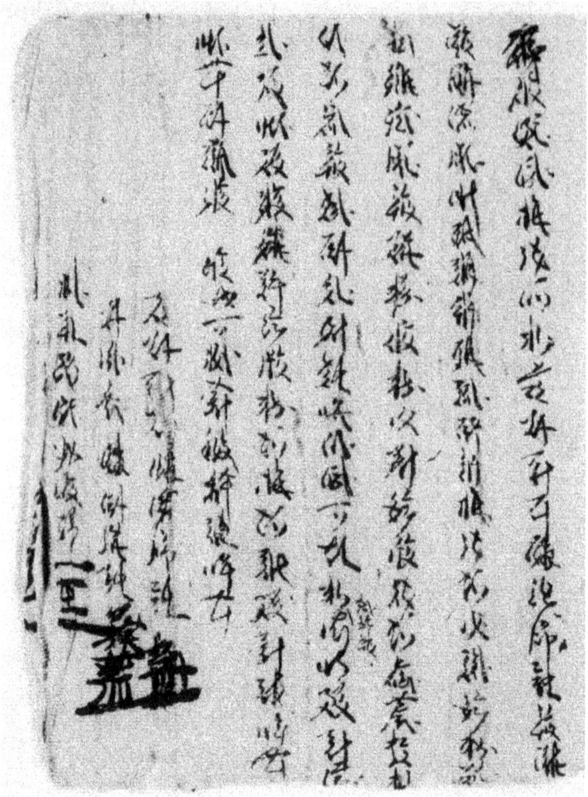

FIGURE 179 Инв. No. 5124-2(2): 24th day of 1st month in Yin year of Tianqing (1194) contract of land lease at fixed price by [illegible]

1. The manuscript Инв. No. 5124-2(2) is a Contract of Land Lease at Fixed Price dated to the 24th day of the 1st month in the Yin Year of Tianqing (1194), which belongs to Su 'The Old House.' It features 9 lines of cursive Tangut in the long scroll of contracts, from the date to the stamp and signature.[231]

Translation:

> On the 24th day of the 1st month in the Yin Year, Contactor Su 'the old house' et al. presently
>
> Lease a patch of land enough to sow 20 *dan* of seeds, in the Left Canal near the end of the Canal belonging to the Pudu Temple,

231 *Russian Collection of Khara-Khoto Manuscripts*, vol. 14, is a scroll of contracts. The previous contract is dated to the [illegible] [ŋwər ljwu le kjiw] (Yin Year of Tianqing). The contract should have been signed in the Jiayin Year of Tianqing (1194).

Where all the cottages and yards are included; the lease is for one year at a fixed price;[232] rent[233] is 10 *dan* 5 *dou* of wheat and
5 *dan* of coarse grains, which is agreed upon. Payment is due by the 1st day of the 9th month.
Past the deadline, for each 1 *dan* of rent, let the payment be 2 *dan*, instead. Heart truly willing.
The party that reneges on the agreement is penalised by 1 *liang* of gold according to the laws. Heart truly willing.

Contract Party: Su 'the old house' ([Tangut characters]) (stamp)

Co-Contract Party: Su 'the prosperous fountain spring' ([Tangut characters]) (stamp)

Witness

…

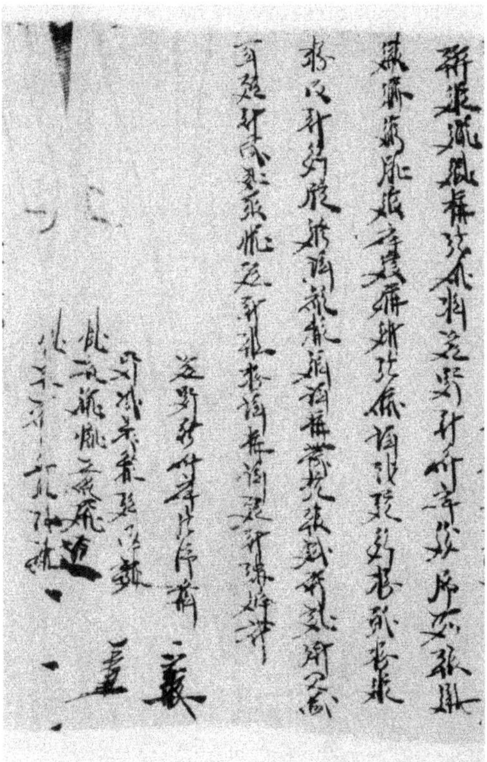

FIGURE 180
Инв. No. 5124-3(3): 29th day of 1st month in Yin year of Tianqing (1194) contract of lease at fixed price by Liang Laofangcheng et al.

232 The Tangut expression is [Tangut characters] [·ja phio] (already leased out [at the fixed price]). The first character is a verbal prefix signifying the state of completion of a particular action. The second character is a loan word from the Chinese 包, which means to rent a patch of land [at a fixed price] to farm.

233 The Tangut expression is [Tangut characters] [lji-. mej], rent paid by the tenants to the landlord.

2. The manuscript Инв. No. 5124-3(3) is a contract of land lease at fixed price dated to the 29th Day of 1st Month in the Yin Year (1194), by [ljow da kia śji-j] et al. It consists of 8 lines in the long scroll of contracts, from the date to the stamps and signatures.[234]

Translation:

> On the 29th Day of 1st Month in the Yin Year, the Contract Party [ljow da kia śji-j] et al., presently
> Lease a patch of land for one year at a fixed price, where 15 *dan* of seeds can be sowed, owned by [ljow lja mja] at the Pudu Temple.[235]
> Both parties agree to set the rent at 6 *dan* of coarse grains and 4 *dan* 2 *dou* of wheat, due by the 8th month,
> 1st day;[236] past that date, double each *dan* in debt. Their own hearts are willing.
> Contract Party: Liang [ljow da kia śji-j] (stamp)
> Co-Contract Party: Son, [ljow ɣwie gia_ phu_] (stamp)
> Witness: [ŋwe mji śjow khjwi-] (stamp)
> Witness: ???? (stamp)

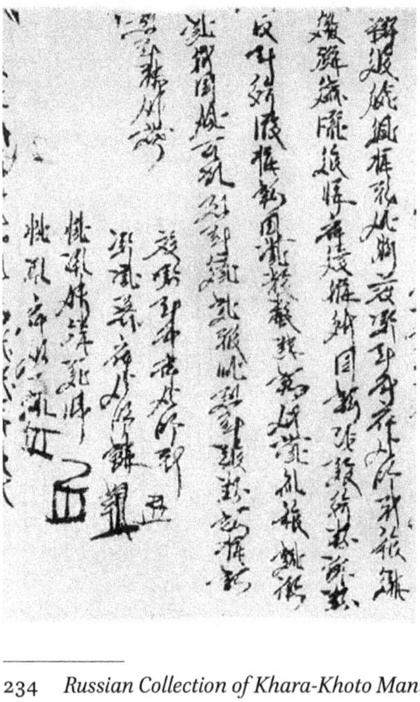

FIGURE 181
Инв. No. 5124-3(5): 29th day of 1st month in Yin year of Tianqing (1194) contract of land lease by et al.

234 *Russian Collection of Khara-Khoto Manuscripts*, vol. 14, p. 15.

235 The leased land could be the same patch of land sold by [ljow da kia ·jiw], fit to sow 15 *dan* of seeds, on the same day.

236 There is a missing character [nji-_] (day) in the original text.

3. The manuscript Инв. No. 5124-3 (5) is a contract of land lease dated to the 29th Day of 1st Month in the Yin Year of Tianqing (1194), by [Tangut] et al. It consists of 8 lines of Tangut in the cursive script in the long scroll of contracts, from the date to the stamps and signatures.[237]

Translation:

On the 29th Day of 1st Month in the Yin Year, Contract Party [Tangut] [ljow da kia ·jiw] et al., presently
Lease a patch of land at a fixed price, where 8 *dan* of seeds are sowed, from [Tangut] [ljow lja mja] at the Pudu Temple,
The rent being 2 *dan* 8 *dou* of wheat and 3 *dan* 6 *dou* of coarse grains, hereupon agreed,
Due by the 1st day of the 8th month. Overdue payment doubles.
Own heart willing.
Contract Party: [Tangut] [ljow da kia ·jiw] (stamp)
Co-Contract Party: [Tangut] [ljow da kia phu_] (stamp)
Witness: [Tangut] [phjij śjo wa śia~] (stamp)
Witness: [Tangut]? [ljow da kia ?] (stamp)

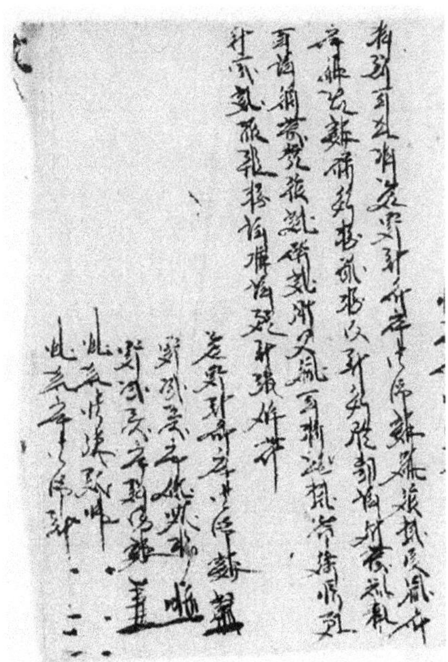

FIGURE 182
Инв. No. 5124-3(8): 1st day of 2nd month in Yin year of Tianqing (1194) contract of land lease by [Tangut]

237 *Russian Collection of Khara-Khoto Manuscripts*, vol. 14, p. 16.

4. The manuscript Инв. No. 5124-3(8) is a contract of land lease dated to the 1st day of the 2nd month in the Yin Year of Tianqing (1194). The land is leased to [illegible] [ljow da kia phu_]. It consists of 9 lines of Tangut cursive in the long scroll of contracts, from the indication of date "on the same day, the first"—which would set the date to the same as the previous contract: first day of the second month in the Yin Year—to the stamps and signatures of the parties involved in the lease.[238]

Translation:

> On the same day,[239] [illegible] [ljow da kia phu_] who sets up this contract, presently from a grain-selling agent at the Temple,
> [illegible] [ljow dow dźjij phu_], lease a patch of land at the agreed rent of 3 *dan* 6 *dou* of coarse grains and
> 1 *dan* 4 *dou* of wheat, due by the 1st day of the 8th month.
> Overdue payment doubles. Heart willing.
> Contract Party: [illegible] [ljow da kia phu_]
> Receiver of the contract: [illegible] [ljow ŋwe mji lji-.]
> Receiver of the contract: [illegible] [ljow ɣwie gia_ phu_]
> Witness: [illegible] [phjij śjo wa śia~]
> Witness: [illegible] [ljow da kia ·jiw]

238 *Russian Collection of Khara-Khoto Manuscripts*, vol. 14, p. 18.

239 The previous contract is dated to the 1st day of the 2nd month in the Yin Year [illegible] [ljow ɣwie gia_ ·jiw], a land sale contract. This contract is signed on the same day.

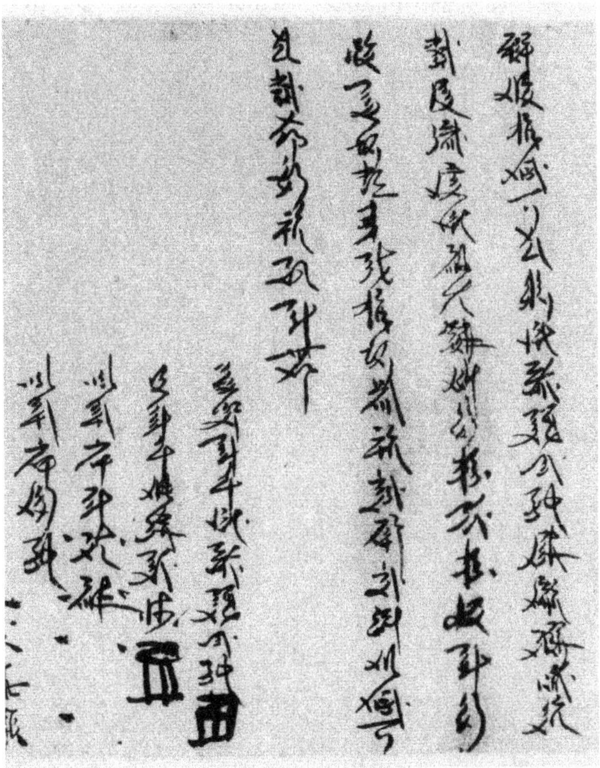

FIGURE 183
Инв. No. 5124-3(2): 1st day of 2nd month in Yin year of Tianqing (1194) contract of land lease at fixed price by [Tangut]

5. The manuscript Инв. No. 5124-3(2) is a Contract of Land Lease at Fixed Price, by a man named [Tangut] [mjadzjwi-], dated to the 1st day of the 2nd month in the Yin Year of Tianqing (1194). It is recorded in 8 lines of Tangut cursive in the long scroll of contracts, from the indication of date to the stamps and signatures, following the standard format.[240]

Adapted Translation:

> On the 1st day of the 2nd month in the Yin Year, [Tangut] [mjadzow pji.phə tśhja wejr] presently from
> A grain agent at the Pudu Temple, [Tangut] [lja mja] and [Tangut] [dow dźjij phu_], lease a patch of land they own at a fixed price; upon mutual agreement, the rent is set
> At 7 *dan* of wheat and 12 *dan* of grains, due by the 1st day of the 9th month. Willing.

240 *Russian Collection of Khara-Khoto Manuscripts*, vol. 14, p. 15.

Contract Party: [mjadzow pji.phə tśhja wejr] (stamp)
Renter: [phjij śjo wa śia~] (stamp)
Witness: [ljow ·jiw ta phiow][241] (stamp)
Witness: [ljow ne_w wejr] (stamp)

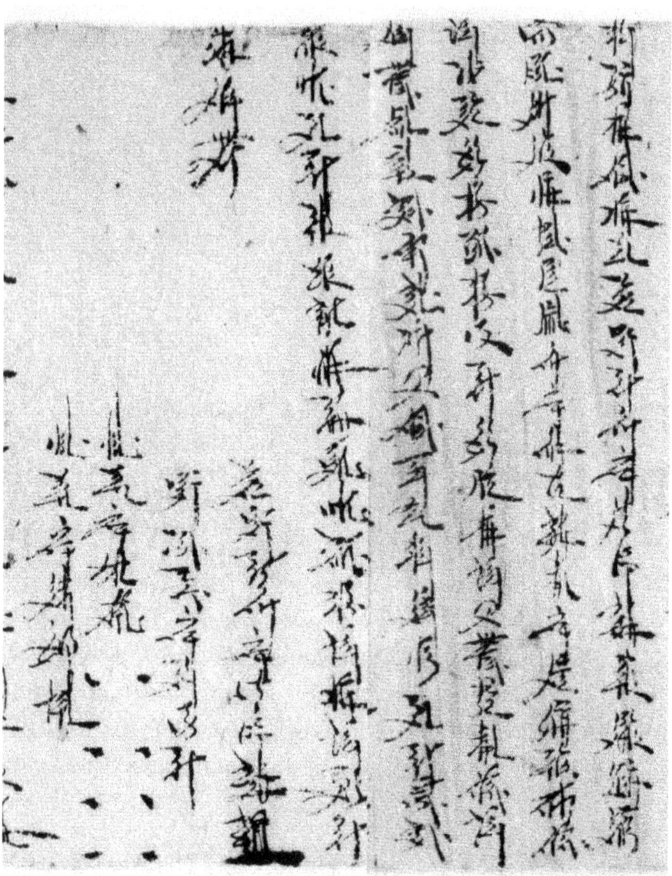

FIGURE 184 Инв. No. 5124-4(1, 2): 2nd day of 2nd month in Yin year of Tianqing (1194) contract of land lease at fixed price by

6. The manuscript Инв. No. 5124-4 (1, 2) is a Contract of Land Lease at Fixed Price dated to the 2nd day of the 2nd month in the Yin Year of Tianqing (1194). The renter is [ljow da kia phu_]. The contract consists of 9 lines in the Tangut cursive, from the date to the stamps and signatures.[242]

241 TN: lit. the white dog in the You year.
242 *Russian Collection of Khara-Khoto Manuscripts*, vol. 14, pp. 18, 19.

Translation:

On the same day: 2nd day of the 2nd month,[243] Contract Party [Tangut] [ljow da kia phu_] et al. from the
Grain agents of the Pudu Temple, [Tangut] [ljow dow dźjij phu_], [Tangut] [ljow lja mja] et al., lease
A patch of land at fixed price, where 5 *dan* of seeds are sowed, at the agreed rent of 2 *dan* 8 *dou* of wheat and 5 *dan*
4 *dou* of coarse grains, due by the 1st day of the 8th month,
Overdue payment is not only prosecuted by law but should also double. Heart willing.
Contract Party: [Tangut] [ljow da kia phu_] (stamp)
Receiver of Contract: [Tangut] [ljow ɣwie gia_ ·jiw] (stamp)
Witness: [Tangut] [ljow wejr śjow] (stamp)
Witness: [Tangut] [ljow ŋwu ne_w mja] (stamp)

FIGURE 185
Инв. No. 5124-4(3): 2nd day of 2nd month in Yin year of Tianqing (1194) contract of land lease at fixed price by [Tangut]

243 Usually, "on the same day" refers back to the same full date, month, and year in the previous contract. There is no need to repeat any bits of information. Still, this contract repeats the precise date, 2nd day of the 2nd month.

7. The manuscript Инв. No. 5124-4(3) is a Contract of Land Lease at Fixed Price dated to the 2nd day of the 2nd month in the Yin Year of Tianqing (1194). The lease, recorded in 9 lines of cursive Tangut in the long scroll, is taken by [ljow ɣwie gia_ phu_]. It begins with the reference to "the same day" and ends with the stamps and signatures.[244]

Translation:

On the same day: 2nd day of the 2nd month, Contract Party [ljow ɣwie gia_ phu_] et al.,
Presently from grain agents of the Pudu Temple, [ljow dow dźjij phu_] and [ljow]
[lja mja] lease a patch of land at fixed price, where 5 *dan* of seeds are sowed, the rent
Agreed upon being 7 *dou* of wheat and 3 *dan* 6 *dou* of coarse grains. Due by the 1st day of the 8th month
Overday payment will double.
Own heart willing.
Contract Party: [ljow ɣwie gia_ phu_] (stamp)
Co-Contract Party: [me_ nja_ ɣwie gia_śjow] (stamp)
Witness: [dju. dju. śja phji wejr] (stamp)
Witness: [phjij śjo wa śia~] (stamp)

244 *Russian Collection of Khara-Khoto Manuscripts*, vol. 14, pp. 18, 19.

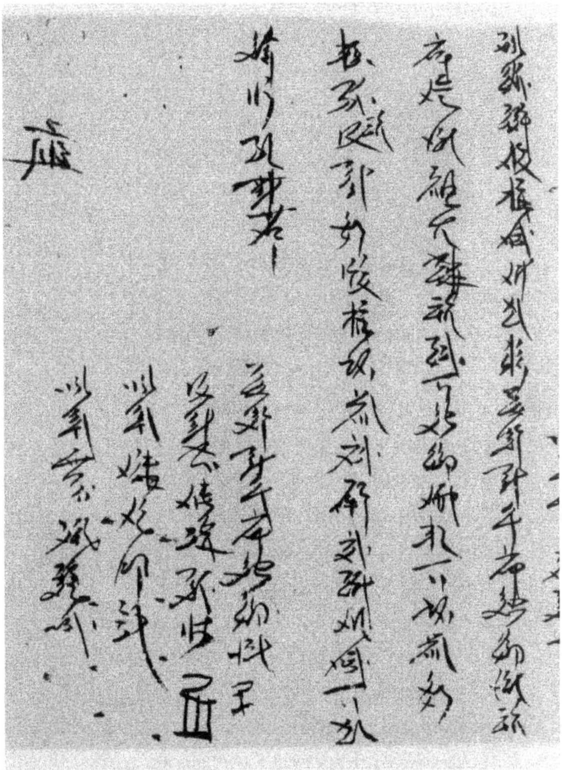

FIGURE 186
Инв. No. 5124-4(7): 6th day of 2nd month, Yin year of Tianqing (1194) contract of land lease at fixed price by 𘝵𗍊𗼻𘀄 et al.

8. The manuscript Инв. No. 5124-4(7) is a Contract of Land Lease at Fixed Price dated to the 6th day of the 2nd month in the Yin Year of Tianqing (1194), recorded in 8 lines of cursive Tangut in the long scroll, from the reference to "the same day" to the stamps and signatures.[245]

Translation:

> On the same day: 6th day of the 2nd month, Contract Party 𘝵𗍊𗼻𘀄 [ljow ŋwu ne_w mja] et al.,
> Presently from the grain agents of Pudu Temple 𘝵𗏁𗵒𘉋 [ljow dow dźjij phu_] and 𘝵 [ljow]
> 𗦳𗴮 [lja mja], lease a patch of land at a fixed price where 5 *dan* of seeds are sowed. The rent is 7
> *dou* of wheat and 3 *dan* 6 *dou* of coarse grains, hereupon agreed, due by the 1st day of the 8th month.

245 *Russian Collection of Khara-Khoto Manuscripts*, vol. 14, p. 21.

Overdue payment should double.
Own heart willing.
Contract Party: [Tangut characters] [ljow ŋwu ne_w mja] (stamp)
Renter: [Tangut characters] [phjij śjo wa śia~] (stamp)
Witness: [Tangut characters] [sji da kia zji] (finger segment printed)
Witness: [Tangut characters] [khjiw khjwi- phə bie_j] (finger segment printed)

4.1.2 The Format and Content of Tangut Land Lease Contracts

4.1.2.1 *Contract of Land Lease at Fixed Price*

The land lease contracts presented and translated above appear to share the same general format as other types of Tangut contracts. Each document begins at the top of the page, without indentation, with the date and the name of the principal Contract Party—the party taking the lease. This is followed by the name of the landowner, the size of the land to be leased, the precise amount of rent, the date by which the rents are due, as well as the terms of penalty for overdue payment. Finally, the contract ends with the stamps and signatures of the Contract Party, co-contract(s) and the witness(es).

At least within the compass of this long scroll of contracts, the Tangut term for the act of 'leasing' or 'renting' is the verb [Tangut characters] [phio], most probably a loan word from the Chinese 包 [pæw] (to reserve and lease at a fixed price). It is likely that the full sense of 'lease at fixed price' did not exist in the earlier Dangxiang language, until the Tanguts branched out from pasturing to farming, and adopted the practice of tenancy. In the contracts, there is usually a 'prefix of completion' before the verbal character [Tangut characters], which signals that the act of leasing is completed.[246]

It often happens that a land lease contract follows immediately a land sale contract, with the same patch of land sold and rented on the same day. Therefore, the lease contract usually simplifies its dating, or refers to the same date, month, or year as the previous contract in the scroll, e.g. "Yin Year …" Here, the Year of Yin refers in fact to the Jiayin Year of Heavenly Celebration (1194 AD). After the year comes the precise date, e.g. "first month, twenty-fourth day." But again, a contract may simply refer to "the same day" for the sake of brevity.

The main "Contract Party," or "the one who makes the contract" here refers to the renter: in Tangut, [Tangut characters] [·jwi-r dźiow wji mjijr], the same four characters as in other contracts.

246 TN: Shi, Jinbo; Li, Hansong. *Tangut Language and Manuscripts*. Leiden: Brill, 2020, pp. 356–393.

Tangut contracts are rarely signed in two copies, each held by one party. Rather, a single copy of the contract remains in the possession of the more dominant party (the property-owner, employer, etc.). Land-lease contracts are also 'unilateral' in this particular sense. The contract is drafted in the voice of the renter—the party which proposes and initiates this legal transaction. The one who holds the contract in possession, however, is the land-owner. The fact that the land-owner is not required to sign or stamp on the contract shows his superior position—rights, advantages, and privileges—in this economic relationship. Due to his economic weakness and vulnerability, the renter is the party constrained by the terms of the contract to fulfil his duties. Therefore, these land lease contracts may be classified as 'contracts of partial obligation.'

4.1.2.2 *Time and Renter*

As mentioned before, the same agents purchase a patch of land and least it out almost immediately. Therefore, these eight land lease contracts share roughly the same dates as the preceding land sale contracts, in the first or second months of that year.

Note that these two months are right in the middle of the hard times in between two autumn harvests. During this interim time, peasants almost always resort to taking loans or sell properties in exchange for foodstuff. It is not enough to manage to feed the family, for they must also start farming now in expectation of a harvest in the autumn. As soon as they lease out a piece of farmland, they have to prepare for tilting and sowing.

There are exactly 8 land sale contracts and another 8 land lease contracts. A quick glance at this scroll is enough to learn the story behind the scenes: representatives of the Pudu Temple, [Tangut] [ljow lja mja] and [Tangut] [ljow dow dźjij phu_], purchased land from impoverished families and immediately lease them out to landless peasants. There is no doubt that the Pudu monastery became a monopolistic land-owner. Exploitative temples do not buy land for direct use, but rather to lease out to peasants who either own little or no land, in exchange for rent.

4.1.2.3 *Land Lease and Land Sale Contracts*

Within the long scroll, it appears that land lease contracts are simpler than land sale contracts. The description of the land leased is less detailed than of the land sold. The precise location of the four bounds are not mentioned here, as in land sale contracts. Sometimes, even the names and identities of the agents involved are abbreviated or outright omitted in the lease contracts. Likewise, financial guarantee is offered in simpler terms than when a sale is involved. In general, fewer signatories are identified on a lease contract. In most cases, only one co-Contract Party suffices, and not as many witnesses are required as in a sale. In fact, a typical land sale contract is almost twice the length of the lease contract, concerning the same patch of land. There are, for example, more than 270 characters in the Инв. No. 5124-2 land sale contract, dated to the 24th day of the 1st month in the Yin Year of Heavenly Celebration. On the same day, the same land which [khjiw bie_j ta] had sold, is leased out to [lhju da kia gji] in the lease contract Инв. No. 5124-3, in about 130 characters. There, even land size is unmentioned. For it is assumed that the holder of the contract would refer to the land size as recorded in the preceding land sale contract: a patch of land large enough to sow 20 *dan* of seeds. On the land lease contract, there is no reference to the agents involved, terms of guarantee, location of the four ends of the land. Signatures are simplified, and the name of only one co-Contract Party is registered. There aren't many witnesses, either.

One obvious reason for the relative simplicity of land lease contracts is that, unlike the land sale contracts whereby a title is transferred from one ownership to another (sometimes called an 'absolute sale'), land lease creates a relationship of tenancy, and involves no change of ownership status. Needless to say, that the volume of transaction in land sale is larger than in land lease. It is for these intuitive reasons that land lease contracts are shorter and simpler than land sale contracts. Even the penalty fee is lower in land lease than in land sale: 1 *liang* versus 2 *liang* of gold.

4.1.2.4 *Renter and the Size of Land Leased*

Most of the tenants in the long scroll are peasants either deprived or short of farmland. They have no choice but to work in the fields of the wealthy, and pray for the harvest to cover the rent and, if all goes well, yield some extra earnings left. The following is a chart that compiles the renter, date, and the land size in the 8 land lease contracts.

The ethnicity and demographics of the renters in these 8 contracts are rather mixed. There is the Dangxiang [mjadzow pji.phə tśhja wejr], the Han, Monsieur Su Laofangzi ([lhju da kia gji]), but the majority are the Liangs, whose identities are not as easy to ascertain. Note that in the third contract, [ljow da kia ·jiw] leased a patch of land fit to sow 8 *dan* of seeds from the Pudu Temple, on the 29th Day of the 1st Month in the Yin Year. Looking for his name in the land sale contracts, we quickly find that he sold his own land, fit to sow 15 *dan* of seeds, to the Pudu Temple on exactly the same day, for which he received a compensation of 6 *dan* of wheat and 10 *dan* of coarse grains. What does he have to pay for the lease, assuming that an autumn harvest will materialise? 2 *dan* 8 *dou* of wheat and 3 *dan* 6 *dou* of coarse grains. Then, in the fourth and sixth contracts, we see that the same

CHART 19 Information and data in the 8 land lease contracts

No.	Date of lease	Renter	Land size
1	24th Day of 1st Month, Yin Year	[illegible] [lhju da kia gji]	For 20 *dan* of seeds
2	29th Day of 1st Month, Yin Year	[illegible] [ljow da kia śji-j]	For 15 *dan* of seeds
3	29th Day of 1st Month, Yin Year	[illegible] [ljow da kia ·jiw]	For 8 *dan* of seeds
4	Same Day (1st Day of 2nd Month, Yin Year)	[illegible] [ljow da kia phu_]	For 10 *dan* of seeds
5	1st Day of 2nd Month, Yin Year	[illegible] [mjadzow pji.phə tśhja wejr]	For 10 *dan* of seeds
6	Same Day 2nd Day of 2nd Month	[illegible] [ljow da kia phu_]	For 5 *dan* of seeds
7	Same Day 2nd Day of 2nd Month	[illegible] [ljow ɣwie gia_ phu_]	For 5 *dan* of seeds
8	6th Day of 2nd Month, Year Yin of Tianqing	[illegible] [ljow ŋwu ne_w mja]	For 5 *dan* of seeds

[illegible] [ljow da kia phu_] leases two patches of land in two consecutive days, one large enough to sow 10 *dan*, the other 5 *dan* of seeds. Moreover, this man is a co-Contract Party alongside [illegible] [ljow da kia ·jiw] in the other contract. More often than not, co-Contract Parties are close family relatives. And given the style of their names, it is easy to tell that they may be brothers. Likewise, [illegible] [ljow ɣwie gia_ phu_], the Contract Party in the seventh contract, is probably a close relative of [illegible] [ljow da kia phu_] to whom he serves as a co-Contract Party in the fourth contract.

4.1.3 Rent

4.1.3.1 *Calculation of the Rent*

Some land lease contracts indicate the land size in precise statistics, usually in the amount of seeds to be sowed; others refer to the land size as recorded in the preceding land sale contracts. Either way, we have data on land size on each patch of land leased. As for the rent, it is often calculated in the mixed terms of fine (e.g. wheat) and coarse grains. Therefore, it is necessary to convert the real currency into a single unit in order to calculate the average rent per unit of land. Fortunatley, we know from Khara-Khoto accounts of grain sales that the price of wheat is around 200–250 mace, whereas the price of millet (a type of coarse grain) is between 150–200.[247] So it is not without reason to set the price of coarse grains at 75%–80% of the fine grains. In this way, it is also possible to convert all rent into the currency of coarse grains, in order to calculate rent per unit of land, as measured by the space fit to sow 1 *dan* of seeds. The summary statistics is presented in the chart below.

CHART 20 Rent statistics in the 8 land lease contracts

No.	Renter	Size of land leased	Total rent in mixed currencies of grains	Total rent in coarse grains	Rent/unit of land for 1 *dan* of seeds
1	[illegible] [lhju da kia gji]	For 20 *dan* of seeds	10 *dan* 5 *dou* of wheat & 5 *dan* of coarse grains	19 *dan*	0.95 *dan*
2	[illegible] [ljow da kia śji-j]	For 15 *dan* of seeds	6 *dan* of coarse grains & 4 *dan* 2 *dou* of wheat	12 *dan*	0.8 *dan*
3	[illegible] [ljow da kia ·jiw]	For 8 *dan* of seeds	2 *dan* 8 *dou* of wheat & 3 *dan* 6 *dou* of coarse grains	7.3 *dan*	0.91 *dan*
4	[illegible] [ljow da kia phu_]	For 10 *dan* of seeds	3 *dan* 6 *dou* of coarse grains & 1 *dan* 4 *dou* of wheat	5.5 *dan*	0.55 *dan*
5	[illegible] [mjadzow pji.phə tśhja wejr]	For 10 *dan* of seeds	7 *dan* of wheat, 12 *dan*	21.3 *dan*	2.13 *dan*
6	[illegible] [ljow da kia phu_]	For 5 *dan* of seeds	2 *dan* 8 *dou* of wheat & 5 *dan* 4 *dou* of coarse grains	9 *dan*	1.8 *dan*
7	[illegible] [ljow ɣwie gia_ phu_]	For 5 *dan* of seeds	7 *dou* of wheat & 3 *dan* 5 *dou* of coarse grains	4.4 *dan*	0.88 *dan*
8	[illegible] [ljow ŋwu ne_w mja]	For 5 *dan* of seeds	2 *dan* of coarse grains	2 *dan*	0.4 *dan*

247 Shi, "Commodity Prices, Transaction Taxes and Loans in Western Xia," 2008.

It turns out that amongst the 8 contracts analysed in the chart, the rent in contract No. 1, 2, 3, 7 are much closer: the renter pays anywhere between 0.8 *dan* and 1 *dan* of grains for each unit of land (to sow 1 *dan* of seeds). In contract No. 5 and 6, however, the rent is much higher, close to or above 2 *dan*. In contract No. 4, 8, on the other hand, the rent is lower than the average: 0.55 *dan* and 0.4 *dan*, respectively. Perhaps a survey of the sale price of the same land would shed some light on the difference in lease price.

CHART 21 Sale price of the land as recorded in the 8 lease contracts

No.	Seller	Land size	Price in mixed grains	Price in coarse grains	Price per unit of land (1 *dan* of seeds)	Asset included in the sale
1	[illegible] [khjiw bie_j ta]	For 20 *dan*	Coarse grains 15 *dan* & wheat 15 *dan*	35 *dan*	1.75 *dan*	A full-set house of 4 cabins & yard
2	[illegible] [ljow da kia ·jiw]	For 15 *dan*	6 *dan* of wheat & 10 *dan* of coarse grains	18 *dan*	1.2 *dan*	House & Yard, trees, stone, stone grave?, etc.
3	[illegible] [dju. dju. śja phji wejr]	For 8 *dan* of seeds	4 *dan* of wheat & 6 *dan* of coarse grain	11.3 *dan*	1.4 *dan*	House of 2 cabins, 5 live trees
4	[illegible] [ljow ɣwie gia_ ·jiw]	Ripe/ unripe land for 10 *dan* of seeds	2 *dan* of wheat, 2 *dan* of millet, 4 *dan* of grains	8.7 *dan*	0.87 *dan*	House & wall
5	[illegible] [khjij śja rjar śji-j]	Ripe/ unripe land for 10 *dan* of seeds	10 *dan* of wheat, 10 *dan* of coarse grain, 10 *dan* of millet	33.3 *dan*	3.33 *dan*	Cottages large/ small, oxen ploughs & tools, stone gate with bamboo fence, pentamerous yokes, tree yard
6	[illegible] [ljow ɣwie ·o bie_j]	For 5 *dan* of seeds	4 *dan* of wheat & 9 *dan* of coarse grains	14.3 *dan*	2.86 *dan*	

CHART 21 Sale price of the land as recorded in the 8 lease contracts (*cont.*)

No.	Seller	Land size	Price in mixed grains	Price in coarse grains	Price per unit of land (1 *dan* of seeds)	Asset included in the sale
7	[illegible] [me_ nja_ dźjwow thja]	For 5 *dan* of seeds	6 *dan* of coarse grain & 1 *dan* of wheat	7.3 *dan*	1.46 *dan*	
8	[illegible] [phjij śjo sjwi sjwi dju]	Ripe/ unripe land for 3 *dan* of seeds	5 *dan* of coarse grain	5 *dan*	1 *dan*	Old house of 4 cabins

Obviously, the land in lease contract 5 and 6 are rented at higher prices for no other reason than that they are worth more, and were acquired by the landowners at a higher cost. Likewise, the rents in contract 4 and 8 are lower because their sale prices are also lower. There are two main factors that determine land prices. First, fertility and convenience of irrigation usually means higher productivity and yield. Second, all the add-on assets which are sold with the land would also factor in the final listed price. In Contract No. 5, for example, the land comes with a whole assemblage of major and minor properties: cabins and cottages large and small, tilting tools for the oxen (ploughs, etc.), stone gate with bamboo or wooden fence, five-branched yokes, as well as a tree yard.

4.1.3.2 *Rent-Sale Price Ratio*

The 12 land sale contracts show that land price in Khara-Khoto is remarkably low, typically around 2 *dou* of coarse grains per *mu* of land. There are multiple reasons for this, chief amongst which is the naturally disadvantageous position of the seller pressed by the urgent need of foodstuff in the underproductive seasons of late winter and early spring. The buyers would then exert pressure on the sellers to further cut the price. Typically, the buyers themselves are both grain monopolists, either Buddhist temples or major landlords in the area. They purchase large chunks of land from grain-deprived in the inter-harvest seasons, in order to maximise profit at the expense of needy peasants. As soon as they buy in new land, the new landowner wastes no time to lease it out to peasants, who either lost or sold their land, to extract rents from the landless, who cannot afford to wait to start farming now. In this second round of bargain, the landowners again stand to gain from the neediness of the peasants, by raising the rent. The chart shows that the total annual rent is nearly half of what it costs to purchase the land in the first place. In other words, in no more than two years, the landlords could earn back their initial investment. By means of lease, the land quickly pays for itself. The speedy transfer and massive concentration of land property into the hands of landowners in the late-Tangut period is a remarkable phenomenon in economic history.

For instance, in the land sale contract Инв. No. 5124-3(3), [illegible] [ljow lja mja] of the Pudu Temple purchased from [illegible] [ljow da kia ·jiw] a patch of land fit to sow 15 *dan* of seeds, at the cost of 6 *dan* of wheat and 10 *dan* of coarse grains. He then immediately leasese the land out, and within a year, he would receive 6 *dan* of coarse grains and 4 *dan* 2 *dou* of wheat in revenue—that is a whopping ⅔ of the purchase cost! In the land sale contracts Инв. No. 5124-3(4, 5), the same [illegible] [ljow lja mja] of Pudu Temple paid [illegible] 4 *dan* of wheat and 6 *dan* of coarse grains for a patch of land fit to sow 8 *dan* of seeds. Here, too, Liang is able to earn back 2 *dan* 8 *dou* of wheat and 3 *dan* 6 *dou* of coarse grains—nearly ⅔ of the buying cost—within just one year. The high rent-sale price ratio speaks volumes to the exploitation of the landless, grainless peasants at the hands of the financiers, whether a temple or a landlord.

4.1.4 Guarantee

Land lease is a form of legal and financial transaction. And for any transaction, there must be a way to guarantee its enforcement. For this reason, Tangut land lease contracts set forth penalties for the violation of the terms. A statement on penalties is usually found immediately after the information on rent.

4.1.4.1 *Penalty for Breach of Contract and the Legal Force of the Contract*

Terms of penalties for breach of contract in land lease are less exhaustive and severe than in land sale. Below is a chart comparing the summary statistics of penalty fees against default, overdue payment, dispute, or renegation, across the 8 land lease contracts.

In land sales, the chief concern of the purchasing party is whether the seller is transferring full and legitimate property right. The contracts seem to suggest that for the buyer to renege on the contract is a way to question or to deny the proper ownership of the seller. Therefore, the contract specifies that in a scenario where property right is under dispute, liability falls on the side of the seller, who is also obliged to pay the penalty fee, usually double the sale price. Otherwise, any party that reneges on the terms of agreement is penalised. The penalty fee varies from 1 to 3 *liang* of gold, depending on the size and quality of land concerned. But in case of land lease, the real source of anxiety and

CHART 22 Penalty fees in the 8 lease contracts compared

No.	Renter	Land size	Overdue payment	Penalty for breaching contract	Penalty for land sale dispute	Penalty for reneging on the land sale
1	[illegible] [lhju da kia gji]	For 20 *dan* of seeds	Doubles (2 *dan* per *dan*)	Penalty Fee of 1 *liang* of Gold	Doubles (2 *dan* per *dan*)	Penalty Fee of 2 *liang* of Gold
2	[illegible] [ljow da kia śji-j]	For 15 *dan* of seeds	Doubles (2 *dan* per *dan*)		Doubles (2 *dan* per *dan*)	Penalty Fee of 3 *liang* of Gold
3	[illegible] [ljow da kia ·jiw]	For 8 *dan* of seeds	Doubles (2 *dan* per *dan*)		Doubles (2 *dan* per *dan*)	Penalty Fee of 1 *liang* of Gold
4	[illegible] [ljow da kia phu_]	For 10 *dan* of seeds	Doubles (2 *dan* per *dan*)		Doubles (2 *dan* per *dan*)	Penalty Fee of 1 *liang* of Gold
5	[illegible] [mjadzow pji.phə tśhja wejr]	For 10 *dan* of seeds	N/A		N/A	Penalty Fee of 3 *liang* of Gold
6	[illegible] [ljow da kia phu_]	For 5 *dan* of seeds	Doubles (2 *dan* per *dan*)		N/A	Penalty Fee of 1 *liang* of Gold
7	[illegible] [ljow ɣwie gia_ phu_]	For 5 *dan* of seeds	Doubles (2 *dan* per *dan*)		N/A	Penalty Fee of 1 *liang* of Gold
8	[illegible] [ljow ŋwu ne_w mja]	For 5 *dan* of seeds	N/A		Penalty fee of 5 *dan* of wheat	

flashpoint of contention is not property right but timely payment of rent. Of course, there is also the question of renegation. So, the contract usually contains two statements on penalties: overdue payment and renegation. Penalty fee for overdue payment is based on the rent. Usually, the fee doubles the rent (i.e. for each 1 *dan* the fee is 2 *dan*). The volume of transaction in land lease is decidedly smaller than in land sale. Therefore, penalty is also less severe. It is generally uncertain what would happen if a party walks back on his promises and breaches the terms of agreement set forth in the contract. Only the first contract offers clear instructions: the penalty fee is 1 liang of gold. None of the other contracts mentions this matter, in particular. It is likely that the landowners are not concerned with the prospect of their tenants ever changing their mind.

4.1.4.2 *Stamp and Signature*

Consistent with the grain loan accounts and land sale contracts, Khara-Khoto land lease contracts also end with signatures and stamps of the parties involved in the transaction. In most cases, each person occupies a separate line. First comes the Contract Party—the principle party which initiates the transaction, in this case the renter, or the tenant farmer—followed by his liability-sharing co-contractor, and finally the witnesses. There is no more than one principle Contract Party, but there may be multiple co-Contract Parties and witnesses. In these land lease contracts, however, there is usually just 1 co-Contract Party, though sometimes there may be 2. In contrast, there are 2 or 3 co-Contract Parties in land sale contracts. Likewise, land lease contracts feature 1–2 names of witnesses, versus 2–3 in land sale contracts. In short, whether it comes to the number of co-Contract Parties or witnesses, land lease contracts tend to be shorter and simpler, because it does not involve the absolute transfer of title in large volume. Below is a chart compiled to compare the forms of stamp and signatures in land lease versus land sale contracts.

Also consistent with the format of land sale contracts in the long scroll, the names of sellers, liable parties, and witnesses are all written in a fluent cursive style by a single hand. The handwriting is also exactly the same as in the main text. Therefore, it must have been a professional scriber who wrote out the entire document (apart from the stamps and finger-segment prints).

As expected, the liability-sharing co-Contract Party is referred to, as usual, as 𘁁𘂚𘃢 [dźiow sa dźjwi-]: the one (also) receiving the document, i.e. the co-Contract Party. But in the fifth contract, the signatory after the main Contract Party is not registered as 𘁁𘂚𘃢, but as 𘄴𘅥𘆖 [phio wji mjijr] (the one taking the lease), or "co-renter." This man, by the name of 𘇇𘈸 [phjij śjo], claims the same status as that of a co-Contract Party, and also shares liability with the main Contract Party. If the main Contract Party delays or denies payment, dies, escapes, or evaporates, the co-Contract Party takes over the legal obligations and shoulders the financial burden. It is worth noting that the co-Contract Parties in lease contracts are not addressed as family relations to the Contract Party (wife, son, etc.). It also shows that, in contrast to the more serious contracts of land sale, land lease contract requires less rigorous vetting and screening.

Witnesses sign as 𘉩𘊚 [nwə dzjwo], literally "the one who knows," i.e. witnesses. It could also be abbreviated into the single-character 𘉩. A point of curiosity is that, whilst the names of the Contract Party and the co-Contract

CHART 23 Stamps and signatures in the 8 land lease/sale contracts compared

No.	Contract party	Co-contract party/ parties	Stamp /Print	Witness(es)	Stamp /Print	Co-contract parties in land sale	Stamp /Print	Witness(es) in land sale	Stamp /Print
1	[illegible] [lhju da kia gji]	1	Stamp	1	Stamp	2	Finger-segment	3	Finger-segment, Stamp
2	[illegible] [ljow da kia śji-j]	1	Stamp	2	Finger-segment	3	Finger-segment	3	Finger-segment
3	[illegible] [ljow da kia ·jiw]	1	Stamp	2	stamp	2	Finger-segment	2	Stamp
4	[illegible] [ljow da kia phu_]	2	Stamp	2	Finger-segment	3	Finger-segment, stamp	2	Finger-segment
5	[illegible] [mjadzow pji.phə tśhja wejr]	1	Stamp	2	Finger-segment	2	Stamp, Finger-segment	2	Finger-segment
6	[illegible] [ljow da kia phu_]	2	Stamp	2	Finger-segment	3	Stamp, Finger-segment	2	Finger-segment
7	[illegible] [ljow ɣwie gia_ phu_]	1	Stamp	2	Stamp, Finger-segment	2	Stamp, Finger-segment	2	Stamp, Finger-segment
8	[illegible] [ljow ŋwu ne_w mja]	1	Stamp	2	Finger-segment	0		2	Finger-segment

Party are written in parallel, the names of witnesses are usually one or a half space higher. This is probably a way to distinguish between two kinds of legal personae: the Contract Party and co-Contract Party share substantive liability, whereas the witnesses are there only to fulfil a legal function. If things go awry, the witnesses may be consulted, but are under no substantive obligation.

There are, as usual, two ways to authenticate the legal document: by stamping a pictorial icon, or by drawing the signatory's finger-segments. Most of the Contract Parties and co-Contract Parties in land lease contracts paint a symbol or icon, but witnesses choose either way. For instance, in contract Инв. No. 5124-3(3) the Contract Party, co-contractor, and one of the two witnesses stamped their symbols, whereas the other witness printed his finger-segments.

Then, in Инв. No. 5124-3(5), all renters, co-renters, and witnesses stamped their symbols. Whereas in Инв. No. 5124-3(2), the co-Contract Party stamped, whereas the both witnesses chose to print their finger-segments.

4.1.5 Features of Tangut Land Lease Contracts

Along with the land sale contracts, Khara-Khoto land lease contracts constitute a major part of the primary sources on the history of socio-economic activities in Western Xia. These manuscripts accurately portray how land was used, farmed, and transacted in rural areas of Western Xia, at the very bottom level of the Tangut society.

4.1.5.1 *Key Materials for the Study of the Tangut Economy*

Khara-Khoto land lease contracts provide fresh, real, and detailed primary materials for the study of the Tangut economy. These texts are also key to any survey of medieval Chinese, East Asia, Inner Asian, and world economic history. For the first time, they make it possible for the academia to gain deep and reliable insights into the distribution, transfer, and use of farmland. Moreover, it is not a single piece, but a batch of documents that are discovered. A connective and comparative reading of these economic records yields new forms of knowledge unimaginable in the past.

4.1.5.2 *Reflection on the Socio-Economic and Living Conditions in Khara-Khoto*

The value of Tangut land lease contracts goes beyond the historical study of land use, per se, but informs a full understanding of the Khara-Khoto socioeconomy and the living conditions of ordinary Tanguts during this period. The contracts show that a number of Tangut peasants lacked farmland, and therefore resorted to land lease. They obtain leases at exorbitant prices, suffering multiple rounds of exploitation, wagering entirely on a harvest to pay for their debt and to maintain subsistence. They gamble it all on the autumn harvest, even though they are fully aware of high risks and uncertainties when it comes to the yield. The fact that in Khara-Khoto, where population was not the densest and arable land not the scarcest, land lease was under such enormous pressure, speaks to the harsh realities on the ground.

4.1.5.3 *Monopolistic Acquisition of Land by Temple Establishments*

The Khara-Khoto land lease contracts also reveal the extent to which Buddhist temples engaged in predatory, monopolistic acquisitions and transactions of scarce farmland. Pudu Temple purchases land en masse at low prices, and lease them out at higher prices to peasants either without or short of land to farm. In two rounds of transactions, the temple is able to extract a huge sum of revenues from the peasants. Purchased and leased, a patch of land typically pays for itself in a year or two.

4.1.5.4 *Land Lease Contract Is Shorter and Simpler than Land Sale Contracts*

Within the long scroll of legal documents, each land lease contract concerns the same patch of land as in the preceding land sale contracts. For this reason, some information is omitted in the land lease contract, under the assumption that the two contracts are kept and read in conjunction. Moreover, given that land lease is not as risky and significant as land sale, there is no need for such details as the four boundaries of the land, tax information, sources of irrigation, etc. Since a lease contract involves no 'absolute sale,' even the terms of penalties are rather succinct. Furthermore, fewer co-Contract Parties and witnesses are involved in land lease than in land sale. These points of comparison show that Tangut contracts are, after all, flexible and practical documents.

4.2 *Land Lease and Livestock Mortgage*

At times, Tangut peasants in Khara-Khoto had to mortgage their livestock in order to secure land leases. This is a further complicated case of an otherwise simple lease of farmland. Such contracts are rare to find. So far, only one has been successfully identified.

The manuscript Инв. No. 5949-30 is a "contract of farmland lease and livestock mortgage" dated to the Chen year of Yingtian (1208 AD). The original piece is a single-page contract of 15 lines in cursive Tangut handwritten on a 21.1 × 45.5 cm hemp paper. The document begins with the date, "Yingtian, Chen Year, Last month, 21st Day" and ends with the stamp and signature.[248]

This contract is written in a remarkably cursive style, with many characters simplified from their standard forms, making it even more difficult to render a clean text. The first two characters in the first line should be, according to conventions, the era title of the year. The first character looks like [Tangut] [ŋwər] (heaven). The second one is decisively unclear, written almost in a single stroke. But we could infer it as [Tangut] [bju] (accord, respond), to make the era title complete. There are several Tangut era titles that begin with the character [Tangut]: [Tangut][Tangut] [ŋwər lji.j] (Tiansheng; Heavenly Prosperity), [Tangut][Tangut] [ŋwər ljwu] (Tianqing; Heavenly Celebration), [Tangut][Tangut] [ŋwər bju] (Yingtian; Heavenly Accord), and [Tangut][Tangut] [ŋwər dzji.] (Huangjian; Imperial Foundation). Given the shape of the second character here, the era title intended in this case could only be [Tangut][Tangut] (Yingtian).

248 *Russian Collection of Khara-Khoto Manuscripts*, vol. 14, p. 92.

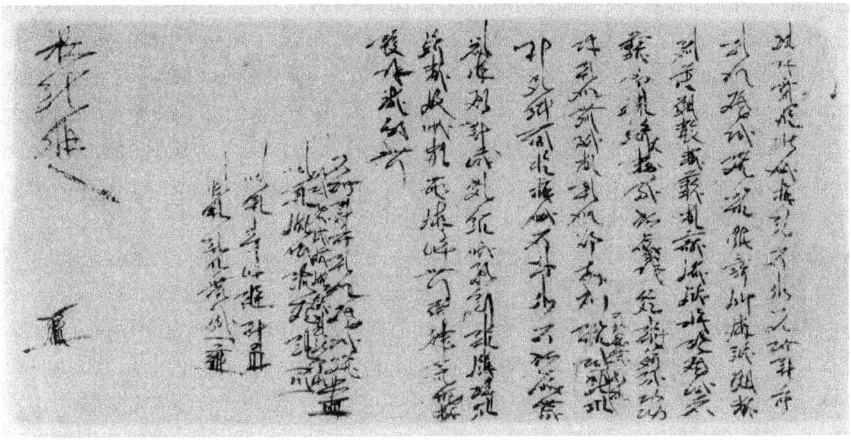

FIGURE 187 Инв. No. 5949-30: Chen year of Yingtian (1208) contract of farmland on livestock, et al. mortgage

We gain a much stronger sense of certainty in our reading of the mysterious character as 瀡, not least because the second character in line 9 of the text is also written in this shape, and in that context, also, the character is best read as 瀡. When the *Russian Collection of Khara-Khoto Manuscripts* was first published, the contract was mislabelled "Tianqing" or "Heavenly Celebration," which should now be corrected to "Yingtian" or "Heavenly Accord." The contract was signed on the 21st day of the last month in year 1208.

Despite the radical cursiveness of the script, it is still possible to interpret the basic meaning of the text as a whole. The contract was signed on the 21st day of the last month in 1208—that is, in the late-Tangut period, less than 20 years before the fall of the empire—by a certain 羖㣍嫒祁殘 [·jaxwa phə phji ta], who leased out a patch of land fit for 1 *dan* 5 *dou* of seeds, on a mortgage of his own donkey. In addition, he has to pay a rent of 1 *dan* 5 *dou* of coarse grains to the land-owner, Yehe Xianling et al., due by the first day of the second month in the following year. Overdue payment will be duly penalised.

Contracts which concern large assets and major factors of production such as land and livestocks are extremely important, and therefore usually wordy, formal, and complicated. The contract is validated by iconic stamps rather than an approximate print of finger-segments. The contract ends with there large characters in ink: 𢆯祁? [ɣa. nji-_?] (two-ten-?), which might be another indication of the date, above the stamps. Given the conventional format of more formal contracts, the space at the end of the document may be reserved for signatories of higher status. If we survey the stamps and signatures here, we see a line written in smaller font: "co-Contract Party, wife Eyi 'the joy of the old house'" was evidently inserted into the text at a later time. So, it seems that the name, which was not there at first, was added at the insistence of the land-owner, to whom the legal presence of a co-Contract Party's signature is not dispensable. This lady, Eyi, is the wife of the Contract Party—the party which takes the lease on livestock mortgage. With her formally involved in the contract, the document is more secure and enforceable. But to look at it from another angle, we see again the indisputable socio-economic status of women, especially if they are female heads of households, in the inner lives of the Tangut society.

Most of the relevant parties involved in the contract, whether it is M. Yehe himself, or his wife Eyi, or still the witnesses Weiyi, Liang, and Yehe, are Dangxiang Tanguts. M. Liang, however, could be either an ethnic Fan or a Han—the exact truth, we shall never know. It shows that a large number of Tanguts engaged in agriculture, including both wealthy land-owners and impoverished peasants.

Contracts of land lease on livestock mortgage are rare finds amongst Tangut manuscripts. To interpret them is as necessary as demanding. There is a lot of room for further studies.

5 Employment Contracts

The broad category of Tangut "employment contracts" includes both human and animal labour contracts. By Contracts of Labour Employment, the employed human beings offer their physical work in exchange for a set amount of compensation. By Contracts of Livestock Employment, those in shortage of draft animal labour hire draft animals from livestock-owners, for which they pay a fee. Both types of contracts were used in Western Xia, and prove important sources to the study of Tangut society and economy.

5.1 *Employment of Human Labour*

Contracts of human labour employment is a key source on the identities of the Tanguts employed for physical labour—their names, socio-economic status, and relationship to the employer. Amongst the copious manuscripts discovered in the city of Khara-Khoto, thus far, only one complete document of Labour Employment Contract has been identified. But to see from the macroscopic temporal horizon, this manuscript is probably the best labour employment contract from the Liao, Song, Xia, and Jin Dynasties. It fills in the void of 11th–13th century Chinese labour contract.

5.1.1 Translation and Interpretation of Tangut Contracts of Labour Employment

The Инв. No. 5949-32 Labour contract is dated to the last month in the Mao Year of Guangding (1219), a single-page, 19.8 × 47.9 manuscript with 15 lines handwritten in the Tangut cursive and standard-running scripts. The first line begins with the date: "Mao Year of Guangding, Last month, Fifth Day" (1219); the contract ends in a standard format, with stamps and signatures.[249]

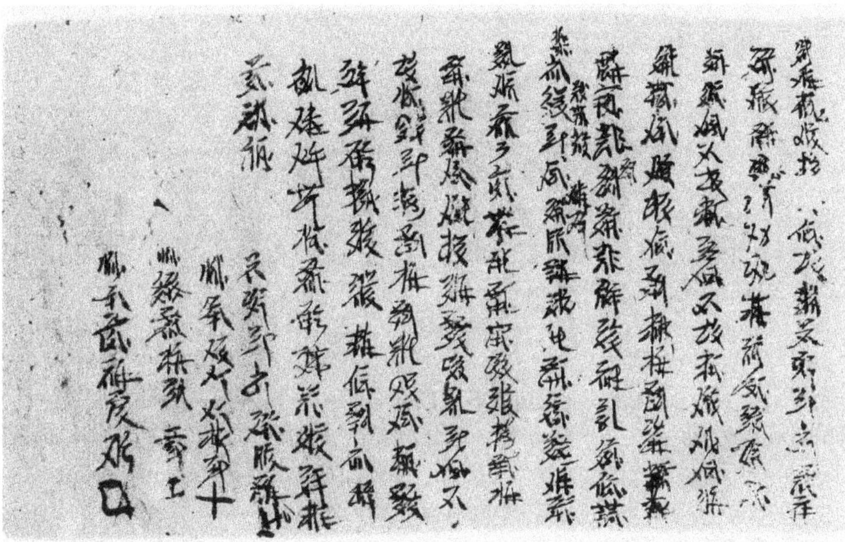

FIGURE 188 Инв. No. 5949-32: Mao year of Guangding (1219) contract of labour employment

Translation:

> On the 5th day of the last month in the Chen Year of Guangding, Contract set by Babe Quan-
> fenmao, presently voluntarily at ???'s place, from
> the 1st day of the 1st month to the 1st day of the 10th month, for 9 months, offers employed
> labour, at the price of 5 *dan*, 2 *dan* of which is paid immediately; in the autumn

249 *Russian Collection of Khara-Khoto Manuscripts*, vol. 14, p. 94.

the other 3 *dan* is paid, along with 3 *zhang* of white cloth for summer clothing. He himself plants 5 *dou*

2 *sheng* of coarse grains, 3 *dou* of wheat, to be certain. Let [illegible] [khjwi- lji- phu_] make his best effort,

Without deceits or evasions; if he acts arbitrarily, or is absent during a busy day, for each day

He has to work for 2 days. If the rest of the wage is not paid by the 1st day of the 10th month,

For each *dan* let the employer pay 2 *dan*. Whoever regrets and reneges on these agreements,

Pays the penalty of 5 *dan* of coarse grains according to the law. But only are the two parties willing in their hearts, but let them enforce the terms herein contained in the document, and according to the circumstances.

Contract Party: [illegible] [khjwi- lji- phu_] (stamp)
Witness: [illegible] [tshja gju_ gju_ rjur ·jiw] (stamp)
Witness: [illegible] [mja dzow kə zji] (stamp)
Witness: [illegible] [·jow dow dźjij lhu] (stamp)

5.1.2 Interpretation of the Basic Content in the Contracts

This important piece of labour contract offers an abundance of information: the time of the contract, the Contract Party (the employed labourer as the primary party that sets up the contract), the employer, the duration of the employment, wage, terms of employment, as well as penalties for default and violations of the contract, followed by the signatures and stamps of both parties. The format is that of a complete contract. Indeed, it is a rich and accurate reflection of labour employment in Western Xia.

The contract must have been negotiated and signed in the Mao Year of Guangding—during the reign of the Shenzong Emperor of Western Xia. There are 13 years in this period, and only one of them is a Mao Year. Therefore, we know almost for certain that the contract was signed in the last month of 1220, towards the late period of the Tangut Empire—only 7 years from its fall.

The reference to the 'maker of the contract'—[illegible] [·jwi-r dźiow wji mjijr]—is the same as in other types of Tangut Contracts. The labourer here who sets up the contract is Babe [illegible] [khjwi- lji- phu_] (the prosperous dog manure). The family name [illegible] [ba be] appears under the section of 'Tangut names'in both the *Assorted Words of the Three Realm* and the *New Collection of Golden Fragments in the Palm*.[250] In the tunnelway of Cave 61 in the Mogao

---

250 *Russian Collection of Khara-Khoto Manuscripts*, vol. 10, pp. 49, 110.

Grottoes of Dunhuang, on the back of the Tejaprabhā Buddha on the Southern wall, there is a portrait of votive Bhikkhunī figure. By its side, one finds her name in both Chinese and Tangut: 掃灑尼姑播盃氏願月明, and [illegible] [tjij njwi-. tji. śjwo mjijr ba be zji-. tji. śji-j swew] (lamp, burn, vow, emanate, person, Ba, Be, name née, wish, become, light). A literal translation of the Tangut is: "The lamp-lighting, vow-taking one, Babe, prays for enlightenment."[251] This nun is most probably an ethnic Tangut woman. The same family name is also found in Tangut documents and seals of military chiefs. Therefore, the employed labourer in this Contract of Labour Employment is a Tangut man of the Babe family. There is also much to be said about his given name. The Tanguts devised diverse names for their children. Some are meant to be auspicious; others indicate the months and years in which the child is born; some feature Buddhist imageries and jargons, others borrow from low-status humans and even animals: "an auspicious dog," "dog of the old house," "the one with a donkey," "the rain-bird," "the benevolent slave," "the slave-treasure," etc. It is possible that these less-than-flattering names were meant to ward off the jealousy of the spirits, making it easier to raise the children to their adulthood. A "dog's manure," otherwise "prosperous," is a fitting example of such a naming strategy. A similar example is a certain witness to a loan-repayment contract, by the name of [illegible] [ljow khjwi- lji-] "Liang 'the dog manure.'"[252] As for the five-character name of the employer in the contract, most of them are blurred, so much so that they can hardly be identified. But it is quite possibly a Tangut name, as well.

The contract is clearly dated to the last month of the Mao Year of Guangding. The labour is employed from the first day of the first month in the upcoming year—that is, the first day of the Gengchen Year of Guangding (1220)—to the first day of the tenth month, a total duration of 9 months that encompass the spring, summer, and autumn. The labourer is to work from the sowing season to the harvesting season.

The Tangut expression for 'offering labour' or 'renting out labour' is [illegible] [ɣie tshwew lho]. This phrase echoes the legal expression in the Tangut *Laws of Heavenly Prosperity*, where the chapter on "Offering Labour" is titled [illegible] [rar ɣie tshwew ɣa] (pawn/rent, labour, offer, gate/chapter/section). The two characters in the middle for "offering labour" is the same as in this contract.

251 Bai, Bin; Shi, Jinbo. "Mogaoku Yulinku Xixiawen Tiji Yanjiu" [莫高窟榆林窟西夏文題記研究]: "A Study of Tangut Inscriptions in the Yulin Cave of Mogao Grottoes" in *Kaogu Xuebao* [考古學報]: *Acta Archaeologica Sinica*, issue 3, 1982.

252 *Russian Collection of Khara-Khoto Manuscripts*, vol. 13, p. 318.

The labourer's wage is 5 *dan* of grains. The contract stipulates, in lucid language, that of the total wage, 2 *dan* is pre-paid at the signing of the contract. The other 3 *dan* is paid only in the harvest season. Apart from the grains, the employers are obliged to offer summer clothings to the employed. The Tangut expression is 𗹙𗖵 [tsja gjwi] (hot, cloth = clothes in the hot season, i.e. summer clothing). These summer clothings will be made out of the '3 *zhang* of white cloth' provided for by the employer. In addition, the employers are allowed to plant 5 *dou* and 2 *sheng* of coarse-grain seeds, as well as 3 *dou* of wheat seeds in a patch of land, out of their own labour and for their own enjoyment. These numbers here measure land size by seeds. The Tanguts measured land by *qing* or *mu*, but also by the amounts of seeds to be sowed. If the land for 1 *dan* of seeds is roughly equivalent to 4 (Song) *mu* ≈ 10 Tangut *mu*, then the labourer concerned in this contract is permitted to farm a little more 3 (Song) *mu* of land, where 8 *dou* of seeds are sowed.

By a stipulation of the contract, the employer also requires that the employee exert his utmost physical power. The requirement of making an effort is in the language of 𗏁𗗙𗡴𗖵𗗘 [źia_ khjow ·ja_r lew dźjwo] (lit. diligent, labour, day, should, devote), that is, the labourer is expected to devote his labour with diligence during the working days. The contract also expects no deceit from the labourer, asking that he not to miss any work for private reasons. Emphatically, the contract makes clear that during the busy season, any work day missed has to be made up for by two additional workdays. The Tangut expression 𗗙𗡴𗂧 [khjow ·ja_r ŋwu] refers to the busy days; 𗗙𗡴𗂧𗹬 [khjow ·ja_r ŋwu rjir] means to leave work undone during the busy days.

But the contract also secures the labourer's right to receive the second payment in the harvest season. If the 3 *dan* of grains are not paid to the worker by the first day of the tenth month, for each 1 *dan* of wage, the employer has to pay 2 *dan*. In general, if either party walks back on the promises outlined in the agreement, the penalty is the standard 5 *dan* of coarse grains, according to Tangut law. Both parties express their willingness to abide by the terms laid out in the contract, and to enforce them according to the requirement of particular circumstances. Overall, it can be said that the contract restrains the economic conduct of both parties: the employing and the employed.

The contract ends with the signatures and stamps of the Contract Parties and the witnesses. Since the family name of the Contract Party, Babe, already appears at the start of the contract, a given name suffices at the end. There are three witnesses, two of which are ethnic Tanguts: 𗦳𗗚 [tshja gju_] and 𗹬𗆗 [mjadzow]; the third, a Yang, is most probably a Han. Given that the handwritings of the four signatories, as well as the main text of the document, are nearly identical, it is possible that a single scriber wrote and signed the entire contract. The 'signatures' are followed by stamps. As discussed before in this book, there are two kinds of stamps: a symbol or a print of the finger-segments. Icons and Images are more formalistic. They are used most often when there are multiple Contract Parties and co-Contract Parties. Finger-segments are usually preferred by the witnesses. Given the importance of this labour-employment contract, all stamps take the form of iconic symbols.

5.1.3 The Economy of Labour-Employment as Reflected in the Contracts

Labour employment is an important issue in socio-economic lives of the Tanguts. There is a long tradition of labour-employment in China, but the practice of hiring workers is seldom documented in conventional historical archives. So far, a small but impressive body of surviving ancient Contracts of Labour Employment, most of which excavated in modern eras, have been identified: Han-dynasty labour employment contracts in Han-slips; Gaochang Labour Employment Contracts in Turfan dated to the Wei, Jin, Northern and Southern dynasties; Labour Employment Contracts in Turfan and Dunhuang dated to the Tang and Five Dynasties, as well as early-Song contracts unearthed in Dunhuang.[253] This manuscript of Tangut Labour Employment Contract, excavated in Khara-Khoto to the northeast of Dunhuang, adds one more temporal geographical perspective to the list.

The contracting party in this Contract of Labour Employment is an ethnic Tangut man. Historically, the first Dangxiang Tanguts engaged in pasturing and livestock-raising. But once relocated to more arable lands, they gradually pivoted to agriculture, hence the significant presence of Tangut peasants in the Khara-Khoto documents. In this particular labour contract, both the employer and the hired, and even the two witnesses, are Dangxiang Tanguts. It shows that in the span of two centuries, some Tanguts became highly-skilled and employable farmers.

By definition, labour contracts reflect the legal relationship in between the employer and the labourer in terms of rights and obligations—that is, one party offers compensations for the service provided by the other. This contractual relationship is founded upon mutual and voluntary agreement. Contract-making is recorded in the chapter on "hiring labour" in the *Laws of Heavenly Prosperity*:

253 Zhang, Chuanxi. *Zhongguo Lidai Qiyue Cuibian* [中國歷代契約粹編]: *An Edited Collection of Contracts in All Chinese Dynasties* (upper tome). Beijing: Peking University Press, 2014, pp. 72–73, 175–177, 369–388, 613–619.

> With the exception of the *shijun*, the wives and sons of the many and of their lords, the men and women of those in government, given mutual consent, and according to texts official or private, may practice of hiring.[254]

That is basically another way of stating that, by Tangut laws, it is legal to hire labourers (lit. to 'pawn' or 'mortgage' labour). The expression for "offering labour" is the same two characters as appears in the labour contract: 𗼇𘟣 [ɣie tshwew].

What are the living conditions and family backgrounds of the particular employer concerned in this contract? For what reasons does he hire additional labour? Is it out of an ordinary shortage of hands, or an over-abundance of land? These 'motives' are not revealed to or hinted at within the compass of the text. Perhaps they are buried in history and never to be known.

The labour is contracted for a span of 9 months, which almost entails a whole-year schedule. It may be considered a 'long-term hire.' There is, after all, little or nothing to do in the fields during the three coldest months in the winter.

In this labour contract, as in most others, the price of labour—or the wage of the hired labourer—is calculated in terms of grains. The compensation is 5 *dan* of grains. With a bit of research, we know that a unit *sheng* of wheat in Western Xia weighs about 1 modern Chinese *jin* (*shijin*). A unit *dan* of grains is, therefore, approximately 100 *jin* in our own terms. But on top of this standard payroll, the employer grants his labourer the right to farm on around 3 (Song) *mu* of land. Given the much lower fertility, hence productivity at the time, one *mu* of land must have yielded no more than a few *dou* of grains, definitely below 1 *dan*. Even if we allow that the high yield of 1 *dan* per *mu* was occasionally possible, the total yield would have been no more than 4 *dan*. That is to say, the total pay for the labourer here is 8 *dan* of grains. His monthly wage then comes down to nearly 1 *dan* of grains. In addition, he receives free summer clothings from the employer. But it is very likely that these clothes would up with wears and tears by the end of the year.

On average, an adult consumes about 5 *dan* of grains per year. Suppose that the labourers are fed at the employer's expense during the workdays. It is very much possible, then, that he would be able to feed one adult and one child in his own family by his annual earnings. Tangut grain loan accounts show that, toward the last few years of Western Xia, a large number of peasants in Khara-Khoto, especially in a state of penury in the interim months between

254 *Revised Laws of Heavenly Prosperity* 11, "On Hired Labour," p. 388.

one harvest and the next, resorted either to taking high-interest loans from exploitative creditors, or to sell their land or livestocks in exchange for foodstuffs. In addition to grains for dietary purposes, the peasants were also in need of seeds to sow in whatever bits and pieces of land that remained in their possessions. Now, this particular labourer is bound to his work all year long. If his family also owns land, no matter how little, he would not be able to plough his own fields. In that case, the optimal solution is to outsource his land to others. Or, perhaps, he could be one of the many landless peasants at the time. It would have been extremely difficult for him to pull it off, if indeed, he had to feed his wife and children by his daily exertion of labour, alone. With the 2 *dan* of grains he procures in the spring, a family of three or four were barely going to make it to the autumn harvest. But if the household was privileged enough to have enjoyed extra labour, then his annual earnings of 8 *dan* or so would be an impressive income.

The labour contract makes an emphatic point about the necessity to make the best effort in the fields. No procrastination is tolerated. Delay and dereliction of duty on a busy work day would result in two additional days of labour as penalty. In a total of about 270 days, regardless of weather at the time and the physical condition of the labourer, he is bound to intensive and endless work. Therefore, despite the seeming 'contractual equality' between the two legal personae, it must be said that the employer is in a position of advantage if not outright domination. There is even a relationship of subordination between the hiring and the hired. The contract makes an explicit reference to penalty in accordance with laws should the terms of the agreement ever be violated. In fact, the Tangut laws go to great lengths to secure the rights of the employers, to the extent of validating unequal terms and conditions:

> If a hired labourer, bound to his service, fails to perform the tasks, and the employer beats him to death, let him be sentenced to one year of imprisonment. If the aggressor uses tools to torture the labourer to death, let the imprisonment be three years. If the death is caused by premeditated murder, let the case be judged according to the laws on premeditated murders.[255]

That is to say, if an employer beats his unperforming worker to death by hand, accidentally and unintentionally, he is to suffer no more than one year in prison. The use of weapon upgrades the manslaughter, resulting in three years of imprisonment. Only when intention and premeditation can be proved,

255 *Revised Laws of Heavenly Prosperity* 11, "On Hired Labour," pp. 388–389.

would the case be tried as a case of murder. Needless to say, the Tangut laws are a product of the feudal time and order. They are therefore sensitive to caste and hierarchy. Offences committed by those of lower status against their superiors are punished much more than if the power relation is the other way around.[256] The Tangut laws are explicit about such structural legal inequalities:

> If the hired labourer rapes the employer's wives, daughters, daughters-in-law, aunts, sisters, etc., let the charge be three levels higher than what is stipulated in Book VIII on the wives of others ...
>
> Let no labourer beat, resist, or verbally abuse the employer. In case of a violation, and if the employer is a commoner, let a labourer who hurled verbal insults suffer thirteen strokes, and let a labourer who launched physical attacks be jailed for one year. If the labourer causes any injury, then let the charge be three levels above the normal charge of physical violence; if a death is caused, let the perpetrator of the crime be hanged. If the labourer verbally insults an office-holder of high status, let him be jailed for one year; if physical violence is involved, let the imprisonment be two years. If any injury is caused, let the charge be five levels higher than a normal charge of physical harm. Should the struggle result in death, let the perpetrator be cut by a sword ...[257]

Rape or sexual harassment committed by the hired to the female members of the employer's household are three levels higher than usual. Any verbal or physical attacks against one's employer also results in much heavier punishments than under normal circumstances—that is, when the socio-legal statuses of the involved parties are equal. Obviously, then, the employers and their employees are in a fundamentally unequal legal relationship. In fact, it is misleading to characterise it as a relationship of employment, for it comes strikingly close to the relationship between a lord and his servants. The *Laws of Heavenly Prosperity* also require that:

> If *Shijun* [semi-slaves], *Nupu* [servants/serfs], *Dianren* [hired men], and the like should steal the written records of their mortgage ... let them be tried according to the laws of theft.[258]

256 *Revised Laws of Heavenly Prosperity* 8, "On Caused Injuries," pp. 296–297.
257 *Revised Laws of Heavenly Prosperity* 11, p. 389.
258 *Revised Laws of Heavenly Prosperity* 3, "Miscenllaneous Crimes of Theft," p. 167.

Neither the semi-slaves of military origin, nor the household servants and serfs owned their own legal persons. They are the Tangut equivalents of the Tangut and Song-era Buqu or Nubi.[259] Here, the Tangut law lists the hired men alongside the serfs and slaves. It is perhaps the most striking testimony to the low social status of hired labour in the Tangut economy and society.

Of course, the contract also seems to have restrained the actions of the employers. After all, according to the terms of agreement, should the employer fail or refuse to deliver the second payment to the labourer in the amount of 3 *dan* of grains, then for each 1 *dan* owed to the employee, he now has to pay 2 *dan*, intead. It should be carefully noted that that such terms are not coercive. Nor do they really impose any pressure or difficulty upon the employers, or at least not at the level enforcement and execution of the rights and duties. Still, in evident contrast to the unilateral nature of grain loan, land sale, or livestock contracts, this document of labour contract at least outlines the contours of bilateral duties, and moreover, the precise terms and forms of penalties for both sides, should either of them ever walk back on his promise. It reflects a certain degree—certainly not a high or adequate degree—of balance between the rights and the duties of both parties.

The stamps and signatures of this contract also testifies to ethnic diversity and cross-ethnic demographics in the rural areas of Khara-Khoto. The employer, the labourer hired, as well as the first and second witnesses, all seem to be Dangxiang Tanguts. The third witness is a certain Yang, most probably an ethnic Han. Since he is invited be a witness to the contract, he must have been a close associate of the labourer concerned. Of course, the close Fan-Han ties shown here is consistent in other economic records of Western Xia, such as grain loan and land sale contracts.

5.1.4 Comparisons with Tang and Song Labour Employment Contracts

Amongst the many social documents discovered in the celebrated Dunhuang library cave, some are clearly labour contracts. Labour contracts in agriculture dated to the Tang, Song, and the Five Dynasties are, however, rare finds. A total of fifteen such contracts are accurately dated, and have well survived. The Tangut labour contract with which we are principally concerned here comes slightly later than this batch of Dunhuang manuscripts, but there is a lot of discernable temporal and geographical continuity there, nonetheless. To start with the obvious, all of these papers originate from the northwestern area of China. Dunhuang and Khara-Khoto are only 1 degree apart in latitude; both

259 Shi, Jinbo. *Xixia Shehui* [西夏社會]: *Tangut Society*. Shanghai: Shanghai People's Press, 2007, pp. 221–227.

cities enjoy an arid inner-continental climate, with much draught, little rain, and cold wintry days. Even today, the difference in the average temperatures of the two is a mere matter of 1 degree Celsius. For these and many reasons, the geographical and meteorological conditions of agricultural production in the two areas are, and still remain, strikingly similar and completely comparable.

Indeed, the format and content of these 15 labour contracts and the Tangut contract share a great deal of similitude. Almost all contracts begin with the date of the contract and the name of the principle party in the contract, then proceed to specify the duration of the employment, the wage, terms and requirements, recompensations for neglected work, penalties for violations of the terms, and end with the stamps and signatures of all concerned parties. Although the Tangut labour contract is written in the Tangut language by Dangxiang-Tanguts, the legal document itself inherits, or imitates, the Chinese tradition of contract. It again shows the profound social, legal, and cultural impact of the migration into the agricultural zones of the Chinese Central Plains on the Tanguts, who had for so long relied on pasturing, hunting, and livestock-raising.

For a thorough analysis of the Tangut labour contract in comparison with the Tang and early-Song (9th–10th centuries) contracts, I have compiled the 15 contracts of long-term agricultural labour in the chart below, alongside the Tangut labour contract.[260]

It is self-evident that employers hire labour only when short-handed. Most Tang and Song labour employment contracts document the precise reasons of the hire: "because the household is short of hands," "since there is a shortage of human labour," "given that the family lacks sufficient labour" etc. Tangut contracts, however, do not contain these expressions. The omission of formulaic, programmatic, and probably superfluous legal language renders the contract much more concise. Not only in the Contracts of Labour Employment, but also in land sale and grain loan contracts, the Tanguts tend to omit these contextual explanations.

There is yet another difference between Tang, Song and Tangut contracts of labour employment. Most of the labour contracts dated to the Tang and Song eras record the precise addresses of the employers and the employees. For example, Linghu Anding's labour employment contract in Dunhuang documents that the employed labourer lives in Longle Village, whereas the employer

260 *Dunhuang Economic Documents*, vol. 2, pp. 55–71. Some of the contracts only indicate the sexagenary cycle but not the era names. See also Zhang, Chuanxi, Upper Tome, 2014, pp. 376–382; 613–620.

CHART 24 Tang, Song, and Tangut labour contracts compared

Register	Title of the contract	Time	Employed labourers	Employers	Duration of hire	Wage	Clothing provisions	Penalty for negligence
1	Linghu Anding of Dunhuang, Contract of Labour Employment	Wuxu Year (878?)	Commoner Long Cong'er	Commoner Linghu Anding	1st to the end of the 9th month	5 *dou* per month	1 pair of spring clothes; shirt; pants and shoes	1 *dou* per day
2	Zhang Naji, Contract of Labour Employment	Jiayin Year (894)	Commoner Jiu Han'er	Commoner Zhang Naji	1st to 9th month	1 load of millet sold per month	Spring clothes; shirt …	missing
3	Kang Baozhu of Dunhuang, Contract of Labour Employment	Renwu Year (922?)	Commoner Zhao Jinjiangnan	Commoner Kang Baozhu	1st to the end of the 9th month	1 load per month	Spring clothes 1 pair; shirt 1; pants 1 set; leather shoes 1 pair	missing
4	Yin Sijia of Dunhuang: Contract of Employment	Fourth Year of Longde in Later Liang (924)	Commoner Yin Sijia	Commoner Zhang Sijia	2nd to the end of the 9th month	1 load over a month	Spring clothes 1 pairs; long-sleeved sacrificial gown; leather shoes 1 pair	2 *dou* per day
5	Han Zhuang'er of Dunhuang: Contract of Employment	Jiashen Year (924?)	Commoner Han Zhuang'er	Commoner Su Liunu	1st to the end of the 9th month	Wheat + millet: 6 loads	missing	missing

CHART 24 Tang, Song, and Tangut labour contracts compared (*cont.*)

Register	Title of the contract	Time	Employed labourers	Employers	Duration of hire	Wage	Clothing provisions	Penalty for negligence
6	Deng Wuzi of Dunhuang, Contract of Employment	Yiyou Year (925?)	Commoner Deng Wuzi	Monk Baoxiang of the Qianyuan Temple	8 months from 12th day of 2nd month	1 load per month	Spring clothes, long-sleeved gown 1, trousers for gown 1 set; leather shoes 1 pair	5 *dou* per day in busy months; 1 *dou* in leisurely months
7	Yao Wenqing of Dunhuang, Contract of Labour Employment	Fourth Year of Tianfu in Later Jin (939)	Commoner Chengyi Shennan	Commoner Yao Wenqing	(since) 1st day of the 1st month	1 load per month	Spring clothes 1 pair; long-sleeved [gown] 1; shirt 1; plain-cloth trousers 1 set; leather shoes 1 pair	2 *dou* per day
8	Li Yuanchang of Dunhuang, Contract of Employment of Peng Zhangsan	Wushen Year (948)	Commoner Peng Zhangsan	Commoner Li Yuanchang	1st month to the end of the 9th month	1 load per month	Spring clothes, shirt 1, pants and long-sleeved gown, leather shoes 1 pair	2 *dou* per day in busy times; 1 *dou* in a leisurely day
9	Ma Yingde of Dunhuang, Contract of Employment	Yimao Year (955?)	Commoner Ma Yingde	Commoner Meng Yading	1st month to the end of the 9th month	8 *dou* per month	Spring clothes; shirt; leather shoes 1 pair	2 *dou* per day on a busy day; 1 *dou* if otherwise

CHART 24 Tang, Song, and Tangut labour contracts compared (*cont.*)

Register	Title of the contract	Time	Employed labourers	Employers	Duration of hire	Wage	Clothing provisions	Penalty for negligence
10	He Baoding of Dunhuang, Contract of Labour Employment	Dingsi Year (957?)	Commoner Long Yuandingnan	Commoner He Baoding	One full year	1 load per month	Spring clothes 1 pair; shirt 1; long-sleeved gown; pants 1 set; leather shoes 1 pair	2 *dou* per day
11	Li Jichang of Dunhuang, Contract of Employment of Wu Zhu'er	Xinyou Year (961?)	Commoner Wu Zhu'er	Commoner Li Jichang	9 months	1 load per month	missing	missing
12	Dou Boti of Dunhuang, Contract of Employment of Deng Yanshou	Jiaxu Year (974?)	Deng Yanshou	Commoner Dou Boti	9 months	1 load per month	Spring clothes 1 pair; shirt 1; pants 1 set; leather shoes 1 pair	2 *dou* per day in busy times; 1 *dou* otherwise
13	Fan Zaisheng of Dunhuang, Contract of Employment of Fan Zaiyuan	Guiwei Year (983?)	Commoner Fan Zaiyuan	Virtuous Commoner Fan Zaisheng	1st day to the end of the 9th month	1 load per month	Spring clothes 1 pair; shirt 1; pants 1 set; leather shoes 1 pair	2 *dou* per day in busy times; (missing below)
14	Deng Handuo Contract of Labour Employment	Dinghai Year (987)	Commoner Geng Handuo	Commoner Deng Handuo	1 full year	1 load per month	Spring clothes ...	

CHART 24 Tang, Song, and Tangut labour contracts compared (*cont.*)

Register	Title of the contract	Time	Employed labourers	Employers	Duration of hire	Wage	Clothing provisions	Penalty for negligence
15	Shi Fansan of Dunhuang, Contract of Employment of Du Yuanchang	Wuzi Year (988?)	Commoner Du Yuanchang	The Liang Household, Shi Fansan	missing	8 *dou* 7 *sheng*? per month	Spring clothes; 1 shirt	2 *dou* per day in busy times; 1 *dou* otherwise
16	Babe Quanfenmao, Contract of Labour Employment	5th day of last month, Chen Year of Guangding	Babe Quanfenmao	Ning Liqing?	1st month to 1st day of the 10th month, duration of 9 months	5 *dan*; land for 8 *dou* 2 *sheng* of grains	Summer Clothes, 3 *zhang* of white cloth	2 *days* of work per day missed.

resides in Hongrun Village. Precise documentation of addresses furnishes the contract with an additional layer of security; perhaps more importantly to modern historians, it makes it possible to study the economic geography of medieval labour relations, and even the human geography and historical geography of the past. In contrast, Tangut Contracts of Labour Employment barely divulge any information on the dwelling places of the employers and the labourer. Tang and Song contracts also provide fuller and more accurate socio-economic identities of the parties involved. Again in the Linghu Andi's contract in Dunhuang, we know the labourer as "commoner Long Cong'er" and the employer as "Commoner Linghu Anding"; in Deng Wuzi's contract in Dunhuang, the labourer is "Commoner Deng Wuzi" and the employer is "Monk Baoxiang at the Qianyuan Temple"; the contract of Fan Zaisheng in Dunhuang registers the employee as "commoner Fan Zaiyuan" and the employer as "A particularly virtuous commoner Fan Zaisheng." Again, barely any identity-markers could be found in Tangut labour contracts.

Most of the Dunhuang labour contracts dated to the Tang, Five Dyansties, and early-Song periods, are drafted in the first or second lunar month of the year. The labourer is hired for about 8 or 9 months. Only two contracts of mark the duration of work as an entire year: (1) He Baoding's Labour Employment Contract in Dunhuang, in the Dingsi Year (957?) is signed on the 7th day of the 4th month, effective for an "entire year"—that is, until the 4th month of the following year; (2) Deng Handuo's Labour Employment Contract in the Dinghai Year (987) is signed on the 23rd day of the 1st month, for the next "full cycle of a year." The Tangut Labour contract is set up in the last month of the previous year. The terms of employment are effective for 9 full months in the following year, from the first day of the first month to the first day of the tenth month. In other words, the labourer has to get started on the very first day of the New Year, missing the opportunity to celebrate the holiday.

When it comes to the wages, there is some variety amongst Tang and Song labour contracts. The Tang contract dated to the Wuxu year features thus far the lowest wage: "5 *dou* per month." Most other contracts indicate a wage around the level of 1 'load' per month—that is, 1 *dan*, or 1 *shuo*. Elsewhere, in two documents, the wage appears slightly less, either 8 *dou* or slightly more. In the Tangut labour contract with which we are presently preoccupied, the employer promises 5 *dan* of grains, and in addition, permits the hired worker to till a patch of land where the seeds of 5 *dou* 2 *sheng* of coarse grains and 3 *dou* of wheat are sowed. The harvest is estimated to be more than 3 *dan* if all goes well. That makes the total payment a little less than 9 *dan*. It is worth remarking that the area of Khara-Khoto is in no scarcity of land, necessarily, although the fertility and unit-productivity of the soil may be suboptimal. The harsh reality faced by any hired labourer is principally the uncertainty of produce and harvest. It can never be safely assumed that 1 mu of land is going to yield anything around 1 *dan* of grains, especially on land tilled for their own enjoyment. Not to mention, of course, that employers have few clothings to offer to their workers. It must be said, therefore, that the wage in the labour employment contract we have from Western Xia is short of impressive. But the low wage rate is also easy to explain in the context of social upheavals, into the final years of the Tangut Empire. The regime was simultaneously battling the Jurchens and suffering Mongol invasions. As a major city along the northern frontier, the Khara-Khoto population proved an easy and natural casualty. Ten years prior to the signing of this contract, the Mongols for the first time breached the walls of Khara-Khoto. There, the Mongol army steered southward to the imperial Capital, the city of Zhongxing. Then, 5 years after this contract, in 1225 AD, Khara-Khoto was once again taken by the Mongols. The second fall of the city unveiled the curtains of the Mongol destruction of Western Xia and started the beginning of the end of Tangut power. It could only be imagined what the circumstances were surrounding the arrangement for this labourer's work in the fields amidst such chaos.[261] It usually happens that during wars and unrests, both land and labour prices fall, whilst the cost of the highest of

261 Wu, Tianchi. Xixia Shigao [西夏史稿], Beijing: Commercial Press, 2010, pp. 111–124.

all necessities, the grains, skyrockets to incredible heights. The fall of the land prices in the late Tangut period has been sufficiently and convincingly demonstrated by the land sale contracts analysed in this book. Now, we point to the data in this labour contract to demonstrate the economic-historical phenomenon of falling labour prices in the last years of Western Xia.

It should also be noted that Tang and Song labour employment contracts tend to be rather detailed and strict in preventive measures against default and indiscreet behaviours. They even elaborate on the consequences of the labourers damaging the farming tools. In the contract of Linghu Anding, dated to the Wuxu Year (878?), for example, it is clearly stipulated that:

> Once the contract is established, let the concerned party enter his duty of work, and let him never abandon his labour. One day of negligence results in the penalty of 1 *dou* [of grains.] Should a matter of life and death emerge, a leave of 3 days is permitted. But thereafter, let him immediately resume work. All the farming tools and other properties are entrusted to Cong'er. Let him not unreasonably beat the cattles and the livestocks. If he does beat them, and thus violate the rules, let him recompensate the owner.[262]

Another example is the labour contract of Deng Wuzi in Dunhuang, dated to the Yiyou Year (925?):

> From the day the labourer enters into his employment, let him diligently proceed to work, day after day, and month after month. Let him never cast aside his work duties. If in a busy season, he leaves one day of work undone, let him pay 5 *dou* as recompensation. If his negligence occurs at a rather leisurely time, the penalty is 1 *dou* instead. Wuzi has entrusted all of his farming tools in his possession to the labourer. If the worker loses them, let him recover the loss. If the worker falls sick, let him be granted five days to deal with the malady. Should he take more days of rest, those days will come at the expense of his wage.[263]

The contract of Ma Yingde of Dunhuang in the Yimao Year (955?) states the following:

262 *Dunhuang Economic Documents* 55, in Zhang, Chuanxi, 2014, Upper Tome, p. 377.
263 *Dunhuang Economic Documents* 70, in Zhang, Chuanxi, 2016, Upper Tome, pp. 381–382.

> The owner of the land has entrusted all the hoes and plows needed for the work to Yingde. Should these tools be lost, let Yingde recompensate the costs. If they are handed to the owner of the household, then let the liability not fall on Yingde. If Yingde casts aside his duty in a busy workday, let him pay 2 *dou* of grains as a penalty; if the day is not so busy, let him pay 1 *dou*, instead.[264]

The Tangut contract is rather terse in such provisions. It urges 𗏹𗼻𗨞 [khjwi-lji- phu_] to make his maximum effort, never to deceive or misrepresent information, or to find pretexts and excuses to neglect his duties. If he were ever to act imprudently or arbitrarily, or fail to show up at a busy time, he is obliged to work for two days to compensate for each day neglected. But here, there is no provision for where liability lies in case the tools are damaged or lost. Nothing is said about sick days, either. It is striking that there is no statement on a three-day or five-day paid-leave, should the labourer fall seriously ill. So, a reasonable absence due to illness or disability would have been treated as absence. Surely, this is not an arrangement that by any minimal standard tends to the basic rights and benefits of the labourers. But in comparison to the Tang and Song contracts, the Tangut contract stipulates a lower rate of compensation for neglected work. In the Dunhuang contracts—depending on whether they operate a legal distinction between 'busy' versus 'non-busy' days—punish each day of neglected work with 2 *dou* or 1 *dou* of grains. In some extreme cases, the penalty on a busy day is as much as 5 *dou* (See the Dunhuang contract of Monsieur Deng Wuzi). The Tangut contract, on the other hand, asks for 2 days of labour to cover each busy day neglected. It is possible that if nobody is in a hurry, then the labourer should feel free to work only 1 additional day to cover each day neglected. Given a monthly wage of 1 *dan* of grains, a penalty of 1 *dou* of grains is worth 3 days of wage; 2 *dou* of grains are the labour costs of 6 days; at the same rate, 5 *dou* of grains are the wage for half a month! Therefore, the '2 days for each (busy) day neglected' requirement is less of a burden than in the Dunhuang contracts.

Every single contract specifies the terms of penalties for default. The Dunhuang contract of Linghu Anding, for example, states that "if one party first breaches the contract, let the penalty be one sheep, to be transferred to the party that does not breach the contract." In the Dunhuang contract of Han Zhuang'er, "the party which first breaches the contract is to transfer two loads of green wheat to the non-breaching party." Again, in the contract of Deng Wuzi, "A party that breaches the contract is punished 5 *shuo* of wheat, to be

264 Ibid.

claimed by the person who does not breach the agreements." It seems that the penalty turns severe over the course of time. So is the case in the Tangut contract, where the party which walks back on its promise has to surrender 5 *dan* of coarse grains, in accordance with the laws. 5 *dan* is a heavy punishment. The contract cites the Tangut laws as a reference. We do find in the *Laws of Heavenly Prosperity*, that:

> Let the many who engage in transactions or loans, as well as other forms of associations with other parties, out of their voluntary will, establish written records, whereupon let them note down the relevant words, concerning the price of transactions, quantity of the money, as well as the conditions ... thereafter, if any party reneges on these words, let him be punished: if he were an office-holder, let him submit the payment directly to the government; if he were a private man, let him transfer the sum privately to the other party.[265]

By this law, labour employment seems to fall into the rather broad category of "other forms of associations with other parties" for a variety of matters. Given the distinction between the public and the private, surely the man hiring another man for agricultural labour falls into the private domain. Therefore, the penalty fee would probably go into the hands of the other party, which does not renege on the agreements.

Expectedly, the contract ends with the stamps and signatures of the concerned parties. The most important, however, seem to be those of the hired labourer. The employer does not actually sign his name or stamp his symbol. In the light of the aforementioned provisions against the theft of legal records in the *Laws of Heavenly Prosperity*, it seems that these types of contracts are preserved in the hands of the employers. It could have been the case also in the Tang and Song contracts. In other words, the contracts are unilateral promises made by the labourers to their employers. There, too, the inequality is self-evident.[266]

In sum, the Tangut labour contract, the only surviving contract of labour employment dated to the 11–13th centuries, reflects the economic activity of hiring labour in the later history of Western Xia. It reveals a wide range of

265 *Revised Laws of Heavenly Prosperity* 3, "Urging the Payment of Debt and Interest," pp. 189–190.

266 Mie, Xiaohong. "Zailun Dunhuang Nongye Gugongqi zhong de Guyong Guanxi" [再論敦煌農業僱工契中的僱傭關係]: "Another Discussion on the Labour-Employer Relationship in the Employment Contracts in Agriculture found in Dunhuang" *Zhongguo Jingjishi Yanjiu* [中國經濟史研究]: *Researches in Chinese Economic History*, issue 4, 2011.

details concerning the economics of labour and employment. It is also a side, sectional, and microscopic view of the Tangut agriculture. The Tangut labour contract receives from and builds upon the Chinese contract tradition. Its further simplification of both format and content, decrease in wage and increase in labour intensity, as well as a more salient relationship of subordination, could all have been the result of socio-economic instability in the last years of the Tangut Empire.[267]

5.2 *Employment of Livestock*

Contracts of Livestock Employment constitute an important legal genre in the economic and legal history of China. Yet, few Livestock Employment contracts survive to the present day. There are a mere 6 contracts of livestock employment from the Tang and Song era. These contracts of camel, oxen, and donkey draft were found in the Cave Library in Dunhuang. Every single one of them is of tremendous historical value. So far, five Khara-Khoto contracts of livestock labour have been identified in the corpus of Khara-Khoto manuscripts. One of them, the document Инв. No. 2996-3 is the tail end of a long scroll. Three others are included within the No. 5124 scroll of contracts. Before each of the three contracts of livestock employment, there is one contract of livestock sale. In fact, the animals being rented out to perform draft labour (per livestock employment contracts) have just been purchased from the hands of impoverished peasants. Another piece is the partially damaged manuscript Инв. No. 19-2. Fortunately, the main content is preserved alright. In most contracts of livestock employment, the term for 'employing' a draft animal is 𗣹 [kwo], which sounds very much like the Chinese 僱 [kuH] (to hire, to employ). Historically, the term 'to employ,' like the verb 'to contract or rent at a fixed price,' is likely to have been a loan word from medieval Chinese. In all likelihood, employment in this sense had not been a socio-legal norm to the Tanguts prior to their reception of Han culture, hence the absence of any vocabulary that denotes it in the Tangut language. But after the migration northward, the Dangxiang people developed more complex modes and relations of production—such as contractual employment of human and animal labour—as the Tanguts were increasingly drawn to and integrated with economy of the Central Plains.

267 Shi, Jinbo. "Heishuicheng Chutu Xixiawen Gugongqi Yanjiu" [黑水城出土西夏文僱工契研究]: "A Study of Tangut Contracts of Employment Excavated in Khara-Khoto" *Zhongguo Jingjishi Yanjiu* [中國經濟史研究]: *Researches in Chinese Economic History*, issue 4, 2016.

5.2.1 Translation and Interpretation of the Contract of Livestock Employment

The format of Livestock Employment Contracts is for the most part similar to that of other contracts in the Tangut period. But unlike contracts of 'absolute sales' such as those of land or livestock sales, whereby the title of the property is transferred entirely from the seller to the buyer, the employment contract sets the terms of a lease for a given period of time. For this reason, the legal language in the narratives of time, penalty fees, and other requirements are usually much more simplified. The following are the translations of 5 pieces of Tangut Contracts of Livestock Employment written in the Tangut script, arranged in chronological order.

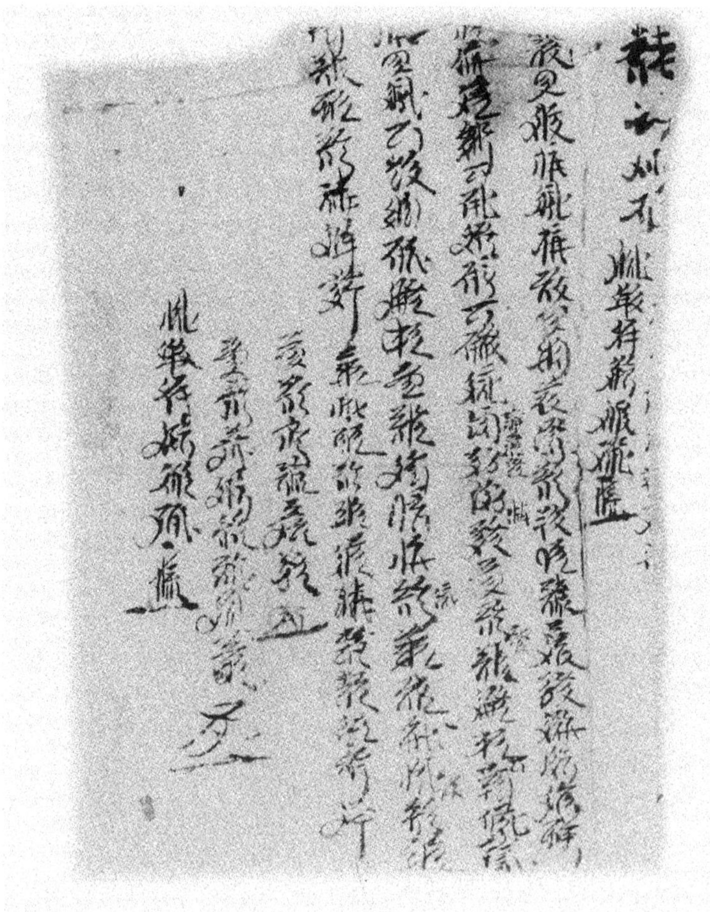

FIGURE 189 Инв. No. 2996-3: Contract of livestock employment for 18 years

1. The manuscript Инв. No. 2996-3 (Eighteenth Year) Contract of Livestock Employment features 8 lines of Tangut cursive handwritten on an 18.7 × 13.4 hemp paper fragment once used as a layering page to a sutra. There are damages on both the upper and lower sections. About 2–3 characters are missing in each line of the upper section. It may be surmised that the contract comes after a few others. The first line of this fragment, with its witness signatures and stamps, seems to be the last of the previous contract. The present document begins only with the second line. It dates the contract to "… eighteenth year, the 28th day of the 2nd month." There are only two 'eighteenth years' in the Tangut chronology: Tiansheng and Qianyou. Therefore, this contract could only have been signed in either the bing-xu 18th year of Tiansheng (1166) or the ding-wei 18th year of Qianyou (1187). Some, if not all of the missing words in the upper section could be inferred from the formulaic language of the law. As usual, the contract ends with stamps and signatures.[268]

Translation:

□□year 18, month 2, day 28, Yehe 'Bore the prosperous' now from Tongpan
?? 'of puppy' voluntarily hires a female mule & ox; labour price: 1 *dan* 5 *dou*.
By 1st day of 8th month, let both livestocks and fees be returned. If overdue,
each *dan* doubles. Hearts willing. Default penalty in wheat, according to the law. Willing.
Contract Party: Bore the prosperous ([illegible]) (stamp)
Co-Contract Party: son ? the prosperous iron-head ([illegible]) (stamp)
Witness: Liang 'the Kind Dog of the Xu Year' ([illegible]) (print)

268 *Russian Collection of Khara-Khoto Manuscripts*, vol. 13, p. 162.

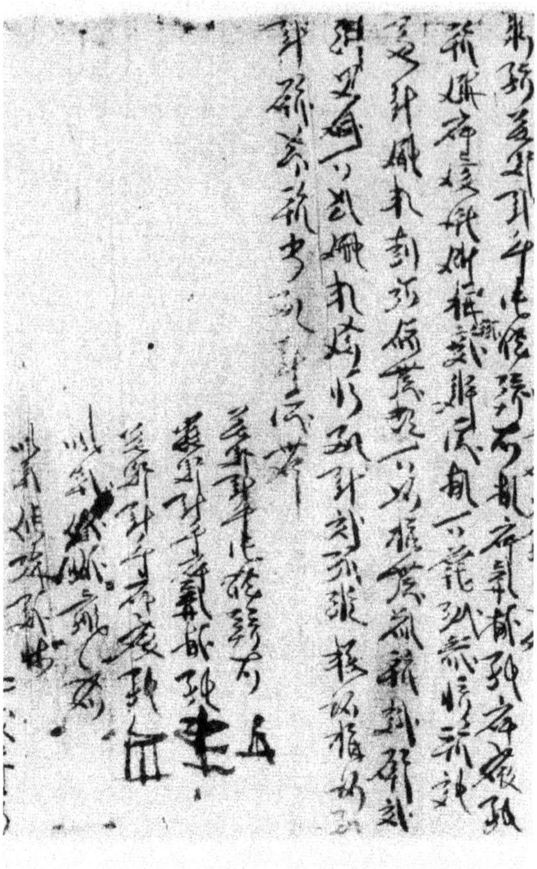

FIGURE 190
Инв. No. 5124-3(6): Yin year of Tianqing (1194) contract of livestock employment

2. The text Инв. No. 5124-3(6): Yin Year of Tianqing (1194) is included in a long scroll of contracts, three of which are records of livestock employment. It features 10 lines of Tangut in the cursive script, as well as signatures and stamps at the end.[269]

Translation:

> On the same day, [Tangut] [dzji. rjir dźjiwu dju] and Liang "The Prosperous Iron"
> Et al., presently have [Tangut] [ljow lja mja]'s 2 cattles and 1 full-teethed black ox
> Employed; labour price: 3 *dan* 5 *dou* wheat + 1 *dan* 2 *dou* coarse grains, agreed.

269 *Russian Collection of Khara-Khoto Manuscripts*, vol. 14, p. 17.

By the 1st day of the 8th month, the fee is to be paid; overdue payment doubles.
The livestock is also to be returned. Willing.
Contract Party: [illegible] [dzji. rjir dźjiwu dju] (stamp)
Contract Party: [illegible] [ljow zjo. dźjo wejr] (stamp)
Contract Party: [illegible] [ljow śjow wejr] (stamp)
Witness: [illegible] [ŋwe mji wa wa dju] (stamp)
Witness: [illegible] [phjij śjo wa śia~] (stamp)

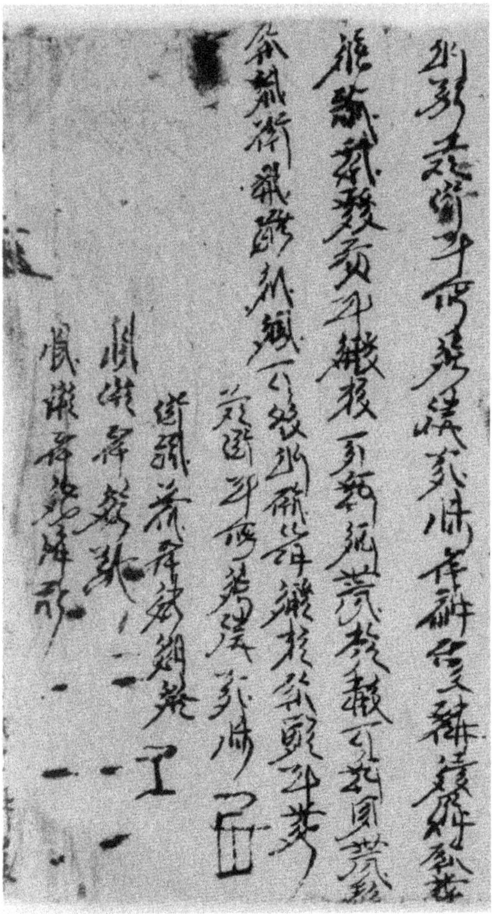

FIGURE 191
Инв. No. 5124-4(4): Yin year of Tianqing (1194) contract of livestock employment

3. The Инв. No. 5124-4(4) Yin Year of Tianqing (1194) Contract of Livestock Employment is the second record of livestock labour in the long scroll of contracts. It features 7 lines of Tangut in the cursive. The text begins with the reference to "the same day"—that is, the same day as the previous contract (a

contract of livestock sale), signed on the third day of the second month in the Yin Year of Heavenly Celebration.[270]

Translation:

> On the same day, the maker of the contract [illegible] [phjij śjo wa śia~], from [illegible] [ljow dow dźjij phu_], [illegible] [ljow lja mja] et al.,
> Hires a mare, at the labour price of 1 *dan* 4 *dou* of wheat and 1 *dan* 8 *dou* of coarse grains,
> Terms are agreed upon. By the due date: 1st day of the 9th month, the livestock is to be returned, and the fee to be paid. Willing.
> Contract Party: [illegible] [phjij śjo wa śia~]
> Co-Contract Party: [illegible] [ljow lji-. we mja]
> Witness: [illegible] [ljow ne_w wejr]
> Witness: [illegible] [ljow da kia ·jiw]

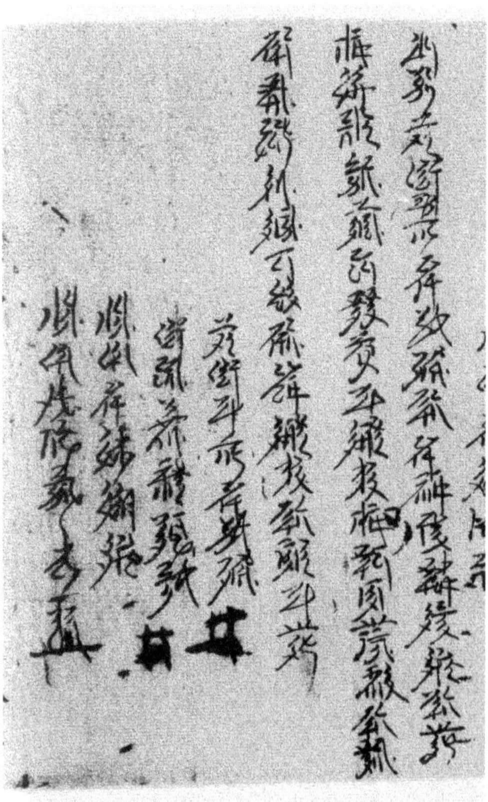

FIGURE 192
Инв. No. 5124-4(5): Yin year of Tianqing (1194) contract of livestock employment

270 *Russian Collection of Khara-Khoto Manuscripts*, vol. 14, p. 20.

4. The Инв. No. 5124-4(5) Yin Year of Tianqing (1194) Contract of Livestock Employment is the third record of animal labour in the scroll of contracts. The text is comprised of 8 lines in cursive Tangut. It, too, begins with the indication of "the same day." In this case, both the two contracts that come immediately before defer to the previous contracts. The next contract further back, a Contract of Livestock Sale, is recorded on the third day of the second month in the Yin Year of Heavenly Celebration. This is, presumably, an accurate dating of the contract with which we are principally concerned in the translation below.[271]

Translation:

> On the same day, the maker of the contract Liang [illegible] [khjwi- wejr] et al., from [illegible] [ljow dow dźjij phu_], [illegible] [lja mja] et al.,
> Hires 1 two-teethed male camel, at the labour price of 1 *dan* 8 *dou* of coarse grains.
> It is agreed upon that by the 1st day of the 9th month, the livestocks and the fee are to be returned and repaid. Willing.
> Contract Party: [illegible] [ljow khjwi- wejr] 'the prosperous dog'
> Co-Contract Party: son, [illegible] [phə zji] 'the Qiangic'
> Witness: [illegible] [ljow lji-. we mja] 'the mother donkey'
> Witness: [illegible] [dzji. rjir wa wa tsji-]

Neither of the three Contracts of Livestock Employment above indicates time in precise terms. All defer to previous contracts by the legal expression "on the same day." The nearest contract accurately dated is the first Contract of Livestock Sale, signed on the 29th Day of 1st Month, in Yin Year of Heavenly Celebration (Tianqing). The second and third contracts are both dated to the 3rd day of the 2nd month, in the same year.

271 *Russian Collection of Khara-Khoto Manuscripts*, vol. 14, p. 20.

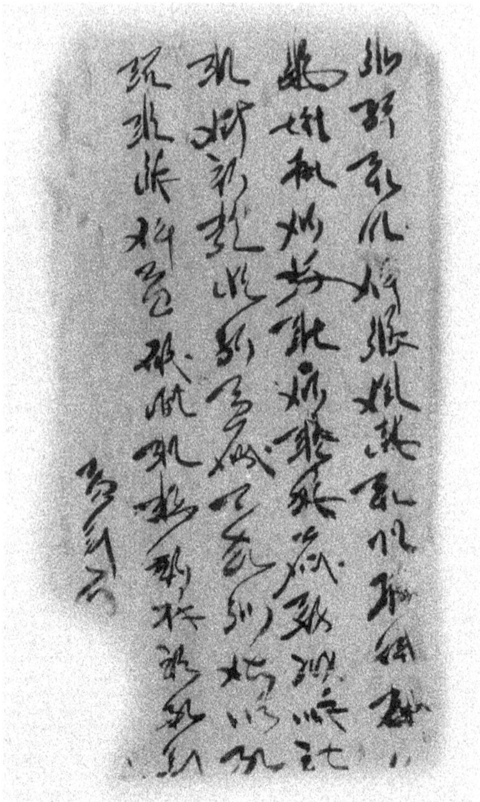

FIGURE 193
Инв. No. 19-2: Contract of livestock employment

5. Инв. No. 19-2: Contract of Livestock Employment is a manuscript fragment with 5 lines of Tangut cursive handwritten on a 24.2 × 13 cm hemp paper, and damages in the lower sections and the back. A few cursive characters remain unidentifiable.[272]

Translation:

> On the same day, Yehe 'the joyful at heart' presently from [illegible] [·jaxwa]??, a female cam[
> el] and a four vertical[-teethed] four male?? Voluntarily … hire
> price: 6 *dan* of wheat, to be gathered by the 1st day of the 7th month in the same year. The day
> passed, first the hiring fee is to be paid, for each 1 *dan*, let 2 *dan* be repaid. Hirer …

272 *Russian Collection of Khara-Khoto Manuscripts* 12, p. 1.

5.2.2 The Relationship between Livestock Employment Contracts and Livestock Sale Contracts

The long scroll Инв. No. 5124 shows that those who hire animals to perform draft labour in the Contracts of Livestock Employment have in most cases sold their own livestocks. They do so not because they have no need for their service, but to obtain more foodstuff in the short run. Once they are no longer starving, they return to the field, short of animal labour, reduced to the position of hiring animal labour to make up for what they have sold out of urgency and necessity. Surely the peasants might have managed to survive. But there is little doubt that from selling to hiring, they incurred tremendous economic losses that are extremely difficult to recover. They have given up ownership rights to the draft animals—much-valued resources in the agrarian economy.

Take Liang in the Инв. No. 5124-4(4) Contract of Livestock Sale as an example. Immediately after selling his camel and horse in exchange for 2 *dan* of wheat and 3 *dan* of coarse grains (roughly 5.6 *dan* of coarse grains altogether), he hired a two-teethed camel from the Pudu Temple at the price of 1 *dan* 8 *dou* of coarse grains. The camel is to be returned, and the fee paid in full by the first day of the ninth month of the year. Clearly, Liang is in need of livestocks. But in between two harvests, short of grains, he has no recourse but to sell his animals to the Pudu Temple, before proceeding to hire another one. Liang lost his two large-sized livestocks. Once the hiring fee is deducted, Liang only receives 3.8 *dan* of coarse grains for the horse and camel—that is, on average, a low price of no more than 2 *dan* of coarse grains per animal. A huge loss in incurred in this "selling-and-hiring" process. A similar situation is found in the Инв. No. 5124-4(5) Land Sale Contract. [illegible] [phjij śjo] sells his two-teethed male camel to the same Pudu Temple in exchange for 2 *dan* of barley and 1 *dan* of millet (3 *dan* of coarse grains, in total). Immediately after, he borrows a mare from the Pudu Temple at the price of 1 *dan* 4 *dou* of wheat and 1 *dan* 8 *dou* of coarse grains (altogether roughly 3.7 *dan* of coarse grains). After the autumn harvest, [illegible] is expected to return the animals along with the fee. But already upon signing the contract, he loses ownership over his own camel. Curiously, it appears that the mare [illegible] [phjij śjo] loans from the Temple is one of the livestocks that Liang had sold to the Temple. And it seems to be the case that the camel Liang ends up borrowing is the one that the Temple purchased from [illegible] [phjij śjo]. Likewise, the 3 cattles hired out by [illegible] [dzji. rjir] and Liang were the exact 3 animals that Weiyi 'the treasure of fortune' had sold to the Pudu Temple on the same day.

The following chart compiles the data on sell and purchase price and employment fee in the 5 Contracts of Livestock Employment and the Contracts of Livestock Sale. Note that where there are more than one kind of grains, I have recalculated the amount in the unit of coarse grains, in order to make it easier to compare. (all the register numbers begin with Инв. No.).

CHART 25 Price of livestock sale and employment

Register	Time	Hirer	Livestock owner	Livestock hired	Hiring fee	Fee in coarse grains	Sell and purchase price	Price in coarse grains
2996-3	Day 28, Month 2, Year 18	[illegible] [·jaxwa parya wejr]	[illegible] ?? [illegible] [thow pha~ ?? kə ta] Tongpan ?? 'the puppy'	1 mare, 1 usable cattle	1 *dan* 5 *dou*			
5124-3 (6)	Same Day (Year Yin of Tianqing 29th day of 1st month (1194)	[illegible] [dzji. rjir dźjiwu dju] & Liang "The Prosperous Iron"	[illegible] [ljow lja mja]	Live & usable cattle + 1 full-teethed black ox	3 *dan* 5 *dou* wheat+ 1 *dan* 2 *dou* coarse grains	≈ 6 *dan*	5 *dan* wheat + 2 *dan* coarse grains	8.7 *dan*
5124-4 (4)	Day 3, Month 2, Year Yin of Tianqing (1194)	[illegible] [phjij śjo wa śia~]	[illegible] [ljow dow dźjij phu_], [illegible] [lja mja], et al.	1 mare	1 *dan* 4 *dou* of wheat+ 1 *dan* 8 *dou* of coarse grains	≈ 3.7 *dan*	1 camel + 1 horse sold for 2 *dan* of wheat + 3 *dan* of coarse grains	≈ 5.7 *dan*
5124-4 (5)	Same Day: Day 3, Month 2 of Tianqing (1194)	[illegible] [ljow wejr khjwi-]	[illegible] [ljow dow dźjij phu_], [illegible] [lja mja]	Two-teethed male camel	1 *dan* 8 *dou* of coarse grains	1.8 *dan*	2 *dan* of barley + 1 *dan* of millet	3 *dan*
19-2	Same Day (illegible)	[illegible] [·jaxwa nji_j lji-.j wejr]	[illegible] [·jaxwa] ??	Female Camel + four-vertical[-teethed] 4 male??	6 *dan* of wheat	≈ 8.5 *dan* of coarse grains		

It is not difficult to tell from the three Инв. No. 5124 Livestock Employment Contracts that the cost of hiring animals from spring up to the harvest season in the autumn is more than half of the money earned by selling the livestocks. In other words, the Pudu Temple earns back the cost of purchase within a mere span of two years. Clearly, the monastic establishment there exploited the need of starving peasants suffering the shortage of grain supplies, acquires livestocks en masse at low prices, and loan them back to the peasants deprived of their animals. The temple is able to achieve profit-maximisation in this 'purchase-and-loan' strategy. In two rounds, either two years or even within a year, the temple is able to recover the investments and start making profits, as if they gained the livestocks for free. Therefore, a comparative and connective reading of Livestock Sale contracts, on the one hand, and Livestock Employment contracts, on the other, reveals the behind-the-scenes financial manipulations of the temples. It also shows that the Pudu Temple, one of the Buddhist temples in the Khara-Khoto area, is deeply engaged in and intertwined with the local economy. It becomes a major owner of land and livestocks, constantly merging, acquiring, expanding, and driving already impoverished peasants onto the path of no return, to bankruptcy and deprivation.

6 Exchange and Mortgage Contracts

Contracts of exchange are rare in the history of social and legal documents. Some of the Khara-Khoto contracts of exchange are single pages. Others are treated as scratch papers, and bound into a book to transcribe Buddhist sutras on their back. On the other hand, contract of grain loans on livestock mortgage are found either in the single-page format, or in scrolls of papers that feature multiple contracts on the same pages. Both types of contracts are fairly complicated in terms of legal arrangements and social relationships.

6.1 *Exchange Contracts*

A class of Tangut contracts is applied in a particular type of transaction: the exchange of livestocks between two parties. The difference in price is compensated for by the transfer of additional grains. There are specialised legal vocabularies in contracts of exchange. In the manuscript Инв. No. 4195, for instance, the verb used to denote the nature of the transaction is [illegible] [ɣwej] (to exchange), and the term, 'to make up for the price difference' is either [illegible] [lhu] (to add) or [illegible] [khjow] (to pay). Stil, other contracts refer to the action of an owner toward their own livestock as either [illegible] [źji.] (to sell) or [illegible] [lwə] (to purchase), but it is important to take note that in this particular legal context, they are meant to convey the sense of 'exchange,' as well. The force of 'sell and purchase' is there, only because one party, whose livestock is in a worse condition, is paying another, who owns a superior animal, to cover the price difference. So, their identities as the 'buyer' and the 'seller' are legal fictions. Surely, there is no reason for why these Contracts of Livestock Exchange cannot be classified as 'Contracts of Livestock Sale.' But they are also clearly much more complicated than simple sell and purchase contracts. Below are the translations of three contracts of livestock exchange with better surviving records of the terms and prices of the exchanges.

6.1.1 Translation and Interpretation of Livestock Exchange Contract

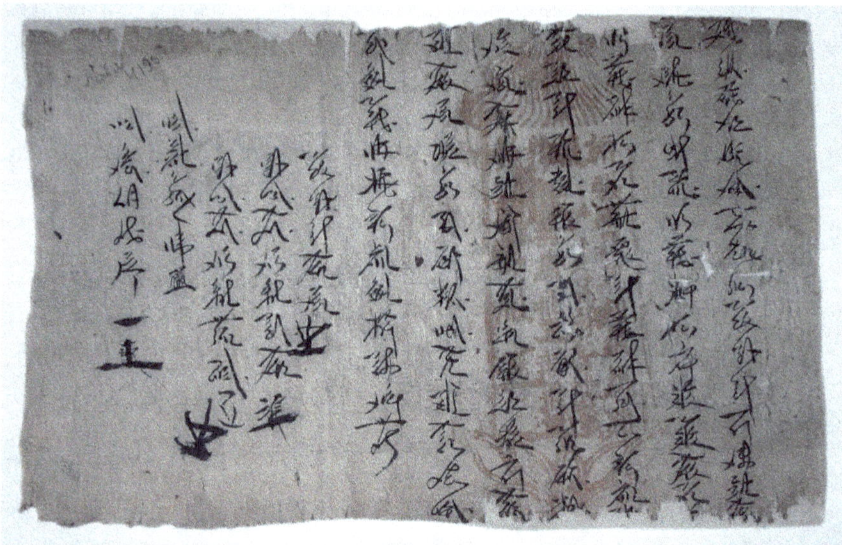

FIGURE 194 Инв. No. 4195: Wu year of Tianqing (1198) contract of livestock exchange

1. Manuscript Инв. No. 4195: Wu Year of Heavenly Celebration (1198 AD) Contract of Livestock Exchange is a single-page contract handwritten on a 23 × 37.6 cm hemp paper, with 12 lines of Tangut in the cursive style. The stamping features a lotus imagery, as well as the official 22 × 7 cm red seal of the Tangut House of Transactions.[273]

Translation:

> On the 10th day of the 1st month, Wu Year of Heavenly Celebration, Contract Party [illegible] [mə zji śjow]

273 *Russian Collection of Khara-Khoto Manuscripts*, vol. 13, p. 195.

[Tangut] [bie_j], has his one full-teethed coloured cow, with [Tangut]? [ljow tśju. ·wejr śjow ?]
's full-teethed white cow exchanged. To the white cow is added 1 *dan* of coarse
grains. The livestocks and grains are delivered, with no debt incurred. If the livestock & grains
are disputed publically or privately by those in the same *chao* or others,
at that time, 'the joyful iron' is liable. If the direct parties renege on the promise or lie,
the penalty is 2 *dan* of coarse grains. The hearts are willing.

Contract Party: [Tangut] [śjow bie_j], the joyful iron (stamp)
Co-Contract Party: son, [Tangut] [lji.j śjow], 'the prosperous iron' (stamp)
Co-Contract Party: son, [Tangut] [śja phji] 'the shining way' (stamp)
Witness: [Tangut] [gu_ wa wa śia~] Wu 'the hidden mount' (stamp)
Witness: [Tangut] [zjwi. khjij da kia] Yiqi 'the old house' (print)

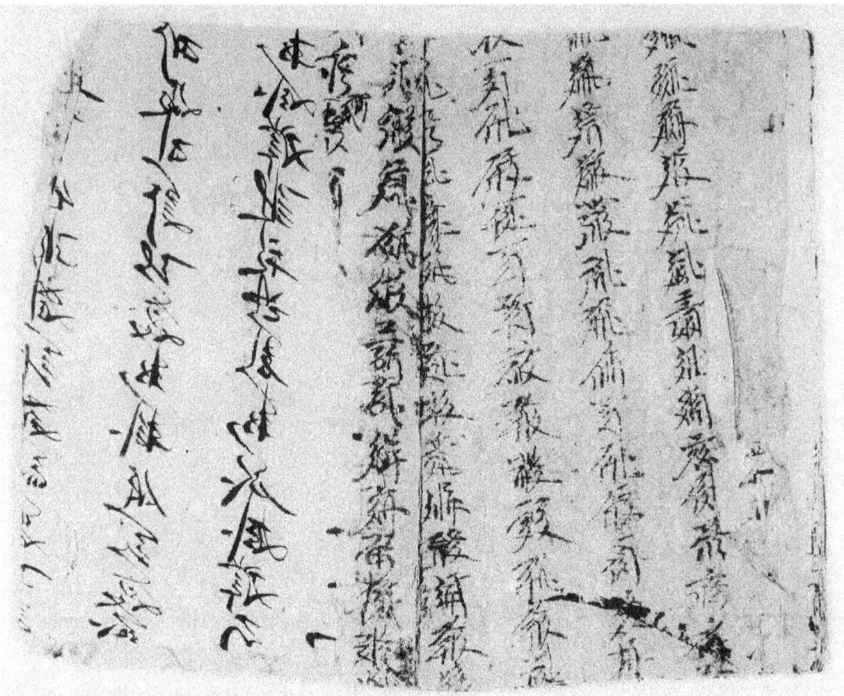

FIGURE 195 Инв. No. 2851-1: Hai year of Tianqing (1203) contract of livestock exchange

2. Инв. No. 2851-1 Hai Year of Tianqing (1203) Contract of Livestock Exchange is a piece of contract found in a volume of books that has been bound by

discarded contracts. On the back of the pages are scripts of Buddhist sutras. 5 lines of Tangut in the running script are handwritten on a 19.8 × 25.7 cm hemp paper, with damages near the end.[274]

Translation:

> Hai Year of Tianqing 19th day of the 1st month, Contract Party Liang ...
> ? presently purchased from Luwo Xianling's 1 horse, 1 mule ...
> Price: to the maroon horse is added 1 *dan* of coarse grains—paid; re: the livestocks et al. (no) debt incurred
> ... and all the concerned parties' affiliates in the same *chao*, dispute (if there is) ...
> ?? is liable. If hereafter any party reneges on the terms, the regretting party is to the not-
> regretting one (pay) 3 *dan* ...

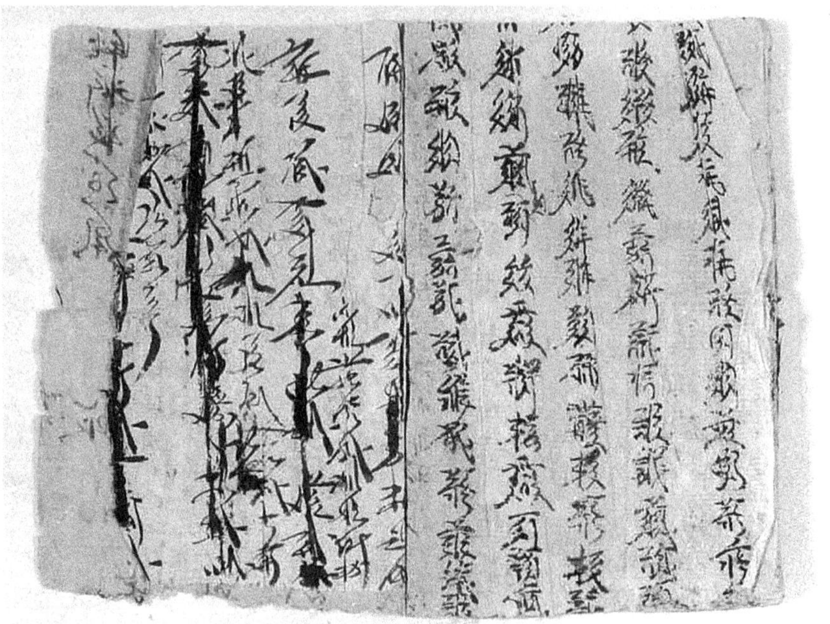

FIGURE 196 Инв. No. 2851-33: Hai year of Tianqing (1203) contract of livestock exchange

3. The manuscript Инв. No. 2851-33 Hai Year of Tianqing (1203) Contract of Livestock Exchange is included in the same volume, handwritten on a 19.8 × 25.7

274 *Russian Collection of Khara-Khoto Manuscripts*, vol. 13, p. 119.

hemp paper with 5 lines of cursive Tangut, with damages near the end. To the left is another official document.[275]

Translation:

> Hai Year of Tianqing, on the 18th day of the 2nd month, the Contract Party?
> ? [illegible] [pie. mja][276] et al., presently have their own full-teethed black male camel
> Voluntarily sold to [illegible] [·jiw dji.j nji_j lji-.j ɣwie]; price: 1 full-
> Teethed male donkey, plus 1 *tuo*[277] of coloured coarse cloth, 1 *dan* 5
> *dou* of coarse grains. One the same day no debt is incurred; if the camel
> …

FIGURE 197 Инв. No. 5120-2: Zi year of Tianqing (1204) contract of livestock exchange

4. The Инв. No. 5120-2 Zi Year of Heavenly Celebration (1204) Contract of Livestock Exchange is a single-page contract of 14 lines of cursive Tangut scribed on a 24.3 × 39.3 cm hemp paper. The first line dates the contract to

275 *Russian Collection of Khara-Khoto Manuscripts*, vol. 13, p. 135.

276 TN: lit. "a female frog."

277 TN: Possibly a Tangut equivalent of the Chinese measure unit 庹: the length of the distance between two arms stretched out.

"24th day of the 2nd month, in the Zi Year of Tianqing" (1204). The document also features stamps and signatures.[278]

Translation:

> On the 24th day of the 2nd Month in the Zi Year of Heavenly Celebration, Contract Party Mingbu
> 'the prosperous donkey' et al., have their own one-toothed horse, with [Tangut] [lwər ze] '? kind iron'
> 's own camel exchanged, on top of which is added?
> 'the kind iron' has to keep; obtain 5 *dan* of coarse grains. Re: the horse, if the many
> In the same *chao* dispute over it, and if any party diverges in their wishes,
> and regret over the terms, the penalty is 10 *dan* of wheat according to law. Hearts willing.
> The terms in actual circumstances are enforced according to the document.
> Contract Party: Mingbu 'the prosperous donkey' ([Tangut])
> Co-Contract Party: Mingbu 'the greatly prosperous elder' ([Tangut])
> Co-Contract Party: Mingbu '?? dog' ([Tangut] ??[Tangut])
> Witness: Xiaoti 'E of the Tenth Month' ([Tangut])
> Witness: Xiaoti 'E of Longevity' ([Tangut])
> Witness: Hun 'the Lucky Treasure' ([Tangut])
> Witness: Yehe 'the Joyful Treasure' ([Tangut])

Of the four Contracts of Livestock Exchange presented above, the first is the most complete, and legible. The second and third both suffer the loss of information near the end. The fourth piece is relatively well-preserved, despite missing or blurry characters here and there in the middle.

6.1.2 Analysis of the Contracts of Livestock Exchange

Compared to simple contracts of livestock sales, these Contracts of Livestock Exchange differ most crucially in the two parties' voluntary conveyance of titles of livestock properties in their respective domains to each other, resorting to grains to make up for any difference in price and qualities. Therefore, the key points here are the reasons for the exchange at all, and the rate at which grains are transacted to cover price differences.

278 *Russian Collection of Khara-Khoto Manuscripts*, vol. 14, p. 8.

In the first transaction—the Contract of Livestock Exchange Инв. No. 4195—Moyi offers his own full-teethed coloured cow in exchange for Liang's full-teethed white cow. An additional *dan* of coarse grains is added to the white cow's end. Although both cows have fully grown their teeth, they are of evidently different prices. The white cow is inferior by 1 *dan* of coarse grains. But why this consensus on the superiority of the coloured cow to its fellow white bovine? It has been discussed before that large-sized Tangut livestocks are not to be slaughtered at will. Only after dying a natural or otherwise necessary death would the cattles offer their meat to human diet. Therefore, the most likely scenario is that one party initiates the exchange in order to enhance the efficiency of his animal labour. The other side of the negotiation table—the party with the stronger cattle—might have had ample draught labour, but intended to hoard up their grains. They did not simply sell their excellent animal, because they still needed some, if not that much, draft labour. But they are perfectly content with an inferior animal, if only the exchange comes with additional foodstuff. Considering then that these contracts are signed in the interim season between the spring and the autumn, the primary incentive to initiate the exchange could be as simple as the lack of food for daily consumption. As a genre of legal writing, therefore, livestock exchange contracts reflect the historical developments of voluntary economic modulations in the private sphere of the economy. The involved parties obtain what they needed and complemented each other's economic activities. Of course, no transaction is free from defects and inequalities.

It should also be noted that the exchange could only take place in the civil sphere and the private market. That is, only privately-owned animals can be exchanged with other animals in private possession. No personal properties can be used to exchange for government-owned livestocks. The *Laws of Heavenly Prosperity* is strict in this restriction:

> The many are prohibited from exchanging superior and inferior livestocks under government ownership. If such exchange takes place against the law, the price at the time of the exchange is to be calculated. If the values of the livestocks exchanged are equal, let the names be recorded, and those implicated in the exchange be sentenced to one year of imprisonment. If the prices of the livestock are unequal, then let the price difference be recorded, let the charge and sentence be exactly one level below theft. If there is bribery involved, compare it to the charge of corruption, and let whichever is more severe be applied to the criminals. If there is room for discussion, let the sentence be communicated to one level

> below the original charge. Let the original livestocks be returned to their previous possessions.[279]

It is worth noting that not only the exchange of government-owned livestocks is punished severely, up to a year of imprisonment, the sentence is even graver if there is a price difference between the livestocks exchanged. For more intuitive comparisons, see the chart below for the data in the three Contracts of Livestock Exchange.

Compared to sell and purchase, the exchange of livestocks is an economic activity that took place with less frequency, and certainly much more rarely documented in contracts, as well. Thus far, only two contracts of livestock exchange have been identified prior to this period. One was unearthed in Tomb No. 39 in the Astana Cemetery. The manuscript, dated to the 11th year of Shengping era in the Former Liang Dynasty (367 AD), records the camel sale by a certain Wang Nian in the Kingdom of Gaochang. In fact, it is a Contract of Livestock Exchange. The text reads:

> On Day 15 of the 4th month, 11th year of Shengping, Wang Nian offers his camel
> to Zhu Yue, and receives in return a camel; no added exchange: simply left to
> right & right to left. If any of the owners regrets, the penalty is 10 fur carpets
> to be offered. Man present at the time: Bo Xianfeng; scriber: Li Daobo; total …
> (lost)[280]

The two concerned parties exchange their camels, with no scheme of compensation to cover the price difference. This is a contract about 670 years earlier than the Khara-Khoto documents. The other surviving piece of livestock exchange contract is the aforementioned contract found in the Dunhuang cave library, concerning an ox-donkey exchange by a monk at the Bao'en Temple.

---

279 *Revised Laws of Heavenly Prosperity* 19, "On the exchange of government-owned or private livestocks," p. 584.

280 Zhang, Chuanxi, 2014, p. 88.

CHART 26 Data in livestock exchange contracts

Order	Register	Time	Party initiating the exchange	Party to exchange with	Livestock exchanged	Price in exchange	Compensation
1	4195	Wu year of Tianqing (1198)	[illegible] [mə zji śjow bie_j]	[illegible] [ljow tśju. ·wejr śjow wa]	1 full-teethed coloured cow	1 full-teethed white cow + 1 *dan* of coarse grains	2 *dan* of coarse grains
2	2851-1	Day 19, month 1, Hai Year of Tianqing (1203)	[illegible] [ljow] ... Liang ...	[illegible] [lu. gjwi-r ljo phji]	1 horse, 1 mule ...	1 maroon horse + 1 *dan* of coarse grains	3 *dan*
3	2851-33	Day 18, Month 2, Hai Year of Tianqing (1203)	?? [illegible] [pie. mja]	[illegible] [·jiw dji.j nji_j lji-.j ɣwie]	Full-teethed black male camel, one	1 Full-teethed male donkey; coloured coarse cloth 1 *tuo*; 1 *dan* 5 *dou* of coarse grains	
4	5120-2	Day 24, Month 2, Zi year of Tianqing (1204)	[illegible] [mjij pu. lji-. wejr]	[illegible]?[illegible] [lwər ze ? śjow]	One-teethed horse	1 camel; 5 *dan* of coarse grains	10 *dan* of wheat

One Yellow bullock, eight years of age (no seal of purchase□) (missing words)
On Day 18, first month of the Yin Year, Bao'en Temple's tenured master, with no ox to use,
□presently offers a 'green-grass' donkey, seven years of age, and 1 *pi* of fine cloth, in
Exchange□□□inn□□(bullock). The cattle, the donkey, and the cloth, etc.
… (missing end)[281]

In this case, a 7-year-old donkey feeding on green pasture is exchanged for a bullock. The price difference is compensated for by the additional offering of fine cloth. This contract predates the Tangut contracts of livestock exchange by about 370 years.

Thus far, the two documents above are the only livestock exchange contracts that came before the Tanguts. This legal genre is altogether rarely found in the seven or eight hundred years after Western Xia. The fact that up to four Contracts of Livestock Exchange have survived from the Tangut era is most extraordinary.

Obviously, all the 6 contracts of livestock exchange, across 3 different historical periods, have their origins in northwestern China. It seems that there was a long-living tradition of livestock exchange in this area, where pasturing and animal-husbandry has been a major pillar of the economy.

6.2 *Mortgage of Livestock in Grain Loans*

The Khara-Khoto contracts show that some peasants developed the practice of depositing their livestocks as mortgage in order to obtain grain loans. It is a much more complicated legal process than in a simple grain loan contract. Most of these contracts stipulate that the titles of the animals be conveyed to the creditors if the debtor fails to fulfil his financial and legal obligations—the timely repayment of both the principle and the interests—after the autumn harvest. At least 8 pieces of such Contracts of Grain Loan on Livestock Mortgage have been identified in the corpus of Khara-Khoto manuscripts. These legal documents can be further classified in the following ways. Below are the selective translations of these Contracts of Grain Loan on Livestock Mortgage.

281 *Dunhuang Economic Documents*, p. 35; Zhang, Chuanxi, 2014, p. 207; Chinese Academy of Social Sciences-Institute for History & British Library (eds.). *British Collection of Dunhuang Manuscripts*. Chengdu: Sichuan People's Press, 1995, vol. 10, p. 208.

6.2.1 Tangut Contracts of Grain Loan on Livestock Mortgage: Translation and Interpretation

Examples of livestock mortgage contracts include: Инв. No. 2996-1, Инв. No. 4079-1, Инв. No. 4079-2, Инв. No. 4079-3.

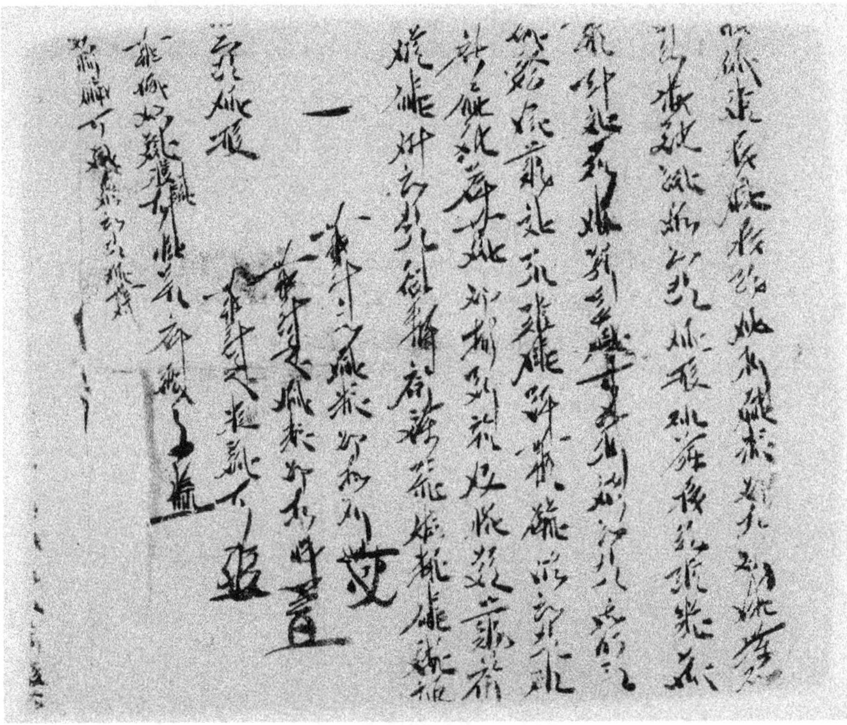

FIGURE 198 Инв. No. 2996-1: Wei year of Tiansheng, contract of grain loan on livestock mortgage

1. The Инв. No. 2996-1 Contract of Grain Loan on Livestock Mortgage in the Year of Wei is a single-page contract handwritten on a 19 × 23.5 cm hemp paper that was used as the layering cover of another text. There are 11 lins of Tangut in the cursive script, with some damages on the upper side. Stamps and signatures are found at the end of the contract. What remains of the first line dates the contract to approximately the "… Wei year, twelfth month, twenty-ninth day." The first character that remains somewhat legible, probably the second character of the era title, survives in half, is likely to be 𗖵 [lji.j] (prosperous). If so, then the era title is in all likelihood 𗼃𗖵 [ŋwər lji.j] (heavenly prosperity). There are, however, two years of Wei within the Tangut era of Heavenly

Prosperity: the Third year Xin-wei of Heavenly Prosperity (1151 AD) and the Fifteenth year Gui-wei of Heavenly Prosperity (1163 AD).[282]

Translation:

Heavenly Prosperity-Wei Year-Month 2, Day 29, [illegible] [lwər ze gju_ rjur ɣwie] (Lüyi now from?

? "the puppy" borrows 4 *dan* of wheat (principle), impawns a two-teethed male camel

By the 1st day of the 7th month in the same year, to assemble and repay 6 *dan* of wheat

? ? overdue, the impawned livestock would cover 6 *dan* of wheat;

? ? 'the lucky force' et all agreed. If reneges

When the penalty fee according to law is 6 *dan* of wheat; enforced according to the circumstances and the legal document.

Borrower: [illegible] [lwər ze gju_ rjur ɣwie]

Borrower: [illegible] [lwər ze gju_ rjur śia~]

Borrower: [illegible] ? [pu. ? dju]

Witness: [illegible] [ljow ...]

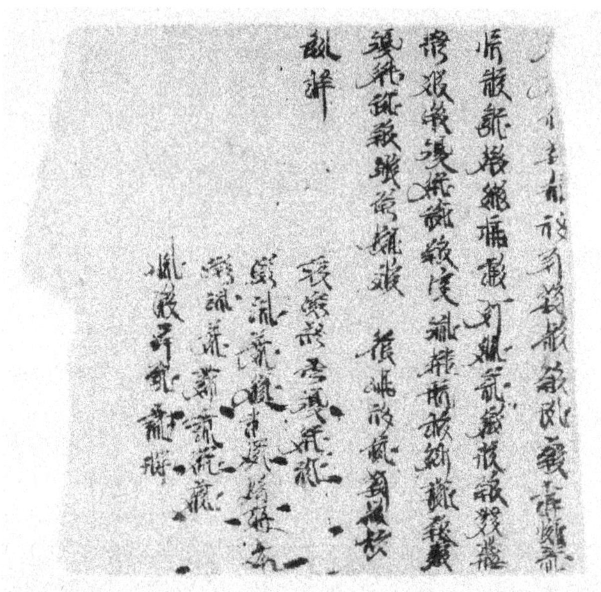

FIGURE 199 Инв. No. 4079-1: Contract of grain loan on livestock mortgage

282 *Russian Collection of Khara-Khoto Manuscripts*, vol. 13, p. 161.

2. The Инв. No. 4079-1: Contract of Grain Loan on Livestock Mortgage is a manuscript of 9 lines of cursive Tangut written on a 21.8 × 22 cm hemp paper, partially damaged at the front. Both the time and the initial indication of the Contract Parties' names are lost. But the signatures at the end have survived. The stamps are done by finger-marks.[283]

Translation:

…
?? 5 *dan* of wheat, 11 *dan* of coarse grains, loaned; whilst full-teethed
Male & female camels 2, and 1 ?-teethed cow are impawned,
Through Intermediaries Jia Laohei et al.; if looted by enemies,
Jia Laohei et al. are liable. For default, the penalty according to law is 15 *dan* of coarse grains
Contract Party: Jia "the old dark one" ([illegible])
Co-Contract Party: Weiyi "iron joyful at heart" ([illegible])
Co-Contract Party: Shijun 'father dog' ([illegible])
Witness: Liang "deer? of Chen-wu" ([illegible])

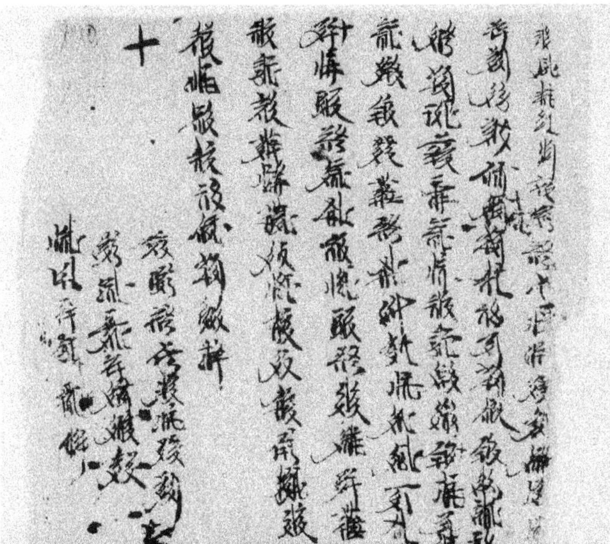

FIGURE 200 Инв. No. 4079-2: Contract of grain loan by pawning livestock

283 *Russian Collection of Khara-Khoto Manuscripts*, vol. 13, p. 181.

3. Инв. No. 4079-2 Contract of Grain Loan on Livestock Mortgage is a single-page contract with 10 lines of Tangut in the cursive handwritten on a 22 × 23 cm hemp paper. The first line gives away the time as the "third day of the last month." The end of document features signatures and stamps.[284]

Translation:

> On the 3rd day of the 12th month, Contract Party [illegible] [pu. kə ta ɣwie] first from??
> From [illegible] [ljow ɣwie rjijr lji-.] borrowed 5 *dan* of wheat, 11 *dan* of coarse grains
> In total 16 *dan*; 2 full-teethed camel, male & female, 1?
> Teethed female camel on mortgage. Due date set on the 1st day of the 9th month
> To be repaid. If the payment is overdue, first the impawned
> Camels would be seized, with no complaint. In case of dispute or default,
> The penalty is coarse grains and wheat in 15 *dan*, according to the law.
> Contract Party: [illegible] [pu. kə ta ɣwie]
> Co-Contract Party: Liang Huihuni
> Witness: Liang? Chenwu

FIGURE 201 Инв. No. 4079-3: Contract of grain loan by pawning livestock

284 Ibid., p. 182.

4. The document Инв. No. 4079-3: Contract of Grain Loan on Livestock Mortgage is a roll of serial contracts. Three texts remain legible, where 15 lines of Tangut cursive are handwritten on a 22 × 23 cm hemp paper, followed by signatures and finger-stamps.[285]

The first document suffers some damage at the beginning, but the second and third are basically intact. The following is a translation of the second contract.

Translation:

> On the same day, [Tangut] [mə dzow gju_ dzjwo] (Mozang "the lucky man") borrows 1 *dan* of wheat; the principle is increased to 1 *dan*
> 5 *dou*, on the mortgage of 1 roll of fur carpet, 1 sheep. By the date agreed upon,
> before August, the sum must be repaid. In case of overdue payment, first to cover the debt
> The [mortage] is seized. There is no disagreement.
> Borrower: [Tangut] [mə dzow gju_ dzjwo]
> Witness: [Tangut] [pha~ gia mji-_ ɣwie]

Here, the mortgage is comprised of not only animals but also a roll of fur carpet.

FIGURE 202 Инв. No. 4079-4: Contract of grain loan on livestock mortgage

285 Ibid., p. 182.

5. The document Инв. No. 4079-4: Contract of Grain Loan on Livestock Mortgage is a 22.2 × 23 cm manuscript on hemp paper, partially damaged. It features 7 lines of Tangut in the cursive. Two pieces of contract are patched into one. The first 3 lines are in fact the signatures lingering from the previous contract. The last 4 lines are the first half of another contract. In the last line, in particular, only the half of the characters—the strokes on the right—have survived.[286]

Translation:

> On the same day, contract set up by [illegible] [tśji- zjwi. me_ ·jiw], now from the official [illegible] [ljow ɣwie rjijr]?
> Borrowed 5 *dan* of wheat, 10 *dan* of coarse grains, and have 1 full-teethed female camel, 1
> 2 vertical (teethed) female camels, 1 tamed male camel mortgaged. Date?
> …

A few other documents, such as the Инв. No. 4079-5 and the 4079-6, all belong to this genre of contract of grain Loan on Livestock mortgage.

There is yet another piece of grain loan contract on mortgage that is even more peculiar and complex. The Or.12380-0023 (K.K.II0283.t) grain loan account, now in Britain, is written on a piece of 19 × 18.5 white hemp paper. It has 11 lines of Tangut in the cursive script.[287] The debtor wishes to take out a loan of 7 *dan* of wheat, 4 *dan* of barley, as well as 4 *dan* of millet. If he fails to repay the debt in full by the first day of the seventh month, then the title of not only camels, but also a *shijun* would be conveyed to the creditor. Thus far, this is the only loan contract whereby both livestocks and living human beings are deposited in the mortgage. Likewise, it is a rare find also in the history of mortgage and transactions of human beings in ancient China. It is also an example of 'real contract': *obligatio quae re contrahitur*, in the history of Chinese contracts.

6.2.2 Analysis of the Contracts of Grain Loan on Livestock Mortgage

The Tangut Contracts of Grain Loan by Pawning Livestock are similar to simple grain loan contracts in two key aspects of the legal documents: the creditors charge interests, asking for the return of not only the principle but also the profits at the end of the term. Also, it is the same in both cases that, overdue payments are penalised with a fee, also in terms of grains. One could not but

286 Ibid.
287 *British Collection of Khara-Khoto Manuscripts*, vol. 1, p. 11.

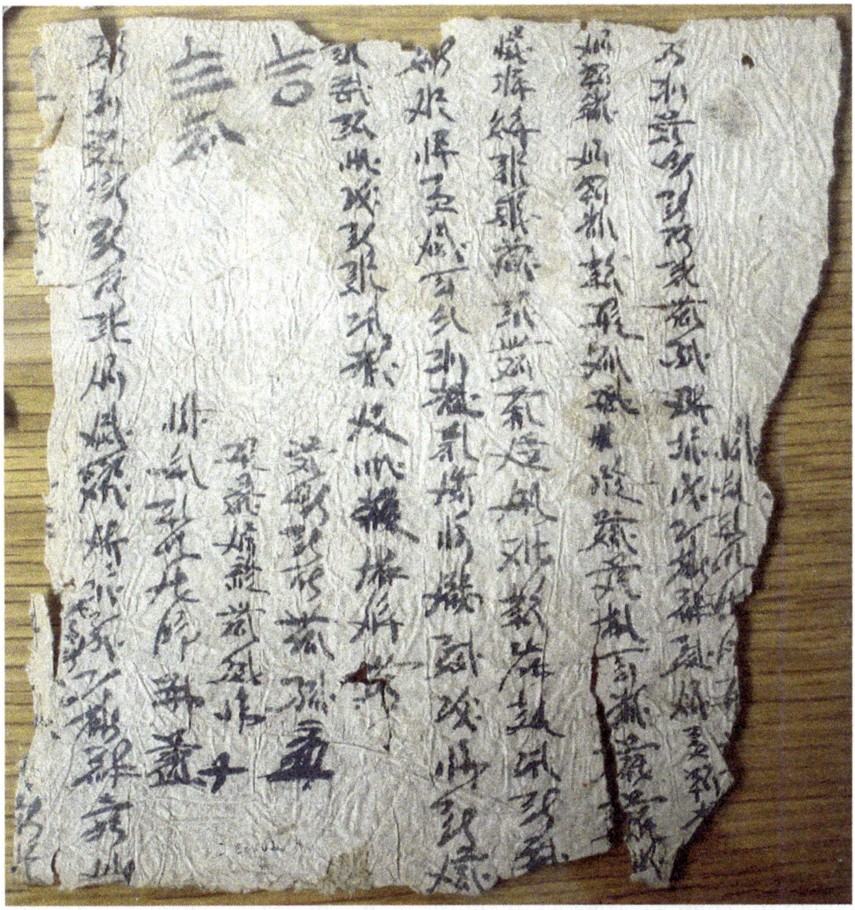

FIGURE 203 British Manuscript Or.12380-0023 (K.K.II0283.t): Contract of grain loan on livestock and human mortgage

wonder how the defaulter could be realistically expected to be able to muster more grains to pay the penalty fee if he fell short of the original sum. The Contracts of Grain Loan on Livestock Mortgage, however, differ form simple grain loan contracts in one key aspect: the borrower has deposited his livestocks as a security upon the signing of the lease. In case of overdue payment or default, the loaners could simply claim the property as their own, according to the terms set in the contract. This form of loan provides a much greater sense of financial security for the creditors. In the document Инв. No. 2996-1: Contract of Grain Loan by Pawning Livestock in the Year of Wei, the debtor deposited a mortgage of a two-teethed male camel in order to take out a loan of 4 *dan* of wheat. When the harvest season comes in the autumn, he is expected to pay 6 *dan* of wheat, at the same interest rate of 50% as in most simple grain loan contracts that we have so far seen. In case of an overdue payment, the creditor may seize the camels to cover the loss. But if the debtor reneges on his obligations altogether, the penalty is another 6 *dan* of wheat.

Because the document Инв. No. 4079-1: Contract of Grain Loan on Livestock Mortgage, has a missing first line, there is no reliable way to establish its date or to identify the contracting parties involved. But near the end, the signatures reveal the main Contract Party as Jia Laohei, who borrowed 5 *dan* of wheat and 11 *dan* of coarse grains, on the condition of depositing 2 camels and 1 cow as mortgage. From the text itself, it seems to be the case that the livestocks are still kept by the debtor, rather than transferred to the guardianship of the creditor, for the time being. So, they are not technically a 'security deposit' in the hands of the loaner. That is why the contract also hypothesises a scenario most intriguing, that if the animals are looted and fall into the dominion of foreign enemies, it is Jia Laohei, the borrower, who bears liability. In addition, the agreement stipulates that in case of default, the debtor pays a penalty fee of 15 *dan* of grains.

The curious reference to the legal complications whereby the camels are looted by the enemies is rarely seen elsewhere in historical contracts. It shows, first of all, that the livestocks were in constant danger of being seized in plunders and pillages. It would not be added into the contract as a clause in peace times. So, although we are still unsure of the precise dating of the contract, it is quite likely that it was signed at a time when the border city of Khara-Khoto was menaced by Mongol arms—that is, toward the end of the Tangut Empire.

A certain co-Contract Party by the name of Shijun Quanfu also signed at the end of the contract. The identity of the man concerned is labelled as Shijun. It is known, of course, that the shijuns constituted a special class of lowly serfs who were legally transacted by their masters. Therefore, the presence of a *shijun*, as a legal persona in the role of the co-Contract Party, is most noteworthy. It shows that, quite possibly, the shijuns had by this period of time achieved a certain kind of legal status in the Tangut society by this period of time. However, it must also be noted that although they are able to perform legal duties as self-owning civilians, the mark of their historically lower status is not altogether easy to erase. That is perhaps why the label "shijun" has to be bound up with the name.

In the document Инв. No. 4079-2: Contract of Grain Loan on Livestock Mortgage, the Contract Party is the pawner Bu who takes out a loan of 5 *dan* of wheat and 11 *dan* of coarse grains from Liang, on a mortgage of livestock. In case of overdue payment, the creditor is legally authorised to appropriate these camels. But if the debtor reneges on his commitments, then the penalty would be 15 *dan* of grains. Near the end of the contract, one finds the names of not only Mr. Bu, but also two other co-Contract Parties. One of them is Liang Huihuni. Huihu (𗶀𗶁) is, of course, also the name of the ethnic Huihu folk. Of course, a sizeable Huihu population lived in the Tangut dominion, whilst other Huihu tribes bordered Western Xia as neighbours. Curiously, "Huihu" is listed as a "Fan name" in the *Assorted Words*. It is well possible that here, the man named Liang Huihuni might have had ethnic Huihu heritage.

Below is a chart that offers a more visual representation of the data in Tangut contracts of grain loans and livestock mortgages:

CHART 27 Data in Tangut contracts of grain loans and livestock mortgages

Register	Date	Pawner	Loaner	Livestock mortgaged	Grain loan	Overdue payment	Default penalty
2996-1	Wei Year: Contract of Grain Loan by Pawning Livestock	𗁀𗁁𗁂𗁃𗁄 [lwər ze gju_ rjur ɣwie]	??𗁅𗁆 [?? kə ta]	Two-teethed male camel	Wheat 6 *dan*	Loaned livestock covers 6 *dan* of wheat	6 *dan* of wheat
4079-1				2 full-teethed male & female camels, and 1? teeth cow	Wheat 5 *dan*; coarse grains: 11 *dan*		15 *dan* of coarse grains
4079-2	Third day of the last month: Contract of Grain Loan by Pawning Livestock	𗁇𗁅𗁆𗁄 [pu. kə ta ɣwie]	𗁈𗁄𗁉𗁊 [ljow ɣwie rjijr lji-.]	2 full-teethed male & female camels, 1? tooth-camel	Wheat: 5 *dan*; coarse grains 11 *dan*	Pawned camels	Coarse grains & wheat: 15 *dan*
4079-3	Same Day: Contract of Grain Loan by Pawning Livestock	𗁋𗁌𗁂𗁍 [mə dzow gju_ dzjwo]		1 cattle, 1 sheep, as security for loan	Wheat: 1 *dan*; to pay 1 *dan* & 5 *dou*	To be seized to cover the debt	

CHART 27 Data in Tangut contracts of grain loans and livestock mortgages (*cont.*)

Register	Date	Pawner	Loaner	Livestock mortgaged	Grain loan	Overdue payment	Default penalty
4079-4	Same Day: Contract of Grain Loan by Pawning Livestock	[illegible] [tśji- zjwi. me_ ·jiw]	[illegible] [ljow ɣwie rjijr]	Full-teethed female camel; 1 two-vertical (teeth) female camel; 1 male camel	Wheat: 5 *dan*; coarse grains: 10 *dan*		

7 Communal Contracts

Societies are a unit of organised community in the civil sphere and at the base level of ancient Chinese societies. Societal organisations have a long history that dates back to pre-Qin eras. They reached unprecedented heights of prosperity in the Tang, the Five Dynasties, and the Song periods. As a primary source, the communal contracts are documents that reflect the content of the historical communal activities. The vivid details contained in these materials are of tremendous historical value. A batch of such documents have been found in the Dunhuang library cave. Since then, Dunhuangologists have conducted systematic studies of these materials, prepared full transcriptions, and published academic literatures on some of the contracts.[288] Amongst them are about 20 or so communal 'charters' or 'constitutions' that enumerate the bylaws and the terms of agreements, designed for the better orgnaisation of these societies. Of these, 10 are official documents, most of which are fragments, whereas others seem to be drafts, copies, and duplicates. The corpus of Khara-Khoto communal contracts, on the other, boast some of the more complete official documents that are of especially great value.

7.1 *Format and Content of Communal Contracts*

So far, two charter-style communal contracts have been identified in the midst of Khara-Khoto manuscripts. They are called 'societies of the many' in Tangut. Although essentially a charter of rules and regulation for the

288 Ning and Hao, 1997.

internal governance of the organisations, such documents are legally binding. Therefore, they may be styled as "Communal Contracts."

7.1.1 The Translation and Interpretation of Communal Contracts

The two Tangut Communal Contracts referred to above are the Инв. No. 5949-31: "Communal Contract in the Yin Year of Guangding (1218)" and the No. 7879 Communal Contract. Both contracts are written in cursive Tangut. In addition to paleographic and calligraphic complexities, the text is not in its optimal state of legibility. Therefore, it is impossible to speak of a high level of confidence in any effort to read, translate, and interpret. For the time being, many questions remain to be tackled. The No. 7879 Communal Contract, in particular, suffers significant loss and damage. Due to poor legibility, it is extremely difficult to sew individual characters into sensible sentences. Therefore, only a literal transcription into Chinese characters is provided in the notes.

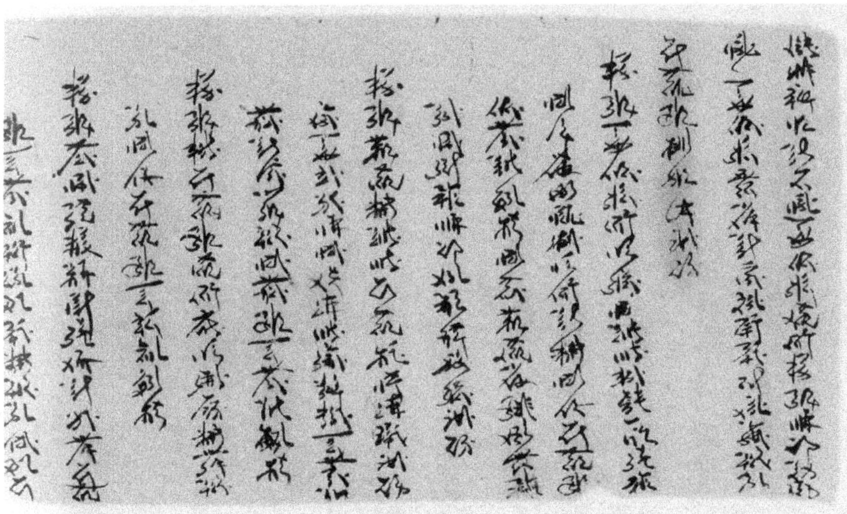

FIGURE 204 Инв. No. 5949-31: Yin year of Guangding (1218) communal contract (1)
Note: TN: The manuscript No. is not 7879.

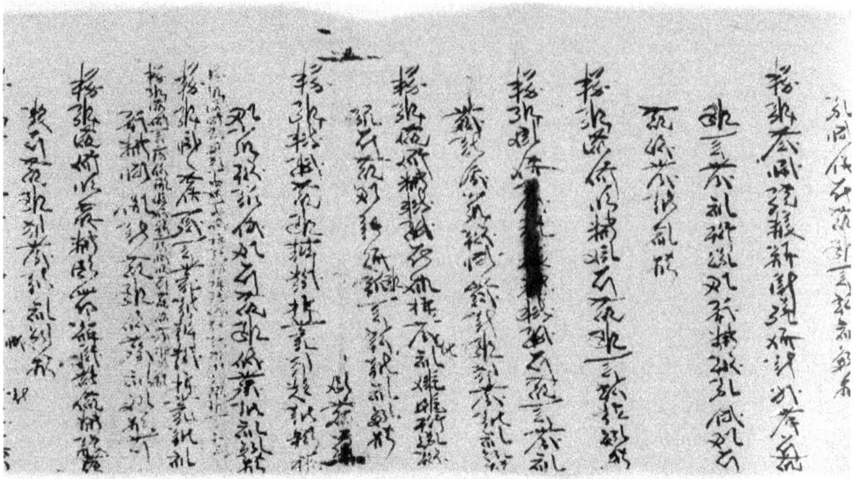

FIGURE 205 Инв. No. 5949-31: Yin year of Guangding (1218) communal contract (2)

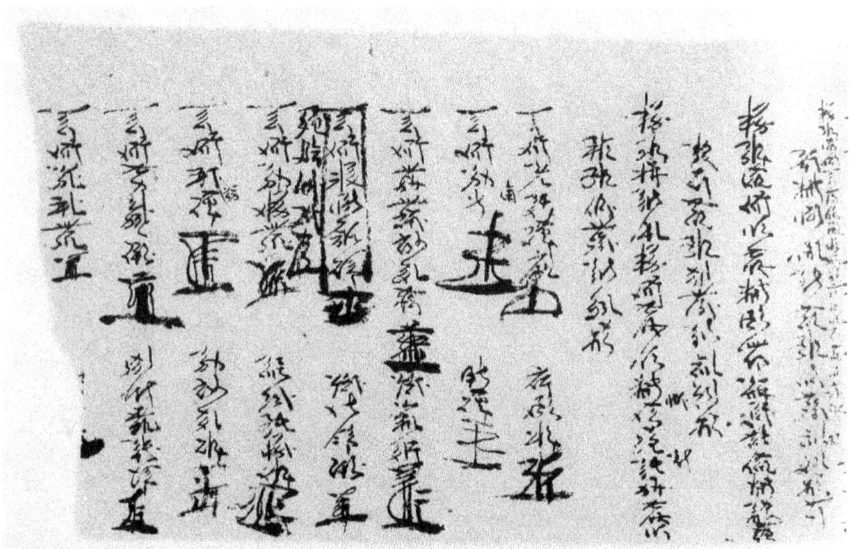

FIGURE 206 Инв. No. 5949-31: Yin year of Guangding (1218) communal contract (3)

1. The Инв. No. 5949-31 Communal Contract is a long, 19.4 × 90.2 cm scroll handwritten on hemp paper, with 40 lines of writings in cursive Tangut. The first line reads, "Guangding, Year of Yin, eleventh month, fifteenth day"—that is, the year of 1218 AD. The contract is signed and stamped, and there are traces of edits and erasures in the manuscript.[289] The handwriting in this manuscript

289 *Russian Collection of Khara-Khoto Manuscripts*, vol. 14, pp. 92–93.

is highly cursive, supplemented by occasional appearances of running-script writings in a smaller font, which are even harder to identify.

Translation:

> On the 15th day of the 11th month, in the Yin Year of the Guangding era, a society is established, whereby its members voluntarily agree to
> gather on the 15th day of each month, hereupon discussed and decided. The first ceremony?
> the persons at the time are to implement the following terms:
> One item: concerning the gathering on the 15th day, unless ill or in long-distance travel,
> (with these exceptions), if members are slack or absent in attending the gathering,
> They are not only punished 5 *dou*, the many? to go engage in merit-making?
> the place of the various bureaus? should? proceed to implement.
> One item: let all visit the severely sick amongst the many at their own place,
> Let members who fail to visit within ten days deliver them medicine and rice instead
> And 1 *sheng* of grains. If they fail to deliver these, the penalty is 1 *dou*.
> One item: all members are to bid farewell to the deceased at the funeral. Amongst them,
> Those who do not attend are penalised by 1 *dan* of coarse grains
> One item: if a member brings a dispute or lawsuit to the bureaus,
> Let there be a penalty of 1 *dou* of coarse grains. If this payment is not delivered,
> Let an additional penalty of 5 *dou* of coarse grains be imposed.
> One item: those who drift away from the gatherings are punished 1 *dan* of wheat
> One item: to a member preparing a funeral for his deceased wife, deliver 1 *dou* of coarse
> Grains. If this amount is not delivered, let there be a penalty of 3 *dou* of coarse grains.
> One item: if the deceased member of the society had ? 2 *dou* of coarse grains
> The extra is to be paid?? If overde, let there be a penalty of 1 *dan* of coarse grains.[290]

290 This line was added later, in a small font. The characters are blurred and almost illegible.

One item: in preparation for a funeral, pay 2 *sheng* & 3 rolls of rice and grains

If overdue or unpaid, let there be a penalty of 5 *dou* of coarse grains.

One item: the society's gathering …

One item: at the monthly gathering, deliver 1 *sheng* of rice/grains, 2 *sheng* of coarse grains

If not delivered, let there be a penalty of 5 *dou* of coarse grains; willing.

One item: gathered society one? no? nobody?? the absent ones are penalised by 5 *dou*

One item: when the society gathers to deliver merit-making ?? where amongst the many? ?

Those who resort to selling are subject to a penalty of 3 *dou* of coarse grains

One item: if two join the gathering not for substantial matters, or if they form a faction

The penalty is 5 *dou* of coarse grains

One member: ?? [illegible] [ta śjow] (stamp) [illegible] [ljow ne_w lji-.] (stamp)

One member: [illegible] [pji-r tsji-] (stamp) ? [illegible] [ta] (stamp)

One member: [illegible] [tśhji- ta~] ??? [illegible] [kie.] (stamp) (Yang)[illegible] [·jow la śiəj] (stamp)

One member: [illegible] [pu.]?? [illegible] [gju_] (stamp)[291] (Yang)[illegible] [da kia]? [?] (stamp)

[illegible] [tow ne_w]? [illegible] [khjwi-] (stamp)

One member: [illegible] (Zhang Ade) [tśjow ·ja te] (stamp) [illegible] [ka]? [illegible] [zji rjijr lji-.] (stamp)

One member: [illegible] [wow swew ta] (stamp) [illegible] (Zhang)? ? [illegible] [tśjow lji-.] (stamp)

One member: [illegible] [tśhio thjij thjij khjwi-] (stamp) ??[illegible]? (stamp)

One member: [illegible] [twu. kji~ te] (stamp) ? ? (stamp)

291 The name here is crossed out.

FIGURE 207 Инв. No. 7879: Communal contract

2. The Инв. No. 7879 Communal Contract is a 19 cm × 48 cm fragment of 19 lines of cursive Tangut handwritten on a piece of hemp paper.[292] Due to excessive damages, the little ink that remains, and overlapping writings on the front and the back of what used to be a sutra, which very much confuse the characters; lots of words remain unidentified. Therefore, only a rough transcription is provided in the notes.[293]

---

292 *Russian Collection of Khara-Khoto Manuscripts*, vol. 14, p. 198.

293 TN: Transcription into Chinese characters with notes:
... One *dou* of coarse grains ...
...? 甲中有身轉者有時尸置上一[泊]? ? (in case of a deceased member of the society)
令音昬以? 其日先如不來與二斗? (members who do not attend the event have to pay 2 *dou*)
不僅庫置中甲中三石布施上? <> 施一?
? 憂四類? 小為當
一條聚日上 ? 處一斗雜施供養為緣因 (1 *dou* of contribution to be paid during the gathering)
一條顯甲會已置日不聚日過時五斗雜? (absence results in a penalty of 5 *dou* of coarse grains)
?? 繳當 (a certain amount to be paid)
一條顯甲中已入中大眾不議過時一??
日? 眾?? 不議因 官依一石麥繳服 (regardless of reasons, to pay 1 *dan* of wheat according to the law)
One member ...(stamp) One member ... (stamp)
... ... (stamp)
One member ... One member ... (stamp)
... (stamp) ...
One member ... (stamp) One member ... (stamp)
... (stamp) ...
One member ... One member ... (stamp)
... (stamp) ...

7.1.2 The Content of Communal Contracts

The two new Tangut charters set out the rules for collective activities that bind the members of the society, whereby participants commit to their solemn pledge of mutual support. The documents are written in the Tangut cursive script. The contract refers to the organisation as a [illegible] [·ji ljwu] (lit. the many, gather; i.e. the gathered many, an organised society). The document ends with the signatures and stamps. By virtue of this format and content, it acquires the legal force of a contract. For this and other reasons, these charters are considered to be communal contracts.

If the Dunhuang library cave furnishes us with a corpus of 10th century medieval communal contracts, then these two Tangut documents fill in the void of the 12th century. The first one, in particular, is preserved almost in its entirety and in excellent conditions.

The No. 5949-31 Communal Contract in the Yin Year of Guangding is almost entirely legible, despite some loss of words near its end. This document suffices to inform us of the basic format and content of Tangut communal contracts. It is written in fluent Tangut on a white hemp paper. The text starts with an opening statement, and a detailed reference to time: "On the 15th day of the 11th month in the Yin Year of the Guangding era" (1218), followed by the characters [illegible], an expression that appears as many as 7 times in the document. The contract then enumerates 11 rules of the society, with two more additional stipulations that appear in a smaller font, making it 13 rules in total. There also seem to be some crossings and erasures. Each item of rule begins with the formulaic expression, [illegible] [·ja tjij] (one item). The gathering activity of the society is referred to as [illegible] [ljwu dzji-.] (gather, assemble; to gather into an assembly), which appears 3 times in the text. The participants in these gatherings are called [illegible] [tha ·ji] (lit. large, many; the many, or the gathered many), which likewise appears 3 times. Finally, there are the signatures and stamps of the members. Due to the damages at the end of the manuscript, it is virtually impossible to know the precise number of members in this society.

This communal contract not only shares the generic features of the many contracts discussed in this chapter, but retains its own characteristics. Therefore, it is better understood as a special contract. As a charter of rules that govern the conduct and activities of a voluntary social organisation in Khara-Khoto, it surely differs from contracts of an economic nature, such as those of transactions, mortgages, loans, and leases, which serve to testify to a set of agreements by the two parties involved in an economic relationship. Rather, the communal contract binds multiple parties to a collective agreement, whereby all members give their consent and mutual reassurance. It is a form of regulation in the private social sphere, at a distance from the laws of the government.

The opening statement of the communal contract makes it clear that the members associate with the society voluntarily. They obviously agree to gather on the fifteenth day of each month. We know, therefore, that the society operates by monthly meetings. Moreover, the constituent members agree to abide by the following rules and regulations.

The first item of stipulation states that all members, except those who fall sick and those who embark on long-distance travelling, are obliged to attend the monthly gatherings on the fifteenth day of each month. Those who are absent without legitimate cause are to pay a penalty fee of grains in the amount of 5 *dou*. Although a private initiative unfettered by governmental regulations, the society obviously enforces its own rules rigorously. Once an individual joins the group, he faces coercive punishment from the organisation for failure to comply with his duties.

The details of the contract all point to the impression that the society is founded on the basis and for the sake of mutual support. According to the second rule, for example, all others are obliged to visit the heavily sick members of the group. Furthermore, "Let members who fail to visit within ten days deliver them medicine and rice instead and 1 *sheng* of grains. If they fail to deliver these, the penalty is 1 *dou*." And under the second rule, if a member passes away, his funeral is attended by the whole group. Those who do not show up have to pay "1 *dan* of coarse grains." According to item 6, when a member prepares a funeral for his deceased wife, others either support him with 1 *dou* of coarse grains, or face a penalty in the amount of 3 *dou*. Likewise, items 7 and 8 also concern spiritual and material support for the funerals of deceased individuals. Visitations by fellow members of the society is a source of consolation, and a positive force in the treatment and recovery processes. Moreover, attendance at the funeral is socially important, and more grains are always most helpful to the survived families. These and such social conducts are a kind of humanitarian support and mutual care. It promotes friendly and fraternal solidarity and communal love within the neighbourhood and across families and households. To some extent, it reflected the tenets of moral teachings and the prevalence of public mores at the time. Whereas it most cases, this layer of morality and sociability is optional, often undertaken by the virtuous and unattained by others, it is an enforceable obligation and procedural necessity for those involved in these organisational societies. Those who do not either live up to this aspiration or fail to comply with their duty face stringent punity in economic terms.

A number of characters in item 4 remain undeciphered. But the undecoded part does not prevent us from understanding the basic meaning of the text. It states something to the effect that, a member implicated in a lawsuit, and possibly incriminated at the court, is also charged with a penalty fee of 1 *dou* of coarse grains. Those who do not comply are further charged with 5 *dou* of coarse grains. In this scheme of double punishment, members are warned not to violate any laws, lest they be both indicted by the government and punished within the society. Objectively, such a measure also reinforces the law and order under the local government. By a mixture of mores and laws, the society supports the political end, as well. Of course, morals and laws are products of their own time. And during this time, both the moral teaching and the legal regime are installed to defend the rights and interests of the powerful, a tool to safeguard and facilitate the smooth operation of the social sphere in its existing order. The Tangut Empire is ruled by its imperial law code. The government enforces these laws to perpetuate imperial rule by the royal elites. The laws are more effective when this regime is capable of normatively shaping the social conduct of its subjects. What is interesting here is that the communal society deters its members from violating the imperial laws by threatening them with the society's by-laws. The force of this deterrence comes from within the voluntarily-formed civil organisation. In this way, the civil is allied with the governmental, the private with the public, and the social with the imperial.

Item 10 in the Communal Contract requires that each member pay a due of 1 *sheng* of rice or grains, 2 *sheng* of coarse grains during the monthly gathering. Failure to do so would result in a penalty fee of 5 *dou* of coarse grains. Therefore, members are not supposed to join the meetings empty-handed.

The signatures and stamps at the end of the text suffice to show that the document is of a legal nature. It should therefore be considered as a proper contract. In the opening statement of the contract, there is no mention of a leader who acts as the legal representative of the society. But it is possible that the first name on the file counts as the head of the organisation. A quick glance at the calligraphic style reveals that the handwriting is consistent from the main text to each of the signatures. There is no doubt that the same person who drafted the document wrote down all the names, as well. But each name is followed by highly varied signs, prints, and stamps. The stamping endows the text with legal force.

The record of individuals who signed and stamped in the contract may not be the full list, given the damage of the contract near the end of the manuscript. What appear on the page now are 17 signatories and their stamps in 8 lines. A certain name was crossed out in line 4, and replaced by another name to its left, which is the 5th line. In other cases, each line contains 2 names, one above and the other below. Further above the name in the upper section, there is a formulaic expression, 㭧 𘝵 [lew ljwu] (lit. one, gathering; one member of the society in the gathering). These two characters are not repeated for the name below. This, again, testifies to the pragmatism of the format.

Another Communal Contract written in Tangut is the Инв. No. 7879 manuscript, which suffers excessive damages. The text is thus barely legible. Still, a bit of information could still be extracted from the modicum of words that lend themselves to a rough translation. In line 7, the opening "One Item" is followed by the expression, [śja kia ljwu] (lit. society, neighbourhood/household; gathering). In line 9, "One Item" is followed by . It is possible that the "Neighbourhood/Household Society" is the name of society concerned.

The contract also specifies that "on the day of the gathering, submit a due provision of 1 *dou* of coarse grains." Whereas in the No. 5949-31 Communal Contract mentioned above, each member pays 3 *sheng* of coarse grains during the monthly gathering. It seems that the dues are higher in the Инв. No. 7879 contract. Note that, as shown in the Инв. No. 7879 Communal Contract, failure to show up at the meeting results in a penalty of 5 *dou* of coarse grains, which is the same amount as the penalty fee for absence as specified in the No. 5949-31 Communal Contract.

7.2 *Communal Contracts and the Tangut Society*

Societies are popular communal groups that formed in the civil sphere, and at the base level of the Chinese society. Some societies wield considerable power and influence in the local area. Communal documents found in the Dunhuang cave library show that societies remained popular in and near Dunhuang from the Tang Dynasty and the Five Dynasties, down to the Song period. Building on this discovery, the corpus of Tangut communal contracts in Khara-Khoto show that communal societies also existed in Western Xia, even in the far-northern city of Khara-Khoto. The new manuscripts that come to light only in recent decades have added new primary materials to Tangut historiography, which enable scholars to dive into the socio-economic base of the Tangut Empire.

The Tangut and Dunhuang communal contracts belong to the same type of texts: charters that set down the rules and bylaws of an organisation. In Chinese historiography, documents referred to variously as *Shetiao* [社條], *She'an* [社案], or *Tiaoliu* [條流] are the basic texts of communal documents. The Dunhuang documents are varied in their lengths and details. Typically, a text begins with the general principles, narrates the purpose of founding such a society, the reasons for the establishment of the rules. It then proceeds to delineate the structure of the society and the substance of its activities, as well as terms and conditions of penalties that deter members from violating the rules. When the text sets out to account for the motifs and purpose of the society, it typically legitimates its raison d'être by the tenets of Confucianism or the doctrines of Buddhism. Under the spirito-ideological guidance of these principles, the society is said to enable friends to form partnerships for mutual support and education, for members to engage in collective sacrificial rituals and to offer aids in their own lives, and also to collaborate on fasts and funerals: there are usually two communal sacrifices, one in the spring and the other in the autumn, in addition to three long fasts.[294] Rules are itemised, each in its own line. Each item starts with the formulaic expression, "One …" which falls in line with the formats of legal writings during this period. Some other communal charters, however, do not itemise the rules. Subscribed members are called the 'many of the society,' or the 'society's many.' They participate in communal affairs under the watchful eyes of the 'head of a society,' 'officer of the society,' and the 'elder of the society' (also called the 'transcriber of the affairs'). These three roles are collectively referred to as the 'three officers,' assigned by popular will. The society operates under the guidance and leadership of these communal 'officers.'

Both Tangut and Dunhuang Communal Contracts are charters of civil societies, voluntarily-formed for mutual help and support, in the private sphere of the medieval society. The Tangut contracts do not elaborate on the fundamental reasons for setting up the society in the first place. There are few, if any moral narratives that justify the establishment of the organisation, or the enactment of the by-laws. The contracts are straightforward about the clear and precise terms: what acts are permitted and what not, and what penalties ensue from the violations of these terms of agreement. In contrast, the Dunhuang documents feature more didactic narratives of moral reasoning. The British manuscript, the Dunhuang S 6537 (back)/3–5 "Charters of a Society founded by Fifteen Individuals" states the following:

> It is heard that in the splendid realm of Dunhuang, the society rests upon the principles of the Three Gems.[295] The customs and mores depend on the support of the wise and prudent … The people live in peace and prosperity, where benevolence and righteousness prevail. No family is in want of reverence for the good order,[296] and all neighbourhoods spread the

294 TN: The Three Fasts [三長齋月] refer to fasts in the first, fifth, and ninth months of the lunar calendar.

295 TN: Of course, the invocation of the "Three Gems" (三寶) is in the Buddhist sense of Pali: tiratana (Sanskrit: त्ररित्न/रत्नत्रय).

296 TN: The loose reference to the order of the more or less dignified and revered (尊卑) could be based on age, gender, and other familial patterns. So, I have refrained from rendering it as simply 'old and young' (長幼尊卑).

> teachings and rituals of filial piety. However, fearing that perchance, tensions may arise and harm, and that the good human sentiments may not persist as in times past; that in these scenarios, disagreements may ensue, and that each party clings onto its own partial view, the fifteen individuals here resolve to form a contract, with a shared mentality and understanding. The elders are to be treated with the same intimacy as parents, and to be provided for all the time. The younger are like loyal sons, and will never change their ways ... To help those in perils and to save the lives at stake; to benefit the dead and to honour those alive; to sacrifice oneself for the good of others, and never begrudge; all must deliberate and negotiate; let the hearts of men not change over the course of time. Because all are of the same opinion, we hereby establish this document as a testimony. We shall thus form a society of fraternal fellowship, which is to be remembered and respected by posterity.[297]

The Dunhuang manuscript Д11038 contains the charter of the Society of the Suowang clans. The document makes clear that,

> The kins of the Suowang ... gradually evolve into divided households. The families have changed their wills in pursuit of their interests, and in so doing, neglected the customs of the good order. The elderly and the young cannot bear to see, and fear that their generation brings shame to the name of their ancestors.[298]

The Tangut communal contracts seem to have inherited the core features and purposes of Chinese equivalents: the defence of the basic social order of the feudal society, and the tradition of mutual help and support. But the Tangut documents significantly reduced the moral teachings. Without the didactic prolegomena, the Tangut texts are simpler and more practical.

With respect to the numbers of rules and items in the contracts, the rather complete Tangut communal contract, Инв. No. 5949-31 in the Yin Year of Guangding contains 13 items. Fewer items have survived in the Dunhuang contracts. For example, due to damages, only two of the additional rules laid down by the head of the society Wang Wu et al. have survived in the P.3544 manuscript, dated to the 29th day of the 9th month, in the 9th year of Dazhong (855 AD); Seven items have survived from the S.2041 manuscript, the charter of the society for the western alley in the 'neighbourhood of Confucian mores,' thrice renewed in the Dazhong era (847–860 AD); the charter of a certain

297 Ning and Hao, 1997, pp. 49–50.
298 Mie Xiaohong, 2008.

Dunhuang-based society, found in the P.3989 mansucript dated to the 10th day of the 5th month in the Third Year of Jingfu (894), does not enumerate its by-laws in a list of separate items; Even the content-rich charter of the society founded by fifteen men—the sample that has been analysed in the S 6537 (back)/3–5 manuscript, only 7 items survive.[299] A quick survey of the Dunhuang corpus shows that none of its communal contract is as elaborate as the Tangut communal contracts.

The communal societies as evidenced in the Dunhuang contracts are diverse in their natures and purposes. Some set their goals as mutual economic help and provision for common livelihood. Others are organised around the Buddhist rituals and worshipping activities. The two identified pieces of Tangut communal contracts both belong to the tradition of mutual economic support. Below are the four main functions of the society:

(a) Periodical gatherings, in this case on a monthly basis. These gatherings are supposed to build personal connections and emotional ties within the society, so that the participating families stay engaged and informed on the situations at other households.

(b) The society pledges spiritual and emotional support to its members in vulnerable positions and under difficult circumstances. Members are obliged to pay visits to the sick and the dead, to show care and pay condolences. Such items suggest that Tangut societies aim not only at the betterment of material conditions but also the promotion of mental, spiritual, and emotional welfare.

(c) But the society is also pragmatic in its approach to support its members. Death of a family member comes with pain but also a significant cost. A funeral always places a heavy financial burden on the survived. So, the provision of foodstuff is a matter of both spiritual and financial support and solidarity. As the communal contract No. 5949-31 in the year of Yin of Guangding shows, a member who suffers the death of a wife claims at least 1 *dan* 7 *dou* of coarse grains from the society. In the case that the member himself passes away; the family is to receive 3 *dan* 4 *dou* of coarse grains.

(d) Members of the society are punished for any conduct in violation of its by-laws. The penalty usually comes in the form of the confiscation of grains. This punitive measure has three ends: to warn and deter members, both the ones guilty and those who are not, from violating the rules in the future; to increase the stockpile of grains; and to establish the dignity and firmness of order in the civil sphere. The society acts as a

299 Ning and Hao, 1997, pp. 1–66.

quasi-government when it enforces its principles by force. In this regard, these non-governmental organisations are a complementary force in concordance with the imperial government. They play a supporting role in guarding the rules and orders of the feudal society.

The materials above outline the basic structure of rights and obligations for those who form or join a communal society.

It is obvious from the Dunhuang communal contracts that the three communal 'officers' lead the societies into various activities, according to the rules laid down in the contract. Candidacies for the officers are proposed and approved by the members of the society. But it also occurs every so often that these positions come to be filled by large clans and powerful families in the area. Some societies are also controlled by the local governments, temples, aristocracies, bureaucracies, and wealthy households, who derive indirect levies and labours from the communities. But the two Tangut communal contracts contain no materials on these subjects, and therefore shed very little light on the possibility that such phenomena might also have been found in Western Xia.

The communal society stockpiles grains from monthly dues (3 *sheng* per member each month). For a society of 17 members, the sum is around 6 *dan* of grains for a fiscal year. As mentioned earlier, the society also accrues grains by means of penalty fees. As for whether these grains are owned by the legal persona of the society, or by the heads of the organisations, or yet, perhaps, owned collectively by all, is not articulated in any legal language. Therefore, there is no reason to exclude the possibility that the leaders of the society might have embezzled common properties.

But the stamps and signatures on the back of the communal contract point to a significant level of collective participation. The by-laws are put forth and signed into effect by all the members as a collective body. They are therefore obeyed, guarded, and accounted for by all the signatories. There is basic equality and collective liability in this arrangement. In this regard, the Tangut and Dunhuang communal contracts share more common ground.[300]

Amongst the identified names of the 17 undersigned in the communal contract Инв. No. 5949-31 in the Yin Year of Guangding, no typical Dangxiang Tangut clan-name has been identified. The Han names are the vast majority: 2 Yangs, 2 Zhangs, as well as Wang, Ge, Liang, as well as 1 Khitan. It is well

300 Meng, Xianshi. "Lun Tang Song Shiqi Dunhuang Minjian Jieshe de Shetiao" [論唐宋時期敦煌民間結社的社條]: "On the Charters of Civil Societies in the Eras of Tang and Song" Ji, Xianlin and Jao, Tsung-I. *Dunhuang Tulufan* Yanjiu [敦煌吐魯番研究(第九卷)]: *Journal of the Dunhuang and Turfan Studies Volume IX*. Zhonghua Book Company, May, 2006, pp. 317–337.

possible that the communal enthusiasts who joined these societies were mainly comprised of Han Chinese, who might have held on to such a tradition. But given Khitan membership, it also seems as if societies in Western Xia broke ethnic barriers. Some of these communal societies might have been properly 'multi-ethnic.' At any rate, these founding documents of civil orgnaisations offer a new perspective on intra- and inter-people conducts in the private sphere, at a distance from the imperial authority. They add a new element of 'multi-ethnicity' to the historical study of communal contracts.

The Tanguts also resorted to crowd-funding to alleviate the plight of poverty. They undertook private initiatives to establish mutual funds for communal support. Such a manuscript that documents the terms of the mutual fund has been found. It is an account excavated in the cave of Xiaoxigou Hills, in Wuwei. The text translates as, "On the 7–5 day of the first month, in the Year of Tiger in Tianqing, [funds] are crowd-sourced at the place of Eming Quanbao. The funding sources are: Elao 'the lady' pledged 150 mace; Wamo Axinji 100; Lingjie Xiaowuyu 150, Eming 'the treasured puppy' 50; Su 'the iron puppy' 50; Mingbu 'treasure of the little house' 50; Eliu 'the uncle's gold' 50; Elao 'guided by the uncle' 50; Wu 'treasure of the dog and the cow' 50; Eming 'the lady' 50; total sum: 750 mace enters the communal account."[301]

The Year of Tiger during the Tianqing era (1194) falls in the late period of Western Xia. The account shows but a modicum of funding. It reflects a particular perspective of mutual economic support in the private sphere of the Tangut society.

8 Features of Tangut Contracts

Amongst the vast number of Tangut social documents, especially those unearthed in Khara-Khoto, the contracts are undoubtedly the most eye-catching and thought-provoking sources. Tangut contracts are large in number and diverse in kinds. Each type of contract is known for its own characteristics.

Tangut contracts are largely similar in format. A contract sets about the transaction with its time, then the names of the Contract Parties, followed by the content of the contract. In most cases, the document includes a clause on potential disputes with relatives and neighbours, and the terms of default and penalty. At the end, the contract is sanctioned and notarised by the signatures

301 Shi, Jinbo. "Gansu Wuwei Faxian de Xixiawen Kaoshi Zhiyi" [甘肅武威發現的西夏文考釋質疑]: "Questions over the paper, 'Critical interpretation of the Tangut texts found in Wuwei, Gansu'" *Kaogu* [考古]: *Archaeology*, issue 3, 1974.

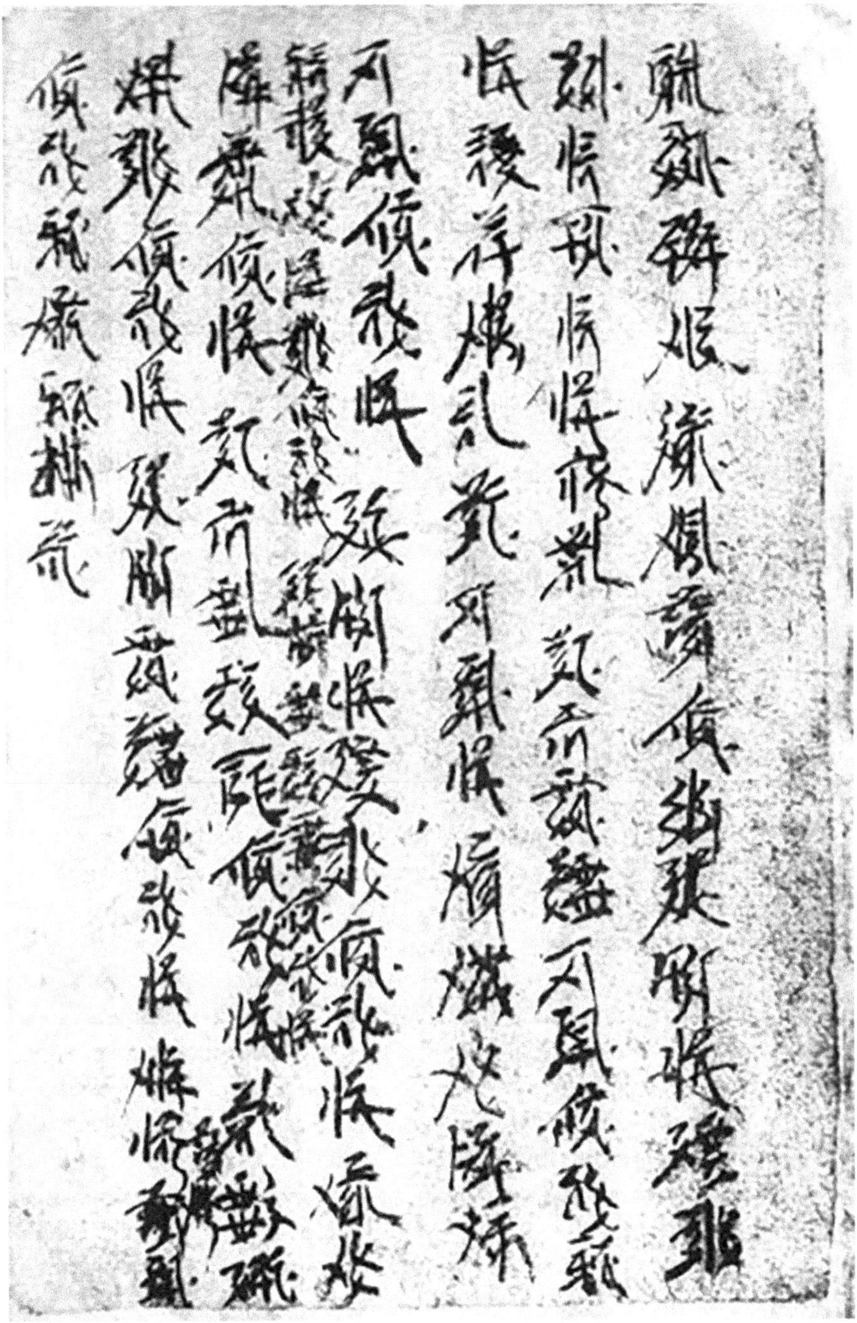

FIGURE 208 Tiger Year of Tianqing: Crowd-funding account, unearthed in Xiaoxigouxian, Wuwei

and stamps of the concerned parties and the witnesses. Tangut contracts do not narrate the causes and reasons for the transaction, as is the tradition of contracts in previous dynasties. The format is largely formulaic and formalistic. The fact that all Contract Parties follow the same legal formula speaks to the maturation of the contract as a legal genre in Western Xia.

Contracts in Western Xia also inherit certain traditions of contracts from Han Chinese practices. These similarities are also shared by the Dunhuang contracts. Although written in the Tangut language, the spirit of the contract reflects a long-standing tradition in the Chinese legal history of contracts.

The rich variety of Tangut contracts showcases the very diversity of the Tangut economic lives.

Grain loan contracts are signed most often in the intervening times between two harvests. These contracts testify to the historical practice of usurious loans, whereby the interest rate reaches as much as 50%, and even 80%, 100% and beyond. These primary materials reveal the heavily exploited lives of the Tangut poor who suffered at the hands of loan sharks. The presence of not only numbers written in characters but also numerical notations speaks to the influence of mathematics in the Central Plains on accounting practices in Western Xia.

A large number of land sales contracts are signed by impoverished Tangut peasants who sold their farmland in exchange for subsistence. Buyers included temples and landlords, who expanded their large possessions of land into farmlands, encroaching upon private lands by a series of acquisitions. To generalise, these economic phenomena take place characteristically towards the end of dynastic empires throughout the long imperial history of China. Such is the case in the land sales contracts of Western Xia. For historians, the contracts contain an enormous amount of data and information on the ownership, management, and transaction of public and private Tangut lands, that have hitherto been unknown to the world. Some contracts also inform us of the boundaries and delineations of land, as well as the locations and distributions of canals for irrigation purposes. The land marked as sold in these transactions sometimes include the abodes of the peasants, which speaks to the historico-anthropologico-ethnographical fact that the Tanguts in Khara-Khoto erected their dwelling places right on their farmland. Rich information with regard to water supply and locations of canals amplifies the historian's understanding of the use of irrigation in Tangut agriculture. For the first time, these contracts reveal to us the price of farmland in Western Xia. It is no overstatement to say that the price of land is critical to any meaningful study of the Tangut economy. Last but not least, the picture of Tangut labour, once entirely invested in hunting and pasturing, and now deeply engaged with agricultural production, reveals the significant extent to which inter-ethnic exchange and migration altered the structure of industries and shifted the modes of production in the progress of time.

Thanks to the Tangut land lease contracts, we are now aware of the surprising extent of land scarcity in Khara-Khoto, a city whose population was not at all dense, and where arable land was far from exiguous. The fact that so many Tanguts struggled to procure farmlands by lease, shows that the peasants must have lost their initial allotment of land to the temples and wealthy financiers. As a result, they are left with no recourse other than to rent back their sold land. The religious establishments of the temples, by a feat of 'asset manipulation' if not 'asset management,' are able to earn back the principle by the lease of a mere two years. That suffices to show how much rent they charged, and how serious a problem these land-monopolists pose to the local community.

An analysis of the livestock sales contracts uncovers the market prices of large livestocks in Western Xia: camels, cattles, and horses, amongst others. Needless to say, the prices of major commodities that are also factors of production in Western Xia are a key route to understanding the Tangut economy. A comparative study of livestock sales by grains and by cash, in Khara-Khoto and in Wuwei, respectively, arrives at the conclusion that the circulation of currency is much more developed in Wuwei than in Khara-Khoto. These contracts of livestock sales also provide us with a vivid testimony to the skyrocketing market prices of livestock in the late imperial era of Western Xia. The high inflation rate is probably due to social instabilities at the gloomy prospect of Mongol invasion.

Contracts of human sales and purchases have filled in the void of our understanding of human transactions in 12th–13th century China. The humans circulated as properties in these contracts are labelled as *shijun* or *nupu*, the semi-slaves of the lowest status in Western Xia. It shows that historically, there was at least a class of the 'enslavable' regularly sold and bought without complete authority over their own free dominion. Correspondingly, there existed a class of *shijun*-buying, and *nupu*-owning class of masters. This would have meant that Western Xia is a 'feudal society with remnant Slavery characteristics.' The contracts also reveal the falling price of humans towards the end of the imperial era. It is most likely due to social instability and external threats in the last two decades that the market of human transactions spiraled down, before an eventual collapse.

The Contract of Labour Employment analysed in this chapter is the only known example of labour employment contract dated to the 11th–13th centuries. It inherits the generally accepted format of labour contract in the Chinese tradition. But on top of it, the Tanguts simplified the content and the format.

The moral persons of the employers and the employed in the legal document seem to exhibit the relationship of the dominus and the subordinate. The employees are required of intense labour, and yet offered a low wage. These and such arrangements reflect the social instabilities of the late imperial period, where means of livelihood was so strained that the few employment providers were able to exploit labour to such degrees of magnitude. The Contract of Livestock Employments, on the other hand, shows how the Tangut poor sell their livestock to the temples under the pressure of sustenance, then immediately rent back their sold animals from the wealthy. The temples acquire livestock at low prices from needy sellers, and then loan the animals back to their former owners at exorbitant prices. This exploitative investment strategy is highly profitable. But it further solidifies a vicious circle, setting the Tanguts already in financial troubles onto the road of perpetual impoverishment. As a result, the poor become poorer.

Contracts of livestock exchange constitute a rather rare genre of contracts amongst the known contracts of ancient times. The genre itself reflects the realities of voluntary economic exchanges of animal labour in the private sphere of the local populace. The end is to make flexible adjustments through temporary and complementary transfers of livestock as a factor of production, for the purpose of mutual benefits and interests. It is also worth pointing out that the grain loan contracts on livestock mortgage differ from simple grain loan accounts. Tangut borrowers resorted to mortgaging their livestock or other properties of equal value, in order to strengthen their case in taking out the loan, and to secure and guarantee the interest of the creditor, who expects to recover the principle and the interest by the due date of the loan.

The two pieces of Tangut communal contracts are a key finding after the discovery of the Dunhuang communal contracts. They fill in the void of communal contracts in the 12th century. Records of communal lives are a key source to historians who try to shed new light on the economic lives at the base level of the Tangut society. By these communal contracts, the Tanguts sought to set the terms for mutual help in their quotidian lives and activities. They are well in line with the tradition of communal contracts in the Central Plains, where local communities seek modes of cooperation in the private realm, in a way that complements, rather than undermines the feudal socio-legal order. Given this particular purpose, communal contracts tend to be simple and utilitarian in nature, without going too much into the tedious narratives of ethical norms and principles of constant virtues. Most participants in the communal contracts are Han Chinese, also in line with the customary practice of forming societies popular in Han Chinese communities. There are, however, a few Khitans in these civil societies. The presence of Khitan names shows that at least some neighbourhood communities in Western Xia could be properly described as 'multi-ethnic.' Such societies would to various degrees of visibility promote inter-ethnic exchanges and fusions in the Tangut Empire.

The form and content of Tangut contracts also vary according to the importance of the document and the transactions specified therein. It is usually the case, for example, that the more important the content is, the lengthier the text tends to be. The more valuable the property concerned is, the more detailed and convoluted the clause on disputes with neighbours and relatives seems to be. If the property isn't all that valuable, it is even possible to omit this bit of information. The penalty fee also varies: the greater the pawn or loan is, the higher the fee is. Likewise, the more there is at stake, the more complicated formalities such as signatures and stamps are. And the more signatories there are, the more formal the stamping format is bound to be. As a result, it often occurs that a quick glance at the outlook of contract suffices to judge its level of importance. A two-line document is probably a simple and straightforward loan record of a few *dou* or *sheng* of grains. Whereas, a contract featuring a dozen or so lines and a few hundred characters, as well as a long list of signatures and stamps, is probably the testimony of a much larger transaction.

The corpus of Tangut contracts is a multi-sector, multi-dimensional, and multi-perspective reflection on the history of the Tangut economy and the economic lives in Western Xia. As invaluable primary sources on Western Xia, the contracts realistically restore the many aspects of the Tangut society. It is a matter of fortune for Tangut history and a gift for all time that the Tangut contracts have survived to see the light of our own day.

CHAPTER 8

Economic Records in Chinese

Kozlov's Khara-Khoto expedition (1908–1909) brought to light large quantities of social documents written not only in Tangut, but also in Chinese, some of which are also economic records of Western Xia. These manuscripts are mostly published in the Chinese sections of the *Russian Collection of Khara-Khoto Manuscripts*. Additionally, a small number of Tangut-era Chinese economic records have been found in the British holdings first discovered by Stein. Most of these texts written in Chinese characters are miscellaneous pages and remnant volumes, which have so far been compiled and examined by experts. In order to present a full account of Tangut economic records, this chapter introduces readers to the Chinese manuscripts which may be studied comparatively with the Tangut texts of similar types and dated to the same period.

1 Markets and Materials

In the eras of the Northern and Southern Song, Liao, Xia, and Jin dynasties, up to the Mongol Yuan dynasty, border-markets functioned as exchange posts that connected the flow of goods and materials across territories of various ethnic regimes. Certain appointed officials presided over commercial activities in these trade markets. With the exception of government-controlled transactions, private merchants had to pay taxes in exchange for an official certificate as a token of approval to trade. Indeed, the Chinese documents provide important information on these trade markets.

1.1 *Market Records*

The twelve pieces of market records are written on the cover pages of the Tangut woodblock print *Mahāvaipulya Buddhāvataṃsaka Sūtra*.[1] When used as a layering paper, the document was cut at the top and the bottom, and thus remains a broken manuscript.

1.1.1 Format and Content

Take Russian manuscript Инв. No. 307, a document of an official in the southern market, as an example. It is 13.2 × 35 cm, and the two sides—both documents

1 *Russian Collection of Khara-Khoto Manuscripts*, vol. 6, pp. 279–286.

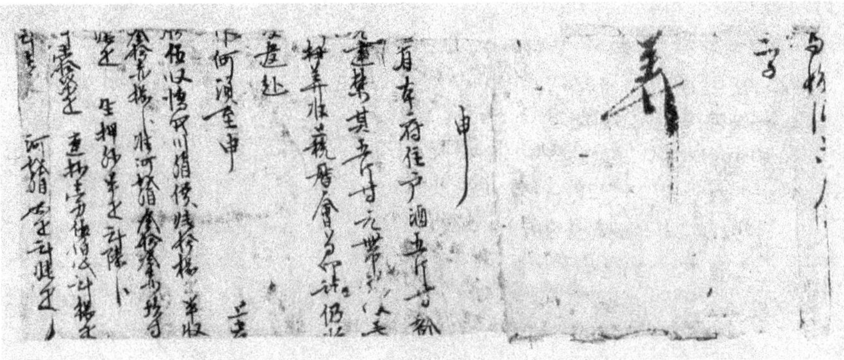

FIGURE 209 Инв. No. 307: application filed by the intendent of the southern market, to the silver medal official, concerning the settlement and tax related to the purchase of goods at government-fixed prices, including five *jin* of alcohol, by residents of this region

FIGURE 210 Инв. No. 307: application filed by the intendent of the southern market to the silver medal official, concerning the settlement and taxes related to the purchase of goods at government-fixed prices by certain residents in Zhendong

Note: TN: It was a common practice in the times of Northern Song that the government would fix commodity prices, and designate individuals or associations to purchase the goods *en masse*. It seems that either the 'purchase' here is in the general sense, or that the Tanguts also practiced price-fixing and government purchase. The fact that the Market Intendents had to report to the Silver-Medal Official speaks somewhat to the official nature of the transaction. But it remains entirely possible that the purchase is normal, and that the reporting is a procedural requirement.

of the same type—are patched together. One side has 14 lines of Chinese, with the top and bottom cut, and the other has nine lines, also in Chinese.[2]

Sun Jimin and other scholars have named the two pages of the document "Application Filed by the Intendent of the Southern Market, to the Silver Medal Official, concerning the Settlement and Tax related to the Purchase of Goods at Government-fixed Prices, including Five *jin* of Alcohol, by Residents of this Region" and "Application Filed by the Intendent of the Southern Market to the Silver Medal Official, concerning the Settlement and Taxes related to the Purchase of Goods at Government-Fixed Prices by Certain Residents in Zhendong." The following is a literal translation:

(1)
...
... Gao
... calculate
... report
... Resident in the same district, alcohol 5 *jin* ...
... No violation of prohibitions, 5 *jin* carried cloth,[3] fur ...
... calculate, raise the taxes, to be stamped, still ...
... distribute, to
... must be reported to higher offices ...
...5 *duan*, fixed-price purchase of Sichuan silk, price 48 *pi*[4] & half, received ...
...30 *chi* 8 *fen*, standard Hebei silk 33 *chi* 9 *cun* ...
...4 *pi*, raw yarn half a *pi*, counted 6 *fen*.
...17 *pi*, *lianchao*[5] 10500 mace, counted 8 *pi* ...
... counted 1 *pi*, Hebei silk 2 *pi*, counted 4 *pi* ...
...
(2)
...
... Intendent application
... head officer: all residential households in Zhendong ...
... search according to law, no violation of prohibition, its ...

---

2 *Russian Collection of Khara-Khoto Manuscripts*, vol. 6, p. 279.

3 TN: "self-carried" (Chinese: 原带) refers to residents of the same district bringing their own cloth for export.

4 TN: 疋 is the equivalent of 匹, a unit of cloth. See *Book of Han* (漢書), "Biography of Shusun Tong" (叔孫通傳), "乃賜通帛二十疋，衣一襲，拜為博士" etc.

5 TN: 連抄 is a type of paper.

... returned goods to be counted by the standard of precedents, registered on tax accounts ...
... The following items □□ to distribute
... to conduct what type of reference, must apply
... yellow cloth 58 *duan*, white cloth 3 *duan*, fur cloth ...
... price 311 *pi*, raise tax on Sichuan Silk ...
... Standard Hebei silk 2 *pi* 7 *chi*[6] 7 *cun* ...
...

Similar manuscripts include Инв. No. 308, 313, 315 (1), 315 (2), 315 (3), 316, 347, 351, 352A, 352B, 353, and 354. These records of market transactions offer a glimpse into the commercial activities across the bounds of the Tangut Empire and Central Plains, and refer to a wide range of commodities. Amongst them, silk products included Sichuan fine silk, Hebei fine silk, *hansha* silk, Sichuan colour-patterned silk, small coloured silk fabric (*shixie*),[7] small aura-silk (*yunxie*), large silky linen, small patterned silk fabric, medium flora-patterned gauze, small thin silk, purple thin silk, yellow light linen, and purple light linen. Fur products included fur cloths (*pinhe*), yellow fur cloth (*huanghe*), white fur cloth (*baihe*), fur yarn (for weaving clothes), fine leather, white ribbon, and otter fur. Condiments included ginger, peppers, honey, tea, etc. Other commonly used commodities included papers, brushes, ink, and 'deer arrows.'[8]

One could easily tell that the lion's share of trade in the market fell within the exchanges of silk, cloth, and fur. Manuscript Инв. No. 308 mentions, "[2]9 *duan*, white cloth 6 *duan*, purchase of Sichuan [silk] at fixed price"; Инв. No. 313 notes, "yellow cloth 16 *duan*, purchase of Sichuan silk at fixed price"; Инв. No. 353 records, "cloth 40 *duan*, white cloth 4 *duan*, purchase of Sichuan [silk] at fixed price." Clearly, the Tanguts traded their own fur cloth products for Sichuan and Hebei silk in these border markets. The Tanguts also imported sauces and spices as well as stationaries from Song; goods included everything from ginger, peppers, and tea to brush, ink, and paper.[9]

Chinese historical archives have documented Tangut trade with Song, Liao, and Jin along the imperial frontiers. In the Fourth Year of Song's Jingde reign (1007), the Song court approved King Deming's request to establish trade posts in Bao'an, commencing the history of large-scale Song-Xia bilateral trade. The Song empire "traded silk fabrics and coloured linens for camels and horses,

6 TN: 赤 = 尺.
7 TN: Chinese: 絁纈.
8 TN: Beyond the obvious literal meaning, the reference to 鹿射箭 remains unclear.
9 Du Jianlu and Shi Jinbo, 2012, pp. 22–30.

cattle and sheep, jade and fur carpets, as well as liquorice plants (*gancao*); Chinese perfume, spices and medical herbs, ceramics, ginger and cinnamon, and other goods were exchanged for *mila* amber, *sheqi* musk, fur and hemp shirts, goat-antelope horns, the mineral *sal ammoniac*, bupleurum herbs, cistanche, safflower, and plume." As these joint market sessions came to an end, the two governments "let the people free to trade amongst themselves."[10] In the Ninth Year of Heavenly Endowed Rituals and Laws and Extended Bliss (天授禮法延祚) in Western Xia (1046), the Song and Xia negotiated a peace settlement. Part of the peace terms were agreements to revive the market in the Bao'an Military District (close to modern-day Zhidan county of Shaanxi province) and to find new ones near the Gaoping Fortresses in the Zhenrong Military District (present-day Guyuan, Ningxia). After the imperial court of the Song Dynasty relocated to the south, the Jin Dynasty emerged as the new main trading partner with Western Xia, after gaining firm ground as a power in the Central Plains. In the second year of Daqing in Western Xia (1141), the Xizong Emperor of Jin, in response to a formal request from Emperor Renzong of Xia, agreed to set up markets along the northwestern Yunzhong area:[11] Guoyaodai, Shang Shileng Po,[12] Tiande, Yunnei, and Yinweng. This region was once a busy trading zone for the Liao and Xia. Besides renewing Khitan-era infrastructures, the Tanguts and Jurchens expanded the scope of their commercial exchange. In around the same period, the Tanguts and Jurchens also established bilateral markets in Lanzhou, Bao'an, and Suide.

To secure robust control over foreign trade, both the Song and Jin Empires established markets, overseen by senior officials and special agencies, just slightly within their own border lines. Western Xia, in particular, designated managers and officers of the markets to be in charge of overseeing commercial activities.[13] There was, in addition, an officer in charge of tax collection. The standard policy was to "raise a limited amount of taxes from Han [merchants] from the imperial region [the Song Dynasty]; raise the normal amount of taxes on Fan merchants in the western territories."[14] This state of affairs remained

10 *History of Song*, Bk. 186. "On Food and Trade" II. 8, "Laws of Bilateral Trade."

11 TN: Yunzhong (雲中) refers to the area of Yunzhou or Yunzhong county (present-day Datong, Shanxi), an administrative region that Song inherited from Tang. The Khitans, however, referred to it as Datongfu.

12 TN: My understanding is that 上石楞坡 is located somewhere near the city of Fengzhen (ᠹᠧᠩᠵᠧᠨ ᠬᠣᠲᠠ) or the county of Zhuozi (ᠵᠦᠸᠧᠽᠢ ᠰᠢᠶᠠᠨ) in Ulanqab (ᠤᠯᠠᠭᠠᠨᠴᠠᠪ ᠬᠣᠲᠠ) in south-central Inner Mongolia.

13 *Zizhi Tongjian*, Bk. 436, 2nd Year of Jiayou in Emperor Renzong's Reign (1057), second month, Renxu.

14 Wen, Yanbo. *Lugong Wenji* [潞公文集], photocopy of the Siku Quanshu edition [四庫全書本], see printed edition by Taipei: Taiwan Commercial Press, 1983; (明嘉靖五刻本, 傳

more or less the same after the Jurchens put an end to the Northern Song imperium. Some of the aforementioned Chinese market records provide detailed accounts of Tangut "levies on Fan merchants."

These documents from Tangut markets make it clear that cross-border trade was conducted under the command and supervision of the Market Officer. Upon the closing of a deal, the Market Officer issued a "reference" document and reported to higher administrative offices in the relevant departments. These official "reference documents" were submitted in the names of the Market Officers, signed at the top by the "Intendent of the Market" or the "Intendent of the Southern Market," followed by the Chinese character "申" and "Silver-Pai Head Officer" or "Head Officer."[15] Whilst taxing Tangut merchants, the officials conducted inspections on the goods and commodities and required the submission of information including addresses, names, types of goods carried, and whether any resupplied cargo contained goods prohibited from transaction. Moreover, the taxes were "counted and raised, officiated with a stamp" and "immediately dispatched for distribution." The second half of the document records the purchase of goods at fixed prices and the tax receipts, followed by the year and printed signatures.

The first half of the document ends with the expression, "In prostration, humbly requesting a reference document; it is necessary to report to higher offices" (Chinese: 伏乞照會作何須至申), which not only points out the nature and purpose of the document but also reflects the standard format of reference notices of the Song and Xia period.

1.1.2 Locations of Inter-State Trade Markets in the Economic Documents

The largest number of market records appear to have originated from the Zhenyi county and the Xiliangfu. The Tanguts established an administrative system of prefectures and commandries. The Su Prefecture (Jiuquan, Gansu), for example, corresponds to Fanhe Commandry, and the Gan prefecture (Zhangye, Gansu) is equivalent to Zhenyi Commandry.[16] This piece of information had been known for a long time solely in the *Book of Western Xia* (*Xixia Shushi*), without any labels or notations of original sources. Therefore, it has been subject to the rightful suspicion of historians. Later, the name "Zhenyi

增湘校本; edited by 四川大學古籍整理研究所) Beijing: Xianzhuang Book Company, 2004; (叢書集成續編. 集部. 別集類 101) Shanghai: Shanghai Shudian, 1994. Bk. 19, "Zou Xixia Shi Zhao Shi" [奏西夏誓詔事].

15 TN: I have translated 銀牌 as Silver Pai, Paiza, or more loosely, tablets, tokens, and medals. These are tablets signaling rank and status, power and privilege.

16 *Xixia Shushi*, Ch. 12.

Commandary" was discovered on a stele inscription in Zhangye, which provided a second layer of historical evidence. Now, with the explicit reference to Zhenyi in market records, the existence of this administrative unit in Western Xia may be properly established beyond doubt.

Xiliangfu is another name for the Liang prefecture (today, the city of Wuwei, Gansu). The government of Xiliangfu was first established in the early Song period, but it later fell to Tibetan invaders. In the aftermath of the Tangut conquest of the Hexi Corridor, Western Xia inherited the title of Xiliang, though sometimes also referred to the prefecture simply as Liangzhou. Such is the expression as it appears in the Chinese text of the renowned "Inscription of the Renovated Liangzhou Pagoda."

No reference to markets in the Hexi Corridor is found in conventional sources such as historical chronicles. The Liangzhou market records mentioned above could fill in this historical gap. Manuscripts Инв. No. 347 and Инв. No. 352B end with the signature "by the Intendent of the Market, the Market Officer of Xiliang, and the Public Notary of Records," which makes clear that the official manager of the market (Chinese: 拘榷) exercises jurisdiction over the Xiliang territory, and also assumes responsibility as the Public Notary, or Record Keeper (簽判).[17] Both positions are related to the government of Xiliang.

The next question is whether the "Southern Market" referred to in manuscripts Инв. No. 315 and Инв. No. 354 are related to the "Southern Realm" administration as mentioned in the *Laws of Heavenly Prosperity*. Amongst the many military supervisory districts of Western Xia, there is a "Military Supervisory District of the Southern Realm," which should have been located in the Prefecture of Liang. The Tangut-Chinese bilingual inscription of the Liangzhou Stele matches the "Southern Realm" with the "Right Compartment."[18] Therefore, in most if not all likelihood, the market of Liangzhou might be none other than the celebrated Market of Lanzhou. Historical chronicles record that in the early period of Western Xia, the Tanguts traded with the Song Empire near the Gaoping Fortresses in the Bao'an and Zhenrong military districts. In

17 TN: 簽書判官廳公事, see Chen, Yanxiao [陳岩肖]. *Geng Xi Shi Hua* [庚溪詩話] Bk. 1. "英宗朝, 自鳳翔簽判滿任, 慾以唐故事召入翰林"; Wu, Zimu [吳自牧]. Meng Liang Lu [夢梁錄], "Shiren Fu Dianshi Changming" [士人赴殿試唱名], "其狀元官授承事郎，職除上郡簽判，榜眼授承奉郎，探花授承務郎，職注中郡或下郡簽判"; Gao Cheng [高承]. *Shiwu Jiyuan* [事物紀原] on 簽判 and Wenxian Tongkao [文獻通考]. For English translations, See Hucker, Charles. *A Dictionary of Official Titles in Imperial China*, p. 154; Zhang, Zhejun and Wang Jing. *Song Dynasty Tales: A Guided Reader*, p. 182n35.

18 Shi Jinbo, 1988, pp. 249, 253; "Xixia Shiqi de Wuwei" [西夏時期的武威] in *Xixiaxue* [西夏學] (*Tangut Studies*) 7. Shanghai: Shanghai Ancient Works Publishing House, Dec. 2011.

late Tangut history, Western Xia and the Jin Dynasty expanded their markets. In addition to the ones in Bao'an and Suide, a new market was added to the eastern end of the Hexi Corridor and in the Lanzhou prefecture, which at that time would have been under the administration and jurisdiction of the "Southern Realm" of Western Xia.

Most of the Tangut economic records mentioned in this book concern transactions within Western Xia. The corpus of Chinese documents, however, preserves a unique source of information on external trade: economic activities between the Tanguts and other people. These two collections of manuscripts are therefore complementary to one another. It also makes sense for the external trade records to be written in Chinese, as bilateral agreements are required to be written in the more commonly used language. A contract signed in Tangut is incomprehensible to Chinese partners, but a Chinese document is used beyond the territories of the Song Empire—such as in Xia to the west and Jin to the north. Chinese characters, therefore, played the role of lingua franca in business contracts throughout east, northeastern, and inner Asia. This is perhaps the reason why no inter-state market records in the Tangut language have been found up to this day. Whenever it comes to external trade, Chinese appears to have been the default language, thanks to its popularity and expediency. From another angle, this also demonstrates that even in the time when China was divided into ethnic regimes, the Chinese language persisted as a medium of economic and cultural exchange in the space between and across empires.

Exactly how these trade records made their way from Liangzhou to Khara-Khoto is a question both worth asking and with no easy answer. Most of these documents are actually patched with the layering paper to the book cover of a Tangut block-printed *Mahāvaipulya Buddhāvataṃsaka Sūtra*. It is very possible that the Khara-Khoto copy of *Mahāvaipulya Buddhāvataṃsaka Sūtra* originally came from Liangzhou. If so, one plausible explanation is that at the time when the sutra's cover was made in Liangzhou, a pile of papers was stacked together as a hard cardboard to provide physical support. Since paper was anything but in excess in Western Xia, those who made the book cover reused expired and long-discarded paper documents from the local market. In this way, these social texts travelled to Khara-Khoto with the sutra. Another hypothesis is that the sutra covers were instead fabricated in Khara-Khoto. This would mean that, since Khara-Khoto fell within the administrative authority of the larger Liangzhou-based government of the Northwestern Strategic and Regulatory Commission, used papers from Liangzhou markets were transported into various localities to be reused for printing purposes. The latter explanation, while certainly plausible, seems less likely to have been the case.

1.2 *Records of Materials and Resources*

The editors of the *Russian Collection of Khara-Khoto Manuscripts* first designated a piece of manuscript dated to the second year of Qianyou as a "Timber Account." Upon closer scrutiny, however, we found several other types of materials and resources in the same document. Therefore, the document is now entitled "account of materials" or "record of resources."

1.2.1 Format and Content

A record of materials in the second year of Qianyou have been identified in manuscripts B61, Дх2828 and Дх10279 at the IOM.[19] The three documents are each in 8, 18, and 4 fragments.

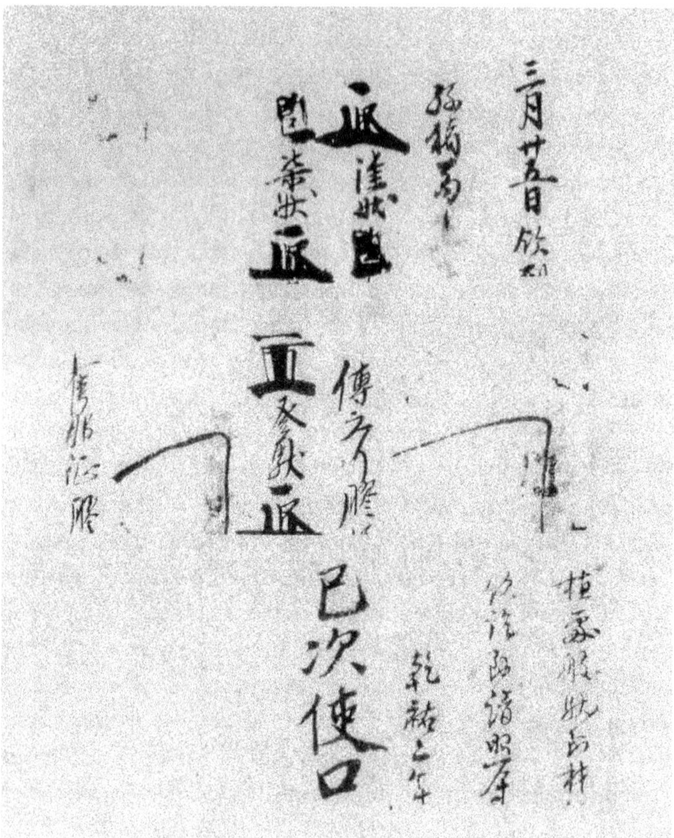

FIGURE 211 Дх2828: Second year of Qianyou (1171) document submitted to the Bureau of Storage, for the handover of timber for transportation (1)

19 *Russian Collection of Khara-Khoto Manuscripts* 6, p. 60, pp. 150–159.

The following is a translated transcription of lines 1, 8, 12, 15, 16, 18 of Дх2828, and line 1 of Дх10279, which are the best preserved and the more legible parts of the manuscripts:[20]

(1)
...
... (signature, stamp) 2 loads (signature, stamp) ...[21]
... Wang Qinlai, sandy earth ...
... (signature, stamp) 2 loads (signature, stamp) ...
... (signature, stamp) 2 loads (signature, stamp), calendar ...
... Fu Chounu, sandy earth ...
... (signature, stamp) 2 loads (signature, stamp) ...
... (signature, stamp) 1 load (signature, stamp) ...
... Cui Nazheng, sandy earth ...
... (signature, stamp) 4 loads (signature, stamp) ...
... (signature, stamp) 4 loads (signature, stamp) ...
...
(8)

Front page:

......
... in Huaiyuan county cut ...
...2 pods, each weighs 4...
... thousands
... each 14 *chi* long
...6 *chi* long, 1 *chi* wide ...
... month day 14...
...

20 See Sun, Jimin, et al. (eds.). *Ecang Heishuicheng Hanwen Wenxian fei Fojiao Wenxian Zhengli yu Yanjiu* [俄藏黑水城漢文文獻非佛教文獻整理與研究]: *Compilation and Survey of non-Buddhist Han Chinese Documents in the Russian Collection of Khara-Khoto Manuscripts*. Beijing: Beijing Normal University Press, 2012, vol. II, pp. 638–641, 662–671, 673–674. The title and the transcription are both based on the version published in that volume, where the first two documents are named "Document submitted to the warehouse office to request the hand-over of timber in the second year of Qianyou (1171) of Western Xia" (西夏乾祐二年付庫司文書為材植交納施行事), and the latter "Document submitted to the warehouse office for the hand-over of clay earth in the second year of Qianyou (1171) in Western Xia" (西夏乾祐二年付庫司文書為交納膠泥土事).

21 TN: All the "loads" (馱) in the translation refer to one unit load of goods onto a pack animal.

Back (written between lines 3 and 4 on the front page):

> … Officer who hand-received the submitted document: Yang Axi …
> (12)

Front:

> …
> … □□length: 14 *chi* …
> …4 *chi*, cun board, 2 pieces, each 6 *chi* long …
> … *cun*.
> …5 materials, 2 pieces□, 1 piece, length: 1? …[22]
> … □ 5 *chi* cun board, 5 pieces, each length: …
> … □ material, 2 pieces, length: 14 *chi* each …
> … length 5 *chi*, width 1 *chi* 5 *cun* …
> … 2 pieces ……
> …

Back (written between lines 4–5 on the front page):

> … day 15, hand-receiver of the materials, Bai Bangou
> (15)

Front:

> …
> Here, there is the footman Li Cai …
> Handover of timber sourced from …
> □ 4 pieces for the purpose of building …
> According to the quantity to be delivered …
> 1 load
> 7 × 5 material 2 pieces …
> cun board, 4 pieces inside …
> 2 pieces …
> 1 piece, length: …
> …

22 TN: This is a two-digit number. The number value of the single digit is missing.

Back page: (written between lines 1–3 on the front page):

It is to Meng Ayong ...
zhiran ...[23]
(16)

Front page:

...
... right footman Li Zhu'er ...
... cut wooden board, 3 loads, each weighs ......
... on behalf of Li, office of the warehouse, deliver ...
... load, 7 × 5 material, joint board, size ...
...7 × 5 material 2 pieces, inside, 1 piece, length ...
15 *chi* long
... wooden board 2 pieces, each 6 *chi* long ...
... load, 7 × 5 material 2 pieces, inside ...
... 1 piece, length: 15 *chi*
4 pieces
...

Back of the page: (written between lines 2–3 on the front page):

...... (signature, stamp) 2nd month, 12th day received ...
(18)

Front page:

...
Right, request to the Warehouse, 2 loads of the above item ...
Timber, to proceed to provide. Second year of Qianyou ......
2nd month, 17th day
...

23 TN: meaning of 只染... unclear due to the missing characters. It could be a term or a name, or yet a reference to the dyeing of the wood boards; or yet stamps and prints.

ДX10279 (1) translated transcription:

...
...9 loads
5 loads (signature, stamp) 5 loads ...
... up 3 wan[24]
... Shiban, load, claysmith ...[25]
...1 load (signature, stamp) 1 load (signature, stamp) 1...
... up 3 wan[26]
... load clay earth ...
...

Both documents, B61 and Дx2828, are dated to the Renzong Emperor's reign, or the second year of Qianyou (1171). The B61 shows "second year of Qianyou, 25th day of 3rd month" whereas the Дx2828 mentions the 2nd, 4th, 5th, and 6th months in the second year of Qianyou. Both records refer to the county of Huaiyuan. The format, timing, and names of persons and places in B61, Дx2828, and Дx10279 suggest that they fit the same type of economic documents: written requests to the warehouse office that were necessary to receive an order of timber. The staff in charge of transferring and transporting the timber wrote down the quantity and quality of the timber in a given order and provided their stamps and signatures. The staff in charge of deliveries (manual labourers tasked with the actual move) also signed and stamped, but on the back of the page, noting down "received according to the number"; "received"; "already received," etc. The dispatchers and the delivery men each signed and stamped. Given this formality, these formal requests may be deemed as 'contracts.'

The 'sandy earth' (漫土) and the 'clay earth' (膠泥土) as mentioned in Дx10279 do not require stamps, signatures, or the acknowledgement of a receipt on the back of the page. One possible explanation is that these two types of materials required extraction on the part of the delivery staff, rather than a simple take-over from the warehouse. Regardless of the types of

24 TN: There does not seem to be a fitting translation for 上叁丸, nor a consensus on its meaning. 丸 could of course be a unit of measurement, but I doubt if a small round object could be relevant to this context. Occasionally, 丸 does also substitute in for 完, that is, xxx goods 'uploaded' (hence the 'up'), where the loading is 'completed.' But that is my own uneducated guess.

25 TN: It is unclear how to punctuate or understand 示般駄塑匠膠 without recovering more missing characters. Out of context, 示般 could only be considered a name of some sort. 駄 is the regular unit of load, again without more contextual information. To me, 塑匠膠 is a claysmith or clay used for a smith's workshop or construction sites.

26 See TN on the previous occurrence of 上叁丸.

accounts and documents, all similar records have to do with the calculation of transportation and labour costs.

1.2.2 The Tangut Economy of Transportation as Reflected in the Records of Materials

The manuscript fragment B61 (6) refers to the "Huaiyuan county" as an administrative region. The manuscript fragment Дx2828 (8) records that the materials are to be "delivered and handed over in the county of Huaiyuan." Of course, the history of Huaiyuan as a county goes back to the Tang Dynasty, when the area fell within the prefectural administration of Lingzhou. In the early period of Song Dynasty, Huaiyuan was downgraded to a town. But Li Deming "established a base in Huaiyuan, renamed Xingzhou,"[27] which Yuanhao remade into Xingqingfu, the legendary capital of the Tangut Empire. However, "Huaiyuan," as a name, did not fall into disuse. Rather, it remained used in popular languages in the imperial capital's vicinities but shifted to refer to an important county near the capital. The Tangut *Laws of Heavenly Prosperity* volume 10, "On the Order of Bureaus and Offices," for example, designated the four counties: Dingyuan, Huaiyuan, Linhe, and Baojing, along with Lingwu and Ganzhou as the Lower Bureaus.[28] Both accounts of timber transportation mention Huaiyuan. These are processed, rather than raw timbers: 'ripe wood' or wooden boards of various sizes: "7 × 5" and "4 × 5" wood materials, or "3 *chi*" and "5 *chi*" *cun* boards, etc. Some are "6 *chi* wide," others "15 *chi* long" or "6 *chi* long, 1 *chi* wide," etc. In general, processed wood weighs less and are therefore easier to transport. Since the documents were found in Khara-Khoto, the timber might as well have been sourced from local areas. These wood materials could have been made from a special kind of timber in the Khara-Khoto area. When the imperial government lays out plans for constructions, they would request that these processed timbers be transported to the vicinities of the capital, such as the Huaiyuan county, for use at construction sites.

The manuscript fragment Дx2828 makes repeated mentions of "footmen."[29] As intuition may suggest, these were transport workers, a profession documented at length in chronicles of the Five Dynasties, Song, and Yuan Dynasties.[30] Names shown on transport records show Sun, Fu, Cui, Wang, Yang, Li, He, Liang, Tian, Bai, and Meng. The all-Chinese team suggests that

27 *History of Song*, Bk. 485 "The State of Xia" Part 1.

28 *Revised Laws of Heavenly Prosperity*, vol. 10, "The Order of Bureaus and Offices," p. 363; see Shi and Li, p. 449.

29 TN: 腳戶, 腳家, or 腳人.

30 *Old History of the Five Dynasties*, Bk. 146, "On Food and Trade"; *History of Song*, Bk. 271, "Biography of Guo Tingwei"; Song, Lian; Zhao, Xun; Wang, Yi, et al. *Yuanshi* [元史] *History of Yuan*. Beijing: Zhonghua Book Company, 1976. Bk. 93, "On Food and Trade."

most Tangut 'footmen' in the business of long-distance transportation were Han-Chinese ethnics. Perhaps because of this oversized representation in the profession and for the sake of expediency, these documents were written in Chinese only. This way, it was easier for the officials to communicate with the Han Chinese 'footmen' and for the workers to sign and stamp, without extra logistical costs and problems that may arise from language barriers.

1.3 *Hay Account*

There is also a number of economic records in the British collection of Khara-Khoto manuscripts, amongst which are four pieces of hay (for the horses). These documents shed light on the conditions of hay supplies and horse provisions in Western Xia.

1.3.1 Format and Content of Hay Accounts

All four pieces of hay records were originally unearthed in Khara-Khoto. For a long time, they were preserved in the midst of fragments in the Or.12380-3178 manuscripts.[31]

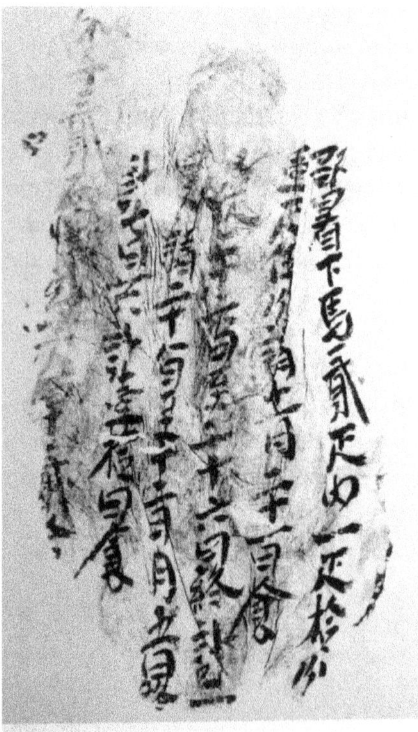

FIGURE 212
British Manuscript Or.12380-3178a (K.K.): Hay account

31 *British Collection of Khara-Khoto Manuscripts*, vol. 4, pp. 33–34.

1. British manuscript Or.12380-3178a (K.K.): Hay Account:

...
For the staff arranged[32] horses 2 *pi*, of which 1 *pi* [of horse] is granted 10 points [worth of ration]
□ 1 [another] *pi* [of horse] 5 points [worth of ration] □ 11th month, 21st day, food
From 26th day, to 26th day, end. Counted: 1...
... request: 28th day, to 12th month 5th day, end.
Counted 7 days, in total □ food for 10 days
... □□ *dan* ...
...

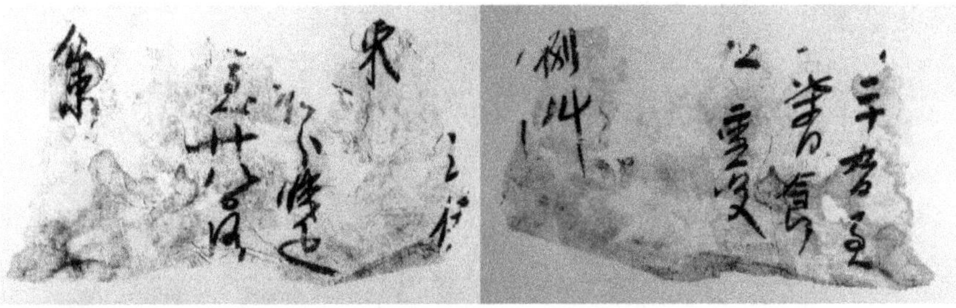

FIGURE 213 British Manuscript Or.12380-3178b (K.K.): Hay account

2. British manuscript Or.12380-3178b (K.K.): Hay Account:

...
... bundle
... □ 4 *pi*
... till day 28, end
... □ bundle
... day 29, till
... food for 7 days
...
... 8 *dou* ...

32 TN: 暑 ought to be 署.

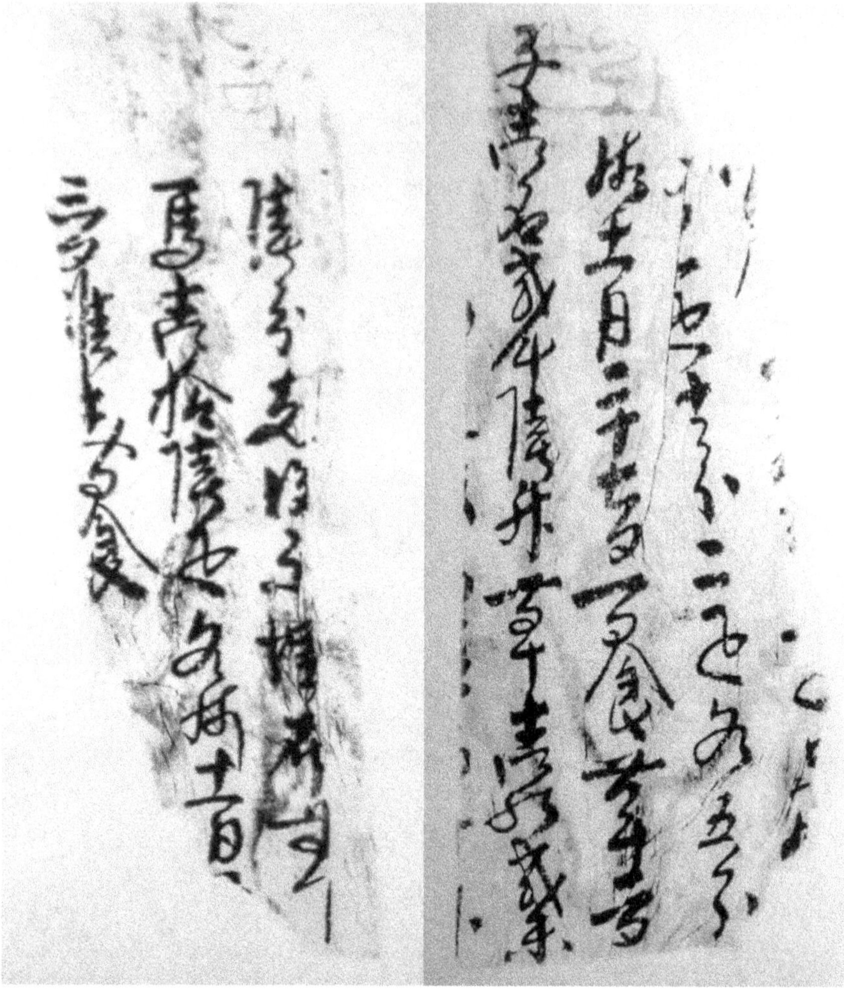

FIGURE 214 British Manuscript Or.12380-3178c (K.K.): Hay account

3. British manuscript Or.12380-3178c (K.K.): Account of Hay (for horses):

> 6 points, provided □□□□ hay
> Horses 16 *pi*, each provided for 11 days …
> 3 days, ration for 20 days
> …
> … 1 *pi* [of horse] 10 points [worth of hay]; 2 *pi* [of horse] 5 points [worth of ration] each
> (on) 11th month, 27th day, hay for one day's provision, 2 days
> … zi 1 *dan* 2 *dou* 6 *sheng*, hay 12 bundles
> …

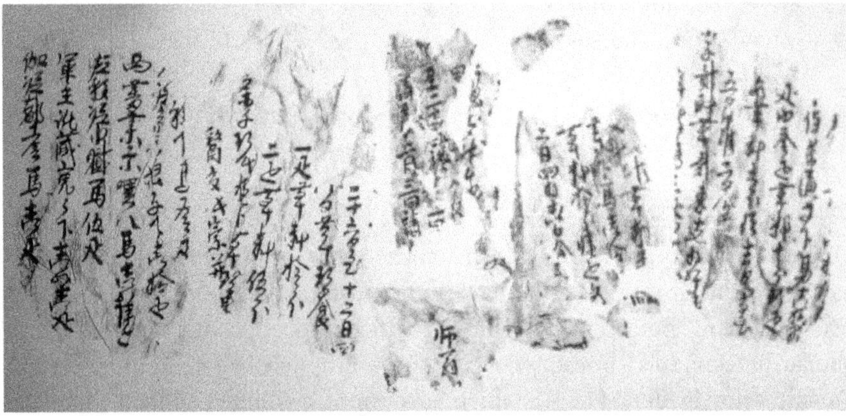

FIGURE 215 British Manuscript Or.12380-3179 (K.K.): Hay account

4. British manuscript Or.12380-3179 (K.K.): Hay Account:

...
... Bao□tong et al., horses 12
pi, including 10 points [worth of] hay for 3 *pi*, 9 *pi*
Each 5 points [worth of] hay, must 12th month 4th day to
5th day, □ approved standard food for 2 days
□ (proso millet) 2 *dou*, hay 2 bundles, provide□□□ ...
... □□ [horses 3 *pi*] ...
□ hay 8 bundles ...
... hay, □horses 10 ...[33]
... hay/forage, 14 *pi*, each ...
Month 2, day 4, food for one day
...
To 20th day ...
Request, to 12th month 3rd day request ...
26th day to 12th month 4...
Hays for 8 days, food for 9 days
First *pi* [of horse], hay 10 points [worth of ration]
Second *pi* [of horse]: hay 5 points [worth of ration]
Proso millet, 9 *dou*□□, hay 9 bundles
...
□□horses 3 *pi*
□□□□xx[34] 10 *pi*

---

33 TN: The single digit may be missing.
34 TN: 子 and 下.

Xi□□shiluoba, horses 16 *pi*
Zuoyi Nijinni, horses 5 *pi*
Military officer Ezang Weiming, 11 *pi*
Ganidu□ horse 1 *pi*
…

1.3.2 Analysis of Hay Records

Of the documents above, the British manuscript or.12380-3179 (K.K.) is the richest in content. It even lists the names and positions of the persons involved: "Zuoyi Nijinni, horses 5 *pi*"; "Under military officer Ezang Weiming, 11 *pi* [horses]"; "Ganidu□, horse 1 *pi*" etc. Chinese chronicles often mention certain Tangut 'army leaders' [軍主], which is certainly a military office in Western Xia.[35] The names of the concerned parties in the documents, such as Ezang, Zuoyi, Gani, and especially Weiming and Ezang, were prominent Dangxiang Tangut surnames. There is no question, even from the content itself, that these records are from the Tangut era.

From the incomplete records above, it is easy to tell that the Tanguts made active distinctions between different horses, providing them with different amounts of hay based on points of five or ten. The Tanguts also supplied horse provisions based on the number of days on a given business trip: 1 day, 2 days, 3 days, 7 days, or up to 20 days. This criterion seems to suggest that the documents were used for the horse provisions of government employees dispatched on official duties. It is illuminating to compare the actual records with the relevant statements in the *Laws of Heavenly Prosperity*. It describes when and where the Court dispatches officers on horses to state-owned pasturing lands for the examination of government-owned livestock:

> The officers sent out from the imperial capital to review and examine the many pasture lands, including the clerks (*antou*), office staffs (*sili*), attendants, as well as juniors acting in the capacity of servants, may procure rations of food for their horses from the government. When they receive the provisions from the pastures, let the precise numbers be calculated, and let anyone be judged and duly prosecuted for any violation of the laws.

> A senior officer enjoys 1 slaughter every 7 days, and 4 *sheng* of rice and flour each day, including 1 *sheng* of rice; of the two horses, one is

35 *History of Song* vol. 5, Chapter 11 on Taizong Emperor, 485: Book on the State of Xia; 7: chapter 11 on Zhenzong Emperor; 492: Book on the Dangxiang.

provided with 7 *sheng*, the other 5 *sheng*. One junior servant receives 1 *sheng* of rice.

Together, the *Antou* and the *Sili* enjoy a slaughter every 15 days; each receives 1 *sheng* of rice per day; their horse is provided with 5 *sheng* of food.

One Keeper of the Rod is allotted 1 *sheng* of rice per day.

One examiner enjoys a slaughter every 15 days, 2 *sheng* of rice and flour per day; his horse is allotted 5 *sheng*.[36]

The Tanguts also laid down exhaustive rules on the allotment of hay to government employees dispatched on horses on official trips:

Provisions to the staff in the Bureaus of Review and Inspection, according to their ranks:

A Senior Official enjoys a slaughter every 10 days, 4 *sheng* of rice or grains per day; of the 2 horses, each one is allocated 7 *sheng*, the other 5 *sheng*; a Junior is allotted 1 *sheng* of rice.

☐ An official such as a Secretary in the Bureau of Review and Censorship each enjoys a slaughter every 15 days, 1 *sheng* of rice per day; 5 *sheng* for the horse; a Junior is allotted 1 *sheng* of rice per day.

Government employees: *Antou* and *Sili* both enjoy one slaughter every 20 days; each of them is allotted 1 *sheng* of rice per day; a Junior and a Keeper of the Rod each has 1 *sheng* of rice.

Provisions granted to the employees in the higher and lower Bureaus of Livestock Review and Inspection, according to ranks:

A senior official enjoys a slaughter every 7 days, 4 *sheng* of rice or grains per day, of which there is 1 *sheng* of rice; food for 4 horses, 7 *sheng* for one horse, 5 *sheng* in case of the 3 horses; for the three children, there is 1 *sheng* of rice per day.

36 *Revised Laws of Heavenly Prosperity* 19, "On the Examination of Livestock," p. 585.

☐ All serving agents in the Bureau of Review and Inspection and others enjoy a slaughter every 15 days, 1 *sheng* of rice per day, 5 *sheng* of food supply to the horse, as well as 1 *sheng* of rice to a single child.

The two lower-level *Antou* and *Sili* officials enjoy a slaughter every 15 days; to each of them, there is a supply of horse food in 5 *sheng*; to each of them there is 1 *sheng* of rice per day; to the one child, there is 1 *sheng* of rice.

Each of the two men receives an allocation of 1 *sheng* of rice per day:
One in charge of the rod.
One in charge of equipment.[37]

In the *Laws of Heavenly Prosperity*, rules on the provisions of meat, grains, and hay to government staff and their retinue (including horses) on official trips are extensive and exhaustive. The Chinese documents transcribed, translated, and discussed above have not only verified the information we find in the law code but also add new insights on the enforcement of the laws. We now know, for example, that the provision of hay had to be approved, according to the different ranks of horses. The quantity of hay is calculated according to the duration of the trip (in days) and again recounted in summary statistics. It is a slight pity, however, that these documents refer only to the allotment of hay for horses, not that of food and meat to the officers and staff.

2 Contracts

Though fewer than Tangut contracts, Chinese contracts in Western Xia are just as diverse and valuable historical sources and economic records.

2.1 *Grain Loan Contracts*

Several Chinese grain loan contracts were discovered in Khara-Khoto and seized by both Kozlov and Stein. These contracts were written on fragments that were used as layering papers of Buddhist sutras. A businessman named Pei Songshou, apparently active in the pawning business, is the protagonist in these contracts. In 1953, Henri Maspero published *The Chinese Documents of the Third Expedition of Sir Aurel Stein in Central Asia* in London, which

37 *Revised Laws of Heavenly Prosperity* XX, "On the Different Degrees of Crimes and Liabilities," pp. 613–614.

contains the Tianqing grain pawning contracts of Western Xia.[38] The contract is included in *Dunhuang Ziliao* issue 1, edited by the Institute for History at the Chinese Academy of Social Sciences and published in 1961.[39] In 1980, Chen Guocan published an article on the subject, "A Restoration of the Grain-Pawning Contracts Fragment in the Tianqing era of Western Xia," based on the material presented in *Dunhuang Ziliao*. What he accomplished was a close examination and interpretation of the 15 pawning Tianqing contracts at the British Library.[40]

Grain-pawning contracts, also dated to the Tianqing era of Western Xia but obtained and preserved by the Russians at the IOM, came into public light in the 1990s, as Chinese and Russian experts collaborated on the publication of the *Russian Collection of Khara-Khoto Manuscripts* (photocopy in Vol. 2).[41] Although the English and Russian manuscripts are from the same period and concern the same Pei Songshou, the grains loaned and the interest rates applied are quite different.

Amongst the 15 documents held at the British Museum, 11 have survived well and remain legible. The first piece, in particular, offers an abundance of evidence:

> Tianqing 11th year, 5th month 3rd day, contract set by Wunü Langsu presently …
> … □fur coat 1 item, from Pei's place …
> … *dou* plus 3 (interest), wheat 5 *dou* plus 4 (interest), principle & interest total, barley …
> … *dou* 5 *sheng*, if pawn not redeemed, till the due time the coming August …
> Let sold, no complaint.
> Contract set by Wunü Langsu (stamped)
> Witness □□ (stamped)

In the light of a comparative analysis with the other 14 contracts, as well as further research and inference, Chen Guocan has surmised some of the

38 TN: French sinologist and philologist Henri Maspero (1883–1945). See, Maspero, Henri (eds.). *Les Documents chinois de la troisième expédition de Sir Aurel Stein en Asie centrale*, London: British Museum, 1953.

39 For the original, see Chinese Academy of Social Sciences-Institute for History (eds.). *Dunhuang Ziliao* [敦煌資料]: *Sources of Dunhuang*, issue 1. Beijing: Zhonghua Book Company [中華書局], 1961.

40 Chen Guocan, 1980.

41 *Russian Collection of Khara-Khoto Manuscripts*, vol. 2, pp. 37–38.

missing characters and filled in the incomplete information. The following is his amended version of the contract:

> Tianqing 11th year, 5th month 3rd day, Contract set by Wunü Langsu, who presently, with her own□□fur coat 1 item, at Pei's place pawned in exchange for wheat 5 *dou*, plus 3 as interest; wheat 5 *dou* plus 4 as interest; principle & interest: 1 *dan* 3 *dou* 5 *sheng* of barley. If the pawn is not redeemed by the due date: 1st day of the 8th month, then let [the fur coat] be sold, and let there be no complaint or dispute.
> Contractor: Wunü Langsu (stamped)
> Witness: Ejing (stamped)

The contract tells the story of a woman who has to pawn her belongings in exchange for subsistence. To pawn fur carpets or fur coats for grains, the interest rate was usually 30% or 40% for three months. If one takes into account the fact that, in most cases, the possession was under-valued by the pawning shop, then the interest rate might as well be around 50%, roughly the equivalent of the rates found in Tangut grain loan contracts.

In the *Russian Collection of Khara-Khoto Manuscripts*, there are 12 page-fragments, registered as TK49P. They are contracts signed by borrowers of grain and by the aforementioned loaner, Pei Songshou in a year of Tianqing. Amongst them, the data in five pieces of contracts remain legible.

FIGURE 216 Russian Khara-Khoto manuscript TK49P: Tianqing contract of pawning wheat at Pei Songshou's place

The following is a translated transcription of one of these contracts:

> On the 16th day of the 4th month in the 6th year of Tianqing, contractor Hu Zhu'er□ ...
> From the place of Pei Songshou, obtained barley in the amount of 6 *dou*, plus 5 as interest; the principle and interest in total are 9 *dou*,
> The loan of barley is due to be repaid by the 1st day of the 8th month. If by the due date it is not
> Repaid, let there be 1 *dou* of penalty per *dou* of loan ...

It is not clear what kind of property is being pawned, except that it is worth approximately 6 *dou* of barley. "Plus 5 as interest" means a "50% interest rate." With a total of 11 pawning contracts signed anytime between the 1st and the 9th day of the 5th month in that year, Pei Songshou loaned out wheat and barley in a total amount of 14 *dan*. Pei was in the pawning business at least from the 6th year (1199) to the 11th year (1204) of Tianqing. He charged exorbitant interest rates during these six years: 50% interest rate in the 6th year of Tianqing, 30% or 40% in the 11th year of Tianqing, etc. All of these pawning arrangements count as usuries. He counted on loans to people who would pawn their clothing in the 4th or 5th months of the year, when there was no longer the need for heavy coats to survive the wintry days. However, it was also a time when leftover grains from the previous year ran out, and new crops were not yet ripe for harvest. The plan was to redeem the pawned properties, albeit at the cost of additional interests, after the harvest. These contracts show the exploitations of the poor at the hands of usurious loaners. It seems that, at least in Khara-Khoto but probably also elsewhere in Western Xia, there existed a class of professional financiers such as Pei Songshou who profited mostly, if not only, from usuries.[42] They issue grain loans in exchange for pawned properties and high interests. It is a peculiar profession in Tangut society and economy.

Pei Songshou arranges for multiple pawning contracts to be written and signed in continuum on the same piece of paper. This format is present in some of the Tangut grain loan contracts, as well.[43] Although squeezed into one single account, each document features the signatures and stamps of its own borrowers and witnesses. So, there is no question that, in terms of legal force, each of them counts as a contract in the proper and accurate sense of the term.

---

42 Du, Jianlu. "Heicheng Chutu de Jijian Hanwen Xixia Wenshu Kaoshi" [黑城出土的幾件漢文西夏文書考釋]: "A Critical Interpretation of Several Chinese documents of Western Xia Unearthed in Khara-Khoto" in *Zhongguoshi Yanjiu* [中國史研究]: *Journal of Chinese Historical Studies*, issue 4, 2008.

43 Shi Jinbo, 2005 (b).

2.2 *Monetary Loan Contracts*

There is a total of three Tangut monetary loan contracts written in Chinese, all preserved at the IOM of the Russian Academy of Sciences: the Инв. No. 7779A, the Инв. No. 7779B, and the Инв. No. 7779E. All three are contract fragments, originally written on layer papers of the Tangut Buddhist sutra *Mahāmāyūri-vidyārājñī-sūtra*.[44,45] The 7779A is cut into two fragments, each 9.6 cm × 29.7 cm. At the joint of the two fragments, half a character is missing. But there is no question when it comes to dating the contract: "□sheng Guiwei 15th year"—obviously it should have been "Guiwei the 15th Year of Tiansheng" (1163 AD). On the back of the cover is a balance sheet account, with statements of incomes and expenditures. The 7779B contract has survived in three separate fragments: (1) 11.2 cm × 7 cm, also dated to "Guiwei 15th Year of Tiansheng" (2) 19.1 cm × 4.6 cm, with the following note: "received on the 8th day, now with money in the amount of 5 *guan wen*" etc. (3) 19.3 × 5.8 cm, with references to "the person who set up the contract" etc. The 7779E contract is 9.6 cm × 7.8 cm, with a note that reads, "20 wen, to be fully [repaid/reimbursed] in 65 nights" etc.

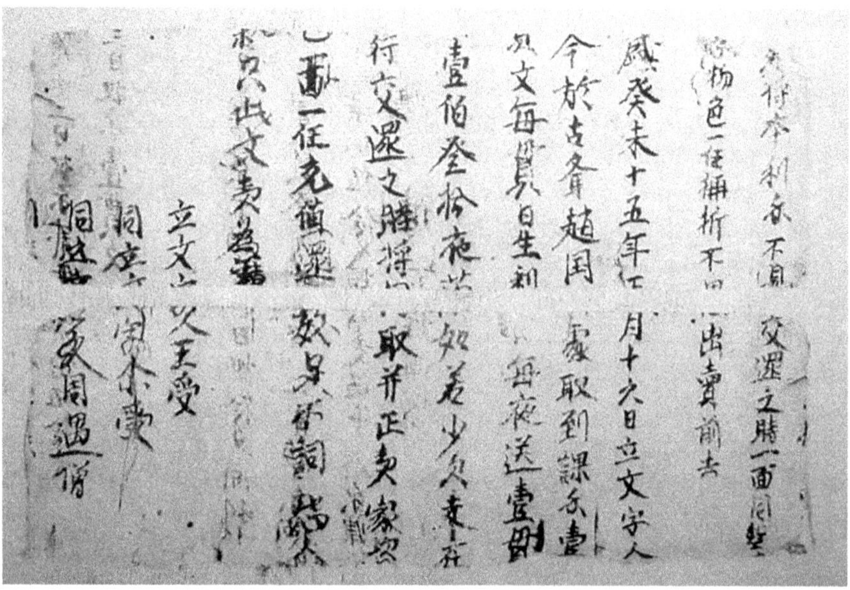

FIGURE 217 Инв. No. 7779A: 15th year of Tiansheng (1163) Wang Shou's contract of monetary loan

44 *Russian Collection of Khara-Khoto Manuscripts*, vol. 6, pp. 321, 322, 325.

45 TN: See Shi and Li, p. 113. Tibetan title: *Rig-sṅags-kyi rgyal-mo rma-bya chen-mo.*

The Инв. No. 7779A is mostly intact and legible. The following is a translated transcription: (the contract begins with the 3rd line as shown in the image):

> ... Tiansheng era, Guiwei 15th year, 1stmonth, 16th day, contractor ...
> ... present, from "ancient Qi & Zhao states" □ place, received monetary loan 1...
> ...... *guan wen*, each *guan* at the interest rate of □, 1 *guan* to be delivered per night ...
> ......130 nights [completed][payment]; in case of insufficient [repayment], at ...
> ...... the time of repayment, will [also] obtain the contract, household property ...
> ...... suffer confiscation as repayment, until the debt is cleared, with no complaint. lest ......
> ... This contract alone serves as testimony.
> Contractor: Wang Shou
> Co-Contractor: Xiaoshou
> Co-Contractor: Zhou Yuseng
> ...[46]

The manuscript Инв. No. 7779A provides the date, month, and year of the contract, the names of the borrowers and the creditor, the size of the monetary loan, terms, interest rates, and penalties in case of default. The contractor (borrower) and the co-contractors (guarantors) all signed but did not stamp the contract. The first two lines, as it appears on the contract, are the ending of a previous contract, which seems to be incomplete and without the proper signatures of names. Given a number of suspicious evidences, the creditor is bizarrely referred to as the "ancient Qi & Zhao states," the loan is in a large quantity, and the borrower is to 'deliver 1 *guan* of interest per night.' The document thus does not seem to be a normal contract and might have been a special kind of document that was written in the contract format.

2.3 *Lease Contracts*

There is a remarkable piece of contract in the Russian collection of Khara-Khoto manuscripts, the Дх18993 contract of bakery shop lease in the 1st month of the 12th year of Guangding, signed by Li Chungou et al. At first, the document was not given a title, and was placed by mistake in the Russian collection of

46 For the transcription, see *Compilation and Survey of Non-Buddhist Han Chinese Documents in the Russian Collection of Khara-Khoto Manuscripts*, vol. II, p. 749.

Dunhuang manuscripts, and included in the published edition of the *Russian Collection of Dunhuang Manuscripts* vol. 17, p. 310.[47] The 12th year of Guangding (1222) fell within the reign of Shenzong emperor, Li Zunxu, near the twilight of the Tangut Empire.

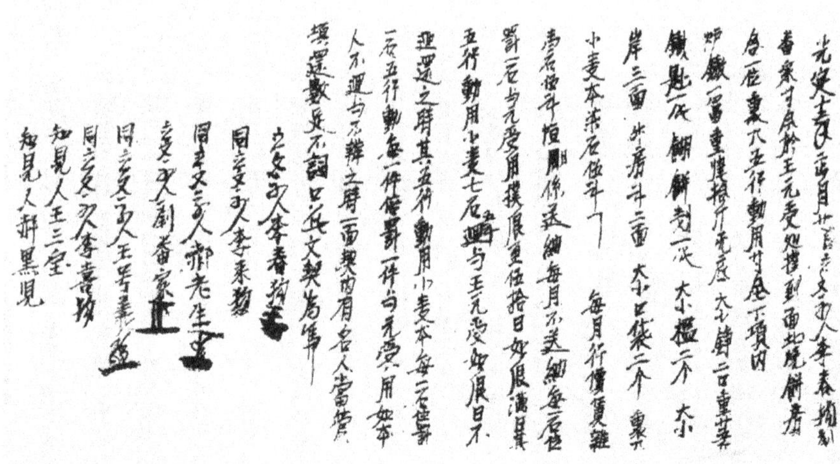

FIGURE 218 Дх18993: First Month, 12th year of Guangding (1222) Li Chungou, et al., lease contract of renting a house for baking pancakes

Translated transcription:

> In the 12th year of Guangding, on the 21st day of the 1st month, Contractor Li Chungou, Liu
> Fanjia, et al., presently received from Wang Yuanshou north-faced flat-bread house
> One lot, *li jiu wu* tools all equipped,[48] the following items

47 Institute of Oriental Manuscripts (IOM), Russian Academy of Sciences in St. Petersburg (Институ́т востокове́дения Росси́йской акаде́мии нау́к, Санкт-Петербургское отделение) & Shanghai Ancient Works Publishing House (eds.) Ecang Dunhuang Wenxian [俄藏敦煌文獻]: *Russian Collection of Dunhuang Manuscripts*, vol. 17, p. 310. Shanghai: Shanghai Ancient Works Publishing House, 2001.

48 TN: 裏九五 could be referring to the size of the shop, or to the tools therein equipped. 行動用 or 動用 definitely refer to the tools to be used. A discussion with Professor Du Jianlu has left it as an open-ended question.

Griddle 1 item, weighs 40 *jin*, no bottom [of pot]. Large and small toasters 2;[49] weighs 25 *jin*.
Iron spoon 1, Spatula 1,[50] large and small cupboards 2,[51] large and small [cutting]boards 3,[52]
Boards 3, *shengfangdou* 2,[53] large and small bags 2, *li jiu*
Wheat and principle, 7 *dan* 5 *dou*; miscellaneous rents on a monthly basis
1 *dan* 5 *dou* of monthly payment. If the monthly rent is not delivered, for each *dan*, there is a
dan of penalty, for the use of Yuanshou. When the lease is due in 50 days, by due date, its
5 tools are used, wheat 7 *dan* 5 *dou*, to be paid back to Wang Yuanshou. When due, if it is not
returned, and if the 5 tools are used, then a penalty of 1 *dan* of wheat applies to each loan of
1 *dan*; each of the 5 tools[54] is penalised with a new one for Yuanshou's use. If the person
himself does not return or cannot be identified, the co-signed parties in the contract ought to
fill in the full sum, without complaint. Let this contract alone be the proof.
Contractor: Li Chungou [stamped]
Co-Contractor: Li Laigou
Co-Contractor: Hao Laosheng [stamped]
Contractor: Liu Fanjia [stamped]
Co-Contractor: Wang Haoyi [stamped]
Co-Contractor: Li Xigou
Witness: Wang Sanbao
Witness: Hao Heijian

This is a rare piece of a fully complete contract, and rare also with regard to the type of contract: a contract of bakery shop lease. It is the only survived

49 TN: 鋢 is a generic, alternative reference to 餅鐺. Not the electric type, of course, but metal pans used to fry and bake cakes.

50 TN: I am somewhat confident that 餬餅剗 refers to a specialised spatula used for lifting and flipping *shaobing*.

51 TN: The 檻 here most probably refers to cupboard or a case.

52 TN: a wild if not impossible guess is that these are cutting boards.

53 TN: The 升房斗 is a measure container of a *dou*, in which there is an attached container that measures a *sheng*.

54 TN: I would fill in "the [damage of] each …"

contract of *shaobing* shop lease from Western Xia. It may be either singular, or 'as uncommon as the phoenix's feather and the unicorn's horn' in the entire history of Chinese contracts.

The contract's reference to "wheat and principle: 7 *dan* 5 *dou*" may be the summary principle that includes both the shop itself and the tools that are included in the lease. The interest is calculated based on this total sum of principle. Therefore, the rent: "1 *dan* 5 *dou* of monthly payment" is basically a monthly interest charged on the principle in the amount of "7 *dan* 5 *dou*." It amounts to a monthly interest rate of 20%. A 5-month lease would yield the creditor a cumulative interest rate of 100%; the rate for a one-year lease would rise up to 240%. We know from the vast number of Tangut grain loan contracts that although some of the interest rates reach up to 100%, most stay around 50% for a duration of three to six months. Therefore, if the agreement between Li and Wang is representative of Tangut shop leases in general, then one could say that the loan of bakery shops charges a much higher interest rate than that of grains. But one would expect this to be the case, given that the *shaobing* shop is a for-profit enterprise rather than a source of simple subsistence.[55]

2.4 *Land Sale Contracts*

In the 1990s, experts from the Dunhuang Academy systematically surveyed the stone caves in the northern zone of the Mogao Grottoes. Amongst their discoveries were a batch of Tangut and Chinese manuscripts dated to the era of Western Xia. One of the Chinese documents is the G11 • 031[B59:1] manuscript found in the 59th cave in the northern zone: land sale contract by Weiming Fabaoda.[56] The manuscript fragment is 18.8 cm × 22.7 cm in size, contains 11 lines of texts, and features four red seals, two of which remain legible.

55 Du Jianlu and Shi Jinbo, 2010 & 2012, pp. 42–48.

56 *Chinese Collection of Tan· [U+00B7, Brill font]ut Manuscripts*, vol. 16, p. 46.

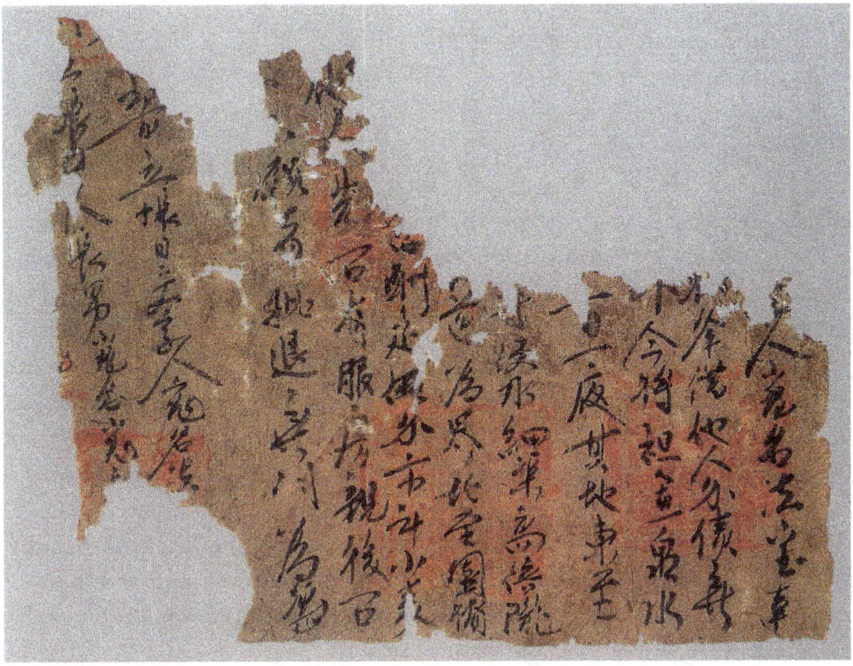

FIGURE 219 Mogao Cave, G11 • 031 [B59:1]: Weiming Fabaoda land sale contract

The following is a transcription of the main text of the document:[57]

... year, setting the account in text person, Weiming Fabaoda
... due to the difficulty and poverty of life? borrow loans from others, no thing to repay? ... □now, to have [on the] plain □ straight-flowing spring (water)
... one day, one night, the land's east end-point
... □makes the water narrow streams on Gaobeilong
... way, as boundaries, bi (north) up to the yard
... □to negotiate on the premise of market price of wheat
... the land unsold? others, first ask the relatives of the same house, then ask the

57 For the transcription, see Luo, Haishan. "Weiming Fabaoda Maidi Wenshu Kaobian" [嵬名法寶達賣地文書考辨]: "A Critical Study of the 'Weiming Fabaoda Land Sale Document'" published in Shen, Zhibei. *San Ge U Ji: Huo Cunfu Jiaoshou Congjiao Sanshinian Jinian Wenji* [3 個U 集: 霍存福教授從教三十年紀念文集]: *Three Us: Collection of Essays in Honour of Professor Huo Fucun's Thirtieth Year of Teaching*. Beijing: Intellectual Property Publishing House Co., Ltd, 2015.

neighbours, unwilling ones rescind, □□have□
… 1st day, contractor Weiming Fa[baoda]
… co-contractor of the account, elder son, Weiming We□
…

This contract fragment on the sale of land features four seal prints in the red colour. The seller of land, namely the "person who sets up the account in text" is listed as Weiming Fabaoda. It is no secret that the Weimings were a large royal family of the Dangxiang Tanguts. It is all the more intriguing then that the purpose of the sale was to compensate for "personal debts of monetary loans from others." Interest rates in Western Xia were notoriously high.[58] The feudal regime assumes as one of its primary duties the guaranteed protection of the interests of the creditors. The laws require that "let all demand and press the debtors for repayments, the failures of which are to be reported to the bureau, in order that force be employed to search, obtain, and interrogate."[59] After its occupation of Dunhuang, the Tangut regime inherited the irrigation system from the Tang and Five Dynasties. References to "springs" and "narrow canals" as endpoints of the region for sale in the contract fragment prove the existence of irrigations in neighbouring areas. By the rule "first ask the relatives in the family, then inquire the neighbours" this legal document affirms what we know to be conventional rights of families and neighbours.

Although a page fragment, this document has gained the attention of a number of Tangutologists and have been subject to many critical surveys. These scholars, however, diverge in their naming, timing, and determination of its properties. Since this document mentions neither names of buyers nor terms of default penalties and also uses the word for 'account' rather than 'contract,' some experts have named it "Account of Land Sale by Weiming Fabaoda." For others, a careful analysis of the format and other aspects of this contract suggests that it might have been a land sale contract by the Tanguts after the fall of the regime, possibly during the Yuan Dynasty years.[60]

58 Du, Jianlu: "Xixia Gaolidai Chutan" [西夏高利貸初探]: "A Preliminary Survey of High Interest Rates in Western Xia" in *Minzu Yanjiu* [民族研究]: *Ethno-National Studies*, issue 2, 1999; Shi Jinbo, 2005 (b).

59 *Revised Laws of Heavenly Prosperity*, vol. 3. "On Urging the Payment of Debt."

60 Luo, Haishan. "Weiming Fabaoda Maidi Wenshu Yanjiu" [嵬名法寶達賣地文書研究]: "A Study on the Document of Weiming Fabaoda's Sale of Land" (unpublished paper).

Epilogue

One of the fundamental areas of historical inquiries is the study of the society and its economy. Revealing patterns of economic practices, regulations, policies, and laws in the past offers both theoretical insights on human conduct and practical lessons on the underlying principles of our own socio-economic activities.

This book is a study of the newly discovered, compiled, and published economic records of Western Xia. The archives that constitute the primary body of materials for this research project are 12th–13th century economic records produced by the Tangut people, which have thus far never been the subject of any monographic study. These primary sources of great academic value proved a pleasant surprise, when first identified at the Institute of Oriental Manuscripts (IOM) in St. Petersburg. And it gives me great joy and satisfaction to share my findings on this rich cultural heritage of Western Xia with my colleagues in Tangut studies and allied fields.

This book is the first focused study on the Tangut economy by way of a systematic analysis of the social documents. It tries to present a new and deeper understanding of the Tangut economy and society, in the following ways:

(A) Household registration, which certifies a natural person's legal status as a civil subject, is an instrumental source of material to any socio-economic research. The corpus of Tangut household registers shows that Western Xia enjoyed an excellent system of household registration, which features diverse types of registers and accounts. The contents recorded in the registers and the *shoushi* self-reports are rich and informative. These demographic records furnish us with the necessary materials to conduct studies on the ratio and proportion of household types, ethnicities of local families, names and name-giving, the practices of inter-ethnic marriage at the basic and bottom levels of the society, and the customs of cross-cousin and polygamous marriages in the area of Khara-Khoto, all of which fill in the gaps and vacuum of our previous knowledge in the Tangut society.

(B) The Tangut tax records reveal to us a fixed system of levying taxes in grains, based on the size of farmlands. In the agricultural areas of Western Xia, peasants paid land, labour, and hay/forage taxes. Receipts of grain taxes and additional bundles of hay taxes, as well as the poll tax, a form of *tributum capitis* levied on each 'head' of a liable subject, are some of the main attributes of the Tangut tax system. The so-called 'water-tax' is a special levy on the use of water for the purpose of irrigation. Among these taxes, survived records of the poll tax and water tax count amongst the finest, rarest, and most valuable primary materials in Chinese history.

(C) Financial and property accounts supply us with the names of the commodities. Given our limited knowledge in the actual lives of the Tangut people, such as their quotidian uses and produces, the abundance of names and features of various goods recorded in these newly-discovered primary sources enlivens our imagination of the daily lives of the Tanguts, and delineates the social contexts of these materials. Some iconic products, such as Fan cloth (made in Western Xia) and Han cloth (made in the Central Plains), are now well-known thanks to these accounts of grains and properties, which are undoubtedly amongst the best primary sources for social historians of Western Xia and of China. That both Fan and Han cloths are mentioned in these accounts shows that the Tanguts produced their own cloth even prior to their arrival in what were Han Chinese territories, and that even after their integration with local Chinese populations, both types of cloth coexisted in households and co-circulated in markets, neither of which had entirely replaced the other. This has, on the one hand, shaken our prior assumptions about the absence of any native Tangut textile industry, and on the other, confirmed our intuition that the Tanguts absorbed Chinese technology in an era of inter-ethnic socio-economic exchanges.

(D) Trade and transaction records not only reflect the status of medieval commerce in and beyond Tangut territories, but also provide us with the most critical sources on the commodity prices in Western Xia markets. They reveal the production costs and market prices of a variety of goods, from livestock, silk to alcohol, that were continually made, sold and exchanged. Besides, there exist a number of transaction taxes, which were also an integral part of the economic lives of the Tangut people.

(E) Each and single one of the contracts prior to the Yuan Dynasty is a gem. Amongst the Tangut social documents, the contracts are most numerous and diverse, numbering up to about 150 registers and more than 500 pieces, which altogether account for the largest portion of Tang and Song contracts (including the contracts excavated in the Dunhuang Grottoes) hitherto identified. Tangut contracts are wide-ranging, including transactions, pawns, loans, as well as employment and exchanges. As the vivid and illustrative saying goes, "The government has its laws, the people have their contracts." Moreover, this corpus of materials adds a large number of important sources to the field of Chinese contract studies. In general, Tangut contracts represent an intermediary stage, in transition from Tang and Song to Yuan traditions.

(F) The Tanguts resorted to block-printing receipts that were used on a large scale, at a high frequency, and in a fixed format. Then, they filled in required information in the empty spaces. Such are the cases in the receipts of grain tax and the additional bundles of hay taxes. In this way, the procedures of issuing these receipts became formalised, operationalised, and greatly expedited, thus the chance of typological errors significantly reduced. To date, this is the earliest example of printed receipt in ancient and medieval economic history, a successful application of the block-printing technique to daily-used documents, and a major step forward in the both the history of printing, and the history of economic documents.

Studying the Tangut economy with the aid of its economic records represents a new approach within the field of Tangutology. This method also extends to a comparative study of the Tangut household registers, accounts, and contracts with the law code of Western Xia, the *Laws of Heavenly Prosperity*. So far, studies show that the *Laws of Heavenly Prosperity* were thoroughly, if not perfectly implemented on the ground level of the Tangut society. Therefore, we are assured that this code of law is a reliable source of historical knowledge.

Another important contribution of the social documents is to Tangut calligraphy and paleography. Upon reading the cursive writings in these documents, I spent a total of 20 years perusing and probing the patterns of cursive strokes, both by comparison and in reference to the Tangut standard script. Up to now, the cursive script of the Tangut writing has been basically deciphered.

Historians bury themselves in archives, not least to use primary historical sources to reconstruct the actual lives of peoples in the past. Indeed, the economic records of Western Xia now allow us to re-imagine the vivid scenes of social lives in the once prosperous city of Khara-Khoto. This book shows, for example, that around 800 years ago, not only Fan (Dangxiang-Tangut) and Han (Chinese), but also Qiangic (which to the Tanguts meant 'Tibetan'), Huihu (medieval Uyghur), Khitan, and even Dashi (Arab) migrants resided on the banks of the Blackwater River. They cultivated and irrigated the fields, planted and harvested wheat, millet, barley, sorghum and beans, lived in houses and yards built on their lands, and raised horses, cows, camels, and sheep in a half-settled and half-pastoral life. Men and women dressed in different ethnic costumes come and go, converse and transact in all places. The commoners wore gowns made of Fan or Han cloths, while the wealthy embellished their dress with silk. Fields were farmed in large numbers, but also taxed by the local government: the 'junior accounting magistrate' waits at the gate of the grain storage site to receive the dues, a process overseen by a supervisory official standing by his side. Upon receiving the taxes, the official hands back receipts into the taxpayer's hands. Besides, some peasants either bore the burden of taxes by their own labour, or paid the dear capitation taxes. For the farmers, diverting water to irrigate their field was also liable for taxation. After a good harvest, the peasants would have paid their taxes, carried grains on carriages, and transited across the busy roads. The common peasants could fill their stomachs when things went well, but would starve should a drought strike the town. In springtime, which must have followed a harsh winter but still anticipated the harvest season, the most impoverished of the peasants suffered a shortage of food, and had no recourse but to take grain loans at a high interest rate, which usually exceeded 50% of the principle loan, and in some extreme cases, as exorbitant as twice the sum due for repayment. Others found a solution in selling parts of their land, or a number of livestock in exchange for the much-needed grains. This, unfortunately, would start a vicious cycle of impoverishment. Many local landlords and temple establishments seized the opportunity to exploit the toiling poor, grab land and expand their estates. Peasants waited in line at temples to borrow grains, vend or lease land, and sell their livestock, ready to imprint their finger segments on the contract. Even worst was the transaction of lowly semi-slaves, and the unfree, contract-bound servants, who were vended and purchased like livestock by their masters.

The Tanguts not only bartered in direct exchanges of goods, but also traded by the medium of widely-circulated currency, including iron and copper coins, as well as gold and silver. Upon the successful completion of a transaction, magistrates in the government's Bureau of Transaction Tax would collect taxes, and register the transaction in the official records. Individuals and social groups, such as families and communities, were organised into *li* and *jia*, somewhat corresponding to the military organisations of *liu* and *chao*. Communal societies, popular amongst the Han Chinese, were also present and known as the 'convention of the many' on the basis of mutual help: if a member's families suffered diseases or deaths, other members of the 'commune' would pay visits, provide moral and financial support, and offer consolations and condolences.

The city of Khara-Khoto and its nearby areas remained under effective Tangut rule until the last years of Western Xia. This in part explains the wealth of official and private documents produced in a relatively stable society over a long span of time. Locals who knew the Tangut script well made a living by writing, constantly preoccupied with producing records and receipts for a variety of purposes. Needlessly to say, the ones that have survived to our day are only a small fraction of the total amount. But in all cases, these texts have not only filled in void of the social history of Western Xia, but also enlivened and, in a way, 'materialised' it. The social and economic records of the enigmatic empire, written in the most mysterious script of a dead language, now permit us to peek into the actual lives of the medieval Tanguts.

Tangut economic documents in the cursive script constitute a reservoir of primary sources for the convenience of those intent on mastering the Tangut cursive writing, and for scholars in need of these materials for their own research.

The translation, interpretation and analysis of the Tangut economic records in this book could at best count as a preliminary and preparatory work. On the one hand, the translations cover only a part, rather than the entire body of available texts; on the other hand, there are still characters and words that remain in question and need further clarification. Additionally, there is still room for more comparative study between these materials and the economic records of contemporaneous, previous and subsequent medieval regimes and dynasties. Indeed, archival work on this corpus of social documents has only just begun. And this book is, says the Chinese idiom, a 'brick cast to invite the jade,' in a long journey of research on the economy of Western Xia.

Bibliography

Primary Sources

Charignon, A.J.H. (ed.). *Le Livre de Marco Polo*. Pékin: Albert Nachbaur, Vol. 1. 1924, Vol. 2. 1926, Vol. 3. 1928.

Chinese Academy of Social Sciences-Institute for History & British Library (eds.). *Yingcang Dunhuang Wenxian* [英藏敦煌文獻]: *British Collection of Dunhuang Manuscripts*. Chengdu: Sichuan People's Press, 1995.

Guo, Maoqian (Song Dynasty). *Yuefu Shiji* [樂府詩集]: *Anthology of Yuefu Poetry*. Sibu Congkan Edition (四部叢刊). Shanghai: Commercial Press, 1922.

Huang, Zhenhua; Nie, Hongyin; Shi, Jinbo (eds.). *Fan Han Heshi Zhangzhongzhu* [番漢合時掌中珠]: *Fan-Han Pearl in the Palm*. Yinchuan: Ningxia People's Press, 1989.

Li, Tao. *Xu Zizhi Tongjian Changbian* [續資治通鑒長編]: *The Extended Zizhi Tongjian*. Emended Critical Edition. Beijing: Zhonghua Book Company, 1979.

Li, Yanshou, et al. *Bei Shi* [北史]: *History of the Northern Dynasties*. Beijing: Zhonghua Book Company, 1974.

Liu, Xu, et al. *Jiu Tang Shu* [舊唐書]: *Old Book of Tang*. Beijing: Zhonghua Book Company, 1975.

Ma, Duanlin (Song Dynasty). *Wenxian Tongkao*, "Tianfukao" [文獻通考·田賦考]: *Comprehensive Examination of Literature* (1317). Beijing: Zhonghua Book Company, 1986.

Shi, Jinbo; Nie, Hongyin; Bai, Bin (eds.). *Xixia Tiansheng Lüling* [西夏天盛律令]: *The Tangut Laws of Heavenly Prosperity. Zhongguo Zhenxi Falü Dianji Jicheng* [中國珍稀法律典籍集成]: *A Collection of Rare and Precious Chinese Codes of Law*, vol. 5. Beijing: China Science Publishing & Media, 1994.

Shi, Jinbo, and Chen, Yuning (eds.). Centre for Tangut Studies at Ningxia University, National Library of China & Gansu-Wuliang Centre for the Compilation of Historical Manuscripts (五涼古籍整理研究中心). *Zhongguo cang Xixia Wenxian* (中國藏西夏文獻): *Chinese Collection of Tangut Manuscripts*. Lanzhou: Gansu People's Press & Dunhuang Wenyi Press, 2005.

Shi, Jinbo; Nie, Hongyin; Bai, Bin (eds.). *Tiansheng Gaijiu Xinding Lüling* [天盛改舊新定律令]: *Revised Laws of Heavenly Prosperity*. Beijing: Law Press of China, 2000.

Shi, Jinbo; Wei, Tongxian; Кычанов, Е.И. (eds.). *Ecang Heishuicheng Wenxian* [俄藏黑水城文獻]: *Russian Collection of Tangut Manuscripts*. Институт восточных рукописей Российской академии наук, formerly the St. Petersburg Branch of the Institute of Oriental Studies of the Russian Academy of Sciences. Institute of Ethnology and Anthropology, formerly Institute of Ethnology of the Chinese Academy of Social Sciences. Shanghai: Shanghai Ancient Books Publishing House, 1996–2011.

Song, Lian; Zhao, Xun; Wang, Yi; et al. *Yuanshi* [元史] *History of Yuan*. Beijing: Zhonghua Book Company, 1976.

Su, Shi. *Dongpo Quanji* [東坡全集]: *Complete Works of Su Dongpo*. Shanghai: Shanghai Ancient Books Publishing House, 1987.

Ta, La; Du, Jianlu; Gao, Guoxiang (eds.). *Zhongguo cang Heishuicheng Hanwen Wenxian* [中國藏黑水城漢文文獻]: *Han Chinese Documents in the Chinese Collection of Khara-Khoto Manuscripts*. Beijing: National Library of China Press, 2008.

Tang, Geng'ou; Lu, Hongji (eds.). *Dunhuang Shehui Jingji Wenxian Zhenji Shilu* [敦煌社會經濟文獻真跡釋錄]: *An Interpretive Transcription of the Original Dunhuang Economic Documents*. Beijing: National Library of China, Quanguo Tushuguan Wenxian Suowei Fuzhi Zhongxin [全國圖書館文獻縮微複製中心], 1990.

Tuo, Tuo, et al. *Liao Shi* [遼史]: *History of Liao*. Beijing: Zhonghua Book Company, 1974.

Tuo, Tuo, et al. *Jin Shi* [金史]: *History of Jin*. Beijing: Zhonghua Book Company, 1975.

Tuo, Tuo, et al. *Songshi* [宋史]: *History of Song*. Emended Critical Edition. Beijing: Zhonghua Book Company, 1977.

Wang, Gong (Song Dynasty). *Wen Jian Jin Lu* [聞見近錄]. Beijing: Zhonghua Book Company, 1984.

Wei, Zheng, et al. *Sui Shu* [隋書]: *Book of Sui*. Beijing: Zhonghua Book Company, 1977.

Wen, Yanbo. *Lugong Wenji* [潞公文集], photocopy of the Siku Quanshu edition [四庫全書本]. Taipei: Taiwan Commercial Press, 1983; (明嘉靖五刻本, 傅增湘校本; edited by 四川大學古籍整理研究所) Beijing: Xianzhuang Book Company, 2004; (叢書集成續編. 集部. 別集類 101) Shanghai: Shanghai Shudian, 1994.

Wu, Guangcheng. *Xixia Shushi* [西夏書事]: *Book of Western Xia*. Fifth Year of Daoguang (1835) printed edition (Beijing: Wenkuitang, 1935; Taipei: Guangwen, 1968).

Xie, Yujie, and Wu, Fangsi (eds.). *Yingcang Heishuicheng Wenxian* [英藏黑水城文獻]: *British Collection of Khara-Khoto Manuscripts*. Second Northwest University for Nationalities, Shanghai Ancient Works Publishing House, and the British Library. Shanghai: Shanghai Ancient Works Publishing House, 2005.

Xue, Juzheng, et al. *Jiu Wu Dai Shi* [舊五代史]: *Old History of the Five Dynasties*. Beijing: Zhonghua Book Company, 1976.

Zeng, Gong (Song Dynasty). *Long Ping Ji* [隆平集] Wenyuange Sikuquanshu edition (文淵閣四庫全書本). Rpt. Beijing: Airusheng, 2009; Taipei: Taiwan Commercial Press, 1983.

Zhang, Chuanxi (ed.). *Zhongguo Lidai Qiyue Huibian Kaoshi* [中國歷代契約彙編考釋]: *Studies and Interpretations of Contracts in All Chinese Dynasties*. Beijing: Peking University Press, 1995.

Zhuang, Chuo (Song Dynasty). *Ji Lei Pian* [雞肋篇]: *Essays: Chicken Ribs*. Beijing: Zhonghua Book Company, 1983.

Secondary Sources

Bai, Bin; Shi, Jinbo. "Mogaoku Yulinku Xixia Ziliao Gaishu" [莫高窟榆林窟西夏資料概述]: "A Summary of Tangut Materials in the Yulin Cave of Mogao Grottoes" in *Lanzhou Daxue Xuebao* [蘭州大學學報]: *Bulletin of Lanzhou University*, issue 2, 1980.

Chen, Bingying. *Xixia Wenwu Yanjiu* [西夏文物研究]: *A Study of Tangut Cultural Relics*. Yinchuan: Ningxia People's Press, 1985.

Chen, Bingying. *Xixia Yanyu* [西夏諺語]: *Tangut Proverbs*. Taiyuan: Shanxi People's Press, 1993.

Chen, Guocan. "Xixia Tianqing Diandang Canqi de Fuyuan" [西夏天慶典當殘契的復原]: "Restoration of the Remnant Pawning Contracts from the Era of the Heavenly Celebration (Tianqing)" in *Zhongguoshi Yanjiu* [中國史研究]: *Journal of Chinese Historical Studies* issue 1, 1980.

Chinese Academy of Social Sciences-Institute for History (eds.). *Dunhuang Ziliao* [敦煌資料]: *Sources of Dunhuang*. Beijing: Zhonghua Book Company [中華書局], 1961.

Du, Jianlu. *Xixia Jingjishi Yanjiu* [西夏經濟史研究]: *A Study of the Economic History of Western Xia*. Lanzhou: Gansu Culture Publishing House, 1998.

Du, Jianlu. "Xixia Gaolidai Chutan" [西夏高利貸初探]: "A Preliminary Survey of Usury in Western Xia" in *Minzu Yanjiu* [民族研究]: *Ethno-National Studies*, issue 2, 1999.

Du, Jianlu. *Xixia Jingjishi* [西夏经济史]: *An Economic History of Western Xia*. Beijing: China Social Sciences Press, 2002.

Du, Jianlu. "Heicheng Chutu de Jijian Hanwen Xixia Wenshu Kaoshi" [黑城出土的幾件漢文西夏文書考釋]: "A Critical Interpretation of Several Chinese Documents of Western Xia Unearthed in Khara-Khoto" in *Zhongguoshi Yanjiu* [中國史研究]: *Journal of Chinese Historical Studies*, issue 4, 2008.

Du, Jianlu, and Shi, Jinbo. *Xixia Shehui Wenshu Yanjiu* [西夏社會文書研究]: *A Study of Tangut Social Documents*. Shanghai: Shanghai Ancient Works Publishing House, 2010 & 2012.

Dunnell, Ruth. "Locating the Tangut Military Establishment: Uraqai (Wulahai) and the Heishui Zhenyan Army" *Monumenta Serica*, 1992, pp. 219–234.

Gernet, Jacques. "La vente en Chine d'après les contrats de Touen-houang (IXe–Xe siècles)" *T'oung pao*, 1957-01-01, Vol. 45 (4/5), pp. 295–391.

Han, Guopan. "Cong Tulufan Chutu Wenshu zhong Xiatian Quanqi lai Tan Gaochang Zudian de Jige Wenti" [從吐魯番出土文書中夏田券契來談高昌租佃的幾個問題]: "A Discussion on Several Issues about Tenancy in Gaochang, based on Farmland Lease Contracts in the Unearthed Turfan Documents," pp. 199–224, Han, Guopan (eds.). *Dunhuang Tulufan Chutu Jingji Wenshu Yanjiu* [敦煌吐魯番出土經濟文

書研究]: *Studies on the Economic Documents Excavated in Turfan and Dunhuang*. Xiamen: Xiamen University Press, 1986.

Huang, Zhenhua. "Xixia Tiansheng Ershiernian Maidi Wenqi Kaoshi" [西夏天盛二十二年賣地文契考釋]: "A Study of the Land Sale Contract in the 22nd Year of Tiansheng," pp. 313–319, in *Xixiashi Lunwenji* [西夏史論文集]: *Collection of Essays on Tangut History*. Yinchuan: Ningxia People's Press, 1984.

Институ́т востокове́дения Росси́йской акаде́мии нау́к, Санкт-Петербургское отделение) & Shanghai Ancient Works Publishing House (eds.). *Ecang Dunhuang Wenxian* [俄藏敦煌文獻]: *Russian Collection of Dunhuang Manuscripts*. Shanghai: Shanghai Ancient Works Publishing House, 2001.

Кычанов, Е.И. Тангутский документ 1170г. о продаже земли, "Письменные памятника Востока.Ежгодник. 1971" М., 1974, pp. 196–203. Е.И. Кычанов Тангутский документ о займе под залог из Хара-хото Письменные памятника Востока. Ежгодник. 1972, М., 1977.

Кычанов, Е.И. Измененный и заново утвержденный кодекс девиза царствования Небесное процветание (1149–1169). В 4-х кн. М.: Издательство «Наука», ГРВЛ, 1987–1989 (Памятники письменности Востока LXXXI, 1–4). Translation and Commentary by Shi Jinbo, Nie Hongyin, Bai Bin. *The Laws of Heavenly Prosperity* in *Zhongguo Zhenxi Falü Dianji Jicheng* [中國珍稀法律典籍集成]: *A Collection of Rare and Precious Laws in China*, edition *jia*, vol. 5. Beijing: Science Press, China. 1994; Translation and Commentary by Shi Jinbo, Nie Hongyin, Bai Bin. *Revised Laws of Heavenly Prosperity* in *Zhonghua Chuanshi Fadian* [中華傳世法典]. Beijing: Law Press, 2000. For the original text, see also Shi; Wei; Kychanov. *Russian Collection of Khara-Khoto Manuscripts* Vol. VIII, Vol. IX, pp. 1–52.

Li, Fanwen, and Museum of Ningxia (eds.). *Xixia Lingmu Chutu Canbei Suibian* [西夏陵墓出土殘碑粹編]: *Inscription Fragments Excavated in the Tangut Tombs*. Beijing: Cultural Relics Publishing House, 1984.

Li, Fanwen, and Nakajima, Motoki. "Computational Analysis of Tangut Literature Zazi," Tokyo: Research Institute for Languages and Cultures of Asia and Africa (ILCAA) at the Tokyo University of Foreign Studies, 1997.

Liang, Jihong. "Wuwei cang Xixixawen Qianding Younian Zengna Caokun Wenshu Chutan" [武威藏西夏文乾定酉年增納草捆文書初探]: "A Preliminary Survey of the Documents on Additional Levies of Hay in Bundles, Written in Tangut, Dated to the You Year of Qianding, Preserved in Wuwei" in *Xixiaxue* [西夏學]: *Tangut Studies*, No. 10. Shanghai: Shanghai Ancient Works Publishing House, 2014.

Luo, Haishan. "Weiming Fabaoda Maidi Wenshu Kaobian" [嵬名法寶達賣地文書考辨]: "A Critical Study of the 'Weiming Fabaoda Land Sale Document'" published in Shen, Zhibei. *San Ge U Ji: Huo Cunfu Jiaoshou Congjiao Sanshinian Jinian Wenji* [3個U 集: 霍存福教授從教三十年紀念文集]: *Three Us: Collection of Essays in Honour of Professor Huo Fucun's Thirtieth Year of Teaching*. Beijing: Intellectual Property Publishing House Co., Ltd, 2015.

Luo, Haishan. "Weiming Fabaoda Maidi Wenshu Yanjiu" [嵬名法寶達賣地文書研究]: "A Study on the Document of Weiming Fabaoda's Sale of Land" (unpublished paper).

Maspero, Henri. *Les Documents chinois de la Troisième Expédition de Sir Aurel Stein en Asie Centrale*. London: Trustees of the British Museum, 1953.

Meng, Xianshi. "Lun Tang Song Shiqi Dunhuang Minjian Jieshe de Shetiao" [論唐宋時期敦煌民間結社的社條]: "On the Charters of Civil Societies in the Eras of Tang and Song," pp. 317–337, Ji, Xianlin, and Jao, Tsung-I. *Dunhuang Tulufan* Yanjiu [敦煌吐魯番研究(第九卷)]: *Journal of the Dunhuang and Turfan Studies Volume IX*. Beijing: Zhonghua Book Company, May, 2006.

Mie, Xiaohong. "Lun Tang Wudai Dunhuang de Minjian Sheyi" [論唐五代敦煌的民間社邑]: "On Civil Societies in the Tang and Five Dynasties" *Wuhan Daxue Xuebao* [武漢大學學報]: *Bulletins of the Wuhan University* (Humanities Edition), issue 6, 2008.

Museum of Gansu. "Gansu Wuwei Faxian Yipi Xixia Yiwu" [甘肅武威發現一批西夏遺物]: "A Batch of Tangut Materials has been Discovered in Wuwei, Gansu" in Kaogu [考古]: *Archaeology*, issue 3, 1974.

Nie, Hongyin, and Shi, Jinbo. "Xixiawenben Suijin Yanjiu" [西夏文本碎金研究]: "A Study of the Tangut *Golden Fragments*" *Ningxia Daxue Xuebao* [寧夏大學學報]: *Journal of Ningxia University* (Humanities & Social Sciences Edition), issue 2, 1995 (a).

Nie, Hongyin, and Shi, Jinbo. "Xixiawen Sancai Zazi Kao" [西夏文三才雜字考]: "A Study of the Assorted Characters of the Three Realms" in *Zhongyang Minzu Daxue Xuebao* [中央民族大學學報]: *Bulletin of the Minzu University of China*, issue 6, 1995 (b).

Ning, Ke; Hao, Chunwen. *Dunhuang Sheyi Wenshu Jijiao* [敦煌社邑文書輯校]: Nanjing: Jiangsu Guji Chubanshe [江蘇古籍出版社] (Jiangsu Ancient Books Publishing House, renamed 鳳凰出版社), August, 1997.

Niu, Dasheng. "Yizuo Zhongyao de Xixia Qianbi Jiaocang—Neimenggu Wushenqi Taoli Jiaocang" [一座重要的西夏錢幣窖藏—內蒙古烏審旗陶利窖藏]: "An Important Tangut Coin Hoard: Depository of Tangut Coins in Uxin Banner, Inner Mongolia" in *Gansu Jinrong Qianbi Zhuanji* (甘肅金融錢幣專輯), 1989.

Niu, Dasheng. "Xixia Qianbi Lunji" [西夏錢幣論集]: "Collected Essays on Tangut Coins" *Ningxia Jinrong* [宁夏金融]: Ningxia Finance, Supplementary Issue, 2007.

Nomura, Hiroshi. "Wuwei Xixia Bowuguan cang Haimudong Chutu Xixiawen Qiyue Wenshu" [武威西夏博物館藏亥母洞出土西夏文契約文書] in *Dongyang Shiyuan* [東洋史苑] Issue 75, July 2010.

Pan, Jie. "Tiansheng Gaijiu Xinding Lüling Cuijiaozumen Yiduan Xixiawen Zhuihe" [天盛改舊新定律令·催繳租門一段西夏文綴合]: "Conjoining a piece of Tangut writing in the Section on Urging the Payment of Taxes in the *Revised Laws of Heavenly Prosperity*" in *Ningxia Shehui Kexue* [寧夏社會科學]: *Ningxia Social Sciences*, issue 6, 2012.

Pan, Jie. "Xixia Zuyicao Kaoshu" [西夏租役草考述]: "A Critical Survey of Tax, Labour, and Hay in Western Xia" (unpublished manuscript).

Qi, Xia. *Zhongguo Jingji Tongshi* [中國經濟通史]: *Complete History of the Chinese Economy*, vol. 11. Beijing: Economic Daily Press (經濟日報社), 1999.

Qi, Xia; Qiao, Youmei. *Liao Xia Jin Jingjishi* [遼夏金經濟史]: *An Economic History of Liao, Xia and Jin Dynasties*. Baoding: Hebei University Press, 1994.

Shi, Jinbo. "Gansu Wuwei Faxian de Xixiawen Kaoshi Zhiyi" [甘肅武威發現的西夏文考釋質疑]: "Questions over the paper, 'Critical interpretation of the Tangut texts found in Wuwei, Gansu'" *Kaogu* [考古]: *Archaeology*, issue 3, 1974.

Shi, Jinbo. "Xixia Minghao Zakao" [西夏名號雜考]: "Miscellaneous Studies on Tangut Titles." *Zhongyang Minzu Xueyuan Xuebao* [中央民族學院學報]: *Academic Journal of the Minzu College (University) of China*, issue 4, 1986.

Shi, Jinbo. *Xixia Fojiao Shilue* [西夏佛教史略]: *A Brief History of Tangut Buddhism*. Yinchuan: Ningxia People's Press, 1988.

Shi, Jinbo. "Xixia Hanwenben Zazi Chutan" (西夏漢文本雜字初探): "Initial Thoughts on the Chinese Miscellaneous Characters in Western Xia" in *Zhongguo Minzushi Yanjiu* (中國民族史研究): *Studies in Chinese Ethnic History*, issue 2. Beijing: Minzu College (University) of China Press, 1989.

Shi, Jinbo. "Yibu You Tese de Lishi Fadian: Xixia Tiansheng Gaijiu Xinding Lüling" [一部有特色的歷史法典: 西夏天盛改舊新定律令]: "A Historical Law Code with Characteristics, the Tangut *Revised Laws of Heavenly Prosperity*" *Zhongguo Falüshi Guoji Xueshu Taolunhui Lunwenji* [中國法律史國際學術討論會論文集]: *Proceedings of the International Conference on Chinese Legal History*. Xi'an: Shaanxi People's Press, Sept. 1990.

Shi, Jinbo. "Xixia Tiansheng Lüling Lüelun" [西夏天盛律令略論]: "A Cursory Discussion on the Tangut *Laws of Heavenly Prosperity*" *Ningxia Shehui Kexue* [寧夏社會科學]: Ningxia Social Sciences, issue 1, 1993.

Shi, Jinbo. "Xixia de Zhiguan Zhidu" [西夏的職官制度]: "The Bureaucratic System of Western Xia" in *Lishi Yanjiu* [歷史研究]: *Historical Research*, issue 2, 1994.

Shi, Jinbo. "Xixiayu de Maimai he Jiaqu" [西夏語的買賣和嫁娶]: "Tangut Words for 'Buy,' 'Sell,' 'marry (to a husband),' 'marry (to a wife).'" *Minzu Yuwen* [民族語文]: *Minority Languages of China*, issue 4, 1995.

Shi, Jinbo. "Xixia Duliangheng Chuyi" [西夏度量衡芻議] "Some Initial Discussions on the Tangut System of Measurement" *Journal of Guyuan Teacher's College* [固原師專學報], now *Journal of Ningxia Normal University*, issue 2, 2002.

Shi, Jinbo. "Xixia Huji Chutan: 4 Jian Xixiawen Caoshu Huji Shiyi Yanjiu" [西夏戶籍初探: 4 件西夏文草書戶籍譯釋研究]: "Some Initial Discussions on the Interpretation of Four Tangut Household Registers in the Cursive Script" in *Minzu Yanjiu* [民族研究]: *Ethno-National Studies*, issue 5, 2004 (a).

Shi, Jinbo. "Guojia Tushuguan Cang Xixiawen Shehui Wenshu Canye Kao" [國家圖書館藏西夏文社會文書殘頁考]: "A Study of Manuscript Fragments of Tangut Social Documents at the National Library of China" in *Wenxian* [文獻] *Documents*, issue 2, 2004 (b).

Shi, Jinbo. "Xixia Nongye Zushui Kao—Xixiawen Nongyeshui Wenshu Yishi" [西夏農業租稅考: 西夏文農業稅文書譯釋]: "Agricultural Taxes in Western Xia: Interpretations of Tangut Documents of Agricultural Taxes" *Lishi Yanjiu* [歷史研究]: *Historical Research*, issue 1, 2005 (a).

Shi, Jinbo. "Xixia Liangshi Jiedai Qiyue Yanjiu" (西夏糧食借貸契約研究): "A Study of Tangut Contracts of Grain Loans" in *Zhongguoshehuikexueyuan Xueshu Weiyuanhui Jikan* (中國社會科學院學術委員會集刊): *A Collection of Papers by Fellows of the Chinese Academy of Social Sciences*, issue 1. Beijing: Social Sciences Academic Press, March 2005 (b).

Shi, Jinbo. *Xixia Shehui* [西夏社會]: *Tangut Society* (vol. 1). Shanghai: Shanghai People's Press, 2007.

Shi, Jinbo. "Xixia de Wujia, Maimaishui he Huobi Jiedai" [西夏的物價、買賣稅和貨幣借貸]: "Commodity Prices, Transaction Taxes and Loans in Western Xia" in *Songshi Yanjiu Lunwenji* [宋史研究論文集]: *A Collection of Papers on Song History*. Shanghai: Shanghai People's Press, July 2008.

Shi, Jinbo. "Yingcang Heishuicheng Wenxian Dingming Chuyi ji Buzheng" [英藏黑水城文獻定名芻議及補正]: "A Preliminary Proposal for Naming and Amending the British collection of Khara-Khoto manuscripts" in *Xixiaxue* [西夏學]: *Tangut Studies*, No. 5, September 2010.

Shi, Jinbo. "Xixia Shiqi de Wuwei" [西夏時期的武威] in *Xixiaxue* [西夏學] (*Tangut Studies*) 7. Shanghai: Shanghai Ancient Works Publishing House, Dec. 2011.

Shi, Jinbo. "Heishuicheng Chutu Xixiawen Maidiqi Yanjiu" [黑水城出土西夏文賣地契研究]: "A Study of Tangut Contracts of Land Sales Excavated in Khara-Khoto" *Lishi Yanjiu* [歷史研究]: *Historical Research*, issue 2, 2012 (a).

Shi, Jinbo. "Xixiawen Junji Wenshu Kaolue: Yi Ecang Heishuicheng Chutu Junji Wenshu Weili" [西夏文軍籍文書考略: 以俄藏黑水城出土軍籍文書為例]: "Studies on Tangut Military Records: Taking the Military Records from the *Russian Collection of Khara-Khoto Manuscripts* as Examples" in *Zhongguoshi Yanjiu* [中國史研究]: *Journal of Chinese Historical Studies*, issue 4, 2012 (b).

Shi, Jinbo. "Heishuicheng Chutu Xixiawen Zudiqi Yanjiu" [黑水城出土西夏文租地契研究]: "A Study of Tangut Contracts of Land Lease Excavated in Khara-Khoto" *Wu Tianchi Jiaoshou Bainian Danchen Jinian Wenji Papers* [吳天墀教授百年誕辰紀念文集]: *Essays Dedicated to the Hundredth Year Anniversary of Professor Wu Tianchi*. Chengdu: Sichuan People's Publishing House, Nov. 2013.

Shi, Jinbo. "Xixiawen Maichuqi he Guchuqi Yanjiu" [西夏文賣畜契和雇畜契研究]: "A Study of Tangut Contracts of Livestock Transaction and Employment" *Zhonghua Wenshi Luncong* [中華文史論叢]: *Series on Chinese Literature and History*, issue 3, 2014 (a).

Shi, Jinbo. "Heishuicheng Chutu Xixiawen Mai Renkou Qi Yanjiu" [黑水城出土西夏文賣人口契研究]: "A Study of the Tangut Contracts of Human Transaction Excavated in Khara-Khoto" in *Zhongguoshehuikexueyuan Yanjiushengyuan Xuebao* [中國社會科學院研究生院學報]: *Academic Journal of the Graduate School of the Chinese Academy of Social Sciences*, issue 4, 2014 (b).

Shi, Jinbo. "Heishuicheng Chutu Xixiawen Zhonghui Tiaoyue (Shetiao) Yanjiu" [黑水城出土西夏文眾會條約(社條) 研究]: "A Study of Tangut Communal Contracts Excavated in Khara-Khoto" in *Xixiaxue* [西夏學]: *Tangut Studies*, issue 10. Shanghai: Shanghai Ancient Books Publishing House, 2014 (c).

Shi, Jinbo. "Heishuicheng Chutu Xixiawen Gugongqi Yanjiu" [黑水城出土西夏文雇工契研究]: "A Study of Tangut Contracts of Employment Excavated in Khara-Khoto" in *Zhongguo Jingjishi Yanjiu* [中國經濟史研究]: *Research in Chinese Economic History*, issue 4, 2016.

Shi, Jinbo; Li, Hansong (transl.). *Tangut Language and Manuscripts: An Introduction*. Leiden: Brill, 2020.

Shi, Jinbo; Bai, Bin; Huang, Zhenhua. *Wenhai Yanjiu* [文海研究]: *A Study on the Sea of Characters*. Beijing: China Social Sciences Press, 1983.

Sun, Jimin, et al. (eds.). *Ecang Heishuicheng Hanwen Wenxian fei Fojiao Wenxian Zhengli yu Yanjiu* [俄藏黑水城漢文文獻非佛教文獻整理與研究]: *Compilation and Survey of non-Buddhist Han Chinese Documents in the Russian Collection of Khara-Khoto Manuscripts*. Beijing: Beijing Normal University Press, 2012.

Sun, Shouling. "Xixia Qianding Shennian Dianmi Qiyue" [西夏乾定申年典糜契約]: "Proso Millet Loan Contract in the Shen Year of Qianding in Western Xia" in *Zhongguo Wenwu Bao* [中國文物報]: *China Cultural Relics News*, issue 5, 1993.

Trombert, Éric. *Le crédit à Dunhuang—Vie matérielle et société en Chine médiévale*. Paris: Collège de France (*Institut des hautes études chinoises*), 1995.

Wu, Tianchi: *Xixia Shigao* [西夏史稿]: *A History of Western Xia*. Chengdu: Sichuan People's Publishing House, reprinted 1983.

Yang, Jiping. "Qushi Gaochang yu Tangdai Xizhou Shazhou Zudianzhi Yanjiu" [麴氏高昌與唐代西州沙洲租佃制研究]: "A Study of Land Lease Contracts in Gaochang of the Qu Family, and Xizhou and Shazhou of Tang Dynasty," pp. 225–292, Han, Guopan (eds.). *Dunhuang Tulufan Chutu Jingji Wenshu Yanjiu* [敦煌吐魯番出土經濟文書研究]: *Studies on the Economic Documents Excavated in Turfan and Dunhuang*. Xiamen: Xiamen University Press, 1986.

Index

www.ingramcontent.com/pod-product-compliance
Lightning Source LLC
LaVergne TN
LVHW021724021026
849161LV00004BA/662
* 9 7 8 9 0 0 4 4 6 1 2 9 1 *